endorsed by
AQA

Applied Business

WITHDRAWN

A2

Tim Chapman   Malcolm Surridge

Stuart Merrills   Gordon McGuire   Neil Buchanan

Collins

William Collins' dream of knowledge for all began with the publication of his first book in 1819. A self-educated mill worker, he not only enriched millions of lives, but also founded a flourishing publishing house. Today, staying true to this spirit, Collins books are packed with inspiration, innovation and practical expertise. They place you at the centre of a world of possibility and give you exactly what you need to explore it.

Collins. Do more.

Published by Collins
An imprint of HarperCollinsPublishers
77–85 Fulham Palace Road
Hammersmith
London
W6 8JB

Browse the complete Collins catalogue at
www.collinseducation.com

© HarperCollinsPublishers Limited 2006

10 9 8 7 6

ISBN 978 0 00 720142 6

Tim Chapman, Malcolm Surridge, Stuart Merrills,
Gordon McGuire and Neil Buchanan assert their moral
rights to be identified as the authors of this work

British Library Cataloguing in Publication Data

A Catalogue record for this publication is available from the British Library

Commissioned by Graham Bradbury

Cover design by Blue Pig Design Limited

Cover picture courtesy of Corbis

Series design by Patricia Briggs

Book design and project management by DSM Partnership

Additional material by Christine Swales

Indexed by Julie Rimington

Picture research by Thelma Gilbert

Production by Sarah Robinson

Printed and bound by Printing Express, Hong Kong

Acknowledgements

The authors and publisher would like to thank the following for permission to reproduce photographs and other material:

Advertising Archives p134, p197.

Alamy p56/7, p87, p100–1, p106, p148/9, p152, p161, p237, p239, p264, p413.

Art Directors p241, p305, p351.

Corbis p59, p164, p173, p194.

Dyson p402–3.

Empics p169, p196, p198, p247, p273, p276, p301, p366, p384, p419.

Sally & Richard Greenhill p255.

RJ Herbert Engineering p354.

Hyundai p354.

KwikFit p379

London 2012 p262, p390.

M&S p8/9, p18, p202.

Steve Moulds p278–9.

Newscast p18.

Nissan p385.

Photos.com p8–9

Rex Features p89, p120, p150, p232, p242, p353.

Roger Scruton p30, p121, p234/5, p324, p328, p362, p353.

Superstock p207.

Tesco p267.

Toyota p375.

Vauxhall p326.

Virgin Mobile p309.

Zara p110.

Every effort has been made to contact copyright holders, but if any have been inadvertantley overlooked, the publishers will be pleased to make the necessary arrangements at the first opportunity.

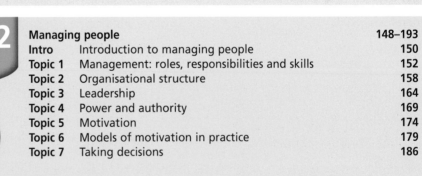

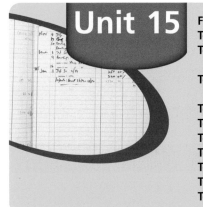

5

Contents

 Marketing route:
Units 9, 10 and 11

 Human resources and
administration route:
Units 12, 13 and 14

 Finance and operations
route: Units 15, 16 and 8

About this book

Welcome to A2 Applied Business. This textbook is written specifically for students taking the AQA Applied Business awards and covers everything you will need to know to complete either the single or double award (see table below).

Single award	
AS-level units	**A2-level units**
■ All units are compulsory	■ Unit 8 (compulsory)
Unit 1 Investigating Business (Internal assessment)	**plus** two more units from 9 to 16 (at least one of the units must be 11, 12 or 15 as these are externally tested)
Unit 2 People in Business (Internal assessment)	
Unit 3 Financial Planning and Monitoring (External test)	

Double award	
AS-level units	**A2-level units**
■ Units 1, 2 and 3	■ Units 8 (compulsory)
■ **plus** three units from 4, 5, 6 or 7	■ **plus** five more units from 9 to 16 (at least one of the units must be 11, 12 or 15 as these are externally tested)
Unit 4 Meeting Customer Needs (External test)	Unit 8 Business Planning (Internal assessment)
Unit 5 Business Communication and Information Systems (External test)	Unit 9 Marketing Strategy (Internal assessment)
Unit 6 Developing a Product (Internal assessment)	Unit 10 Promotional Activities (Internal assessment)
Unit 7 Career Planning (Internal assessment)	Unit 11 The Marketing Environment (External test)
	Unit 12 Managing People (External test)
	Unit 13 Managing Information (Internal assessment)
	Unit 14 Managing Change (Internal assessment)
	Unit 15 Financial Accounting for Managers (External test)
	Unit 16 Managing Resources (Internal assessment)

■ To gain a single award you must successfully complete three AS-level units plus three A2-level units, which must include the compulsory units.

■ To gain a double award you must successfully complete six AS-level units plus six A2-level units, which must include the compulsory units.

Your teacher will explain the combination of units you require to complete the award for which you are studying.

The assessment of your knowledge and understanding of the different units will be follow the same pattern as your AS-level award:

■ an assignment that is written and marked by your teacher (internal assessment)

■ a written examination lasting one and half hours, which is written and marked by AQA, your awarding body (external test)

Collins Applied Business A2 for AQA is divided into nine units and each unit in this book corresponds to a unit of the AQA A2 Applied Business award. The units in this book are divided into topics and each topic provides a manageable chunk of learning covering the subject content of an AQA A2-level unit. The contents list at the beginning of this book and at the start of each unit will show you how the topics correspond to the AQA Applied Business A2-level specification.

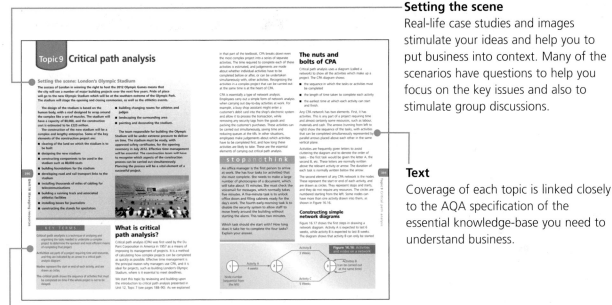

Setting the scene

Real-life case studies and images stimulate your ideas and help you to put business into context. Many of the scenarios have questions to help you focus on the key issues and also to stimulate group discussions.

Text

Coverage of each topic is linked closely to the AQA specification of the essential knowledge-base you need to understand business.

Key terms

The specialist terminology used in business is explained in simple terms.

Business practice

A variety of case studies based on real-life business, followed by questions on the key issues, allow you to apply your newly acquired knowledge.

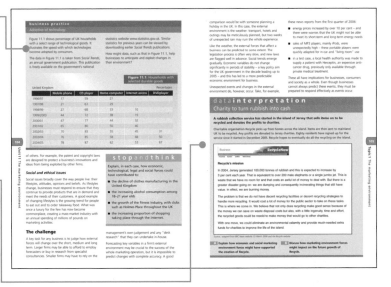

Assessment practice

A variety of investigative and active learning exercises, which include internet-based research, small-scale research projects and information gathering activities to help you extend your knowledge and skills.

Good luck with your GCE A2-level studies. This book provides you with interesting, supportive and motivating learning materials that we hope will help you to succeed in your applied business course.

IN THIS UNIT, WE INVESTIGATE WHY MARKETING ACTIVITIES are vital to the achievement of business aims and objectives. You will develop an understanding of marketing strategies and the marketing tactics designed to implement these strategies.

This unit helps you to consider the research and planning behind any successful marketing campaign. You will investigate how market research helps businesses to select their best marketing strategy and to develop a mix of marketing activities capable of meeting the needs of their target markets.

The assessment for this unit requires you to produce a marketing strategy, and associated marketing mix, for a new or existing business. The business can be a company, a partnership or a sole trader, or a not-for-profit business (such as a charity or a public sector organisation).

At the end of each topic, there is an assessment practice section. The guidance given in each assessment practice is there to help you build your plan of a marketing strategy as you work through the unit. Your teacher will provide further guidance on how to present your plan of a marketing strategy.

Marketing strategy

Business aims and marketing objectives

Setting the scene: marketing the Victoria and Albert Museum

The Victoria and Albert Museum (V&A) is based in South Kensington, London. The museum contains artefacts from many of the world's richest cultures, including ceramics, furniture, fashion, glass, jewellery, metalwork, photographs, sculpture, textiles and paintings.

This extract from the V&A's website describes the marketing challenge facing the museum, and the marketing objectives that the museum has set. After reading the extract, consider why marketing might be an essential activity for the museum. What difficulties might it face in achieving its marketing objectives?

Marketing the V&A

Marketing a museum is the process of identifying the needs and wants of the visitor and delivering benefits that will satisfy or enhance their experience. Marketing also helps maximise the performance of the museum. It is a complex activity requiring extensive creativity, planning, organisation and problem-solving.

At V&A South Kensington, the process is mostly handled by the marketing department and press office working together, led by the Director of Public Affairs. They act as a public voice for the V&A, communicating with many different audiences, including tourists, colleges, schools, families and adults (individuals and groups). Together they promote, or advise on the promotion of, the V&A's permanent collections and galleries, major exhibitions, contemporary programmes, and a wide range of displays, events, activities and courses.

The V&A has several key marketing objectives:

- to increase visitor numbers
- to build the V&A's brand (the values that the V&A wants to be known for)
- to increase public awareness of services and events
- to increase revenue through temporary exhibitions
- to attract new audiences.

The museum also has commercial objectives to increase revenue through a variety of different sources, including the museum shops, publications, events and catering.

Source: www.vam.ac.uk

Business aims

All businesses – whether for-profit enterprises or not-for-profit concerns – have specific aims and objectives. A business aim sets an overall target to be achieved by the business. Business objectives are the steps that a business needs to take in order to achieve a particular aim. In Unit 1 of the AS textbook (see pages 12–13) we introduced a number of typical business aims: survival, meeting stakeholder needs, maximising sales revenue (or income), maximising profit (or surplus), and growth.

The Victoria and Albert Museum, as a not-for-profit business, aims to:

- survive, by ensuring that it has enough finance to cover the costs of providing its services

- meet stakeholder needs, including those of a diverse visiting public, academic institutions (universities) and the UK government, which provides grants to fund the V&A

- grow, by for example using ICT to develop the V&A's website and its online services.

Achieving a set of aims is a complex and challenging task for any business. The V&A faces severe competition, both direct and indirect, from a wide range of leisure and entertainment providers. It relies heavily on government grants, which come attached with targets set by the Department for Culture, Media and Sport. It has a complex product which has the potential to excite, inform and entertain but which needs to be presented in accessible ways.

To achieve these aims the V&A, and any other for-profit or not-for-profit business, should identify a set of relevant marketing objectives. One of the V&A's marketing objectives (see the extract opposite) is "to increase visitor numbers". This objective would be a key "stepping stone" towards achieving the first two of the V&A's aims as set out above. It is a marketing objective because it focuses on an aspect of the V&A's market – that is, to increase the number of customers visiting the V&A.

SMART objectives

One of the keys to a successful marketing campaign is selecting a realistic and appropriate set of marketing objectives. These marketing objectives must have a direct relationship to one or more business aims – if you can't see how a particular marketing objective contributes to achieving a business aim, it should not

be listed. Marketing objectives should be practical.

- The business should have the resources to carry out marketing activities capable of achieving the objective.

- These marketing activities should be capable of sufficiently altering the buying behaviour of current and potential customers.

- They should have the potential to deliver results within an appropriate time frame.

Marketing objectives should be SMART: that is, they should be specific, measurable, achievable, relevant and time-specific. Before committing to a particular marketing objective, a business should test it against the SMART criteria. It is not likely that a business will reveal its SMART marketing objectives to the general public, but key personnel within the business should be given marketing objectives which, at the very least, are practical and relevant.

The V&A's marketing objective of increasing visitor numbers is a summary of a potentially SMART objective. In reality, this marketing objective will be communicated in a SMART way to key V&A personnel. It would be:

- specific – in terms of a percentage increase in visitors per day, week or month

- measurable – by counting the number of visitors

- achievable – considering the potential size of the market, the resources available to V&A personnel and the number of visitors which can be handled

- relevant – linked to its overall aims, as by increasing the number of visitors the V&A may well be meeting government targets (contributing to meeting stakeholder needs) and will hopefully increase shop and catering purchases (contributing to survival)

- time-specific – in terms of a percentage increase in visitors by a particular date.

Marketing objectives

Marketing is a complex process because it aims to reinforce or alter the buying behaviour of current and potential customers. As such, it has to take into account the many forces that impact on the behaviour of these customers, including:

- the mass media – TV, radio, newspapers, magazines and the internet

- friends, family and other opinion formers (such as celebrities and the people we work with)

- each individual's internal view of the world – his or her fears and hopes, desires and daily concerns

- competitor actions – their marketing activities, including promotional activities, product ranges and prices

- the state of the economy – local, national and, perhaps, international economic activity as it impacts on the behaviour of the business's customers.

It is not surprising, then, that a wide range of possible marketing objectives are available to businesses, including:

- successfully targeting a new market or part of an existing market (market segmentation)

- achieving or maintaining a particular share of the market

- developing a suitable range of products (product mix)

- increasing the profit (surplus) received on products (contribution)

- positioning the product in a more favourable segment of the market (product positioning).

We shall consider each of these general marketing objectives in terms of their practicality and relevance.

1 Targeting a new market

The idea of customer segmentation was introduced in Unit 4 (see pages 154–7 of the AS textbook). By analysing the characteristics of customers, it is possible to define different types of customer needs and target those needs accordingly. In this way, markets can be segmented.

The market for cars is usually segmented according to the benefits different customers are seeking to gain from their purchase, such as safety, speed, status, economy or reliability. Individual customers place a different emphasis on each of these benefits, making it possible for manufacturers to segment the market. So, for example, some cars are marketed on the basis of their status, some on the basis of their reliability, some on the basis of their affordability, etc.

In practical terms, small and medium-sized organisations do not have the resources to target large markets or multiple market segments. For these organisations it is crucial to select the most appropriate market segment. For example, a sole trader starting an interior design service will, of necessity, have to target a narrowly defined market segment capable of generating sufficient revenues. A key aspect of the interior designer's business plan would be a careful description of the customers likely to place sufficient value on this service. The marketing objective would then be expressed in terms of targeting this market segment – say, high income earners who are cash-rich but time-poor. As the business develops and takes on more staff, the marketing objective might broaden to target different segments, such as commercial properties like retail outlets.

2 Gaining market share

Market share represents the fraction of the total market serviced by a business. It could be measured by volume for a particular time period (such as one year or one month):

$$\frac{\text{number of products sold by the business}}{\substack{\text{total number sold by all businesses} \\ \text{in the market}}} \times 100$$

It could also be measured by value for a particular time period:

$$\frac{\text{revenue made by the business}}{\substack{\text{total revenue of all businesses} \\ \text{in the market}}} \times 100$$

Achieving a particular market share might be a relevant marketing objective if the business needs to gain a degree of dominance in the market. This might be a business aim if the market is so competitive that profit margins are too low for a small business to survive. Alternatively, it might be an aim because the business its a public limited company (plc), and its shareholders expect the higher dividends that could be obtained if the company achieves a greater market share.

For most small and medium-sized organisations, their objectives are likely to be limited to maintaining their existing market share, particularly in situations in which new competition has entered the market. An independent high street retailer, for example, might have this as a marketing objective if a new store opens in the immediate area which is serving similar customer needs.

If maintaining or increasing market share is a marketing objective, the business must have some way of calculating its market share. Quantifying market share is often difficult. A business will have records of its own sales – by volume and value – yet it will not be immediately aware of the sales made by other businesses in the market. Secondary research data is available but this can be for one or more years in the past and is relatively expensive for smaller businesses to purchase.

3 Developing a product mix

The mix of products offered by a business is obviously an essential element of its marketing mix. The range of needs held by the target market of a business may be varied, and a comprehensive product mix would be essential if the business is targeting a number of market segments.

Product mix can be measured in terms of:

- **width**, the number of different types of products (product lines) offered by a business – a pub's product lines might be alcoholic drinks, food and entertainment
- **depth**, the number of different products within each product line – in the pub's case, one measure of depth would be the range of alcoholic drinks it offers.

business practice
Mazda's market share

Car sales in the UK, either new or second-hand, are recorded as part of the vehicle registration process. The website of the Society of Motor Manufacturers and Traders Limited (www.smmt.co.uk) provides free monthly data on the market share of all car manufacturers trading in the UK.

Individual car manufacturers trading in the UK market also regularly publish market share data. The following extract is adapted from a press release published by Mazda, a Japanese car manufacturer. What does it reveal about Mazda's possible marketing objectives?

Mazda reaches all-time record market share

Highest Mazda monthly market share ever – 2.7 per cent

Most successful January ever – 4,400 sales

Mazda is officially Britain's favourite sports car brand – 13.8 per cent segment share

Mazda is celebrating two landmarks for sales this month as the recently published SMMT (Society of Motor Manufacturers and Traders) sports car segment figures for 2005 confirm that Mazda is now Britain's favourite sports car brand with a market share of 13.8 per cent, representing 10,153 sports car sales. Mazda's share of the sports car segment was followed by premium car brands Porsche at 10.9 per cent and Mercedes-Benz at 10.6 per cent.

Sales director Jeremy Thomson commented on this record sales month: "We are delighted to reach a 2.7 per cent market share for the first time. Sales of our volume family and company car models Mazda3 and Mazda6 continue to grow in popularity, while the success of our sports models Mazda MX-5 and RX-8 go from strength to strength."

Source: Mazda news brief, 6 February 2006 (www.mazda.co.uk)

Developing the product mix is not always a sensible marketing objective. Each product added to the mix must improve the capability of the business to meet customer needs. The added product must not detract from the main trading purpose of the business or reduce the sales of the other products offered by the business. If a new product line presents a poor overall image of the business, or a new product within an existing product line simply replaces sales, scarce resources would have been wasted for no return.

Small-scale businesses may see the addition of a new product line – or a new product within an existing product line – as a quick route to increased sales and profitability. Every sole trader will keep a keen eye on new ways of meeting customer needs, but the decision to offer a product should be based on an understanding of how it might affect customer opinions of the business as a whole. If a new product inadvertently targets a different market segment, current customers could take their business elsewhere. For example, the customers of a quiet country pub might not appreciate the introduction of Sky Sports or a pool table, but they might appreciate an improved dining experience.

4 Increasing product contribution

The contribution a product makes to the overall profit of a business can be defined as the sales revenue generated by the product less the costs incurred in producing and selling the product. The costs incurred when selling the product include:

■ the cost of the business purchasing, or producing, the product

■ sales costs of promotional activities directly related to the product, such as the costs resulting from any merchandising and personal selling.

Both production and sales activities are related to marketing, and gaining higher product contributions would obviously help to achieve wider business aims such as survival or maximising profits.

This marketing objective is closely related to the objective of developing the product mix. Indeed, one way to increase the contribution made by products is to manage the product mix. Selecting the best product mix, then, might not be solely in terms of choosing the "best sellers", but of selecting the most profitable products. Selling one high-contribution product is possibly a more achievable and successful approach than selling thousands of low-contribution products – although, in practice, this depends on the nature of the target market and the expertise of the sales personnel within the business.

5 Repositioning a product

This marketing objective is closely related to the objective of increasing product contribution. If a business sets itself an objective of increasing product contribution, then one way to achieve this is to reposition one or more of its products.

Products are positioned in relation to the market segment at which they are aimed. For example, an interior design business might be finding it difficult to generate enough contribution on each job because it is selling to the wrong market segment – it might be targeting customers that are either unable or unwilling to pay a high price for the business's services. Relaunching its services, and targeting a market segment with greater interest in the product (or greater bank balances), might result in fewer sales but a higher total contribution.

It can sometimes be profitable to move down-market – to reduce the contribution made on each product, but significantly increase the volume of business. For example, a restaurant might find it profitable to reduce the quality and variety of ingredients if potential customers in the area want "good basic food". This might result in the restaurant losing some of its customers, but this could be more than compensated by an increase in sales volume.

This marketing objective of repositioning products has the potential to radically improve the profitability of a business and to increase its ability to meet stakeholder needs. However, the difficulty, and inherent risk, is in selecting the new market segment: understanding the market and its needs is essential.

assessment practice
Starting work on your marketing strategy

For this unit the awarding body, AQA, requires you to produce a marketing strategy and associated marketing mix for a new or existing business. At the end of each topic in this unit, there is an assessment practice section to help you gradually build up your portfolio.

These sections provide guidance to help you develop your marketing strategy and associated marketing mix as your work through the unit. Your teacher will provide guidance on how to present your marketing strategy.

As part of your marketing strategy for a new or existing business you are required to explain:

■ the marketing strategy

■ the target market

■ the marketing aims and objectives.

Start by identifying the business that will be the focus of your marketing strategy. It is recommended that you do not choose a large, well established business, such as Cadbury or Coca-Cola. It may well be more appropriate to select a smaller, local business. Remember, the business can be a profit or not-for-profit business, a new enterprise or an established company. Your teacher might be able to suggest suitable businesses.

You might be currently working on ideas for Unit 8 (Business Planning), and this could be an opportunity to develop the marketing elements of your business plan.

A Carry out research into your business to find out:

- ■ its main activities
- ■ its main aims
- ■ the range of products it offers
- ■ the market segments it targets
- ■ the degree of competition in the markets in which the business trades.

Note that if you have selected a new business, your research should take care to identify likely competitors.

B Use the findings from your research to produce a profile of your business on a single page of A4. This profile should cover:

- ■ the activities of the business and its product mix
- ■ the market segments the business targets
- ■ the business's main competitors.

C Using this profile of the business, produce a five-minute presentation, titled "Three next steps", which identifies three possible marketing objectives consistent with the aims of the business.

Marketing strategies and tactics

Setting the scene: responsibletravel.com

Responsibletravel.com is an online travel agent based in Brighton, England. It was launched in 2001 for travellers who want more real and authentic holidays that also benefit the environment and local people. Responsible travel is a new way of travelling for those who've had enough of mass tourism. It's about respecting and benefiting local people and the environment – but it's about far more than that.

If you travel for relaxation, fulfilment, discovery, adventure and to learn – rather than simply to tick off "places and things" – then responsible travel is for you. Responsible travel is about bringing you closer to local cultures and environments by involving local people in tourism. It's about doing this in a fair way that helps ensure that they will give you an even warmer welcome. For example, local guides from the destination will open your eyes to their cultures and ways of life far better than a guide from your own country could ever do – they will also earn a much needed income from you.

The responsible traveller prefers smaller groups, and to meet some local people rather than be surrounded by thousands of people from back home. They don't like being herded about in a large crowd like nameless faces, and they understand that travelling in smaller groups makes local people and cultures more accessible. At the same time, the responsible traveller understands that some cultural experiences are best kept private, and that their visit would be an intrusion. They believe that travelling with respect earns them respect.

Source: Online Travel Agency www.responsibletravel.com

Marketing strategies

A marketing strategy describes how a business plans to achieve its marketing objectives. It sets out the overall approach of the business's marketing, and informs the choice and mix of marketing activities as well as the market segments to be targeted. The concept of the marketing mix was introduced in Unit 1 of the AS textbook (pages 32–9). The concept of market segments was introduced in Unit 4 of the AS textbook (see pages 154–7).

Responsibletravel.com would appear to have adopted a focused marketing strategy aimed at increasing the contribution received on each holiday it sells. It could also have some non-financial objectives such as "reducing the negative impact of tourism on developing economies". However, as a private business, it has to generate sufficient contribution to

KEY TERMS

Marketing strategies set out how a business intends to achieve its marketing objectives.

Marketing tactics are the particular marketing activities that will be used to implement a marketing strategy.

Marketing warfare strategies are marketing strategies that result from aggressive conditions found in competitive markets. It is unlikely that all businesses in the market can achieve their aims without contesting for sales.

Competitive position strategies are approaches taken by businesses operating within competitive markets. In competitive markets, for example, market followers yield to the dominance of the market leader.

break even and meet the financial needs of its owners. The plan of action adopted by responsibletravel.com could be described as a niche

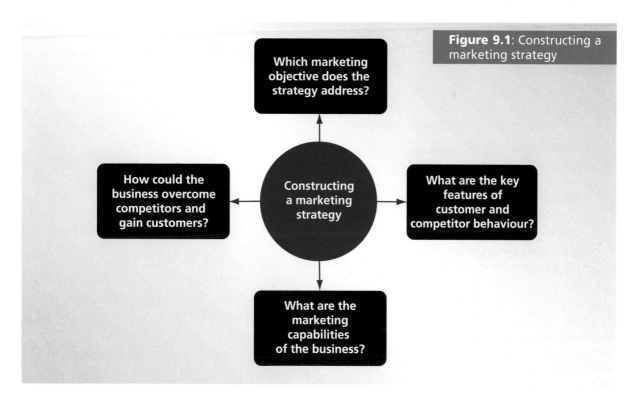

Figure 9.1: Constructing a marketing strategy

- Which marketing objective does the strategy address?
- What are the key features of customer and competitor behaviour?
- What are the marketing capabilities of the business?
- How could the business overcome competitors and gain customers?
- Constructing a marketing strategy

strategy: it targets the needs of a market segment which is currently not being met by the dominant businesses in the travel industry, offering a unique holiday experience sympathetic to its ethical values.

Without a marketing strategy, marketing activities carried out by a business are at risk of being counterproductive. Just as a building should be constructed on solid foundations, marketing activities should be based on a sound marketing strategy.

Figure 9.1 illustrates some of the questions that might be asked when constructing a marketing strategy. These four questions are essential.

- **Which marketing objectives?**
  Without clear marketing objectives, a marketing strategy will have no direction.

- **What are the key features of customer and competitor behaviour?**
  The marketing strategy will be misguided if the business does not understand how customers and competitors might respond to its marketing activities.

- **What are the marketing capabilities?**
  The business should have the marketing resources to carry out the marketing strategy, including expertise and finances.

- **How could the business overcome competitors?**
  A marketing strategy's primary goal is to defeat competitors and win over customers.

The last question indicates that any marketing strategy should aim to achieve victories. Successful marketing strategies gain prizes for businesses, and it is this "battling" aspect of marketing which led marketing theorists to identify similarities between marketing and warfare.

Marketing warfare

Overcoming competitors and gaining customers is the essential purpose of any marketing strategy. At times, the focus will be on gaining customers; at other times, it will be to defeat rival competitors. The similarities between warfare and business are striking – in both situations groups of people are striving to achieve dominance and gain valuable rewards. In each case a strategy, defining how the battle should be fought, is essential. This is especially true when a business is operating in a market which is not growing and which contains several competitors. In this situation, each business is literally fighting for orders from customers – as one business succeeds another will lose out.

In markets that are growing rapidly, it is possible for a temporary peace to exist. In these markets it is pointless battling it out when each business has more than enough opportunities to sell and is actually struggling to keep up with the level of demand. Ultimately, however, one or more businesses will establish a degree of dominance. For example, a

This article from *The Scotsman* newspaper illustrates a contemporary feature of marketing warfare: the battle for the UK groceries market.

Residents in one of Scotland's most affluent districts are at the centre of a store war which could threaten the future of small traders, after Marks & Spencer announced that it was buying the local Iceland shop. M&S will sell ready meals, fresh produce, sandwiches, wine, flowers and basic groceries to consumers in Morningside, Edinburgh. The move comes as Tesco prepares to open a Tesco Metro at nearby Holy Corner.

John Drummond, chief executive of the Scottish Grocers' Federation, said: "Clearly we are not excited about the big guys moving into our marketplace, wherever that happens – be it a Tesco Metro, a Sainsbury's Local, or a Marks & Spencer Simply Food. We do think that we offer a good, friendly local service that can be more easily tailored to the needs of the community, but the arrival of large multiples is rarely good in terms of diversity on the high street."

M&S said its Simply Food brand, which already has two stores in the centre of Edinburgh, was a "very popular and profitable" concept.

Source: adapted from The Scotsman, 18 January 2006

The marketing strategy being adopted by Tesco and Marks & Spencer could be described as offensive. This is not because the marketing strategy offends local shopkeepers, but because it is an aggressive strategy. In military terms, Tesco and Marks & Spencer are taking the battle to the high street in an offensive campaign designed to capture market share.

How can independent high street stores respond? These smaller businesses do not have the resources to directly combat the activities of Tesco and Marks & Spencer. In military terms, the smaller businesses need to choose different battlegrounds, carry out surprise attacks or retreat to fight another day.

As indicated by the article, the smaller businesses could consider their marketing capabilities and develop a marketing strategy based on the perceived weaknesses of Tesco and Marks & Spencer. This strategy would be based around offering "a good, friendly local service that can be more easily tailored to the needs of the community". However, if customers in the local area are not prepared to pay the higher prices that this level of service requires, the battle for the high street may already be lost.

stop and think

How have the actions of larger retail organisations, such as Tesco and Marks & Spencer, affected smaller retailers in your area? To what extent can your local smaller retailers survive? Justify your answer.

business might establish a superior product mix and consequently gain a larger share of the market. This business now has greater influence in the marketplace, as well as greater marketing capabilities, and might adopt a strategy of targeting the markets of the smaller businesses.

Marketing warfare strategies

Marketing warfare strategies explicitly recognise the confrontational nature of competitive markets. These strategies can be grouped under four headings.

Offensive

These are marketing strategies which, as illustrated by the activities of Tesco and Marks & Spencer in

Edinburgh (see "The battle for the high street" box), are designed to attack competitors head-on. This strategy would deliberately target customers of competing businesses in the belief that they could be won over by offering a superior deal. This is the rationale behind Marks & Spencer's Simply Food retail outlets.

Defensive

These are marketing strategies which focus on keeping a share of the market or maintaining the contribution made on sales. Small high street retailers might adopt this kind of strategy when faced with the "offensive" strategy of larger retailers. A market position, however, can only be defended if you have strong enough defences, such as a reputation for good customer service or a unique product mix.

Flanking

If it appears impossible to defend a market, a possible approach is to find a new market which is not under attack. This marketing strategy could be adopted by small high street retailers. It might mean physically relocating their businesses or repositioning their products in a more favourable segment of the market.

Guerrilla

These are marketing strategies which rely on an element of surprise. This approach might be suitable when a smaller business faces new competition from a larger business. Neither defence nor attack is possible, and the smaller business does not want to leave the current market. In this situation, the business needs to identify the larger business's potential weaknesses and attack these in short bursts,

Figure 9.2: Competitive positions and marketing warfare strategies

Competitive position	Description	Marketing warfare strategy
Market leader	The dominant business, with the highest market share	Capable of adopting offensive strategies to protect or enhance its dominant position. Faced with a competitor wishing to challenge for market dominance, the leader might consider a defensive strategy. However, the best form of defence is to remain proactive and offensive. Flanking strategies might apply if market conditions change: for example, if leadership in a particular market segment looks in danger and the segment is not valuable enough to be worthwhile defending. Guerrilla strategies could also apply if the current leadership position is fragile.
Market challenger	Non-market leader which is striving to become the market leader	Needs to adopt an offensive strategy. These offensive strategies should focus on the weaknesses of the market leader. However, if other challengers exist in the market, defensive strategies might need to be used at times of intense competition. Guerrilla strategies could be appropriate if the business is not yet recognised as a challenger but wants to announce itself as one.
Market follower	Low market share competitors without significant marketing resources and no desire to challenge the leader	With a desire for a "quiet life", market followers are content to survive in the shadow of the market leader. Defensive marketing strategies might have been used in the past to establish and maintain their current position. However, they are continually under threat as their market share can appear attractive to both challengers and the market leader in times of slow market growth. In these circumstances, flanking strategies might seem attractive as they possibly have very little genuine customer loyalty and certainly have insufficient resources to mount any counterattacks.
Market nicher	Businesses focusing on specific segments of the market and offering a restricted product mix	Possibly a market follower that has adopted a flanking strategy, the market nicher does not have the resources to carry out offensive or defensive strategies. By focusing on an area of the market not contested by either the leader or challengers, the nicher can develop a profitable business without having to invest in a large product mix. If another similar-sized business attempts to enter the niche market, the business might adopt an offensive strategy. However, with limited resources, it would have to rely mainly on the loyalty of its customers and the inability of the challenger to meet their needs.

perhaps through public relations events or temporary price discounts. The aim is to repeatedly inconvenience the larger competitor, forcing it to move on to other markets or to cease its offensive marketing strategy. Guerrilla marketing strategies, however, will not succeed unless the business has some loyal customers to begin with.

The marketing warfare strategies adopted by businesses partly depend on their position within the market and, in particular, how dominant they are. Businesses with significant market shares are likely to adopt very different strategies compared with businesses that have a low market share. As Figure 9.2 illustrates, by categorising the businesses within a market according to their degree of dominance, it is possible to consider which marketing warfare strategies each business might adopt.

stop and think

How might marketing warfare strategies be used in these markets: (a) ice cream sold along a popular sea front, (b) takeaway food in your area and (c) charities in your local area? Do these strategies have to be confrontational?

Marketing tactics

A marketing strategy describes how a business plans to achieve its marketing objectives. Marketing tactics grow out of this overall approach and provide a detailed action plan for implementing the strategy.

This action plan will describe the exact marketing mix capable of achieving the strategy's marketing objectives – that is, the combinations of product, price, promotion and place which put the strategy's battle plan into action.

Figure 9.3 illustrates the relationship between a business's aims, objectives, marketing strategy and tactics. This diagram also illustrates some of the complexity of marketing – the marketing mix does not come from nowhere. A successful marketing mix relies on a business having a very clear set of objectives and a rational plan in mind. Whether the business employs three or 3,000 people, the issues are the same:

■ objectives – what am I trying to achieve

■ strategy – what is the general plan of attack

■ tactics – how do I turn the general plan into practice?

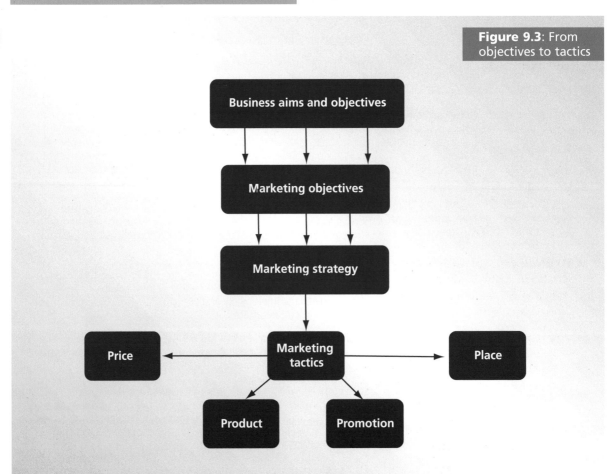

Figure 9.3: From objectives to tactics

Business aims and objectives

Marketing objectives

Marketing strategy

Price ← Marketing tactics → Place

Product   Promotion

A sole trader operating a landscape gardening business faces declining orders because of a new competitor in her local market. Her current market area is defined as 15 miles from her home address and, including the new competitor, this market is served by four other landscape gardening businesses.

She thinks that she is the leader in the local market, but this is difficult to quantify. The new competitor, located 2 miles away, is undercutting her prices by roughly 30 per cent. Her order book, compared with last year, shows a 10 per cent decline in the number of customers for the next three months. However, this seems to be mainly smaller jobs. Compared with the previous year, she is still gaining the same number of high-value orders from customers requiring major landscaping of their gardens. Roughly 80 per cent of her profits come from these high-value orders.

The sole trader has set a business objective of increasing her annual profit by 5 per cent. Assuming that she is at the start of her financial year, what marketing warfare strategy would you recommend, and how might she use the marketing mix to implement this strategy? Justify your answers.

assessment practice
Possible marketing strategies

From the assessment practice activities in Topic 1, you should have an idea of:

- the aims, activities and product mix of your chosen business

- the market segments the business currently targets

- the business's main competitors

- three possible marketing objectives consistent with the aims of the business.

In this practice assessment, you should think about possible marketing strategies, based on the your three marketing objectives, and the marketing activities which could implement these strategies.

A Using Figures 9.1 and 9.2, identify which marketing warfare strategies might be appropriate for your business. Justify your answer.

B For each marketing warfare strategy you selected in 1, outline the marketing tactics capable of implementing the strategy. You should consider:

- which market segments are being targeted

- what practical product, price, promotion and place activities might be used to implement the strategy

- how your business's competitors might react to your marketing tactics.

Choosing a strategy: Ansoff's matrix and the Boston matrix

Setting the scene: retail buyers

Retail buyers buy goods such as clothes, food, wine, furniture and electrical goods. The goods have to be bought at the right price, quality and quantity to meet the needs of the customer.

Retail buyers are employed by department stores, supermarkets, high street retailers and mail order companies. According to the "jobs4u" careers website, there are around 12,000 retail buyers in the UK, and competition for jobs is fierce.

The "jobs4u" careers website also provides a more detailed job description and person specification. Retail buying may involve:

- planning and selecting the range, type and quantity of goods to buy
- searching out new products
- meeting and negotiating with suppliers
- keeping up to date with market trends and reacting to changes in demand
- monitoring how goods and merchandise are selling
- attending trade fairs or fashion shows.

A retail buyer should:

- have strong business skills and be commercially aware
- have a fine sense of the price and value of goods

- have good ideas and be creative
- be a skilled negotiator
- be well organised and able to work well under pressure
- be able to work in a team
- have an interest in the retail sector they wish to join.

Do you think an understanding of a business's marketing strategies is essential for a retail buyer? Would retail buyers help to determine a business's marketing strategies or its marketing tactics?

Source: job descriptions from www.connexions-direct.com/jobs4u

Segmentation and product mix

The work of retail buyers is an essential aspect of any marketing strategy – they help to implement the strategy and they have the potential to inform future marketing tactics. The work is connected with the implementation of two key aspects of marketing strategy:

- segmentation
- product mix.

Segmentation is a vital aspect of an effective marketing strategy. By splitting a diverse market into smaller groups, a business can select the most

KEY TERMS

Segmentation strategies involve dividing markets into separate groups of customers.

Ansoff's matrix is a marketing tool that considers likely marketing strategies by focusing on the extent to which a business might develop its markets and develop its product mix.

The Boston matrix is a marketing tool that considers likely marketing strategies by assessing the performance of the different products within the business's product mix.

appropriate marketing strategy for each segment. If the business is not aware of its customers' diverse buying behaviour, its marketing strategies and activities are likely to be very "hit and miss", and they will only work for some customers.

Segmentation helps a business to focus on market opportunities, and it should inform its marketing strategy. It is valuable for smaller businesses because they are unlikely to have the capability to reach the whole market – they can choose to ignore some market segments and focus on others, or even just a single segment.

The choice of marketing strategy is inextricably linked to the segmentation strategy adopted by a business. For example, focusing on one narrowly defined segment might imply a flanking strategy and a desire to become a market nicher. Alternatively, targeting several market segments may well be an approach used by a leader or challenger using offensive marketing strategies.

A business's choice of product mix might be seen as a tactical decision, as part of the marketing mix designed to implement a marketing strategy. However, the products sold by a business go a long way to define what a business is about and help to form both customer and competitor attitudes towards it. In this way, the product mix is an essential part of any business's marketing strategy.

Segmentation and product mix decisions help to define the ways in which a business plans to deal with competitors and gain customers. Whichever marketing warfare strategy is adopted, the business will need to consider its approach to segmentation and the product mix. Two tools to help businesses clarify their thinking about these issues are:

■ **Ansoff's matrix**
  (Ansoff's competitive strategy matrix)

■ **the Boston matrix**
  (the Boston Consulting Group product portfolio analysis).

Ansoff's matrix

As Figure 9.4 shows, Ansoff's matrix identifies four possible strategies a business could follow when seeking to achieve marketing objectives. Each of the four strategies focuses on different aspects of a business's market and product mix.

■ **Market penetration** – increasing the sales of an existing product in its current markets and taking sales away from competitors. For example, Tesco might increase the frequency of its television advertising or reduce prices on a standard range of products within its stores.

■ **Product development** – launching a new or improved product to existing markets. Tesco's introduction of financial services was, at the time, product development – it was selling a new product to its existing customers.

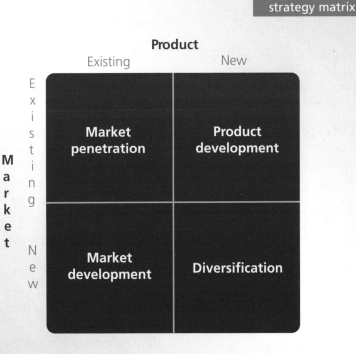

Figure 9.4: Ansoff's competitive strategy matrix

Ansoff's competitive strategies	Offensive marketing warfare strategies	Flanking marketing warfare strategies
Market penetration	**Appropriate** The leader and challengers aim to gain market share, and market penetration might be seen as the least complex way of attacking market share.	**Inappropriate** The aim is to get out of a market segment, and a flanking strategy would not consider contesting market share.
Product development	**Appropriate** Challengers could steal customers by introducing a new or improved product that has a greater ability to meet the needs of the leader's customers. The market leader could improve its position by widening its product mix, enhancing its ability to meet customer needs, and stealing customers from challengers.	**Inappropriate** The aim is to get out of a market segment and a flanking strategy would not consider product development in an existing market.
Market development	**Possibly appropriate** If the new market is being targeted by a competitor, then this could be a way of taking the battle to the competitor. Otherwise inappropriate.	**Appropriate** The aim is to find new market segments, and market development focuses on this without the need to develop new products.
Diversification	**Inappropriate** Unless this represents a market segment/product combination of a competitor, this would not be a direct assault.	**Appropriate** The aim in flanking is to find new market segments – that is, diversification. However, perhaps only suitable for larger organisations as new products need to be added to the product mix.

- **Market development** – finding new markets for existing products. Tesco has made acquisitions in Europe and Asia to establish a presence in these markets. While product ranges differ, the core product – groceries – remains the same.

- **Diversification** – entering new markets with new products. Nokia, the mobile telephone manufacturer, has implemented a successful diversification strategy: the company initially operated in the wood pulp and paper industry.

Ansoff's matrix should be used to consider whether a business's marketing strategy might focus on new market segments or new additions to the product mix. Figure 9.5 shows how Ansoff's competitive strategies relate to offensive and flanking strategies – two of the marketing warfare strategies discussed in Topic 2.

stop and think

Construct a table similar to Figure 9.5 but focusing on defensive and guerrilla marketing warfare strategies. Compare the two tables. What are the similarities and differences?

The Boston matrix

The Boston matrix is a tool for analysing the suitability of a business's product mix. From this analysis a business can have a better understanding of whether it should alter its product mix. It can also help when considering the suitability of marketing warfare strategies. Figure 9.6 illustrates the key features of the Boston matrix tool.

As we saw in the introduction to this topic, a retail buyer has to have in-depth knowledge about the business's product mix, and must also understand product and consumer trends in the market. For example, buyers need to know which products are fashionable and are likely to "fly off the shelves", and which might prove difficult to sell.

The vertical axis of the Boston matrix – market growth – would be a familiar concept to a retail buyer. It is measuring the current popularity of a product in the market as a whole. This looks at the prospects for growth in demand for a product, such as the percentage growth in sales of LCD televisions in the UK. This is measuring total market demand, and does not concern itself with the market shares of individual businesses. The horizontal axis – market share –

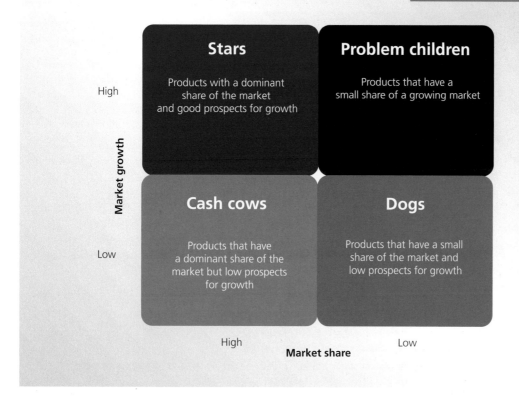

Figure 9.6: The Boston matrix

Stars

Products with a dominant share of the market and good prospects for growth

Problem children

Products that have a small share of a growing market

Cash cows

Products that have a dominant share of the market but low prospects for growth

Dogs

Products that have a small share of the market and low prospects for growth

Market growth — High / Low

Market share — High / Low

measures how well a business's version of the product is doing in the market. For example, it would record the percentage of LCD televisions sold by Sony.

In both cases, two simple options are allowed – high and low. These are likely to be subjective assessments, and they will depend on the state of the market and the number of competitors. For example, a car manufacturer that has a 15 per cent share of the compact car market (smaller vehicles) would probably consider this to be a high market share, as several manufacturers produce cars in this segment of the car market. Furthermore, if the market for compact cars was growing rapidly, the business would probably classify its compact cars as "stars".

business practice

Sony's Boston matrix

Figure 9.7 contains a number of extracts from news reports in January 2006 concerning products sold by the electronics business Sony. The Boston matrix can be used to analyse these news reports.

The Walkman products might be seen as "dogs" or "problem children" as Sony's Walkman products have "fallen behind rivals". Digital personal music players are a growing market, but the 25 January article could be referring to CD players as opposed to digital players. Either way, Sony would seem to have a problem in relation to its personal music players, and its future marketing strategies might need to consider how this situation could be reversed. On the other hand, these news reports indicate two possible "stars": LCD televisions and hand-held games consoles (Sony's PSP).

The 26 January report also indicates an interesting alliance between Samsung and Sony, two companies which are normally competitors. This shows that strategies can, at key times, include cooperative agreements when it is clear that both parties will benefit.

Consider the other products mentioned in the reports. Is Sony's movie division a "dog" or a "problem child"? Which of Sony's products – perhaps not mentioned in the articles – might it view as its "cash cow"?

Figure 9.7: Sony news reports

Date	News report
10 January 2006	Better supplies of Sony PSP consoles have helped computer games retailer Game Group to enjoy outstanding sales over the Christmas period. Game said it had secured a much improved supply of the consoles in the days before Christmas, and sales of PSP hardware and software had been strong.
	In 2006, Game said it expected rapid growth in sales of both the Sony PSP and Microsoft Xbox 360, and was also looking forward to the expected launch of the Sony PlayStation 3 and Nintendo Revolution in the second half of the year.
25 January 2006	Japanese electronics firm Sony will stop domestic production of its Walkman products and shift manufacturing abroad as it looks to revive its business.
	Sony said it will halt production at its plant in Saitama, bringing to a close an era that started in 1979. Even though Sony led the way with its personal stereos, it has fallen behind rivals, as firms like Apple focused on producing digital players.
26 January 2006	Electronics giant Sony, whose products include flat-screen televisions and PlayStation games consoles, has reported a surprise jump in third-quarter profits. The results were lifted by sales of the PlayStation Portable games console, offsetting losses at its film division.
	Sony saw strong sales of flat-screen LCD televisions, with Japanese press reports saying it will meet rising demand for the screens by building a new factory in South Korea with another manufacturer, Samsung.
	A lack of blockbuster movie success hit its movie division, where it made a 400 million yen loss, compared with a 18.6 billion yen profit a year earlier.
	Sony is due to launch its latest PlayStation 3 (PS3) games console in the spring, about six months behind Microsoft's rival Xbox 360 player.

Source: BBC News website

assessment practice
Competitive strategies

In this assessment practice, you should use Ansoff's matrix and the Boston matrix to reflect on and develop the marketing strategies you proposed in the exercise at the end of Topic 2.

A Which of Ansoff's competitive strategies apply to the marketing warfare strategies that you outlined in the Topic 2 assessment practice? Justify your answer.

B Carry out research into your business's product mix to identify the market growth and market share for each product. You need only estimate these in terms of "high" and "low", as it's unlikely that you will have access to detailed data. If your business sells multiple products, focus on its product lines.

C Present your findings in the form of a Boston matrix diagram. Provide a commentary explaining your choice of stars, cash cows, dogs and problem children.

Choosing a strategy: customer needs and competition

Setting the scene: Primark's strategy

Primark is a fashion retailer and a leading player in the high street. At the end of 2005, it had 123 shops in the UK and had plans to open more UK branches in its bid to become a dominant presence on the high street.

Primark's success is interesting because it came at a time of slow market growth. Rivals such as BHS, Next and Matalan were being squeezed by competition, a slump in consumer confidence and falling growth in clothing sales.

Retail analysts, however, felt that the economic climate in 2005 was perfect for Primark. Although interest rates and utility costs were rising, people still needed to buy clothes. In particular, it was felt that women wanted their fashion fix and Primark was offering a combination of low prices and fashionable clothing.

It takes, on average, just six weeks for a Primark item of clothing to go from concept stage into the shops, irrespective of whether it is a Kate Moss style waistcoat or a Sienna Miller boho style skirt. The volume of turnover also means that Primark can negotiate cheap prices from its manufacturers in China

and Eastern Europe. Primark keeps prices low by working to a smaller profit margin per item than some other high street stores.

Consider what marketing strategies Primark might have used in its efforts to become a leading player in the high street. Why might Primark have to adopt different marketing strategies in order to continue being a leading player?

KEY TERMS

Segmentation by customer characteristics is a means of segmenting the market according to specific characteristics of customers, such as by age or by lifestyle.

Segmentation by benefits is a means of segmenting the market according to the different benefits demanded by customers.

Differential advantage is obtained if a business is able to meet customer needs in a way that is unmatched by its competitors.

Marketing SWOT analysis considers the marketing strengths and weaknesses of a business in order to reflect on its marketing opportunities and threats.

Putting strategies into practice

The rise of Primark illustrates marketing strategy in action. No matter how clever a business might be at thinking about its marketing strategies, these have to be put into practice and executed with precision. Primark would appear to have done this in 2005. Despite the difficult trading environment with a lack of consumer confidence, the business pursued an offensive marketing strategy in an attempt to gain a degree of market dominance. It would appear to have used both market penetration and product development strategies. At the time, Primark was also using a market development strategy by entering the Spanish market. It might also be safely assumed that Primark would regularly review its product mix and sort out the "cash cows" and "stars" from the "problem children" and "dogs".

Recall Figure 9.1 (see page 16). Two of the essential questions any business must ask itself before constructing an effective marketing strategy are:

■ what are the key features of customer and competitor behaviour

■ what are the marketing capabilities of the business?

Successful marketing strategies respond to customer needs, and the strengths and weaknesses of competitors, by making effective use of the business's marketing capabilities. Primark's offensive marketing strategy was successful because it understood customer needs and it had the marketing capabilities to turn this knowledge into a competitive advantage – by producing fashionable clothes at reasonable prices. Primark understood its products and its customers.

Meeting customer needs

Unit 4 in the AS textbook considered the issues businesses need to consider if they are to meet the

Figure 9.8: Methods of market segmentation by customer characteristics

Method	Description	Example
Age groups	The market is segmented according to age. For example, under 13, 13 to under 18, 18 to under 60, 60 and over.	Cinemas will target films at particular age groups, as well as charging different prices and using alternative promotional activities.
Socioeconomic groups	The market is segmented according to the occupational, educational and/or income characteristics of customers. For example, it might be divided into people with professional, skilled, semi-skilled and unskilled occupations.	Sporting and leisure services and goods might be targeted at particular occupational groupings. Statistics indicate that people in professional occupations may participate in walking, swimming, cycling and jogging but are less likely to play darts or football
Lifestyle groups	The market is segmented according to how people live and spend their time; the importance of work, home and community in their lives; their attitudes and beliefs in relation to themselves and others.	Any system of lifestyle, psychological or mixed profile segmentation needs to characterise what it is that's similar about the people in each segment. For example, a common lifestyle grouping is "Dinkie" (or "Dinkys"), standing for double income, no kids. This lifestyle group is likely to respond to aspirational marketing, such as selling a sophisticated lifestyle for busy professionals.
Psychological profiles	The market is segmented according to psychological profiles of attitudes towards consumption. For example, early adopters are consumers who instinctively purchase the latest versions of products.	The ACORN classification system categorises all 1.9 million UK postcodes into different lifestyle and mixed profile segments by "using over 125 demographic statistics within England, Scotland, Wales and Northern Ireland, and 287 lifestyle variables". According to the ACORN website, this makes it a "powerful discriminator, giving a clearer understanding of clients and prospects".
Mixed profiles	The market is segmented according to a complex mix of customer characteristics – ranging across aspects of age, income, occupation, lifestyles and culture. The ACORN system (www.caci.co.uk/acorn) is an example of this type of segmentation.	

needs of their customers. In summary, these issues are:

- who are our customers and should they be segmented
- what does each segment need
- how can we meet the needs of each segment?

Figure 9.8 illustrates some common methods of market segmentation. These methods look at how particular customer characteristics can be used to place customers in different segments. The basic principle is that if people have the same characteristics, they will want similar things. With this knowledge, a business can choose to enter a new market segment, improve the way it meets the needs of a current market segment, or opt to ignore a market segment. In other words, an ability to segment the market allows a business to make informed decisions about its marketing strategies.

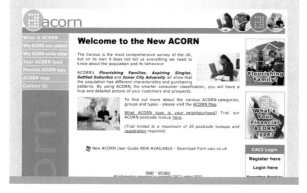

While it is common to segment markets by customer characteristics, it is questionable as to whether it is effective. Customers with similar characteristics may well not want the same things, and changing patterns of behaviour can reduce the predictive power of characteristics such as occupation, location and age. Our society is becoming increasingly fragmented – just because two people are the same age, have similar types of jobs and live in the same area, it does not mean they will have the same outlooks on life and buyer behaviour.

An alternative approach is to segment markets according to customer needs and expectations. Benefit segmentation adopts this method and segments markets according to the benefits customers want from their products. For example, a supermarket could analyse its loyalty card data to identify different benefit segments. For example, it might decide to segment the market according to customers' desire for benefits such as:

- speed of service
- value of products
- range of products
- quality of products
- in-store services.

The supermarket could investigate further how different customers might respond to different benefits through the use of consumer panels (see page 27 of the AS textbook). It could then consider its own internal marketing strengths and weaknesses, and the marketing opportunities and competitor threats it faces. The marketing strategy that results from this analysis might be an offensive one which deliberately focuses on just two of the benefit segments – some customers might be lost, but this could be more than compensated for by attracting customers from competitors. Alternatively, the supermarket might recognise the need for a defensive approach which stresses the ability of the supermarket to meet the needs of a wide range of benefit segments.

It is likely that an analysis of "what customers want" will result in segments that cut across traditional characteristics such as age, occupation and housing type. Paradoxically, this is the biggest problem with benefit segmentation – you can end up identifying segments which might consist of very diverse people who are difficult to target.

In practical terms, market research should be carried out which identifies:

- key characteristics of customers, such as age, occupation, location, family structure and education
- benefits customers want from particular products – for a food product, benefits might include taste, texture, shelf life, quantity versus quality, and ease of preparation.

From these two sets of results, both segmentation by customer characteristics and benefits could be carried out.

Dealing with competition

Being better than the competition is a priority for many businesses. Primark's superiority in 2005 seemed to be based on its ability to provide the latest fashions at a bargain price. This was Primark's differential advantage. A business possesses a differential advantage when its marketing mix meets customers needs in a unique way – that is, it meets customer needs in a way that is not matched by any of its competitors.

Differential advantages can be real or perceived. It might be the reputation of a business rather than its actual performance which sets it above the rest. The promotional activities carried out by a business might be a way in which a differential advantage could be

Figure 9.9: Using SWOT analysis to evaluate marketing strategies

Strengths and weaknesses	Opportunities and threats
Analysing the strengths and weaknesses of the business's product mix in relation to: - the needs of identified market segments - the ways in which competitors are meeting the needs of these market segments - the marketing capabilities of the business.	Using the results of the analysis of the strengths and weaknesses to identify: - threats in terms of competitors developing or possessing a differential advantage, and ways in which these threats could be dealt with through marketing strategy - opportunities in terms of possible offensive or flanking marketing strategies designed to establish a differential advantage.

established. However, it would have to have product features that backed up the promotional messages.

By carrying out a SWOT analysis, a business can identify ways in which a differential advantage might be established. This is an essential component of an effective marketing strategy. As Figure 9.9 shows, a SWOT analysis brings together most of the key issues involved in constructing a marketing strategy (see Figure 9.1, page 16). In the next two topics we will use this framework to carry out and analyse the research needed to inform a marketing strategy.

assessmentpractice

Segmentation and competition

The nature of your marketing strategy partly depends on how your chosen business might segment its market and deal with competition. These tasks are intended to make you think about some of the problems you might face when carrying out research into segmentation and dealing with competition.

Figure 9.10: Setting out data requirements (see Task C)

Data required	How the data might be collected
Age profiles	The business – interview or website Customers – observation or interview/questionnaire
Direct competitors	The business – interview Website searches and Yellow Pages Customers – interview/questionnaire
Strengths and weaknesses of the business's marketing capabilities	The business – observation and interview Customers – interview/questionnaire

A **Outline the data you would need to collect in order to analyse how your business might:**

- **segment its market**
- **deal with competition.**

B **Suggest ways in which you might collect the data identified in Task A.**

C **Present your findings in the form of a research plan using the format shown in Figure 9.10 (three rows have been completed as examples).**

D **Produce a spider diagram of the benefits customers might want from the products sold by your business.**

E **Produce a short questionnaire to find out which of these benefits customers consider important. Trial this questionnaire on a representative sample of 10 customers and assess the suitability of the questions.**

Preparing for market research

Setting the scene: Key Note reports

Key Note has been providing commercially relevant industry analysis reports to businesses, libraries and academia for almost 30 years. Having published almost 1000 reports spanning 30 industry sectors, Key Note boasts one of the most comprehensive databases available to corporations in the UK.

The company claims that it has over 4,000 clients already using its market intelligence and more than 250,000 end users, securing it an "outstanding reputation within the business information marketplace". Figure 9.11 describes four of Key Note's main products. This is how they are advertised on the company's website:

The Key Note Advantage

Our acclaimed range of consumer, financial, industrial, business-to-business and lifestyle titles, combined with a team of professional consultants committed to a superior standard of customer service, will ensure you have the support you need to make informed strategic business decisions.

Use Key Note reports to help maintain the competitive edge needed to succeed in your marketplace. Keep a close eye on competitor activity, pinpoint opportunities, and be prepared for an uncertain market.

Source: www.keynote.co.uk

Examples of these reports are available as free downloads from the Key Note website. Look at a sample Key Note report to assess how it might inform the marketing strategy of a business. Consider to what extent they would be relevant for smaller businesses.

Figure 9.11: Selected Key Note products		
Title	**Description**	**Price**
Key Note Market Reports	Invaluable aids to anyone needing to gain a highly detailed understanding of a specific market for more informed decision-making.	£420
Key Note Market Reports Plus	Concentrating on more dynamic consumer markets, these offer the same incisive market intelligence as Market Reports but include additional chapters and primary research data.	£550
Key Note Market Reviews	Focusing on the bigger picture, Key Note Market Reviews are designed to inform you of developments and opportunities across entire industry sectors.	£680
Key Note Market Assessments	Providing in-depth strategic analysis and including primary research, these premium reports examine the scope, dynamics and shape of UK and European markets, with a focus on financial services, consumer and lifestyle sectors.	£840

Source: Key Note Limited, Field House, 72 Oldfield Road, Hampton, Middlesex, TW12 2HQ, Tel: 020 8481 8750, Fax: 020 8783 0049 www.keynote.co.uk

Market research plans

This topic is designed to help you prepare the market research necessary for an informed marketing strategy. It will help you define research objectives, specify data requirements and decide on research instruments. In other words, it will help you determine the components needed to write a market research plan.

At the outset, it may be worth refamiliarising yourself with the basic differences between primary and secondary research. The concepts of primary and secondary research were introduced Unit 1 in the AS

Research objectives set out the purposes of market research. They should be expressed in terms of specific questions that need to be addressed, such as what is our market share?

Data requirements are the specific data needed to achieve the research objectives. For example, a business would need to find out the total sales in the market if it wanted to compute its market share.

Research instruments are the methods by which data will be collected , such as a questionnaire or a web search.

Sampling frame is a list of all people who might be asked to part in a survey (also referred to as the population). For example, a research organisation might obtain the names and addresses of people living within a town prior to undertaking a survey for the council.

Random samples are made such that every person from the sampling frame has an equal chance of being selected in the sample.

Stratified random samples partition the sampling frame into subgroups and then select at random from these subgroups. For example, a researcher might split the sampling frame into age groups and then select at random from each age group.

Representative sample is a sample of people which is likely to reflect the views of the population (sampling frame).

Sampling bias occurs if the sample has not been selected at random. Any findings are unlikely to represent the views of the population (sampling frame).

---

textbook (see Topic 4, pages 26–31). Key Note reports, for example, are a form of secondary research. They may be a valuable source of data capable of informing a business's marketing research. However, without knowing the particular information a business needs for its marketing strategy, it is impossible to comment on the usefulness of a Key Note report. Many small businesses would need some convincing to spend £420 on a Key Note Market Report. However, for some larger businesses, spending £840 on a Key Note Market Assessment report could be extremely cost-effective.

Exactly how you use the ideas in this topic depends entirely on the business you have chosen to base your assessment around. However, the general framework will apply to every student in your class.

In preparing any market research, three key questions need to be answered.

■ What am I hoping to find out about customers and competitors?
These are the research objectives.

■ What data will I need to collect?
These are the data requirements.

■ How will I collect this information?
These are the research instruments.

Research objectives

As we have discussed in previous topics, market research is necessary to inform a marketing strategy in two key respects. First, market research is needed to help a business understand the key features of buyer behaviour:

■ the characteristics of customers

■ the benefits they seek from the product(s) sold by the business

■ their attitudes towards the product(s) offered by the business and by its competitors.

Second, market research can add to an understanding about the marketing activities of the business and its competitors:

---

stop and think

Recall the work you completed for your assessment practice tasks from Topic 1. You should be able to state:

■ the business you are investigating and its activities

■ the marketing objective(s) your marketing strategy will be based on.

At this stage you might want to change the marketing objectives, but you must have at least one clear marketing objective. Using the Abigail's Restaurant example as a template, define your own set of research objectives. Compare these with the research objectives of other students in your class.

- how the business is currently attempting to meet the needs of its customers

- the business's marketing capabilities

- the ways in which competitors are attempting to meet customer needs.

Each objective needs to be tailored to your own investigation – to the specific circumstances of your business and the overall objectives for your marketing strategy. For example, suppose Abigail's Restaurant has a marketing objective of increasing market share. The panel on this page sets out the specific research objectives that you might set to inform a marketing strategy for this restaurant. The information in bold indicates features specific to this investigation.

These research objectives provide clear guidelines for the next step in preparing for market research. This next step involves setting the data requirements of the market research.

Data requirements

After making a list of research objectives, you need to brainstorm the data required by each objective – that is, the facts and figures you will need to collect in order to answer the questions posed by your research objectives. This is likely to be a mix of quantitative and qualitative data.

For example, the research objectives for Abigail's Restaurant require you to collect:

- quantitative data – prices set by each restaurant

- qualitative data – customer attitudes towards an evening meal.

For quantitative data you will need to specify units, such as the price for a standard two-course evening meal. In this case, you just need to make sure that you collect prices on comparable meals. This is relatively easy to define.

For qualitative data, however, you must take care to define the meaning of the data. For example, it is too vague to simply state collect data on "customer attitudes towards an evening meal" – this needs further definition. You may need to define the experience further, so that you get separate data on customer attitudes to the quality of the food, the prices charged, the quality of service, the atmosphere in the restaurant, etc. You may need to state how attitudes are to be measured, perhaps by asking a sample of customers to rate each feature of the meal in terms of four-point scales with:

1 – Excellent

2 – Good

3 – Satisfactory

4 – Poor

Note that it might be impossible to determine what are the dimensions of "attitudes towards an evening meal" until you have some answers to the research objective addressing the "benefits they seek from an evening meal". In other words, market research

---

Research objectives for Abigail's Restaurant

1 To understand the key features of buyer behaviour:

- the characteristics of customers

- the benefits they seek from an **evening meal at any restaurant**

- their attitudes towards the evening meals offered by:
  - **Abigail's Restaurant**
  - **Peter's Brasserie**
  - **Chez Terry's**

2 To understand the marketing activities of the business and its competitors:

- the current marketing mix of **evening meals** at **Abigail's Restaurant**

- the marketing capabilities of **Abigail's Restaurant**, to include:
  - **the style and quality of food it can offer**
  - **the ability of the business to design and deliver promotional activities or fund external agencies to carry this out**
  - **the extent to which the business could carry out product development**
  - **the funds available for improvements to the exterior of the building or its internal décor**

- the ways in which **Peter's Brasserie** and **Chez Terry's** are attempting to meet customer needs, to include:
  - **the menus offered for evening meals and their prices**
  - **particular features of each restaurant, such as entertainment and décor**
  - **the promotional activities carried out by each restaurant**

sometimes has to take place in stages, with earlier stages helping to determine the data requirements of later stages.

Whenever you come across a data requirement with a definition that seems to depend on another research objective, you must split your research into stages.

s t o p a n d t h i n k

Recall the work you completed for your assessment practice in Topic 4. Here you began to identify data that you needed to collect. Use that work to help you with this task.

Brainstorm the data requirements of the research objectives you completed in the previous Stop and Think exercise. Produce a spider diagram for each objective. Do not be overly concerned about accuracy at the moment; the purpose of the exercise is to begin to define the type of data you need to collect and spot any difficulties in terms of measuring the data.

To what extent do your spider diagrams indicate the need to split your research into different stages?

Research instruments

Once you have an idea of what data you need to collect, you can then think about how this data will be collected. In other words, you can begin to define your research instruments. These research instruments range from direct observation to paying for professional market reports. Some of the research instruments you can use to collect data were briefly described in Unit 1 (see pages 27–8 of your AS textbook).

We can categorise data collection into primary and secondary research methods. Most of the time, secondary sources are likely to be more reliable than primary sources. If you can get access to an up-to-date Key Note report on your business's market, this would be ideal. However, you – and your business – will often not have access to these types of secondary sources, and other sources must be identified.

When choosing how you will collect your data, you must consider whether the research instrument will provide data that is:

- timely – refers to current market conditions and is not several years out of date

- accurate – measured in a way that avoids misinterpretation by the individuals completing the research instrument, and produces unambiguous results

- valid – representative of competitor or customer behaviour and not prone to bias.

Figure 9.12 lists some research instruments and summarises their ability to be accurate and valid. Whether a method is timely simply depends on when the data was collected.

s t o p a n d t h i n k

In the first Stop and Think on this page you are asked to identify your data requirements. Now identify which of these data requirements might be met by carrying out a survey.

There is good advice on constructing surveys available on the internet. For example, look at the material posted by the US research company, Creative Research Systems (www.surveysystem.com/sdesign.htm). Using this advice, construct three survey questions that target some of your data requirements.

Sampling techniques

In surveys, the need for representative samples is crucial to ensure validity. The results of a survey are not likely to be valid if they are based on a biased sample of the population. The most representative sample possible is 100 percent of the population – that is, ask everyone. However, not only is this simply impractical in most cases, you do not need to ask everyone to get reliable results. What you need to do is use a sampling technique that provides a good cross-section of people to survey.

Stage 1 – set up the sampling frame

The sampling frame is simply a list of people you would like to select from. It isn't the final list of people you will survey, just a list of desirable people.

The simplest situation is when you have the possibility of selecting from the entire population – in other words, when you have a list detailing everyone you'd ever want to question. In this case, the sampling

Research instrument	Accuracy	Validity
Surveys For example, a face-to-face questionnaire	Depends on how the individual questions are constructed. Genuine potential for ambiguity and a lack of accuracy, especially if these are online or postal surveys. In general, closed questions – selecting from options – should be used.	Depends on the sample size – the numbers that completed the survey – and whether they were representative of the market as a whole. To avoid bias, a reasonably large representative sample of the population should be used. This can be expensive to define and carry out.
Observations For example, in-store observation of buyer behaviour	Relies on the observer accurately recording the behaviour of customers. In addition, the observer could alter customer behaviour if he or she is obtrusive.	Clear potential for bias to be introduced – the observer must record objective events and not be asked to interpret the behaviour of customers. Also depends on when and where the observations take place. Repeated observations at different times and, possibly, different locations required to avoid bias.
Consumer panels For example, a small cross-section of consumers discussing the benefits of a new product	Relies on the skill of the interviewer and the interview questions and/or scenarios presented to the panel. The interviewer can clarify questions and ensure accurate responses.	The selection of the consumer panel is crucial. If one or more members of the panel consciously or subconsciously distort outcomes, then the results will be biased. However, if the panel is representative of the target market and the panel members do not interact in ways which distort outcomes, it will produce reasonably valid results.
Government statistics and reports For example, *Social Trends*	Likely to be accurate but often data is at least one year old. Provides an idea of general trends but needs to be followed up with more in-depth primary research or purchase of commercial research reports.	This is likely to be as valid as the sampling methods used to obtain the data. The selection of people and businesses that are questioned in government surveys needs to be a representative sample of the population.
Media reports For example, BBC News website	Can provide specific insights into buyer and competitor behaviour. However, the accuracy of reporting must often be questioned, and it is important to seek additional articles not based on the initial report. This is often a problem with the internet news sites.	Possibility of bias is very strong, and this research instrument must not be used on its own. As a method of investigating trends and opinions it has some validity.
Commercial research reports For example, Key Note Market Review	Yes, as the reputation of the business producing the results depends on accuracy. This is precisely why the best research companies charge so much for their reports. In addition, the data is likely to be as timely as is possible considering that wide-ranging research usually needs to take place.	Yes, as the reputation of commercial research organisations similarly depends on validity. If a research company produced reports with invalid data, it would soon lose its customers.
Internal business data For example, customer records	Depends on the methods of data collection used by the business. Potentially a source of accurate data. However, a business's records may not be comprehensive, and some useful data might not be collected at all.	In terms of the business's customers, this is likely to be an extremely valid source of data. However, this will not capture the opinions of consumers who are not customers of the business.

frame is that list. This might be the case if you wanted to carry out a survey of Year 13 students in your school. It should be possible to obtain a list of student names from the head of Year 13.

However the situation is much more difficult when you do not have a list of everyone you'd ever want to question. This is where bias begins to creep in! How do you know who you should be sampling? For example, who would be in the sampling frame of the current and potential customers of a local pub? How could this list be created without leaving out some current or potential customers?

Stage 2 – select from the sampling frame

Once you have the sampling frame – the list of people who should have the chance of being surveyed – you then need to select a sample of people. You don't need to ask everyone on the list, just a representative sample from that list.

If you think everyone on the list has similar characteristics, then you will obtain a representative sample by simply selecting names at random. For example, you could put all the names in a hat, or some kind of lottery machine, and pick names at random. Everyone on the list has an equal chance of being selected. You could use a computer to do this, but note that even computers don't select at random: computer-generated random numbers are actually "pseudo" random numbers – seemingly random, but a pattern does exist.

If people in the sampling frame do not have the same characteristics – if, for example, you expect people of different age or occupational groups to have different opinions about the products and the businesses you are researching – then you should stratify the list. This involves dividing the list into subgroups defined by these differentiating characteristics. For example, you might divide a list of potential customers into subgroups defined by age groups. You then build up your overall sample by taking a random sample from each subgroup. The number you select (randomly) from each subgroup would depend on its relative size. If, for example, 50 per cent of the sampling frame are aged between 16 to 18, then 50 per cent of your random sample should come from this subgroup. This way you will get a representative sample.

How many people should I sample?

Given a reasonably large and representative sampling frame, you can receive reliable results with a 10 per cent random sample. The exact size of the sample depends on how confident you want to be in your results and the size of the sampling frame. As the sampling frame increases in size, you need to sample a smaller percentage of the population. If you want to increase the confidence in your results – to reduce the chance of being wrong – you need to sample a higher percentage. Again, Creative Research Systems can assist here: visit this page on the company's website (www.surveysystem.com/sscalc.htm) to see how the numbers work.

Validating sample data

Sampling is a difficult activity. Even professional organisations get it wrong from time to time: for example, some have failed to forecast the results of general elections from their exits polls. If the sampling frame is biased, it doesn't matter how many people you sample – you could sample everybody on the sampling frame and the results would still be biased.

The harsh reality is that your own primary research could be based on a biased sampling frame. It is best therefore to recognise this fact, and appreciate the importance of gathering secondary data – from the business, for example – which might help to validate your results.

stop and think

Explain how you might establish a representative sampling frame – the list of people you select random samples from – in each of these scenarios:

- a survey on healthy eating, targeting children of primary school age in your local area

- a survey on which forms of entertainment might be introduced in a pub, targeting actual and potential customers in the immediate area

- a survey on charitable giving, carried out by a group of charities, targeting adults living in the south-east of England.

In each case describe how the sampling frame might be stratified. Justify your answers.

assessment practice
A market research plan

In this assessment practice, you need to produce a research plan which will help you to collect all the primary and secondary data required to inform your marketing strategy. This is a very important exercise. You should keep a record of all work you carry out in this assessment practice as it will form part of the appendices to your marketing strategy.

You should seek advice from your teacher(s) whenever you come across difficult or complex decisions: you will not be penalised for seeking this advice. However, if you produce an ill-considered research plan and/or only partially implement your plan, your marketing strategy will suffer.

Figure 9.13: Constructing a research plan (see Task A)

Research objective	Data requirements	Possible research instruments	Selected research instrument
The benefits people want from an evening in a local pub	A list of benefits from people which I can then group into 5–10 general benefits. I will then use these benefits in a later survey.	1 Survey of current and potential customers – not just those using the pub, but people living in the local area. 2 Interview the owner and/or staff if this is acceptable. 3 Media reports if available – would these be relevant to my local area? 4 Commercial reports – if these can be accessed for free and are relevant to my local area.	Options 1 and 2 might produce some timely and accurate results. Option 2 could be used to check the validity of option 1.

A Using your answers to the Stop and Think exercises in this topic and your responses to previous assessment practices (in Topics 1 to 4), construct a research plan using a table structure similar to Figure 9.13.

B Using the research plan, decide how you will collect your data. Determine your research instruments and provide detailed specifications for any survey format, interview questions, web search criteria, etc. In each case, you must check whether the research instrument can produce timely, accurate and valid results. In particular, check the structure of your survey questions.

C Trial your research instruments. Carry out test runs to ensure that they are capable of collecting your data requirements. Modify any survey or interview questions which are potentially ambiguous or confusing.

D Carry out your market research. Try to reduce bias in your primary research by using representative samples, but recognise and be explicit about the bias that is present.

Analysing market research

Setting the scene: Wealth of the Nation 2005

CACI is an international marketing solutions and information systems business. Its UK division offers a variety of "smart solutions for intelligent marketing and information systems" and provides the ACORN classification system (see page 29).

One of CACI's market research activities is an annual report of incomes within the UK entitled *Wealth of the Nation*. The report analyses household income data gathered across the UK and allows CACI to estimate "gross household income right down to the level of postcode".

Figure 9.14 is a table presented in the summary of the 2005 report, which can be downloaded from CACI's website (www.caci.co.uk). Consider how this type of analysis of household income data might help a UK pensions business to develop a marketing strategy.

Figure 9.14: UK areas with highest percentage households earning more than £100,000

Postcode sector	Location	Total households	Households earning more than £100,000
GU51 1	Fleet	1144	15%
KT19 7	Epsom	608	12%
TN15 9	Sevenoaks	635	12%
E14 2	London	599	11%
WD3 4	Rickmansworth	1413	11%
CR3 7	Caterham	767	11%
SW13 8	London	924	11%
SL9 8	Gerrards Cross	1761	11%
SL9 7	Gerrards Cross	1928	10%
E1W 2	London	2251	10%

Source: Wealth of the Nation 2005

Data analysis

The *Wealth of the Nation* report illustrates how raw data – individual earnings of people living in the UK – can be analysed to produce useful information. It is not sufficient to turn quantitative data into simple tables and bar charts, the data must be grouped and investigated so that patterns can be identified. Qualitative data should also be analysed to gain insights into buyer and competitor behaviour.

Figure 9.14 orders the data by the percentage of households in a postcode area earning more than £100,000 a year. The data would have been grouped by postcode and then analysed according to how many households, in each postcode, earned over

£100,000 a year. This then allowed a subset of data – the "top 10 postcodes in the UK" – to be extracted and displayed as a table. This is potentially useful information. The analysis transformed the data into information.

Analysing market research data, in order to develop a marketing strategy, requires you to:

■ group data to establish patterns of behaviour

■ identify possible segmentation strategies

■ use analytical tools to identify potentially successful marketing strategies.

As in Topic 5, this structure is meant to provide a framework for your own investigation. It is up to you to apply this framework to your own unique business situation. However, it is strongly recommended that you carry out all of your market research before starting this topic.

Grouping data

Your market research will hopefully have generated a wide range of quantitative and qualitative data. At this stage it is very easy to get confused and dispirited. It helps to initially order your findings into basic categories:

■ **customers** – findings that relate to customer opinions, characteristics and behaviour

■ **business** – findings that relate to the marketing activities and capabilities of the business you are investigating

■ **competitors** – findings that relate to the degree of competition and the activities of competitors within the market

■ **other** – any other data you've picked up on the way which doesn't seem to fit neatly into the other three categories.

For each category, you should identify possible ways in which the data can be grouped. This is essential if you are to identify meaning from the data – if you are to turn data into information. Consider, for example, data you have placed into the customer category. Here you should be able to group answers to survey questions according to customer characteristics, such as age group, location, occupation or other aspects such as "number of times I visit the bistro bar each week".

After you have grouped survey responses according to a characteristic, look at the responses to other questions such as "what I want from a visit to a bistro bar". You can then produce tables which cross-reference one set of data with another. From these tables, you can begin to identify possible patterns of behaviour enabling you to make some general predictions.

For example, if you are developing a marketing strategy for a local cinema, with an objective of increasing its market share, you might be able to produce a table of grouped data like Figure 9.15. This table, and others like it, could help you consider the segmentation strategies the local cinema might adopt.

This process of grouping data does not have to be restricted to quantitative data. You can perform a similar task on qualitative data by identifying links. For example, in your competitors category, you might have collected local news reports or observations on rival business's marketing activities. Perhaps you have collected print advertisements from each competitor. You can now look for similarities and differences in the promotional messages and, perhaps, prices and product mixes. You could produce a table to summarise your observations. From this exercise, you could then establish patterns in competitor behaviour and, perhaps, identify which competitor businesses are adopting offensive marketing strategies and which might be adopting flanking or guerrilla strategies.

Identifying possible segmentation strategies

Once you have categorised and grouped your data, and analysed patterns in order to produce information, you are in a position to consider the segmentation strategies your business might use. In Topic 4 we considered several segmentation strategies available to businesses. One of the decisions you will have to make is whether segmentation by

Figure 9.15: Frequency of visits to cinemas in the local area during June 2006

Age group	Did not visit	Once	Twice	Three times or more
15–19 year olds	3	9	15	6
19–23 year olds	8	16	18	15
23–27 year olds	11	12	16	18

characteristics or by benefits is more appropriate. You will only be able to make this decision after analysing the buyer behaviour of the customers you surveyed. You might also have collected some secondary data that will help you take this decision.

Segmenting a market is only appropriate after a number of questions have been satisfactorily answered.

- Is it possible to segment the market?

- Is it potentially worthwhile segmenting the market?

- Could the business exploit the opportunities segmentation might offer?

The key question to ask is whether the analysis of your data reveals a difference in the way groups of consumers behave. Segmentation is only appropriate if you can answer yes to this question. If your analysis of your data does not reveal differences in the way groups of consumers behave, then it is not sensible to recommend a segmentation strategy, and your marketing strategy should be based on targeting the market as a whole. However, if you can perceive patterns in the behaviour of distinct groups of consumers, you should consider recommending segmentation as part of your marketing strategy. The degree to which you strongly recommend this depends on how confident you are in your results. This depends on the accuracy and validity of your research findings.

If you are confident about a particular segmentation strategy – by characteristics or benefits – your next question should be "would it be worthwhile targeting this segment or segments?" The answer to this question depends on the initial marketing objective(s). For example, if the objective is to increase contribution, and you have identified how the market could be segmented by income, then the business might adopt a strategy of targeting higher-income groups. It could adopt this strategy because your research describes the buyer behaviour of higher-income customers, and it allows you to recommended marketing activities which will attract these higher-income buyers. If you can't demonstrate this through your research, then do not recommend segmentation as a strategy.

You then need to consider whether the business has the resources and marketing capabilities to target the market segment(s) in a way which would achieve one or more of the marketing objectives. It is of limited value knowing (or suggesting) marketing activities that will attract the particular market segment, if these are not within the capabilities of the business to

carry out. For example, it is useless to suggest that a local corner shop should advertise on television – it would not have the financial resources to buy any advertising time. You have to convince yourself that the target market can be reached by the business.

stop and think

You should have collected data on the marketing capabilities of your business. Using this data, to what extent do you think your business has the ability to exploit any market segmentation opportunities? Justify your answer.

Do you think any segmentation opportunities exist? Does you customer data indicate this is a possibility?

Analytical tools

Topics 3 and 4 introduced a number of theories which you can use to make sense of your market research findings. These analytical tools will help you to identify possible marketing strategies for your business. You have already considered one aspect of your marketing strategy – segmentation – and these analytical tools should help you consider other aspects:

- Ansoff's matrix (introduced in Topic 3)

- the Boston matrix (introduced in Topic 3)

- marketing SWOT analysis (introduced in topic 4).

Ansoff's matrix

All three main categories of data – customers, business and competitors – can be analysed using Ansoff's matrix. In terms of identifying marketing strategies, Ansoff's matrix suggests four possible routes.

- **Market penetration** – an offensive marketing strategy, with an objective of increasing market share or contribution, which alters price and/or promotional aspects of the marketing mix but does not alter the product mix or attempt to enter new markets (perhaps by altering the place aspect of the marketing mix).

  Analyse your data: see if the market can be contested by your business – are customers dissatisfied with competitor provision, are competitors struggling and does your business have a competitive advantage but has failed to promote this sufficiently? Does your understanding of the market lead you to think that your business could reduce its price but increase overall contribution because demand would increase significantly? Does this strategy fit with the business's marketing objective(s), or is the business attempting to establish a niche market?

■ **Product development** – an offensive marketing strategy but one which also has the potential to be defensive in that it could consolidate the market position of a business. New products are introduced to existing markets. This is likely to be a possible strategy for a number of business situations. However, adding to the product mix can be potentially damaging.

Analyse your data: see if potential gaps in the market exist by comparing the needs of customers against what they are currently being offered by your business and its competitors. If customers are looking for product benefits not met by the products sold by the businesses in the market, perhaps scope exists for product development. However, check your research on the marketing capabilities of your business – would the business be able to successfully introduce and market the new product?

■ **Market development** – the same products are offered to new markets. This could be considered as a flanking strategy with a business making a move out of its existing market. This could be achieved by altering the place and promotion aspects of the marketing mix, such as by selling through mail order or starting an e-commerce operation.

Analyse your data: has your business expressed an interest in selling to new markets? Have you collected any media reports indicating new markets in this product area? Does your business have the marketing capabilities to enter new markets. This can be very expensive and requires specific knowledge of the new market.

■ **Diversification** – a new product in a new market. This could be either the act of a successful business seeking new growth opportunities, or a flanking strategy by a business wishing to exit a market which has become too competitive.

Analyse your data: has your business expressed an interest in growth through diversification or a need to find a niche market? Does your customer and competitor data indicate that the business has no

competitive advantages and that it might struggle to retain customers in the current market? Does your business data indicate that it has the ability to diversify?

stop and think

Are any of Ansoff's strategies appropriate for your marketing strategy? Justify your answer, referring to your market research findings and the business's marketing objectives.

The Boston matrix

You can use the Boston matrix to analyse your customer, business and competitor data. The aim here is to assess the suitability of your business's product mix. This could help you to make decisions concerning the appropriateness of Ansoff's competitive strategies. Analyse your data by placing your business's products into the four possible categories within the Boston matrix.

■ **Stars** – in general these are increasingly popular products which produce a relatively high market share for the business. This could be a key element of any market penetration or development strategy.

Analyse your data: see if your customer data indicates the increasing popularity of the product. Media or commercial reports might provide confirmation. Does the business see the product as a star product? Does your competitor data indicate that rival businesses are struggling with this product – that they might classify it as a problem child?

■ **Cash cows** – products which have steady sales in general and which produce a relatively high market share for the business. In terms of marketing strategy, nothing needs to be done with these cash cows apart from using the revenue they generate to fund any product and market development activities.

Analyse your data: does your business have sufficient "steady earners" to fund any expensive marketing strategies? This is part of the key marketing capabilities question. If your business is short of cash cows, you might want to avoid suggesting any marketing strategies that require significant levels of funding, as this approach could be too risky.

- **Problem children and dogs** – products which detract from the profitability of the business's product mix. Problem children are increasingly popular in the marketplace, but the business is not penetrating the market with its version of the products. Dogs have an overall market which is stagnant, and the business has a low share of this market.

- **Analyse your data:** as part of your marketing strategy, you might suggest a fresh look at the product mix. Does your business, customer and competitor data indicate any products which the business would do well to remove from the product mix? Are resources being wasted on certain product lines?

SWOT analysis

A marketing SWOT analysis will help you to bring together a number of findings so that you can get an overview of the business's marketing strengths and weaknesses. It also allows you to outline possible threats you might have identified from your customer and competitor data. These include ways in which competitors might develop or exploit a differential advantage. On the basis of these strengths, weaknesses and threats, you might identify possible opportunities that your business could exploit.

stop and think

Carry out an initial marketing SWOT analysis using your customer, business and competitor data. This does not need to be detailed at the moment. Given your general understanding of your findings, what are the marketing strengths, weaknesses and threats? In turn, what marketing opportunities and strategies would seem to be available to your business?

assessment practice
Analysing your research

In this assessment practice, you are required to analyse the results of your market research. This analysis will provide you with the evidence needed to develop the marketing strategy for your business.

You should keep a record of all the work you carry out in Tasks A and B of this assessment practice. This will form part of the appendices to your marketing strategy, and it contributes towards part C of this unit's portfolio requirements. Task C forms the introduction to your marketing strategy and meets requirement A of this unit's portfolio requirements

Before you start the tasks you should review all the previous topics and their assessment practices. You should seek advice from your teacher(s) whenever you come across difficult or complex decisions: you will not be penalised for seeking this advice.

A Analyse your market research findings to answer the research objectives you set yourself in Topic 5's assessment practice.

B Use appropriate analytical tools to recommend a number of marketing strategies that your business could adopt to achieve its marketing objectives. This should also include reference to any segmentation strategy and the markets which will be targeted.

C Select the most suitable marketing strategy and produce an executive report which thoroughly explains the marketing strategy, its target market(s), and business aims and marketing objectives. You should use realistic and detailed examples – drawn from your research – to illustrate your report.

Developing a marketing strategy

Setting the scene: the UK coffee bar market

The UK coffee bar market includes well-known brands such as Starbucks and Caffè Nero as well as smaller independent retailers. The market also includes businesses that run coffee bars to complement their other services, such as internet cafes and bookshops.

Figure 9.16 shows one way in which the differences between the various businesses in the coffee bar market can be illustrated. It shows how selected coffee bar businesses have positioned themselves in the market. This positioning map measures two characteristics of each business:

■ the range of coffees offered to customers

■ the extent to which each business focuses on speed of service or a comfortable environment.

Figure 9.16 is taken from the Foundation Degree South West website, a course developed by Bournemouth Media School, part of Bournemouth University and the University of Plymouth. Below the map is an extract of how the course authors have analysed the diagram.

Positioning maps are useful tools both for existing businesses in the market and for any company trying to break into a new market. Can you see how a business entering the UK coffee bar market could use the positioning map to help it develop its marketing strategy? Consider how existing coffee bar businesses, such as Caffè Nero, might use the map.

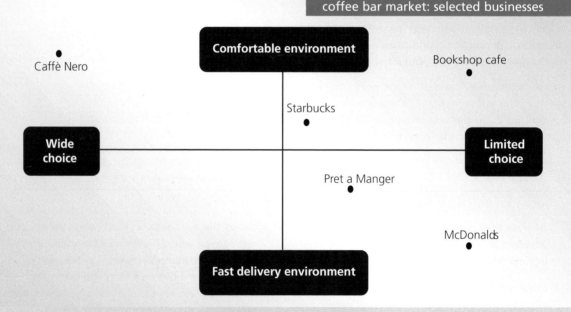

Figure 9.16: Positioning map for the UK coffee bar market: selected businesses

Source: Foundation Degree South West, ©Bournemouth Media School and the University of Plymouth

This positioning map is suggesting that two of the important criteria used by consumers when making judgements in this marketplace are the type of environment created in the premises and the range of coffees on offer. It has then plotted a number of businesses by judging where they would be positioned in a consumer's mind when considering these two criteria. We can see that McDonald's is considered the fastest delivery environment but with very limited choice, whilst Caffè Nero creates a much more relaxing environment in which to choose and consume one of the many different coffees offered. Consumers make their preferences known by deciding which coffee bar to frequent.

Source: media3.bournemouth.ac.uk/marketing/index.html, Richard Scullion, Mike Molesworth and Janice Denegri-Knott

Positioning maps are graphical representations of a business's position in a market according to specific customer benefits. For example, in the market, for fast food, these might be speed of service and quality of food.

Marketing mix is the specific combination of product, price, promotion and place used by a business to implement its marketing strategy.

Repositioning is a strategy that attempts to alter customers' perceptions of a business by modifying aspects of the marketing mix. For example, a business might attempt to move "up-market" by launching a high-quality product line.

Product differentiation is as trategy of modifying the characteristics of a product, or products, in order to meet the needs of particular market segments.

The three Cs are cost, competition and customer value. They help a business determine the prices it charges for its products.

Promotional mix is the particular combinations of promotional activities designed to communicate the benefits of a business's products.

Above-the-line promotional activity is promotion carried out through independent media such as advertising.

Below-the-line promotional activity is promotion carried out by the business itself, such as personal selling.

Distribution channels are the means of distributing a business's products to its consumers.

Marketing tactics

In Topics 5 and 6, we have considered how market research can be planned, executed and analysed. Using the results of market research, a business should be able to identify an appropriate marketing strategy. This will include a segmentation strategy and an initial understanding of the marketing activities that have the potential to meet the needs of the target market or markets. In this topic, we investigate some of the issues faced by businesses when developing a range of marketing activities, and we look at the marketing tactics needed to implement a marketing strategy.

The introduction to this topic illustrates how businesses in the UK coffee bar market can differentiate themselves through offering different levels of benefits, such as speed of service or choice of coffees. Each business's marketing strategy is implemented in practical ways:

■ Caffè Nero provides comfortable leather sofas and a wide variety of coffees

■ McDonald's focuses on speed of service and offers a single coffee product.

Each business has its own combination of marketing activities. Given their marketing objectives and strategy, each business selects particular combinations of product mix, pricing, promotional activities and methods of distribution to suit their target markets. This combination of marketing activities is called the marketing mix.

Before reading further, it is recommended that you review Topics 5 and 6 of Unit 1 (see pages 32–9 in your AS textbook).

The marketing mix

In Unit 1 of the AS textbook you looked at the marketing activities – the four Ps – available to businesses that combine to produce the marketing mix. These are:

■ product

■ price

■ promotion

■ place.

Marketing tactics use the four Ps to turn theory into practice: by mixing the four Ps into specific combinations of marketing activities, a business chooses the tactics that will achieve the objectives of the marketing strategy. At the centre of the marketing mix is the product decision – without an effective product mix, the business has nothing to market. Price, promotion and place support the marketing of the product mix.

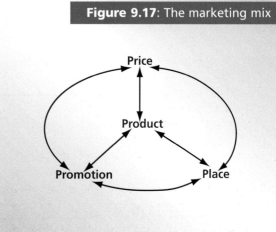

Figure 9.17: The marketing mix

It is through the marketing mix that a business communicates with customers and competitors. Consider, for example, the situation of a market nicher protecting its position when faced with a new entrant into the market. In this situation, you might see the business making extensive use of promotional activities to communicate its differential advantage and, perhaps, adding to its product mix in order to enhance this differential advantage. It might also maintain the prices of its products but, using promotional activities, emphasise how these are a result of the unique products being offered by the business. Perhaps, if the new competitor distributes its products in an alternative way, the market nicher will develop a new channel of distribution.

The individual elements of a marketing mix – the specific characteristics of the four Ps – should support each other. As the marketing mix is communicating the benefits of a customer using a business's product, the messages transmitted by the individual elements of the marketing mix should be consistent. This consistent message will help to establish and maintain, in the minds of customers, an appropriate image of the business. The aim should be that when the name of the business is mentioned, customers will have in mind characteristics and benefits which the business wants to portray.

Perceptual maps

In order to implement a marketing strategy, a business's marketing mix should convey the right image. This image is created by three groups – the business, its customers and its competitors. A business's marketing image is determined by the

46

stop and think

To what extent do you think that these two businesses have a consistent marketing mix? In each case, justify your answer.

■ The Natural Soap Company (www.naturalsoap.co.uk)
A UK soap manufacturer targeting consumers looking for handmade soaps, that positions itself at the "higher end" of a very competitive market.

■ BSkyB (www.sky.com)
The dominant business in the UK subscription and pay-per-view television market.

interaction of these three groups. Customers are the final interpreters, but they base their perceptions on the actions of the business and its competitors.

The perceptions that customers have of the businesses within a market can be illustrated through the use of perceptual maps. For example, the BBC commissioned a survey of viewer attitudes towards the four terrestrial television broadcasters in the UK: the BBC, ITV, Channel 4 and Channel 5. Interviewees were given a list of 15 adjectives, such as impartial, cutting-edge and entertaining, and were then asked to state which descriptions could be applied to the respective four terrestrial television broadcasters. The survey was undertaken by MORI, a specialist market research agency. Figure 9.18 presents the results as a perceptual map. This plots the overall interviewee

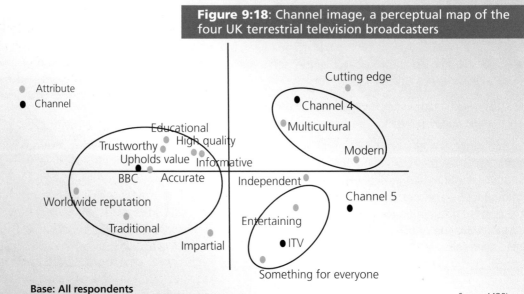

Figure 9:18: Channel image, a perceptual map of the four UK terrestrial television broadcasters

Base: All respondents

Source: MORI

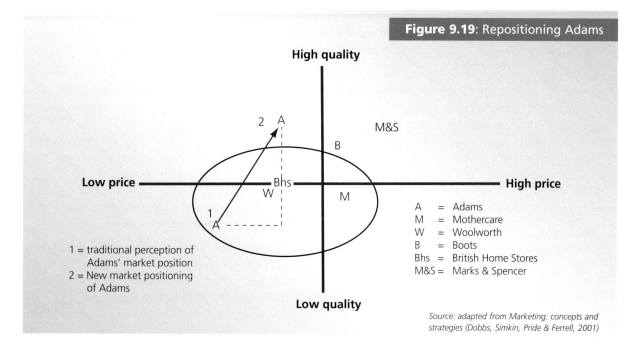

High quality

Low price

2 A

B

M&S

Bhs
W

M

1
A

High price

Low quality

A = Adams
M = Mothercare
W = Woolworth
B = Boots
Bhs = British Home Stores
M&S = Marks & Spencer

1 = traditional perception of
Adams' market position
2 = New market positioning
of Adams

Source: adapted from Marketing: concepts and strategies (Dobbs, Simkin, Pride & Ferrell, 2001)

perception of each channel by showing the relationship between each of the 15 adjectives and the four broadcasters.

So how does the BBC come out of this exercise? The main aim of the BBC is to "inform, educate and entertain", but the BBC Charter Review White Paper contains government proposals to extend the organisation's remit to include:

■ sustaining citizenship and civil society

■ promoting education

■ stimulating creativity

■ reflecting the identity of the UK's nations, regions and communities

■ bringing the world to the UK and the UK to the world

■ building digital Britain – where the BBC will act as a "trusted guide".

The perceptual map shown in Figure 9.18 would seem to indicate that the BBC has, through its marketing mix, created an image capable of achieving these aims and objectives.

Perceptual maps are also referred to as positioning maps because they help to position a business, or its products, in relation to competitors. Figure 9.16 (see page 44) is an example of a positioning map for the UK coffee bar market. A business's marketing mix should be used to position the business in the most appropriate area of the perceptual map. It would seem that, for example, both the BBC and Caffè Nero

are positioned appropriately. Caffè Nero's website states that:

> Our aim is to provide a European-style coffee house experience offering premium espresso-based gourmet coffee, authentic Italian food products and a relaxing atmosphere in every store.

If customers do perceive Caffè Nero as a "comfortable place to consume a wide range of coffees", then this is in line with their stated aim. However, it is worth pointing out that the perceptual map in Figure 9.16 is

(see page 44)

s t o p a n d **t h i n k**

Given your analysis of your own market research that you carried out in Topic 6's assessment practice exercise, how might you use a perceptual or positioning map to compare the image customers have of your business with that of its competitors?

Draw a positioning map showing your assessment of how your business and its main rivals would be judged against two key factors. For example, if you are investigating the fashion retail market, the x-axis might measuring price (high/low) and the y-axis might represent quality (high/low). For the broadband internet providers market, the x-axis could represent reliability and speed of connection, and the y-axis could show price.

47

Topic 7 Developing a marketing strategy

not based on market research (unlike Figure 9.18): it represents the opinions of the authors of the material on the Foundation Degree South West website.

Positioning maps can be used to identify the marketing mix appropriate for a particular marketing strategy. One of the useful things about a positioning map is that it combines all three aspects of the market research you carried out in Topics 5 and 6, bringing together findings about the business, its customers and its competitors. This means that they can be used as a tool to consider how the business could use the marketing mix to follow one of two options.

- **Maintain a favourable position**
  The business is positioned in a way which is consistent with your marketing strategy, and so the marketing mix should be used to consolidate this image of the business.

- **Move the business away from an unfavourable position**
  The marketing strategy would indicate that the business should be positioned differently. The marketing mix should be used to reposition the business by creating an image consistent with your marketing strategy.

Figure 9.19 illustrates how, within the UK market for children's clothing, Adams repositioned itself. Having found itself in an unfavourable position – as far as customer perception was concerned – Adams consciously repositioned itself by modifying its marketing mix. It sought, through a combination of adjusting its price, product, promotion and place, to communicate a more up-market image. In turn, this allowed Adams to generate a higher contribution on each product sold, ensuring the survival and profitability of the business.

Using the marketing mix

A business communicates with its customers through its marketing mix. The marketing mix is the "voice" of the business, and the only opportunity it has to influence the behaviour of customers. Other external forces will impact on the behaviour of customers: the marketing mix of a competitor, the opinions of customers' friends and families, how rapidly the local economy is growing and many other factors completely outside the control of the business.

Each business must carefully select the elements of its marketing mix. This will be done by taking into account the results of market research – similar to the research you carried out in Topics 5 and 6. When

selecting the elements of a consistent marketing mix, a business needs to consider its product differentiation, price decisions, promotional mix and choice of distribution channel.

We shall consider each of these marketing activities in turn below. However, it is important to remember that an appropriate marketing mix must be capable of communicating the central message of the marketing strategy. This message is the product of detailed market research and a careful analysis of the business's market position. As such, in deciding whether and how a particular marketing activity should be used, consider three factors.

- **The ability of the activity to communicate the marketing strategy's central message**
  Example: for a flanking strategy, with a business entering a new market, this might be a promotional activity to announce the arrival of the business and communicate the specific benefits of the business's products.

- **The ability of the activity to support and work in conjunction with the other components of the marketing mix**
  Example: a high price, selected because it reinforces a prestige message, would be consistent with a promotion campaign designed to communicate an exclusive image.

- **The ability of the business to deliver the marketing activity**
  Example: proposing that a business should, as part of a market development strategy, develop an e-commerce website would not be appropriate if implementing this would use most of the resources available for the marketing strategy.

Product differentiation

As Figure 9.20 shows, products are comprised of three aspects – core, augmented and actual:

- **core product is the basic product function** – for example, the core product of an iPod is its ability to play music

- **actual product is the additional features of the product on top of its basic function** – for example, an iPod has the capability of storing music in an electronic format and replaying tracks in an order determined by the user

- **augmented product is the support aspects of the product** – for example, if the plastic screen of an iPod cracks, then the warranty covers its repair.

Each aspect in turn provides benefits for customers.

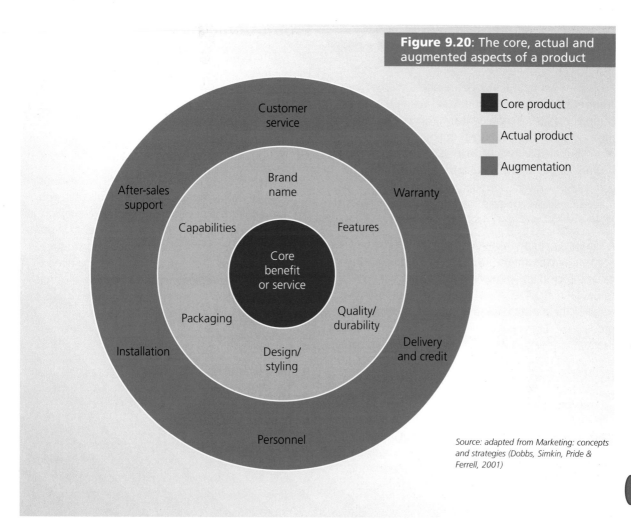

Figure 9.20: The core, actual and augmented aspects of a product

Core product

Actual product

Augmentation

Customer service

After-sales support

Brand name

Warranty

Capabilities

Features

Core benefit or service

Packaging

Quality/ durability

Installation

Design/ styling

Delivery and credit

Personnel

Source: adapted from Marketing: concepts and strategies (Dobbs, Simkin, Pride & Ferrell, 2001)

For example, The Body Shop's core benefits might be viewed in terms of natural products which make the consumer feel "at one" with nature as they are made from ingredients which do not damage the environment or infringe animal rights. The products are created through extensive laboratory research. They are high quality, and they are associated with an internationally known brand name and sold in a range of sizes with the minimum of packaging. The augmented benefits associated with The Body Shop's products include the advice sheets which are available in the shops, the product knowledge of the staff and the recycling of containers.

A business can modify any or all of these aspects in order to differentiate its product so as to meet the needs of a market segment. Whether this is an appropriate action obviously depends on the chosen marketing strategy and associated target markets. It also depends on the ability of the business to carry out product differentiation. It should be remembered that products refers to both goods and services. The business you are investigating might be providing services, and these can also be analysed in terms of their core, actual and augmented components.

stop and think

Consider how your business might be able to differentiate its products by altering (a) the core product, (b) the actual product and (c) the augmented product.

To what extent does your marketing strategy and research findings indicate that product differentiation would be a key component of your suggested marketing mix?

Price decisions

A business's products should be placed at the centre of its marketing mix. However, the price decision is crucial as it conveys a message to customers and also helps to determine the contribution made on each product sold. The price decision, in general, should be based on three forces -- the "three Cs" of cost, competitors and customers.

A business needs to consider the **cost** of the product and, in turn, the unit contribution the business intends to make on the product. As cost increases and/or intended unit contribution increases, the price charged for a product will be forced up.

A business needs to consider the prices charged by **competitors** for similar products. The influence competitors' prices have on it own prices depends on the amount of competition in the market, the position of the business within the market and the marketing strategy of the business. A high degree of competition and the adoption of an offensive marketing strategy would force the price of a product down.

A business needs to consider the value placed on the product by **customers**. To what extent do customers value the product – how high a price are they willing to pay? An increase in customers' perception of the value of the product will tend to force the price of a product up. The link with promotional activities and product differentiation is obvious: if you can construct a "high-value" image, underwritten by a product with significant core, actual and/or augmented product benefits, you can get away with a high price.

The three Cs cover the essential aspects of any marketing strategy – the marketing objectives and capabilities of the business, the marketing activities of competitors and the behaviour of customers. Your own market research should have provided you with a range of information about these three Cs, and this will help you to decide on the price element of the marketing mix.

You should attempt to balance the sometimes opposing forces of the three Cs when selecting prices for your businesses products. However, it's important to remember the tactical role that price plays in implementing your marketing strategy. It is a key weapon in any marketing warfare strategy, be it offensive, flanking, defensive or guerrilla. To continue the warfare analogy, it is also important to recognise that price is possibly the sharpest weapon available to a business and it should be handled with care – get the price right and the strategy will work, get it wrong and the whole strategy will come to nothing.

s t o p a n d t h i n k

To what extent does your market research findings and your chosen marketing strategy make a case for altering the prices of your business's products? Use the three Cs to justify your answer.

Promotional mix

The promotional activities used to communicate the central message are key to any effective marketing mix. If customers are unaware of what the business has to offer, then the product mix and price decisions are irrelevant. A business must ensure that the benefits offered by its product and price combinations are clearly understood by the intended audiences.

Unit 10 provides a systematic approach to developing an effective promotion campaign. For this unit, you are not required to develop a promotion campaign for your marketing strategy. You could, however, choose to develop this element of your marketing strategy in Unit 10. As far as this unit is concerned you need to understand the components and significance of the promotional mix:

- merchandising
- personal selling
- sales promotion
- advertising
- public relations.

These promotional activities were introduced in Unit 1 (see page 37 of the AS textbook) and are covered in greater detail in Topic 3, Unit 10 (see pages 66–71 of this book). You should read these pages now.

A business will select a mixture of these promotional activities so as to communicate with the target market in the most cost-effective way. One decision businesses need to make when selecting promotional activities is whether to use above-the-line or below-the-line methods:

- above-the-line promotional activities is a promotion that is carried out through independent media that enable a firm to reach a wide audience easily, such as advertising and public relations
- below-the-line promotional activities is a promotion over which the firm has direct control, and includes methods of promotion like personal selling, merchandising, and sales promotion.

Using below-the-line methods to communicate directly with the target audience is preferable to above-the-line methods. However, if the message needs to broadcasted to the general public, then above-the-line methods are more appropriate. For example, a business might deliberately use above-the-line methods when implementing an offensive marketing strategy, such as a public relations blitz to announce the opening of a new retail outlet close to a competitor's location.

Choice of distribution channel

The distribution channels available to a business were covered in Unit 1 of the AS textbook (see page 38). Irrespective of the size of the business, place can be an important element of the marketing mix. You might be developing a marketing strategy for a small retail business that currently sells directly to customers through a single outlet. Even in this situation, place may be an important element of your marketing strategy. For example, you might be considering a market development strategy, and this could be achieved by establishing an e-commerce website.

Your business might be a manufacturer which currently distributes its products through wholesalers and retailers. Given an objective of increasing contribution, direct sales could be an additional distribution channel appropriate to your business.

In both these cases, the choice of distribution channels – either in terms of adding or reducing the number and/or length of channels – should be determined by your research findings and marketing strategy. In particular, your findings in relation to the marketing capabilities of the business are crucial – modifying or adding channels of distribution is not something that should be suggested without firm evidence that the expense involved will be more than justified by increased revenues and efficiency savings.

In addition, the choice of distribution channel should support the other elements of the marketing mix. For example, if a niche strategy is adopted, then the ability to precisely target a small market segment would be crucial. Products with considerable actual and augmented benefits, a relatively high price, and supported through the use of below-the-line promotional activities are likely. These three Ps would seem to imply that the business should use a direct sales channel if the marketing mix is to be consistent. However, perhaps the use of a limited number of retail outlets – in locations which the targeted market segment is known to prefer – might be an option. The deciding factor would be the ability of the business to communicate directly with the market segment: if this is not possible, then relying on the expertise of a number of select retail outlets would make sense.

assessment practice
Identifying marketing activities

In this assessment practice, you should identify the possible marketing activities capable of implementing your marketing strategy.

In order to complete this assessment practice, you should have access to all your work from previous assessment practices and from the Stop and Think activities in this topic. As in the previous end-of-topic exercises, you should seek guidance from your teacher(s) as you work through these tasks.

A Using your research findings, produce at least three product positioning maps to illustrate the perceptions customers have of your business and its competitors.

B To what extent do your product positioning maps indicate that the business should reposition itself? Justify your answer with reference to your marketing strategy and its objectives.

C Using your answers to Tasks A and B, and for each element of the marketing mix, outline possible marketing activities for your marketing strategy. At this stage, do not concern yourself with the mix of marketing activities, just identify and describe suitable marketing activities. For example, you might suggest product: adding to the product mix; price: offering price reductions; promotion: using point-of-sale display materials; place: introducing a home delivery service.

Recommending a marketing strategy

Setting the scene: marketing strategies for small businesses

The Chartered Institute of Marketing has a comprehensive website providing support for its members. The "Knowledge Hub" section of its website provides a wide range of marketing intelligence.

This extract is taken from one of the many fact files that can be found within the Knowledge Hub. The fact file provides advice on marketing strategies for small businesses.

| The Chartered Institute of Marketing | About CIM | Knowledge Hub | Professional Development | News and Events | Marketing Shop |

The Chartered Institute of Marketing
Welcome to the world's leading professional marketing organisation

Adopt lower-risk strategies

When you are operating with limited resources, it makes sense to look at lower-risk strategies first.

Avoid moving into new markets too rapidly

Far too many small businesses get carried away with the excitement of new horizons and forget to fully exploit their existing markets before moving on. You may have a very good reason for looking at new markets if your existing market has dried up or has undergone a downturn, but remember, the further you move away from your existing market, the risk and cost of marketing increase. This is because you know far more about your existing market and have far more information upon which to base your decisions.

Check your need to increase your customer base

In many cases, micro-businesses and some small businesses are operating with a customer base that is far too small. This imposes undue risk, because the sales from one customer can account for a substantial proportion of total revenue. Consequently, the loss of a customer could have a major impact on your business, and in some cases result in its demise.

Stimulate referrals

Recommendations and referrals from existing customers form a substantial source of new customers for many small businesses. This has the advantage of being cost-free, but the downside is that over-reliance on word-of-mouth promotion is risky. You can reduce this risk and take control by actively encouraging referrals.

Source: www.cim.co.uk

Consider the reasons why a small business's marketing strategy might be risky. Are these risks always reduced when a business increases its size?

Making choices

In previous topics you have investigated how marketing strategies are constructed. We have seen that an effective marketing strategy is based on:

- SMART marketing objectives

- timely, accurate and valid market research into the business's marketing capabilities and the behaviour of its customers and competitors

- a segmentation strategy that identifies target markets providing the best opportunities for the business to achieve its marketing objectives.

The marketing strategy is put into action through a considered mix of marketing activities. This marketing mix is designed to favourably position the business in relation to its target markets and competitors.

In this final topic, we look at some of the issues faced by businesses when choosing a marketing mix and recommending a marketing strategy.

Assessing market research findings

The advice from the Chartered Institute of Marketing (reproduced in the introduction) indicated one of the problems faced by small businesses when adopting a market development or diversification strategy: does the business know enough about customers in the new market segment?

Topic 5 covered the steps required for effective market research. These are:

- define the research objectives
- identify the data requirements
- design the research instruments.

Each step contains its own "risks", which can reduce the quality of the market research.

Research objectives

A framework was provided in Topic 5 to help you to identify possible objectives for your market research. A list of general objectives was provided (see pages 73–4) and it was stated that "each objective needs to be tailored to your own investigation".

Identifying research objectives can be a difficult task for market research professionals, let alone students following an A-level course in applied business. With the benefit of hindsight, most people can identify mistakes at the research objectives stage: it is often easy to identify gaps in your market research after you have carried it out.

You should make reference to missing research objectives when recommending a marketing strategy. You should make it clear what additional research might be required and the extent to which these gaps

in research increase the risks associated with your recommended strategy. Possible gaps include:

- failing to identify potentially suitable market segments

- underestimating or overestimating the importance of a competitor's marketing activities

- overlooking a key aspect of consumer behaviour or focusing too much on one particular behavioural characteristic.

Each of these gaps could significantly increase the risk associated with your recommended strategy and its marketing mix. The Chartered Institute of Marketing makes this explicit by suggesting that small businesses should be advised to avoid risky strategies such as a niche strategy. By requiring a business to reposition itself in a distinctly different area of a perceptual map – to, in effect, enter the unknown – there is a risk that the strategy could threaten the entire enterprise if it doesn't prove to be successful.

Data requirements

It is possible, indeed likely, that you failed to adequately specify the data required to fulfil the research objective. You may have forgotten to collect some key data or you may have collected the wrong data. The most common errors come from:

- failing to define the meaning of the data – for example, by stating that you will collect data on customers' opinions of the "quality of service" rather than speed of service, friendliness of staff, availability of staff, and so on

- failing to recognise the need to collect some key data – for example, by not recognising that data on competitor promotional activities should be collected.

Omissions in terms of data requirements will reduce the accuracy and validity of your research findings. In turn, this will result in uncertainties and leave you guessing as to what might be the best strategy and marketing mix. This then will increase the risk of the marketing strategy.

As before, you should be clear about these problems and include this risk assessment in your marketing strategy report. This assessment should have some impact on your final choice of marketing mix. For example, when faced with uncertainty, you might decide to minimise possible risks by adopting a more cautious approach to marketing activities. In other words, you might take the view that it is often better to "stick with what you know".

Research instruments

Figure 9.12, and the discussion on sampling techniques in Topic 5 (see pages 35–7), addressed the issues of the accuracy and validity of market research instruments. Review these items now. Considerable uncertainty can be introduced by poor choice, construction and/or use of research instruments. For example, uncertainty can result from:

■ using an unreliable secondary source of data, such as an inaccurate or out-of-date website

■ failing to validate primary research through the use of reliable secondary sources, such as not checking the results of a questionnaire against government or commercial reports

■ poor construction of survey questions, such as vague or compound question structures like "why do you buy your favourite products?"

■ using a biased sampling frame and/or biased sampling from the frame, such as interviewing friends and family.

These errors and omissions will generate uncertainties in your findings that could introduce critical risks into your marketing strategy.

Assessing risks

The marketing environment is often full of uncertainties and risks. If it wasn't, then we would all be able to set up and run successful businesses. New markets, such as those for technology products, can present golden opportunities for people with technical knowledge but little marketing expertise. However, most markets are reasonably mature and are for products that meet everyday needs. Businesses within these markets are successful because they manage the market's uncertainties and risks.

Your marketing strategy, and its mix of associated marketing activities, should take account of uncertainties and risks. This can be done through a risk assessment which isolates key areas of risk and identifies possible actions that need to take place to minimise the cause and/or effects of these risks.

Consider, for example, a marketing strategy based on product development. This might be the result of recommending an offensive strategy for a business which was identified as being a market challenger aiming to increase market share. This is an inherently risky strategy because of the potential uncertainties relating to consumer and competitor behaviour.

How could this risk be minimised? You have already considered the influence and consequences of poorly constructed market research. Either new market research takes place, which reduces uncertainty, or the strategy is reviewed, which reduces the risk associated with the uncertainty. This might result in recommending a market penetration rather than product development strategy. Alternatively, product development is kept but the scale of the operation is reduced by, for example, focusing new development on product lines which are more familiar to the business.

stop and think

Search the internet for stories about bad market research. Type "bad market research" into Google or some other search engine, making sure to include the quotes. Do not restrict your search to UK websites. What factors contributed to the research being assessed as "bad"?

assessment practice
Recommending marketing activities

In this final assessment practice, you should detail the marketing activities required by your marketing strategy.

In order to complete this assessment practice you should have access to all of your work from previous end-of-topic exercises. As in the previous assessment practices, you should seek guidance from your teacher(s) as you work through these tasks.

These tasks contribute to parts B, C and D of this unit's portfolio requirements.

A Assess the timeliness, accuracy and validity of your market research by considering any errors or omissions you might have made regarding the:

- research objectives
- data requirements
- research instruments.

B Using your assessment of your market research, list the possible risks associated with the marketing strategy, and associated segmentation strategy, you chose in Topic 6's assessment practice.

C Assess the significance of the risks you identified in Task B, and suggest how these might be reduced.

D Assess the suitability of the marketing activities identified in Topic 7's assessment practice, taking into consideration:

- your marketing objectives and marketing strategy
- your analysis of your market research
- the reliability of your market research – that is, the extent to which it was timely, accurate and valid.

E Using your assessment of the suitability of the marketing activities, select the marketing activities which will make up a consistent marketing mix capable of implementing your marketing strategy. Justify your choice of marketing activities.

IN THIS UNIT WE INVESTIGATE HOW BUSINESSES select and deliver promotional activities. You will develop an understanding of the relative advantages and disadvantages of different types of promotional activities. This unit is a very practical one, and you are encouraged to think about how promotional activities are used by a range of different businesses.

The assessment for this unit requires you to produce a plan of a promotion campaign, working within a realistic allocated budget, for a new or existing business. This business can be a company, a partnership or a sole trader, or a not-for-profit business (such as a charity or a public sector organisation).

At the end of each topic, there is an assessment practice section. The guidance given in each assessment practice is there to help you build your plan of a promotion campaign as you work through the unit. Your teacher will provide further guidance on how to present your plan of a promotion campaign.

Promotional activities

Setting the scene: Health Promotion Agency

The Health Promotion Agency for Northern Ireland (HPA) is a government organisation. Its main responsibility is to provide leadership and support to people and organisations involved in promoting health in Northern Ireland. Its mission statement is "to make health a top priority for everyone in Northern Ireland".

In November 2004, the HPA launched a promotion campaign to raise awareness about the dangers of passive smoking, the damage caused by indirectly inhaling the smoke produced by other people's cigarettes. The campaign had two phases, with each phase having a separate aim, and targeted different groups involved in this health issue.

Phase 1 ran from November to December 2004. Its aim was to make smokers and non-smokers aware of the health effects of passive smoking and, in turn, to encourage smokers to stop smoking in the company of others or to quit for good. The primary target groups were smokers and parents (both smokers and non-smokers); the secondary target group was the general public.

Phase 2 ran in January and February 2005. Its aim was to encourage workplaces to introduce a no-smoking policy (in the absence of legislation outlawing smoking in public places). The primary target group was employers; the secondary target groups were employees and the general public.

The campaign had several objectives:

- to increase knowledge of the major health effects of passive smoking
- to encourage smokers not to expose others to the damaging health effects of their smoking
- to support employers wishing to implement a no-smoking policy in the workplace
- to encourage non-smokers to be less accepting of passive smoking
- to promote the smokers' helpline service
- to increase the number of smokers seriously considering quitting or making a quit attempt
- to encourage ex-smokers to "stay quit".

The campaign used a range of promotional activities to achieve its objectives, including television advertising, posters, leaflets and information packs. The television advertisements can be viewed on the HPA website.

For more information, visit www.health promotionagency.org.uk/

KEY TERMS

Promotion campaigns are a mix of promotional activities aimed at achieving specific objectives.

Promotional activities include sales promotion, merchandising, personal selling, exhibitions, advertising and public relations.

Target audiences (or target groups) are the subgroups of the population that are the focus of a promotional activity. Target audiences are usually defined by characteristics such as age, sex, income levels and location.

Media are the platforms used to deliver a promotional activity, such as cinema, leaflets and web pages.

Mass media are media which have potential to reach large audiences, such as television and radio.

Promotional activities

Promotion campaigns, such as the one carried out by the Health Promotion Agency of Northern Ireland (see above), consist of a series of carefully chosen and timed promotional activities. In this unit, we will investigate the promotional activities carried out by businesses and how these are used in promotion campaigns.

Promotion is one element of the marketing mix: the four Ps of price, product, promotion and place. The four Ps are covered in Unit 1 (see pages 32–9 of the AS textbook), and you should ensure that you are familiar with the concept before studying this unit. Promotion communicates the benefits of products or actions to potential and current customers. It can be very general, such as an advertising campaign warning people about the dangers of drink driving. However, it can also be very specific, such as a "buy two, get one free" sales promotion.

In the passive smoking campaign, the HPA used television advertising, posters, leaflets and information packs to communicate its message. The promotion campaign was communicating the benefits of stopping smoking by focusing on the harm smokers inflict on the people around them. In general, organisations can draw on a wide range of promotional activities when designing a promotion campaign.

- **Sales promotions** – providing customers with a direct incentive to buy products, such as an offer of a free cinema ticket when purchasing a meal in a fast-food restaurant.

- **Merchandising** – the use and arrangement of in-store display equipment to communicate the benefits of a product and/or present the product in a favourable way, such as product display units in a fashion shop.

- **Personal selling** – personal, face-to-face communication aimed at informing and persuading customers. For example, salespersons in retail outlets are able to give information about products.

- **Exhibitions and trade fairs** – a display of several businesses' products intended to communicate the benefits of products to potential customers. Venues like the National Exhibition Centre in Birmingham and Olympia in London are regularly used for trade fairs.

- **Advertising** – communicating with customers through mass media, such as television, radio and newspapers.

- **Public relations** – raising awareness through obtaining favourable publicity in the media. For example, a retailer opening a new store might arrange a launch event to get coverage in local newspapers.

- **Sponsorship** – improving the image of a business and/or product by funding unrelated activities. For example, many businesses sponsor football teams, allowing the business to put its name or logo on the team's kit and giving it good publicity.

Another key promotional activity is direct marketing. In recent years, this has become an essential part of many businesses promotion campaigns. In direct marketing, a business communicates directly with

stop and think

What promotional activities might a fitness centre use as part of a campaign to encourage 16–19 year olds to become members.

specific customers. The form of communication can vary – from telephone calls to direct mail leaflets – but the intention is to develop a one-to-one relationship between the business and its individual customers.

This leaflet from Sky is a typical example of direct marketing. It contains information about Sky's range of digital television services and the price the company charges for each service. The leaflet also contains contact details for potential customers wishing to subscribe to a service.

The leaflet has the potential to carry out two essential aspects of promotion: informing and persuading. It informs readers about the technical aspects of the product – the channels available, prices charged and equipment required. It attempts to persuade readers to purchase a subscription and does this by using well-known cartoon characters from *The Simpsons* and *Finding Nemo*. Note that the leaflet incorporates a sales promotion technique – a free installation offer – aimed at persuading readers to buy from Sky.

Aims and objectives

All business organisations need objectives. Business objectives define the direction of the organisation and allow it to measure its success. In Unit 1 of the AS textbook, you studied SMART objectives. These are objectives which are specific, measurable, achievable, relevant and time-specific. They are clear objectives, such as to increase sales by 10 per cent in the next six months, or to raise £500,000 in charitable donations within a year.

The Health Promotion Agency of Northern Ireland (HPA) has a general mission statement. This informs people about the organisation's aims, which focus on specific public health issues such as alcohol-related illnesses and the health benefits of physical exercise. Any campaign that the HPA carries out to promote healthier lifestyles has campaign objectives. These are necessary to ensure that its promotion campaigns are focused and capable of achieving their aims.

In this topic, we have used a not-for-profit organisation, the HPA, to illustrate the aims, objectives and activities behind a promotion campaign. The same principles apply to profit-making businesses: whether a business is large or small, profit-motivated or has some other mission, its promotional activities must have clear objectives that help to achieve its business aims and objectives. For example, a corner store might have a business objective to increase the revenue from its film rental service by 20 per cent within six months. Any promotional activities carried out to support this objective must have clearly defined promotional objectives that are capable of assisting in increasing rental revenues over a six-month period. For example, the corner store may use leaflet advertising in the first three months of the campaign with the promotional objective of raising customer awareness of the film rental service.

Figure 10.1 illustrates the type of objectives usually set for promotional activities. The exact objective will depend on the particular role played by the promotional activity in the overall campaign.

All promotion campaigns need to have clear objectives. A campaign might have one or two aims, but it should have several specific objectives that are capable of supporting this aim. This is illustrated by the HPA campaign to raise awareness about the dangers of passive smoking. Each phase of the campaign had clear objectives and a clear target audience.

Promotional activities can be expensive, and it is important to justify their use. An entertaining, professionally produced television advertisement is useless if its intended message is not delivered effectively or is misinterpreted by the target audience. By setting specific objectives for particular promotional activities, it is more likely that their messages will be received and understood.

stop and think

Visit the HPA website (www.health promotionagency.org.uk) and investigate a health campaign other than passive smoking. Identify the aims and objectives of the promotion campaign, and explain the suitability of its associated promotional activities. Why is it important for promotion campaigns to have aims and objectives?

Figure 10.1: Objectives for promotional activities

Objective	Example
Improving customer awareness and knowledge of a product	A full-page advertisement in a Sunday newspaper colour supplement magazine providing information about a new, environmentally friendly car
Improving the image of the business	A public relations press release announcing a £200,000 charitable donation by a large international software manufacturer
Generating or increasing sales	A "50% off" end-of-season sales promotion by a small fashion retailer
Improving customer loyalty to a product or business	An increase in the number of customer service staff employed by a fitness centre
Altering customer perceptions of a product	The use of an interactive visual display unit to communicate the different functions performed by a multimedia home entertainment system

Planning a promotion campaign

The assessment for this unit requires you to produce a plan of a promotion campaign, working within a realistic allocated budget, for a new or existing business. As part of your plan, your are required to explain:

- the main objectives of the promotion campaign
- the range of promotional activities available to the business
- the characteristics of the target customers.

You are required to demonstrate other evidence, but this will do for now! Remember, the assessment practice sections are there to help you gradually build up your portfolio.

A The promotion campaign can be for a new or an existing business. So start by identifying a suitable business. Your teacher might be able to offer suggestions. If you have completed Unit 9, Marketing Strategy, this could be an opportunity to develop the promotional activities element of the marketing strategy.

B Consider the overall aims of the promotion campaign and describe these in short, specific paragraphs. Use the HPA aims for its passive smoking campaign as a guide.

C Make an initial assessment of the objectives which could help to achieve the campaign's aims. Describe these objectives, and explain how they help to achieve the aims of the promotion campaign. You will probably modify these objectives as you develop your plan.

D Consider the range of promotional activities that your chosen business could realistically use. In part, this will depend on the budget allocated to the promotion campaign. Your teacher will help you to set a realistic budget. If you have chosen a new business, make a list of promotional activities and, as you work through the topics in this unit, keep returning to this list to alter your original ideas. If your chosen business is already established, research the range of promotional activities it traditionally uses.

E Describe the types of customers and other stakeholders that will be the focus of the promotion campaign. What is their age, sex, location and socioeconomic profile? Use Unit 9, Marketing Strategy, for guidance (see in particular, Topic 4).

Topic 2 | Budgets and campaign plans

Setting the scene: recycle – the possibilities are endless

Recycle Now is a UK government campaign that aims to increase the percentage of waste recycled by the general public. The advertisements illustrate the many products that can be made from recycled waste, and the campaign slogan is: recycle – the possibilities are endless.

A website (www.recyclenowpartners.org.uk) assists key stakeholders in delivering the campaign. These stakeholders include local authorities, and one section of the website is devoted to helping local government departments budget for and plan Recycle Now campaigns. It offers this advice.

Tips for planning

■ Things take longer than you think. Make sure you have sufficient personnel (in-house and external) to deliver the campaign within your campaign's time frame.

■ Create your main action plan, and develop mini-plans to support each area of activity.

■ Build in contingencies for problems such as sickness, redoing work and unforeseen circumstances.

■ Build in contingencies for promotional activities that can be expanded if further funding becomes available, or reduced should the campaign cost more than anticipated.

■ From the outset involve the right people (in-house and external). Involve marketing professionals from the outset or at least from a very early stage.

Tips for budgeting

■ Be realistic when setting a budget. Communication materials and services are not cheap. Realistic projections are required to ensure an appropriate and successful campaign is developed.

■ Have a flexible strategy that allows areas to be expanded or condensed to allow for a range of financing options.

■ Look at your objectives. Work out which strategy will take you there, which activities need to be completed as part of a strategy, and then cost it up.

■ Seek competitive quotes at all key stages.

Which tip for planning and which tip for budgeting do you think are most important for the success of a local authority's Recycle Now campaign?

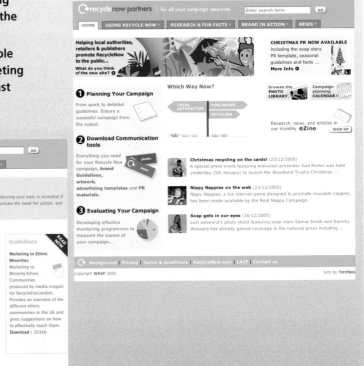

Gantt charts are a diagrammatic method of scheduling tasks to complete an activity.

Budgets

The resources available to a business play a central role in shaping its promotion campaigns. The range and extent of promotional activities available to a business will be shaped by the availability of human, physical and financial resources.

1 Human resources

The advice on the Recycle Now website emphasises the importance of involving the right people when planning the campaign. Assessing the human resources available to a business is an essential step which must be carried out when planning a promotion campaign. Producing and delivering effective promotional activities requires significant skills, such as:

- communications skills, such as the ability to construct compelling messages that favourably alter the behaviour of targeted customers

- design skills, such as the ability to compose attractive page layouts in printed advertisements that grab the attention of targeted customers

- organisation skills, such as the ability to co-ordinate and monitor the publication and delivery of key promotional activities

- technical skills, such as the ability to produce print and IT media efficiently and accurately.

Although these skills might be present within many organisations, they may not be available for immediate use on the campaign as employees will be applying these skills to activities directly related to the business's core purpose. So, when planning a promotion campaign, decisions have to be taken about which parts of the campaign will be carried out in-house and which might be best carried out externally by specialist professionals. For example, the Recycle Now website contains a range of design templates for leaflets and advertisements which local authority staff can download and quickly adapt. In this case, employees can complete the design of the communications in-house at little expense and without needing to bring in specialist design skills. However, it does not follow that communications will be printed in-house, as the authority might not possess the appropriate physical resources.

2 Physical resources

Promotional activities require physical resources such as print and IT equipment, distribution systems and specialist display equipment. In many cases, a business will not have the required specialist physical resources, so either the work will be contracted out to an external supplier or the necessary equipment will need to be purchased. Suppose, for example, that a promotion campaign requires the production of an illustrated product catalogue on DVD. While most businesses have the ability to copy DVDs in small quantities, they will not be able to:

- copy large volumes of DVDs

- produce, to a professional standard, the original images required for the catalogue

- produce the illustrated catalogue using specialist multimedia software

- create attractive packaging at a low unit cost.

Unless the physical resource provides wider benefits within the business, or the promotional activity is ongoing, most businesses will choose to contract out the DVD's design and production. However, before making this decision, a business should review both its physical and human resources to calculate the cost of producing the promotional activity in-house. This provides a benchmark to compare the quotes from external providers, and allows an informed decision to be made after taking into account any quality issues.

3 Financial resources

The budget allocated to any promotion campaign will depend on the financial resources available to the business. If a business's profits are falling, then the budget allocated to promotional activities is often the first to be cut. As the real benefit of promotional activities is often hard to prove, owners and managers would rather cut this cost than lay off employees or look for savings elsewhere in the business.

> **stop**and**think**
>
> One of the aims of your school or college's website is likely to be promotional: it will seek to communicate the benefits and effectiveness of the institution. Find out which individual or company produced and maintains your school or college's website. Do you think the website is an effective promotional activity? How might it be improved, and should this improvement be carried out in-house or externally?

Planning promotion campaigns

Any budget allocated to a promotion campaign has to be fully justified. Specific aims and objectives should be identified and the campaign outlined. The promotion campaign should operate within the allocated budget, allowing a margin for increased costs.

A plan of a promotion campaign should specify:

■ the promotional activities forming the components of the campaign

■ the timing of each promotional activity – when they will be delivered

■ the cost of each promotional activity

■ the objectives each promotional activity is designed to achieve.

Considerable research and analysis must be carried out before a promotion campaign plan can be produced. Later topics in this unit will help you recognise what information needs to be collected, and understand how to make decisions on the choice of promotional activities.

Once the research and analysis has been carried out, and decisions have been made regarding the choice of promotional activities, a Gantt chart can be used to illustrate the timing of the promotional activities (see AS textbook pages 233–4). Gantt charts are a good way to show the activities that make up the promotion campaign, and they can also be used to fine-tune their delivery. In addition, a Gantt chart can be used to monitor the delivery of the promotion campaign by checking off the actual dates for the start and end of each promotional activity against the planned dates.

Figure 10.2 shows a simple Gantt chart, or calendar, used in planning the Rethink Rubbish Lancashire campaign. This Gantt chart, together with many other tips for planning a promotion campaign, is from *Setting Timetables and Budgets*, a document which can be downloaded from the local authorities section of the Recycle Now website (www.recyclenow partners.org.uk.)

The simple Gantt chart helps the organisation to view, at a glance:

■ the range of promotional activities that form part of the campaign

■ the duration of each promotional activity

■ the sequence of the promotional activities

■ the busy and quiet times during the campaign.

The Gantt chart can be used at the planning stage to consider the suitability of the sequence and duration of the promotional activities. Busy times, such as the

Figure 10.2: Rethink Rubbish Lancashire project planning chart

	December 2	9	16	23	30	January 6	13	20	27	February 3	10	17	24
Research	■	■							■	■			
Launch event			■										
Regional launches			■										
Billboard advertising			■	■	■								
Ad-van			■										
Green Santa			■										
Bus advertising						■	■	■	■				
Media partners	■	■	■	■	■	■	■	■	■				
Pantomime	■	■	■	■	■	■	■	■	■				
Roadshows						■	■	■	■				
Patron support			■	■	■	■	■	■	■				
Competitions						■	■	■	■				
Rubbish United		■	■	■	■								
Christmas features			■	■	■								
Other features						■	■	■	■	■	■	■	■

Source: www.recyclenowpartners.org.uk

last week of January, can be anticipated and resources allocated. The logic of the sequencing can be checked to ensure that, for example, roadshows don't occur before the public is generally aware of the campaign.

Simple Gantt charts, of the type in Figure 10.2, can be constructed using a spreadsheet program such as Microsoft Excel. The chart can be developed to include financial information. For example, costs could be added for each row, and total costs of the campaign could then be calculated by inserting a formula.

Setting out Gantt charts in a spreadsheet allows planners a simple method of undertaking what-if calculations. For example, if the campaign is coming in over budget, you might reduce the duration of one or more promotional activities, which would then be reflected by reducing the costs of those activities. A number of what-if calculations could be carried out until the final cost of the campaign came within the allocated budget. In this way, planners can quickly look at the financial implications of different combinations and durations of promotional activities, and hopefully arrive at the best mix and sequencing of activities that can be achieved within the budget.

stop and think

Use a spreadsheet to create the Gantt chart illustrated in Fig 10.2. Add a column at the end of the chart to show the cost of each promotional activity. Insert a formula to show the total cost of the promotion campaign (the sum of the costs of all the activities). How might you alter this spreadsheet for your own promotion campaign? What other formulas and data might you add to the spreadsheet?

assessment practice
Resource planning

To produce your plan of a promotion campaign you will need to analyse the resources available to your business.

A Research the key human, physical and financial resources available to your business. For example, do any employees have skills relevant to the design, production and/or delivery of promotional activities; what relevant technology does the business posses; what budget is the business likely to be able to allocate, and could this be increased?

B Using your findings from task A, analyse how the resources available to the business might shape your promotion campaign. As you learn more about the range of promotional activities available to the business you may want to revisit this analysis.

C Produce a spider diagram illustrating the resources available to your business which also shows the impact this could have on your promotional activities.

Setting the scene: store layout

Successful retailers understand the importance of store layout. Figure 10.3 indicates the typical routes taken by shoppers in convenience stores.

Figure 10.3: Store layout and customer routes

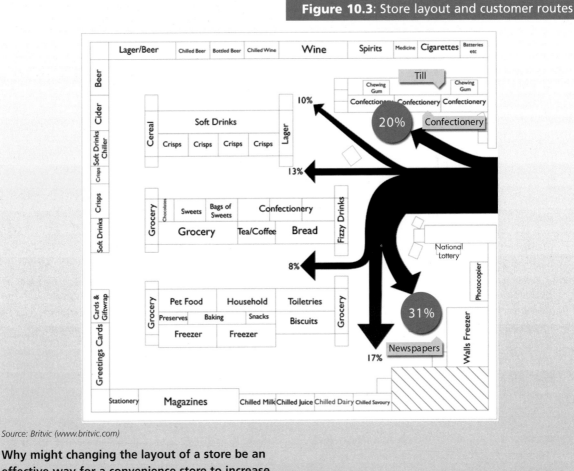

Source: Britvic (www.britvic.com)

Why might changing the layout of a store be an effective way for a convenience store to increase its sales revenue?

Types of promotional activities

Topic 1 introduced you to the range of promotional activities generally available to businesses. In this topic, we consider in greater depth the ways in which these promotional activities can help businesses achieve the promotion campaign objectives.

1 Sales promotion

Sales promotion acts directly on buyer behaviour by offering a financial incentive for the buyer to purchase the product. It is a simple and direct form of promotion. Figure 10.4 illustrates the variety of incentives that can be offered to customers.

In itself, a sales promotion is unlikely to turn a disinterested individual into a customer. However, in competitive markets in which several businesses are apparently offering very similar products, the effective use of sales promotion techniques can help to "win" a sale.

One of the most common forms of sales promotion is the use of coupons and money refunds. These, typically, offer discounts on the promoted product

Sales promotions are a direct financial inducement or promise of added value that encourage the purchase of a product. Examples include the use of coupons or free samples.

Point-of-sale materials are any physical items used to enhance the display of a product within a retail outlet or to provide additional information about the product.

Merchandising is the use of the retail environment – including the arrangement of stores and the use of point-of-sale material – to communicate the product benefits and present products in a favourable way.

Personal selling is the process of informing customers and persuading them to purchase products through personal communication.

Exhibitions showcase the products of several businesses. They usually cover a specific type of products – for example, there are separate trade fairs for cars, holidays and office equipment – allowing potential customers to compare a range of products at a single event.

Advertising is a paid form of non-personal communication transmitted through mass media.

Sponsorship involves the support of an event, individual or organisation by a business in return for the prominent display of the business's name or brands

Public relations (PR) is a co-ordinated effort to ensure that key stakeholders, such as customers, employees and suppliers, adopt and maintain a positive view of a business.

Figure 10.4: Sales promotion incentives and techniques

when presented at a retail outlet. Coupons are distributed in a variety of ways and may appear as:

- inserts placed in newspapers and magazines – known as free-standing inserts or FSIs

- direct mail and leaflet drops

- printed advertisements

- point-of-sale material in retail outlets.

Price-off offers are an obvious direct incentive to purchase. However, this type of sales promotion should be used with care as the image of the product might be damaged if it appears to be constantly on offer. In addition, a business may simply be losing sales revenue if it is offering discounts to customers

that might have purchased the product without the coupon.

Sales promotion techniques are also used to persuade retailers to purchase a supplier's products. In general, free merchandise and point-of-sale materials are often used to convince a retailer to take on a particular product or product range. For example, a supplier might offer the retailer a 10 per cent discount (or an attractive in-store stand to display the products), if the retailer agrees to stock the supplier's products.

2 Merchandising

In the context of this unit, merchandising refers to the techniques used by manufacturers, distributors and retailers to display products effectively within trade and retail outlets. In its simplest form, merchandising is the shelving used to display products to customers. Both the display units themselves, and the way in which products are displayed within shelves and cabinets, impact on buying behaviour.

Taken to the next level, merchandising covers the use of sophisticated display units and the careful arrangement of the overall layout of a store. "Visual merchandising" is crucial for some products. In fashion retailing, for example, the techniques used to display clothes in attractive and engaging ways play a vital role in driving sales.

Store layout is also a key aspect of effective promotion. Identifying the best layout depends on the type of products stocked, the routes taken by customers as they enter and leave the store, and the physical limitations of the store. Altering the layout of a store, and the style of shelving used, can often have dramatic effects on sales.

business practice
retailing bottled water

Even the seemingly simple task of selling bottled water can be enhanced by detailed attention to merchandising. Highland Spring, the UK's leading bottled water supplier, offers this advise to retailers on its corporate website (www.highland-spring.com).

Retailers can enhance their merchandising by ensuring that they stock the leading brands that are recognised and trusted by consumers. A common mistake is to stock too many brands, which can confuse consumers. Some tips include:

- *place key brands at eye or grab levels*

- *ensure shelf edge labels are visible and show current price and special offers*

- *use vertical brand blocking to create impact and ease shopping*

- *separate still, sparkling, functional and flavoured products so consumers can quickly identify their preferred product type*

- *make effective use of point-of-sale materials and signposting to communicate key messages and generate sales*

- *site bottled water alongside other healthy products to drive sales*

- *place kids' bottled water alongside the adult range.*

What do you think is the reasoning behind each of the display tips given by Highland Spring?

3 Personal selling

Personal selling is a highly individual activity. Individual salespersons differ in their approach to customers, and individual customers seldom agree on the attributes of a good salesperson.

Personal selling has much to do with psychology. A good salesperson will approach and communicate with each customer differently, depending on how the salesperson assesses that the customer perceives themselves. If you have ever attempted to chat up someone you are attracted to, you will appreciate the art and difficulty of personal selling.

Most sales staff go through several distinct steps when attempting to make a sale.

1 **Prospecting and evaluating**, through identifying potential customers and selecting likely buyers.

2 **Preparing** prior to the sales pitch, by identifying the individual needs of customers and some of the key issues which will determine whether they purchase or walk away.

3 **Approaching the customer**. The key issue here is how to make the first contact with the customer. The hardest approach is the "cold call": here the salesperson contacts a potential customer without any prior invitation or approach. In many sales situations, a cold call must be made. However, it is sensible to use this initial contact to gather information rather than to attempt a sale. Getting success at this stage – through gaining some interest from the potential customer rather than a direct rebuff – is one of the key attributes of a good salesperson.

4 **Making a presentation**. A sales presentation or a product demonstration allows a salesperson to sell the benefits of the product to the customer. However, as with any effective communication, this stage is about listening as well as talking. The customer should be drawn into the transaction, so that he or she feels that purchasing the product is a sensible and/or desirable decision.

5 **Overcoming objections**. Although effective presentation is essential, the ability to overcome customer objections to purchasing the product is another sign of an effective salesperson. This requires understanding the personality type of the prospective buyer – different approaches will be required depending on the attitude of the buyer. For example, in some cases the "brutally honest" approach will work, while in other cases the salesperson will have to flatter the buyer.

6 **Closing**, by getting the prospective customer to purchase the product. Some salespersons are adept at steps 1 to 5 but find this stage challenging. Sometimes the salesperson simply fails to recognise when the customer is ready to buy the product. An effective salesperson will gently question the customer throughout steps 3 to 5 in order to gauge how close the customer is to purchasing. In some cases all that is necessary is to complete step 3: the customer wants to buy the product and was just waiting to be approached!

7 **Follow-up**. This is not necessary in all situations. However, if the product is expensive and, perhaps, requires delivery and installation, then a follow-up call could help to ensure repeat business in the future. If no call is made, a customer may assume that the salesperson's interest only extends as far as making a sale, and this is unlikely to encourage repeat business. After all, effective personal selling is about building relationships with customers.

4 Exhibitions

Effective personal selling relies on the ability of a salesperson to communicate the benefits of a product to a potential customer. Allowing the customer to view and try out the product can facilitate the sales process. If the product is attractively presented, then it is conceivable that it could sell itself. Exhibitions provide an opportunity for customers to interact with a range of products. Coupled with personal selling, taking space at a trade exhibition can be an effective way for a business to promote its products and achieve sales.

An exhibition allows a business to add to its database of potential customers. Although potential customers might not commit to a purchase at the exhibition, a salesperson can request permission to take a note of any potential customer's contact details. This will certainly help with step 3 of the personal selling process.

Failure to attend an exhibition can be damaging. If a business's main competitors have set up stalls and display units, brought in their top sales people and presented their latest products, then failing to attend the event will project a poor image. Many businesses selling high-value products find that it is essential to attend the major exhibitions and trade fairs in the UK and mainland Europe. This is seen as contributing to building and maintaining brand awareness. However, each business needs to weigh the cost of attending an exhibition against the benefits gained. Some exhibitions and venues can lose their appeal and, if major competitors begin to withdraw from particular exhibitions, a business should perhaps reconsider its presence.

5 Advertising

Advertising is undoubtedly the main form of promotion that we encounter. Advertising is all around us – on television and radio, in magazines and newspapers, on billboards and bus shelters and, increasingly, through the internet. The primary purpose of advertising is to inform and persuade current or potential customers. Figure 10.5 illustrates some specific uses of advertising.

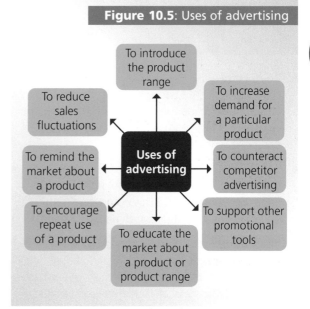

Figure 10.5: Uses of advertising

- To introduce the product range
- To increase demand for a particular product
- To reduce sales fluctuations
- **Uses of advertising**
- To counteract competitor advertising
- To remind the market about a product
- To support other promotional tools
- To encourage repeat use of a product
- To educate the market about a product or product range

Consider the typical structure of a printed advertisement. We'll use as an example a Vodaphone advert for a new generation mobile phone (shown overleaf on page 70).

- **Headline** – this is the first text noticed by the reader. The headline needs to convey the main message as quickly as possible. Most readers will ignore the rest of the advert unless the headline appeals to them. Vodafone's headline – Video calling, Live it – aims to grab readers' attention.

Video calling. Live it.

- **Body copy** – the main message of the advertisement. The body copy might attempt to inform or persuade the reader. Here the body copy ends by suggesting an action – to visit the Vodafone website.

- **Signature** – a recognisable logo or text identifying the business. The signature should be distinctive and easily recognisable. This advert carries the Vodafone logo and the brand name – "live!"

- **Illustration** – the visual elements of the advertisement. This could provide additional detail about the product or act as an emotive, persuasive element of the message. Vodafone's advert has both a picture of the product and also an emotive picture of someone using the product.

6 Sponsorship and public relations

One of the purposes of promotion is to raise a business's profile – to increase awareness and create a positive image of the business and its products. Sponsorship and public relations are often used for this purpose.

Sponsorship can be in the form of a financial grant, such as a £1000 donation given to a local performing arts group in return for some acknowledgement in the art group's publicity or programmes. It can also be in the form of other types of material support, such as providing free sports equipment to a school or community centre. Many entertainment events now receive sponsorship in some form. In particular, important artistic and sporting events are often sponsored by major corporations.

Figure 10.6 shows the total financial value of sports sponsorship by corporations and indicates the number of businesses that now provide sponsorship. The table indicates that the value of sports sponsorship is increasing, but the number of corporations carrying out this sponsorship has declined from a peak in 1999. Sports sponsorship tends to be dominated by companies in a relatively small number of sectors. The main sponsors (by number of involvements) are banks and insurance companies, although hotel and travel companies, sports goods firms, car manufacturers and beer companies also have a substantial presence.

On a smaller scale, many sole traders, partnerships and small private limited companies provide sponsorship of some form. Combined with public relations, sponsorship can raise the profile of a business and establish favourable connections between a business and the sponsored event or activity.

Public relations activities make use of the mass media to get publicity and to communicate positive news stories about the business's activities. Public relations activities which are single events are referred to as PR events. Sustained activities, combining several events over a period of time, are referred to as

Year	1997	1998	1999	2000	2001	2002	2003
Expenditure (£ millions)	322	353	377	401	421	429	411
Number of sponsors	995	969	1172	859	698	656	516

Figure 10.6: Sports sponsorship

Source: Marketing Pocket Book 2005

PR campaigns. A business carrying out a PR event or running a PR campaign will aim to get publicity in various ways, including by:

- holding press conferences

- getting feature articles about the business or its products in newspapers and magazines

- securing product endorsements by key stakeholders

- issuing press notices that get widely noted and/or quoted

- getting captioned photographs of the business, its staff or its products in the media.

assessment practice
Developing your mix of promotional activities

The assessment practice in Topic 1 asked you to consider the range of promotional activities that your chosen business could use. What other promotional activities do you think your business could *realistically* use? In order to complete this activity you need to carry out some additional research.

A Find out how businesses similar to your chosen business use any of the promotional activities covered by this topic. Collect examples of these activities and describe their features.

B Research your chosen business's use of promotional activities in more detail. For example, consider the role of personal selling and, if possible, interview a salesperson to establish some of the challenges your business faces when selling products to potential customers. Is merchandising a key promotional activity? Is store layout a significant feature? Try to cover all six promotional activities.

C If your chosen business is a new business, consider how it might, for example, use personal selling by explaining some of the issues you think its salespersons could face. Again, try to consider all six promotional activities.

Communicating with target customers

Setting the scene: McDonald's Salads Plus

The BBC News online magazine has a regular Ad Breakdown feature which reviews advertising campaigns, identifying key features of advertisements and analysing the thinking behind them. Here are extracts of its review of McDonald's 2004 campaign for its Salads Plus range.

The brief: Attract people who would never eat a Big Mac and large fries.

What's going on: After a rundown of the menu, including Caesar salads, Quorn, yoghurt, "or even a crunchy apple", the voiceover says: "These girls are also new in McDonald's. Impatient Sophie, sensible Charlotte, and ... Joanna, who's always late! New food – new people, Salads Plus."

Reasons: Recently the company recorded the first loss in its history, possibly due to a consumer trend towards healthier diets. So salads were introduced, designed to be "contemporary and relevant", ideal for appealing to "ladies who lunch", and to mums taking their children for a Happy Meal. The tactic seems to be working. In April 2004 the company reported a 56 per cent increase in first quarter profits – in spite of newspaper reports that a crispy chicken Caesar salad has more calories (when served with dressing and croutons) than a Big Mac.

Media: Initially a television campaign, McDonald's is now focusing its efforts on putting these adverts in women's magazines, on websites and on the radio. One of the advertisements, placed in a women's health magazine, reads: "Aromatherapist Anna is typical of the new breed of customer attracted to McDonald's. Anna hates football, but loves Thierry Henry. She hates alcohol but loves bars ... she hates her job but loves her boss."

Source: adapted from BBC News website, 19 May 2004

Effective communication

Effective communication occurs when a message being sent is understood by the person receiving it. The receiver will also know how and when to respond to the message. Figure 10.7 illustrates the key elements of communication.

As Figure 10.7 shows, any communication can be broken down into several distinct components.

- **Sender** – the individual, group or organisation wanting to communicate ideas about the product.

- **Message** – the use of text, images, sounds, etc. to convey ideas and information about the product.

- **Medium** – the platform used to deliver the message, such as television, radio, magazines, the internet and face-to-face communication.

- **Receiver** – the individual, group or organisation the message is intended for. The receiver interprets the message and attempts to understand its meaning.

KEY TERMS

Feedback is the response to a message. Feedback can use a variety of different media or may be absent if the message is not understood or does not interest the person receiving it. It may take the form of an action, such as purchasing a product.

Noise is anything that gets in the way of the receiver understanding the message, such as conflicting information or an inability to believe the message.

Buyer behaviour describes the way individuals make purchasing decisions. Buyer behaviour is affected by a complex range of influences. These can be grouped under three headings: social, psychological and personal influences.

- **Feedback** – the receiver's response to the message. This could be made using a variety of different media or might simply be an action (including ignoring the message).

- **Noise** – anything that gets in the way of the receiver understanding the sender's true message.

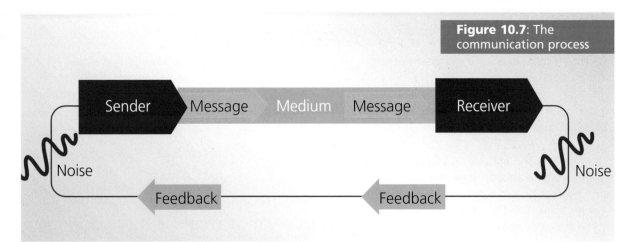

Figure 10.7: The communication process

Sender → Message → Medium → Message → Receiver

Noise

Feedback ← Feedback

Let's see how this communication model applies in a real situation. Alpro manufactures soya drinks, desserts and dairy-free alternatives to single cream and yoghurts. This advertisement for Alpro soya™ appeared in the June 2004 issue of the *Waitrose Food Illustrated* magazine.

Look at the communication elements in Alpro's advertisement.

- **Sender** – Alpro, which wants to communicate the benefits of its soya milk drink.

- **Message** – the advertisement uses text and images to communicate the health benefits and versatility of the soya milk.

- **Medium** – the advertisement was placed in a colour magazine published by a major supermarket chain.

- **Receiver** – readers of the supermarket's magazine might interpret the advert as saying that Alpro soya™ is good for your health and can also be used for making fruit smoothies.

- **Feedback** – readers might purchase the product, call the freephone number provided, visit Alpro's website for more information, or ignore the message.

- **Noise** – readers might be uncertain about what soya is or might believe that it is no substitute for traditional dairy products that are essential for good health.

For effective communication to take place, any business needs to ensure that its promotional activities deliver messages which:

- help to achieve business objectives

- target the intended audience

- are capable of being understood by the target audience

- promote positive feedback from the target audience.

Promotional activities that do not consider the key elements of the communication process are likely to be ineffective. An advertisement might be entertaining and amusing, but it will be ineffective if it attracts the wrong target audience or fails to promote positive feedback.

stop and think

Which target audience do you think the Alpro advertisement is aimed at? Do you think the Alpro soya™ advertisement has the potential to communicate effectively with its target audience?

Look back at the McDonald's Salad Plus campaign (see above). How is McDonald's communicating with its target audience? What assumptions is McDonald's making about the motivations of its target audience?

Buyer behaviour

Promotional tools are designed to communicate effectively by providing information to potential customers. In addition, they attempt to affect buyer behaviour by:

- creating and raising awareness
- creating, enhancing and/or changing the product's image.

In both cases, the focus is on perception. The promotional campaign aims to shape customers' perceptions of a business and its products. In other words, promotional tools are being used to influence the purchasing decisions of consumers by creating a favourable view of a business and its products.

Making purchasing decisions is a complex process. Figure 10.8 illustrates the three main influences on buyer behaviour. It indicates that the decision to purchase a product can be a very complex one, especially if the product is expensive (such as a house) or of significant interest to a consumer (such as buying clothes to wear at a party).

Promotional tools, such as advertising and sales promotion, need to focus on some of the influences listed in Figure 10.8 if buyer behaviour is to be altered. The choice of influence depends on the product being promoted and the audience being targeted.

Sometimes promotional tools will be used in emotive ways, by acting on our feelings and targeting emotions such as fear and happiness. At other times, promotional tools will be used to inform rather than persuade, to provide rational facts and figures rather than appeal to our emotional identity.

A fashion clothing business such as French Connection UK, launching a new range of clothes, would possibly focus on these aspects of buyer behaviour:

- **social** – focus on the attitudes of friends and use advertising showing groups of people with apparently similar age and background characteristics
- **psychological** – communicate the values represented by the range of clothing and to which the buyer might aspire, such as "independent", "edgy" or "casual"
- **personal** – promote key aspects or benefits of the product likely to appeal to the target age group, such as price ranges or the style of the clothing.

When promoting a new range of fashion clothing, it's likely that the social and psychological factors will be most important; psychological factors are likely to be most dominant because fashion is often based an abstract ideas – "style" or "cool" – rather than a functional product.

Figure 10.8: Influences on buyer behaviour

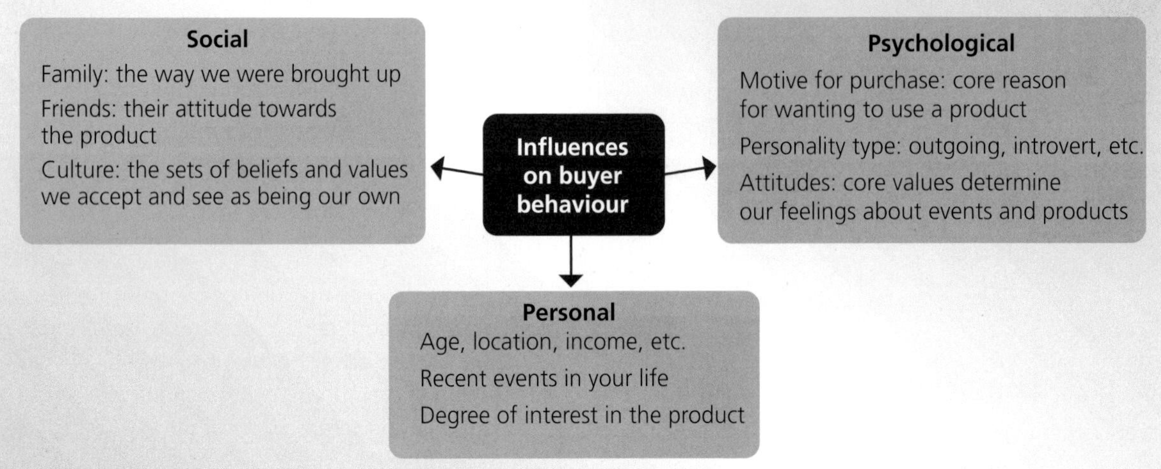
Social
Family: the way we were brought up
Friends: their attitude towards the product
Culture: the sets of beliefs and values we accept and see as being our own
Influences on buyer behaviour
Psychological
Motive for purchase: core reason for wanting to use a product
Personality type: outgoing, introvert, etc.
Attitudes: core values determine our feelings about events and products
Personal
Age, location, income, etc.
Recent events in your life
Degree of interest in the product

Identify which of the influences on buyer behaviour in Figure 10.8 might be most important when using a promotional tool to:

■ encourage students to enter post-16 education in a school or FE college

■ increase the number of chocolate bars sold by a confectionery manufacturer such as Cadbury

■ increase donations to a charity such as Oxfam or Shelter.

assessment practice
Assessing the effectiveness of communication

This assessment practice requires you to consider how you might communicate effectively with your targeted customers.

Using evidence you collected in the previous assessment practice – the examples and illustrations of promotional activities carried out by your chosen business or a similar business – analyse the effectiveness of your business's (proposed or current) communication with its target customers.

A Use Figure 10.7 to identify examples of effective communication and examples of poor communication.

B Interview a small sample of the target customers to gauge their opinion of the business's promotional activities.

C Using your findings from task B, and considering Figures 10.7 and 10.8, produce a single A4 page document summarising what you consider to be the do's and don'ts of communicating effectively with your business's target customers.

Promotional media

Setting the scene: "POW!"

Posters On Wheels (POW) claims to be the UK's mobile billboard advertising specialists. This is how the company sells the benefits of mobile billboards.

Imagine an advertising medium that will attract a customer's eye just by the way it looks. Then imagine coupling this medium with your stunning creative message and running rings around your competitors. That's what mobile advertising is all about – it's a unique way of delivering your message directly to your target market.

POW mobiles' unique and unusual appearance demands attention and each has in-built public address systems and stadium-quality loudspeakers. They are also equipped with bright lights for early morning and night time use.

On the road, the medium is a moving billboard. Stationary, it continues to broadcast your message. The result is media exposure close to 100 per cent of the time

You can find out more about mobile billboards by visiting Posters On Wheels' website at www.postersonwheels.com. Consider why a mobile billboard might be an effective promotional medium. Apart from the cost of hiring the vehicle and driver, what other costs might be involved in producing a mobile billboard?

Production requirements and costs

Decisions about which media to use in a promotion campaign involve balancing several factors. The effectiveness of any particular medium has to be weighed against the costs of using that medium. In this topic, we consider the production requirements, costs, and benefits and limitations of three important groups of promotional media:

- print media

- audiovisual media – film, video, television and radio

- new media – websites, e-mail and mobile phones.

1 Print media

Print media covers a wide range of promotional materials. As Figure 10.9 shows, this includes advertisements in newspapers and magazines, leaflets, brochures and direct mail, and billboards and other outdoor sites.

Production requirements

Posters on Wheels offers an interesting platform for displaying printed media. However, the business does not provide a design service – the customer must supply the poster design in an electronic format, either on disc or uploaded to the Posters on Wheels website. The website (www.postersonwheels.com)

Graphic designers produce artwork using desktop publishing and graphic design programs. Graphic designers require professional training: having a graphic design program on your computer does not make you a graphic designer.

Desktop publishing programs enable graphic designers to lay out a document ready for sending to a professional printer. The most commonly used desktop publishing packages are QuarkXpress and Adobe InDesign.

Graphic design imaging programs enable graphic designers to produce images which can be imported into a desktop publishing program or sent to a printer. Commonly used imaging programs are Adobe Illustrator, Adobe Photoshop and Macromedia Freehand.

Drafts are initial versions of a document. A proof is the finished version of a document. The perfect proof is the final version of the document.

Straplines are phrases, usually at the end of promotional material, that summarise the benefits of the product or help to define the product's image. Straplines often aim to exploit the target audience's psychological reasons for purchasing the product.

Scripts set out the words (including any dialogue) used in audio and moving-image promotional materials. Storyboards outline the sequence of images/events in films and videos.

An audio or moving-image promotion (such as a television advert) moves through several stages during the editing process. A **rough cut** characterises the initial stages; the **final cut** represents the finished product.

Web servers are computers that provide information to users' computers when they browse a business's website. The web server can be located within the business or managed by a specialist web hosting business.

Figure 10.9: Print media

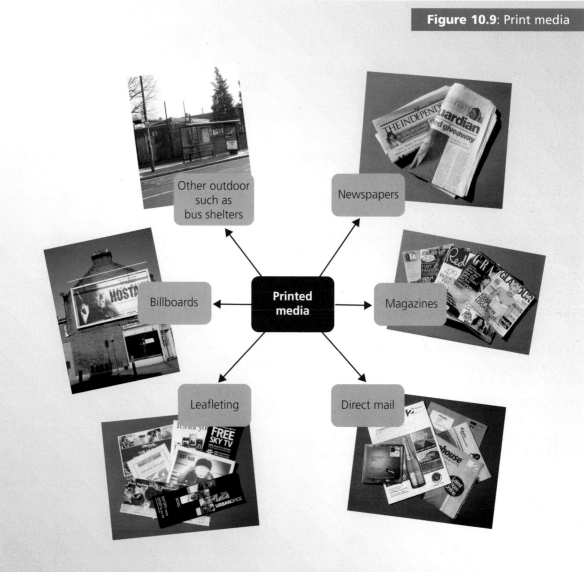

Other outdoor such as bus shelters

Newspapers

Billboards

Printed media

Magazines

Leafleting

Direct mail

details the requirements of any electronic file sent to Posters on Wheels. It also provides templates – blank documents – which can be opened by computer design software such as QuarkXpress and Adobe InDesign.

Any business wishing to produce printed promotional material – whether designing a leaflet, newspaper advertisement or a billboard – needs to follow four steps once it has developed a rough outline or idea for the material.

Step 1 Identify the design requirements of the organisation printing the promotional material. Often work must be submitted using particular software and/or templates; if colour printing is being used, additional design requirements will be stipulated

Step 2 Produce first drafts of the material. This work can be done in-house by the business or can be undertaken by a design agency. A design agency should certainly be used if the business has no staff with graphic design qualifications and experience.

Step 3 Produce a proof version. Check the draft for content accuracy and visual appearance. It might take several drafts before the designers produce an acceptable proof.

Step 4 Approve a perfect proof. Check the initial proof version for errors to produce a perfect proof. It is the responsibility of the business to check the accuracy of the perfect proof before it is printed.

Costs

Print costs depend on several factors. These include:

- the use of colour – black and white is less expensive than full colour, but the price gap has fallen in recent years

- the size of the print run – the larger the print run (the number of copies printed), the cheaper the unit cost (see Figure 10.10 for an example)

- the size of the promotional material – the cost of a 48-sheet billboard is obviously much higher than an A4 leaflet; a full-page advert in a national newspaper is more expensive than a small listing in a local newspaper

- the use of design and/or advertising agencies – costs can be reduced considerably if design work is carried out in-house, although the quality and effectiveness of the finished promotional material is likely to suffer as a consequence.

Figure 10.10: Costs of printing a two-sided, A4, full-colour leaflet		
Print run	**Total cost**	**Unit cost**
1,000	£154	£0.15
5,000	£219	£0.04
10,000	£338	£0.03
50,000	£1,112	£0.02

Note: Trade prices from Imex Print, as at January 2005, based on using lowest weight paper

stop and think

Visit the website of a professional printing business, such as IMEX Print at www.trade-print.com, and look at the production requirements. Find out which design software is accepted, how the files are to be delivered and any issues relating to colour. Why might many businesses choose to use a design agency to develop work for print rather than attempt to produce the material in-house?

stop and think

Newspapers calculate the cost of an advert by the amount of column inches or column centimetres it occupies. If the column centimetre rate is £10, then an advert which is 5 cm in height and 2 columns wide will cost £200 (= 5 x 2 x £10). Visit websites of local and national papers, such as the *Eastern Daily Press* (www.edp24.co.uk) and *The Guardian* (www.guardian.co.uk), and find out their advertising rates. How much more expensive is it to advertise in the national press?

Benefits and limitations

Figure 10.9 illustrates some of the different media available for printed promotional materials. The true cost of printed promotional material is not only determined by the design and printing costs. A business needs to consider the costs of distribution, of sending promotional materials to customers or buying advertising space (in, say, newspapers or on billboards). A vital consideration is the coverage and frequency of the printed promotional material.

Coverage is measured by the proportion of the target audience that views the promotional material; for example, the number of people within the targeted age group who buy a particular magazine compared with the total population in that targeted age group. Frequency is the number of times the promotional material might be viewed; for example, the number of times an advert is carried by a newspaper.

Ideally, to produce a useful cost indicator, the total cost of designing, printing and distributing any promotional material should be divided by the number of people viewing the material. For example, hiring Posters on Wheels to drive around a city centre during peak shopping times might have a high cost, but the coverage and impact could be much greater than distributing leaflets to local housing estates.

The wider the coverage and the greater the frequency, the greater the possible impact of any promotional material. However, wide coverage and high frequency usually come at a price, driving up the total cost of producing and distributing the promotional material. The final choice of print media depends on the business's objectives and the amount of money allocated to the promotion campaign. Figure 10.11 summarises the key benefits and limitations of some print media.

2 Audio and moving images

The most high-profile use of audio and moving images in promotional media is in radio, television and cinema advertising. However, promotional activity in this area isn't limited to paid advertising. Many businesses produce promotional videos and DVDs for direct distribution to customers or for use in installations in retail shops and at exhibitions and trade shows. An increasing number of businesses also use audiovisual elements on their websites.

Production requirements

Promotional campaigns using audio and moving images require careful planning. As with print media, a systematic approach to planning and executing the campaign is essential. This is certainly the case when producing moving-image promotional media, such as television and cinema advertisements.

It requires a variety of demanding skills to produce audio and moving images. In general, therefore, all audio and visual work is likely to be carried out by specialist agencies. However, any organisation commissioning an audiovisual promotional campaign needs to manage and control the process, and it should ensure that these stages are followed.

- A rough outline of the promotion should be produced. This needs to take into account the overall objectives of the campaign. This should help to determine the messages that need to be conveyed, and the characters and events that might be involved.

Figure 10.11: Benefits and limitations of some print media

Print media	Benefits	Limitations
Newspapers	Many people read newspapers. Can define the type of person reading the newspaper by age, income group, etc. Adverts can be placed without too much notice, say one to two weeks. Published daily or weekly.	Discarded very quickly. Limited printing capabilities – quality of graphics can suffer and limit the design of the advertisement.
Magazines	Easy to identify the readership of magazines, especially with specialist publications. Good printing capabilities with high-quality graphics possible. Kept for long periods resulting in repeated exposure.	High initial advertising costs compared to other print media. As most are monthly publications, advance notice needed when placing an advert. Could be kept for too long, resulting in out-of-date promotional messages
Billboards and other outdoor sites	Low cost given repeated viewing. Can be located close to where target market lives, works or travels. Always displaying the message.	Message can't be complicated, as only a few seconds devoted by the reader. Doesn't often gain full attention. Can't easily control who views the message.

- A script (audio) and storyboard (moving image) should be produced. These are used to direct the production of the soundtrack and/or moving image.

- The audio or moving-image piece needs to be recorded and edited. A rough cut, or draft version, is then reviewed by the customer. A final cut is then produced.

- The final cut is stored using an appropriate format such as DVD, web server, digital audio tape, film and video tape.

- The finished product is distributed to appropriate locations, such as particular radio stations, television channels and cinemas, and/or uploaded to websites. Broadcast time slots, if required, should have been booked in advance.

Costs

The cost of producing and broadcasting promotional material using audio and/or moving images depends on factors such as:

- the quality of the final production

- the length of the final production

- the delivery method

- timing and location.

High-quality radio, television and cinema advertising is much more expensive to produce than material intended for more limited distribution across the internet or on a video display unit in a supermarket. Production standards are much higher for television and cinema advertising, and the editing and image processing costs are also higher. Note that as the running time of the material increases, so will the final cost of production. These costs can escalate, and it's vital that the production has clear targets regarding content and duration.

Advertising rates depend on the platforms being used. The internet presents an almost costless platform (if the company runs material on its own website). By comparison, advertising on television seems expensive. Distributing material on DVD is relatively inexpensive, even after original production (filming) costs are taken into account, and can be an attractive option.

Advertising rates also depend on the timing and location of the broadcast. Advertising on radio or television at peak listening and viewing times costs more than at periods when the audience is much smaller. Similarly, showing advertisements in busy, inner-city cinemas is more expensive than running a campaign in rural cinemas.

Benefits and limitations

As with printed promotional materials, the true cost of a particular distribution channel for audiovisual promotional material depends on coverage and frequency. Although it is possible to produce audio and moving image material inexpensively and distribute it at virtually no cost across the internet, the coverage (the percentage of the target audience viewing the website hosting the material) and the frequency (the number of times the website is viewed) may be low.

For television and radio advertising, it is sensible to think in terms of the cost per 1000 viewers of, say, placing 30-, 15- and 5-second adverts. In this way, true comparisons can be made. Figure 10.12 shows the average cost per 1000 potential adult viewers of a 30-second advertising slot using different UK television channels.

Figure 10.12: The cost of television advertising (2003)

Channel	30-second equivalent per 1000 viewers
ITV	£6.86
Channel 4	£6.96
Channel 5	£4.09
GMTV	£3.75
Satellite	£3.99

Source: Marketing Pocket Book 2005

Data on the coverage (or reach) of individual television channels is available from Barb, the Broadcasters' Audience Research Board. (Visit Barb's website www.barb.co.uk for more information.) Radio Joint Audience Research Limited – commonly known by its acronym Rajar (www.rajar.co.uk) – performs a similar function for radio. The Advertising Association (www.adassoc.org.uk) provides detailed information on how to assess the true cost of radio and television advertising.

Figure 10.13 summarises the key benefits and limitations of radio and television media. Note that for many smaller businesses with limited promotional budgets, the use of radio, cinema and television advertising might be prohibitively expensive. The high initial cost of most cinema and television advertising will rule these methods out for many businesses.

Method	Benefits	Limitations
Radio	Readily accessible by target audience, at home or on the move. Relatively low cost compared to television and cinema, a 30-second slot on a national station might cost around £1,500 for a peak listening time slot. Message can be quickly modified. Plenty of regional stations.	Obviously limited to audio messages. Prestige of the medium has declined. Attention span of listener is limited – people listen to the radio and do other things at the same time. Once the audio message has been played, it's gone – message does not persist.
Television	Reaches a very large audience. High initial cost, but low cost per viewer. Benefits from using sound and vision – some adverts can be highly memorable. High prestige. Regional television stations afford some selectivity of audience. Stations also have some age group and income level selectivity – compare, say, Channel 4 to ITV1.	High initial cost. As with radio, a "perishable" message. Audience size can fluctuate. Space extremely limited during peak viewing times. Increasing use of videos and other recording technologies means that viewers can skip adverts. Viewers can also switch channels during the advertising breaks.

stop and think

What do you think are the benefits and limitations of cinema advertising? Visit Carlton Screen Advertising's website (www.carltonscreen.com) to develop your ideas. In answering the question, think about:

- the classification system (U, PG, 15, 18, etc.) used for films
- the quality of the audio and visual systems
- the target audience.

3 New media

Businesses are always looking for new and more effective ways to get promotional messages across to their target audiences. The technologies underpinning the internet, e-mail and mobile phones offers new avenues for promotional activities.

Websites

The science fiction movie *Minority Report*, released in 2002, featured interactive video advertising screens. These screens, located in public places, had the ability to identify individuals and address them by name. Now, e-commerce websites can perform a similar, if less spectacular, task by using small files, or cookies, stored on our PCs. The technology works as follows.

- When you visit a website you have previously visited, your cookie file is read and your identity is revealed to the website.

- The website uses this information to communicate with the central web server, drawing down a profile of your buying behaviour.

- The web server can then deliver individual promotional messages which it hopes are tailored to your interests – for example, Amazon's website does this with the message: "We have recommendations for you".

Web servers can also record the particular web pages that users browse or click through. Promotional materials appearing on web pages, or as separate pop-up windows, encourage you to click on them to get more information; the web server then records these events for later analysis.

This analysis helps to build a profile of individuals' interests and browsing habits. In turn, businesses can use this information to improve their online promotional activities and their understanding of buyer behaviour. Double Click is a business that specialises in this type of analysis and technology. You can find out more by visiting the company's website at www.doubleclick.com.

E-mail and mobile telephone technologies

E-mail and mobile telephone text messaging can provide very accurate channels of communication. Businesses can purchase lists of e-mail addresses covering a particular target group, such as a list of individuals within a certain age and income group that have bought particular products in the past. These lists can be used to bulk e-mail carefully designed promotional messages to people who should be interested in the offer.

The success of this approach depends on the accuracy of the e-mail address list. If it is inaccurate, or too general, then the promotion campaign will be ineffective. To counteract this problem, many businesses use opt-in lists. These e-mail lists are comprised of users who have actively agreed (or opted in) to receive further e-mail communications.

Bulk text messaging is also being used to send promotional messages to target audiences. Given the use of text messaging by teenagers and young adults, this is likely to be an effective medium for products targeted at these age groups. Now 3G networks also makes it possible to use picture messaging.

The production requirements and cost of new media vary according to the scale of the operation and particular technologies used. It is virtually costless for a business to place promotional messages on its own existing website – the website has already been established and promotional graphics for web pages are not difficult to produce. However, it does cost time and money to establish a website, as well as to gain the skills and technologies needed to target website users with specific promotional messages.

Delivering e-mails and text messages to your target audience is not very expensive (see Figure 10.14). It can, however, be expensive to obtain accurate e-mail and telephone lists. Bulk e-mails also suffer from a "junk mail" problem. Text messages lack any real visual impact, but this can be overcome by using newer picture messaging.

Figure 10.14: The cost of bulk texting

Volume of texts	Cost per message
1–999	£0.060
1,000–4,999	£0.055
5,000–9,999	£0.052
10,000–24,999	£0.050
25,000–49,999	£0.048
50,000–99,999	£0.046
100,000–149,999	£0.044
150,000–249,999	£0.042
250,000–499,999	£0.039
500,000–1,000,000	£0.038

Note: Prices, exclusive of VAT, as at January 2005
Source: www.zimepl.com

assessment practice
Costing your promotional activities

You will need to research the cost of producing and delivering the promotional activities you intend to use in your promotion campaign.

A Review the evidence you have gathered in previous assessment practices. By now you should be getting an idea of the types of promotional activities you will use in your promotion campaign. Make a list of the promotional activities involving: print, audio, moving images, and websites and e-mail.

B Estimate the likely size and characteristics of each promotional activity you listed in task A.

For print, specify the size of leaflets, advertisements and coupons, the use of colour and quality of paper etc; decide which individuals or companies will design, print and deliver the materials.

For audio, specify duration of the piece; decide which radio stations are to be used; determine who will produce and edit the advertisement.

For moving images, establish the format and purpose (television advert, in-store promotion, DVD, etc.); specify the duration and delivery (for example, a 30-second advert on a regional television station); determine who will produce and edit the material.

For a website, specify the number of web pages; determine who will produce the website, etc.

C Estimate the cost of each of your promotional activities. Some of the information in this topic may help you estimate these costs, but you will probably need to undertake additional research.

D Present your results using a spreadsheet. Use formulas as much as possible to allow you to calculate how the total cost of a promotional activity might change if you have to alter your plans or change some of your assumptions.

Researching and analysing customer attitudes

Setting the scene: selected newspaper readership profiles

Each of the UK's national newspapers attract readers with a different range of characteristics. This means that newspapers, such as the *Daily Mail*, have distinct readership profiles. This can be illustrated by looking at two ways of profiling customer characteristics: by socioeconomic group (see page 155 of the AS textbook) and by age.

Figure 10.15 below shows the average daily circulation in 2004 (number of newspapers sold) of three UK national daily newspapers – *The Sun*, *Daily Mail* and *Daily Telegraph* – together with their readership profile by socioeconomic group and by age, both expressed as a percentage of each newspaper's circulation. Consider how a business that intends to advertise in a national newspaper could use the information contained in Figure 10.15.

Figure 10.15: Readership profile of three UK newspapers

	Readership profile by socioeconomic group (percentage of circulation)					
	Circulation	A	B	C1	C2	DE
The Sun	3,157,000	1	9	26	29	34
Daily Mail	2,302,000	5	26	36	19	14
Daily Telegraph	870,000	15	45	28	7	6

	Readership profile by age (percentage of circulation)					
	Circulation	15–24	25–34	35–44	45–54	55–64	65+
The Sun	3,157,000	20	20	20	14	12	14
Daily Mail	2,302,000	9	10	15	18	20	27
Daily Telegraph	870,000	8	7	13	16	20	36

Source: Advertising Statistics Yearbook 2005
Note: Circulation figures relate to 2004

The importance of customer attitudes

All promotional activities rely on effective communication. It is important in planning promotional activities and deciding on the appropriate media to use in a campaign that businesses consider the attitudes of their target customers. If businesses get the tone of the message wrong, or use an inappropriate medium, then the target group is unlikely to "hear" the message and the communication will be ineffective. Understanding customer attitudes is crucial, therefore, in any promotion campaign.

Tone, structure and content

It is important to ensure that the tone, structure and content of any message is appropriate. For example, the tone and structure of a printed advertisement designed to create a sale will be very different to one that aims to alter customer perceptions of a product. The promotional activity should always be designed to achieve specific promotional objectives.

Selecting appropriate media

The message of a promotional activity needs to be delivered to its intended audience. The promotional activity should therefore be delivered through media most likely to target the intended audience. The chosen medium should be cost-effective and capable of delivering the promotional activity's message.

Suppose that a business wants to promote its sale, in which it is offering 50 per cent price reductions on some goods. This could be delivered by e-mai,l or the business could place adverts in national newspapers. E-mail might be appropriate if the offer is restricted to a few products aimed at a niche market. A national newspaper might be appropriate if the offer applies to several products and is pitched at a mass market.

For guidance on designing effective communications, and the strengths and weaknesses of different media, look back at pages 211–15 of the AS textbook.

Engaging the audience

Individuals increasingly face information overload. During our waking hours we are subjected to a large volume of messages. To cope with this excess of information, we subconsciously reject messages that appear either irrelevant or unappealing. Suppose, for example, you receive a text message promoting the launch of a new product. Two to three seconds might be devoted to scanning this text message before deciding to keep or delete it.

Most people need an immediate incentive before they consider that a message is worth reading or interpreting. Promotional messages need to engage with the target audience and attract their interest and attention. Messages aimed at young people might "say" save money, appealing directly to their wallets, but they are just as likely to be effective if they "say" have fun or experience something new.

business practice

Dr Pepper campaign

In order to demonstrate the effectiveness of cinema advertising, Carlton Screen Advertising frequently carries out audience surveys. This assessment of a Dr Pepper campaign is from Carlton's website (www.carltonscreen.com). The campaign's objective was to increase awareness of, and likelihood to try, Dr Pepper amongst the key 15–24 target audience. The main results reported by Carlton were:

- recall at the cinema was above average, a huge 85 per cent of cinema goers could recall seeing the advert compared to 63 per cent of non-cinema goers

- over half of cinema goers spontaneously recalled the advert's strapline – What's the worst that could happen? – compared to a quarter of non-cinema goers

- depth of communication amongst cinema goers was far higher than that of control sample – those seeing the ad on the big screen were able to recall over four different aspects, compared to under two mentions for the average television viewer (see Figure 10.16)

- cinema goers were also more likely to find it funny and enjoy watching the advert.

When using moving images to communicate a promotional message, why might cinema be more effective than television? Under what circumstances would television be more appropriate?

Figure 10.16: Impact of Dr Pepper advertisement

Spontaneous descriptions of ad	Cinema goers	Non-cinema goers
Boy picked up his date	75%	20%
Girl comes downstairs	52%	15%
Dad and boy wrestled	50%	11%
Mention of date/prom	76%	20%
Mention of offering – Dr Pepper and strapline	46%	15%
Average number of mentions	4.28	1.69

Source: www.carltonscreen.com

The willingness to interpret a message also depends on the environment in which the promotion is delivered. This might influence whether people are in the mood to receive the message. Entertainment events, such as a party to launch a new product, can be appropriate vehicles for some promotional activities as they create a more receptive atmosphere and individuals are more likely to "receive" the promotion's messages.

business practice

IGD

IGD is a registered charity that promotes education and training for people working in the food industry. To fund IGD's charitable activities, a trading company – IGD Services Ltd – carries out a range of commercial activities, including market research. The company publishes market research findings under its Shopper Insight brand. This is an extract from an IGD brochure promoting its insight report into promotional activity. The Shopper Insight report on promotional activity costs £500 (£350 for IGD members).

Promotional Activity

Advertising, direct mail, BOGOFs, price reductions, extra free, coupons, in-store media… Various promotional techniques are used by retailers and manufacturers to build awareness of their offer and influence shoppers to purchase.

Promotions can build loyalty to a brand or retailer, or can result in shoppers being less loyal as they shop around for the best offer. The type of promotional activity is dependent on the [product] category, the target audience and the objective that it seeks to achieve.

IGD's Shopper Insight report on **Promotional Activity** explores shoppers' attitudes to the various promotional activities employed by retailers and manufacturers in the food and grocery industry.

Promotional Activity will:

- provide you with a deeper understanding of your shoppers' mindsets, their motivations, behaviours and values

- clarify what promotional mechanics encourage shoppers to try new products

- explain how responses to promotions could be different depending on the [product] category being promoted

- investigate whether different promotions are preferred by different types of shoppers.

You can use this information to make informed business decisions and develop successful strategies to meet shoppers' needs.

For retailers, manufacturers and media companies, this report will be an invaluable source of primary research intelligence you won't find elsewhere.

Research methodology

Shopper Insight is based upon unique, original primary research.

Qualitative research provides a detailed understanding of the beliefs and attitudes driving shoppers' needs, enabling us to identify any changes in opinion. Eight focus groups are conducted, each comprising eight main shoppers from different life stages and socioeconomic groups from different regions around the UK.

Quantitative research allows us to substantiate the prevalence and strength of specific attitudes and behaviour across a representative sample. Demographic and regional differences will be highlighted in each report as well as variations by main supermarket used.

Source: IGD Services Ltd (www.igd.com)

Suppose the owner of an independent corner store wants to increase her sales revenue by 20 per cent during the next six months. Last year her sales revenue was £150,000 and, after allowing for a personal income of £20,000, she made a profit of £10,000. She is considering purchasing IGD's Shopper Insight report on promotional activity. Do you think this would be a worthwhile purchase? Justify your answer.

Research and analysis

In developing a promotion campaign, market research should be carried out to provide information on customer attitudes towards promotional activities and media. This could involve both primary and secondary market research. (Look back at pages 26–31 of the AS textbook if you need to revise these concepts.)

Secondary market research should be considered first as, given reliable sources, this information will be immediately available, and key trends will have been identified by researchers and analysts. However, secondary sources have potential drawbacks:

■ a business might have a unique target audience which secondary sources fail to profile

■ the only secondary information available may be out of date and the business feels that it needs up-to-date, information

■ the price of the secondary information is high in relation to the business's financial resources.

If any of these circumstances apply, then primary research should be considered. Some businesses will, in any case, be forced down the primary research route because the information they require is very specific and will not be available from secondary sources.

Primary research should be considered if a business wishes to verify the validity of secondary research in relation to its target customers' attitudes. It is also a good option if the business has a source of internal customer data, such as customer sales records, which could be analysed to provide useful information.

If primary research is required, the business should consider how the data will be collected. In the context of promotional activities, these methods are particularly important:

■ customer questionnaires – using, for example, closed questions to rank the relevance of particular sales promotion techniques

■ consumer panels – for example, organising several panels, each with particular socioeconomic and age groupings, to discuss the impact of a planned advertisement

■ personal interviews – using, for example, open-ended questions to reveal attitudes towards the use of particular imagery and cultural references within a moving-image advertisement.

Once the primary data has been collected, it should be analysed to identify key trends and patterns. The grouping of data by customer characteristics is particularly important. Without this level of analysis, primary research into customers' attitudes will be of little value, as a business would not be able to relate any findings to specific customer groups that may be the target audience for individual campaigns.

assessment practice
Researching customer attitudes

In Topic 1 you considered the characteristics of your business's target customers. This assessment practice requires you to research your target audience's attitudes towards promotional activities.

A Construct a questionnaire and/or an interview sheet. This should be designed to collect the following data on your target customers.

 i Some indication of their socioeconomic profile. This is a sensitive area, and you will need to collect information which allows you to make an assessment of each respondent's socioeconomic group. Your teacher will help you to construct these questions.

 ii Their use of media such as television, newspapers and magazines. For example, ask questions about favourite television channels and programmes, times when they listen to the radio, which newspapers they read.

 iii Attitudes to promotional activities and media. For example, do they prefer "50% off" or "buy two, get one free" promotions? Do they read leaflets posted through the letterbox? Ensure that you cover a range of promotional activities and media. You might base some questions on specific examples by, say, showing them copies of printed adverts.

B Present your findings in the form of a 10-minute presentation on "attitudes towards promotional activities". This should include a handout of no more than two A4 pages, containing tables and charts illustrating your findings, and identifying the promotional activities and media likely to be positively received by your target customers.

The promotional mix

Setting the scene: Finding Nemo

In 2003 a campaign used to promote the animated film *Finding Nemo* (Walt Disney/Pixar) targeted three separate groups: children, their parents and 15–24 year olds. Different promotional activities were aimed at each of these groups.

For children, for example, there were *Finding Nemo* themed lunch bags, which offered a discount on the movie on collecting four bottle tops from Robinson's fruit drink bottles.

Promotional activity aimed at parents included a prominent advert placed in the sports pages of newspapers on the day of an important football match between England and Turkey. The advertising copy read:

> **Things to do today**
> Catch Fish
> Take the kids to see Finding Nemo –
> programmes start from 12 pm
> Stuff Turkey
> Home in time for kick-off at 6 pm

To reach 15–24 year olds, teams of people were hired to promote the film at Reading and Leeds music festivals by distributing promotional postcards to the target age group.

The promotion campaign used a wide variety of promotional activities and media, with messages tailored to specific target audiences. The campaign was successful as it appealed to all target audience groups. In 2003, *Finding Nemo* was the number one box office film – grossing over £38 million. It attracted not only its core market (children and their parents) but also a significant audience in the 15–24 age group.

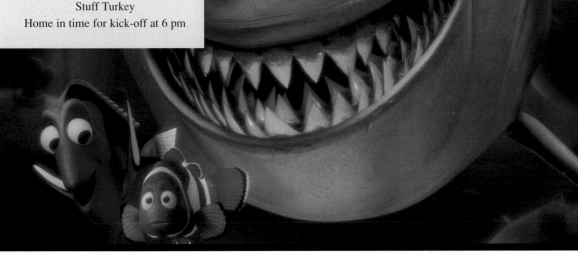

Getting the right mix

The promotion campaign surrounding *Finding Nemo* is a good illustration of the way in which a business can use a variety of promotional activities to communicate with its target customers. By using several promotional activities, it was possible to target different segments of the market for the film.

The specific combination of promotional activities within a single campaign is known as the campaign's promotional mix. Sophisticated marketing campaigns will use many different promotional activities within

the mix. However, any campaign's promotional mix can draw from a range of promotional activities, including:

- sales promotion
- merchandising
- personal selling
- exhibitions
- advertising
- public relations.

You have already looked at these promotional activities in some detail (in Topic 3) and considered the costs of delivering these promotional activities through different media (in Topic 5). The challenge is to get the mix of promotional activities right. This is a crucial element of a successful promotion campaign. The exact make-up of a campaign's promotional mix requires careful consideration: rely too much on one type of promotional activity and the message might only reach a relatively limited range of customers; use too many promotional activities and the message might be confusing and difficult to decode.

Several factors help to determine the nature of any campaign's promotional mix. These include:

- the objectives of the campaign
- the campaign's budget
- the target customers' attitudes towards different promotional activities.

An effective promotional mix will balance the demands of these factors. The objectives of the campaign are paramount, but the choice of promotional activities will be heavily influenced by the size of the campaign budget. The attitudes of particular customer segments will also influence the choice of promotional activities and the media used to deliver them.

The choice of the most appropriate promotional mix should be made after considering these competing factors. Careful analysis and evaluation, based on valid research of promotional activities and customer behaviour, is required if the promotional mix is to support the campaign's objectives. In this topic we consider the importance of the campaign's objectives and its budget. In Topic 8 we investigate the significance of the target customers' attitudes towards different promotional activities.

Campaign objectives

Any promotion campaign has one or more objectives. As we showed in Topic 1, typical objectives include:

- improving customer awareness and knowledge of a product
- improving the image of a business
- generating or increasing sales
- improving customer loyalty to a product or a business
- altering customer perceptions of a product.

To achieve any of these objectives, customer attitudes towards a business and/or its products have to be altered. It is unlikely that any single promotional activity will achieve a campaign objective – a promotional mix is required.

When outlining a promotional mix, it is sensible to consider a variety of promotional activities that might be available to the business within the budget. The final selection and sequencing of promotional activities will depend on the budget and customer attitudes. However, initially it is sensible to think in general terms and outline a number of different promotional mixes.

These mixes will differ because they use different promotional activities, and/or they present the promotional activities in a different sequence. For example, a campaign whose objective is to raise awareness about a new product might use an exhibition and a PR event. However, which should come first? Should the activities take place simultaneously? Should the PR event act as an initial message, to gain interest in the product, with the exhibition providing detailed product information to interested potential customers?

Campaign budget

Topic 5 set out some typical costs of delivering various promotional activities. However, the overall cost of any promotional activity will be determine by its detailed

The Xbox 360, a new version of Microsoft's video game console, was launched in the USA towards the end of 2005.

The day before the consoles went on sale, a launch party was held in the Mojave desert, a few hundred miles from Microsoft's headquarters in Redmond. Three thousand Xbox gamers had the opportunity to meet Microsoft executives and play on Xbox consoles connected to high-definition screens.

Tickets for the event could only be obtained by entering prize draws through affiliated websites such as Game Pro (www.gamepro.com). These websites displayed advertisements for the Xbox 360 along with articles speculating on the capabilities of the product.

Similar events were held in European cities. Just as in the USA, events were scheduled just

before the official product release in each major European country. The promotion campaign had a

clear plan: the Xbox 360 was to go on sale shortly after the publicity and buzz generated by each launch party.

Unfortunately, the supply of Xbox 360 consoles could not meet the demand and many potential customers were disappointed. News reports suggested that Microsoft had brought the launch date forward in order to release the Xbox 360 before competitors, such as Sony, launched their latest consoles.

Microsoft's campaign utilised launch events, PR and web-based advertising. What other elements do you think that Microsoft could have used within its promotional mix when launching the Xbox 360? Would you consider the Xbox 360 launch campaign to be successful? Give your reasons.

specification: the particular medium used, the duration of the activity, the design costs (including labour costs), the channels used to deliver the activity (such as poster vans, local or national newspapers), etc.

The size of the campaign budget inevitably has a considerable influence on the types of promotional activity selected in a campaign's promotional mix. Given a limited budget, difficult choices have to be made, and expensive media may be immediately ruled out of consideration. Even when a budget seems generous, often the objectives of the promotion campaign are such that substantial promotional effort is required if they are to be achieved. This means that, while the size of a campaign budget might dictate which types of promotional activities can be used, difficult decisions have to be made irrespective of how much money has been allocated. In all campaigns, the marketing team will be looking to use promotional activities which make the most impact and deliver the best value for money.

It is sensible to complete a detailed budget for a promotion campaign (see Topic 2) which sets out the method, timing and cost of each element of the campaign's promotional mix. In order to carry out what-if calculations, the budget should be constructed using a computer spreadsheet.

Using spreadsheets to plan campaigns

Spreadsheets are useful because they can be set up to carry out what-if calculations. For example, what if a decision is made to use a national newspaper to carry an advert rather than a local newspaper? If the spreadsheet is set up correctly, all that would need to be altered would be the daily rate charged by the newspaper. The impact on the total cost of the campaign would be automatically calculated.

The cost of each promotional activity can be split into fixed and variable costs (see Unit 3 in the AS textbook). Spreadsheets can simply calculate the variable cost by multiplying the unit cost by the number of times the promotional activity is used. For example, if the daily rate for placing a half-page advert in a local newspaper is £250 and the campaign is based on ten placements (say, every Friday and Saturday for five weeks), then the variable cost would be £2,500 (£250 x 10). The fixed cost – in this case, the cost of designing the advertisement – would have to be researched. This would involve getting a quote from a graphic designer or an advertising agency, or, if the advert is to be produced in-house, by estimating how many hours it would take to produce, and multiplying this by the hourly wage rate of the employee producing the advertisement.

The estimated total cost of the promotion campaign would be calculated by adding up the total costs (fixed plus variable) of the campaign's individual promotional activities. It would also be sensible to budget for contingencies such as increased design or labour costs. A spreadsheet could do this very simply, by calculating the contingency as a certain percentage (say, 10 per cent) of the budget. The total cost of the promotion campaign, including the contingency, is then compared with the allocated budget. The aim is to balance the two.

Consider, as a further example of its usefulness, how a spreadsheet could be set up to take into account discounts for bulk orders. For example, you might get a 10 per cent discount if more than 1000 A5 fliers are ordered from a printer. Again, it is straightforward to enter a formula so that a spreadsheet applies a discount when a particular threshold is reached.

assessment practice
Using spreadsheets

The assessment practice at the end of Topic 5 asked you to estimate the cost of your promotional activities and present these in the form of a spreadsheet. This assessment practice requires you to develop the spreadsheet set up in Topic 5's assessment practice and to carry out some what-if analyses as part of an initial assessment of the suitability of your campaign's promotional mix. In doing so, you should appreciate how you can use a spreadsheet to plan your business's promotion campaign more effectively.

A Recall the spreadsheet you set up for the assessment practice in Topic 5. Develop this spreadsheet by entering formulas to calculate:

- the fixed, variable and total costs of each promotional activity

- the total cost of all your promotional activities, including an allowance for contingencies

- the gap between the total cost of your promotional activities and the allocated budget – in other words, calculate budget minus total cost.

Get your teacher/lecturer to check the accuracy and functionality of the spreadsheet.

B Use the spreadsheet to carry out a number of what-if analyses. This requires you to alter key aspects of your promotional activities and to assess the impact of these changes on the total cost of your promotional mix.

Each time you change an aspect of a promotional activity you should ensure that you stay within your budget. For example, if you increase the number of free products you give to customers, this will increase the cost of this promotional activity, and you will have to reduce the cost of some other promotional activities to stay within budget. Which promotional activities would you change and why?

C Produce a single-page A4 document summarising the results of your what-if analyses. This document should present an initial assessment of the suitability of your promotional mix.

Attention, interest, desire, action

Setting the scene: Campaign targets student drinkers

A nationwide campaign is being launched to warn students of the dangers of excessive alcohol. The drive, headed by the National Union of Students (NUS) in conjunction with the drinks company Diageo, aims to promote sensible drinking.

The union will place beer mats and stickers in student bars giving young people tips on how to keep their drinking within reasonable limits. Tips appearing on the beer mats include having something to eat while drinking, having soft drinks in between alcoholic ones, and drinking plenty of water.

NUS spokesman Nick Emms told BBC News the traditional image of the hard-drinking student was "no more", with 25 per cent of them not drinking at all. He said students were much more interested in their own health and fitness than they had been in the past. Mr Emms said students would appreciate the informative tone of the campaign, which would not sound "preachy" or "lecturing".

The government has also launched a campaign to tackle binge drinking. It includes a graphic poster campaign warning of £80 on-the-spot fines for being drunk and disorderly. Posters warn "get drunk and disorderly, get arrested, get an £80 fine", with one spelling out £80 in vomit.

Source: BBC News website, 15 November 2005

Note: the posters from the government campaign can be downloaded from www.gnn.gov.uk

KEY TERMS

AIDA is an acronym for Attention-Interest-Desire-Action. These are the stages and individual needs to be taken through before purchasing a product.

Promotional mix is the specific combination of promotional activities used within a promotion campaign.

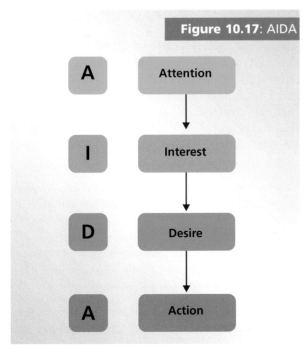

Figure 10.17: AIDA

Altering buyer behaviour

Promotional activities attempt to influence the decisions of consumers by creating a favourable view of a business and its products. A systematic approach to altering buyer behaviour can be taken by using the AIDA model (see Figure 10.17). Used chiefly within advertising, AIDA is a way of thinking about the key steps an individual needs to take before purchasing a product. It can be applied to all promotional activities, and helps when considering the timing of promotional activities in a promotion campaign.

Consider what each AIDA stage means in terms of buyer engagement by looking at a campaign to promote a new nightclub:

- **attention** – gaining an initial awareness of the product and establishing knowledge about the product, for example by using a PR event to announce the opening of a new nightclub

- **interest** – moving from awareness of the product to establishing a willingness to investigate purchasing the product, say by half-page advertisements in a local newspaper

- **desire** – moving from a general interest in the product to an intention to purchase, perhaps linked to coupons on A5 leaflets distributed to homes for free drinks on opening night

- **action** – closing the sale by turning an intention to purchase into a confirmed sale through, in this case, personal sales outside the nightclub on opening night.

In the responsible drinking campaigns (featured above), both the NUS and the government had the same intention: to promote the sensible use of alcohol. However, the campaigns adopted very different approaches. The NUS adopted an informative approach which did not preach, or lecture, to its audience. The government used fear to communicate a harsher message – drinking to excess is harmful to your wallet and your stomach!

In terms of the AIDA model, the government campaign was more likely to gain the attention of the reader. The approach taken by the NUS might have been more successful in establishing a willingness to listen to the message. Taken together, the two approaches could take the target audience through the stages of attention and interest. It is likely that additional promotional activities would be required to alter behaviour in the long run – to take the audience through the stages of desire ("I really shouldn't drink to excess") and action ("Never again!").

stop and think

Why do you think the NUS attempted to communicate in an informative way, while the government used posters adopting a more aggressive tone? What other promotional activities might the NUS have used in its campaign to warn students of the dangers of excessive alcohol?

Identify a promotion campaign which took you through all four AIDA stages, from gaining your attention to purchasing the product (or altering your view). How did the campaign's promotional activities do this?

Using AIDA

Any promotion campaign relies on an effective promotional mix. The AIDA model helps in selecting the best combination of promotional activities. In particular, it provides a procedure for ensuring that the final promotional mix takes into account the target customers' attitudes towards different promotional activities.

1 Attention

If the target audience is not aware of the product and/or business, it is essential to gain the target audience's attention. The first element of an effective promotional mix is a promotional activity (or set of activities) that can get attention for the product or business. This promotional activity will "kick off" the campaign, and it will be the first entry in the campaign's Gantt planning chart.

As this promotional activity, or set of closely connected activities, will set the tone for the rest of the campaign, you need to carefully consider:

- the tone and content of the message being communicated

- the type of promotional activity best suited to gaining the attention of the target audience

- how the promotional activity will be delivered – the medium or media that will be used

- how often to repeat the message – the frequency of the promotional activity.

The choices you make in each case will be determined by the objectives of the promotion campaign, the nature of the product, and the target customers' attitudes towards different promotional activities.

If a product has a mass market appeal, and the target audience spans a wide range of socioeconomic groups, then the message should be universal. In this case, advertising on television and/or in national newspapers would appear to be appropriate. As the message may well be a simple one, frequency would not have to be high if the advertisement delivered its message forcefully by, for example, using humour or fear.

If a product has a less universal appeal and is designed for a niche market, then a more targeted approach to gaining attention is required. Direct mail could be appropriate if a reliable mailing list is available. The message would have to appeal to the concerns of the target customers and rely more on information than emotion, although the exact nature of the product would be crucial here.

Whatever the nature of the product's market, however, the aim here is to get the attention of the target audience. This means a focus on activities that can spark that interest. Some promotional activities are unlikely to be appropriate when attempting to gain the attention of the target market. These include sales promotion, merchandising and personal selling.

These promotional activities address target customers who are already aware of the product. They work best when potential customers already have an interest in finding out more about the product. For example, while "cold calling" can sometimes work, personal selling is far more effective when the customer approaches the salesperson by, for example, walking into a store and requesting assistance, or ringing a customer helpline.

Exhibitions, advertising and PR are often more appropriate when the objective of the promotional activity is to gain the attention of the target market. Advertising and public relations are particularly suited to this stage of the AIDA model. An exhibition, while capable of gaining the attention of the target audience, relies on individuals attending the event and therefore assumes a level of awareness which might not be present. An advertising campaign followed by an exhibition, however, would be appropriate.

2 Interest

The AIDA model illustrates the importance of sequencing promotional activities. This is certainly the case when moving the target audience from the attention stage to the interest stage.

To move an individual to the interest stage requires promotional activities that appeal to the personal, psychological and social influences on an individual's buying behaviour (see Figure 10.8, page 74). Understanding the motives behind a potential buyer's behaviour is crucial for this stage of the AIDA model.

At this stage, PR events may be less successful than more focused activities such as direct mail shots and exhibitions. Personal selling could be highly effective if the target audience initiates contact with the sales force: if, for example, potential customers respond to an advertisement which successfully gained their attention, and provide a telephone or e-mail contact. Merchandising, in the form of in-store displays, could perform a similar function, but sales promotions assume a high level of interest by the target customers and are more appropriate for the desire and action stages of the AIDA model.

3 Desire

At this stage the focus should shift from establishing a willingness to investigate the benefits of a product to providing genuine incentives to make a purchase. The promotional activities should be very focused and address specific influences on buyer behaviour. The message should be about why purchasing would provide very real benefits. The promotional activity should aim to convince potential customers that they will lose out if they do not purchase the product.

Advertising can be effective at this stage of the AIDA model. It can instil a degree of urgency in the target market. However, personal selling, sales promotions and merchandising are ideal ways to establish the desire to purchase a product – given a willingness to investigate purchasing a product, these promotional activities can communicate specific benefits and address the particular needs of individual customers.

4 Action

The final stage of the AIDA model focuses on the task of convincing the target market that they should purchase the product. The desire to purchase should have already been established, so the final elements of the promotional mix aim to turn this desire into a financial transaction, a change in behaviour or a change in attitude towards a product or business. Sales promotion, merchandising and personal selling are all capable of achieving this change. They are focused promotional activities which can be designed to provide that final push to get customers to commit to the purchase.

stop and think

Identify two promotional activities which convinced you to purchase a product or altered your attitude towards a product or business. In each case, describe the features of the promotion – the type of activity, the content of the message, any incentives provided, etc.

assessment practice
Developing your campaign using AIDA

This exercise requires you to develop your promotion campaign's promotional mix.

Using the AIDA model, assess whether the promotional mix you outlined in Topic 7's assessment practice is capable of achieving your promotion campaign's objectives. You should consider the order of your promotional activities as well as the type of promotional activities used.

Recommending a promotional mix

Throughout this unit, we have investigated the factors which help to determine the promotional mix of a promotion campaign. These factors include:

- business and marketing aims and objectives – the overall direction of the business and how it is intending to use marketing activities to achieve its aims and objectives (see Topic 1)

- the objectives of the promotion campaign – the specific targets set for the promotion campaign, such as raising product awareness or increasing product sales (see Topic 1)

- customer attitudes – the importance of customer attitudes towards different promotional activities and how to communicate effectively with the target audience (in Topics 4 and 6)

- the budget allocated to the promotion campaign – the importance of working within a campaign budget and using various techniques (such as Gantt charts and spreadsheet models) to plan the elements of the campaign's promotional mix (in Topics 2 and 7).

The core of the unit (Topics 3, 5, 7 and 8) introduced a range of promotional activities available to businesses, allowing you to investigate their advantages and disadvantages, to appreciate their typical costs, and to understand how they could be combined into a promotional mix.

Constructing an effective promotional mix, as we have seen, is not a simple matter. Information about the target audience has to be researched and analysed. The cost of different promotional activities needs to be considered, including the extent to which the activities are produced and carried out by the business or by an external agency. The timing and balance of the various promotional activities must be considered. And all of this has to come within the allocated budget.

The case study that follows is taken from a real promotion campaign – the Get On campaign. The background material and illustrations are sourced from www.dfes.gov.uk/get-on unless otherwise stated. The study is intended to help you review all the ideas presented in this unit before you consider

how you might recommend a promotional mix for your own promotion campaign.

The Get On campaign

The Department for Education and Skills (DfES) is the government body responsible for all aspects of education, training and learning. The DfES is keen to promote the idea of lifelong learning – that learning should not end after we finish our time in formal education at 16 or 18. Through its Skills for Life initiative, the DfES is working with key stakeholders (such as colleges and employers) to improve adult literacy and numeracy.

For many adults lacking basic numeracy and literacy skills – for example, those with an inability to read or write – the thought of "going back to school" is terrifying. Through fear and embarrassment, adults lacking basic skills have traditionally never spoken about their problem: they struggle in silence.

The Get On campaign's main aim is to encourage this target market to take that first step – to pick up the telephone and call the Get On hotline.

The target audience

The Get On campaign's target audience are those adults who lack basic literacy and numeracy skills. At a public relations event held in August 2003, a government education minister said:

> Millions of adults in the UK do not have the skills of an average 11-year-old. This lack of basic skills affects many areas of their lives – from how much they get paid, to being unable to help their children with homework. Many people with poor basic skills will see their own children or other young people getting their GCSEs later this week – something they feel they could never achieve themselves. Tackling the problem of adult basic skills is a key priority for the government, and we are determined to help 1.5 million adults improve their reading, writing and maths by 2007.

The 2004/5 campaign made very effective use of the advertising signature shown at the top of page 95.

Get rid of your gremlins and (get on) 0800 100 900

The gremlin theme has become a distinctive feature of recent Get On campaigns. Stuart Barnes, from the advertising agency St Luke's, explains the reasoning behind the gremlin theme:

> The Get On campaign to promote awareness and take-up of adult basic skills learning opportunities was the result of careful research by St Luke's. The research showed that people with poor reading, writing, spelling or numbers skills felt that it was their own personal issue which only they could fix and only when they felt it was right for them. They couldn't be told or even encouraged to learn, either by advertising, by an organisation, and often not by friends or family.
>
> Nearly everyone we spoke to with poor literacy or numeracy had the same emotional response. They felt very frustrated with themselves when they were unable to complete tasks they thought they should be capable of. They were scared of being found out and were afraid of the severe impact on their self-confidence that would result. This is where the idea of the gremlins came from.
>
> The gremlin personifies this emotional response as a third party. It appears when you are confronted with a task involving reading, writing or numbers. The gremlin is the thing which stops you being able to do things – it undermines your confidence, it mocks your mistakes and always threatens to embarrass you.

Additional research carried out by St Luke's showed that people with poor literacy or numeracy skills do not see it as a problem as long as they can adopt coping strategies to get through everyday activities. The lack of literacy and numeracy skills did not make them any less of a person and did not impact on their social and family lives.

St Luke's concluded that both humour and fear would be essential parts of any advertising campaign capable of breaking through the barriers put up by people with poor literacy and numeracy skills: humour to get the attention and interest of the person; fear to generate desire and action.

Promotional activities

The script for a 40-second television advertisement produced by St Luke's for the Get On campaign is shown on page 96. Note that "super" means superimposition and refers to the telephone number and Get On logo – the signature of the advert – that were displayed on screen at the end of the advertisement.

In addition to advertising, the Get On campaign has used several other promotional activities including:

- **public relations exercises** – for example, the campaign has used celebrities such as Phil Tufnell to publicise the campaign

- **direct mail** targeting key stakeholders and raising awareness of the campaign

- **personal selling** through encouraging key personnel in contact with the target audience to deliver the message – these front-line personnel include GPs, health visitors, counsellors, prison officers, probation officers, immigration officers, Jobcentre Plus personal advisers and social service staff.

New drive against learning gremlins

The Department for Education and Skills says the latest figures show that since the Get On campaign began two years ago, some 320,000 people have gained a reading, writing or maths qualification, and millions more have started courses. A new series of adverts will build on the previous theme of the campaign and feature people being tormented by a little gremlin – their embarrassment over a lack of basic literacy or numeracy skills.

Among those in the new campaign is former cricketer and *I'm A Celebrity Get Me Out of Here* winner Phil Tufnell. "When I was growing up all I thought about was cricket, so it's fair to say I wasn't too hot at things like spelling," he says. "But just because you missed out on a chance to learn first time around, doesn't mean you can't go back into learning and knock your own gremlins for six."

Source: BBC News website, 18 August 2003

Open on a man sat at a table in a factory rest area. In front of him on the table we see a large envelope, which he's looking at slightly anxiously.

After a short while, we suddenly see a gremlin appear from behind the table.

GREMLIN: OH NO, NO, NO, WE DON'T WANT TO OPEN THAT. WE'LL JUST BE DISAPPOINTED.

We then see the gremlin and the man sat on some steps together.

GREMLIN: LET'S FACE IT, YOUR ENGLISH IS ABOUT AS GOOD MY TAP DANCING.

We then see the man and the gremlin in the washroom, the guy splashes his face with water while the gremlin files his nails.

GREMLIN: I TOLD YOU YOU'D NEVER PASS THAT COURSE. YOU KNOW WHAT PEOPLE CALL YOU BEHIND YOUR BACK?

We see the man walk through the corridor, gremlin following.

GREMLIN: IT'S FAILURE, FAILURE, LOOK AT YOU, YOU'RE A FAILURE!

We see the man pick up the envelope and start to open it. We see the gremlin fold his arms in annoyance.

GREMLIN: GO ON THEN. SEE IF I CARE.

As the man looks at the contents of the envelope, we see the gremlin look at himself and realise that he's shrivelling and shrinking. As he does so, he speaks in an ever higher pitch of voice until he's really tiny.

GREMLIN: URGHH. NOT THE QUALIFICATION. I HATE QUALIFICATIONS.

We then see the man accidentally tread on the tiny gremlin. The confident man puts up his feet on the table. On the sole of one of his shoes we see a squashed tiny gremlin.

GREMLIN: I'LL BE BACK. THIS ISN'T THE LAST YOU'VE HEARD FROM ME!

Cut to the man using the side of the table to scrape the gremlin off his shoe. As the gremlin lands in a wastepaper bin we here a small thud.

VOICE OVER: GET RID OF YOUR GREMLIN. CALL 0800 100 900.

SUPER: 0800 100 900 and Get On logo.

GREMLIN: I WANT MY MUMMY!

Promotional media

A wide range of promotional media has been used by the Get On campaign. This perfect proof for a printed advertisement shows a continuation of the "get rid of your gremlin" theme. While focusing more on humour than fear, it reinforces the main message delivered by the televised adverts.

- Get On pencils – white pencils with the Get On logo and 0800 100 900

- CD-ROMs – electronic copies of the templates and pictures

- video – motivational video designed to engage potential learners.

Radio advertisements have also been broadcast, and they used the same combination of humour and fear. You can listen and view radio and television advertisements by visiting the campaign's promotional website at www.dfes.gov.uk/get-on and clicking on the download menu button.

The campaign also makes use of various print and IT media in the form of:

- balloons – white, with blue Get On logo and 0800 100 900

- postcards – three different gremlin designs, with top tips and space for local details

- gremlin masks – available in both paper and plastic

- beer mats – gremlin branded on the front with the 0800 100 900 on the back

- posters – available in A2 and A3, the smaller posters have space for local information

- bookmarks – gremlin branded with the 0800 100 900

- notepads – yellow pads with the Get On logo and 0800 100 900

- stickers – single gremlin window stickers and smaller sets of Get On and gremlin stickers

- scratch cards – types available include workplace, sports, personal finance, family learning

Finally, key stakeholders (such as schools and colleges) can download templates of posters and logos, along with clip art, to help them to put together their own printed promotional materials. Here (above and below) are some examples of the clip art available for download.

Assess the suitability of the promotional mix used by the DfES in its Get On campaign by considering:

- the extent to which the campaign considered the attitudes of the target audience

- the suitability of the promotional activities and media used by the campaign

- the ability of the campaign to achieve its aim – to get adults lacking basic numeracy and literacy skills to call the Get On hotline telephone number.

Evaluating a promotional mix

Any promotional mix is only as good as the assumptions it is based on and the media it is delivered through.

Assumptions

In selecting the elements of the promotional mix, various assumptions will have been made, including assumptions about:

- the attitudes of the target audience towards various promotional activities

- the appeal of the product to target customers

- the ability of the business to produce and deliver promotional activities.

In the Get On campaign, the DfES employed an advertising agency to research and specify the ways in which the campaign message would be communicated. Various aspects of the campaign were devolved to key stakeholders. For example, the agency produced poster templates that could be downloaded and used by, for example, schools and colleges. Nevertheless, given the size of the Get On campaign, external agencies would have carried out much of its planning and implementation.

It is likely that the promotion campaign you have been investigating in the assessment practice activities is on a much smaller scale. If this is the case, then it is likely that the business will have to produce and deliver most of the promotional activities. It is, therefore, crucial that you have made realistic assumptions about the ability of the business to undertake these tasks in-house. Incorrect assumptions here would result in a promotional mix that looked fine on paper but would be difficult to implement.

Have you made reasonable assumptions about the attitudes and motivations of the target customers? Are these assumptions based on some valid research? If not, then it would be impossible to judge the suitability of the campaign's promotional mix. While you will not be able to carry out research on the scale implemented for the Get On campaign, you should endeavour to carry out sufficient research so that you can make some valid working assumptions about the attitudes and motivations of your target customers.

Media selection

In Topic 8 you looked at how the AIDA model could help you to analyse a campaign's promotional mix. While it is important to justify the choice of promotional mix in terms of the promotional activities, a more practical issue is the media used to deliver these activities. In addition, the timing and location of promotional activities must also be considered.

The Get On campaign used a variety of different media. Both radio, television and print were used for the central advertising campaigns, while PR was directed at mass media communications such as national daily newspapers and internet news sites. Personal selling was also part of the campaign. As the target audience was reluctant to engage initially with schools and teachers, the campaign had to consider suitable personnel who were likely to have some contact with adults who might lack basic numeracy and literacy skills. The Get On campaign solved this problem by using Jobcentre Plus personal advisers and social service staff.

Your promotion campaign is likely to be allocated a limited budget. If this is the case, then your choice of media will be a difficult one to make. Judging which media to use for particular promotional activities will require you to balance the suitability of the media against its cost of production and delivery. Devoting a large proportion of your budget to a radio or television advertising campaign could be sensible, but you will have to clearly demonstrate that this promotional activity and its particular delivery is capable of taking the target audience through all stages of the AIDA model. In all likelihood, the use of one promotional activity, delivered via an expensive medium, will not be sensible and will not achieve the campaign's objectives.

If you have completed all the assessment practices in this unit, you should have:

■ a set of objectives for your promotion campaign and an allocated budget

■ an analysis of the target market – who they are, what motivates them, and their attitudes towards various promotional activities

■ an understanding of the promotional activities available to your business – and the ability of the business to produce and deliver these activities – and their costs

■ a spreadsheet outlining your campaign's promotional mix, including timings and costs

■ an analysis of the suitability of your promotional mix in terms of the AIDA model.

For this final assessment practice you are required to review your promotion campaign.

Using all of the above outcomes, evaluate the suitability of the campaign's promotional mix by assessing:

■ the ability of the campaign to achieve its objectives

■ the extent to which the promotional mix takes into account the attitudes of target customers

■ the cost of promotional activities compared with the resources available to the business and your allocated budget.

IN THIS UNIT WE INVESTIGATE HOW THE MARKETING ENVIRONMENT helps to determine the marketing strategies of profit and not-for-profit businesses in national and international markets.

You will develop an understanding of the different aspects of the marketing environment and how changes in it can alter the degree of competition within a market. You will investigate how businesses gather and analyse marketing environment data. Finally, you will explore ways in which businesses alter their marketing strategies given changes in the their marketing environment.

This unit is externally assessed. The assessment practices at the end of each topic are designed to develop your ability to analyse and evaluate the impact of the marketing environment on marketing strategies.

The marketing environment

The marketing environment

Setting the scene: tackling traffic congestion

This article, taken from the BT Group's website, introduces a report produced by the telecommunications company on how modern communications could be used in tackling traffic congestion. The report can be downloaded from www.btplc.com.

BT • | Home | | Search | ⊙ Just this Section ⊙ Whole site | Go ▶ |

| About BT Group | Investor centre | News & media | Society & environment | Innovation | Careers |

Society & environment

The UK suffers from the worst traffic congestion in Europe. But replacing just one in ten of our journeys could change all that. Current thinking revolves largely around measures which tackle the symptoms of the problem such as road widening, building new roads and congestion charging. However, we also need to look at the root cause of the issue – we are making too many journeys. Travel substitution is part of the answer.

BT's report *Broadband – the role of communications in beating congestion* analyses the growth in UK and regional traffic, which has seen an average growth of 19 per cent in the past decade, and is a call to action for those involved with traffic management, employers, commuters and shoppers.

With broadband communications available to 99.6 per cent of the population by summer 2005, it is clear that there is significant potential to make a real impact on congestion. The report brings together contributions from business, motoring, academia and BT to suggest a way forward. International comparisons show that the task is achievable and realistic. It shows how business can become more profitable and productive while individuals can lead more fulfilling lives.

Source: www.btplc.com

How might BT exploit opportunities arising from increasing traffic congestion in the UK?

Marketing revisited

As this unit builds on the basic knowledge of marketing developed in Unit 1 of the AS course, it is worth revisiting the main concepts that underpin the marketing model.

Marketing is a continuous process. The basic elements of the process, often called the marketing model, are:

■ deciding on marketing objectives and priorities

■ finding out what the customer wants through a process of market research

■ designing and producing suitable goods and services (or modifying existing products)

■ informing customers about products, and motivating them to commit to purchase

■ ensuring that products are available when and where consumers wish to buy.

A key part of this process is the use of review and feedback to adjust the process at all stages. For example, a mobile phone services provider may test=market a new ringtone but find that initial sales are very disappointing. This may well cause the

The **marketing environment** is the range of forces, outside the direct control of a business, which affect buyer behaviour and competition within markets. These include economic, technological, legal and regulatory, and social and ethical forces.

Economic forces are changes in economic variables, such as taxation, which alter consumers' spending and/or alter the prices set by businesses for their products. For example, an increase in value added tax (VAT) would increase the price of, and reduce the demand for, some products.

Technological forces are developments in technology that alter the ways in which businesses produce and/or sell products, For example, internet technology has made it easier for businesses to sell products directly to consumers.

Legal and regulatory forces are laws or government regulations that constrain business practices. For example, consumer protection legislation restricts the way any business can promote and advertise its products.

Social and ethical forces arise from the attitudes generally held by society, or sections of society. For example, changing public attitudes to the environment are forcing businesses to demonstrate greater environmental responsibility. Changing attitudes towards financial debt is having an impact on credit sales.

company to revisit its market research. Were there weaknesses in the initial analysis of data? Were sound sampling techniques used?

Marketing strategies

Strategies are long-term plans to ensure that key aims or objectives are achieved. They are often contrasted with tactics, which are short-term measures designed to achieve strategic objectives.

Marketing strategies should be closely related to overall corporate objectives. For example, a business might set itself an objective to increase the profitability of its overseas operations. An appropriate strategy may be to launch a new product in one or more countries, either simultaneously or in a planned sequence. A possible tactic, designed to implement the strategy, might be the modification of one of the business's products to cater for different cultures.

The marketing environment

Marketing is a practical activity, and marketing departments must respond to the world as they find it – not as they might wish it to be. There are several forces or factors which are beyond the direct control of any business. These forces are sometimes referred to as the marketing environment of business. This unit looks at the impact on marketing strategy of the most important of these external forces.

Economic factors

Key economic statistics, like inflation, unemployment and the exchange rate, are called "variables" by economists. This is simply a shorthand for "things that may change" – you may also have come across this term in mathematics. Changes in economic variables tell us something about the general state of the

economy, and this needs to be taken into account when taking marketing decisions.

Economic statistics are published by both central and local government. They may refer to the nation as whole or to particular regions, such as the Midlands. Many firms will also be interested in data from other countries or transnational economic zones such as the European Union. The impact of changes in economic variables will be considered in detail in Topic 3.

Technological factors

Technology is often the factor that changes most quickly, making decision-making difficult for individuals as well as businesses. Consider, for example, how quickly information and communication technology develops. Software is rapidly updated, computer hardware can become quickly obsolete, games consoles are usurped by the latest models.

Many businesses have problems deciding when to adopt new technology, given that even the latest systems may suddenly be rendered obsolete by a new breakthrough. On an individual level, digital camera technology is a good example of how a product can develop very quickly, causing current models to become out of date within a few months.

Legal and regulatory factors

Laws exist to protect people from the harmful actions of others. The same principle applies laws that regulate and impact on business. Most laws relating to business concentrate on the protection of stakeholders, such as consumers, employees and shareholders, from the potentially harmful actions of a firm. For example, there are regulations that prevent businesses misleading consumers by publishing false information in promotional materials. However, there are also laws that protect businesses from the actions

Figure 11.1 shows percentage of UK households with a select range of technological goods. It illustrates the speed with which technologies become adopted by consumers.

The data in Figure 11.1 is taken from *Social Trends*, an annual government publication. This publication is freely available on the government's national statistics website www.statistics.gov.uk. Similar statistics for previous years can be viewed by downloading earlier *Social Trends* publications.

How might data, such as that in Figure 11.1, help businesses to anticipate and exploit changes in their environment?

Figure 11.1: Households with selected durable goods

United Kingdom   Percentages

	Mobile phone	CD player	Home computer	Internet access	DVDplayer
1996/97	17	59	27		
1997/98	21	63	29		
1998/99	27	68	33	10	
1999/2000	44	72	38	19	
2000/01	47	77	44	32	
2001/02	65	80	50	40	
2002/03	70	83	55	45	31
2003/04	76	85	58	48	50
2004/05	78	87	62	53	67

of others. For example, the patent and copyright laws are designed to protect a business's innovations and ideas from being exploited by other firms.

Social and ethical issues

Social issues broadly cover the way people live: their lifestyles, attitudes, opinions and beliefs. As lifestyles change, businesses must respond to ensure that they continue to provide products that are in demand and meet the needs of their customers. A good example of changing lifestyles is the growing trend for people to eat out and to order takeaway food. What was once a luxury for the few has now become commonplace, creating a mass-market industry with an annual spending of millions of pounds on marketing activities.

The challenge

A key task for any business is to judge how external forces will change over the short, medium and long term. Larger firms may be able to afford to employ forecasters or buy in research from specialist consultancies. Smaller firms may have to rely on the

stop and think

Explain, in each case, how economic, technological, legal and social forces could have contributed to:

■ the decline of clothes manufacturing in the United Kingdom

■ the increasing alcohol consumption among 18–21 year olds

■ the growth of the fitness industry, with clubs such as Holmes Place throughout the UK

■ the increasing proportion of shopping taking place through the internet.

management's own judgement and any "desk research" that they can undertake in-house.

Forecasting key variables in a firm's external environment may be crucial to the success of the whole marketing operation, but it is impossible to predict changes with complete accuracy. A good comparison would be with someone planning a holiday in the UK. In this case, the external environment is the weather: transport, hotels and outings may be meticulously planned, but two weeks of unexpected rain may ruin the whole experience.

Like the weather, the external forces that affect a business can be predicted to some extent. The legislation process is often very slow, and new laws are flagged well in advance. Social trends emerge gradually. Economic variables do not change significantly in periods of stability – a key policy aim for the UK government in the decade leading up to 2005 – and this has led to a more predictable economic environment for business.

Unexpected events and changes in the external environment do, however, occur. Take, for example, these news reports from the first quarter of 2006:

- energy prices increased by over 10 per cent – and there were worries that the UK might not be able to meet its short-term and long-term energy needs

- sales of MP3 players, mainly iPods, were unexpectedly high – these portable players were quickly adapted for in-car and "living room" use

- in a test case, a local health authority was made to supply a patient with Herceptin, an expensive anti-cancer drug, previously only available through private medical treatment.

These all have implications for businesses, consumers and society as a whole. Even though businesses cannot always predict these events, they must be prepared to respond effectively as events occur.

data **interpretation**
Charity to turn rubbish into cash

A rubbish collection service has started in the island of Jersey that sells items on to be recycled and donates the profits to charities.

Charitable organisation Recycle picks up from homes across the island. Items are then sent to mainland UK to be recycled. Any profits are donated to Jersey charities. Eighty residents have signed up for the service since it started in December 2005. Recycle hopes to eventually do all the recycling on the island.

Business	RecycleNow
Welcome | Contact Us | News	User: [_____] Password: [_____]
Household Business Symbols Other Services	

Recycle's mission

In 2004, Jersey generated 100,000 tonnes of rubbish and this is expected to increase by 3 per cent each year. That is equivalent to over 200 male elephants or a single jumbo jet. This is waste that we have no room for and that costs an awful lot of money to deal with. But there is a greater disaster going on: we are dumping and consequently incinerating things that still have value. In effect, we are burning money.

The problem is that we do not have decent recycling facilities or decent recycling strategies to handle more recycling. It would cost a lot of money for the public sector to take on these tasks. This is where we come in. We believe that not only does recycling make good sense because of the money we can save on waste disposal costs but also, with a little ingenuity, time and effort, the recycled goods could be resold to make money that would go to other charities.

With one move, we could eliminate an environmental calamity and provide much-needed extra funds for charities to improve the life of the island.

Source : adapted from BBC News website 13 March 2006 and the Recycle website

A Explain how economic and social marketing environment forces might have supported the creation of Recycle.

B Discuss how marketing environment forces might impact on the future growth of Recycle.

Competition

Setting the scene: competition in the cinema market

In 2005, Vue Entertainment Holdings (UK) Limited was the third-largest operator of cinemas in the UK. On 29 April 2005, it acquired the Ster Century (UK) Limited chain of cinemas. Ster, prior to being acquired by Vue, owned and operated multiplex cinemas at Basingstoke, Cardiff, Edinburgh, Leeds, Norwich and Romford.

Vue already operated a multiplex cinema at Basingstoke, and the acquisition of Ster now meant that Vue owned two multiplex cinemas at Basingstoke. These cinemas are located 1.5 miles apart.

On 23 September 2005, the Office of Fair Trading referred Vue's acquisition of Ster to the Competition Commission. This is the government organisation that carries out investigations into mergers and other anti-competitive business practices which might be against the interests of consumers. On the 24 February 2006, the Competition Commission made a ruling (extract opposite) on the case.

The Competition Commission ruled that Vue's acquisition of the cinema in Basingstoke led to "higher prices". Why did it reach this view? Why do you think the CC ruled that Vue should sell one of its Basingstoke cinemas to "a cinema operator with the resources, expertise, incentive and business plan to operate it as a multiplex cinema showing mainstream films"?

> The Competition Commission (CC) has decided that Vue Entertainment Holdings must sell one of the two cinemas it currently runs in Basingstoke to another cinema operator in order to preserve competition.

It has concluded that the completed acquisition of the Festival Place cinema in Basingstoke by Vue Entertainment Holdings (UK) Limited would substantially lessen competition, leading to higher prices and reduced choice for customers.

Vue will now be required to sell either the Leisure Park cinema, which it already owned, or the Festival Place cinema. The sale must be made to a cinema operator with the resources, expertise, incentive and business plan to operate it as a multiplex cinema showing mainstream films.

The full transcript of the findings can be found on the CC's website, www.competition-commission.org.uk.

Degrees of competition

An important feature of the particular markets in which a business operates is the degree of competition it faces from rival enterprises. Marketing planners need to be aware of the competition facing their business, and design marketing activities that they believe will give their business a competitive advantage.

The level of competition faced by a business is determined by several factors, including:

- the number of businesses in the market – that is, the number of direct rivals

- the attitudes and values of decision-makers in competitor businesses

- the nature of the product being sold and the size of the market.

Each market is different. However, markets can be broadly classified into one of four types, each with different structures and different levels of competition. These types are:

- monopoly
- oligopoly
- monopolistic competition
- perfect competition.

Monopoly

Monopoly, strictly defined, is a market in which only one business operates. In a monopoly market, the business – that is, the seller – is in an enviable position. It would not, by definition, face competition, and it would have significant control and power to set prices because consumers would not have an alternative supplier.

Even if a business does not have 100 per cent of the market, a business with a significant market share can exert considerable power. In these near-monopoly conditions, a dominant business is called a "price maker" as it has significant control over the prices it can charge customers for its products.

Governments have recognised the potential dangers of monopoly situations: consumers get a raw deal, and there is little competitive pressure to force the dominant business to become more efficient or to be innovative. All market economies have laws and regulations to prevent monopolies or near-monopoly situations coming about. If a near-monopoly situation exists, the market is usually regulated by a government agency to protect consumer interests and to ensure that businesses do not abuse their position.

In practice, although there are several heavily regulated industries, there are few pure monopoly markets in the UK. Perhaps the best example is the supply of mains water and sewage services, as households cannot choose the company that provides their water supply. Precisely because this is the case, all water companies in the UK are heavily regulated.

Under UK law, any business with more than 25 per cent share of any market is considered to have the potential to exercise monopoly power. The Office for Fair Trading (OFT) aims to make markets work well for consumers, and it enforces competition and consumer protection law. The OFT has the power to refer proposed mergers between companies to the Competition Commission where it believes that there may be expected to be a substantial lessening of competition in a UK market if a merger or acquisition takes place. For more information on the role of the OFT, see the introduction to Topic 4, page 117.

As we saw in the introduction to this topic, the Competition Commission can rule that a merger or acquisition – or part of a planned acquisition – should not go ahead. However, as the example below illustrates, an investigation does not always result in action. Not all mergers are seen as being against the interests of consumers. The ruling in the Heinz and HP case states that the companies were, on the whole, operating in separate markets. Indeed, it might be that the merger could actually help Heinz to produce HP's range of sauces at a lower cost, leading to lower prices for customers.

Oligopoly

In an oligopolistic market, there are usually a few large dominant businesses. There may also be smaller businesses, but it is the presence and behaviour of the few large businesses which attract the attention and shape the competitive landscape. There are many examples of oligopolistic markets in the UK, including motor vehicle manufacturing, food and household supplies (dominated by supermarkets) and banking.

The behaviour of businesses in oligopoly is unpredictable. Even if there are only two businesses in the industry, competition may be fierce. However, there is a widely held view that businesses in

On 22 February 2006, the Competition Commission published its provisional findings on the proposed acquisition of HP by Heinz.

Both Heinz and HP produce ketchup, brown sauce and barbecue sauce. Heinz also produces baked beans and tinned pasta products, while HP-branded baked beans and pasta products are currently produced by Premier Foods plc under licence from HP.

In its report, the commission concluded that the acquisition may not be expected to result in a substantial lessening of competition within the markets for the supply of tomato ketchup, brown sauce, barbecue sauce, tinned baked beans and tinned pasta products in the UK.

It provisionally concluded that there was very limited, if any, competition between Heinz and HP products in the supply to retail customers, so in spite of the increased size of the merged company, it did not expect a substantial loss of competition or an increase in prices to result from the merger. In investigating the markets, it found that ketchup and brown sauce were in separate markets for a number of reasons: these included their characteristics and uses, which differed in the customer profiles and the usage on different host foods of the two products.

In the case of ketchup, brown sauce, baked beans and pasta products, the Competition Commission found that Heinz and HP products were not acting as a competitive constraint on each other. It therefore did not expect an increase in prices to result from the merger.

As for barbecue sauce, although there was some evidence of competition between the HP and Heinz products, it found that the barriers to new providers were lower than with other items, and that barbecue sauce isn't viewed as a "must-stock" item by retailers, which means that the merged company's ability to raise prices for this product would be constrained.

The commission also looked at the food service market such as supply to restaurants, where HP only competed with Heinz on a very limited basis, so again it concluded that there would be no damage to competition.

Source: www.competition-commission.org.uk

In recent years, some new companies such as Hyundai and Kia have entered the UK car market. How might the arrival of new competitors affect the marketing mix of businesses in an oligopolistic market such as the car market?

oligopolistic markets tend to avoid competition, especially on price.

A key feature of oligopoly markets is interdependence. Each business in the oligopolistic market knows that its actions will affect the others, and that it can expect a reaction to any decision it makes. For example, a business that pursues an aggressive pricing strategy knows that it may provoke a reaction which could lead to a price war. In the end, prices will be driven down and every business in the market will suffer. So, instead of competing on price, businesses may choose to compete in other ways. Two common marketing approaches in oligopolistic markets are product differentiation and advertising.

Advertising may be informative, by giving the consumer facts about the product, or persuasive by trying to influence the consumer's feeling about the product. Advertising is often used as part of the process of product differentiation: businesses selling similar products try to convince consumers that their version is in some way preferable. Consider television advertising for instant coffee. Adverts tend to make vague references to taste or the mood-enhancing qualities of the particular brand of coffee – price is rarely mentioned. Successful marketing will lead to clear and effective product differentiation, which will play a significant role in creating customer loyalty.

Both advertising and distinct product differentiation have the further advantage for businesses already in the market of creating barriers to entry. It is more difficult for a new business to enter these types of markets because they face potential high advertising costs to generate a presence and a challenge to create a product that is sufficiently differentiated from those already in the market. A key task for the marketing department of any new entrant will be to overcome these barriers. Of course, existing businesses may seek to develop further barriers to entry in order to preserve their market share and maintain profitability.

Trying to create artificial barriers to entry would be an anti-competitive practice. In general, the law tries to prevent actions which deliberately reduce competition in a market. The most extreme example of anti-competitive practice is collusion between businesses. This is a situation in which businesses have agreements, usually unofficial and "off the record", to control the output and prices of certain products. The media uses terms like "price-fixing" to describe this behaviour. The agreements have to be unofficial, as most aspects of collusive behaviour are illegal in the UK. Any reputable company would seek to avoid any accusation that it was involved in collusive or blatantly anti-competitive practices.

Perfect competition

Perfect competition is the complete opposite of a monopoly. In a perfectly competitive market, there are many businesses competing to supply goods to numerous consumers. Intense competition drives prices down to a minimum, and there would be no customer loyalty, as all products would be identical and consumers would know – and would always shop with – the business that offer the best – that is, the lowest – price.

Examples of industries that have all the conditions necessary for perfect competition are difficult to find. However, in the UK, the wholesale fruit and vegetable markets and the market for shares have some of the features of perfect competition.

Businesses in perfectly competitive markets are described as "price takers". Because of the high degree of competition, no business in the market has the ability to control prices. If a business increases its prices, customers would simply go to a competitor. This is because there is no differentiation between products, so any customer, it is argued, would be irrational to pay a higher price for the same quality of product.

The lack of customer loyalty and lack of any price-setting power makes it difficult for businesses to survive in perfectly competitive markets. Changes in the marketing environment are likely to impact severely on perfectly competitive businesses, as each individual business has no way of differentiating what it offers. The only way to survive is to reduce costs of production – to become more efficient than your competitors.

Monopolistic competition

Monopolistic competition has much more in common with perfect competition than it does with a monopoly. Indeed, the only difference between perfect competition and monopolistic competition

relates to the nature of the product or service supplied. In the case of monopolistic competition, the product is differentiated. For example, in a town there may be a number of builders, all offering a similar service. Over time one or two builders may gain a reputation for quality and reliability, while others become known as "cowboys" that offer a cheaper service if you are prepared to take the risk. Gradually the services are differentiated in the minds of the customer, and demand for the services of the reputable builder will rise. As the reputable builder's profits rise, more resources can be devoted to activities such as marketing.

The typical size of a business in a market characterised by monopolistic competition tends to be small, and the scope for marketing is limited. Marketing activities may involve placing small advertisements in local papers, or leafleting. Extensive research and planning would not be practical. However, some small businesses may form associations which enable them to undertake more expensive marketing activates on a collective basis. Examples of these types of association are the Londis chain of convenience stores and the Federation of Master Builders.

Businesses in these types of markets can cope with changes in the environment by altering their marketing activities. These businesses have some ability to set prices and can enhance this ability by modifying the product, place and promotion aspects of their marketing mix.

stop and think

Classify the degree of competition you think is present in each of these markets:

- window cleaners
- convenience stores such as local corner store
- broadband internet services
- fast food
- book retailers (including internet retailers)
- new housing developments
- rented accommodation.

In each case, focus on the market in you local area. Compare your answers with other students in your class – be prepared to justify your decisions.

Marketing practice

In practice, every industry is different and many may not fit neatly into the market structures outlined in this topic. Nevertheless, the ways of characterising different market structures are important for marketing practice – a general sense of the degree of competition in a market should influence both strategy and tactics. Key questions relating to competition are:

- what are the resources available for marketing
- how will other businesses respond to any marketing activities
- how do businesses usually compete in this industry
- do barriers to entry have to be overcome or created
- are any planned marketing activities within the law?

The term "high street fashion" refers to designs that have been taken from the catwalk and copied by department stores and fashion shops that are accessible to everyone.

One reason why the high street is successful is the sheer speed with which it can "translate" hot fashion trends. High street stores make cutting-edge clothes available very quickly after the original has been exhibited at a fashion show. This process gets faster each season, partly due to the ready availability of images in magazines and on the internet.

Although nobody admits to direct copying, sneaking into shows for "inspiration" or "research" has been going on for many decades. This activity has often been cited as a form of spying in order to quickly make mass-produced copies of exclusive designs.

An action group in the UK called Acid (anti-copying in design) has campaigned on behalf of designers to combat the growing trend for plagiarism. Set up in 1996, Acid has established a voluntary code of conduct for retailers to acknowledge and protect the intellectual property rights of designers.

This code of conduct has been relatively successful. However, UK consumers are so fond of a bargain that this is never going to be quite enough. People are used to seeing cheaper versions of exclusive designs, and they get a thrill from the idea of paying less, even if the quality is inferior. High street fashion stores such as Topshop, Topman, Mango, Zara, and Burton provide an affordable way to wear the latest catwalk trends without blowing an entire month's wage.

Many designers have now decided that if they can't beat the retailers, they'll join them. Some, like Vivian Westwood and Paul Smith, have opened more of their own boutique shops. Others, like Zandra Rhodes or Antoni and Alison, opt for showcasing limited ranges within selected department stores or shops.

Source: British Council website

A Using the article and your own internet research, describe the degree of competition present in the high street fashion market.

B Explain why UK designers established the action group Acid.

C State two actions independent designers could take to reduce the degree of competition in their market. Justify each action.

Economic and technological forces

Setting the scene: the Chinese economy

China has been one of the world's success stories since its government began introducing economic reforms in 1978. Official figures show that national income has grown on average by 9 per cent a year over the past 25 years.

A growing share of China's economic growth has been generated by the private sector as the government has opened up industries to domestic and foreign competition. However, the role of the state in ownership and planning remains extensive.

China's economic and social development challenges remain huge. These include reforming poorly performing state-owned industries, restructuring the financial sector and raising the incomes of China's rural population.

China's leaders have launched a campaign to develop the country's western regions, as well as a drive to rejuvenate the old industrial bases in the north east. These campaigns are part of an effort to slow down the widening income gaps between China's more developed areas and the interior.

Figure 11.2 shows some key economic data for China and the UK. In 2004, the UK's economy (as measured by national income) was larger than China's. However, by 2006 China had overtaken the UK and it is now the world's second biggest economy, second only to the United States.

Why might UK businesses be interested in the development and performance of the Chinese economy?

Figure 11.2: Economic and demographic data, China and the UK

	Population (2004)	National income (2004)	Growth of national income (2004)	Exports as a % of national income (2003)	Imports as a % of national income (2003)
China	1,300 million	$1,600 billion	9.5%	34.3%	25.1%
UK	59.4 million	$2,100 billion	3.1%	31.8%	28.1%

Sources: UK Trade & Investment and the World Bank

KEY TERMS

National income is a measure of the value of goods and services produced by a nation over a period of time.

Economic growth is a measure of the increase in a nation's national income. For example, the UK national income grew by 5.4 per cent in 2004.

Unemployment level is a measure of the number of people who are out of work and are actively seeking employment. In the UK, unemployment fell from a peak of 3 million in 1993 (about 11 per cent of the working population) to 1.5 million (about 5 per cent) in 2001.

Interest rate is the return a financial institutioon (or an individual) receives for lending money to a borrower. The interest rate can be used to calculate the cost of the loan to the borrower.

Fiscal policy is a statement of how a government intends to finance its spending through taxation. This is done through a mix if direct taxes (such as income tax) or indirect taxes (such as VAT and duty on fuel, alcohol and cigarettes).

Exchange rates specifies the value of one nation's currency in terms of another nation's currency also referred to as foreign exchange rates. If the exchange rate between the UK and the USA ise £1:$1.60, then you can get $1.60 for every £1.

Barriers to trade are any monetary or non-monetary action which makes trade between nations more difficult. For example, a government might place a limit on the number of motor vehicles that can be imported from other nations.

Economic forces

There are many features of the economy that may influence the marketing process. It is important that marketing professionals understand economic conditions and that they appreciate the impact that changes in the economy can have on their markets.

National income

National income is a measure of the value of goods and services produced by a nation over a period of time. This period is usually one year: note that the national income figures for China and the UK in Figure 11.2 cover one year's production (2004). There are other measures of a nation's output: gross national product (GNP) and gross domestic product (GDP) are the most commonly used alternatives to national income. There are technical differences between the three terms, but they are closely related.

Rising national income is an indicator of prosperity. Periods of rising national income are known as economic growth. The government expects national income to rise by about 2 per cent every year in the UK. When economic growth rises above this trend, the economy is said to be in a "boom" period. If national income falls for two consecutive quarters, then the economy is officially in "recession".

In the past, the UK and other economies moved between periods of boom and recession in an economic cycle. Figure 11.3 shows the traditional pattern of the economic cycle. However, the last recession in the UK was in the early 1990s, and some

economists believe that economic growth will be much more stable in the long term.

Marketing planners need to consider the impact of changing levels of national income on the demand for products. If national incomes are rising, businesses may have increased opportunities to market their products. Consumer spending is likely to increase and, as a result, companies in business to consumer (B2C) markets should anticipate an increase in sales.

stop and think

How might an increase in the growth of UK national income in the UK from, say, 2 per cent to 4 per cent affect the marketing activities of:

- supermarkets such as Tesco and Sainsbury

- car dealers such as Perrys (www.perrys.co.uk)

- house builders such as Bovis (www.bovishomes.co.uk)

- multiplex cinemas such as Vue (www.myvue.co.uk)

Unemployment

The significance of unemployment levels to a business will vary according to the nature of its products. Demand for some products, such as cheap clothing, may actually rise during periods of higher unemployment. In general, businesses would expect high or rising unemployment to affect consumer

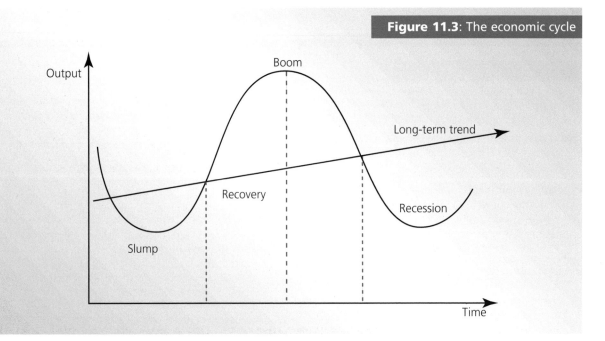

Figure 11.3: The economic cycle

confidence and so reduce demand for luxury goods or non-essential purchases.

In recent years, UK unemployment figures have been stable and relatively low. One consequence of low unemployment is that some businesses may face labour or skills shortages, which may cause difficulties in supply. There is little point in running a successful marketing campaign if production cannot be increased to meet the additional demand.

Interest rates

Interest rates in the UK are based on the Bank of England's base rate. At April 2006, the Bank of England's base rate was 4.5 per cent. Savers may receive less than this rate, borrowers should expect to pay higher interest rates on their loans.

Demand for products that tend to be purchased with the aid of loans, such as cars and expensive furniture, is especially sensitive to interest rate changes. Perhaps the impact of interest rates is most keenly felt in the housing market.

Fiscal policy

The government spends large amounts on services such as education, health and defence. This money is largely raised through taxation, such as income tax and VAT. Collectively, a government's spending and taxation plans are known as fiscal policy. Each year the government announces its spending proposals and its decisions on taxation through the Budget and other economic statements to Parliament.

Changes in government spending can create opportunities and threats for businesses. Some industries are heavily dependent on government contracts as their main source of revenue; others businesses benefit indirectly from government spending. An academic book publisher is likely to be pleased if the government announces it is increasing university spending, providing more places for students, whereas shipbuilding and aerospace businesses are unlikely to welcome cuts in defence spending if these reduce orders from the armed forces for ships and aircraft.

business practice
The UK housing market

As this extract from Social Trends shows, there is a declining proportion of first-time buyers in the UK housing market. This is a key factor in the marketing environment for any business involved in the housing market, such as estate agents, house builders and mortgage providers.

> Steep increases in house prices have made affordability a particular concern to first-time buyers. House prices impact disproportionally on first-time buyers because they need to fund deposits from savings, gifts or loans rather than being able to do so from the profit made from the sale of an existing home. In 2004 the average deposit paid by first-time buyers in the United Kingdom was 21 per cent of the purchase price, compared with only 10 per cent in 1996.

> Since the late 1990s, the proportion of first-time buyers entering the housing market has fallen sharply. In 2003 and 2004, 29 per cent of new mortgage loans in the United Kingdom were to first-time buyers, an all-time low since records began in 1974. The highest proportions of first-time buyers

occurred in 1993 and 1994 at 55 per cent.

> Another factor contributing to the fall in the proportion of new mortgages obtained by first-time buyers has been the substantial increase in the buy-to-let market. This is where houses are bought by landlords who then rent the houses to tenants. By the end of 2004 there were over 525,000 buy-to-let mortgages in the United Kingdom, more than seven times the number at the end of 1999.

Adapted from Social Trends 36

Is the current situation sustainable? A declining proportion of first-time buyers is potentially disastrous – all house sellers rely on new buyers to "kick-start" the house-selling chain. If buy-to-let investors are purchasing the typical first-time buyer properties – pushing up demand, and hence contributing to higher prices – how is any first-time buyer expected to get on the property ladder? Consider how house builders and mortgage providers might respond to the problem of the declining proportion of first-time buyers.

Direct taxes are those which are levied on an individual's income (income tax) or a business's profits (corporation tax). Raising direct taxes tends to reduce the total demand for goods and services in the economy, as it reduces the total income of both individuals and businesses: conversely, reducing direct taxes should increase demand.

Indirect taxes are taxes on spending. Essentially, a proportion of the amount spent on goods or services is taken as tax by the government. The most ubiquitous indirect tax is value added tax (VAT), which is applied to most products, though many foods, children's clothing, books and some other goods are exempt. Some products, such as alcohol and tobacco, have separate indirect taxes, known as duties, outside the VAT system. Changes in indirect taxation tends to impact on the overall level of demand in the same way as direct taxation.

Exchange rates

The exchange rate is the price of one currency expressed in terms of another country's currency. The value of the pound, for instance, can be shown against a variety of other currencies such as the dollar, the yen or the euro. At the end of April 2006, one pound sterling was worth:

- 1.44 euros
- 1.78 US dollars
- 2.36 Australian dollars
- 203.8 Japanese yen
- 13.2 Swedish krona

Businesses that import raw materials, components and goods for retail, and those that export their goods and services, are particularly affected by changes in exchange rates. The exchange rate can change the domestic prices of internationally traded goods and services. If international trade plays a significant part in a business, managers must take account of the possible impact of exchange rate movements on costs and prices.

Take a UK firm that imports wine from France to sell in the UK. If the wine costs 9 euros a bottle (wholesale) in France, then at an exchange rate of 1.5 euros to the pound, the UK firm will be paying £6 per bottle for the wine. If the exchange rate falls, and the firm only gets 1.4 euros to the pound, then each bottle will cost £6.43. The price in France has remained unchanged, but the firm's costs have increased. A falling exchange rate, therefore, can increase costs for importers.

A firm exporting suits to France would benefit from the same exchange rate change. A suit priced at £200 in the UK would be valued at 300 euros in France at an exchange rate of 1.5 euros to the pound. If the rate falls to 1.4 euros to the pound, the firm could charge 280 euros for each suit and still receive £200. It could lower its prices in France without losing any income, which should help to increase demand for the suits.

The euro

In 1999, 11 of the then 15 member states of the European Union adopted the euro as their currency, thereby electing to give up their own currencies. Greece joined the eurozone in 2001, leaving only Sweden, Denmark and the UK opting to retain their own currencies. Some UK politicians have indicated a willingness to join the euro at a future date, and the government's position (as at 2006) is that it will recommend that the UK adopts the euro if it is clear that the UK economy will benefit as a result. Any decision would have to be ratified by a referendum.

For businesses trading in Europe there are three main benefits of being in the eurozone:

- it removes transaction costs – that is, the cost of changing one currency into another

- it promotes price transparency – differences in the prices and costs of products across member countries can be clearly seen

- it eliminates exchange rate uncertainty – reducing the fluctuations described above.

The business arguments against adopting the euro are more complex. Some businesses are concerned that:

- the UK would lose control over economic policy issues, such as the level of interest rates

- the euro exchange rates with other major trading partners, such as the US and Japan, might not be as favourable as current UK exchange rates

- the single currency would make it easier for customers to compare prices of UK products with those of other European businesses – in other words, they fear the transparency that others would welcome.

Barriers to trade

Some countries seek to restrict the free movement of imports and exports, usually to help businesses within their own country. For example, some countries impose tariffs (a tax) on imports. In theory, this makes imports more expensive and it is therefore easier for domestic firms to compete against foreign competition.

There are other methods of restricting trade, through a variety of non-tariff barriers. These include:

- subsidising domestic firms to allow them to charge lower prices

- insisting that complicated import documentation must be filled in before products are allowed to enter the country, causing delays in delivery

stop and think

Give examples of two types of UK businesses which you believe benefit from free trade in Europe. Explain why you think they have benefited.

- imposing unreasonable quality or safety standards before goods are allowed to be imported.

Technological forces

New technology offers many opportunities to businesses. For many, it allows them to be efficient and to adopt cost-effective methods of production. More directly, it offers an array of new product areas. As a result, sales of some products will decrease – music companies no longer produce audio cassettes, for example – but on balance new technology has led to a growth in product sales.

Information and communication technology (ICT) has changed the way many firms undertake their marketing. Databases relating to existing and potential customers can be used to tailor products to match consumer wants and needs. For example, Tesco uses its Clubcard loyalty scheme to provide detailed information on the buying habits of its customers, which it can then exploit through the way it structures its promotional campaigns and the way it organises the goods within its stores.

ICT also offers new ways of communicating with customers: firms can easily and cost-effectively communicate through text messages, e-mail, personalised mail shots and websites. Marketing departments have to decide which combination of communication methods is likely to be the most cost-effective.

All firms seek to gain competitive advantage through technology. Cheaper production methods, better knowledge of the market and products with unique features can give a business an advantage over its rivals, for a period of time at least. ICT may both create and break down the barriers to entry to a market. For example, any firm patenting a new invention is creating a legally enforceable barrier to entry which can be sustained over a period time. Intel has legitimately created a market barrier by patenting its Pentium computer chips.

Technology may allow entry to markets previously dominated by a few oligopolistic firms. The vehicle insurance industry is a good example of how this can happen. At one time, an insurance firm needed an extensive and expensive branch network to handle the paperwork associated with providing car insurance. However, recently new internet-based providers have emerged that can cut these office costs and, as a result, they are often able to offer lower premiums to customers.

Recorded music sales continue to dip

Sales of recorded music continued to fall worldwide in 2005. The International Federation of the Phonographic Industry (IFPI) said the fall continued despite a rise in online and mobile music store revenues. Chairman John Kennedy said global music retail revenues fell by about 2 per cent in 2005.

The overall sales decline came despite a threefold increase in digital music revenue, while illegal file-sharing volumes changed little, according to a separate IFPI market report. Recorded music businesses are now having to look beyond piracy to explain the latest decline in revenues, which have fallen by around 20 per cent globally since 1999.

EMI chairman Eric Nicoli said: "Piracy in all its forms has been the major factor, but not the only one. Twenty years ago there were no mobile phones, no DVDs, no computer games to speak of."

A number of record companies are also pressing Apple to allow more pricing flexibility on its iTunes music store, which currently charges the same rate for any downloaded song. They have argued, so far without success, that they should be able to charge more for the most sought-after hits.

Apple's iTunes accounts for around 70 per cent of US and British online music sales. This popularity is widely credited with halting the growth of piracy, but record companies complain that it has come at a cost – with a loss of control over their own pricing and marketing.

Source: adapted from BBC News website, 23 January 2006

A Using the article, describe two changes in the recorded music industry's marketing environment.

B Explain why record companies have complained about Apple's iTunes music store.

C Discuss how recorded music businesses such as EMI could alter their marketing activities in order to increase their music retail revenues.

Legal, regulatory, social and ethical forces

Setting the scene: Office of Fair Trading

The Office of Fair Trading (OFT) is a government agency tasked with ensuring that markets work well for customers. The OFT monitors the degree of competition present in markets, and intervenes when necessary.

The Competition Act 1998 gives the OFT the power to investigate any business that is found to have entered into agreements between itself and competitors:

- on the prices to be charged for products
- on which customers or areas in the country they will supply products to
- to deliberately limit the supply of products, so as to artificially increase prices.

In addition, the Competition Act 1998 allows the OFT to investigate businesses that might be abusing their dominant position in the marketplace. Businesses with a market share of over 40 per cent could be considered as having a potentially dominant position, but this also depends on the number and size of competitors in the market, and the barriers to entry – the ease with which other companies can enter the market. Examples of abuse of a dominant position include:

- charging excessively high prices
- refusing to supply an existing customer without good reason

- charging different prices to different customers where there is no difference in quantity, quality or other characteristics of the products.

Representatives of the OFT can enter a business's premises without a search warrant and require managers to produce documents and information relevant to the particular investigation. The OFT can order that any offending agreements or anti-competitive behaviour be stopped.

Businesses that contravene the Competition Act face legal penalties. These include fines of up to 10 per cent of a business's UK sales for up to three years. Individuals found, by a court, to be dishonestly involved in price-fixing agreements can be fined and imprisoned for up to five years.

Can you think of any markets in the UK that are dominated by one or two businesses? Consider ways in which the Competition Act 1998 might constrain the marketing activities of these businesses.

KEY TERMS

The **Office of Fair Trading** is a UK government body that seeks to protect the consumer from anti-competitive practices. It can impose significant fines on businesses that are found to be harming consumer interests through anti-competitive practices such as restricting supply or fixing prices at an artificially high level.

The **Competition Commission** is an independent body responsible for investigating mergers, market shares and conditions, and the regulation of businesses in the UK.

The **Advertising Standards Authority** is an independent body responsible for regulating broadcast and non-broadcast advertising in the UK.

Ethical values are sets of beliefs that define what society, or a group within that society, considers as acceptable behaviour.

Legal and regulatory forces

There are many laws relating to the activities of business. Health and safety legislation, alone, involves several major Acts of Parliament. Most laws that regulate business activities are designed to ensure fair competition in markets and to protect individuals and other companies from the potentially harmful actions of any firm.

Consumer protection

There is a considerable body of legislation that offers rights to consumers. This has grown in recent years as a result of public pressure for better standards of quality and service. The law protects consumers against businesses giving false or misleading information about products, businesses adopting unfair trading practices, such as a supplying a smaller quantity than advertised on the packaging, and businesses supplying unsafe or faulty products.

These rights are enshrined in consumer protection legislation. These are some of the main laws that apply in any business transaction.

- **The Sale of Goods Act 1979**
  This states that goods must be of merchantable quality (work properly and not be broken), fit for the purpose and as described by the manufacturer. It was not until much later that a law relating to the quality of services provided was introduced.

- **The Weights and Measures Act 1986**
  This states that weights and measures used in trading must be guaranteed in terms of accuracy.

- **The Trade Descriptions Act 1968**
  This makes the misleading description of goods and services an offence.

Although these laws have now been on the statute book for more than 20 years, consumer protection law is still evolving. Pressure groups such as the Consumers' Association, publishers of *Which?*, are continually monitoring business practices, and pressing for new legislation where necessary.

Regulation

Legislation provides the backbone of consumer protection and competition policy in the UK. However, the law is generally used as a last resort. Regulation is the process whereby organisations – usually set up by government – monitor business behaviour, listen to issues raised by consumers and negotiate with the businesses to resolve problems. These regulatory bodies can use the courts if necessary to force businesses to comply with the law, but they often try to resolve disputes and consumer grievances through negotiation and mutual agreement.

Office of Fair Trading

This agency oversees consumer protection in the UK on a national level, offering advice to consumers and, when necessary, prosecuting companies that are thought to be adopting unfair practices.

Competition Commission

The Competition Commission was established by the Competition Act 1998. It has a responsibility to ensure that businesses in the UK operate in a competitive environment, and it works closely with the Office of Fair Trading. One of the commission's main roles is to

prevent the creation of oligopolistic or near-monopoly markets that may operate in an anti-competitive way (see Topic 2). When a company announces plans to acquire (or merge with) another business that might create a dominant player in the market, the case may be referred to the Competition Commission. The commission may refuse to allow the takeover if it feels that it would be against the public interest.

Advertising Standards Authority

Advertising Standards Authority (ASA) monitors all advertising media, except that on television and radio. Its responsibility is to ensure that advertising is "legal, decent, honest and truthful". The ASA responds to complaints from the public and has, on occasions, forced companies to withdraw or modify advertising campaigns. The Independent Television Commission (ITC) fulfils a similar role in relation to advertising on television and radio.

Industry regulators

The government has set up regulators in several industries that are dominated by a small number of large companies. These tend to be industries which by their nature allow only limited competition or which provide essential services. There are regulators for all the major utilities, including gas and electricity, water and sewerage, and telecommunications.

Self-regulation

Many industries have developed their own voluntary codes of practice or "customer charters" to set standards for the quality of their goods or services. These codes serve two purposes: they are designed to provide protection to consumers, and they show government that the industry can regulate its own affairs. Many codes of practice go beyond the minimum standards set by the law, and they are often heavily publicised as part of a promotional package.

stop and think

Explain how legal and regulatory forces might impact on the marketing activities of:

- companies offering ringtone and other mobile download services, such as Jamster

- BSkyB, the satellite television broadcaster

- fashion retailers, such as Topshop and Next

- car manufacturers, such as Ford and VW

- budget airlines, such as Ryanair.

Unit 11 The marketing environment

Social forces

Society is in a continuous process of change. Some changes are gradual; others may take place fairly quickly. Here are a few examples of these changes:

- over the past 200 years there has been an almost continuous increase in the standard of living

- at one time most people lived in rented accommodation, now most are owner-occupiers

- there are many more one-parent households than in previous generations

- most adults now have access to a motor vehicle

- smoking in public is now much less acceptable.

Obviously, this list could be extended to cover many other changing facets of UK life. The key point, however, is that each trend results in changing patterns of consumption. Businesses will try to anticipate these trends and respond to them. Larger firms may be able to commission specialist research to identify emerging trends in society. Businesses must be sensitive to changes in society by, for example, avoiding causing offence to certain groups in the way they promote their products.

Ethical forces

Ethical behaviour is that which is deemed to be morally acceptable by the standards of the society of the day. These standards are influenced by many factors, such as parents, politicians, religion and the media. The boundary between ethical and unethical behaviour is often unclear. One person may regard an action as acceptable, another may not. As society changes, so do ethical values. Consider these statements from your own ethical standpoint.

- It is unacceptable to sell cigarettes to children less than ten years of age.

- It is acceptable to sell military aircraft to other countries.

- It is unacceptable to buy products that have been manufactured by children in the developing world.

These statements illustrate the difficulties faced by businesses. Some issues are fairly clear cut – most would agree with the first statement – others are not. In some areas, legislation governs ethical behaviour. However, in many areas there are no guidelines. For this reason, many firms have drawn up codes of practice to make their own ethical standards clear.

business practice
Grey power

The population of the UK is ageing. There will soon be as many people aged over 65 in the population as people aged 16 and under. This has significant implications for many businesses. This extract from an article published by the research firm Mori in 2003 analyses some of the marketing implications.

> We are already seeing a more hedonistic approach to life among retirees. Our data suggest that this trend is only going to be magnified. Baby boomers (those born in the late 1950s and early 1960s) expect to take part in more leisure activities as they get older. It would appear that the retirement envisioned by the majority of them will revolve around leisure and culture.

> A significant growth area would appear to be in travel. Four in five baby boomers expect to take more holidays and short breaks after they retire. This does not mean that people are expecting to spend all their money on travel, and will have none left for other activities – after all, what happens when they get to their holiday destination?

> It does have an impact on marketing, though. Visitors will be spending large amounts of their free time (and money) on travelling further afield, so leisure providers will have to look harder for custom. There will be influxes of people visiting from further afield, so traditional forms of marketing may pass them by. The internet would appear to be the ideal medium: older people already spend longer online, visit more sites, and have a higher dwell time.

> These results are based on a snapshot of current opinions and attitudes. Only time will tell if our baby boomer generation will turn out to do all the things they claim they are planning to do. One thing is clear, though: given their history of social activity, it is unlikely that they will decide to grow old gracefully and spend all their time in the garden. Baby boomers are going to make very active and very demanding retirees over the next few years, so be prepared.

Source: Ipsos MORI. www.ipsos-mori.com

assessment practice
Survey confirms 24-hour drinking is urban myth

Not one single pub will open for 24 hours, according to a new national survey by the British Beer and Pub Association (BBPA). The survey of BBPA members, who own over 30,500 pubs and bars in England and Wales, confirms that not one intends opening for 24 hours once the Licensing Act 2003 is implemented in late 2005.

"As we have said for some time, no pub intends opening for 24 hours and none of our customers want to drink for 24 hours. What pubs want is the flexibility to provide more choice after 11 pm," said Mark Hastings, the BBPA's director of communications.

"At present the only choice you have at 11 pm is to go home or go to a noisy nightclub. Following the introduction of the Licensing Act 2003, pubs will be able to apply for variations in their opening and closing times. Our survey shows that we will experience a variation in closing times, as many have predicted, and that the majority will occur between 11 pm and 2 am.

"Just because pubs may want to stay open a little later, does not mean that they can," continued Mr Hastings. "All applications have to be approved by local authorities. The police and the local community can object to any application, particularly where a pub has caused or is causing problems.

"The implementation of the Act will provide choice for customers and a greater variety of late-night venues, which no longer have to provide music or dancing. With the removal of the restrictions required under existing law, our towns and city centres will cater for a much wider age range than at present," said Mr Hastings.

The results of the survey, which focused on opening hours and closing times, show that some businesses will apply for variations in their licences. The only days on which pubs are looking to extend their hours are Friday and Saturday, with the majority (58 per cent) expecting to close at 1 am. Some will apply for a closing time of 2 am to allow flexibility on special occasions.

Neil Sullivan of The Hermit in Winwick said: "We're certainly not going for 24 hours. Our customers want an extra hour on Fridays and Saturdays. We have a very busy restaurant, and at the weekend we have people coming in at 10 pm to eat. It means they don't have to rush and can stay a bit longer. It also means we won't lose trade to the local town."

Alison Smith of Bar One Nine in Keynsham said: "We are probably only looking to open up until midnight on Thursday, Friday and Saturdays. But this is a 'nice-to-have' rather than a 'must-have'. We are 50 per cent food, and that's what's driving this. People want to linger over a meal, not to be rushed out of the door."

Source: British Beer & Pub Association press release, 24 January 2005

A Using the BBPA press release, explain how pubs and bars in the UK plan to alter their marketing activities after the introduction of the Licensing Act 2003.

B To what extent will the Licensing Act 2003 have a major impact on the marketing activities of pubs and bars in England and Wales? Justify your answer.

Unit 11 The marketing environment

Scanning the marketing environment

Setting the scene: Mintel reports energy drink sales to reach £1 billion

Mintel is a market research and consumer intelligence organisation. The research agency can help businesses discover opportunities, monitor competitors, develop products and services, and hone their marketing and advertising efforts.

Mintel regularly issues press releases about its latest research activities. This extract is from a press release promoting a report on the market for energy drinks. This market includes well-known brand names such as Red Bull and Lucozade Energy. The full report is available from Mintel priced at £995.

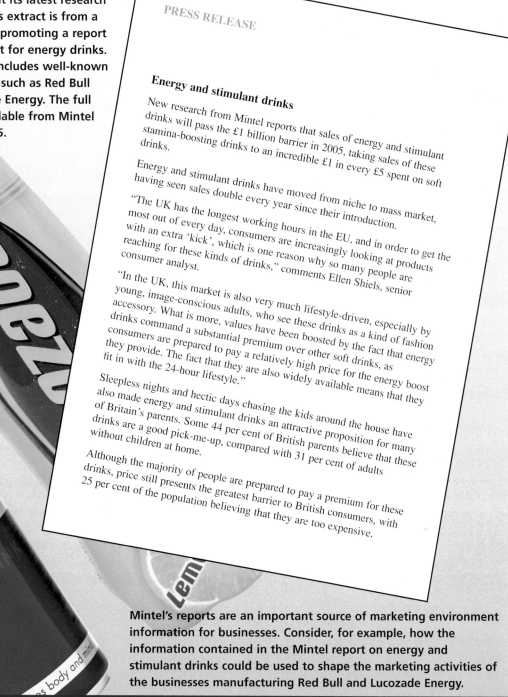

Source: adapted from Mintel press release
(reports.mintel.com)

PRESS RELEASE

Energy and stimulant drinks

New research from Mintel reports that sales of energy and stimulant drinks will pass the £1 billion barrier in 2005, taking sales of these stamina-boosting drinks to an incredible £1 in every £5 spent on soft drinks.

Energy and stimulant drinks have moved from niche to mass market, having seen sales double every year since their introduction.

"The UK has the longest working hours in the EU, and in order to get the most out of every day, consumers are increasingly looking at products with an extra 'kick', which is one reason why so many people are reaching for these kinds of drinks," comments Ellen Shiels, senior consumer analyst.

"In the UK, this market is also very much lifestyle-driven, especially by young, image-conscious adults, who see these drinks as a kind of fashion accessory. What is more, values have been boosted by the fact that energy drinks command a substantial premium over other soft drinks, as consumers are prepared to pay a relatively high price for the energy boost they provide. The fact that they are also widely available means that they fit in with the 24-hour lifestyle."

Sleepless nights and hectic days chasing the kids around the house have also made energy and stimulant drinks an attractive proposition for many of Britain's parents. Some 44 per cent of British parents believe that these drinks are a good pick-me-up, compared with 31 per cent of adults without children at home.

Although the majority of people are prepared to pay a premium for these drinks, price still presents the greatest barrier to British consumers, with 25 per cent of the population believing that they are too expensive.

Mintel's reports are an important source of marketing environment information for businesses. Consider, for example, how the information contained in the Mintel report on energy and stimulant drinks could be used to shape the marketing activities of the businesses manufacturing Red Bull and Lucozade Energy.

Market research is the systematic collection and analysis of data to enable a business to make better marketing decisions.

Primary research involves gathering information directly from customers within the target market.

Secondary research involves gathering information from already published data such as government statistics.

Market research

The external environment can have a considerable impact on business activity, as the previous two topics have demonstrated. Many businesses scan this environment on a regular basis. They may be looking for business opportunities or trying to anticipate threats to their current market position. Businesses may also undertake more focused research in, say, testing a new product idea. Customers are another important area of research. Many businesses undertake regular customer opinion surveys. Some businesses seek to add value to their customer base through relationship marketing.

Market research has already been investigated in Unit 1 (see pages 26–9 of your AS textbook). Primary research involves obtaining information directly from consumers through techniques such as surveys, observation, consumer panels and test marketing. Secondary research relies on information that has already been obtained by another party. Useful sources of secondary information include government statistics, commercial research reports (from companies like Mintel) and a business's own records.

Customers' views and feelings are very important to businesses. Attracting new customers is often difficult and expensive – all the more reason then for any business to make the most of its existing customers. Businesses may seek to establish some kind of relationship with their customers in order to find out the kind of products they would like in future.

One practical difficulty of customer opinion research is finding a method that customers do not find annoying or intrusive. Simple analysis of past purchases and complaint levels avoids this problem, but may not give the qualitative information, such as detailed views on the level of service provided by staff, that a business wants. Questionnaires may be used, particularly if they are part of an after-sales customer follow-up survey. Sometimes a business offers a small inducement, such as entry into a prize draw, to encourage participation. However, consumer goodwill will soon be lost if a survey goes beyond a few questions, and some researchers believe that providing rewards for respondents can distort their views. In short, valid information about customer opinions is difficult to obtain, but if it is available it can form a useful basis for staff training programmes and future product development.

Maven Management is a market research agency that specialises in customer and employee satisfaction surveys. This is an extract from its website (www.maven.co.uk) which explains how the company undertakes customer loyalty measurements for its clients.

Customer loyalty measurements

Before setting about the improvement of customer satisfaction and loyalty, Maven helps clients with some vital initial steps, and assists in developing a customer retention strategy.

First, using customer satisfaction surveys and other methods, we measure the loyalty rate as it stands now, before the process of improvement starts. We also establish the different loyalty rates of various customer types – males and females, different age groups, or customers for different types of products and services. Our surveys can determine drivers within the loyal groups to create satisfaction targets to drive loyalty.

Second, we also measure the cost of customer disloyalty to your organisation, again for the various customer types.

When we use these two measures together, we can then provide you with a valuable predictor of the return that each percentage point of improvement in customer loyalty will make to your profitability. These measures establish the base line for improvements over time, allowing meaningful targets to be set and business reviews to be conducted.

Why might it be sensible for a business to use an external agency, such as Maven Management, to carry out and analyse the results of a customer satisfaction survey? How might the results modify the marketing activities of the business?

Observation of market activities

For a long time, there was an unwritten agreement that firms would not denigrate or even refer to a competitor's product in their marketing campaigns. This still holds true in many industries, but some businesses are now prepared to comment on competitors' products as part of their advertising.

The fact that a business does not comment on its competitors should not be taken to imply that it does not keep a close eye on their activities. Most want to know about new product innovations in their industry and any areas where rivals seem to be successful. This information can be obtained by:

- trawling websites and obtaining published data on competitors such as their annual accounts

- monitoring the national and trade press for information about rivals

- purchasing or commissioning reports on market segments from agencies such as Mintel

- visiting rival premises that are open to the public – in effect, using the "mystery shopper" technique.

Market intelligence, gathered by monitoring newspaper reports and other media, is an essential source of information on a business's marketing environment. Many websites – some free, some only accessible via a subscription payment – provide a useful short-cut service by collecting together articles from different media sources on a particular market or industry. These websites, in effect, do the monitoring for a business. For example, the Association of Convenience Stores' website (www.thelocalshop.com) helps convenience store owners to keep up to date with changes in their marketing environment.

Government publications

The UK government collects and publishes a range of social and economic data that may be downloaded free from its websites. Its main statistics portal – www.statistics.gov.uk – provides access to databases and reports, containing detailed quantitative and qualitative information on the economic environment.

Two key reports, published each year, are *Social Trends* and *Regional Trends*. In *Social Trends* you can find a wide range of marketing environment data covering the economy, and social and ethical issues. There is data on:

- changes in the structure of the UK population

- structure of households – marital status, number of children, etc.

- employment and unemployment – numbers of people in work, numbers seeking work

- income and wealth of different types of households

- spending patterns of households

- lifestyles and participation of citizens in social and cultural activities.

Regional Trends contains a smaller range of economic and social data, but presents the data by geographic region. So, for example, you can obtain data on the South East or Yorkshire and Humberside. The government's statistics portal also provides neighbourhood profiles. By entering the postcode of an area, you can obtain a range of socioeconomic data that could be of use to a business when deciding on appropriate marketing activities in that area.

The importance of scanning

A useful analogy to use when trying to understand the role of market scanning is that of a modern fishing vessel. It will set off with destination in mind, based on research and past experience. The captain will have to be aware of legal issues: where it is permitted to fish, and the species and quantities that can be landed. Once on the fishing grounds, the vessel will continue to monitor its environment with all its "senses": radar, sonar, contact with base and other vessels, weather reports, and observations by the crew. A successful trip will depend on good intelligence, the judgement of the crew and the vessel having the flexibility to take opportunities as they arise. In other words, any business must scan its marketing environment to ensure that it has up-to-date intelligence on key economic, technological, legal, social and ethical trends. Without this information, its marketing activities are likely to be inappropriate and potentially detrimental to its future survival.

Go-Kart Party is a business providing safe go-karting experiences for children using electrically powered go-karts. It operates through a franchise system, and Figure 11.4 shows a summary description of the business.

Figure 11.4: The Go-Kart Party business

Business description	Children's entertainment
Season	All year round, outdoor or indoor halls (no fumes nor noise)
Target market	Children aged between 4 and 9 years, suitable for boys and girls
Market size	There are more than 4.3 million children in the UK
Market value	Around £216 million is spent annually on children's parties and entertainment
Opportunities	Birthday parties, carnivals, fun days, sports days, traffic education, etc.
Locations	Shopping centres, local authority sites, fetes, fairs, holiday locations, etc.

Source: adapted from www.go-kartparty.co.uk

This article by a Go-Kart Party franchisee has been adapted from the Franchise Direct website. This is a resource for franchisees and franchisors, and includes information on local and international franchise opportunities available in the UK and Ireland.

Call Us: 0870 116 2000   **Go-Kart Party** The most fun kids can have   Email Us

Home | UK Franchise Ops | Overseas Franchise Ops | Book a Party | Members

A phenomenal success

Clive Matkin, from Oxfordshire, tells how he and his family have made a phenomenal success of their Go-Kart Party franchise in just 12 months.

"I never expected it to take off the way it did," remarks Clive. "And certainly not in such a short space of time. It was March 2005 that we started up, and in March 2006, just 12 months later, I did 34 birthday parties in that month alone, and 44 different events in April. It's become my main business."

Although birthday parties are his best source of income, Clive also does corporate events, carnivals, school fetes and air shows, and is now at the point where he is taking bookings several weeks in advance. Having devoted enormous time and effort to finding suitable venues, he currently has a base of 15 different leisure centres from which he operates, meaning that he can offer his services to almost the entire Oxfordshire area.

"Leisure centres make a fantastic venue, as they have a lot of walk-through traffic, and once people see Go-Kart Party in operation, they're sold. Obviously we do a lot of advertising, but the business is really self-promoting. We're at the stage now where we can hardly keep up with demand, so we may have to look at expanding next year."

Source: www.franchisedirect.co.uk

A Using the article, describe two factors which might have contributed to the success of Clive Matkin's Go-Kart Party franchise.

B Give two reasons why it would be important for Clive Matkin to gather information about his business's marketing environment prior to expanding the business.

C Which sources of marketing environment data would you advise Clive Matkin to access prior to expanding his business? Justify your answer.

Analysing marketing environment data

Setting the scene: UK household expenditure

Figure 11.5 is taken from *Social Trends 2006*. It summarises the spending patterns of UK households. The data is grouped by broad product types and the occupation of the main earner within each household.

The table presents a range of data, and it is important to scan its contents before attempting to use the information it contains. What unit or units is the data measured in? What is the importance of the footnotes? What time period does the data cover?

After answering these questions, Figure 11.5 can be interrogated to extract useful information. For example, what does the table say about the pattern of spending on different products for "all households"? What can be understood by comparing the patterns of spending between households whose main earners have different types of occupations?

We could also consider how the data might be presented in different ways. For example, some aspects of the data might be presented as pie charts or bar charts. Some data could converted into percentages. Would this be a more helpful presentation?

Figure 11.5: Household expenditure[1] by socioeconomic classification[2], 2004/05

United Kingdom

£ per week

	Occupations			Never worked[3] and long-term unemployed	All households[4]
	Managerial and professional	Intermediate	Routine and manual		
Food and non-alcoholic drink	53.80	49.60	45.90	34.40	44.70
Alcohol and tobacco	13.80	13.00	13.40	10.60	11.30
Clothing and footwear	35.30	27.70	25.50	23.30	23.90
Housing, fuel and power[5]	49.40	42.30	43.70	57.20	40.40
Household goods and services	46.10	34.70	28.80	15.40	31.60
Health	7.60	4.50	3.70	1.60	4.90
Transport	95.60	71.00	61.30	27.10	59.60
Communication	15.00	13.60	13.70	10.80	11.70
Recreation and culture	84.60	60.10	63.30	31.10	59.00
Education	14.00	5.20	1.70	33.40	6.50
Restaurants and hotels	55.70	42.60	37.30	28.40	36.10
Miscellaneous goods and services	53.80	37.70	33.00	15.00	34.90
Other expenditure items	121.80	82.20	64.80	19.80	69.70
All household expenditure	646.40	484.30	436.00	308.20	434.40
Average household size (number of people)	2.7	2.7	2.8	2.6	2.4

1 Expenditure rounded to the nearest 10 pence.

2 Excludes retired households.

3 Includes households where the reference person is a student.

4 Includes retired households and others that are not classified.

5 Excludes mortgage interest payments, water charges and council tax. These are included in other expenditure items.

Source: Social Trends

KEY TERMS

Rate of change is a measure of how rapidly a variable is changing, usually calculated as a percentage. For example, if the population of a town was 50,000 in 2004 and 55,000 in 2005, then the annual rate of change in the town's population between 2004 and 2005 would have been 10 per cent [(55,000 – 50,000)/50,000 x100].

Mean is the arithmetic average of a set of values calculated by dividing the sum of the values by the number of values. To calculate the mean of this data set {3; 6; 10; 12; 18}, sum the values (the answer is 49) and divided by 5 (the number of values): the mean is 9.8 (49/5).

Median is the middle value within an ordered data set. The median of {3; 6; 10; 12; 18} is 10. Note the median does not have to equal the mean.

Mode is the most frequently occurring value within a data set.

Index numbers indicates change in a time series of data. The current value of a variable (such as prices) is compared with its value at some specified time in the past.

Line of best fit is the line that best represents the apparent relationship between two variables when values for both are plotted as a scatter graph.

Interpreting data

As you have seen from our discussion on Figure 11.5, it is important to interpret data carefully. With any table of figures (or diagram), read the main heading, column headings, axes labels and any other background information carefully. Take care to check if the information is in actual, percentage or index form (index numbers are explained later in this topic). The aim of this process is to gain an overview of the information and to avoid fundamental mistakes.

Figure 11.6: Monthly change in Megacorp sales, quarter 1 2006

Month	Jan	Feb	Mar
Change in sales (%)	10	5	4

One common error is to confuse absolute (actual) figures with data that shows percentage changes. For example, consider the data in Figure 11.6. Reading this table, it is very tempting to say that sales have been falling. In fact, sales have been increasing throughout the period but the rate of increase has slowed down. If the actual sales figures are calculated, as Figure 11.7 shows, they are actually increasing in each month.

Figure 11.7: Megacorp sales, Dec 2005 – March 2006

Month	Dec	Jan	Feb	Mar
£'000	100,000	110,000	115,500	120,120

The source for the information in Figures 11.6 and 11.7 has not been given. Checking the source of information is an important part of establishing its reliability. These figures could be historical data from reliable company records or the optimistic forecasts of an ambitious marketing executive. However, the important lesson here is that percentage calculations can cause difficulties – both for those carrying out the calculations and those interpreting them.

Figure 11.8: Average daily flow of motor vehicles (Great Britain; thousands of motor vehicles)

	1998	2001	2004
Motorways	68.7	71.6	74.9

Source: Social Trends

Tabulated data

Tables of information often contain some form of average or provide the basic data that can be analysed by calculating averages. The most frequently used averages are the mean, mode and median. It is useful to understand the benefits and limitations of using each form of average. Before considering each in turn, note that calculating averages, particularly for large sets of grouped data, can be quite an involved process, although the calculations are easier using the tools available in a spreadsheet package.

Mean

The mean – sometimes referred to as the arithmetic mean – is the most commonly used average. If the word "average" is used in connection with a data set, it can be assumed that reference is being made to the mean unless there is an explicit reference to the mode or median.

To calculate the value of the mean, the values of all items in a data set are added together and divided by the number of items in the data set. (The total number of items in the data set is sometimes called the population.) The mean can be expressed as a formula:

$$\text{mean} = \frac{\text{sum of items}}{\text{number of items}}$$

Study the data in Figure 11.8. This is an extract from a larger table of data in Social Trends. The first point to note is that the figures are measuring average daily figures on all motorways in Great Britain. On a particular day in 2004, the M25 may have had traffic flows of 150,000, considerably in excess of the 74,900 average; equally, the M69 might have had a flow of say 40,000 vehicles.

The second feature to note is the time periods used to represent these average daily flows. Three measurement periods are given: 1998, 2001 and 2004. In each of these three years, an estimate of the annual flow of motor vehicles would have been made and then divided by 365 to produce an average daily figure. However, we do not know what happened to traffic flows in 1999, 2000, 2002 and 2003. It would be incorrect to assume a simple increase during these "hidden" years.

It is useful to think about how these estimates of traffic flows were made. With the increasing positioning of CCTV on motorways, it is reasonable to assume that some accurate estimates could be made for motorway traffic flows.

Figure 11.8 could be used by road construction businesses to produce a crude forecast of the motorway traffic flows in 2007 and 2010. Between 1998 to 2001, traffic flow increased by 4.22 per cent $[100 \times (71.6 - 68.7)/68.7 = 4.22]$. Between 2001 to 2004, traffic flow increased by 4.61 per cent $[100 \times (74.9 - 71.6)/71.6 = 4.61]$.

So it would seem that there is an increase in motorway traffic of around 5 per cent every three years. A conservative estimate of future traffic flows (working to an accuracy of one decimal place) might be:

2007: $74.9 + (74.9 \times 0.5) = 74.9 + 3.7 = 78.6$
78,600 motor vehicles a day

2010: $78.6 + 78.6 \times 0.5) = 78.6 + 3.9 = 82.5$
82,500 motor vehicles a day

These figures suggest that motorways will become increasingly congested. Will the government tackle congestion by building additional roads? That will depend on its transport and environmental policy, and perhaps on the availability of finance through private finance initiatives and taxation. However, as a minimum, a road construction business could assume that increasing traffic will create a greater need for motorway maintenance and repair work.

What additional data on motorway traffic flows might a road construction business collect? Visit the Department for Transport's website (www.dft.gov.uk) to identify the range of data available.

The mean is a useful measure of a set of data: it is generally well understood and it reflects all values in the data. It can provide a good benchmark to compare with the individual members of a population. For example, the average sale per store can be used as a benchmark against which the performance of an individual store of a retail chain can be judged.

The main problem with the mean is that it can be distorted by extreme values. If a retail chain has a large London store, the takings from this store may be so great that it distorts the mean takings of all stores in the chain. This problem can be compensated by calculating means for percentiles, such as the average pay of the top 10 per cent of earners in the UK.

Care must be taken not to read too much into a mean figure. The head office of the retail chain might consider that the average takings per store are very acceptable. However, this mean value might mask the fact that one or two stores performed very badly, and that some had exceptional sales performance.

Median

The median is the middle value in any data set when the values are arranged in ascending (or descending) order. It divides the population into two halves. One strength of the median is that it is not distorted by extreme values, but its weakness is that it does not take account of all values in a data set. It could be appropriate to use the median when awarding bonuses to sales staff: a bonus could be paid to staff achieving above median sales for the month or year.

Mode

The mode is the most frequently occurring value in a data set. Like the median, the mode is not distorted by extreme values but it does not take account of all the data. A further issue with mode is that, on occasions, there may be two (or more) values that occur with the highest frequency. One use of the mode may be when trying to make decisions about forecast data. For example, internet research may

	Jobs ('000)	Median pay	Mean pay	Mean pay of highest earners (top 10%)	Mean pay of lowest earners (bottom 10%)
Males	10,547	£418.60	£524.40	£888.50	£232.50
Females	6,780	£354.60	£420.10	£689.00	£209.10

Source: Annual survey of hours and earnings 2005, www.statistics.gov.uk

reveal over a hundred forecasts for the growth in UK national income for a 12-month period. The modal value would tell the researcher which was the most commonly held view.

stop and think

The government conducts an annual survey of earnings. Figure 11.9 shows some results from the 2005 survey. What does this data say about the pay of full-time employees in the UK in 2005? Why is it significant that mean pay is higher than median pay?

Index numbers

Index numbers give the researcher a picture of the average change in a group of variables over time. The group of variables is called the target population or, simply, the index. Each variable may be referred to as a constituent or member of the index. For example, the FTSE 100 index measures changes in the share prices of the largest 100 public limited companies in the UK. In this case, each public limited company in the FTSE 100 is a constituent of the index, and the 100 top companies are the target population.

Most indexes use the number 100 as a starting point. If, on average, the values of the constituents are increasing, then the value of the index will move above 100. If the values of the constituents are falling, then the index will move below 100. Some index numbers use 1000 as a starting point. The FTSE 100 is an index that uses 1000 as the starting point – the 100 in the name merely refers to the number of companies in the index. In February 2006 the FTSE 100 index stood at 5800, showing that the value of the top 100 shares had increased by a factor of more than five since the index was devised in the 1980s.

Index numbers can be devised for almost any target population. Information contained within the data like "1995 = 100" is a clear indicator that indexed values are being used. Care should be taken when using index numbers. Individual constituents may not follow the trend shown by the group as a whole. Some index numbers may also be rebased (reset to 100 or 1000) from time to time.

Figure 11.10 shows the volume of spending on goods in the UK – that is, the effects of inflation have been taken out. The base year is 1971 – all the index numbers for 1971 are 100. In 2004, the index for food and non-alcoholic drink was 143. This means that between 1971 and 2004 there was a 43 per cent increase in the amount of food and soft drink bought by households. Contrast this with the index number for alcohol and tobacco. The value of 92 in 2004 indicates an 8 per cent decline in the volume of alcohol purchased since 1971. This index increased between 2001 and 2005. This would indicate that consumption (in volume terms) is increasing but it has not yet reached levels seen in 1971.

Figure 11.10: Volume of household expenditure (indices 1971 = 100)

	1971	1981	1991	2001	2004
Food and non-alcoholic drink	100	105	117	137	143
Alcohol and tobacco	100	99	92	88	92
Restaurants and hotels	100	126	167	193	202
Recreation and culture	100	161	283	548	683

Source: Social Trends

Pie charts and bar charts

It is very common to present data in pie charts or bar charts. These forms are well understood and easy to follow. Pie charts are useful for showing how a total can be divided up between its components. For example, a pie chart could show the contribution to total profit made by different product lines.

Bar charts are useful for showing change over time. One point to watch with a bar chart is the choice of units used for the axes. The visual impression of changes can be magnified or diminished according to the scale chosen by the creator of the chart. Three different types of bar charts are commonly used:

- vertical bar charts, such as Figure 11.11
- horizontal bar charts
- stacked bar charts, such as Figure 11.12

Forecasting and X/Y graphs

Forecasts are often based on time series data, such as annual sales over a period of several years. The aim is to make predictions about the future based upon what has happened in the past. A clear pattern of change is usually referred to as a trend. Researchers are often looking for repeated patterns (or cycles) in the data which may alter the trend in a predictable way. These variations are known as cyclical fluctuations. Fluctuations that are related to the time of year are known as seasonal fluctuations.

Scatter graphs are another technique used in forecasting, particularly when researchers are trying to find links between variables. For example, they may use a scatter graph to explore the relationship between website hits and the number of purchases made by consumers. Data for a number of time periods would be plotted on the X axis (website hits) and Y axis (number of purchases). Once enough data is available, researchers may attempt to insert a line of best fit if it appears that there is a linear relationship between the two variables. Researchers would be seeking to identify the nature of any relationship, or correlation, between the two sets of figures.

Good forecasters should always look beyond trends and simple correlations to consider possible reasons for the patterns in the data. If possible, ideas should be tested against additional data before any reliance can be placed upon the research. Any forecaster is aware that the past is not necessarily a guide to the future. The fact that there appears to be a correlation between two variables does not prove causation – that one value (say purchases) is a result of another (number of hits on a website). But there may be a third factor, such as television advertising, that is causing a rise in both website hits and customer purchases. If a new innovative competitor arrives in the market, both variables may decline significantly.

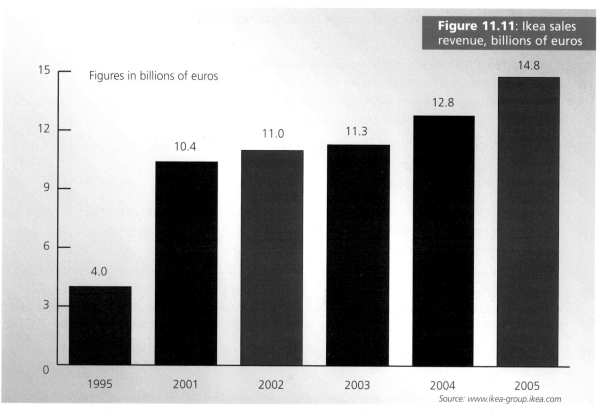

Figure 11.11: Ikea sales revenue, billions of euros

Figures in billions of euros

Year	Value
1995	4.0
2001	10.4
2002	11.0
2003	11.3
2004	12.8
2005	14.8

Source: www.ikea-group.ikea.com

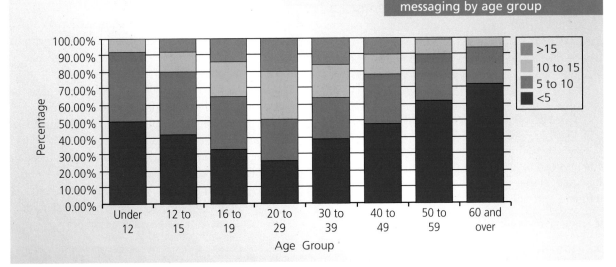

Figure 11.12: Frequency of text messaging by age group

assessment practice
Retail trends 2005

GVA Grimley is one of the UK's leading property advisers. By providing information on retail trends, the company helps its clients to identify profitable retail outlet development opportunities. This article, which provides an overview of retail trends, was published on the company's website (www.gvagrimley.co.uk).

Retail trends: first quarter 2005

The latest UK retail sales figures clearly show the weakening of consumer spending with a slowdown in the underlying annual growth rate of retail sales volumes to 4.3 per cent from 7.1 per cent six months ago.

Poor sales levels have increased the pressure on retailers to cut prices, resulting in value growth underperforming volume growth for all retail sectors, and even more so for non-food retail sectors. Food retailers and department stores performed well in January, seeing increases in their underlying growth rates, in contrast to other non-food sub-sectors.

Average annual rental growth in January was 3.9 per cent for all retail, with retail warehouses showing strongest growth at 6.1 per cent, compared with high street retail units, where rents increased by 2.3 per cent.

Consumer confidence has been affected by the housing market, and despite a slight growth in house prices in January (month-on-month), the overall trend continues to be one of declining year-on-year growth rates.

A Using the article, describe three key trends in the retail market which would be of interest to property developers.

B For each trend, explain why you think it would be of interest to property developers.

C Identify three other specific types of marketing environment data which might be of interest to property developers. Justify your answer.

SWOT analysis

Setting the Scene: marketing plan for Northern Ireland tourism

As part of its marketing plan for 2006, the Northern Ireland Tourist Board (NITB), identified the region's strengths, weaknesses, opportunities and threats in terms of its attractiveness as a tourist destination. Figure 11.13 shows a summary of this SWOT analysis. Consider how this analysis might help the NITB to establish Northern Ireland as an attractive tourist destination. The full report can be downloaded from the NITB's website (www.nitb.com).

Figure 11.13: SWOT analysis of Northern Ireland as a tourist destination

Strengths

Tourism Ireland Ltd provides a shop window to promote Northern Ireland in 21 countries.

Excellent access from Great Britain and major European cities, plus New York and Toronto.

Northern Ireland has a diverse tourism product, which has seen significant investment in recent years in accommodation, entertainment venues and conference facilities.

Northern Ireland is an ideal destination for short breaks – it is compact in size with a wide range of good-quality products such as golf, fishing, walking and cycling.

People are vibrant, warm and friendly.

Opportunities

Maximisation of effective communication channels such as customer relationship marketing (CRM) and web technologies will assist in building one-to-one relationships with the most lucrative customers.

Maximise opportunities which will arise as a result of Ireland hosting the Ryder Cup in 2006, London hosting the Olympics in 2012, and associated opportunities with other high-profile events.

Unlock the potential of the Giant's Causeway and the Antrim and Causeway Coast, Walled City of Derry and St Patrick's Signature Projects in our priority markets.

Use the Belfast Waterfront Hall as a centrepiece to grow business tourism.

Weaknesses

Northern Ireland tourism does not have a unique, stand-alone brand.

The structure of the tourism industry is fragmented.

Marketing and internet investment by the private sector is limited.

There are major product gaps in the tourism offering, such as a lack of family leisure hotels.

The public transport infrastructure for tourism is lacking.

The weather is unreliable, even in peak season.

Threats

Northern Ireland will fall behind competitors if the industry does not respond to changes in how consumers plan and purchase travel.

European Union funding is coming to an end, and without new funding streams, marketing and development initiatives will be curtailed.

The strong pound against the US dollar and euro makes Northern Ireland a more expensive destination.

Strong competition exists from the Republic of Ireland and close-to-home markets in terms of competitive pricing, last-minute offers and marketing visibility.

Increased direct access to the Republic of Ireland from other countries, especially Great Britain, widens competition.

Source: Northern Ireland Tourist Board

SWOT explained

Strengths, weaknesses, opportunities, threats: SWOT is a well-known acronym and the techniques involved in this process have widespread application in many fields. The SWOT analysis summarised in Figure 11.13 was carried out by the Northern Ireland Tourist Board (NITB) to help it to understand the key elements of its marketing environment. In turn, this should help the NITB to provide effective marketing advice to the Northern Ireland tourism industry.

The strengths and weaknesses of a SWOT analysis focus on the current market position of a business in relation to its:

- customers – is the business meeting the needs of its target markets

- competitors – is the business offering a better way of meeting customer needs compared with its competitors

- internal resources – is the business making effective use of its internal resources to meet customer needs and deal with competition?

The opportunities and threats of a SWOT analysis focus on the future market position of a business. Given an analysis of the business's strengths and weaknesses, and considering its marketing environment, what marketing strategies and activities should it adopt?

For a SWOT analysis to be effective, the relationship between the components of the exercise needs to be understood. The strengths and weaknesses must be identified before considering the opportunities and threats. These opportunities and threats must be rooted in the current marketing experiences of the business. They should grow out of an objective consideration of the real strengths and weaknesses of the business.

Unit 11 The marketing environment

stop and think

Carry out your own personal SWOT analysis in terms of your ability to earn income through paid employment or self-employment (such as enterprise activities). You should consider the strengths and weaknesses of your current position, and the opportunities and threats for your future earnings potential after you have finished your current sixth-form education.

As you might appreciate, carrying out a SWOT analysis is difficult because specific information on the business and its environment must be collated before the process begins. For example, it requires access to sales figures, customer feedback information, and examples of successful marketing activities and unsuccessful ones. Participants must adopt an objective view, avoiding any personal bias towards past marketing activities – so, for example, sales personnel need to be honest about the success and failures of past sales campaigns.

Why undertake a SWOT analysis?

The main purpose of a SWOT analysis is to identify appropriate marketing strategies and activities. It is an essential analytical tool which helps a business to make sense of its marketing environment.

A SWOT analysis can serve other purposes. A SWOT analysis may be conducted:

- to avoid complacency – some firms carry out a SWOT analysis as part of a regular programme of self-review

- as a safety check before embarking on a major new project

- as a response to change – a new marketing director might initiate a SWOT analysis to gauge the qualities of the marketing department.

Figure 11.14 sets out the issues that might typically arise when carrying out a SWOT analysis. Note that, in a sense, weaknesses could be a lack of any of the identified strengths. Care must be taken to identify weaknesses that may be hidden by temporary success. An excellent product or service may succeed despite, rather than because of, the marketing effort.

Undertaking a SWOT analysis

There is no set procedure for carrying out a SWOT analysis. It may be carried out by a small senior management group, or the exercise may be extended to include all the employees of a firm. In a small business, it may be an individual exercise undertaken by the owner or senior manager.

At its worse, SWOT analysis can be a sterile, form-filling exercise which occupies a two-hour session and is then forgotten. A more positive approach – and one adopted by many firms – is to involve as many employees as possible. For this to work, SWOT analysis must be given a high priority to avoid being marginalised by the pressures resulting from employees' day-to-day workload.

Figure 11.14: Issues typically raised by a SWOT analysis

Strengths

Campaigns and other activities that have gone well in the past

Any aspect of work which has been given recognition by the firm, industry or customers

Specialist personnel, equipment or techniques

Evidence of being copied by competitors

Group qualities – meeting deadlines or good communication, for example

Creativity and flair

Opportunities

Can value be added to the existing product range?

Is the business's internal research and development generating new product ideas to be marketed?

Can the ideas of rivals be copied or, preferably, bettered?

Could the marketing department benefit from further training in the use of marketing techniques?

Weaknesses

Marketing campaigns that are not seen as being cost-effective

High staff turnover and high levels of absenteeism

High levels of complaints from customers and/or senior management

Loss of clients

Reluctance to change and innovate

Threats

Competitors, particularly those who have strengths in relation to the firm's identified weaknesses

Complacency and missed opportunities, such as failing to develop value added for a product – a competitor may do so

Any unanticipated changes in the legal, social or economic environment (see earlier topics)

Poor ethical decision-making, such as alienating of potential customers through insensitive advertising

Allowing sufficient time to think through all the issues and to generate constructive and practical ideas is crucial. If a business is serious about SWOT, it might organise an "away day" or residential weekend for the marketing department to allow staff to develop their analysis. Smaller teams, such as employees who mainly carry out market research, may undertake their own SWOT analysis in informal groups.

In planning for a SWOT exercise:

- a clear timetable must be devised and notice given so that employees have time to think and prepare for the SWOT analysis

- clear channels of communication should be established to ensure that the work of any subgroup is shared with appropriate personnel

- the commitment of key senior personnel to the process must be demonstrated, preferably through active participation – for example, the marketing

director might spend an hour with each subgroup during an away day.

Besides looking at their own work areas, teams might consider other aspects of the business – for example, the marketing group may give its views on the production process. This encourages new ideas and may be used as a part of a process of triangulation, in which the views of different groups are compared to find common ground on key issues and topics.

The outcomes of the SWOT analysis must be well publicised. If it is to be useful, it ideally should have a genuine long-term effect on the activities of the firm or department. Even if changes are not made, a rationale should be offered to demonstrate that the views of the working groups have been properly considered. This is especially important if the firm wishes to make SWOT analysis a regular part of its activities.

Marks & Spencer has turned around its falling sales, announcing a rise for the first time in nearly two years. In the third quarter of 2005 sales of clothing stabilised, and food sales showed a healthy increase. Total group sales were up 3.3 per cent, with same-store sales in general merchandise (clothing and homewares) down just 0.2 per cent against an 11.2 per cent decline in the first quarter of 2005. Same-store food sales were up 2.7 per cent.

But the good news is dampened by the announcement that George Davies, consultant to the firm's Per Una business, has resigned. In a statement, M&S said that Mr Davies had a 12-month notice period "and will remain committed to the Per Una business for that period to ensure an orderly transition". Per Una has been one of the biggest areas of sales growth for M&S. As well as Mr Davies, the division's finance director Andrea White and head of merchandising Melanie Davies also resigned.

M&S celebrated its first quarterly rise in sales following seven straight quarters of falling sales. "This is an encouraging performance, but there remains much to be done," said chief executive Stuart Rose. He warned that the trading environment remained difficult ahead of the crucial Christmas period, but was confident M&S "would deliver".

The latest figures are being seen as the first set to be the full responsibility of chief executive Stuart Rose, as they are a reflection of his ideas and sales lines, rather than those of the previous management. Rebecca McClellan, a retail analyst, said: "M&S's efforts to focus on the core older customer have clearly borne fruit. They've been on a mission to de-clutter the stores, and the advertising has been good, too."

Source: adapted from BBC News website, 11 October 2005

A Describe the strengths and weaknesses of Marks & Spencer's market position as at October 2005.

B Given these strengths and weaknesses, discuss Marks and Spencer's possible market opportunities and threats in 2006.

My Autograph

Ian Wright
by David Bailey

Stripe jacket £59
Fine stripe shirt £25
Slim black tie £9.50
Straight leg jean £35

YOUR M&S
www.marksandspencer.com

An introduction to marketing strategies

Setting the scene: Ealing Community Transport

Ealing Community Transport (ECT) is a not-for-profit organisation with unrivalled experience in developing innovative transport and recycling solutions and in implementing projects effectively. Its web address is www.ectgroup.co.uk.

ECT began life as a project of the Ealing Council for Voluntary Service in West London in 1979, becoming an independent organisation in 1987. It was set up, as the name implies, as a community transport scheme. In 1982 ECT had an annual turnover of around £30,000, and 64 per cent of its income was derived from grants. By 2004, ECT employed over 600 people with an annual turnover approaching £24 million – of which just over 1 per cent is in grant aid.

This growth has come through diversification – through winning and delivering household waste and recycling contracts for local authorities, recycling material that would otherwise be either incinerated or sent to landfill. Around 5 per cent of ECT's income is derived from minibus transport, with a similar proportion from vehicle maintenance contracts. The remaining 90 per cent is from recycling services delivered under contract to ten London boroughs, two districts in Oxfordshire and one district in Warwickshire. Since April 2003, ECT has also run the franchise for the 195 London bus route in West London, which a mere seven months later was voted one of the most reliable bus services anywhere in the country.

In May 2004, ECT branched out further by entering a partnership with Dartmoor Railway in Devon. Dartmoor Railway is a unique operation. It is the first independent "community railway" in the UK, and it has secured the future of a rural railway with no central government funding by developing sustainable tourism traffic and retail activities. By bringing its expertise in business systems and its experience of community engagement, ECT will give the railway the strength to develop the tourism and community rail services increasingly needed by the people of this picturesque, rural area. ECT also sees this as an exciting learning opportunity, providing the potential to understand how to replicate Dartmoor Railway's success by expanding community rail services in other areas of the country, thereby enhancing its community transport portfolio.

Source: adapted from a National Council for Voluntary Organisations case study, (www.ncvo-vol.org.uk)

KEY TERMS

Segmentation strategies involve dividing markets into separate groups of customers.

Competitive position strategies are approaches taken by businesses operating within competitive markets. In competitive markets, for example, market followers yield to the dominance of the market leader.

Integrated growth strategies are ways in which a business expands its operations through acquiring other businesses.

Ansoff's competitive strategies describe how a business can increase sales through developing its products and/or its markets.

Marketing strategies

A marketing strategy is a medium- or long-term plan of how the firm's key marketing objectives are to be achieved. Each strategy should be unique, designed meet the needs of the business and its customers in a given set of circumstances.

Marketing strategies take many forms. They may be bound documents running to several pages, or they may simply consist of some notes scribbled on the back of an envelope. Strategies may even be unwritten, and just be held in the memory of key individuals. It may be desirable, but it is not necessary, to have knowledge of business theory to devise a strategy. Some marketing managers develop strategies intuitively: indeed, they may not use the term strategy to describe their actions. Nevertheless, some form of planning usually accompanies successful marketing.

As individuals, many of us frequently use strategies without necessarily knowing that we are doing so. For example, when planning a journey to France, say, most people will check the route in advance. They will compare the prices of ferries with the Channel Tunnel, consider whether to drive or use other transport options, look at alternative routes of getting to their final destination, and decide whether they need to book accommodation or complete the journey in a single day. In short, a strategy will be devised. Ultimately, the journey may not be as smooth as planned. Several factors such as traffic, the weather and underestimating journey times may cause the strategy to be revised along the way to achieve the desired goal. However, the ideas and information gathered in the planning stage usually help to solve problems as they arise.

A business, then, needs a strategy or "road map" to help it achieve its marketing objectives. Both the objectives and the strategy can be informed by a SWOT analysis. They will often be strongly influenced by the market environment faced by the firm. One of the reasons for scanning the marketing environment (see Topic 5) is to identify opportunities around which strategies can be based. For example, a business might base its marketing strategy on the idea of trying to be an early adopter of new technology. This is a high-risk strategy, as money could be wasted on ideas that ultimately prove to be unsuccessful. However, there are substantial commercial benefits from being the first to exploit a new technique, or being the first to market with a new product type.

Ealing Community Transport, the not-for-profit organisation featured in the introduction to this topic, has a focused marketing strategy. It understands that its key strengths relate less to the markets in which it operates and more with the organisation's ability to "get things done". It has a track record of effective communicating with key stakeholders within local communities and an ability to turn ideas into practice. ECT's strategy could be described as diversification – serving new customers with new products.

In this topic, we introduce four approaches to marketing strategies:

- segmentation strategies
- competitive position strategies
- integrated growth strategies
- Ansoff's competitive strategies.

Each approach is introduced below, but in the final two topics of this unit, we examine how businesses can put these general ideas into practice.

Segmentation strategies

The idea of marketing segmentation, subdividing a market into customer groups with similar characteristics, was introduced in Unit 4 (see pages 154–7 of your AS textbook). Typical categories used for segmentation are age, gender, lifestyle and socioeconomic factors. Segmentation has been adopted by many firms as a marketing strategy. It works on the principle that if a product can be more closely tailored to a person's needs and desires, then the value added by the product, as far as the individual is concerned, will be greater – and this should increase sales. High value added can also support a policy of premium pricing, in the short term at least. One example of this type of marketing approach was the launch of ice-cream bars, such as Mars Ice Cream in the 1980s. These were premium-priced products aimed particularly at adults, a distinct segment of the overall ice cream market.

Competitive position strategies

There is competition in most markets, even those considered to be oligopolistic (see page 107). A key influence in shaping the marketing strategy will be how the business chooses to initiate or respond to competition. Essentially, businesses can adopt – or seek to attain – four types of competitive position within a market.

- **Market leader**
  This is the dominant company in the market – usually the firm with the highest sales. It will seek to maintain this position in the face of changes in the marketing environment.

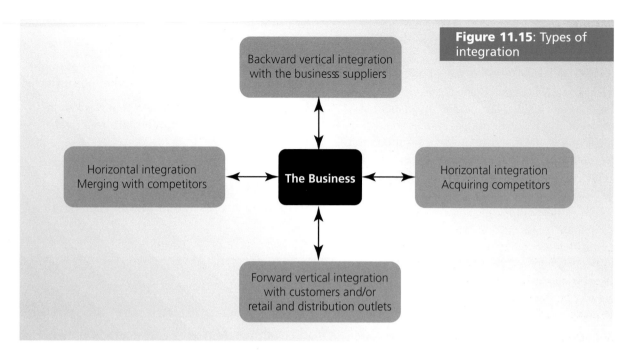

Figure 11.15: Types of integration

- Backward vertical integration with the businesss suppliers
- Horizontal integration Merging with competitors
- The Business
- Horizontal integration Acquiring competitors
- Forward vertical integration with customers and/or retail and distribution outlets

- **Market challengers**
  These firms have high sales and have enough market power to possibly become market leader. Their marketing strategies may well focus on this goal.

- **Market followers**
  These are firms that seek a "quiet life". Knowing that they lack the size or drive to become market leaders, they seek to make enough profit to survive, often by following general market trends.

- **Market nichers**
  Smaller but sometimes very profitable businesses that operate in a narrowly defined segment of the market. Their aim is to dominate their niche rather than the whole market.

All businesses must consider their competitive position strategies. Of course, some businesses may ignore this aspect of their competitive environment and, as a consequence, may unwittingly find themselves in a market-follower position. If this is not their real intention or goal, then these businesses are unlikely to achieve their aims and objectives. Regardless of whether a business wants to be a big fish in a small pond or a major player, it must be conscious of the reality of operating within a competitive market: this is, that competitors can never be ignored.

Integrated growth strategies

Integration means joining together. As similar firms combine, they may achieve economies of scale. This is known as horizontal integration. Firms may also integrate forward or backwards, taking control of

retail outlets or suppliers of their raw materials and other resource inputs. This may give them a competitive advantage, as the profits previously made by different operators within the supply chain are eliminated. This process of supply chain rationalisation is known as vertical integration.

Ansoff's competitive strategies

This is a formal model that analyses the strategy choices facing many firms. It is summarised in Figure 11.16. The choices shown by the model can be related to the level of risk the firm is prepared to accept in developing new strategies. The different elements of the matrix will be considered in Topic 10.

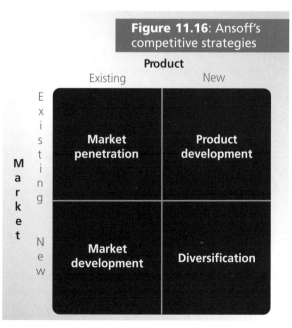

Figure 11.16: Ansoff's competitive strategies

	Product	
	Existing	New
Existing	Market penetration	Product development
New	Market development	Diversification

(Market / Existing-New on vertical axis)

Whatever approach is chosen in planning and drawing up a strategy, the pace of change in modern marketing will demand that review and change become an essential part of any process. Becoming a leading brand has been likened to trying to walk to the centre of a large, fast-moving roundabout in competition with other people: even as you approach the centre of the roundabout, there are strong forces trying to push you back out to the edges. Marketing strategy has to be pragmatic, responding to changes as they arise.

stopand**think**

Explain which approach these businesses might best use to reconsider their marketing strategy:

■ a large supermarket chain that has lost its dominance in the marketplace to a rival

■ a high-street electrical retailer facing increased competition from online firms

■ a UK clothing manufacturer facing a rapid decline in sales due to overseas competition.

assessmentpractice
Caffè Nero

Caffè Nero operates a chain of coffee bars and has established itself as one of the UK market leaders. This an extract from an independent financial report on Caffè Nero by the analysts Collins Stewart Ltd. The full report can be downloaded from the Caffè Nero website (www.caffenero.com).

Coffee market and retail environment

The UK branded coffee bar market continues to thrive despite the generally tough retail environment. Allegra Strategies is forecasting 10 per cent growth per annum over the next few years, and against this backdrop Caffè Nero continues to gain market share.

All three of the leading brands (Caffè Nero, Costa Coffee and Starbucks) are continuing to grow and, given the current retail environment, this suggests that the branded coffee bar market is driven by more than just general consumer trends.

In our opinion, a key driver behind the success of the branded coffee bar market is changing lifestyle patterns, both in terms of leisure and in the workplace. While there is no doubt that coffee has become a more popular beverage in the UK over recent years, the coffee bar environment itself is an equally (if not more) important factor. This trend shows little sign of abating, and given that the most developed coffee bar market in the world, the USA, is still showing good growth, it is clear that the UK market is not saturated.

Strategically, the focus in the near term will remain the UK, where we are forecasting a further 41 new openings during 2005/06. The expansion includes further development of partnerships with groups such as House of Fraser, and branding opportunities with organisations such as the Royal Shakespeare Company and the Tate art gallery.

Source: Collins Stewart Limited, September 2005

A Using the article, identify and describe the key elements of Cafe Nero's marketing environment.

B Discuss the suitability of the marketing strategy outlined in the last paragraph of the article.

Segmentation and competitive position strategies

Setting the scene: is a ban on smoking good for pubs?

This newspaper article is adapted from the Evening Standard. Jim Armitage, the journalist, considers the possible impact on English pubs of a ban on smoking in public places. He reviews the evidence from Scotland where smoking in public places had been banned, as well as evidence from Ireland.

Smoking ban cuts pub takings

Some Scottish pubs have seen takings crash by 50 per cent since the smoking ban came into force, highlighting the potential impact of a ban in England. The leisure industry is watching Scotland's experience closely for clues but early indications have been mixed. Sophisticated city-style bars with outside space and strong food offerings say takings have risen slightly since the ban, while more old-fashioned drink-led pubs appear to have suffered.

The *Morning Advertiser* – the pub trade newspaper – conducted an informal poll of 25 pubs in Edinburgh and found trade in 10 had fallen since the ban, five saw an increase and a further 10 reported no change.

A manager of Edinburgh's Quarter Gill pub, who declined to be named, said takings were down by about 50 per cent. The Quarter Gill does not sell food and is on a street with a narrow pavement. He said: "It's been a disaster. Customers, especially our older ones, don't want to stand outside in the cold with all the buses racing past." He claimed many other pub and bar managers in the city were suffering equally badly, but had been told by their bosses not to speak out publicly. Neither the British nor the Scottish Beer and Pubs Association would comment on the first fortnight of trading.

The impact in England is likely to be less marked than in Scotland because south of the border more pubs sell food. Bigger pub companies have for several years been moving away from the traditional ethos of the working man's pub.

At The Crown gastropub in the village of Thornhill, Perthshire, Peter Mulholland claimed the ban had been positive for business. "Our restaurant area was already non-smoking, but smokers from the public bar have either given up or are going outside where we've built a sheltered area with heating. Non-smokers who previously didn't want to go into the bar now like it because it's not smoky any more."

In Ireland, which banned smoking two years ago, figures last July showed Dublin bar takings were down 16 per cent after the first year. About 600 pubs have closed since the ban, according to the Vintners Federation of Ireland.

Source: Evening Standard, 7 April 2006

Consider how this change in the marketing environment could affect the marketing activities of pubs in England.

Segmentation strategies

Environmental scanning can reveal opportunities for businesses to win new customers and warn of the decline of established markets. This is illustrated by the impact of legislation to ban smoking in workplaces in England. Clearly any legislation will affect pubs, clubs and other businesses in the leisure industry. The threat to the traditional English pub, already hard-pressed by other factors such as the cut-price alcohol available in supermarkets, is obvious. However, there is clearly an opportunity for any business that can find a way of legally catering for people who wish to smoke, drink and socialise simultaneously.

The proposed ban raises broad issues – of both segmentation and ethics – for the major pub chains. Should they continue to target smokers and look to find ways around the legislation? Some have proposed establishing open-air pubs, with drinks and cigarettes served through vending machines. Some pubs may explicitly target non-smokers, perhaps promoting an ethical stance on the issue of smoking,

Segmentation strategies are not only appropriate for large corporations such as Mars. This article illustrates how a decision to target particular groups of consumers can be a profitable marketing strategy for smaller manufacturing organisations operating in developing economies.

Albanian tailor sells to Harrods

When Arben Xibri was a young, trainee tailor, he sewed suits for the top leadership of Albania's Communist Party. Now Mr Xibri is running his own textile business, making shirts for some of the leading Italian and British brand names and selling his goods to leading European department stores, including Harrods in London.

For Mr Xibri it has been a long, tough road from apprentice tailor under the communists – a regime which kept Albania virtually cut off from much of the outside world for more than 40 years – to factory owner. When the communist leadership was swept from office 1991 Mr Xibri, like hundreds of thousands of his fellow Albanians, escaped abroad, working at a clothing factory in Vincenza in Italy. He won a EU fabric design competition and used the prize money to send himself to one of Italy's top textile institutes.

In 1994 Mr Xibri returned to Albania. Together with an Italian partner, he invested in a small factory premises, using savings of $15,000 to buy second-hand German and Italian textile machinery. "The business grew quickly. At first we were making T-shirts and low-cost goods but three years ago I bought new machinery, including special washing machines for processing the shirts, and we

have moved upmarket. We have very good designers and textile specialists in Albania. My aim is to focus on quality and style. Before too long I want to establish my own special brand to compete with the big Italian, French and British names. More and more people will realise that the 'Made in Albania' label is a mark of excellence."

Mr Xibri employs 100 young women at his Intertex company factory. "We produce about 5,000 shirts a week," says Mr Xibri. "Like other countries in Europe we are facing stiff competition from China, but so far we are ahead on quality and can compete on price. Also we are able to deliver our goods to shops in Rome or London in a matter of days. Shirts from China take six weeks to reach the marketplace."

Source: adapted from BBC News website, 27 July 2005

Arben Xibri has adopted a segmentation strategy. He pitched his products at the higher end of the market, making high-quality, stylish garments, targeting higher income buyers in developed economies such as the UK. His marketing environment was conducive to this strategy – he had a skilled workforce, had access to modern machinery, and operated in an economy where wage rates, by our standards, are low.

In the future, Arben Xibri plans to brand his products. Whether this strategy will work depends on his ability to find retailers willing to stock his products rather than those of the "leading Italian and British brand names". Why might this be difficult? How could he make buyers in the UK realise that the "Made in Albania" label is a mark of excellence?

and emphasising other features, such as meals and leisure facilities, to attract customers.

Forward-thinking businesses will have been researching alternatives for a considerable period, as the likelihood of an eventual smoking ban has been evident for some time. There will almost certainly be niche markets for new types of entertainment venues and for new types of products, such as legal services advising landlords and pub businesses as to their position under the new laws.

The legislation on smoking is linked to a long-term social trend: changing attitudes to health and growing public disapproval of smoking. Even so, for many businesses the legislation will come as a sudden and dramatic change in the marketing environment. Other changes in markets, however, happen more gradually.

Consider the market for ice cream bars based on chocolate confectionery products. These were introduced in 1980s, and they were originally marketed as ice creams for adults, designed for impulse purchases and with an appropriately expensive price tag. The success of the original product lines, such as the Mars Ice Cream, surprised even the manufacturer, and the idea was soon copied. With hindsight it is possible to see how changes in the marketing environment contributed to the success of this new product. Improved technology made it possible to manufacture, store and retail the new product at reasonable cost. Rising affluence and falling family sizes also meant that even parents on below-average wages could afford these minor luxuries on a regular basis. Over the years, the product has moved from its luxury niche to a mass market product that is often sold in multi-packs at heavily discounted prices. The fact that many consumers have freezers and the means to transport frozen products in bulk from supermarkets to their homes – another change in the marketing environment – has allowed the market to develop further.

Competitive position strategies

Scanning the marketing environment is also critical for any business developing a marketing strategy based on its competitive position. The first challenge is to identify competitors, because many businesses face competition not just from direct rivals – those firms offering similar products – but also from indirect rivals that may offer very different products but are competing for the same broad group of customers.

There are, for example, many different industries competing for the "leisure pound": sports centres, cinemas, ice rinks, holiday companies and computer game manufacturers provide very different products and services but all are competing for a share of the public's spending on leisure activities. In effect, all are competing for a slice of the same pie. If one industry grabs a larger share of the leisure market, others will lose out. Some analysts attribute the fall in sales of music CDs to increased spending by young people on mobile phones and related services.

Most firms will attempt to find out the strengths, weaknesses and strategies of the competition, both their immediate rivals and the indirect competitors. This may be difficult as firms will naturally try to conceal successful tactics and to keep future plans under wraps. Some secondary research may be useful, but this information tends to be available to all firms in the market and therefore is unlikely to yield insights that can be used to gain a unique competitive advantage. Once a business has built up information on the competition, it can plan and implement a marketing strategy based on its existing competitive position in the market and its longer-terms aims.

Market leaders

Market leaders will seek to defend their position and take steps to frustrate the ambitions of competitors. This might include tactics such as patent enforcement, predatory pricing and expensive marketing campaigns.

Another, perhaps less obvious, defensive strategy is brand proliferation. This involves the market leader offering several versions, or brands, of what is essentially the same product or service. They justify such behaviour on the grounds that it helps them cater for different market segments – so, for example, they might offer budget, middle market and premium versions of their products. However, the increased product range also makes it more difficult for a new entrant to establish a brand name and gain a viable market share. The market for soap powder is a good example of a market with many brands, but it is dominated by two major companies, Unilever and Proctor & Gamble. Consumers might think that they are being offered a wide choice, but this type of brand proliferation strategy helps market leaders to maintain their market share.

Another option for a market leader is to increase the size of the market or develop related product lines that allow them to exploit existing market power. As the leading producer, a market leader should have the most to gain from any growth in the market. The one danger of this approach may be that by generating increased demand for a particular product types – say by increasing the size of the market for particular foods by stressing their health benefits – a market leader may be providing free advertising for rival producers. This is another reason why product differentiation through branding is so important to many producers.

Market challengers

Market challengers can adopt a variety of strategies in their attempts to become market leaders. The success of these strategies will depend on close monitoring of the market environment.

One approach is product development: challengers may seek to offer an improvement in the product, or the way the product is delivered, that is distinctive in the mind of the consumer. Other challengers may seek to grow in size, perhaps by taking over or merging with other challenger firms, so that they have the resources to match the marketing effort of the market leader.

Another form of challenge may be mounted through the courts or the media if the challenger feels that the market leader has undue market power. An example

business practice
Groupe Danone

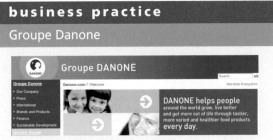

Fresh dairy products is a sector in which consumption varies greatly by market. Groupe Danone has a dominant position in this sector: first place. We are highly successful in all the countries in which we are present. And the key factor is innovation.

Groupe Danone supplies the whole world with superior quality fresh dairy products… while at the same time respecting the tastes and dietary habits of each country. How? By developing local brands.

Actimel is marketed in 35 countries. More than 1.5 billion little bottles are consumed. Actimel is a fermented milk to be drunk. As well as the two traditional ferments of yoghurt, it contains a specific probiotic the Lactobacillus casei Defensis (a living ferment bringing health benefits) developed from the research carried out by Danone. The regular consumption of Actimel contributes to preserving the good balance of intestinal flora, essential for a good state of health, and helps to reinforce the natural defences of the organism.

Drinkable yogurt, a product that responds to the latest trends in snacking, is a key element in the growth of the group's fresh dairy products business: Drinkable Bio in Spain, Danimals Drinkable in the USA, Danonino in Mexico and Drinkable Petit Gervais in a number of other countries.

Source: www.danone.com

stopandthink

Danone, the French based food manufacturer, has particular strength in the fresh dairy product market. The business practice (above) is an extract from its international website (www.danone.com). What marketing activities is Danone using to maintain its "dominant position"?

of this approach is the pressure that has been put on BT by other telecommunications companies to allow them access to BT's fixed_line network at reasonable cost.

A feature of most aspects of challenger behaviour is the fear of retaliation. They will not expect a market leader to accept any challenge to its position passively. Indeed, significant marketing effort may have to be used to counter the initiatives of a market leader or rival challengers. Survival may be more of a problem than expansion. In the worst-case scenario, the responses of a market leader to a campaign mounted by a challenger may actually leave the challenger in a weakened position.

Market followers

If the prospect of mounting a challenge to the dominant firms in the market is too daunting, a business may decide to adopt strategies associated with market followers. This is an essentially cautious approach.

Market followers may simply monitor the market and copy other products or services. For example, many low-cost airlines have set up modelling themselves on the format pioneered by easyJet. Market followers may seek to avoid any initial mistakes made by the innovative firms that first introduced new products and services. However, research indicates that followers find it difficult to challenge the initial dominance of "first movers" into a market such as easyJet, Amazon and Apple.

Many followers may not seek market power, as they may be engaged in a process known as satisficing – making enough profit to be comfortable without having to work too hard or to take too many risks. In this situation, a business will not seek to initiate competition with potentially powerful rivals. It may even play down its success in order to discourage new entrants into the market.

Market nichers

Most of the points made about market leaders, challengers and followers apply to niche marketing strategies. Superficially the niche player may seem to be in good position: the only provider of a specialist service. Inevitably though, success will attract competition, either from new firms or existing firms wishing to diversify their operations. The successful niche business is the market leader in that niche and often faces similar issues to mass market producers in maintaining its dominant position against the efforts of competing firms.

A common niche strategy is to develop a profitable business and then sell the business to a larger operator. Some small niche producers, like some market followers, may choose to remain relatively small, to maintain the distinctive appeal of their product. Specialist organic food producers sometimes adopt this approach.

assessmentpractice
UK clothing industry

The UK clothing industry faces intense competition from overseas producers, particularly from companies based in China and India. Figure 11.17 indicates the scale of the recent decline in this industry, and compares the trend in output of the clothing industry with that of all UK manufacturing industries.

Figure 11.17: Output of the UK production industries

	All manufacturing industries		Textiles, leather and clothing	
	Index, 2002=100	Percentage change, latest year on previous year	Index, 2002=100	Percentage change, latest year on previous year
2001	103.2	-1.3	108.1	−10.8
2002	100.0	-3.1	100.0	−7.5
2003	100.1	0.1	98.1	−1.9
2004	101.8	1.7	87.5	−10.8
2005	100.7	-1.1	85.6	−2.2

Source: National Statistics

A Using Fgure 11.17, describe the trend in output of the UK textiles, leather and clothing industry between 2001 and 2005. Compare this trend with that shown by all UK manufacturing industries in Figure 11.17.

B Which of the strategies covered in this topic do you think should be adopted by UK clothing businesses if they are to survive the challenges posed by foreign competition? Justify your choice of strategy.

Integrated growth strategies and Ansoff's competitive strategies

Setting the scene: First Choice Holidays plc

First Choice Holidays plc is an international leisure travel business which has grown by a series of acquisitions since its inception in 1994. The business operates from 17 countries and employs nearly 14,000 people. These employees are located across the wide range of brands owned by First Choice.

The company has a range of brands within its product portfolio. It offers:

- mainstream holidays – through First Choice Holidays, "whether it's summer sun, Tropical, Florida, Villas, Winter Sun or Ski, First Choice Holidays has got a holiday to suit everyone"

- travel – through First Choice Airways which boasts "the greatest seat pitch of all the UK's charter airlines on the majority of its long-haul flights"

- specialist holidays through companies like Signature Vacations, Canada's leading package vacations company, and the Italian tour operator I Viaggi del Turchese

- activity holidays – through brands like Clubs Sunsail and The Adventures Company.

By ensuring it has access to a range of target markets, through its various travel agencies, and control over aspects of the supply chain (such as airlines and access to accommodation), the business stands a better chance of dealing with a notoriously difficult marketing environment.

First Choice has grown through the use of integrated growth strategies. It is the careful use of these strategies which has ensured the survival and profitable growth of the business.

Integrated growth strategies

Growth is usually a source of increased market power. It is usually measured by the increase in sales revenue and market share: these are important statistics for many businesses. There are also other measures of corporate growth such as profitability, capital employed and numbers of people employed in the business. While growth is a common business objective, it needs to be seen in the context of the market environment: the expectations of a business launching a new product during an economic boom will be different from a business marketing a mature product in a recession.

Integration can help businesses to grow in several ways. One benefit of integration is that it creates a larger business that may benefit from economies of scale and a fall in the unit cost of output. This could be achieved through horizontal integration, by merging with (or acquiring) competitors (see Figure 11.15, page 137). In 2005, the UK's largest cable television company NTL acquired its main rival

Telewest. The new company should be able to benefit by rationalising some of its office functions, enabling it to cut costs and compete more effectively with other players in the subscription television market.

Horizontal integration can also provide the business with access to new markets. This was the case for NTL, as Telewest had a strong customer base in UK regions where NTL had little penetration. An additional benefit of horizontal integration is that each takeover removes a potential competitor. However, if the new company that results from the takeover is too large and could exploit a dominant market position, the acquisition may be referred to the Competition Commission (as we saw in Topic 2).

Vertical integration takes place when a business acquires either a supplier (backward integration) or a distributor of its products (forward integration). First Choice Holidays plc is a good example of a company that has grown by both forwards and backwards integration. It has acquired an airline (backward integration, as transport is a part of the supply chain) and travel agents (forward integration, as travel agents are part of the distribution chain).

Through vertical integration, a business can control costs and ensure that its marketing messages are communicated sympathetically. Without control of airline costs or travel agent sales messages, First Choice Holidays is exposed to a wider range of marketing environment forces. By taking control of aspects of both its supply and distribution chains, a business can reduce risk and uncertainty. It can also help a business to maintain quality standards at each stage of the production process.

A fully vertically integrated operation would own and control all aspects of production – from obtaining raw materials, through processing to the distribution of its products to consumers. Some oil companies come close to this model, by controlling all aspects of their supply chain, from drilling and extraction, to refining the oil and selling petrol on the forecourt. As well as ensuring control, the companies benefit from retaining all profits at each stage of the process.

There are several advantages to extensive integration when considered from the point of view of a manufacturer:

- the quality, availability and price of inputs can be more easily controlled – this will be particularly attractive to businesses that have lean, just-in-time production systems

- the profits that would be earned by suppliers and retailers are retained within the business

- the business will be able to be keep full control of its brand identity – products are not always marketed by retailers in a way that is acceptable to the manufacturer.

Despite the potential benefits, integration is not always successful. A business may be moving outside its original area of expertise: the qualities that make a good food retailer may not necessarily transfer well to farming or food-processing. A business that has core expertise in manufacturing may lack the skills to be a successful retailer.

If the components of the expanded business fail to integrate, successful parts of the business may be held back, or may be forced to cross-subsidise less successful areas. When the mobile phone company O_2 was demerged from the BT Group, one of the reasons given that was that the move would "increase shareholder value" – that is, BT would be more profitable without O_2.

A more general problem may be diseconomies of scale, a situation where efficiency begins to fall once the business grows beyond a certain size. Businesses that are "too big" may experience problems with

communication, motivation and organisation. Some businesses that have been formed from mergers or acquisitions can suffer from internal power struggles between employees of the once separate businesses as they compete for power and influence. In the worst case, employees may be pleased to see another area of the business struggling.

Nevertheless integration, particularly in the context of global markets, is an increasing phenomenon. The minimum size needed to be internationally competitive seems to be increasing for most companies.

Ansoff's competitive strategies

Ansoff's matrix (see Figure 11.16, page 137) is a planning tool. It is a way of summarising the possibilities open to the business rather than offering new strategies. It well may be used in the early stages of the planning process, when aims and methods are being decided upon and potential risk is weighed against potential reward. Using Ansoff's matrix may help business decide on its general direction; the operational detail will come later.

Market penetration

Market penetration is the least adventurous approach. It involves trying to sell more in an existing market, using such techniques as product differentiation. For many businesses, marketing activities related to market penetration approaches will be a continuation of the processes that they already employ. For example, Tesco might increase the frequency of its television advertising or reduce prices on a standard range of products within its stores.

Product development

Product development involves the marketing of new or significantly modified products within the existing market. The investment required to develop and market new products means that this is usually a higher-risk option than market penetration in the short term. In the long term, product development is essential to the survival of most businesses. For example, Tesco's introduction of financial services was, at the time, product development – it involved selling a new product to the company's existing customers.

Market development

Market development occurs when a business tries to reach new markets with existing products or services. One obvious way of achieving this objective is through developing an export trade by marketing its product in different countries. It could expand its export trade through integration, by buying (or merging with) local suppliers. Alternatively, the company could set up operating branches in various countries with some staff recruited locally. In either case there will be a period when the initial investment required to break into the new market will outweigh the short-term returns.

Market development can be risky as it requires the business to carry out research into the specific needs of the new market prior to establishing a presence in that market. For example, Tesco has made a number of acquisitions in Europe and Asia to establish a presence in these markets. While product ranges differ, the core product – groceries – remains the same. However, it can't be assumed that because Tesco has been successful with its business model and marketing strategy in the UK, it will be successful in, say, the Czech Republic.

Diversification

Diversification is concerned with the marketing of new products in a new market, and may be seen as the strategy choice that carries the highest level of risk, as the business is moving into a field where it has little or no experience. Diversification can be a valid exit strategy from an overly competitive market or a market which is declining due to changes in customer needs. It can be a way of using the cash reserves of a

business to ensure a future stream of profits, especially when the profitability of the business's current markets is declining or static. Nokia is an obvious example of diversification – it initially operated in the wood pulp and paper industry!

stopand**think**

You might think that cigarette manufacturers would have focused on a strategy of product diversification as the prospect for future sales growth in developed economies looks increasingly poor. Interestingly, cigarette manufacturers have actually been engaged in aggressive market development in developing economies where controls on the consumption of tobacco are much less prevalent.

Visit the website of British American Tobacco (www.bat.com) to investigate the marketing strategies used by the business when faced with what would seem an unfavourable marketing environment. Do these strategies suggest that BAT thinks that its marketing environment is unfavourable?

It should be remembered that Ansoff's matrix is a model. It is a useful method of summarising some strategy options, but businesses are not bound to follow its structure rigidly. Businesses must take advantage of opportunities as they arise. A business may have planned to launch a product in the UK, but if there is evidence that demand is strong in other EU countries then why not expand into those countries immediately?

A key factor in the choice and implementation of marketing strategy will be the character and attitude of management, together with the corporate culture prevailing in the organisation. These qualities vary from company to company, and they are as different as the personalities of the students in a business studies class. It may be that the response of one or a few key individuals to the marketing environment determines the business's choice of strategy.

Finally note that, important as they are, marketing theory and market research information can only take a business so far. These are resources that are generally available to all professional management groups. The key to any successful business is timing: being in the right place at the right time to provide the products that meet customer wants and needs.

assessment practice
Alan Sugar's Ansoff's matrix

Amstrad plc was founded by Alan Sugar in 1968. It has a long history, and Figure 11.18 picks out some of the key events in the company's development.

Figure 11.18: Amstrad's history

Year	Event
1968	Amstrad is founded by the present chairman Alan Sugar. It sells electrical goods.
1970	First manufacturing venture. Lower prices were achieved by injection moulding plastic hi-fi turntable covers, severely undercutting competitors who used the vacuum forming process. Manufacturing capacity is expanded to the production of audio amplifiers and tuners.
1984	Amstrad launches the first mass-market home computer package (CPC range). Designed by Amstrad engineers in the UK, this product captures the market from the existing players Commodore and Sinclair.
1985	Amstrad launches the first mass-market dedicated word processor (PCW 8256). This product opens up a previously untapped market.
1986	Amstrad launches the first mass-market IBM-compatible PC (PC 1512). At £399 this unit is less than a quarter of the price of established market leaders. Within six months of its launch, Amstrad captures 25 per cent of the European personal computer market.
1989	Amstrad launches the first mass-market satellite receiver/dish package for Sky TV and becomes the European number one supplier of satellite receivers. Amstrad launches the first combined fax, telephone and answering machine, acquiring 52 per cent of the personal fax market.
1993	Amstrad acquires Dancall Telecom (for around £8 million), a Danish dedicated telecommunications manufacturer specialising in cordless phone technologies: CT0, CT1, GSM, PCN and NMT450. The acquisition facilitates access to the Scandinavian market.
1996	Amstrad launches Dancall GSM mobile phones.
1997	Amstrad launches Dancall dual band mobile phone. Amstrad sells Dancall Telecom to German telecoms manufacturer Bosch Telecom for approximately £96 million. Amstrad awarded a contract to supply advanced interactive digital set-top boxes to British Sky Broadcasting plc.
2003	Amstrad signs two separate new manufacture and supply agreements with BSkyB, the first for Sky+ set-top boxes and the second for a new Sky-branded combined keyboard and remote control unit.
2004	Amstrad announces an order to supply digital satellite set-top boxes to the Italian broadcaster Sky Italia. First shipments commence ahead of schedule

Source: adapted from www.amstrad.co.uk

A Using Figure 11.18, describe the range of marketing strategies employed by Amstrad between 1968 and 2004.

B Analyse how changes in Amstrad's marketing environment might have determined the marketing strategies it employed.

C Discuss the marketing strategies Amstrad might use in the future.

Topic 10 Integrated growth strategies

MANAGING PEOPLE IS AN ESSENTIAL ELEMENT OF a manager's work. Managers can be responsible for large groups of people with very diverse skills, experience and attitudes. However, there is a certain core knowledge which is essential to understanding the effective management of people within a business. This unit provides you with this essential knowledge and builds upon the work of Unit 2 from the AS course.

This unit explores the characteristics of different organisational structures and how these structures affect employees at all levels within an organisation. It also explores the skills that a manager needs and the different types of decisions that managers take to carry out their role effectively. You will consider the nature of leadership and why it is important to a business as well as learn the difference between power and authority. Finally we examine how managers motivate people and the importance of empowerment in this process.

This unit is assessed by an external examination based on a series of short case studies. The examination last for one and a half hours.

Managing people

Introduction to managing people

This unit looks at businesses from the point of view of those who have to manage people. It considers, in particular, the roles and responsibilities of business managers and leaders. These two key groups both manage other people, but their roles are different to some extent.

Leaders

A leader is someone who sets the business's overall goals and targets for other people. Leaders guide, encourage and inspire their staff towards achieving these goals. Strong leaders define and shape an organisation's culture.

Bill Gates famously founded Microsoft. He was chief executive of Microsoft from the time it floated in 1986 until 2000. He is now the company's chairman and chief software architect. He has played a key role in setting Microsoft's objectives, has shaped the way the company operates. and continues to be an inspirational figure in the company's commercial and technical success.

An important role for leaders is communicating their ideas and vision to other people in the organisation, especially managers

Managers

A manager sets goals and targets for the aspects of the business for which he or she is responsible. The manager uses the financial, physical and human resources which are available to achieve these goals as efficiently as possible. In many cases, people are the most important resource for which managers are responsible.

Leadership and management skills

As well as looking at the roles and responsibilities of managers and leaders, this unit also examines the skills that they require to be successful. What has made Bill Gates, Stelios Haji-Ioannou (the founder of easyJet) and Richard Branson successful leaders? Are they the same types of leaders and is that why they are successful? This unit will classify leaders according to styles, and consider the circumstances in which these styles may be successful.

We also consider what makes leaders and managers powerful and what gives them authority. What is authority and how does it differ from power? This unit will help you distinguish between these two terms. It focuses on what makes people powerful within a business and how they use that power within the business by, for example, taking decisions.

Leaders and managers have to motivate workers to achieve the organisation's goals and objectives. Motivation is simply the desire to do something. How do managers increase the desire of employees to work harder and to help achieve the organisation's goals? Can particular leadership styles encourage (or inhibit) motivation)?

Numerous leadership theories have been proposed in an attempt to answer to these questions. We review some of these theories and attempt to assess their value to modern managers and leaders. We will help you relate theory to the practical issues within a business, to the practical actions and decisions that managers and leaders can take.

Organisational structure

Not all business are organised in the same way. In large businesses, particularly public limited companies, the roles of managers and leaders are clearly defined and separated. However, in small businesses the roles of managers and leaders may become blurred as it is common for the same person to carry out both roles.

Some businesses are very formally organised with managers of different levels of seniority all reporting to up a clear management chain. Other organisations do not rely strongly on formal structures.

Google, the company that created and owns the popular internet search engine, does not run on formal lines. Teams work independently, and decisions can be taken by many people within the organisation. It is a very informal company. It employs 5000 people

worldwide, but gives its staff a great amount of freedom within the workplace. For example, many of its staff are allowed to spend some time researching private projects in the fields of information technology and the internet. By encouraging its employees' creativity, the company expects to benefit in some way from these private research projects.

Using other real examples, we will look further at how organisations can structure themselves, and will consider the implications of these different structures for those within the business, as well as the business itself.

Decision making

Finally, the unit looks in some detail at decision-making. This is one of the major roles of managers and leaders, and most senior managers will make decisions every day. Some are major decisions, with long-term consequences, while others are small and relatively unimportant. For example, in 2005 Tesco, the UK's largest supermarket chain, agreed to buy 21 petrol retailing stations from Morrisons, one of its rivals. The deal is thought to be worth about £60 million. This is a major decision. In contrast, a manager in an individual supermarket store might be continually making a range of minor decisions, such as arranging and authorising overtime for some employees to cover a particularly busy period.

The unit will help you to assess the different types of decisions that have to be taken within businesses and to evaluate a number of techniques that can be used by leaders and managers to help with decision-making.

How is this unit assessed?

This unit is assessed by an external examination.

- The examination lasts one and a half hours with a maximum mark of 80.

- The examination paper comprises three or four short case studies giving a small amount of information about specific businesses.

- A series of questions is asked about each case study. The first questions are relatively straightforward, the later ones are more demanding.

- The questions will range widely over the subject material covered by this unit.

At the end of each section in this unit you are given an opportunity to tackle questions similar in style to those you will face in the examination. Completing the questions in these assessment practice sections is an important part of studying Unit 12.

Management: roles, responsibilities and skills

Setting the scene: managing a shop selling fashion clothes

If you want to be the manager of a London-based fashion shop (earning about £30,000 a year), then you will be expected to carry out a wide range of responsibilities.

This list (adapted from a real job description) shows the diverse roles and responsibilities of a modern fashion store manager. They are:

- manage staff, recruiting new employees as necessary
- train new and existing staff
- develop an effective team within the store
- meet targets for sales performance
- develop new plans for the business to increase sales

- manage the shop's stock to ensure maximum possible sales
- maintain good communication within the shop and between the shop and head office
- maintain the shop in excellent order and ensure health and safety standards are met
- carry out administrative duties effectively and promptly
- make sure the shop's security is maintained at all times.

Adapted from www.fashionunited.co.uk

What do managers do?

The management theorist Mary Parker Follet defined management as "the art of getting things done through people". What does this mean in practice? All managers have to carry out certain roles and to meet their responsibilities. These roles and responsibilities are normally set out in job descriptions which are given to managers when they are applying for posts or when they are first appointed.

Roles are the duties or tasks that a manager has to carry out as part of the job. For example, a production manager in a food processing plant would have to order stock and draw up work schedules for production line employees. These are some of the duties that make up the role.

Responsibilities are slightly different. They relate to managers being accountable for their actions and decisions. Thus, the production manager's responsibilities are likely to include manufacturing food of sufficient quality. If the quality falls below expected standards, the manager will be expected to put things right and, possibly, to explain why the problems occurred in the first place. The job description for most positions will state to whom a manager is responsible and accountable.

The main duties or roles of managers

The precise roles carried out by managers vary according to their seniority, the size of the business and the type of business. A small printing firm, for example, may only have a single manager (who may also be the owner). This manager will necessarily carry out a wide range of duties because there is no other manager in the firm to whom he can delegate some managerial tasks. A manager in a large business is likely to have a more specialised role. For example, most universities are likely to employ a human resource manager whose duties include planning for future staffing needs, and overseeing recruitment, training and related activities.

However, all managers' jobs have common elements. These are illustrated in Figure 12.1.

1 Planning

A key management role is to look ahead. Planning helps to co-ordinate a business's activities so that it is moving forward in a focused and coherent manner. Managers draw up plans at different levels. Businesses have a strategic plan, usually drawn up by the most senior managers, which sets out how the business will fulfil its objectives. Once this plan is complete, more junior managers can begin the process of planning. Their plans should complement the strategic plan, and set out in some detail how their areas of responsibility will contribute to achieving the business's overall objectives.

Planning can entail a broad range of duties. These include:

- setting targets, goals or objectives for the future

- forecasting likely sales over some future time period and assessing how production might need to be adjusted

- planning marketing actions for the future, such as new markets to be entered and promotional campaigns

- estimating the expected labour requirements of the organisation, including overall numbers, where workers need to be located, and the skills the workforce will require

- financial planning by examining the business's need for long-term capital and short-term cash, and making arrangements to ensure these needs are met

- planning resource needs by detailing the business's likely needs in terms of offices, factories, shops, machinery, vehicles, materials and components.

Through planning in this way, managers aim to work towards strategic objectives and to minimise the chances of the business failing. Most businesses also undertake some form of contingency planning, a specialised form of planning that attempts to forecast, and makes preparations to overcome, any potential crises or emergencies that a business might face.

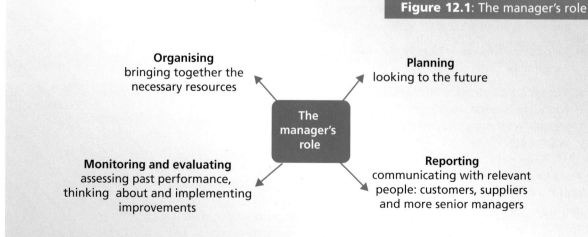

Figure 12.1: The manager's role

Organising
bringing together the necessary resources

Planning
looking to the future

The manager's role

Monitoring and evaluating
assessing past performance, thinking about and implementing improvements

Reporting
communicating with relevant people: customers, suppliers and more senior managers

stop and think

What planning activities might these two managers undertake as a normal part of their role?

- A senior marketing manager at Sainsbury's head office.

- The manager of a small nightclub in a seaside resort.

business practice
Managers plan for bird flu

Concerns about a bird flu pandemic have led to calls for businesses to plan for large-scale absences as their employees succumb to the illness. The research firm Gartner has warned that businesses should not wait until bird flu becomes a problem because they will not have enough time to prepare. Gartner warns that a pandemic could limit travel, disrupt supply chains and hit staff attendance, leading to businesses being unable to maintain production of goods and services.

Gartner advises that managers should plan for a pandemic in which travel may be curtailed and businesses may not always be able to open. Key actions could include:

- keeping staff informed about what is happening so they know when to travel to work and when not to do so

- placing a senior manager in charge of the business's response to the bird flu pandemic

- updating contingency plans especially to cope with large-scale staff absences

- helping staff to work from home, for example by ordering laptops in advance

- increasing the amount of business that is conducted online since it involves less travelling by customers and, possibly, employees.

Assume you are a manager of a Tesco superstore. Write a list of the actions you might take in advance to prepare for an expected outbreak of bird flu in your locality.

2 Organising

Managers have to bring together a range of resources to meet a business's objectives. This can entail considerable organisation. For example, a manager appointed to a fashion shop (see the introduction to this topic) would need to:

- ensure that the shop had sufficient well-trained staff available throughout its opening hours

- have enough supplies of high-fashion stock to satisfy consumers' needs

- make sure that suppliers are paid promptly to ensure continued supplies of stock

- keep accurate records of sales, employee performance and attendance, and the financial performance of the shop

- be aware of customers' views on the shop's stock and on trends in the fashion market to ensure popular products are purchased from suppliers.

This management role requires a substantial amount of organisation. Managers are also expected to use the minimum amount of resources necessary to meet the business's objectives. This can place further pressure on organisational skills.

3 Monitoring and evaluating

Monitoring the effectiveness of the business, and evaluating the impact of individual management decisions, is vital if managers are not to repeat mistakes. As Figure 12.2 shows, this is the final stage in a series of management activities relating to decision-making.

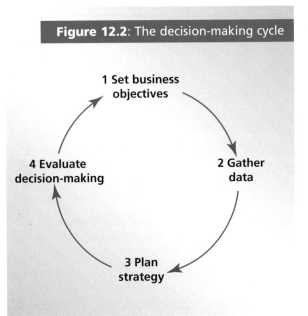

Figure 12.2: The decision-making cycle

1 Set business objectives

2 Gather data

3 Plan strategy

4 Evaluate decision-making

Monitoring can also help managers to improve the business's performance. In 2005 the Sickness Absence Management (SAM) project was launched in Scotland. This project aims to assist businesses in reducing the financial losses (estimated to be £11 billion for UK businesses each year) associated with staff absences. The project is assessing the value of computer software which can be used by managers in all businesses to record and monitor staff absences. It also offers advice on how to reduce absence levels.

4 Reporting

Reporting can provide important information that managers can use in decision-making and planning. The reporting function for managers can take a number of forms.

Annual report and accounts

Senior managers prepare the annual report and accounts. There is a legal requirement for companies to publish an annual report and accounts, but sole traders and partnerships have to report on profits or losses to allow HM Revenue and Customs to assess tax liability. A company's annual report and accounts sets out its profits and losses as well as the value of its assets and liabilities. In addition, the report also gives a range of information about the business's activities over the past year. Suppliers, shareholders and potential investors are all likely to be interested in the financial performance of the business.

Other financial information

Managers are likely to report on whether they have kept within their budgets over the past year. For example, a marketing manager might have to give information to a senior manager about expenditure on advertising, so that the senior management team can compare advertising spend against the advertising budget that was granted at the start of the business's financial year.

Market research

Managers may investigate customers' views in order to gain a fuller understanding of trends in the market. These findings are likely to form the basis of a report for other managers within the business, including those responsible for finance and production.

Employee performance

Reporting on the performance of employees can encompass a range of data. Human resource (HR) managers might provide information on productivity, absenteeism, wage costs and training costs. They may also have responsibility for writing reports on health and safety, identifying areas where action is needed. For example, managers in the leisure industry have reported on the increased chance of bar staff in pubs and clubs suffering hearing impairment as a result of loud music and longer working hours. These reports will be used to help businesses in the industry decide what action to take to tackle the problem.

Key management skills

A manager needs a wide range of skills because managerial jobs are very complex. All managers need the ability to see the organisation as a whole, even if they are in relatively junior positions. They must understand how their section or department fits into the business, so that they can assess the impact of their decisions on other areas of the business. As managers are promoted, the ability to think strategically and consider the long-term needs of the entire organisation become more important. However, there are a number of vital skills that all managers need to possess to carry out their roles effectively.

1 Technical skills

A manager's specific role within the organisation will determine the need for a particular range of technical skills. A marketing manager, for example, needs to have the skills to design an advertising campaign or to develop a successful strategy for researching a particular market. A marketing manager would also need some skills in handling statistical data to interpret the results of market research. In contrast, production managers need skills relating to stock control or scheduling production.

Some technical skills are common to managers throughout a business. Junior and middle managers are likely to need analytical ability and problem-solving skills. Conceptual and strategic skills will become more important as managers are promoted and they have to develop medium- and long-term strategies for large parts of the business.

2 Communication skills

Managers need a range of communication skills to carry out their jobs effectively. They need to be able to articulate their ideas and vision and to convey enthusiasm. Good managers may, at times, need to be able to argue points cogently and to persuade people to their point of view.

However, good managers appreciate that communication is a two-way process, and that listening is an important element of communication. Listening to the views of others can help to test ideas as well as to develop new products and methods of production.

Meetings are the most common forum in which managers are required to communicate. It is important for managers to plan for meetings, whether with a single person or with a group. Managers should restrict those attending meetings to keep numbers to a minimum. They should have a clear agenda for discussion and should exercise tight time controls to prevent meetings dragging on. Managers should enter each meeting with a clear idea of what they want it to achieve. At the end of a meeting it is good practice to summarise what has been agreed and what is expected to happen in the future.

One criticism of UK managers is that relatively few speak a second language fluently. This can cause obvious problems for businesses that trade in a global market. Research suggests that UK companies lose around 13 per cent of the international deals they try to complete due to "communication problems".

Managers also need effective written skills if they are to carry out their jobs effectively. The ability to quickly summarise key points in the form of a report for others in the business is of real value. So is the skill of reading a report written by someone else and being able to draw out the important elements.

These skills should not be taken for granted. Many managers require training in written and oral communication skills, and many businesses would benefit from employing managers who speak at least one other language.

stop and think

Why might a manager working for Shell have to rely more on written communication than a manager in a very small business?

3 Organisational skills

Managers have to organise people and other resources effectively to be successful. Organisational skills can take a number of forms.

Setting achievable targets

Managers have to set targets for themselves and others. These targets should be challenging to stretch employees, but not impossible or they will demotivate staff. Targets can take many forms: they could be a financial sales target, a benchmark for reducing the number of faulty products manufactured, or a time scale within which a project must be completed.

Planning workload

Managers frequently have much more work than they can complete in the time available. They must decide what work is to take priority and what work can be delegated to more junior employees. Well-organised managers do this at the beginning of each week (or at the start of each day) to ensure that they keep up to date and on top of their jobs.

Time management

Having decided which tasks are to be priorities, managers must ensure that they do not spend too long on them. Managers can adopt simple techniques to help make effective use of their time such as imposing deadlines on meetings, dissuading colleagues from "dropping in", and being tidy so that it does not take valuable time to find documents.

Creating effective teams

Many businesses rely heavily on teams to supply goods and deliver services. For example, the pensions and insurance company Standard Life uses teams throughout its organisation. Picking team members who are complementary but have different and supporting skills is an important skill for a manager. Having created effective teams, managers may be more prepared to delegate work.

4 Interpersonal skills

Good interpersonal skills are necessary if a manager is to work successfully with other people. If managers lack interpersonal skills, then they are likely to be of limited effectiveness in their role. Managers with effective interpersonal skills can motivate others and can co-ordinate the work of their employees. To do this, managers may need to coach and encourage employees as well as solving disputes and, perhaps more importantly, preventing conflict.

As well as their own staff and direct subordinates, managers have to work with other people too. They interact with customers, more senior managers, suppliers, trade union officials, government officials and the local community. Managers need to be comfortable in the company of diverse groups, and they need to able to communicate formally when required and to engage in informal small talk.

Assessing interpersonal skills at Mobil

Mobil, one of the world's largest multinational oil companies, asks potential managers a series of questions in an attempt to discover the extent of their interpersonal skills.

- Describe the achievement you were most pleased with while holding a position of responsibility. What happened? What role did you play?

- Describe a situation from your work history where you have used your own initiative to achieve success. What did you do?

- Describe what you consider to be one of your most challenging situations. Detail how you

became involved, and the key steps you took to reach a satisfactory conclusion. What was the final outcome?

- Give an account of a difficult situation you had to deal with which with hindsight you could have handled more effectively. What was involved? What were your key learning points?

The fact that a major employer such as Mobil asks this number of questions suggests that the company considers interpersonal skills to be an important element in successful management.

assessment practice
McAlpine manager wins construction manager of the year

John Roper has won the 2005 Construction Manager of the Year award for his outstanding work leading the McAlpine team that bid for and built the Paul O'Gorman building at Newcastle University. According to the judges, John "demonstrated an excellent understanding of how the project could be successfully delivered within a challenging, live, inner-city environment".

John led McAlpine's bid team, working closely with the building's designers. One of his many achievements was to instigate a series of exercises which reduced costs by 10 per cent without sacrificing quality. Putting John at the helm of the team, with his obvious dedication, gave the client great confidence, leading to McAlpine's appointment to construct the Paul O'Gorman building even though they were not the lowest bidder.

John was then asked to lead the construction team for this very complex project. He introduced a variety of programming techniques, including detailed resource monitoring, to ensure the project developed on track. Employing his own direct workforce gave him close control and allowed him to monitor efficiency in great detail and carry out cost-value exercises, an approach now adopted by all McAlpine sites in the region.

Chris Blythe, chief executive of the Chartered Institute of Building, commented: "John Roper's work on the successful bid was so impressive that his employer, and the client, gave him the job of building it. His total dedication to the project resulted in a world-class building that exudes quality at every level."

Source: Chartered Institute of Building news release, October 2005

A Identify and explain two ways in which John's communication skills might have helped him during the bidding and building stages of this project.

B Describe fully one other management skill which you think was important to John.

C Explain the managerial responsibilities that John Roper may have had during the construction of the Paul O'Gorman building.

D Do you think that John would immediately be a successful manager of a large supermarket? Justify your view.

Organisational structure

Setting the scene: changed company structures make fraud easier

Companies in the UK are more vulnerable to fraud following the introduction of flatter or delayered organisational structures. The increasing popularity of machines such as iPods has also added to the risk.

This combination of MP3 technology, which can be used to download vast quantities of corporate information (as well as music), and lower levels of supervision has allowed some disgruntled employees to obtain large amounts of company information such as databases of customers. This data is then sold or used to start-up a rival business.

Staff who have been given the sack or missed out on promotions are the most likely to turn to this type of fraud. They may be supported by criminal gangs who use employees as insiders to extract information, but even in these cases the insiders are more likely to be disgruntled employees who want to punish their employer.

Andrew Clark, head of fraud investigations at KPMG, said data theft was an increasing problem. "Data is valuable, and companies don't always realise that. These thefts can happen because there is a reliance on automated processes and there are fewer middle managers after 10 years of delayering."

Source: Adapted from www.guardian.co.uk

Understanding organisational structures

An organisational structure is the particular way in which a business is arranged in order to carry out its activities. The organisational structure illustrates a number of important features of the business:

- the routes by which communication passes through the business

- the structure of authority within the organisation

- the roles and titles of individuals within the organisation

- the staff to whom individual employees are accountable

- the units and divisions for which individual managers are responsible.

Businesses change their organisational structure rapidly and regularly; some entrepreneurs believe that they should be continually reorganising their businesses to keep them flexible, efficient and responsive. A principal reason, therefore, for the regular change in organisational structures is that changing external factors frequently force businesses to respond to new environments.

KEY TERMS

Levels of hierarchy refer to the number of layers of authority within an organisation.

The **span of control** is the number of subordinates reporting directly to a manager.

Centralisation places decision-making powers firmly in the hands of senior personnel (often at head office).

Decentralisation is the opposite – it gives decision-making powers to those at lower levels in the organisation and to employees in branch offices and other locations.

Delayering is the removal of one or more layers of hierarchy from the organisational structure.

Another reason is operational efficiency. All businesses have to ensure that they are able to compete with rival firms. Keeping costs to a minimum is an important part of a successful competitive strategy and a common reason for businesses to change their organisational structures. In 2005, businesses such as Barclays Bank and Cadbury Schweppes announced major changes in organisational structure in an attempt to maintain profitability and competitiveness.

There are two key elements that are vital in understanding an organisation's structure:

- levels of hierarchy

- spans of control.

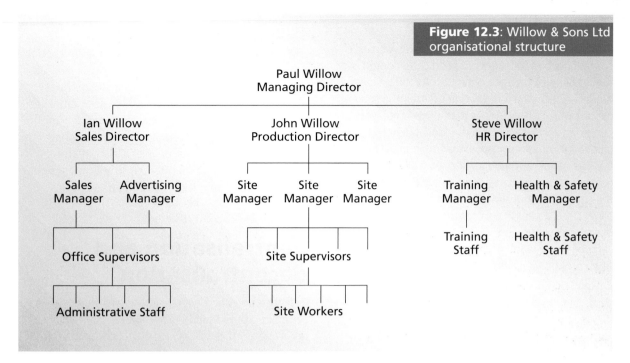

Figure 12.3: Willow & Sons Ltd organisational structure

Paul Willow
Managing Director

Ian Willow
Sales Director

John Willow
Production Director

Steve Willow
HR Director

Sales Manager — Advertising Manager

Site Manager — Site Manager — Site Manager

Training Manager — Health & Safety Manager

Office Supervisors

Site Supervisors

Training Staff — Health & Safety Staff

Administrative Staff

Site Workers

Levels of hierarchy

The number of layers of authority within an organisation define the levels of hierarchy. Figure 12.3 shows the organisational structure of Willow & Sons Ltd, a family-owned house-building firm. This firm has five layers of hierarchy.

Paul Willow, the managing director, has authority to control the whole business. Below him, his three sons have authority over different divisions of the business: production, personnel and sales. In turn, each of these three directors has appointed managers with particular responsibilities such as training employees, looking after health and safety, and managing one of the building sites. The company's managers have supervisors to look after particular areas of responsibility and particular groups of junior employees.

Note that although the bottom tier of employees – the administrative staff and site workers – are not responsible for managing any staff, they will have responsibility (and authority) for carrying out their duties in their particular functional areas.

Spans of control

A span of control is the number of people reporting directly to a manager. Paul Willow has three people reporting directly to him and, therefore, a span of control of three. Steve Willow has a span of control of two.

The balance between spans of control and levels of hierarchy determines whether a business's

organisational hierarchy is flat or tall. There is an inverse relationship between the average span of control and the number of layers of hierarchy within an organisation. So an organisation with a wide span of control will have few layers of hierarchy; it will be the flat organisation in Figure 12.4. On the other hand, tall organisations have many layers of hierarchy, but narrow spans of control.

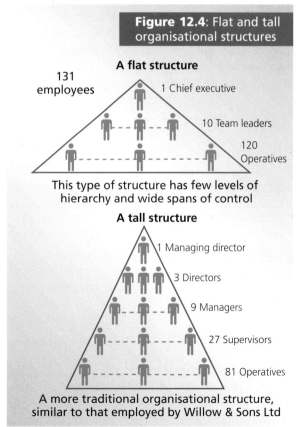

Figure 12.4: Flat and tall organisational structures

A flat structure

131 employees

1 Chief executive

10 Team leaders

120 Operatives

This type of structure has few levels of hierarchy and wide spans of control

A tall structure

1 Managing director

3 Directors

9 Managers

27 Supervisors

81 Operatives

A more traditional organisational structure, similar to that employed by Willow & Sons Ltd

Flat or tall?

A tall organisational structure, with narrow spans of control, enables managers to keep close control over the activities of their subordinates. As the organisational structure becomes flatter, the span of control widens. This means that junior employees are permitted a greater degree of independence in their working lives, as it is impossible for an individual manager to closely monitor the work of a large number of subordinates. Some managers believe that the span of control should not exceed six people, to allow close supervision of juniors. However, in business environments where subordinates are carrying out a range of broadly similar duties, a span of control of 10–12 is common.

It is normal for a span of control to be narrower at the top of organisation. This is because senior employees have more complex and diverse duties, and are therefore more difficult to supervise effectively.

In recent years, as businesses have sought to control or cut their wage costs, it has become increasingly common to introduce flatter organisational structures. (This trend goes back at least as far as the early 1990s.) Many businesses have achieved flatter organisational structures by removing management levels or layers of hierarchy. This process is known as delayering. When companies decide to delayer, it is often middle-ranking managers who lose their jobs. For example, in 2000 Barclays Bank delayered, reducing its workforce by 10 per cent and making many middle managers redundant in the process. The popularity of delayering indicates that it has numerous advantages, but there are many associated drawbacks too. Figure 12.5 sets out arguments for and against a delayering strategy.

The trend towards flatter organisational structures has meant that junior employees have become empowered. This means that they have more control over their everyday working lives, principally because they take more work-related decisions themselves rather than relying on managers. Decisions are taken further down the organisational structure, making communication of instructions easier as they have to be passed through fewer people. It also creates a need for upward communication, so that more senior managers are aware what has been decided.

Centralisation and decentralisation

Centralisation and decentralisation are opposites. A centralised organisation is one where the majority of decisions are taken by senior managers at the top (or centre) of the business. Centralisation can provide rapid decision-making, as few people need to be consulted because all decisions are made by a small number of managers, possibly working at the organisation's head office. Centralisation is one way of ensuring that the business pursues the objectives set by senior managers.

Decentralisation gives greater authority to staff lower down the organisational structure, to employees in branch offices and other locations. The recent trend in the UK has been towards greater decentralisation, and it can offer businesses a number of advantages.

- Decentralisation can improve motivation as junior employees are given greater authority. This can lead to improved performance and foster employee loyalty to the organisation.

Figure 12.5: The pros and cons of delayering

Advantages	Drawbacks
Delayering can improve the competitiveness of a business by reducing wage costs, especially as middle managers often earn high salaries.	The experience and knowledge of middle managers may be missed in an organisation that has delayered.
Delayering often gives junior employees a wider range of tasks and greater responsibility, which may help to motivate them.	Employees may not perform well in a delayered organisation if they fear that future organisational changes may put their jobs at risk.
It is easier for junior and senior employees to communicate in a delayered organisation, and this may result in new ideas and perspectives.	An organisation's training expenditure is likely to increase substantially after delayering as staff have to be prepared to take on new and more demanding roles.
	Wide spans of control give many staff a very heavy workload which may impair their efficiency.

- Senior managers can benefit from a policy of decentralisation as it reduces their workload because more decisions are taken lower down the organisational structure.

- Many junior employees get a better understanding of operational matters following decentralisation. This can help them to gain promotion to more senior posts.

Decentralisation can also improve communication, as many decisions are taken lower down the organisation, making it easier and quicker to inform the employees affected by any decision. However, there is a need to ensure that senior managers are aware of the results of decentralised decisions so that a business's overall performance can be co-ordinated.

Decentralisation can assist businesses in introducing new products and entering new markets because it allows decisions to be made closer to the customer. This is why decentralisation is attractive to many large multinationals. They are simply too big and too diverse for the majority of decisions to be made by senior managers.

Decentralisation can create problems for businesses, however. It can result in a lack of communication and co-ordination. Northern Foods plc is one of the UK's largest manufacturers of chilled foods. It supplies about 34 per cent of Marks & Spencer's ready meals. However, the company has blamed disappointing performances on decentralisation. It said that decentralisation had increased costs and had not helped communication or consistent decision-making.

business practice
Offshoring

Major British companies such as Lloyds TSB, HSBC and Norwich Union have transferred call centre and IT jobs from the UK to Asia in recent years in the hope of reducing costs. This process is called offshoring. In 2005, experts forecast that offshore outsourcing of call centre work could grow by 25 per cent in the next five years.

Put yourself in the position of a senior manager at Norwich Union responsible for its call centre operations. How might the policy of offshoring affect the flow of information

- **within the area of the business for which you are responsible**
- **within the whole of Norwich Union?**

stop and think

Imagine you are a manager for Coca-Cola with responsibility for selling the company's products in Germany. What benefits might you gain if the company introduces a policy of decentralisation? How might the company benefit if you have greater authority to take decisions?

business practice
Pernod Ricard

The French-owned company Pernod Ricard is the second largest producer of wines and spirits in the world. Founded in 1975 by the merger of two businesses, the company's brands include Malibu, Beefeater gin, Havana Club rum, Stolichnaya vodka, Jameson whisky and Mumm champagne. Pernod Ricard is a dominant presence in markets throughout the world, from Europe to Asia Pacific and North and South America.

The company has benefited from decentralisation as it has expanded its range of products and the markets in which it operates. It allows its managers considerable freedom in decision-making.

The company's chief executive Patrick Ricard says: "We have local roots but global reach. Pernod Ricard is a very decentralised group – we try to make decisions as close as we can to consumers."

Figure 12.6: A matrix structure

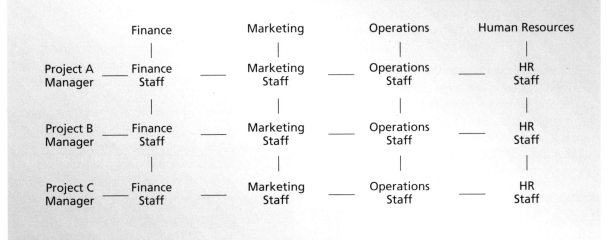

Chief Executive

Finance   Marketing   Operations   Human Resources

Project A — Finance — Marketing — Operations — HR
Manager   Staff   Staff   Staff   Staff

Project B — Finance — Marketing — Operations — HR
Manager   Staff   Staff   Staff   Staff

Project C — Finance — Marketing — Operations — HR
Manager   Staff   Staff   Staff   Staff

Matrix structures

A matrix structure is a fluid one in which teams of employees with appropriate skills are assembled to carry out particular tasks. A matrix structure embodies flexibility, allowing individuals to use their skills to best effect. Project managers bring teams together for a relatively short time until the task is complete. Individuals may be part of two or more teams simultaneously. A matrix structure is often used by businesses such as marketing agencies and management consultancies that manage a number of different projects at one time. Figure 12.6 illustrates a typical matrix structure.

Matrix structures focus on the task in hand – launching a new product, opening new retail outlets, closing down factories or entering overseas markets for the first time. Project groups often have a strong sense of identity in spite of being drawn from various areas in the business. This is because they are pursuing a clearly defined objective, providing team members with a sense of purpose and responsibility. Matrix structures can assist in improving communication within an organisation as they bring together teams of people drawn from all areas of the business. This enhances communication between different levels in the organisation as well as horizontal communication between those at the same level in the business.

Matrix structures bring problems with them. Employees can find it difficult having two managers (project managers and departmental managers) because of divided loyalties. They can be uncertain about which parts of their work to prioritise, and conflict can result. Matrix structures have a reputation for being expensive to operate: administrative and secretarial staff can be costly when used in support of a number of projects.

The John Lewis Group is UK's largest department store chain with a network of shops stretching from Aberdeen in north-east Scotland to Bristol in south-west England. The company has twenty-six department stores with over five million square feet of space, as well as its Waitrose chain of 160 supermarkets.

The company is also Britain's biggest and longest surviving example of worker co-ownership. All 60,000 of John Lewis's permanent staff are partners in the business and share in its profits.

Figure 12.7: The organisational structure at the John Lewis Group

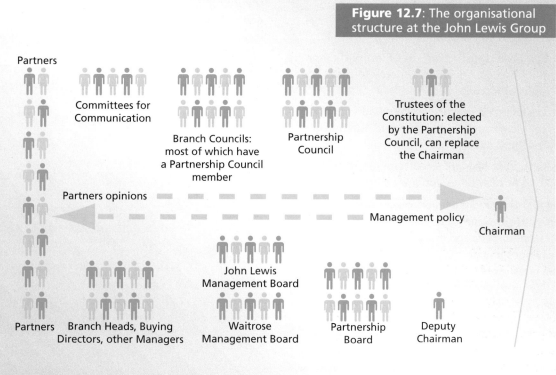

Source: Adapted from The John Lewis Corporate Brochure

A John Lewis operates a relatively tall organisational structure.

i What is meant by a "tall organisational structure"?

ii Explain how this might affect the business's ability to communicate effectively.

B Assume the John Lewis Group is considering implementing a policy of decentralisation. Assess the likely effects of this on:

i the flow of information throughout the business

ii its ability to assemble teams to manage projects (such as introducing new ranges of products to its stores).

Leadership

Setting the scene: the legendary Jack Welch

Jack Welch is arguably the best known leader of a business in the world. He was employed by the giant American corporation General Electric (GE) for 41 years, and was the company's chief executive for more than 20 years. GE produces a wide range of products including jet engines, equipment to generate power, and insurance.

Jack Welch has clear, but tough, views on leadership. Watch out for three things, he says, and success will follow.

- **Employee satisfaction** – at GE every six months the firm's staff filled in a survey to check for signs of discontent,

- **Customer satisfaction** – every half year the conglomerate's customers were asked to give feedback as well,

- **Cash flow** – ignore short-term profitability, as long as cash flows you are doing fine.

He wants to see managers create something, grow the enterprise, take care of their staff, train up new leaders, and make customers happy. So how does one do it? Go to business school? Read the latest books on good management?

"Go with your gut instinct, you've got to act on your gut," Mr Welch says. Yes, some management theory can provide useful tools, but gut feeling and the ability to recognise patterns in your business are the best assets a manager can have.

Jack Welch was certainly a tough manager. When he was running GE, every year the top 20 per cent of his managers were amply rewarded with bonuses and stock options, the middle 70 per cent benefited from the growth of the firm, and the bottom 10 per cent were axed.

Source: adapted from BBC News website

What do leaders do?

The precise duties that fall to a leader depend on the type and size of business as well as the preferences and working style of any individual leader. However, it is possible to identify a number of common features that make up the workload of a leader.

- Leaders set objectives and a direction for the business. They must have vision and know where the business is going. This vision is most effective when it can be expressed in terms of targets for subordinates to achieve.

- Leaders should set standards for the business. They can lead by setting an example in terms of commitment, professionalism and ethical behaviour.

- Leaders need to recognise the skills that exist within the organisation and to make effective use of the human talent available to them.

- Leaders help to shape the culture of the business (the way in which it operates) as well as its organisational structure. (Microsoft, for example, adopts a very informal approach at its Seattle headquarters.) Some leaders prefer tall organisational structures with narrow spans of control. Others do not.

- Leaders may become role models for individuals within the organisation and may choose to build alliances of senior individuals to protect their position.

The demands placed upon leaders have increased over recent years. The increasing use of information technology has meant that senior managers have much more information available to take decisions. This can help them make better informed decisions but it can also risks information overload: leaders can have difficulty in selecting the key elements and trends from a multitude of data.

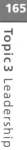

Styles or types of leadership

There is a broad spectrum of leadership styles.
However, it is possible to identify five distinct styles.
These are:

- autocratic or authoritarian leadership

- paternalistic leadership

- democratic leadership

- participative leadership

- laissez-faire leadership.

Figure 12.8 illustrates how these styles relate to one
another and the degree of freedom which each gives
to junior employees. This figure is based on the work
of Tannenbaum and Schmidt.

1 Autocratic leadership

Autocratic leaders are also sometimes called
authoritarian leaders. People who use this style of
leadership exhibit several common characteristics.

- They give little freedom to junior employees to
  take decisions, preferring to retain control.

- Communication tends to be downwards; they give
  junior employees instructions and tasks.

- Autocratic leaders state objectives they expect
  employees to pursue; in other words, they allocate
  tasks and demand that subordinates act on their
  decisions.

Autocratic leadership can have drawbacks. Employees
in an autocratically led organisation often become
very dependent on their leaders. Staff do not have the
information, support and confidence to act on their
own initiative. This can make the organisation less
responsive and slow down decision-making, as junior
employees are reluctant to take action alone.

Organisations managed in an authoritarian style may
face other difficulties. Autocratic leaders are often
harsh critics of other people's work. If subordinates
make mistakes, or are perceived to have performed
poorly, they can face criticism and, sometimes,
disciplinary action. This can result in staff trying to
avoid "putting themselves on the line" – matters to
be decided are either passed up for decisions to be
made at a higher level, or decisions are made by
committees to avoid any individual responsibility.
Senior managers tend to be overworked, and it is not
unusual for staff turnover to be high.

However, autocratic styles of management do have a
part to play in modern businesses. An autocratic style
might be appropriate in the several circumstances.

- When a quick decision is needed. This might be
  necessary, for example, if a company is facing a
  crisis. In 2004, Coca-Cola bosses took a rapid
  decision to withdraw its new bottled water
  (Dasani) from the market because it infringed
  health regulations. Senior managers decided not

**Manager-centred
leadership**

**Employee-centred
leadership**

Figure 12.8: A spectrum
of leadership styles

**Amount of control over
decisions retained by leaders**

**Degree of freedom given
to employees by leaders**

| Autocratic leadership style | Paternalistic leadership style | Democratic leadership style | Participative leadership style | Laissez-faire leadership style |

to attempt to modify Dasani to make it comply with the regulations, because the product had attracted too much adverse publicity.

- When it is important that a uniform message is expressed by all employees, in an attempt to be convincing and to restore public confidence.

- When managers are responsible for a large number of relatively unskilled subordinates.

The term autocratic leadership can be applied to the extremely forceful approach used in the armed forces as well as to the softer but still largely autocratic style known as paternalistic leadership. We consider this approach to leadership next.

---

business practice

Morrisons attracts criticism

Sir Ken Morrison has been chairman of the Morrisons supermarket group since 1956. The company has been highly successful for many years with Sir Ken at its helm. Recently Sir Ken has come under pressure as the company has had to announce that its profits are significantly lower than expected. So what has caused this change?

Problems have arisen because of Morrisons' £3,000 million takeover of its former rival, Safeway, in 2004. At that time analysts thought it was a good decision and a triumph for Sir Ken. Morrisons was gaining control of a larger company, and it had done so before major rivals such as Tesco and Sainsbury could act.

The acquisition seemed an ideal marriage in that Morrisons was dominant in the north of England while Safeway owned many stores in the south. However, the businesses were different in many other ways – different cultures, different customers and different accounting systems.

Problems soon occurred, and the autocratic Sir Ken came in for the majority of the criticism.

Why might Sir Ken's leadership style not have been appropriate for the new enlarged business?

2 Paternalistic leadership

Paternalistic leadership is broadly autocratic, but paternalistic leaders take the interests of the workforce into account when making decisions. They consult with junior employees over decisions and take some notice of the views expressed by subordinates. However, paternalistic leaders retain control over most decision-making and only delegate minor decisions (and little freedom) to subordinates.

Paternalistic leaders regard their staff as part of an extended family. They feel they have a duty of care to their employees. Traditional UK companies, like the chocolate manufacturer Cadbury (now part of Cadbury Schweppes plc), have often adopted this approach in the past. Businesses using this style of leadership consider it important to meet the social and leisure needs of their staff. In the 1950s and 1960s, for example, many companies set up sports and social clubs for employees as part of their approach to leadership and motivating employees.

Paternalistic leaders often have loyal subordinates. Because staff feel protected and cared for, they are likely to show strong loyalty to the company. It is not unusual for paternalistically led businesses to have a low rate of labour turnover. This can help to reduce recruitment costs and improve competitiveness.

However, paternalistic leaders do not encourage their employees to use their creative and imaginative skills, nor do they encourage the use of initiative. This can mean that the business does not make the most effective use of its human resources.

3 Democratic leadership

Democratic leadership is a broad-ranging term covering a range of similar styles of leadership. In its most extreme form, it shades into full participative leadership (see opposite) in which some employees play a full role in decision-making. More generally, democratic leaders allow subordinates some role in decision-making. Some organisations with democratic ledarrive at decisions through a form of voting, but most take decisions on a more informal basis.

There is no fixed pattern to democratic leadership, but typically leaders:

- delegate some decision-making powers to subordinates (which can help to develop managerial skills in junior employees)

- encourage junior employees to express views and ideas which can help enhance the creativity of the management team

- listen to junior employees' views and explain why particular decisions have been taken.

Successful democratic leaders normally possess excellent communication skills and encourage effective communications up and down the organisation's structure. A considerable amount of a leader's time may be devoted to communication.

Employees working for democratic leaders frequently offer constructive and imaginative ideas and suggestions. This can raise staff morale and motivation, and most democratically-led employees gain high levels of satisfaction from their work.

As businesses have become larger and more complex to manage, some form of democratic leadership has become more common. This trend has been accelerated by delayering (see topic 2), which has resulted in relatively junior employees being given a greater role in decision-making. Modern businesses are often large and complicated organisations, and the environment in which they operate is dynamic and changes rapidly. Leaders in these businesses are likely to need the support that democratic leadership can provide.

Democratic leadership does have some drawbacks. It can result in slower decision-making, as consulting with other employees can take time. Furthermore, it can allow some managers to absolve themselves of some of the responsibility for taking decisions. It may result in less consistent decision-making in pursuit of the business's corporate objectives.

4 Participative leadership

Participation is a style of leadership in which business leaders fully involve one or more employees in determining what to do and how to do it. This is a highly democratic leadership style, giving employees a high degree of control over decision making and their working lives.

This style of leadership has similar advantages to democratic leadership, but arguably the benefits are more pronounced. It allows managers to utilise the talents and creativity of subordinates to the fullest extent. This can benefit the organisation both in developing new ideas and approaches as well as in increasing the skills and confidence of junior managers. Participative leadership is most valuable when businesses are required to take complex decisions requiring a range of specialist skills.

The downside is similar to democratic leadership too. Slower decision-making and less consistency may be a price that has to be paid for the benefits of this style.

5 Laissez-faire leadership

Laissez-faire literally means "leave alone", and this accurately describes this style of leadership. This can be regarded as the most extreme type of democratic leadership. Laissez-faire leaders have a relatively small say in the management of the business. Subordinates are empowered to take many decisions without any reference to their managers. This means that businesses with laissez-faire leadership can lack co-ordination, and possibly a clear sense of direction. They can sometimes neglect the planning process.

The laissez-faire style of leadership sometimes exists because of the failings of the individual leader. The leader may not be confident enough or able to carry out the duties associated with the role. However, some determined and confident managers may use this style to utilise their employees' talents as fully as possible. It shows a degree of trust and respect for their employees. It may be an appropriate style to use when leading a highly creative and committed team.

Laissez-faire leadership can be successful in certain situations, such as when:

- the leader or manager leads a well-qualified and experienced team of employees

- subordinates are highly motivated and supportive of the manager

- the leader and the employees are all pursuing the same objectives.

stop and think

Identify three situations in which laissez-faire leadership might be most suitable. Justify your decisions.

The skills of leadership

John Gardner, a US writer, studied a large number of North American organisations and leaders and came to the conclusion that there were some qualities and attributes that appeared common to good leaders. This suggests a leader in one situation could lead in another. These qualities and attributes include:

- physical vitality and stamina

- intelligence and judgement

- eagerness to accept responsibility

- understanding of subordinates and their needs

- skill in dealing with people and the capacity to motivate people

- courage and resolution

- trustworthiness

- decisiveness

- self-confidence and assertiveness

- adaptability and flexibility.

Style versatility

It may be that the best leaders are those who adopt a style appropriate to the situation that they face. The most talented are arguably the most versatile, able to call on one or more of the styles we have discussed, having assessed the demands of the situation.

A versatile manager might adopt a democratic approach when reaching a decision on an advertising campaign with a small group of highly skilled and experienced writers and artists. In contrast, the same manager might deploy a more paternalistic style when deciding on methods of production to be used to supply an urgent large-scale order.

Victor Vroom and Paul Yetton, two US scholars, have taken this approach further. Their model of leadership assumes that leaders are adaptable and versatile. They say successful leaders should act according to the situation in which they find themselves. Their model concentrates instead on the degree of involvement that subordinates should have in decision-making, and relates this to the circumstances surrounding the decision.

If it is true that the most effective leaders are versatile, then this has a number of implications.

- Businesses may need to place greater emphasis (and spend more money) on training managers. It is unrealistic to expect managers to recognise the different needs of varied situations and how to respond most effectively without some training. In particular, managers will need training to help them move away from their "natural" style of leadership.

- A more flexible business culture may be required to cope with versatile management styles. For example, a business with a formal culture may experience difficulties adopting and maintaining a policy of delegating authority to more junior employees, particularly when a complex and challenging decision needs to be made.

- Junior employees may require support and training to work with a manager who uses different leadership styles according to circumstances. Subordinates may require training to enable them to carry out duties requiring higher degrees of independence.

assessment practice
Amazon's leader

In 1994, a thirty-year-old New Yorker called Jeff Bezos read about the internet. He moved to California and in a year had set up an online bookshop. When the orders came in, he packed and posted books from his garage. By 2005 Amazon.com was the world's largest online retailer. Its sales in 2004 were over £4500 million.

Jeff Bezos is an outwardly friendly character, but this hides a steely determination to achieve the highest possible rates of growth for Amazon. He even chose the name because of its association with size. Bezos has faced a lot of criticism, but has maintained a consistent leadership style since 1995. He imposes his style and approach on others, and this has succeeded even as the company has grown and expanded into other countries such as Germany and Japan.

A Some observers think that Jeff Bezos is a paternalistic leader. What are the key features of this leadership style?

B In what ways might Jeff Bezos have had to change his leadership style as Amazon.com has grown?

C Discuss the case for and against Jeff Bezos encouraging all his managers to adopt versatile leadership styles according to circumstances.

Power and authority

Setting the scene: football club chairman calls new owner a dictator

The former chairman of a major Scottish football club has labelled the new owner a dictator. George Foulkes had been the long-serving chairman of Heart of Midlothian Football Club, and initially welcomed the arrival of Lithuanian banker Vladimir Romanov as the club's major shareholder and, effectively, its owner.

Foulkes resigned in October 2005 after Heart of Midlothian's chief executive Phil Anderton was sacked, their departures coming just 10 days after manager George Burley left the club "by mutual agreement". Many of the club's supporters supported Foulkes, seeing Romanov as abusing his power and wealth.

Foulkes said: "Romanov is behaving like a dictator and if he continues there will be a revolution against him. Phil Anderton has only been there six months and has done a very good job – ask anyone in Edinburgh, ask anyone in Scotland. Not only were we top of the Scottish Premier League, our season tickets sales had doubled and we were planning ground expansion."

These events took place as Vladimir Romanov increased his shareholding in the club to 75 per cent, confirming his control of the business. Other shareholders who have sold out to Romanov hold a different view of his leadership style. He is seen as being a strong leader who has not misused his power, but is decisive in pursuit of his aim of making Hearts a top European club.

Vladimir Romanov has appointed his son, Roman, to be the new chief executive. Roman will rely heavily on his father's position for his authority.

Source: adapted from BBC News website, 31 October 2005

KEY TERMS

Power exists when one person can get another person to do something that otherwise they would not want to do.

Authority is a special form of power, in the sense that it gives people the right to give commands which others accept as legitimate.

Distinguishing between power and authority

Power and authority are very important topics in understanding the management of people. A manager has power over someone when he or she can get that person to do something that otherwise they would not want to do. Managers exercising power can get staff to act in a way that they want, irrespective of the subordinates' views on the matter.

The most obvious source of power is control over something of value to someone else. In business, an important source of power for some managers is control over the jobs and wages of employees and the influence they can exert on promotion decisions.

Authority is important too. It is a special form of power in the sense that it implies voluntary agreement by subordinates who recognise the legitimate right of their superiors to give orders. Writing nearly 100 years ago, Max Weber identified three forms of authority:

- traditional
- charismatic
- rational/legal.

Traditional authority

Some people have authority because of tradition or custom. The most obvious examples are royalty: they have authority by custom and tradition, with succession arranged through birthright (because of parentage) rather than any particular innate ability. Many entrepreneurs have appointed their sons and daughters to senior posts within their businesses, often when relatively young. For example, three of Rupert Murdoch's children have held senior posts within the media business he has built up and controls. His son James, who became chief executive of satellite broadcaster BSkyB at the age of 30, is expected to become the next chief executive of News Corporation, though this appointment may prove controversial.

Charismatic authority

Charismatic authority arises out of an individual's personality. An example of a leader noted for his charisma is Michael Grade, the chairman of the BBC. This type of authority is based on followers' assessment of the person's abilities. In many cases, charismatic authority supplements other forms of authority, such as rational and legal authority.

Rational/legal authority

Max Weber associated rational and legal authority with bureaucratic businesses. This form of authority relates to someone's position within the organisation, rather than the person as such. An important source of authority comes from the way in which a person is selected for office. For example, a chief executive might be selected following a lengthy selection process. The legitimacy of the chief executive comes from the belief that he or she was selected in a fair competition. Usually this requires that the post is advertised so anyone could apply, reasonable criteria are used in deciding who would be suitable, and fair methods are used to determine which of the applicants best meet these criteria.

Managers who are perceived to lack authority are likely to experience difficulty in leading and controlling subordinates. Specifically:

- subordinates may question leaders' decisions and spend long periods arguing about instructions

- subordinates may waste time criticising their manager rather than carrying out their duties

- junior employees may ignore managers' decisions and take actions independently, resulting in a lack of co-ordination and weakening a business's general sense of direction.

Sources of power

There are numerous sources of power. Here we consider five specific sources of power, and look at how staff may respond to each type of power and how it may affect the relationship between managers and subordinates.

1 Coercive power

Coercive power is based on the subordinate's fear of the leader. This form of power is normally maintained by the use of threats and punishment. Managers may exercise coercive power through the frequent use of reprimands and a hostile attitude, threatening subordinates with the loss of status, the loss of their jobs or, in extreme cases, physical force. Aggressive language or a powerful and dominant physical presence are other forms of coercive power. This form of power is often linked to the most extreme form of autocratic leadership.

Staff can be scared of a manager whose position is based upon coercive power. They may be afraid of being shouted at, of suffering financial loss due to demotion, or of being sacked. Coercive managers use this fear to ensure that their orders are carried out.

Unsurprisingly, coercive power has many drawbacks. Many people do not perform well in this kind of environment. Few people respond to an approach that is all stick and no carrot. Employees cannot develop their skills and use attributes such as creativity when controlled by a manager exercising coercive power. Some will simply not tolerate it, and coercive power can result in high labour turnover.

More generally, coercive power does not encourage open communication between subordinates and their managers. Subordinates will be unwilling or feel unable to communicate freely with managers, they will not offer suggestions and ideas or use their initiative for fear of upsetting their manager. Communication is limited to managers passing instructions down to subordinates.

2 Reward power

The ability to provide rewards for followers gives leaders a form of power. Subordinates comply with a manager's requests because they expect to benefit through improved pay, promotion or recognition as a consequence. Rewards can be anything that a person values, and some leaders offer quite subtle rewards to get their way, using praise, compliments or flattery to reward subordinates for undertaking particular actions or tasks. In some senses, reward power is the opposite approach to coercive power in that it encourages good performance through incentives rather than threats.

Reward power can be built into the culture of the business and its approach to leadership and management. The high street chemist, Boots, offers all staff rewards in the form of discounted products and a range of other benefits.

Other businesses pay employees through commission which is related to the achievement of key targets. Employees selling financial services are often rewarded in this way.

Reward power is more likely to be associated with a democratic style of leadership. Many staff respond positively to the exercise of reward power, though the precise motivational impact of specific rewards varies between individuals. The next topic on motivation (see page 174) considers this issue in more detail.

Managers using reward power may find that staff respond positively and are willing to offer ideas and suggestions as well as to take on additional duties and responsibilities. This source of power can be effective in a variety of circumstances. It can be particularly useful in situations in which employees are required to show initiative, or where staff do not work under close or direct supervision.

3 Expert power

Possession of particular expertise, skills and knowledge can give power. Leaders with these

Norwich Union Life has offices in 13 main locations around the UK and offers a wide range of products covering pensions, investments, life assurance and healthcare insurance. Norwich Union Life has around six million customers and employs over 14,000 people.

Norwich Union offers staff rewards as part of its VIP awards programme. Employees who are considered to have shown particular merit can be nominated by their colleagues throughout the year to receive a bronze, silver or gold VIP award. These awards reflect the differing levels of achievement by individuals or teams. Each award is worth a number of value points, which can be redeemed on a discount shopping website. Award winners also receive formal recognition of their contribution through, for example, a listing in the company's staff magazine.

Why might a provider of financial and insurance products such as Norwich Union chose a system such as its VIP awards which are based on rewards as a source of power?

attributes have the power to make decisions, as subordinates are likely to recognise the leaders' expertise and be willing to follow suggestions. The more important and unusual the expertise, the greater the power associated with it.

Expert skills can give a leader legitimacy. However expert power also derives, in part, from the difficulty of finding replacements if "experts" leave an organisation, and so experts can be perceived as being invaluable to the business. Senior figures such as professors at universities and very experienced chief executives can exercise expert power. Some more junior employees may also do so as a result of long experience with a particular aspect of the business. For example, experienced personal assistants may have a degree of expert power due to their knowledge of the business, the relationship they have built up with important clients, and their understanding of the market generally.

Managers with expert power may seek to prevent other employees acquiring their particular knowledge and skills. In this way, they can maintain their power base. They may offer subordinates some elements of their particular knowledge and skills to gain their support or to get agreement on a particular course of action. Staff are likely to be willing to accept instructions from an "expert" so long as the expert maintains their respect and is not seen to abuse the power that the expertise confers.

4 Legitimate (position) power

Legitimate power derives from a person's position or job in an organisation. Legitimate power increases as you go up an organisation's hierarchy: a director would normally exercise more legitimate power than a middle manager. However, some managers are more likely to try exercising legitimate power than others. For example, some managers will respond to any questioning of their decisions with a curt "I'm the boss" – an appeal to their legitimate power – whereas other managers may try to direct subordinates using other forms of power.

Organisations vary in the extent to which they emphasise and reinforce legitimate power. At one extreme are Britain's police forces, which have many levels of command, different uniforms to denote various levels of authority, and rituals such as calling senior officers sir or ma'am to highlight the relative power of individuals. In contrast, some modern businesses such as Microsoft operate relatively flat organisational structures, place little emphasis on job titles, and strongly value talent and creativity over hierarchical positions.

Legitimate power does not always result in effective and flexible organisations. It gives employees power because of their roles, rather than because they have particular skills and talents. However, many people are used to accepting (and using) legitimate power. Research in multinational companies shows that employees say that legitimate power is the major reason why they follow their bosses' orders.

stop and **think**

To what extent might the organisational structure of a business reflect the importance of legitimate power in the firm?

5 Referent power

Referent power derives from a leader's charisma. People are more likely to follow the lead (and instructions) of someone they like and admire. Many employees identify with managers who hold referent power, seek their approval, and use them as role models. Strong interpersonal skills may allow managers using referent power to have influence across the business. This can work outside the usual channels of legitimate authority, reward and coercion.

Referent power can be potent. Subordinates identify with a charismatic leader, and they are more likely to follow instructions and to believe in – and work hard to achieve – the leader's policies and goals. This gives charismatic leaders considerable power because their employees have a belief in what they are doing – they are not merely following orders to receive rewards or to avoid punishment. And, as employees and leaders share the same values, it encourages interaction between managers and subordinates.

Of course, anyone in a business may have charisma and be well liked, irrespective of their status and position within the organisation. This means that referent power can be exercised by people at all levels within the organisation.

stop and **think**

Can you think of any managers in the public eye that exercise referent power? What are the qualities that make them successful?

What works in the long term

A series of studies of organisations of all types has shown that coercive power and reward power have a fairly limited lifespan. Legitimate power doesn't really last either. After a while, people start to want more in a leader than just a title. The most long-lasting forms of power, the ones that bring the most change, are based on a leader's expertise and charisma, and the qualities they express.

assessment practice
Bernie Ebbers and WorldCom

Bernie Ebbers was both feared and admired during his period as chief executive of WorldCom, the US telecommunications company which collapsed following financial mismanagement and fraud by its senior managers. A big man, Ebbers had a number of jobs including spells as a nightclub bouncer and a basketball coach before his business career.

Ebbers used a mixture of ruthlessness and charisma to achieve a series of deals which made WorldCom one of America's largest telecom companies. Under Ebbers' control WorldCom pursued an aggressive strategy, taking over 50 small telecommunications businesses. Ebbers made his name as a successful and ambitious manager when sealing the deal which saw WorldCom buy a major rival (MCI) for $40,000 million, one of the largest corporate deals in history.

Some reporters writing about the collapse of WorldCom have suggested that it was Ebbers' aggressive management style that was the basic cause of the company's troubles. Some who knew Ebbers described him as brusque and short-tempered with a reputation for throwing unprepared colleagues out of meetings. Yet he was also charming and caring at times. He opened shareholder meetings with a prayer, could charm important people, and was not worried about eating meals in WorldCom's cafeteria amongst junior staff.

At the trial which followed the collapse of WorldCom, Ebbers maintained that he was not aware of the fraud being perpetrated at the company which eventually cost its shareholders an estimated £120 billion. Despite this, Ebbers was found guilty and sentenced to 25 years in jail.

A Bernie Ebbers exercised power and authority. What is the difference between these two terms?

B Explain the sources of power that Bernie Ebbers may have drawn upon during his time as chief executive at WorldCom.

C Discuss how Ebbers' use of power might have affected WorldCom's employees and the efficiency with which they carried out their jobs.

Setting the scene: report says employees think colleagues are lazy

A survey for Investors in People by YouGov has found that most people think that their colleagues do not pull their weight in the workplace. The survey uncovered that three quarters of UK bosses and 79 per cent of their employees thought some colleagues were lazy and that they underperformed. About 50 per cent of employees said they worked closely with someone they think is "deadwood". Nearly 40 per cent of the employees interviewed said that managers did not take action to improve the performance of poor workers.

The Investors in People survey revealed that the problem of poorly performing employees was more common in larger organisations. The survey showed that 84 per cent of workers in organisations with more than 1,000 employees thought they had an underperforming colleague, compared with 50 per cent in firms with under 50 workers.

The survey found that the employers and employees agreed that the top three indicators of employees "not pulling their weight" are:

■ prioritising personal life over work

■ refusing extra responsibility

■ passing off colleagues' work as their own.

Both employers and employees also agreed that the major reason for someone failing in their job was sheer laziness. Employees reported that they had to work longer hours to cover for shirking colleagues, and felt undervalued as a result. Ultimately, working alongside a lazy colleague could prompt workers to look for a new job, the survey found.

Ruth Spellman, chief executive of Investors in People UK, commented: "This survey lifts the lid on an issue that bosses have shied away from traditionally. It's clear from the findings that UK managers are aware that deadwood is a problem that can damage their organisation – but are failing to do anything about it. However, left unchecked, staff who don't pull their weight can breed resentment amongst colleagues and cripple productivity. It's vital that managers are equipped with the skills and confidence to tackle the issue before it becomes a problem."

Source: Investors in People press release, 19 August 2005

Models of motivation

Motivation can be defined in two ways. Some writers believe that motivation is the willingness to achieve a target or gaol. This assumes that employees require some external factor or stimulus to motivate them. Other writers define motivation as the will to work because of enjoying work for its own sake. (Such people might talk about "loving their job".) This view of motivation suggests that motivation comes from within an individual employee.

However one defines motivation, it is undoubtedly important to all businesses, and especially those in the service industry. Business with highly motivated workforces benefit in several ways.

■ Worker absenteeism is likely to be low, ensuring that the supply of goods and services is not interrupted.

■ The workforce is more likely to be highly productive and to supply a high-quality product with few errors. This can make the business highly competitive.

■ Motivated employees are more likely to offer ideas and suggestions to improve the production process and the business's goods and services.

■ Labour turnover is more likely to be low, because motivated employees are more likely to experience job satisfaction. This can help a business to avoid the substantial costs incurred in recruiting and training new employees.

There are many models or theories of motivation. We consider two models, based on the work of Abraham Maslow and Frederick Herzberg, in some detail. Maslow's and Herzberg's models are similar in the sense that they both consider the psychological

stop and think

Imagine you are a manager of a large hotel in central London. What benefits might you find (as a manager) from having a workforce which is highly motivated?

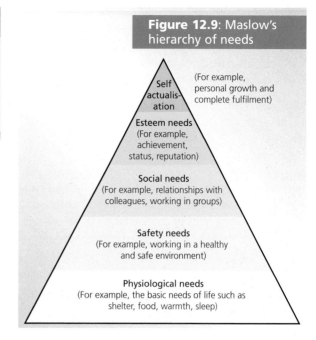

Figure 12.9: Maslow's hierarchy of needs

- Self actualis-ation (For example, personal growth and complete fulfilment)
- Esteem needs (For example, achievement, status, reputation)
- Social needs (For example, relationships with colleagues, working in groups)
- Safety needs (For example, working in a healthy and safe environment)
- Physiological needs (For example, the basic needs of life such as shelter, food, warmth, sleep)

aspects of work. By examining the psychological needs of workers, Maslow and Herzberg argued that managers should see employees as individuals with different needs, hopes and personalities. Their models highlight the fact that because people are different, and have varying needs, different techniques will be required to motivate them. It is from this standpoint that Abraham Maslow devised a model of motivation based on meeting people's needs in the workplace.

1 Maslow's hierarchy of needs

Maslow (1908–70) was a lecturer in psychology at Brandeis University in the USA. His main ideas are set out in two publications *Motivation and Personality* (1954) and *Toward a Psychology of Being* (1962). Maslow's hierarchy of needs sets out the five levels of need which he believed every employee wants

satisfied through work. Maslow famously presented his hierarchy of needs as a triangle, with basic needs shown at the bottom and higher needs at the top.

Maslow's argument was straightforward. He argued that employees want to have several needs met through employment. Maslow put these needs into

business practice

Vodafone

Vodafone's call centres offer a range of customer services, such as help with lost or stolen mobile phones, registration of new customers, and top-up services for subscriber credit. Call centre staff work shifts to ensure the service is available for long hours each day. Figure 12.10 shows how a manager of a Vodafone call centre might use Maslow's principles to motivate staff.

Figure 12.10: Using Maslow to motivate call centre staff

Maslow's level	Examples	Satisfying needs of call centre staff
Physiological needs	Food, shelter, heating	Through a pay system which is fair and affords a good standard of living
Safety needs	Safe, healthy working environment for employees, job security	Giving employees permanent contracts of employment so that they have some job security and the expectation of a regular income
Social needs	Interacting with other employees	Offering the call centre staff the chance to work in teams, and providing staff social facilities for use during breaks and after work
Esteem needs	Promotion, recognition and status	Allowing teams within the call centre to take some decisions themselves, for example drawing up rotas, identifying and meeting training needs
Self-actualisation	To use individual talents to their fullest extent	Giving staff the opportunity to develop new skills and to suggest means of improving the service provided by the call centre

175

Topic 5 Motivation

five categories. What was unique about Maslow's model was that he believed these needs formed a hierarchy. Maslow argued that only once a lower-level need has been met would employees want to have needs higher up the hierarchy satisfied.

Maslow's central point was that managers can motivate employees by providing the chance to satisfy needs at work, but they need to do this by satisfying basic needs and then continuing the process of motivation through offering the chance to satisfy the next level of need in the hierarchy. So a manager can start to motivate employees by offering a fair rate of pay which allows staff to pay for the basic necessities of life: food, shelter, heating, etc. Further motivation would depend upon the manager providing a safe and secure working environment. Employees might be further motivated by the provision of a permanent contract of employment. This would give some guarantee of employment for the foreseeable future.

At a higher level, an employee might have social needs met by working as part of a team. Further motivation could be provided by the offer of team leadership. This could allow the employee to fulfil esteem needs such as responsibility and recognition.

Maslow's model has attracted much attention ever since it was published. It gives managers in the workplace a range of ideas on how to improve the performance of their subordinates. Maslow's achievement was that he encouraged managers to think about employees as individuals, to move away from the sole use of money as a motivator, and to think about the design of jobs as a primary method of improving the performance of individual employees and the business's workforce as a whole.

2 Frederick Herzberg's two-factor theory

Writing in the 1950s and 1960s, Frederick Herzberg was the first researcher to show that satisfaction and dissatisfaction at work arose from different factors. Herzberg's two-factor theory, drawn originally from an examination of the working lives of engineers and accountants and later from sixteen other studies investigating other professionals, suggests that the factors that determine job satisfaction (and serve to motivate employees) are completely different from the factors that create job dissatisfaction.

Herzberg found that the factors that might enhance job satisfaction and motivation include:

- achievement
- recognition for achievement

- work itself
- responsibility
- growth
- advancement.

Herzberg's view was that managers should seek to motivate people by giving opportunities for achievement, and that they should recognise and celebrate achievement by employees. Using Herzberg's "motivators" can help individuals to enjoy and grow in their jobs.

A fundamental finding of Herzberg's work was that the design of jobs has the biggest impact on levels of motivation. Jobs should be designed to allow employees to achieve personal targets and goals, and there should be opportunities to offer praise and recognition. Jobs should be designed to help employees develop an interest in their work by, for example, allowing them to concentrate on aspects of the job in which they have genuine interest and expertise.

The second key element of Herzberg's two-factor theory is the finding that there are many factors in the workplace that do not actually motivate staff, but which can lead to employee dissatisfaction if they are inadequate. Herzberg's research identified the factors most likely to cause dissatisfaction. He called these "hygiene factors", and they include:

- company policy
- administration
- supervision
- interpersonal relationships
- working conditions
- salary
- status
- security.

Herzberg's research classified pay as a hygiene factor and, therefore, he argued that pay was not able to motivate staff. This is perhaps Herzberg's best-known finding: employees cannot be motivated by pay. Herzberg's research highlighted other factors that may cause dissatisfaction. For example, he recommended that managers should minimise the unnecessary paperwork, rules and regulations that employees often encounter during their working lives.

Herzberg believed that any attempt to improve the workplace through either boosting motivators or tackling hygiene factors should be done

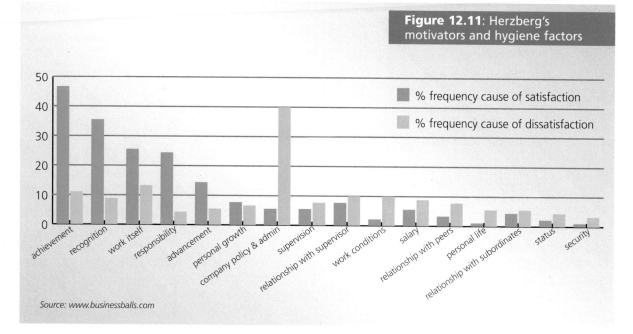

Figure 12.11: Herzberg's motivators and hygiene factors

■ % frequency cause of satisfaction

■ % frequency cause of dissatisfaction

Source: www.businessballs.com

simultaneously. Managers should avoid actions and circumstances that cause employee dissatisfaction, while seeking to create jobs and projects that contain motivators to stimulate employees.

3 Douglas McGregor's Theory X and Theory Y

Douglas McGregor was, like Maslow and Herzberg, a psychologist. He published his most famous book, *The Human Side of the Enterprise*, in 1960, and even though he died over 40 years ago his ideas continue to influence management thinking.

McGregor's theories, though included in this section, are not theories of motivation. Instead McGregor examined how managers view their subordinates. His work helps to inform us how different types of managers and leaders might set about motivating employees. However, McGregor's work does not identify explicitly techniques that may be used to enhance the performance of employees by improving their motivation.

In investigating the attitudes held by managers towards their employees, McGregor discovered that the different views held by managers placed them into two broad categories. He memorably labelled these categories Theory X managers and Theory Y managers (see Figure 12.12 on page 178). McGregor developed this insight by setting out the assumptions that underlay the attitudes of the two types of manager that he had identified.

McGregor argued that Theory X managers would carry out their work based on the belief that:

- the average employee dislikes work and will avoid it if he or she can

- unsupervised employees will not perform efficiently

- employees are motivated by money

- the average person prefers to be told what to do, and wants to avoid responsibility

- employees are not ambitious.

In contrast, managers with Theory Y beliefs and attitudes make entirely different assumptions about their employees. These are that:

- effort in work is as natural as work and play

- employees are able to work efficiently without constant supervision

- commitment to objectives is a function of rewards associated with their achievement

- employees usually accept and often seek responsibility

- most employees possess ingenuity and creativity, and they want to use these skills in their work

- employees seek satisfaction from work and not merely financial rewards.

McGregor's work is a simple reminder of the natural rules for managing people, which under the pressure of day-to-day business are all too easily forgotten. It is a principle from which to develop positive management styles and techniques. We shall consider the application of McGregor's ideas, as well as those of Maslow and Herzberg, in the next topic.

Figure 12.12: McGregor's Theory X and Theory Y

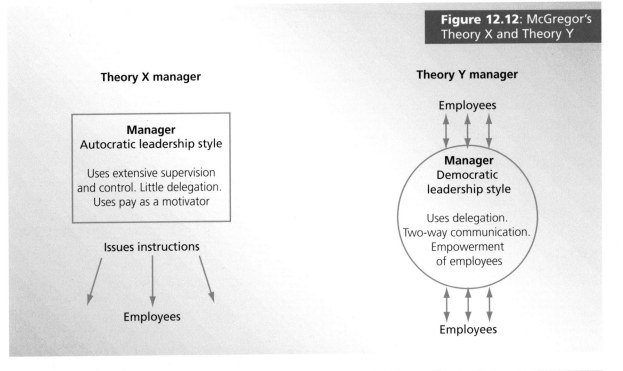

a s s e s s m e n t p r a c t i c e
Nissan's motivated workforce

In 2005, the Japanese-owned car maker Nissan announced that over four million cars had been produced at its Sunderland factory. This represented a major milestone for Europe's most efficient and productive car manufacturing plant. High levels of employee motivation and efficiency have contributed to the success of the Sunderland factory. In 2004 alone, the factory manufactured 320,000 cars.

Nissan operates an extensive training scheme for its employees, which lasts 20 months in total and is delivered through a mix of training and work experience in the factory. In recent years the company has offered its employees extended holidays; however, wages are lower than in other car factories elsewhere in the European Union. There is a good pension scheme, although workers appointed after September 2003 are offered a less attractive pension package.

The company's managers have expressed praise for the efforts of the workforce and have stressed how important the committed and highly motivated workforce has been in making its Sunderland factory highly productive. Nissan has supported its workers on the production line with significant investment in technology.

A What is meant by "a highly motivated workforce"?

B What evidence is there that Nissan's managers have based their approaches to motivation on Herzberg's two-factor theory?

C Nissan has a productive workforce because it designs jobs to motivate its employees. Discuss the case for and against this view.

Models of motivation in practice

Setting the scene: stress in the workplace damages employee motivation

A survey by the employment specialists, Kelly Services, of 19,000 workers across Europe has revealed that many employees face high levels of stress in the workplace. The survey showed that 20 per cent of UK workers who were surveyed said their jobs were "too stressful" or "far too stressful". Male employees, older workers and those in senior positions with high levels of responsibility face the highest levels of stress, according to the survey.

Steve Girdler, Kelly Services' UK marketing director, warns that workplace stress can have a significant impact on individuals and their performance at work. "A certain amount of stress can be a good thing as it pushes people beyond their comfort zone to work harder and smarter. But high levels of prolonged stress are not good because they impact on productivity and are associated with physical and emotional illness."

Stress levels were much higher for workers aged 45 and over with greater levels of responsibility and for those who had held jobs for a considerable period of time. Girdler commented that "workers facing ... high levels of stress are not performing to their optimum, while their own situation is probably impacting on colleagues, customers or others in the organisation".

Girdler concluded that it was important for employers to design jobs that achieved the right balance between challenging and stressful work. He said that the survey revealed that people are happiest when they are given tasks that stretch them and encourage them to develop new skills and competencies, but that the work must not be too demanding.

Source: Kelly Services media release, 18 October 2005

Motivation models and individual employees

One important and common theme to emerge from the models of motivation created by Herzberg and Maslow is that employees need different factors to motivate them at different times and in different circumstances. The theories challenge managers to consider the needs of their employees in the workplace and to design jobs and create environments that allow work to be more fulfilling.

1 Motivating skilled and unskilled employees

Skilled employees are only able to carry out their jobs effectively when they have acquired the necessary skills and knowledge; this usually requires considerable training. Skilled workers – like electricians, website designers and accountants – are likely to be in demand by businesses and many will receive good salaries and have a permanent contract of employment. In terms of Maslow's model, their

KEY TERMS

Empowerment is the process of allowing subordinates to have greater control over their working lives by, for example, letting them make many of their own decisions.

Delegation is the passing down of authority to a junior employee for a particular task. This is often limited to specific tasks and activities; in contrast, empowerment is a more general philosophy of passing down authority and control.

Job enrichment is the process of designing jobs containing tasks of varying complexity that allow employees to use their abilities to a greater extent.

Job enlargement extends the range of duties associated with a particular job.

physiological and security needs have been met. The key to motivating skilled workers, therefore, might be to design jobs and the working environment to allow workers to fulfil their higher needs.

Maslow's model suggests that to motivate skilled employees businesses should consider:

- organising work in teams to allow employees to interact and to meet social needs

- offering employees the chance of promotion and also recognition for successes in their working lives

- enriching jobs by making tasks more complex and demanding and giving workers more responsibility, perhaps by giving teams responsibility for organising their working day, managing budgets or appointing new staff.

Herzberg's model would encourage a similar approach, except that he placed little emphasis on teamworking.

Employees with fewer or no skills are likely to receive much lower rates of pay than skilled workers. Low-skill workers may be on piece rates: that is, they receive a certain amount of pay for each unit of output they produce. For example, telephone sales assistants' pay may be related, in part at least, to the number of sales they achieve. Some low-skilled or unskilled workers may also not have a permanent contract of employment; some work in difficult and dangerous environments (agricultural workers, for example). Maslow's model suggests that low-skilled workers may be motivated through ensuring that their lower needs are met. Herzberg would disagree to some extent. His model simply predicts that increasing pay, improving job security and personal safety would reduce job dissatisfaction, but not improve motivation.

2 Manual workers and knowledge-based employees

Manual work involves some kind of physical labour. Manual workers include plumbers, production line workers, car mechanics and gardeners. One problem with manual work is that it can become repetitive, especially in a factory environment. This can result in boredom and demotivation.

Managers need to recognise that they could increase the motivation of manual employees by extending the range or complexity of tasks that they are required to carry out. Simply extending the range (or diversity) of tasks that employees carry out, but not making them more complex, is termed job enlargement. Redesigning employees' jobs to make them more demanding is called job enrichment. Figure 12.13 illustrates this distinction.

Some manual employees might be motivated through offering them a broader range of tasks. For example, production line workers could be required to carry out a range of tasks, rather than carrying out a single task repetitively. Ford uses this approach successfully in a

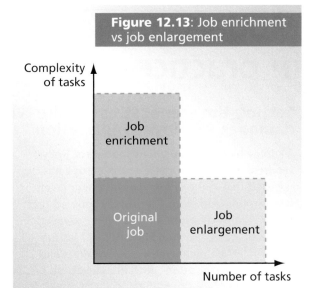

Figure 12.13: Job enrichment vs job enlargement

number of its car manufacturing plants. However, although this approach is used widely in practice, it would not necessarily motivate according to Maslow's and Herzberg's models. Their theories would require that workers are also given greater responsibility, perhaps for ordering materials or for quality checking, if their motivation is to be enhanced.

Knowledge-based employees – like solicitors, teachers, journalists and many managers – use predominantly mental rather than physical effort at work. Stimulating a knowledge-based worker will almost certainly require jobs to be designed to incorporate Herzberg's motivators or to allow Maslow's higher needs to be met through work. One approach could be job enrichment. A junior manager might be motivated by being given responsibility for a particular project such as developing new publicity materials for the business. Further motivation could be achieved by his or her line manager offering praise and according recognition if the project is successfully completed.

Job enlargement is unlikely to be a successful strategy. Offering a broader range of tasks is less likely to motivate knowledge-based workers. Teachers may not want to teach a greater variety of subjects, but they could be motivated by being given greater responsibility for teaching one particular course. Recognition, in the form say of becoming a course leader, may be an effective motivator for teachers.

3 Motivating staff of different ages

The models of motivation developed by Herzberg and Maslow do not specifically take account of an employee's age. However, younger people normally hold more junior positions within businesses, often on temporary contracts of employment, and they usually receive lower rates of pay. Maslow might suggest that designing jobs to ensure that lower needs are met as fully as possible might be the best way to motivate younger employees.

Older employees may be more senior and they are more likely to be financially secure, so Herzberg's motivators will be essential elements in improving performance of the older sections of the workforce. Older workers sometimes feel that age discrimination limits their chances for any further promotion, so ensuring that promotion is clearly based on merit and not age will be an important aspect of managing this age group successfully. Redesigning jobs to offer more responsibility, as well as greater diversity, may also help to raise the performance of someone who has been in the same job for many years and may be becoming stale.

However, it important for managers to realise that they should not stereotype workers according to age. Many young workers are likely to be enthusiastic and keen to progress. They may be motivated by the work itself, and offering them a chance to take responsibility early in their careers may be a successful strategy. If younger staff have the ability and confidence to handle responsible positions, then the company and the individual employees may benefit. Older workers may not want greater responsibility; security may be more important to them. Some older workers fear losing their jobs, and coping with new positions can be difficult later in life.

4 Paid and voluntary work

Paid employees receive wages or salaries as a reward for their efforts in the workplace. However, some people undertake voluntary work for no pay. Many staff used by the Samaritans, for example, are unpaid. Voluntary workers do a job for many reasons, but clearly pay is not a motivation as they do not receive any financial reward for their work. Some voluntary workers are motivated by the desire to help others; some take voluntary roles because the work fits in with their political beliefs; some volunteer because they have retired from paid work and want to keep active. The voluntary sector is fairly substantial, and examples of voluntary work include:

■ working in charity shops

■ working in hospitals, such as providing drinks and snacks for patients' relatives and visitors

■ environmental work, such as clearing litter from places of natural beauty.

Voluntary workers are likely to be motivated by factors such as meeting social needs. Achievement is a particularly important motivator. If voluntary workers can see that their efforts are achieving desired goals, they are likely to be fulfilled in their work. For example, a volunteer in a charity shop may gain great satisfaction at the end of the day from totalling the shop's takings and seeing that it amounts to a considerable sum. A wise manager might make sure that this is part of the volunteer's duties. Praise and other forms of recognition of achievement are also important motivators in the absence of financial rewards. Of course, these factors are important to those in paid jobs, but they must be underpinned by suitable financial rewards and job security, as both Herzberg and Maslow recognised in their models.

Leadership styles and motivation

In Topic 3, we looked at the range or spectrum of leadership styles. These vary from highly autocratic leaders who like to be in total control and offer little freedom, to laissez-faire managers who give employees a very high degree of control over their working lives. Figure 12.14 links this spectrum of leadership styles to the models of motivation and leadership developed by Abraham Maslow, Frederick Herzberg and Douglas McGregor.

1 Autocratic and paternalistic leaders

Although autocratic and paternalistic approaches are rather different leadership styles, these leaders are likely adopt some common techniques in motivating employees. Autocratic and paternalistic leaders like to be in charge and to retain control, even though paternalistic leaders may seek to hide this fact. This greatly limits the range of techniques they will use to motivate employees.

These leaders have a (McGregor's) Theory X view of their subordinates: they believe that staff do not seek responsibility and need close supervision if they are to work efficiently. The prime motivational technique used by this group of managers is money. They use financial incentives and bonus schemes to get the best out of their workforce and delegate little, if any, authority to their subordinates. Autocratic and paternalistic leaders want to take decisions themselves, and this rules out any attempt to motivate junior employees through allowing them substantial amounts of decision-making power.

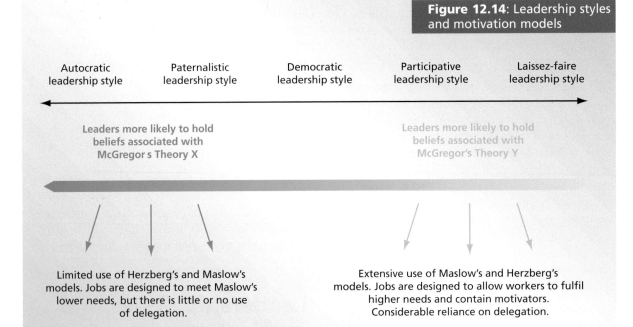

Figure 12.14: Leadership styles and motivation models

| Autocratic leadership style | Paternalistic leadership style | Democratic leadership style | Participative leadership style | Laissez-faire leadership style |

Leaders more likely to hold beliefs associated with McGregor's Theory X

Leaders more likely to hold beliefs associated with McGregor's Theory Y

Limited use of Herzberg's and Maslow's models. Jobs are designed to meet Maslow's lower needs, but there is little or no use of delegation.

Extensive use of Maslow's and Herzberg's models. Jobs are designed to allow workers to fulfil higher needs and contain motivators. Considerable reliance on delegation.

Lincoln Electric is a US company that relies heavily on piece-rate pay to reward and motivate its employees. The company manufactures welding equipment, and all employees in the company, apart from the five most senior directors, have a substantial part of their pay linked to performance. This suggests that the company's managers have a Theory X view of their employees.

2 Democratic, participative and laissez-faire leaders

Arguably this group encompasses an even wider range of leadership styles. However, as with autocratic and paternalistic leaders, it is possible to draw out some common aspects of motivation that this group of managers believe in and use.

This group of leaders believe that subordinates are keen to take responsibility and have the capacity to enjoy work for its own sake. Employees do not need close supervision to work efficiently, and they are not solely motivated by financial rewards. If managers and leaders hold this Theory Y view of subordinates, they are likely to make substantial use of Herzberg's and Maslow's models. In particular, these leaders believe in the use of delegation, sometimes using this approach as a fundamental tool of management. This entails giving subordinates considerable control over their working lives. This approach is called empowerment, and we look at this further at the end of this topic.

Delegation involves giving subordinates responsibility for carrying out specific tasks, providing staff with

opportunities to set and achieve particular goals, and ensuring that all employees receive recognition for their achievements. By designing subordinates' jobs to incorporate as many of these features as possible, this means, in practice, that managers are using Herzberg's motivators and Maslow's higher needs as motivational factors.

Motivation and organisational structures

The organisational structure operated by the management team has significant implications for the range of techniques that are likely to be used to motivate employees. The organisation's structure will also reflect the dominant leadership style used within the business. As a rule of thumb, leaders at the democratic end of the leadership spectrum are more likely to use flatter or matrix structures.

1 Flat and matrix organisational structures

A flat organisational structure has relatively few layers of hierarchy, but will operate with wide spans of control. This has been a popular option for businesses over recent years and has frequently been achieved through a process called delayering. Delayering is removing one or more levels of hierarchy from the structure of the organisation. In many cases, this is achieved by removing layers of middle management.

The shops might look like shoe repairers, key cutters and engravers, but they are also information and help centres – Yellow Pages are kept in every branch, they never say "no" to pleas for change for meters, and customers can use their toilets and even their phones.

Timpson has its headquarters in Manchester and operates 568 branches or shops. Because its 1,684 staff are spread across so many branches, internal communications are important. "You say" provides a chance for employees to do the talking in their meetings with managers. There are also lunches, update videos, newsletters and roadshows. The message is getting through – almost 70 per cent say their manager shares important knowledge and information with them.

Average pay for a branch colleague is £14,948, while only 10 people earn more than £45,000. A substantial proportion would like more pay – just 60 per cent believe their pay fairly reflects their responsibilities.

However, large numbers of staff like it so much they stay and stay – 778 Timpson employees have been with the firm for five or more years, 362 of them for 10 years or more.

The founder and owner of the business, John Timpson, offered this advice in an article he wrote for the BBC News website. "Top managers have to free up the organisation by giving everyone the authority to speak their mind. You need to give people the authority to innovate and you must not have any rules that stand in the way of progress."

KEY DATA

Annual sales	£96.1 million
Staff numbers	1,684
Staff turnover	28%
Earning £35,000+	2%
Typical job	branch colleague
Long service	40% of employees with more than five years' service
Pensions	non-contributory or firms pay double staff contribution
Gym	on-site or subsidised for off-site

What type of leadership style do you think that John Timpson uses? Explain your view. What techniques might his shop managers use to motivate their branch colleagues?

Sources: The Sunday Times 100 Best Companies to Work For (business.timesonline.co.uk) and BBC News (news.bbc.co.uk)

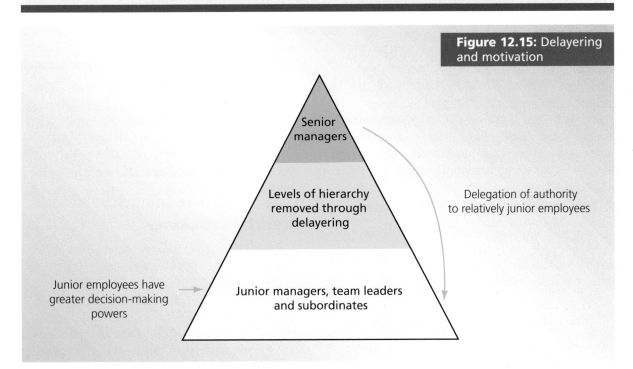

Figure 12.15: Delayering and motivation

Senior managers

Levels of hierarchy removed through delayering

Delegation of authority to relatively junior employees

Junior employees have greater decision-making powers

Junior managers, team leaders and subordinates

Figure 12.15 illustrates how the process of delayering commits senior managers to granting greater freedom to relatively junior employees. In most organisations it would be impossible for a small group of senior managers to have complete control over all decision-making. Many powers that previously lay with middle managers have to be transferred further down the structure. So, with a flat organisational structure, junior managers and team leaders may be given responsibility for managing budgets, appointing staff members and organising production.

This type of structure is likely to encourage the use of motivational techniques associated with Maslow's higher needs and Herzberg's motivators. Junior employees will take on additional responsibilities, have the opportunity to develop managerial skills, and should get recognition for achieving goals and targets.

Many businesses have opted for delayering in an attempt to improve competitiveness by cutting wage costs, but as a consequence they have had to use different techniques to motivate subordinates. It has forced a move towards techniques associated with Maslow's and Herzberg's models of motivation.

The effects of operating a matrix structure are similar, but possibly more calculated. A matrix structure is based on independent teams which are formed for specific tasks and projects before being dismantled once the specific task is completed. They are very task-oriented, and the rewards for attaining the team's goals are recognition, achievement and possibly future promotion. Most employees in a matrix structure have jobs which are complex, challenging and likely to be fulfilling.

As an example, consider the research and development department within a pharmaceutical company that operates a matrix structure. Teams would be assembled to conduct given projects, such as developing a new drug to treat a specific condition. There would be a high degree of empowerment for the teams and significant rewards for successfully developing new products. The motivational techniques and the organisational structures go hand-in-hand.

2 Tall organisational structures

Tall organisational structures are the opposite of flat ones: they have many layers of hierarchy but narrow spans of control. In this type of structure, managers retain high levels of control over subordinates, and the narrow spans of control permit close supervision. In these circumstances relatively few techniques of motivation may be used. Financial rewards are most commonly utilised, possibly in the form of bonuses.

stop and think

Which leadership style or styles are most likely to be associated with a tall organisational structure? Why might you, as a middle manager in such an organisation, be unwilling to delegate significant amounts of authority to junior employees?

Tall organisations can place great emphasis on status and job titles, and career advancement and promotion may be used as techniques to motivate subordinates. However, it is difficult to fully implement the motivational techniques set out in the Maslow's and Herzberg's models within a tall organisational structure. The structures make it difficult to delegate to any great extent, and delegation is at the heart of the two theories.

Motivation and empowerment

Empowerment can be viewed as an extreme form of motivation. A business that has an empowered workforce is engaging in more than just delegation. Delegation is giving authority to juniors for a specific task; empowerment is granting junior employees a high degree of control over their working lives on a permanent basis. Empowerment gives employees the opportunity to decide how to carry out their duties and how to organise their working day. They have the opportunity to decide what to do and how to do it. It is a philosophy that relates to an entire organisation.

Empowerment is based on the models drawn up by Maslow and Herzberg. It is based on the beliefs that employees want to work, that they seek responsibility and enjoy the opportunity to achieve and receive recognition. Empowerment is most likely to be implemented by managers who take a theory Y view of leadership.

Potential problems

As with any management technique, empowerment has advantages and disadvantages. It works better in some circumstances than in others. If a workforce is used to delegation and possesses some of the necessary skills to work with some independence, a move to empowerment might not be too great a shock. For employees used to autocratic management and being tightly supervised and directed, the change might be considerable. In this case, some time and resources will need to be put into training employees and managers alike if the policy is to succeed.

Some managers are reluctant to genuinely empower their subordinates as this involves a loss of control on their part. Some managers may not be prepared to give up power to junior employees. This is especially true of managers used to exercising coercive power. If workforce empowerment is to be successful, all managers must participate fully.

In most businesses the real benefits of empowerment can only be seen in the long term. In the short term, the disruption, uncertainty and the adverse effects of any redundancy and retirement (as a result of delayering, for example) may detract from organisational performance. Empowerment represents an investment that does not generate a quick return.

A manager considering implementing a policy of empowerment may benefit from thinking about the issues on this check list.

Check list for empowerment

- Are senior managers committed to this approach and prepared to empower those below them? Are they good role models?

- Does the organisational structure fit in with this policy? A matrix or flat structure is most likely to complement empowerment.

- Have staff the desire to take greater control of their working lives? This desire may be based on confidence.

- Does the prevailing culture encourage empowerment? Even if senior managers are committed to the approach, empowerment may not work if other managers are seeking to retain power and control.

- Are all elements of the business to be empowered? Does the nature of the work carried out by some departments mean that some employees should have less control?

assessment practice
Troubled times at Microsoft?

Microsoft has 60,000 employees and is one of the most successful technology companies in the world. The company receives over 40,000 applications from job hunters every month. Few applicants turn the company down if they get the chance; over 90 per cent accept a job with the company if it is offered.

Microsoft is well known for providing generous benefits. In return, staff tend to be loyal and willing to work long hours. However, the company has removed some of the perks it previously offered. Some staff have criticised these cuts, arguing that they are unnecessary and would only result in minor savings for the enormously rich company. Perks that have been cut include:

- options to buy the company's shares at predetermined prices

- free health scheme – employees are now asked to make contributions towards the scheme

- generous leave entitlements for new parents – these have been reduced from previous levels.

Traditionally Microsoft employees have been free to be creative and to do "great work". The workforce was liberated and creative. However, as Microsoft has grown, there is evidence that some employees are becoming frustrated by the company's bureaucracy. Today, the various groups which make up the business (computer games, search engines, operating systems, etc.) need to liaise regularly. As a result, employees spend more time in meetings ensuring that product developments are compatible. They need to prepare regular reviews for senior managers, again leaving less time for the more interesting work of creating new technologies and products.

A How might Herzberg have explained why some staff are unhappy at the loss of some perks?

B Explain why empowerment was an effective strategy with Microsoft's skilled workforce.

C Discuss whether employee motivation at Microsoft might improve if the company is split into, say, four separate companies.

Setting the scene: British American Tobacco's decision

One of the world's largest tobacco producers, British American Tobacco (BAT), announced in July 2005 that 530 jobs were being axed at its Millbrook factory in Southampton after 80 years of production. BAT claimed that a number of reviews had found that the factory was not viable.

About 24 billion cigarettes a year are manufactured at the factory, most of which are exported. Manufacturing is being transferred to factories in Poland, Romania and Switzerland, and elsewhere in Europe.

Mike Budd, regional officer for the trade union Amicus, said he was far from happy with BAT's decision-making process. "At the end of the day, the company has gone away, made its decision to close and presented its proposals to the board without including us in that process – and we're extremely unhappy."

Many employees feel that the decision-making process was flawed and that they should have been involved. "A lot of our members are still very sore and shocked and taking it all in," Mike Budd said. He added there would be many meetings with BAT over the next 90 days to try to come to an agreement over the job losses.

Allan Short, head of UK and Ireland operations for BAT, told BBC News: "Obviously it's been a dreadful week for all of us here in Southampton, a lot of shock. We have a good relationship with Amicus and we expect the meetings to be constructive and businesslike."

Mr Short said it would take between 18 and 24 months for manufacturing to cease at the factory and that for now it was "business as usual".

Source: adapted from BBC News website, 15 July 2005,

Types of decisions

When managers make decisions, they have to make a choice between two or more options. Decisions can be particularly difficult for managers to make when:

- they do not have enough information on which to base a decision

- they lack experience in the area in which the decision has to be made

- a decision is needed quickly.

Nearly every decision made by managers affects the employees of the business. For example decisions to produce new products or scrap old products, introduce new technology, or implement new working practices all impact on an organisation's employees. Jobs may be lost or transferred to different locations, new skills may be needed, or established working groups may be split up.

Before looking at some of the techniques and models that managers can use in decision-making, we first consider the different types of decisions that have to be made. It is possible to classify decisions into several distinct types.

1 Routine and non-routine

Routine decisions are ones that are taken regularly. They are also decisions that are not unexpected, so managers expect and are prepared to make them as part of their regular duties. For example, routine decisions that would be taken by a branch manager of the retailers WH Smith might include:

- agreeing staff rotas for the coming weeks

- appointing new part-time staff to work in the shop at weekends

- ordering stock for the shop

- making minor changes to the layout of the shop to help boost sales

- reducing the prices of some goods by making special offers if they are not selling well.

Routine decisions are normally low-level decisions that can be taken by relatively junior staff. These decisions can often be delegated to more junior employees. So, the assistant manager of the WH Smith branch, or a head of section, might be given the task of drawing up the staff rota for the next month, especially if this normally does not provoke controversy.

However, some routine decisions can be major ones, and they will need to be taken by senior managers in the organisation. Many financial decisions have to be taken on a regular basis: for example, most businesses prepare financial plans, or budgets, on a regular (often quarterly) basis. Although a number of junior and middle managers may be involved in drawing up these plans, the budgets are unlikely to be implemented without senior manager approval.

In some industries products typically have short life cycles, so decisions have to be taken regularly about when to launch new products. This is the case in the technology industry, where new versions of products such as MP3 players are launched routinely. Senior managers will normally take these decisions, because they can be crucial to a business's future prospects.

stop and **think**

Give examples of the routine decisions that the manager of a Premiership football club might have to take. Are these all easy decisions, just because they are routine?

Non-routine decisions, by definition, occur irregularly, and may be needed because of some unexpected event. These can be taken by managers at all levels within an organisation. Here are four examples of different types of non-routine decisions.

■ Deciding how to respond to an emergency, such as a fire or a break-in at the business's premises.

■ Making location decisions. For example, many financial services companies like Norwich Union have decided to move some of their call centres from the UK to countries such as India where staff costs are lower.

■ Deciding to cease production of a well-established product which has generated sales for many years. Television companies have to take decisions to stop making popular programmes such as Friends or Frasier at some point.

■ Taking a decision to enter a new market. In 2004 Tesco took the decision to open supermarkets in eastern China. This followed many years of planning, and was not routine in any sense as it entailed an investment of £140 million.

It is the nature of the non-routine decision that determines at what level it is made in the organisation. If a decision will affect the whole

enterprise, then it is more likely to be made by senior managers. For example, the non-routine decision to relocate part of all of the business will be taken at senior level. However, deciding how to respond to a break-in at one of the company's offices may be dealt with by more junior employees.

2 Tactical and strategic decisions

Tactical decisions are based on short-term factors. For example, a business might decide to reduce the price of a product if its sales are below the budgeted or expected figure. This price cut would only be for a short period of time. Similarly a decision to increase overtime pay rates might be made if the business faces a large and unexpected order from a major customer. This enhanced rate of pay might only be offered for a few weeks until the order is complete.

Tactical decisions are normally taken by middle managers, although they may be taken by senior managers if there are significant cost implications or impacts on a large section of the business. So a decision by a retailer to reduce prices on all products in the run-up to Christmas would be taken by senior managers because of the considerable financial implications, even though the decision only involves a short-term pricing policy.

Strategic decisions are those that have long-term implications, often for the entire business. Here are four examples of some strategic decisions taken by well-known UK-based businesses in recent years.

■ In 2002 Dyson, the manufacturer best known for its vacuum cleaners, decided to move its manufacturing facilities from the UK to Malaysia.

■ Monsanto, the US biotechnology company, decided in 2004 to close its European cereal business (based in Cambridge) which had been working on genetically-modified crops.

■ In 2005 Britain's biggest cable company NTL bought rival operator Telewest for £3,400 million. The deal created the UK's largest cable television company.

■ British Airports Authority (BAA) announced in 2005 that it was cutting 700 jobs as part of a move to reduce costs. This is expected to save the company about £45 million a year.

Strategic decisions are made by senior managers because they have far-ranging implications for the businesses concerned. Decisions are normally only taken following prolonged discussion, and after gathering and analysing relevant data.

3 Proactive and reactive decisions

A proactive decision is one taken in advance of events. Managers at all levels in the organisation can take proactive decisions. Junior managers might decide to hold extra stocks of popular products in case of a sudden rise in demand. Senior managers may decide to keep some of last year's profits in a contingency fund to deal with the consequences of a natural disaster such as a severe storm.

Most chief executives (81 per cent according to a 2005 survey) think their businesses are vulnerable to crisis factors such as terrorism, epidemics, accounting scandals and natural disasters. One type of proactive decision is putting in place contingency plans to deal with and mitigate these threats before they occur. However, the survey revealed that only 50 per cent of businesses questioned had any sort of contingency plan in place.

Proactive decisions are taken by enterprising and innovative firms that want to be market leaders and to shape market developments. Apple has manufactured a special version of its popular iPod which will show television programmes and music videos as well as having the usual functions to play music. In the UK the company announced that owners of the video iPod will be able to download BBC television programmes. This is a risky decision by Apple. Time will tell whether this product will be popular with consumers and whether being proactive will pay dividends in this case.

Reactive decisions are taken when businesses respond to events rather than trying to shape them. Apple's rivals will have to decide how to respond to the launch of the video iPod. Manufacturers such as Sony may decide to bring out a rival product or they may choose to keep out of the market as miniature televisions produced in the 1980s did not sell well. In this situation reactive decisions can be less risky, but also less profitable. Apple has taken the risky proactive decision here and, if it is successful, may reap high profits by being first in the market with a new type of product.

Reactive decisions are taken at all levels in the organisation and by all types of businesses. The manager of a café may decide to match a price cut introduced by other cafés in the locality. Senior managers at the Ford motor company may respond to an announcement of a major marketing campaign by Volkswagen by offering interest-free deals on its cars.

Decision-making models

There are a number of decision-making models and techniques that managers can use. In this section we review and assess the value of three of the most common techniques: critical path analysis, statistical process control and decision trees.

1 Critical path analysis

The intention here is to explain the use of critical path analysis and make some assessment of its value. In Unit 16, Managing Resources, we look at the technique in more detail, including how to draw a critical path network.

Critical path analysis (CPA) is one type of network analysis. It is a method of calculating and illustrating how complex projects can be completed as quickly as possible. CPA shows:

■ the sequence in which the tasks must be undertaken

■ the length of time taken by each task

■ the earliest time at which each stage can commence.

A CPA network has two elements, activities and nodes. Activities are the separate parts of a project, that require time and (probably) resources. In a CPA diagram, activities are represented by arrows. They are

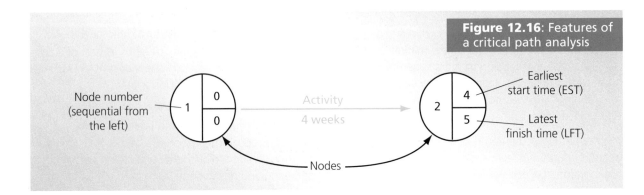

Figure 12.16: Features of a critical path analysis

Node number (sequential from the left)

1 | 0 | 0

Activity
4 weeks

2 | 4 | 5

Earliest start time (EST)

Latest finish time (LFT)

Nodes

frequently given letters, so that each activity can be easily identified. The duration of each activity is written below the arrow. The arrows (running from left to right) show the sequence of the activities necessary to complete the project. Note that in a typical project some, though not necessarily all, activities cannot be started until others are concluded.

Nodes are the start or end of each activity, and they are drawn as circles in a CPA diagram. Each node is numbered in the left-hand segment; the top right-hand segment gives the earliest start time (EST); the lower right-hand segment gives the latest finish time (LFT). The EST is the first time at which an activity can be started, and the LFT states the time by which the activity must be finished if the entire project is to be completed on schedule and not to be delayed.

Using CPA to take decisions

It is easiest to illustrate the use of CPA through an example. Suppose a retailer is planning to open a new flagship store in central London as part of a major promotional campaign. The company has bought a warehouse and plans to redevelop the space to create a light, airy and large new shop. The new store needs to be ready to open in 40 weeks if it is to be part of the campaign.

The directors of the company need to decide whether the opening of the new store should feature as a central element of the promotional campaign. This hinges on whether the store will be completed and ready in 40 weeks. A building firm has been hired to redevelop the warehouse, and Figure 12.17 lists the major activities that have to be undertaken with the firm's estimate of the time it will take to complete each activity.

The activities in Figure 12.17 cannot be undertaken in any order. You can only install the new shop fittings (activity H), for example, after the design (A) and the major construction work (activity F) have been

Figure 12.17: Activities in the warehouse redevelopment

Activity	Expected duration (weeks)
A Design the interior of the new store	6
B Obtain planning permission	4
C Renovate exterior of building and landscape grounds	17
D Carry out internal demolition	3
E Order construction materials	2
F Carry out construction work	18
G Decorate interior	2
H Install shop fittings	4
I Train staff in new techniques	4

undertaken. Here is a complete list of the activities that are order-critical.

- Activity A is the start of the project, it must be undertaken first

- B starts when A is complete

- C, D and E follow B

- F follows D and E

- G and H follow F

- I follows G & H

Figure 12.18 shows the CPA network for the development of the new store. The critical path shows the sequence of activities that must be completed on time if the whole project is not to be delayed. This critical path is indicated by two small dashes across the relevant activities. In Figure 12.18 the critical path is A–B–D–F–H–I.

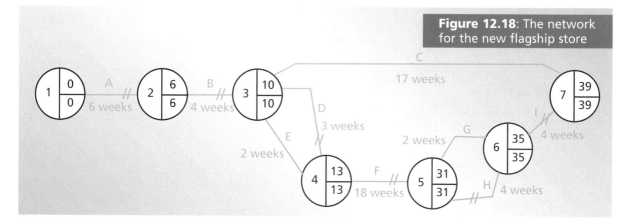

Figure 12.18: The network for the new flagship store

This analysis helps managers in deciding whether a project can be completed within a certain time period. In this case, the directors can see that the project should be finished within 39 weeks, just within the required timescale, though there is very little margin to catch up if any activity on the critical path gets delayed.

Advantages and disadvantages of critical path analysis

There are several reasons why managers might use CPA as a central part of the decision-making process. The technique helps managers use time efficiently by showing which tasks can be carried out simultaneously, helping to minimise costs and reduce the time a project takes to complete. By planning the start times of individual tasks, the resources needed for each activity can be made available at the appropriate time, thus reducing storage and other upfront costs.

The major benefit of CPA is that it helps managers to make informed decisions about project timings, as in the example above. So, CPA can help a manager decide whether a particular process or event can be completed by a certain date. If delays and problems do occur, the CPA network assists managers in deciding on the best solution to rectify the problem.

But as with many techniques in business, there are disadvantages and challenges in using CPA. Complex activities, such as building the new Olympic stadium in London, may be difficult or even impossible to represent on a network. External factors may change, such as the lack of availability of crucial resources, meaning that the information on the CPA network is

not accurate. More fundamentally, the accuracy of the whole CPA network depends on the time durations allocated to the various activities. If these are inaccurate, the whole network will give an incorrect answer.

In general, the benefits often outweigh the drawbacks, and CPA is particularly suited to assisting managers to plan the quickest way to complete a project or to assess whether a particular event or project will be completed within a given time period.

2 Statistical process control

Statistical process control (also known as control charts) uses monitoring systems based on statistics to make sure that production is efficient and meets quality standards.

Two examples are given below to show how statistical process control (SPC) can be used in different circumstances.

The airline

Many airlines monitor passenger satisfaction. It is not unusual for airlines to select a random sample of customers who have flown in the last month and ask them to complete a brief questionnaire about the quality of the service that they have received.

Suppose the final question in the customer questionnaire is: "Would you fly with this airline again?" The responses to this question could be used as a basis for SPC. The airline management may expect that some (though hopefully not too many) customers are likely to respond "no" to this question, perhaps because they have experienced delays or

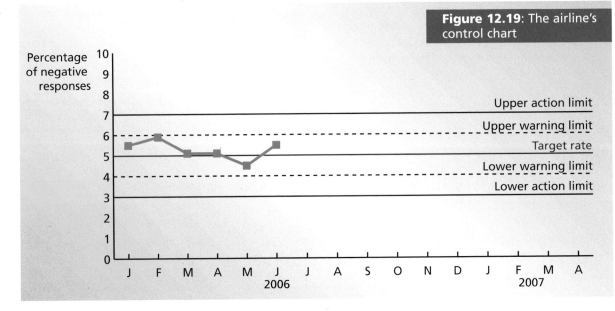

Figure 12.19: The airline's control chart

because their baggage was lost. If a negative rate of 5 per cent is a target for this question, SPC can be used to monitor whether this rate is achieved regularly.

The results each month can be presented on a control chart, such as Figure 12.19, which show the questionnaire responses in relation to the target figure. Upper and lower limits are often added to the chart, providing warning limits (when managers become aware that a problem is arising) and action limits (when a decision is needed).

Figure 12.19 shows data for the first five months of 2005. It can be seen that the level of negative responses is within the acceptable boundaries, and managers could use this information to decide that the current level of customer service provided by its staff is satisfactory and no corrective action is necessary. If the levels of negative responses rise above the upper action level of 7 per cent, a decision would have to be made about what action to take. This might, for example, involve increasing staffing levels on flights or giving staff additional customer service training.

The fundamental weakness of this method is that the survey might not be representative. If all passengers are questioned, a higher (or lower) percentage might say that they will not fly with the airline again. Although it is possible to use statistical techniques to judge how representative a sample is likely to be, this remains a weakness.

A food canning factory

Using samples as a basis for SPC is a potential weakness. However, technology can help address this problem. The managers in a food canning factory can use lasers and bar-coding systems to check every product. The lasers can read the bar code on every can as it comes down the production line. In this way, managers can monitor the rate of production. If this rate falls below an agreed figure (say 50 cans per minute) an alarm bell can ring, alerting managers to a potential problem and inviting them to take the necessary decisions to correct it.

Different technology can be used to monitor the quality of the product. For example, scanners could check the shape of the cans to confirm they are not damaged in any way. Once again an alarm could sound if the number of damaged cans moves outside agreed tolerances.

It is this combination of technology and statistics that is characteristic of statistical quality control. It is a powerful tool that can be used to alert managers to possible quality problems before they become too serious. This allows remedial decisions to be taken at an early stage, ideally before products reach customers. However, implementing SPC can be expensive, and some employees may resent what they perceive as an electronic spy checking up on their work.

3 Decision trees

Decision trees are a more general technique that can help managers take decisions. Decision trees can help to reduce the amount of uncertainty in any decision, giving managers much more confidence in the choices they make.

Decision trees use a combination of financial data and probability theory to give expected values to each of the choices that a manager faces when taking a decision. These expected values can then help the manager in taking the decision. The expected value of an outcome is calculated by multiplying the probability of an outcome by the benefit the business can expect if it happens.

As an example, suppose a retailer is considering whether to open a new shop. If the shop succeeds, the retailer forecasts that the new shop will make £1.0 million profits annually. The retailer estimates that the new shop has a 0.6 (60 per cent) probability of success. So, the expected value from the new shop is:

£1.0 million x 0.6 = £600,000

A manager needs to take a series of steps to construct a decision tree.

1   Identify the options available to the business.

2   Assess the likely outcomes of each option.

3   Calculate probabilities for every option that the business faces.

4   Forecast the expected financial returns from each course of action.

5   Calculate the expected value of each course of action.

6   Choose the course of action generating the highest expected value (although a manager may use other data to help take the decision).

An example: Tom's decision

Tom Dix owns and manages a small farm in Norfolk. The farm produces a variety of fruit and vegetables which Tom sells to a range of customers, including a small supermarket chain. He is, however, dissatisfied with his profit levels and is considering ways to improve his profits.

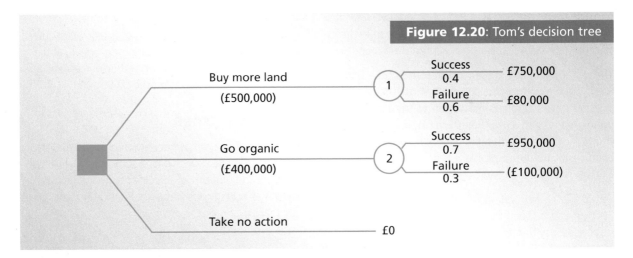

Figure 12.20: Tom's decision tree

Tom has reduced the decision to three choices:

- buy more land and expand production – this might enable him to supply a larger supermarket chain

- go organic – this would enable him to charge higher prices

- do nothing – if this appears to be the best option.

Tom has drawn the decision tree to help him make this particular decision. He has forecast costs and revenues over a five-year period, enabling him to calculate the additional profits each option might make. Figure 12.20 shows Tom's decision tree:

- a decision point is indicated by a square

- costs associated with decisions are shown next to the decision in brackets

- circles represent alternative outcomes

- probabilities of each outcome are shown by decimal figures on the appropriate line

- forecast additional profits are listed on the right-hand side of the decision tree.

To calculate the outcome of any option, Tom has to add the total expected value of the course of action (the expected value of the course of action being a success plus the expected value of the course of action failing) and subtract the cost of the course of action.

The outcomes for the three options available to Tom and illustrated in Figure 12.20 are as follows.

- Buy more land
  (0.4 x £750,000) + (0.6 x £80,000) – £500,000
  = (£152,000)

- Go organic
  (0.7 x £950,000) + (0.3 x £100,000) – £400,000
  = £235,000

- Do nothing = £0

Buying more land has a 40 per cent chance of success and Tom calculates it would generate additional profits of £750,000 over a five year period. However, if this approach was unsuccessful (maybe Tom might fail to get a big contract from a large supermarket), he forecasts that it would only generate £80,000 in additional profit of £80,000 over the five years – he has termed this a failure. Success or failure, the option will cost an estimated £500,000 for the extra land and equipment. The value of this option is therefore:

(0.4 x £750,000) + (0.6 x £80,000) – £500,000
= (£152,000)

The expected outcome is a negative figure. This means the cost of this option exceeds the expected returns. This makes it very unattractive. Clearly Tom would make more profit by doing nothing, and he is best advised to keep his farm as it is.

The second choice is to go organic and produce chemical and additive-free fruit and vegetables. This is less costly (£400,000) and should produce high profits if the venture is successful. However, if it is unsuccessful (say Tom cannot find enough customers), then it will reduce the profits of the business by £100,000 over the five-year period. The value of this option is £235,000, given by:

(0.7 x £950,000) + (0.3 x –£100,000) – £400,000
= £235,000

The third option, doing nothing, obviously leaves his forecast profits for the next five years unchanged. So, using the decision tree alone, Tom should choose to go organic as this gives the highest expected value. Indeed, it is the only option that would fulfil the original objective to increase profits. However, Tom should take other factors into account before he makes a final decision, such as the likely future demand for organic fruit and vegetables and the degree of competition he would face in this market.

Suppose the cost of buying new land is lower than Tom originally expected, and this option would only cost £300,000 rather than £500,000 to implement. Recalculate the expected return of the "buy more land" option and say what decision Tom should take now.

Advantages and disadvantages of decision trees

As with the other decision-making techniques we have considered, decision trees have advantages and disadvantages. On the plus side, the use of decision trees encourages managers such as Tom to be logical and to consider all the possibilities, and it discourages managers from relying too heavily on hunches or instinct. If a manager has access to accurate data, then decision trees can be particularly valuable.

Decision trees are probably most useful when making routine decisions for which financial data and probabilities are likely to be known. It is very difficult to get accurate data – especially relating to probabilities – when taking a major decision which may involve a step into the dark. For example, Tesco would have faced problems constructing an accurate decision tree to help it to decide whether or not to expand into China. Decisions of this type involve too many unknowns.

Decision trees can also be problematic if the business environment is too changeable. This makes it very difficult to assess the various outcomes (and the associated probabilities and financial returns) with any degree of confidence.

assessment practice
Nestlé launches fair-trade coffee

Nestlé has recognised the growing importance of the fair-trade market and has followed a number of other businesses in launching its own fair-trade coffee. Nestlé confirmed that it would be buying its fair-trade coffee from poor farmers in El Salvador and Ethiopia.

Fair-trade products are designed to support producers in less developed countries. Manufacturers such as Nestlé pay higher and guaranteed prices to suppliers (in this case coffee farmers), helping to improve their businesses and enhance their standard of living.

The fair-trade market is now 3 per cent of total coffee sales, and growing. Fair-trade products appeal to ethical consumers who don't want to buy products that exploit producers in poorer economies.

The launch of Nestlé's fair-trade coffee has been endorsed by the Fairtrade Foundation following an approach by the company's senior managers. Many large businesses have been considering launching fair-trade brands, and there is an increasing trend for big business to endorse more ethical products and practices.

Nestlé new *Partners' Blend* (due to be launched in 2006) will only form a small part of the company's production and sales of coffee. Observers think that the multinational wants to present a more "friendly" image, and that this is a major reason behind the decision.

A Classify Nestlé's decision. Was it routine or non-routine, strategic or tactical, proactive or reactive? Explain your choices.

B Explain how Nestlé might use statistical process control to help monitor the quality of the fair-trade coffee that it sells.

C Nestlé could have used decision trees or critical path analysis (CPA) to help with this decision. Which technique would have been more suitable in these circumstances? Explain your decision.

IN THIS UNIT WE INVESTIGATE HOW A BUSINESS COLLECTS, collates and stores the vast amount of information that comes in from all functional areas of the business as well as from stakeholders and the external environment. We examine how a business uses this information to support decision-making throughout the organisation.

The assessment for this unit requires you to propose an information system to co-ordinate and support a complex business activity. Your proposal should explain the information and data requirements of the activity. You need to set out how this information should be collected and collated, you need to develop an outline of the information system, and you need to evaluate its suitability.

At the end of each topic there is an assessment practice. The guidance given here will help you build up the details of the information system for the business activity. Your teacher will provide further guidance on the type of business activity or organisation you should choose.

Managing information

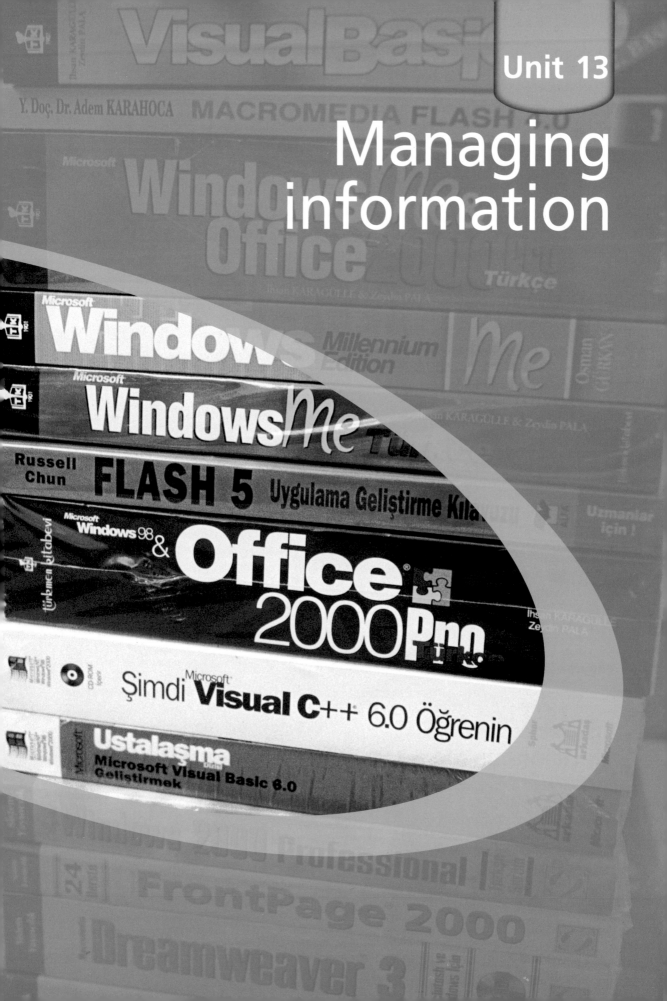

Information and data requirements in business

Setting the scene: Microsoft Xbox 360s

In the run-up to Christmas 2005, high street retailers such as HMV and Dixons ran out of supplies of Microsoft Xbox 360s. Microsoft did not build up a sufficient stock before launching the new model of the Xbox worldwide in an attempt to compete with Sony's new PSP. The severe shortage meant that many consumers were unable to purchase the product until after Christmas, resulting in loss of sales for retailers and for Microsoft.

Consider this situation from an information perspective. Microsoft is launching worldwide using a massive advertising and promotion campaign in an attempt to beat its rivals. It needs to manufacture, stock and supply the Xbox to retail outlets. Production plays a key part in this process, as well as Microsoft's finance function, which needs to provide the funding for the manufacturing effort and the promotion campaign.

You, the customer, go to your local store expecting to find the new Xbox. But you don't! So there's now a disgruntled customer that might purchase a rival product, possibly a disgruntled retailer (if you decide against any substitute purchase), and a major company, Microsoft, that is very unhappy about the potential lost sale.

Microsoft is also likely to be unhappy about the damage to its reputation both in the eyes of the customer and the retailer, and it will not welcome

the unfavourable publicity that the botched Xbox launch gained in the media. Moral of the story? Management needs to match marketing effort to supply throughout the entire logistics and production chain.

How could information have helped management in this scenario? Well, communication between functions could make sure that supply meets demand. This needs co-ordination between sales forecasting, planning of promotion campaigns, production timelines, supply of raw materials, staffing, and a host of other issues. This case shows that even in an organisation the size and sophistication of Microsoft, information problems can arise – perhaps wrong information was given by production or marketing to management – and a poor management decision was made to proceed with the launch.

Information and decision-making

Managers require high-quality information at the right time if there is to be effective decision-making throughout the organisation. Information is required to support management decisions in all functional areas: marketing and sales, personnel, administration, finance, and production and operations. Any organisation – regardless of its structure and particular business – requires information from all these functional areas and from its external environment. Let's look more closely at what information each function might need to inform decisions.

Sales and marketing

Marketing needs to know the target customers and what they want to buy. This information comes from market research, and from the previous buying behaviour of existing customers. This helps a business determine what to advertise, and where and to whom it should pitch its advertising campaigns.

But in shaping a marketing strategy, a sales and marketing department has to answer many other questions. It needs to know how much the advertising will cost? How to measure the effectiveness of a promotion campaign? How much does the sales force cost? How effective is the sales force? What are competitors doing? What they are charging for what products? Are they changing their prices – and if so, should we respond? Is there a price war with other rivals? What is happening in the external environment to affect demand? What are the views and requirements of the business's stakeholders? Are there new government or EU regulations that will impact on the business? The answers to these and similar questions provide more information.

The marketing function should receive and collate information about market and industry trends, the business's competitors including their products and main activities, and the planning and analysis of promotion campaigns. The sales function receives and processes customer orders, produces invoices, keeps customer details, and maintains records of selling activity.

stop and think

In April 2006, Sony announced that it was lowering the price of its PlayStation console in the United States (but not the UK). How do you think Microsoft will respond in its pricing of the Xbox?

Finance

A finance department needs information on all incomings and outgoings of the business. How many items are sold, and when? When does the money come in? How many staff are needed for manufacturing and sales? What are their costs? What are the costs of raw materials and other production resources? What are the credit terms offered by suppliers? What are the credit terms and discounts given to customers? What is the cash flow forecast for the next quarter? What are the costs for overheads, premises, IT, insurance? The list is seemingly endless.

Finance produces sales, purchase and nominal ledgers, operates the credit control system, manages the

The bakery market in the UK has three main competitors: Hovis the market leader, Lancashire-based Warburtons that is gaining market share in the south, and Kingsmill, the bakery division of Associated British Foods.

Kingsmill's sales have fallen due to poor management and a disastrous advertising campaign based around Elvis Presley and devised by J Walter Thompson. Although Kingsmill has moved its advertising to M&C Saatchi, and is monitoring costs closely, it has been forced to close one factory and others may be affected.

However, Kingsmill's problems provide an opportunity for its rivals to capitalise on the situation and increase their market share.

payroll, and maintains records on payments in and out, budgets, projections and accounts. It also will have access to historical financial records. It holds VAT and tax records.

Personnel and administration

Personnel needs to know the staffing requirements of the business. How many staff does the organisation need? In which functional departments are they required – or, for larger organisations, in which branches? These requirements should be expressed is terms of required skills, experience and training. What does it costs to recruit new staff at what level? What are the most effective ways of recruiting and training staff? What are the costs of advertising in the local and national newspapers? Or should the business go through a recruitment agency? What is happening in the external environment that will affect demand and supply of staff? Administration needs to know the costs of insurance, the cost of the premises and related running costs.

Personnel and administration functions hold records on all employees, pension and health scheme details, employment contracts, etc. They will also hold the business's records of board meetings and annual general meetings. Personnel records held for each employee include name, home address, telephone number, national insurance number, education and qualifications, employment history, plus details of an employee's training, promotions and job descriptions since joining the business.

stop and think

A car manufacturer would know that there will be many highly trained engineering staff looking for work after Peugeot announced plans to close its car manufacturing plant in Ryton by 2007 with the loss of 2,300 jobs. Should it see this as an opportunity to "refresh" its workforce?

Production and operations

Production needs to know the detailed specifications for the business's products. It needs to know when products are required. It needs to schedule manufacturing, manage distribution and storage, and deal with raw material suppliers. What are the logistics of ordering and stocking components? What are the ordering and stocking requirements of retailers and distributors? What are the logistics of distribution? What inventory of raw materials and stocks of finished products should be held? What are the implications for manufacturing and warehouse space required?

The production and operations functions hold information on stock control (sometimes called inventory control), purchasing, work scheduling, job costings and delivery.

Organisation flows

With all these questions that are asked and answered in each functional area as they carry out their day-to-day tasks, you are perhaps starting to see the extraordinary amount of information that is both required and generated by a business.

Obviously information must be structured, collected, stored and managed in some kind of system. This system needs to be accessed by the individual users to get the particular information that they want and also

stop and think

Think about the chain of events that might have been triggered by an attempt to buy an Xbox from Dixons for a Christmas present. The customer was responding to the advertising campaign, and decided this was the right product in the marketplace. Suppose the customer was lucky and made a purchase before Dixons' stocks ran out. The purchase reduces the retailer's stock, which then triggers reordering from the manufacturer. Perhaps this information is directly sent from the retailer's checkout till through an electronic data interchange (EDI) system.

We know that in the run-up to Christmas the orders mounted. Eventually, the manufacturer could not cope, and was unable to fulfil these orders in time for the last-minute pre-Christmas rush. Production, marketing and finance functions all feel the pinch, and managers start asking questions.

Where was the failure? Did marketing get the promotion wrong? Or did production get its figures or timing wrong? Did it have enough staff at all stages of production? Or was there a failure with supply of components, or with the shipping and warehousing of finished products? We'll never know, but managers must find out what happened so they can prevent this situation happening again and damaging Microsoft's reputation and customer brand loyalty.

to deposit their own data. The system must have four separate elements:

- collecting or receiving and collating
- storing
- processing and using
- communicating and disseminating.

Throughout the organisation, information is flowing backwards and forwards, upwards and downwards. All functions need information to operate but they must also supply information for overall business control and senior management decision-making. Let's look at some details of these flows.

- Personnel to finance: reports of recruitment, details of new staff including salaries, national insurance numbers, etc., but not all details of past employment history or references.

- Sales to production: sales made, full details on orders (colours, sizes, etc.) and delivery times required.

- Sales to finance: reports of sales made, delivery dates, discounts offered, details of customers, but not specification of the products sold.

- Sales to marketing: information about what is happening in the marketplace, new products, new competitors, customer attitudes and opinions.

- Production to finance: cash required for purchasing raw materials and components to meet production schedules.

External sources

Information is not simply generated from a business's internal functional areas. In any business information flows both in and out of the organisation through its contact with external stakeholders.

Customers – these may be end users, retailers, distributors, individuals, companies or public bodies. All customers need to know about the business and its products, and the business needs to know about customers and their buying behaviour. This interface is with the sales part of the company.

Competitors – a business needs to know about its competitors, including what they are doing in the marketplace, what they are selling, at what price, and to which customers. This interface is with the marketing function.

Suppliers – a business need good relations with all suppliers, whether they are supplying raw materials for manufacturing, finished products to sell on, or equipment and supplies to run the business. It needs details about what suppliers can provide, when, and on what credit terms. They need specifications from the business about what it wants to purchase and when, and how it is going to pay. This interface is with production, administration and, perhaps, finance.

Banks and other lenders – a business will need access to money and lenders will need to know how much, when and what for, and how it is going to pay any loans back. This interface is with finance.

Accountants – external qualified accountants are required to audit the financial accounts each year. They may also prepare annual accounts for the business's shareholders and manage its dealings with HM Revenue and Customs. This interface is with finance.

HM Revenue and Customs – this government department needs official financial information about employees' PAYE contributions and the business's profits to calculate its tax liability. It also need details of VAT on sales and purchases. This interface is with finance.

Insurers – businesses must have insurance for employees, and they may choose to take out professional insurance covering buildings, stock, loss of profit, litigation for faulty products or services, and loss of business if there is a disaster. This interface is with finance and administration.

Lawyers – a business might use lawyers to deal with contracts for supplies or sales, subcontracting work, and employment issues. This interface is with personnel, production and finance.

Shareholders – shareholders need information about dividend payouts, the business's financial performance and its policies and practices. This interface is with finance.

Consultants – a business might use outside consultants for public relations, recruitment, advertising, market research and other functions. This interface is with finance, personnel and administration, and marketing.

Local authorities – a business will deal with local government departments over business rates, planning and environmental issues. This interface is with finance and administration.

Government and industry bodies: a business needs to know the rules and regulations governing its activities. It needs to monitor market industry trends. This interface is with personnel and administration, and marketing.

The public – the public may have views about the industry and the business itself, including its products, ways of operating, and its impact on the global, national and local environment. These will be probably be channelled through opinion polls, focus groups, surveys and questionnaires. This interface is with marketing.

Information will be transferred by a variety of formal and informal ways: face-to-face as in meetings, by telephone, by electronic means such as e-mail, the internet and company intranets, EDI in a supply chain, and by numerous print documents such as memos, letters, order forms, purchase orders, reports and advertising material. For more information on the means of exchanging information see pages 211–5 in your AS textbook.

As you can see from Figure 13.1, there is an extraordinary number of directions of information flowing around the business. This flow needs managing otherwise there will be chaos. A business needs to look at the information coming into the organisation, and the information it generates internally. It needs to consider who needs what information where, and it should then use the organisational structure to devise an information flow.

The aim is to provide staff within each department and function with the relevant information that they need to do their job. Generally speaking, decisions are usually made at the top and passed downwards, and information needed to make those decisions is passed upwards from the bottom. Note that the decision-makers may be in a different location from the implementers.

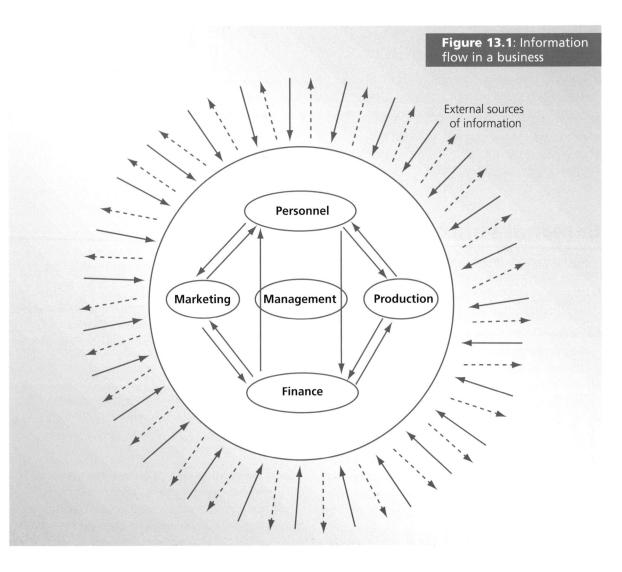

Figure 13.1: Information flow in a business

External sources of information

Personnel

Marketing   Management   Production

Finance

assessment practice
Planning your portfolio

Talk to your teacher about a business activity that could form the basis of your assessment portfolio for this unit. (You might be able to use the business proposal for which you are required to produce a business plan in Unit 8, if you have started this work.)

Identify the detailed market research that you will need to carry out and what data you will need about your target customers, about the environment that you are operating in, and about the industry. Start accumulating the different facts and figures that relate to the different functions of your business idea or activity.

assessment practice
The Cottage Loaf

Friends Katie and James used to live on Pret a Manger sandwiches and coffee when they were both at university. Now back in their home market town, there was nothing like this available. Katie's family have had experience in the catering and bakery business, and with their business studies and legal education respectively, could Katie and James establish something similar to a Pret a Manger with the help of their families?

Katie and James had both worked in bars and restaurants during their university life, so they started thinking about a small café with a takeaway section on the market square. The Cottage Loaf was born. They had in mind starting with a small premises that had kitchen facilities, an open-plan area for customer seating, shelves where customers could help themselves to sandwiches and cold drinks, and then a counter serving customers directly, with one checkout till taking the money.

They started by putting together their business plan. They drew on family help, advice from their local Business Link, start-up information from their bank, and discussions with a family accountant. They began with some market research to identify who their competitors were, and to find out what products they were offering and at what prices. They also started looking at the legal status of the café.

They decided who was going to take responsibility for each aspect of the business. James's father was to be the finance director, as he was lending them some money and was keen to monitor the financial side of the business. They were to be joint managing directors, with James having additional responsibility for marketing and Katie for production. They would have to hire additional staff to help make the food and help out with other parts of the business. Initially, they would be buying in bread and some cakes from Katie's father's bakery business to help them get started. They may decide to make more products in-house when the business is well established and they know which lines have been successful.

A What would Katie and James need to find out from their market research? This should inform their decisions about where to locate and what to sell, for example.

B Start identifying all the activities that they will need to think about in setting up the business, and all the information they will need to function effectively.

C Draw up the responsibilities of staff. Set out the information each would need, and suggest from where this information might be sourced.

Topic 2 | Types of information used in decision-making

Setting the scene: Marks & Spencer Group plc

When he was appointed in 2004, Stuart Rose, the new chief executive of Marks & Spencer, needed to turn round the fortunes of the retail giant, reversing its declining sales and improving its poor public image.

M&S needed to make big changes in marketing and manufacturing. It introduced new fashion lines, changed store layouts, adjusted prices in line with competitors, and launched a very expensive television and newspaper advertising campaign using celebrities and sports stars. The campaign's focus was on "your M&S". The company also promoted its new approach to fair trade, and its greater social and ethical responsibility.

Consider what information Stuart Rose would need to start making these major decisions. How would he know whether he had achieved success? He would need detailed internal data on sales and costs across different stores and product lines. He would need external data on trends in the high street fashion business, including competitors' products and prices. He would need to know more about M&S's existing customers and about why potential customers were put off by the store in the first place.

Stuart Rose sums up his approach as offering better value, better buying, and better styling and quality. The effects can be seen in the sales figures, and in the rise in the company's share price as the City becomes more confident in his ability to make M&S successful again. First quarter 2006 sales in the UK were up by 9.1 per cent in total, with general merchandise up by 9.9 per cent and food up by 8.4 per cent. The share price was up too.

The company's interim results, published in November 2005, reported:

■ improving sales trends
■ margin and cost savings on track
■ strong profit performance
■ strong free cash flow
■ acceleration of capital spend.

Has Stuart Rose changed customer attitudes about M&S? Think about what kind of questions you would ask customers about the new stores, the clothes, the different ranges, and their attitudes to the advertising campaign. If you were conducting a survey, think about what data would you also need about each interviewee, such as their socioeconomic group and buying behaviour.

Information and data

Different types of businesses have different types of information requirements and gather different types of data. A doctor's surgery needs to keep detailed patient records that must be easily accessible and brought up to date at each visit. The doctor would normally input the data on the patient's condition during the consultation, and make a record of, and print out, any prescription (if required). There is no clerk to do this data inputting, and possibly introduce errors from a handwritten document.

Estate agents must keep details of the properties on their books, with room layouts, photos and perhaps videos. They will have details of prospective customers with their house requirements. They also need to keep records of viewings, offers and communications with buyers, vendors and solicitors.

Supermarkets have massive stock control operations, with perhaps 30,000 product lines which need pricing and replenishing at each store as customers remove items from the shelves. This information may go directly back to the suppliers, linked electronically

KEY TERMS

A **budget** is a financial plan for the future operations of the business. Budgets are used to set targets to monitor performance and control operations.

Variance analysis is one of the methods used to monitor company performance. It is the comparison of what actually happened with what the business budgeted (planned to happen).

Ratio analysis is a method of examining financial data. It provides a means of interpreting financial data by measuring aspects of a business's performance.

from the checkout till, to ensure that they replenish stock to the warehouse.

Compare this approach with a market stallholder who sells fruit and vegetables, or a small greengrocer. They will not have sophisticated point-of-sale systems with instant weighing, pricing and inventory control. They will be weighing goods on a scale, which may or may not be accurate, and work out in their head (or using a calculator) the total price owed by customer.

They will replenish displayed stock when they see it going down, probably from a very small stock behind the stall or in a back room, and then order more stock when they get down to the last box. And the ordering is probably done on a daily basis by going to a supplier that gets in new stock every day from the major wholesalers and markets. Orders might be made using a printed order form or simply verbally at a wholesale market. There would be little point in having any type of stock control system, whether manual or computerised, which monitored the precise number of apples sold, as the rest of the operation couldn't match and make use of that level of detail.

stopandthink

Do you think that there is likely to be a big difference between the information requirements of a retail business that sells goods and a business that provides services? Justify your answer.

Information and decisions

Managers needs information to make decisions about planning (environmental and organisational) and control (current performance compared against targets). How do they access this information? Some information is available from the organisation's performance indicators and some from ongoing performance data.

Let's look at each of these sources in turn, and make some links with the organisational functions we consider in Topic 1. First, consider organisational performance indicators. These are generated from several areas of a business. For example:

- marketing provides details about sales revenue and advertising costs

- production provides details about production output and costs

- finance provides details about cash flow, the balance sheet, costings, profit margins, the profit and loss account, and cost analysis

- personnel provides information about salaries and pensions, levels of staff, absence rates, and training and recruitment costs.

Organisational performance data is also generated throughout a business. Marketing and sales provide sales forecasts, based on historical data, trend analysis, market research, and experience and knowledge of market and customers. Marketing also provides expenditure budgets that estimate the marketing and sales expenses for a particular period or product. Production provides production and manufacturing forecasts. Finance provides cash flow forecasts, master budgets (forecast profit and loss accounts that combine all the functional budgets), breakeven charts and financial ratios.

Variance analysis

All budgets can be used to monitor performance, both within functions and for the business as a whole. This is done by comparing actual performance with forecast performance. A favourable variance occurs when results are better than expected. An adverse variance occurs when results are worse than expected.

A favourable or adverse variance does not necessarily mean a good or bad performance respectively. The cost of sales may have gone down, showing a favourable variance, but this may have occurred simply because the business made fewer sales and so there were fewer associated expenses. The cost of labour may have gone up, showing an adverse variance, but this may be because there was more output and more sales.

Variance analysis identifies problem areas both within functions and in the business overall. Management is then able to make decisions on better information.

Financial statements and ratio analysis

Final accounts, such as the profit and loss account and the balance sheet, are used for three main purposes:

- financial control
- planning
- accountability.

The profit and loss account measures the profitability and financial performance of a business over a particular period of time, usually one year. The net and gross profit figures can be compared with previous years, and also compared with competitors' results. This can pinpoint problem or good areas in the business, and inform management decisions. There are a number of ratios that are useful performance indicators:

- gross profit ratio
- net profit ratio
- asset utilisation ratio
- return on capital employed.

Solvency, liquidity and gearing can be investigated using the current ratio. There are a number of other useful ratios:

- earnings per share
- dividend cover
- dividend yield
- price earnings ratio.

Ratio analysis can help in interpreting financial information as they enable managers to compare "like with like" at a glance and to compare different periods, businesses and industries. However, they sometimes can need specialist interpretation.

Figure 13.2 sets out the formulas of key performance ratios. Liquidity ratios tell us about a business's cash situation and whether it needs to do anything about its cash or borrowing requirements. Profitability ratios tell us about the business's profit situation. Efficiency ratios tell us how well the business is operating.

stop and think

Look at the M&S interim results, published on 8 November 2005. These can be found at www.2.marksandspencer.com, the company's corporate website. Can you identify the performance data that Stuart Rose would have used to inform his decisions?

Figure 13.2: Performance ratios

Liquidity ratios

$$\text{current ratio} = \frac{\text{current assets}}{\text{current liabilities}}$$

$$\text{acid test} = \frac{(\text{current assets} - \text{stock})}{\text{current liabilities}}$$

$$\text{gearing} = \frac{\text{long-term liabilities} + \text{preference shares}}{\text{total capital employed}} \times 100$$

Profitability ratios

$$\text{gross profit margin} = \frac{\text{gross profit}}{\text{turnover (sales)}} \times 100$$

$$\text{net profit margin} = \frac{\text{net profit}}{\text{turnover (sales)}} \times 100$$

$$\text{sole trader ROCE} = \frac{\text{net profit}}{\text{capital employed}} \times 100$$

$$\text{limited company ROCE} = \frac{\text{net profit before interest and tax}}{\text{total capital employed}} \times 100$$

Efficiency ratios

$$\text{stock turnover} = \frac{\text{cost of goods sold}}{\text{average stock}}$$

$$\text{debtor collection period} = \frac{\text{debtors}}{\text{credit sales}} \times 365$$

$$\text{creditor payment period} = \frac{\text{creditors}}{\text{credit purchases}} \times 365$$

$$\text{return on net assets} = \frac{\text{net profit before tax and interest}}{\text{net assets}} \times 100$$

assessmentpractice
Portfolio work

Building on the work you undertook in the assessment practice at the end of Topic 1, identify the facts and figures that you need for your business idea or activity. Now start to identify the internal data that is likely to be generated as each function carries out its organisational activities, such as details on sales, customers, products and outputs.

Start to consider how this data can be analysed and presented as useful information for management decision-making. Remember that not all functions need exactly the same information or the same level of detail.

assessmentpractice
The Cottage Loaf

The Cottage Loaf is now up and running, and has been operating for a few months. Katie and James have rented premises in the market square. This store was previously a delicatessen, so it has a kitchen, and they were able to buy some of the refrigerators and display cabinets from the outgoing tenants.

They already have many regular customers, they have established suppliers, and they are working to develop their product range. Katie and James have been experimenting with different breads and sandwich fillings, different pastries and other cakes. They have been finding out what customers buy, what products are easy to make without buying special equipment, what is cheap to make, and what supplies are easy to source. They have money coming in, mainly cash, but they have regular expenses, including the wages of their part-time staff. They have other legal, contractual and financial obligations.

A Identify the key issues that Katie and James must closely monitor to make their business a success. What records do they need to keep on a daily, weekly or monthly basis?

B How do they start organising all this information so it informs what they do in the short term and long term? What should they be comparing on a daily, weekly or monthly basis to monitor their performance?

Issues and pitfalls with information

Setting the scene: error strikes BBC climate model

Just because a project is financially sound, and is backed by major sponsors, doesn't mean that the information that it generates is foolproof. Sometimes rather embarrassing things happen when you are dealing with information and computer systems.

A "major error" was discovered in the world's biggest online climate prediction project, backed by the BBC. The fault in a Climateprediction.net model launched in February causes temperatures in past climates to rise quicker than seen in real observations. The program aims to generate forecasts of climate change. The error in the climate model has been traced to a file that is responsible for introducing data on the amount of manmade sulphate emissions into the atmosphere.

Some of the participants in the project have questioned why the model was not tested thoroughly before its release. The team behind the model says the error was introduced by a minor last-minute change to the program, which made it easier to download.

Source: adapted from BBC News website, 19 April 2006

Problems with information

In today's world, there is an enormous volume of information available on a daily basis from all kinds of sources. A business has to manage the information that it generates internally and that it receives from its external environment. It needs to able to understand and interpret this information appropriately, and access it with the right level of detail. But it must also treat the information with a degree of caution.

It is easy for recipients to misuse information. It needs to be the right level of detail to inform. It is pointless sending daily or weekly sales reports to a managing director who is about to make a decision on whether to open a new factory. The managing director needs the bigger picture, say quarterly sales figures with forecasts and projected profit and loss accounts, and estimates of the additional staffing requirements, together with an analysis of the potential impact of the increased manufacturing capacity. Without this information, it would be very difficult to take a longer-term view. In short, the managing director needs a properly worked-up proposal.

Information being sent by a business to the outside world also needs careful attention. A company is legally required to produce financial statements, and most businesses produce extensive marketing and sales information. According to accountants Grant Thornton, advertisements published by UK financial service companies are often misleading. The firm claims that 76 per cent of a sample of adverts it examined failed the standards set by the Financial Services Authority (FSA).

A business's analysis of its performance – both actual and forecast – can often be tweaked to give a better picture by making comparisons, say, with a previous year in which profit margins were poor rather than a year in which the company performed well.

stop and think

You can use a spreadsheet to build a model or simulation of a business activity such as a promotion campaign. This makes it easy to model "what-if" scenarios. However, if there are any errors in the underlying data used by the model, or if inaccurate assumptions are used in the modelling exercise, then the what-if analysis will produce misleading and erroneous information. A company might actually use the analysis to take a decision that might leave it with a cash flow problem or very poor cost-effectiveness.

To be useful for decision-making, information has to pass five tests. It needs to be up to date, relevant, accurate, complete and timely.

Up to date

Information needs to be as up to date as possible. Using last year's prices – for advertising in the local paper, for printing posters, for buying external public relations services – will produce an inaccurate budget for this year's promotion campaign.

Relevant

Too much irrelevant information can be distracting and lead to information overload. A sales manager doesn't need to receive the production manager's report on the malfunctioning of a machine on the factory floor. The sales team only needs to know whether the business is still able to produce sufficient goods to meet customer demand.

Accurate

Inaccuracies can be introduced into data in several ways. The method of data collection can be biased. If some market research only interviews a sample of men, it would make little sense to use the results to inform a decision about a new product that was aimed solely at women.

Any data needs to be entered correctly. This applies to both manual and computerised systems. This may seem a fairly obvious point, but many people don't check figures after they have entered them into a spreadsheet, or have any kind of monitoring system.

Other errors can arise if you make some invalid assumptions when using the data in, for example, a market model to estimate sales.

Complete

Partial data can be misleading. The first results obtained in a survey, or experiment, don't always reflect the final result. A pharmaceutical company or a cosmetics business would wait for the full results of health, safety and effectiveness tests before releasing new products.

Timely

Information is of no value if it arrives after the decision has been made. If the monthly sales figures take too long to produce, production may have to place orders with suppliers for the next month's components and raw materials before they arrive. There is little point is supplying personnel with a Gantt chart setting out the staffing requirements for a production run if there is not enough lead time to hire or train the personnel required.

Presentation and interpretation

However good the underlying information, it is not very useful unless it is presented in the right way. Numerical information is more easily assimilated if it is presented as pie and bar charts, tables and graphs.

Look at Figure 13.3 on page 208, which illustrates the impact of Marks & Spencer's new "better product" approach. This graph clearly shows the decline in the percentage of products returned to manufacturers,

stop and **think**

Suppose you are the sales manager of a garage selling second-hand cars. You estimate that if you take on an extra salesperson, you can increase sales by 10 per cent. Using a spreadsheet, you can adjust your sales figures and expenses to illustrate this result for your boss. However, if your estimate of a 10 per cent increase in sales is wrong, the presentation of the figures may look good but the information is of little value.

Suggest why it might be a bad idea to simply estimate the increased sales that could be generated by adding a new member of the sales team by extrapolating the sales figures of the current salespeople?

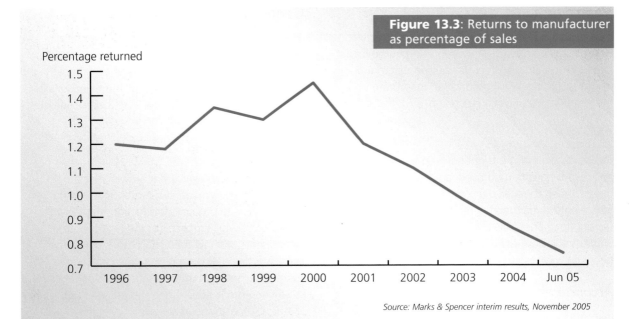

Figure 13.3: Returns to manufacturer as percentage of sales

Percentage returned

Source: Marks & Spencer interim results, November 2005

but think about why the company used the scale since 1996 and not say 2000, or even 2004, which is when there was a big change within the company. Some presentations can distort the information by adjusting the scales.

Figure 13.4 is a good visual presentation of comparative data using a pie chart. It shows that Marks & Spencer's has reduced its sourcing of materials from the Far East from 54 per cent in 2004/5 to 44 per cent in 2005/6, matching this with an increase in the UK and Europe, with supplies from the Indian subcontinent staying the same. This is all part of its "better buying" policy.

Using different graphics

You can use graphics software to represent data in a variety of different formats. For example, Figure 13.5

Figure 13.5: Sales of one of The Cottage Loaf's product lines

Month	Sales
Jan	240
Feb	251
March	80
April	205
May	278
June	329

has sales figures for one of The Cottage Loaf's products. As Figure 13.6 shows, you can present this in many different versions. Which do you think is the most effective? You should use the one that best demonstrates the effects that you are trying to illustrate.

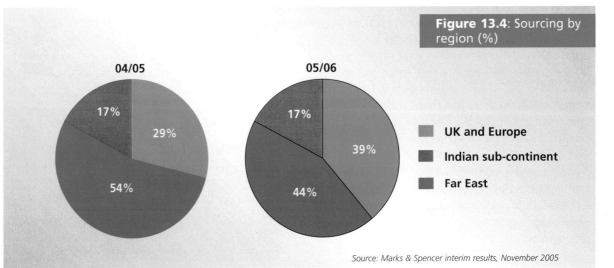

Figure 13.4: Sourcing by region (%)

04/05: 17%, 29%, 54%

05/06: 17%, 39%, 44%

UK and Europe
Indian sub-continent
Far East

Source: Marks & Spencer interim results, November 2005

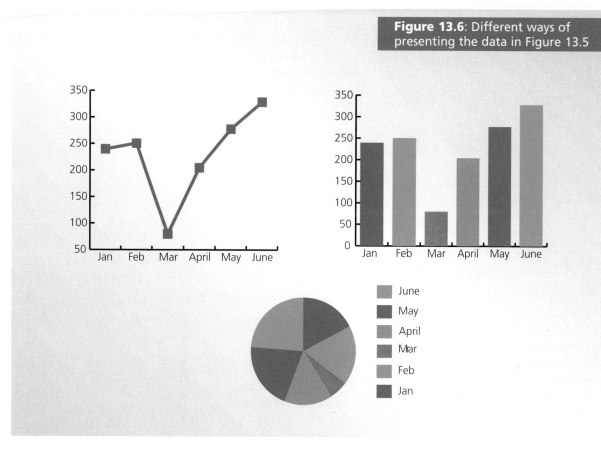

Figure 13.6: Different ways of presenting the data in Figure 13.5

What happened in March: did the café introduce another product that directly competed with this one? Or was there a problem with supplies? Or a problem with staffing – perhaps a key member of staff was ill? There are many issues that might need addressing.

Using spreadsheets

Spreadsheets can be used to process data to produce information. Data is input into rows and columns; the box at which a row and column meet is a cell. The software enables the contents of the cells to be manipulated.

Spreadsheets are useful at all levels of business and decision-making. They can be used in finance for the presentation of accounts and the display of projected figures. They can be used to undertake what-if analysis – for example, if you change the advertising costs of a promotion campaign, what difference does it make to the overall picture. They can be used for cash flow forecasting, financial planning and budgeting. At an operational level they can be used for costing, scheduling and planning.

There are presentational advantages in using spreadsheets. They allow the user to present plans quickly and clearly, with results displayed in different ways. Output can be numbers, text, graphs or charts.

Information overload

There is so much information that is readily accessible today. We know about the environment, about government activities, about all the internal functions of the business, etc. It is easy to overload staff's desks with printed materials, their PCs with e-mails and downloadable files, and their brains by giving them too many things to think about.

Managers don't need to receive information about every aspect of the company. Reports take time to read and digest; e-mails have to be opened and read. And what about storing all this information? It all needs to go somewhere, whether it's on a manager's office shelf, or straight in the wastepaper basket, or filed somewhere on computer. The information system within a business needs to be able to summarise potentially useful information for different parties that they can then access if they need more details.

It is all too easy to copy in the entire company on an e-mail with a report attached and think that you are doing your job well. However, it is simply wasting other people's time and resources if it is not useful and relevant. E-mail traffic has risen enormously – if a member of staff has hundreds of e-mails a day, then they are wasting valuable time and may miss or delay an important task.

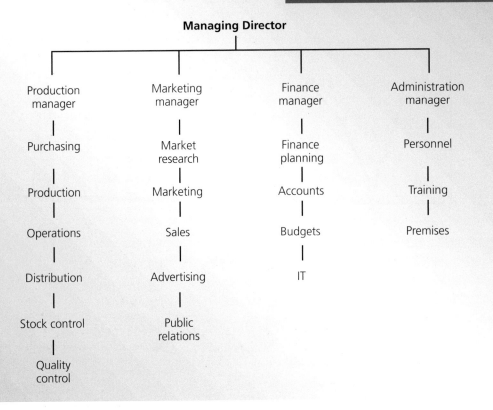

Figure 13.7: Organisational structure for a manufacturing company

Managing Director

Production manager	Marketing manager	Finance manager	Administration manager
Purchasing	Market research	Finance planning	Personnel
Production	Marketing	Accounts	Training
Operations	Sales	Budgets	Premises
Distribution	Advertising	IT	
Stock control	Public relations		
Quality control			

Information needs managing so that:

- the volume provided is not counterproductive – "I can't cope with my inbox on a Monday morning, so I just delete everything and wait for people to follow up important messages"

- information is relevant to needs – production doesn't get unwanted sales reports and vice versa

- its value justifies the effort of generating and disseminating the information – a very expensive national survey may not produce much that is relevant to a small business

- it is presented so that it is quickly and easily assimilated.

Organisational structures and information flow

Every organisation needs a structure, regardless of its size. The organisational structure can dictate how the information flows around the company. Let's consider a manufacturing company, headed by a managing director, and with four main functional areas that have a director or manager – production, marketing, finance and administration. Figure 13.7 represents its structure in a chart.

- The production manager is responsible for purchasing, production, operations, distribution, stock control and quality control.

- The marketing manager is responsible for market research, marketing, sales, advertising and PR.

- The finance manager is responsible for finance planning, internal financial bookkeeping and accounts, budgets and information technology.

- The administration manager is responsible for personnel, training and premises.

In each functional area, managers will communicate *up* with the managing director, *down* with their staff, *across* other departments and *externally* as part of their job function. By identifying the responsibilities of each person in the organisation – their job function and who they report to – you can identify the levels in the organisation and the information that they require. In a larger company, perhaps, there is likely to be a director over the managing director, managers in charge of departments within a function, and then supervisors at a lower level. In a small company, there may be a doubling-up of job functions and fewer levels of hierarchy. The information flow between all areas will be through regular meetings, e-mails and reports.

assessment practice
Portfolio work

Devise some documents, such as customer or patient records, order forms and purchase orders, estimates, schedules and budgets, that could provide templates for a manual for a computerised information system for your business idea or activity. Bear in mind who needs what level of information, and who is receiving the raw data.

Think about the data that is required for spreadsheets across each function, what data needs to be input, and what information outputs are required. Don't worry too much about the detail of all the performance ratios and accounting figures, concentrate more on the basic data that you will need to collect about the business – sales, expenses, customers, suppliers, stock, etc.

assessment practice
The Cottage Loaf

Katie and James need to think about the information needs of their café and bakery business. When do they place the bread order? When will it be delivered? When will the staff arrive to make the sandwiches and baguettes? When will the ingredients for the fillings arrive? What products or other supplies can they order in larger quantities at less frequent intervals and are not perishable?

What documentation do they need for finance and the accountant? What information do they need to give to suppliers? What instructions do they need to give to staff to make the sandwiches in the right way? What information do they need to describe the products to customers?

A Suggest a system of ordering supplies to link with production and staffing. Make sure that data is acquired at each stage that will be appropriate for all relevant functions.

B Devise some procedures for the business to follow. Outline the accompanying documentation so anyone coming into the business knows how it all works.

Setting the scene: shops record Easter sales decline

Read through this report about consumer trends in the UK retail market over the Easter weekend, April 2006. It provides detailed information on the market, making numerous comparisons with previous years.

A sluggish bank holiday weekend has left retailers wondering what lies in the quarter ahead, as shoppers ditched the high streets for their gardens and leisure activities, according to a new report.

Latest figures from retail analyst FootFall show that the volume of shoppers visiting the nation's high streets on Easter Saturday declined 3.3 per cent compared with last year's holiday. Still, the disappointing figure marks a substantial improvement over Good Friday's year-on-year figure, which fell 4.3 per cent over 2005.

FootFall attributes the Saturday rebound to last-minute gift shopping and preparations for the long weekend in driving shoppers to the high streets. Last week's warming weather, as well, proved more enticing than retailers' numerous discounts, the report said. While the bounce-back offers some hope for retailers, it can only offer so much in terms of long-term confidence, the company warned.

"The decline in the number of high street shoppers of 4.3 per cent compared to Good Friday 2005, suggests that tough trading conditions are continuing to hamper retailers," said Natasha Burton, spokesperson for FootFall.

Source: www.startups.co.uk, 18 April 2006

For a major high street trader such as Marks & Spencer, this information is useful as it illustrates an important trend. For a small business, with just one store on the high street, it is possibly not very useful unless the report was based on its particular location.

However, even M&S would want to know more about how the data that these figures are based on was collected. What shops were monitored? And in which locations? And how did trade compare with a "normal" Saturday in April? Notice how the comparisons between years are taken at face value. Might other factors have influenced shopping patterns between the different years?

Data or information?

Data is raw facts and figures. Data is directly collected by a business from a variety of internal and external sources. Information is based on data, but it usually involves results from "processing" the data in some way to provide results in a more usable form. Because there is this process, data and information are not exactly the same.

Consider, for example, how the research company FootFall would have collected the data on which to base the report discussed in the introduction to this topic. It would need to measure the number of shoppers in exactly the same way in each survey location, so the data it collected could be analysed and compared. Its researchers might register the numbers entering the same sample of shops at the

KEY TERMS

Data is raw facts and figures, and descriptions of things, events and activities.

Information is data that has been processed to provide some useful intelligence. Information is subjective: one person's (or one organisation's) useful information may be another person's meaningless data.

Information systems comprise hardware, software, people, procedures and processes. Even though most data processing is computerised, people are still the key part of any information system.

same time of day to get comparable year-on-year figures. This would provide the raw data. The data is absolutely fixed but, as a figure on its own, it may be fairly meaningless – say, 22,000 shoppers on Easter

Figure 13.8: From data to information

Figure 13.8: From data to information

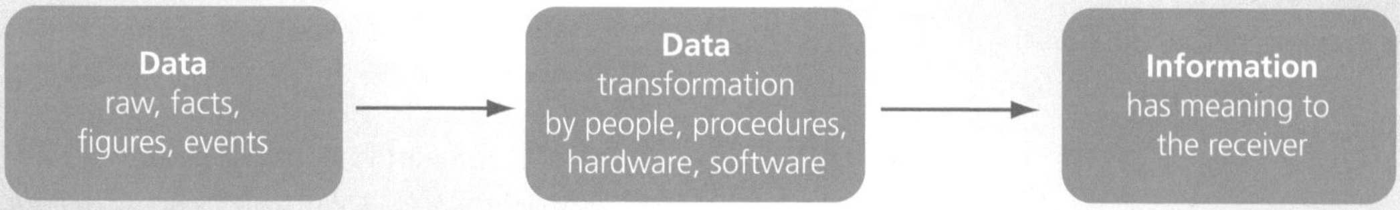

Saturday 2006. It is only when this figure is compared with the previous year to provide a trend, expressed as a percentage decline (or growth), that information is produced. The data has been manipulated and is subject to interpretation. It results in information – useful to some such as M&S perhaps, but not to others, and it still may need viewing with caution.

When data is collected internally and externally in a business, it may be unclear exactly how the data might eventually be used. People at different levels of the organisation have widely differing information requirements for decision-making. At a senior level, the managing director needs a broad view of the organisation in making long-term, strategic decisions. At an operational and functional level, managers need much more detail related to their relatively narrow areas of interest. Production, for example, needs very precise specifications on each product.

With modern information technology, more information may be available to a business than may ever be used. For example, the details held by a business on individual customers is unlikely to be used by the company in a decision-making context. But it may be easier just to log this data continuously, rather take a judgment about what data to collect or not. Sales may need to know something about a particular customer one day, and there might be some useful general information or categorisation that could be extracted from the complete customer database.

Internal data sources

Data is collected by businesses as part of their normal day-to-day activities. Most hold details on their customers, for example. Banks hold all customers' personal and account details in a database. They know exactly who their customers are from the original forms that they filled in and signed when they opened the account. Banks customers have to supply some "official" documentation such as a passport or driving licence, and also have to provide a proof of address in accordance with the latest money

laundering regulations. The design of the customer application form is important to ensure that the bank captures all the data it needs. If a customer fills it in incorrectly then that customer's details will be wrong in the database.

Your school or college holds your personal details and has a record of the courses that you are taking. Perhaps you filled in an enrolment form at the beginning of term, with your name, address, telephone number, date of birth, sex, e-mail address, next of kin for emergency contact, etc.

stop and think

Obtain a blank copy of your school's (or college's) enrolment form. Is it well designed? Would an applicant be able to fill in all the boxes easily, or are some questions ambiguous? Is the space provided big enough to allow you to provide the requested information? Suggest ways the form could be improved.

There are many other ways in which a business acquires data during the course of its daily operations. Again, it can be useful to consider this process on functional lines.

Sales might generate data on what products were bought (and when and for how much) through sales invoices, customer orders or records from the sales force. It might have data on how many products were returned. Were any faulty? It might have data from customer feedback forms.

Production might generate data on how many items were produced for each product line – when, and for what cost. It might have data on how many finished goods are in the warehouse. It might have records of raw materials, components and work-in-progress.

Personnel might generate data on staff, including salary, joining date, training requirements, home contact details, background, job description, and absence and sickness record.

Finance might generate data on the flow of money in and out of the business, credit terms of suppliers and customers, etc.

External data sources

Market research can be used to gather data about customer attitudes and buying behaviour, about competitors and their activities. Industry data can be accessed from trade associations and government bodies. Product data can be accessed through research and development. Health and safety and legal and statutory requirements can be accessed from local and central government. EU regulations can be accessed from the European Commission.

Sources of information

Information flows into and around the business through the interaction of human, written and information technology sources. Staff assimilate information from their working environment through discussions and contact with colleagues, the media, customers and suppliers. Most of this isn't recorded – it is stored in people's heads – but staff might make a note of something they've learnt that's really useful. They retrieve it when it might provide an extra piece of information to help in decision-making. Some information obtained in this way may be recorded using a formal process, such as by writing the minutes of a meeting with a supplier.

Information technology provides data through the business's database and through government and industry databases, and the internet has now become a major source of external information. Despite the widespread use of information technology, written materials still supply a considerable amount of information in the form of reports, forms and handwritten notes.

Some businesses still use a written appointments book for bookings and to hold client details. Your hairdresser might write in appointments in pencil, which can then be rubbed out if changes are made, and ticked when the customer arrives for the appointment. A restaurant might record bookings and table reservations in a book or on a board. Though these systems are popular, they are not always convenient if the book goes missing or is in another room when a member of staff is taking a call from a potential client.

Structuring information

If we want to manage information in a business, then we need to first understand where and how the data comes into the organisation. We know that data comes from many internal and external sources, but how do we link it to the information required in other functions? We need to consider how this data relates to the business and how it can be used to support decision-making. These issues will affect content, data processing and the way that the information is presented to meet the identified needs. By considering these issues, it is possible to specify the components of the information system, which might be developed in-house with the help of different IT suppliers, or commissioned from outside experts and consultants.

For each function, a business can identify the data that is acquired in routine operations, and it can consider how this data can be used within the function or for wider decision-making within the organisation. Let's look first at customer information. How does customer information help a business make decisions about its future plans? Consider a small tile manufacturing company that keeps details of existing and potential customers on a database. Data on existing customers is obtained from actual sales, and includes name of company, person to contact, address, telephone number, e-mail address. It might also include the size of the company, the size of its order, and how often it repeats the order. A survey might have indicated what other lines, styles and uses individual customers are interested in, and also their satisfaction with products, prices and service.

All this information could be used to manage the business and to inform decision-making. For example, marketing might prepare a proposal to extend the product lines to include some modern tile designs for kitchens and bathrooms. Senior managers might want to see the results of the customer satisfaction survey. If this indicated that many tiles were breaking when laid, it might ask production for a report on manufacturing and quality control procedures. Perhaps changes would be needed in the production process. Sales and marketing might propose that customers who complained about breaking tiles could be offered some discount on future orders.

Details of prospective customers could have been put together by the marketing team. They could have sourced this information from external databases, industry sources and the local chamber of commerce. Marketing could then use this information to put together a promotional campaign, perhaps advertising in local papers and by direct mail to these companies.

stopand**think**

Loyalty cards enable a store to accumulate information about its customers and their buying habits. Suggest ways that this information could be used by a retail business.

Using information technology

Most businesses use computers and a range of software for different tasks. Individual software applications are designed to undertake (or speed up) particular functional processes. Some applications link with others in the business, others might be stand-alone systems.

Large software developers such as Microsoft can supply an array of applications to meet many requirements. There are the main office applications – word processing, spreadsheets and basic database management – as well as more complex accounting and payroll packages, customer relationship tools, supply chain and logistics management, and sales packages that can be customised to a business's individual requirements. Other suppliers offer applications for particular industries. There are software packages specifically written for businesses in building construction, estate agency, publishing, advertising – and many more sectors. There is a

bewildering array of solutions, and indeed you will find the word "solution" regularly used in IT companies' promotional material. It's all very well offering a solution, but you need to be very clear about what the problem is in the first place.

Any business planning to set up an information system needs to draw up a detailed idea of what it actually wants to achieve. This is regardless of whether it plans to develop the system in-house, to commission it directly from a supplier, or to bring in outside expertise to help build this system. To obtain this clear vision of what it is trying to achieve, a business needs to answer a number of questions to outline its information requirements. Figure 13.9 sets out a specification check list that can help in this process.

At this specification stage, it is important not to get too involved in the technology. The focus should be on the overall outcomes, in terms of what the business wants at each level of operation and management, and what is possible for it to access in terms of the initial data. It must balance all parts of the system. It is pointless having sophistication and speed at one point, if this cannot be maintained throughout the system. It is also pointless having an elaborate system if it can only be used by very skilled staff which the business cannot afford to employ. If a standard spreadsheet package will do what the business wants to achieve, then it doesn't need to develop (or buy) a fancy database solution.

Figure 13.9: Establishing the requirements of an information system

What is the nature of the business?
    Retail   Service   Manufacturing   Other

What is its sector and what are its main products?
    Industry   Product range

What is the scale of operation?
    Turnover   Staffing   Locations   Branches

What operational systems exist?
    List the functional departments, and what they do

What is the organisational structure?
    Structures and hierarchy
    Who makes the decisions and where are they made?

What information flow systems exist?
    Does this link in with the organisational structure?
    Is information upwards and are decisions downwards?
    Is there any centralisation of information?

What are you trying to achieve that you don't achieve now?
    What outputs/decision-making information is required by whom, where?
    What data processing might be required?

What and how much data is captured?
    What is automatic?
    What needs to be input?
    What do you do now?

What IT, hardware, software, training, documentation, policies and procedures do you have now?
    What manual systems do you have in place?

What security systems do you have for equipment and data?

Do you have an IT or IS department or officer?

Portfolio work

Draw up a specification for an information system for your business idea or activity. This should be written as if you are preparing a brief for an external consultant to design your system.

Start by looking at the data collected by each function. Consider the information required within each function and by the senior management. What data processing is required to generate this information? Combine this with your organisational structure and information flow, so you can provide details on the personnel involved in the information system.

assessmentpractice
Choosing an IT supplier for The Cottage Loaf

As a new IT system can be a significant investment, it's important to choose the right system and supplier. Business Link (www.businesslink.gov.uk) suggests that before any business chooses an IT supplier it should:

- find out whether the supplier can provide all the hardware, software, services, support and maintenance needed

- get details of what exactly is included in the supply contract, and ask whether upgrades and fixes to software are included in the price

- check whether the supplier will install and configure the system so it's fully operational

- ask whether the supplier is happy for the business to test the proposed system, perhaps under a non-disclosure agreement

- find out if the supplier will accept payment for the system only when it is installed and working satisfactorily

- confirm what frontline support the supplier can provide, such as a telephone helpdesk

- ask whether the supplier can provide training and whether it will provide written documentation that will help staff understand the system

- investigate what sort of maintenance contracts are provided and find out what sort of warranty is offered

- ask the supplier to provide references from other similar companies it has helped in the past

- decide whether the supplier understands the needs of the business and has any experience of working in the industry in which the business operates

- find out whether the supplier is financially viable and able to meet requirements in the foreseeable future.

A **Modify this list to include extra questions that would relate to choosing an external IT consultant or an information systems supplier for The Cottage Loaf.**

B **Given the relative inexperience that Katie and James have in running a business, how would you recommend that they source an information management system for The Cottage Loaf, given its possible size and complexity?**

Dealing with data and information

Setting the scene: The US National Map

The National Map is a consistent framework for geographic knowledge. Funded by the US government, it provides access to high-quality geospatial data and information to help support decision-making by resource managers and the public.

The project is designed to enhance the United States' ability to access, integrate and apply geospatial data. One of the key partners is the US Geological Survey. Its vision is to ensure that the United States has "access to current, accurate and nationally consistent digital data and topographic maps derived from those data".

This geographical data has been collected, organised and made available for various users. That does not mean, however, that the information held within the database is necessarily acted on.

For example, it might be argued that the extent of devastation from Hurricane Katrina could have been reduced if government agencies had used the geospatial data on low-lying districts in the New Orleans area to provide a fuller risk assessment. This could have enabled better

preventative measures to be in place to reduce the threat to life and property from hurricanes.

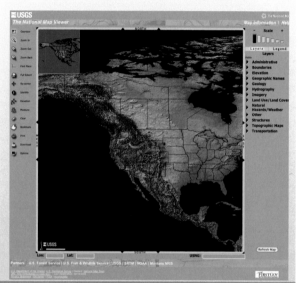

KEY TERMS

Quantitative information is measurable. It is obtained from raw data (facts and figures) that can be analysed numerically.

Qualitative information is obtained from data on people's attitudes, tastes and opinions.

Information systems comprise the hardware, software, data, procedures and people that combine to generate, collect, collate, retrieve, store, process, analyse and disseminate information.

Wireless systems are networks which use no physical connections. Computers and peripherals are linked together using cellular technology.

Local area networks connect computers and peripherals together. They cover a relatively small area, such as the computers within a single building or within a school.

Wide area networks connect computers and peripherals over a larger geographical area.

Collecting, collating and presenting information

Different information requirements dictate what type of data is collected, how that data is processed, and how the resulting information is presented and made available to users. One key distinction is between qualitative and quantitative data, and this has important implications for the design of an information system. The US National Map, for example, is based on quantitative data (given its geographical nature), and that will have helped to determine how the database was designed.

Quantitative data is recorded raw facts and figures. The data has definite values that can be measured, such as the quantity of sales, the number of items produced in a seven-hour shift, the amount of money flowing in and out of the business, and the cost of advertising. This kind of data is sometimes called "hard data" and it is much easier to manipulate and process. Much numerical data is likely to come into a business as part of its routine functional activities, so it can be cheap to collect. It can be stored manually or automatically, and computers can speed up processing and analysis.

Numerical information can show trends, daily variations in sales and production, and the size of market share, for example, and it can be extrapolated to show future likely outcomes. For example, a business might forecast its future sales on the basis of historical data, which will enable it to take decisions on whether it needs to hire new staff or make redundancies, and whether to increase or decrease production. Numerical information lends itself to statistical reports, performance appraisal, comparative analysis, projections and forecasts.

Qualitative data cannot be expressed numerically. It consists of data which cannot be reduced to a set of numbers, such as the attitudes and opinions of customers, stakeholders and society. This kind of data is often called "soft data". It can be collected through customer and employee questionnaires and surveys, through public opinion polls, through consumer and industry focus groups and through observations from the media.

The method used to collect qualitative data is important and may affect the results. Suppose you pay an agency to monitor media reports on behalf of a business. The usefulness of the information provided by the agency would depend on which newspapers and business journals it monitored. And given that you are paying for a service and would want to see something for your money, this might encourage the agency to flag up reports which have marginal relevance to your business.

Collecting qualitative data through questionnaires and other instruments is a manual process, although coded forms could be used to input the final data into the system. The information may be expensive to obtain, especially if large-scale surveys are carried out. As the data does not have numerical values, it is hard to process and is more open to interpretation. However, qualitative information is invaluable. It enables a business to keep in touch with the views of its key stakeholders. It can be used for comparative purposes: you might undertake surveys to find out what consumers thought about the company before and after it undertook a major promotion campaign.

Data input

As computers are inflexible, it is necessary to provide precise instruction for data collection and input. Data entry forms are commonly used to organise data. Data entry can be labour-intensive, requiring manual input through devices such as keypads and handheld terminals. This is why businesses are increasingly looking to use automatic data capture methods. These methods include:

- laser scanners and light pens that can read barcodes at, for example, supermarket checkouts
- page scanners that can input whole pages of text or graphics
- automatic tellers that read data from magnetic strips
- sensors and counters that can be used to collect data in manufacturing processes.

Developments are happening all the time in this area. In April 2006, "smart" meters to measure gas and electricity usage are being trialled in 3,000 UK homes. These consist of a screen in each home and a central monitoring device. The system enables customers to see how much energy they are using, but its primary attraction for utility companies is that, if successful, it means that they would no longer need to employ staff to visit customers, read the meters and key in the reading on a handheld device.

Information systems

As we have discussed, every business needs information to function. To collect, collate, store and process data, and to retrieve and disseminate the resulting information, a business needs an information system. The main objective of any information system is to supply information that enables users to make better – that is, more informed – decisions.

Information systems have been around for centuries. In medieval times, traders and barterers used ledger books and scrolls to record and store the data, and processed this data using an abacus and by doing sums in their head. The very first computerised systems were stand-alone applications for payroll, accounts payable, accounts receivable, inventory, etc. They were used in each functional area, and there was little organisation-wide data sharing. Some businesses still use this approach.

All information systems – regardless of the technological platform – have the same basic features. They collect data, store data and process that data into usable information – and they provide a means of retrieving and disseminating that information. To ensure that the information is accurate and reliable, the system also needs validation and verification.

Although all systems have the same features, the specific characteristics and architecture of an information system will depend on the use to which it will be put. In other words, it will depend on the system requirements.

System requirements

Operational systems usually involve routine activities and applications such as stock control, order processing, retailing systems and share dealing. These are relatively straightforward systems: they are critical to the organisation. As they concern transactions, these systems are often called transaction processing systems (TPS).

At a more complex and higher organisational level, management information systems (MIS) supply information for decision-making within the organisation at a functional level. These might involve monitoring financial budgets, pricing levels, human resourcing, production planning, stock level planning, supply chain management, etc.

At a slightly more senior level, strategic information systems are required to inform long-term policy decisions of the business. These decisions might concern the types of products and services, the location of manufacturing facilities, export distribution planning, 5–10 year investment plans and research and development schedules. Strategic information systems are more likely to require data from external sources, such as interest rates, currency exchange rates and commodity prices, and they need the capability to model sophisticated scenarios. These strategic systems are sometimes called decision support systems (DSS). They are designed for decision-makers and managers, and combine models and data to solve problems.

At the highest level, executive support systems (ESS) support chief executives and senior managers. These are only found in large organisations.

Computerised systems

Complex management information systems enable multiple users to access a central database that stores and processes data, providing information appropriate for the users in different geographical and functional areas. With the progress in computer technology, it is now possible to do many applications, and store a vast amount of data, on single personal computer – previously sufficient power was only available through expensive mainframe computers. Personal computers can be networked into a company intranet, or a local area network (LAN) or wide area network (WAN), so they can "speak" to each other and access the same material.

A computer-based information system is made up of:

- hardware – devices such as processors, monitors, printers and keyboards – the means by which data is input and information is accessed

- software – programs that instruct the hardware to process the data, ranging from simple word processing and graphics to more sophisticated accounting, payroll, production and planning applications

- databases – collections of related files that store the data

- networks – connecting systems to link computers within a business or across different locations to enable sharing of the data – these can be hard-wired or wireless

- procedures – instructions for combining the activities necessary to take data through the system and provide appropriate output

- people – involved at all stages of collecting and (perhaps) inputting the data and using the output information.

Most schools and colleges have a computer-based student record system. It requires teachers (people) to enter data (a student's name, course and course results) into a database following certain procedures. Different teachers can enter and access data at their own PCs through the school or college intranet or a local area network that connects the system and enables users to share information.

The hardware consists of the personal computers and peripherals such as printers, monitors and keyboards. Software manipulates the data and prints out a record sheet and other information. It might e-mail students to tell them their results, again following a predetermined procedure on the instruction of a class teacher or an administrator. The data could also be used by the school management to compare, say, the pass rates in different years, trends in student achievement in particular courses, or the performance of particular students over the years.

Manual or automated systems?

We know that computers store large volumes of data easily. They can process data quickly, copy the data and move it to different locations accurately, and communicate the data to other computers, printers and output devices. So a computerised information system can speed up operational activities, improve information flow, and enable access to many users and access for decision-makers. However, it can also cost a substantial amount of money to develop, and some businesses may not have the resources to establish a company-wide system.

A business needs to consider the costs of the hardware, system analysis and design, developing software or purchasing off-the-shelf applications, installation and testing, implementation, maintenance, updating and staff training. The list seems never-ending, and as users make more demands, a business can find that its IT budget is never large enough to satisfy all requirements.

Manual information systems can have a place in business. These are clearly inappropriate for some businesses, such as those that conduct business on the internet or that handle high volumes of data. However, if a business only has a few transactions then all it might need is a manual system and, say, a few minutes of the owner's time every day with a calculator. However, it is likely that a computer could help it somewhere, so combining a manual system with some electronic information systems may be the best option for smaller companies and some types of businesses.

By taking advantage of readily available software applications, many operational processes and procedures can be undertaken efficiently and relatively cheaply. And using spreadsheets will give some of the benefits of data processing that can be achieved with a fully customised and computerised information system. Remember, though, that data will need to be stored in paper form for the manual parts of the system and filed so that it can be easily retrieved.

A manual system may also generate more errors than a computerised system as there are more stages involving people – the most common source of mistakes. Let's consider a manual card-based stock control system. A card is kept for each stock item, which records numbers in and out, and the date and

the supplier. The warehouse manager may misread the delivery note and enter the wrong figures on the card; he may add up the figures wrongly at the end of the week; he may lose or misplace a stock card. It is time-consuming to look through all the cards to see the level of stocks and to assess what needs reordering. A computerised system would improve stock control because:

- errors would be reduced as there would only be one data entry point

- data would be updated instantly and there would be no calculation errors

- stock items could be automatically reordered when they had reached the reorder level

- the system would allow analysis of monthly sales patterns, stock usage over the year, etc.

- stock data could be combined with other information such as delivery times on orders.

Cost-benefit analysis

Any decision on implementing a computerised information system needs to based on an analysis of the costs and benefits. The costs include:

- initial set-up costs of analysis and design

- hardware

- software

- software development

- system implementation

- staff training

- onward cost, including system maintenance, and upgrading and replacement costs

- any cost implications for customers and suppliers.

The benefits of using information technology are that it can:

- automate some processes, saving time and reducing labour costs

- reduce errors, improve quality and provide a consistent service and product to customers

- increase efficiencies in the supply chain

- increase the available information to the business

- manipulate the available information to inform decision-making at all levels more effectively.

stop and think

Think about a computer-based system that you use, perhaps using a PC at home to do some research on the internet for your homework. Think about all the costs involved for your parents – the PC, the internet connection, the phone line, etc. What about the benefits? Can you equate these costs and benefits? What would be the alternatives?

business practice
Nike

You should never underestimate the amount of testing required for any computerised system, especially if software has been customised.

In 2001, Nike in the US installed very expensive supply chain management software designed to forecast sales, and the demand and supply of raw materials and finished trainers. The software was required to forecast styles, colours and sizes in various locations.

Customised software was used that was not tested. As the result, the company over-bought raw materials, inventory was in the wrong place, and wrong lines were manufactured. Nike suggested that these failures cost the company $100 million in lost sales in the third quarter of 2001.

assessment practice
KnowledgePool Group

KnowledgePool, the learning services company, found that using CourseBooker it was able to reduce administration overheads and develop an online booking system. CourseBooker from CS Group is a complete software package for anyone who sells or delivers training. It combines course booking, scheduling and invoicing with a highly functional customer relationship management (CRM) and marketing database.

KnowledgePool had used three separate databases to manage its course bookings. Each had been developed in-house to meet different needs of the business. One system dealt with sales and bookings of large-volume training projects, another dealt with the administration of public scheduled courses, and the third was for other small project work. The three systems couldn't share information.

By combining the three systems, the company was able to standardise systems and processes and use one approach to manage all bookings across the different areas. Simon Matthews, KnowledgePool's business systems director, said: "CourseBooker has delivered a stable platform that integrates with our day-to-day operations, enabling us to build on our core business, extend our online activities and continually add value for our customers." Simon Matthews, Knowledge Pool Business Systems Director.

Source: www.trainingzone.co.uk

A What data would KnowledgePool have input into its three systems? How could this be combined together for the information needs of the new system?

B What features of the system would enable booking to be carried out online?

Setting the scene: behind-the-scenes technologies are all the rage

Small businesses in the UK have realigned their priorities when it comes to investment, according to a new survey. According to Cisco Systems, real company kudos comes from investment in practical and advanced technologies rather than company cars and executive toys.

A poll of 400 small and medium-sized enterprises (SMEs) conducted by Cisco revealed that most would look to invest in information technology before anything else – indicating its importance in the pursuit of success. Asked how they would spend £20,000, 37 per cent said they would buy new servers and 34 per cent opted for new staff PCs, while just two per cent said company cars.

Bernadette Wightman from Cisco said: "The results show that a surprising number of small businesses are investing in high-performance, advanced technologies – technologies that have a major impact on business productivity and competitiveness."

There are a number of ways in which small businesses can improve their productivity and performance through a relatively low-cost investment in technology. These include investment in broadband, in VoIP services (telephone services over the internet) and mobile devices. Some 38 per cent of SMEs in the Cisco survey had ploughed money into remote workforce technologies.

So if you are looking to show off the signs of your business success, wave goodbye to swanky office furnishings and sleek company cars, and start demonstrating your IT capability.

Source: BT, www.btbroadbandoffice.com, 20 April 2006

Keeping information systems up to date

As the introduction shows, all businesses are using more and more technology, not just large corporations. But how do companies keep not just the technology but the rest of the information system up to date?

Remember that the system is made up of hardware – like the servers that manage the network connections between computers – software, people, procedures and data. All aspects of the system will need monitoring once it is installed. This means having procedures in place to ensure data security and safety, and ensuring that there are processes and procedures for when things go wrong, such as through hardware failure, attack from software viruses, malicious damage, and fraud.

Organisational responsibilities

In a large organisation, there is likely to be an information systems department (perhaps within an information technology department) and employees with specific responsibility for the information system. The information systems department may have a chief information officer at a high level of seniority, reflecting the importance of the information function to the business. These departments and individuals would have responsibility for the more technical aspects of the system, and the shared information resources that are used throughout the business. End users in functional departments may have responsibility for the system within their functional department.

The division of responsibility between the IS department and the end users in other functional departments and management can be tricky. The functional departments needs systems that undertake their routine operations satisfactorily, and they may not be interested in developments or changes that might affect how their data is processed and used by other departments or by senior management. They may be reluctant to keep updating their transaction processing system if it means continually retraining staff or changing their procedures. They may not appreciate having to change hardware or software in their department simply because there have been advances in technology or alterations in the company's processes elsewhere in the organisation.

The information systems department needs to review advances in technology, and advise management at a strategic level of the opportunities to enhance the business's information systems. It needs to consider the whole business, taking into account the needs of individual functions as well as senior managers. It also needs to keep up to date with the systems used by suppliers, clients and competitors. Consider the car insurance industry. If one company can offer immediate quotations, either online or by telephone, then it may start taking customers from other businesses in the sector. If one bank is offering online banking facilities, then all banks are eventually forced to offer an online service as well.

Small businesses

In small businesses, information systems are likely to be much simpler and much easier to maintain and keep up to date. Responsibility might perhaps lie with the finance director, who would keep overall responsibility for the system. Individual users would need to advise on their needs and keep their own data up to date. The individual who has responsibility for the information system needs to build and maintain relationships with suppliers of hardware, software applications and security systems. Of course, system suppliers will be anxious to keep clients informed of new developments and products, so this is hardly a big problem, but it can be extremely time-consuming.

Small businesses can encounter problems if their information systems are incompatible with those of their suppliers or their clients. Consider the situation of The Cottage Loaf, the business we have been reviewing in the assessment practice exercises at the end of each topic. If one of this business's suppliers is a large food manufacturing company that uses sophisticated supply chain management software in managing its dealings with large supermarkets, then there might be problems if it tried to deliver to The Cottage Loaf. It is unlikely that the information systems of the manufacturing business and The Cottage Loaf would have the right interface. In practice, this situation is unlikely to arise as The Cottage Loaf would be dealing with small suppliers, but it illustrates a problem that can occur.

Some large corporations – the utility companies and banks, for example – have solved this problem by designing systems that can accommodate different types of customers. They have the flexibility to be able to offer different services and different ways of

communicating and dealing with individual customers and small businesses, and their large corporate customers.

System implementation and maintenance

A business needs to consider not only which individuals (or departments) should be responsible for the design and implementatiom of its information system, but also who should be responsible for systems maintenance and updating. Someone has to take responsibility for briefing external consultants (if required), for liaising with external suppliers, for co-ordinating the system requirements and managing the financial and logistical issues.

A business's senior managers and/or owners need to give authority to an IS department or individual to take responsibility for these various issues. There are also many policy and procedural issues that need to become part of the business's infrastructure.

Hardware

The key task here is the installation, operation and maintenance of hardware. You wouldn't expect end users to understand the complexities of their PCs and peripherals, or be able to set them up correctly themselves. They might even need a guide on how to use the printer, and a business doesn't want everyone running back to the IS department because they haven't cleaned the print nozzles properly. Individual departments are unlikely to have received the manufacturer's instructions if all printers have been purchased centrally by the IS department.

Training issues

This covers both hardware and software. Operational staff and managers are likely to need training on software and hardware, as well as on the business information system procedures and practices. Again, some documentation is likely to be required.

Software

Software needs to be installed, maintained and upgraded (where appropriate) across the business. You don't want end users to be downloading new versions on to their own PCs. You want to maintain consistency across the business. You will also need a manual for usage in the context of the business.

Security

There need to be firewalls in place, virus protection software to protect users and the system, and data protection procedures. This will affect, say, how a user signs into the system with passwords, and needs to be a co-ordinated policy across the company. These issues are considered more fully in the rest of this unit.

Other issues

The department or individual responsible for the information system also needs to consider:

■ procedures for data collection or input, and data processing

■ legal and regulatory requirements on the collection and use of data (see Topic 7)

■ co-ordination of information requirements of different functional areas.

---

assessment practice
Portfolio work

For your business activity or idea, draw up a list of issues that need addressing in implementing, maintaining and updating the information system. Allocate these issues to a department or individual within the business. Check that the organisational structure and hierarchy, and the information flow, will enable this department or individual to undertake this responsibility.

---

assessment practice
The Cottage Loaf

The Cottage Loaf is growing fast. It is now delivering bulk orders for lunch to local offices. The order must be phoned or e-mailed through before 11 am, and then it can be picked up or eaten at The Cottage Loaf. Large orders are delivered by a local courier company to premises within a radius of five miles of the café.

Katie and James are also looking at the supply side of the operation. They are wondering whether to combine their ordering systems with Katie's father's bakery. Perhaps a direct link to make orders would be helpful too?

A James has taken responsibility for the business's information system. Identify James's responsibilities for the information system as it grows and develops.

B What research should he be doing to find out about how best to meet the business's needs? What questions should he be asking suppliers and customers about their needs?

C What questions should he be asking information technology suppliers about what they can provide? What are the ongoing implications about using externally provided software and hardware?

Data security issues

Setting the scene: Information Commissioner's Office (ICO)

The Information Commissioner's Office is the UK's independent public body set up to promote access to official information and to protect personal information.

It regulates and enforces the Data Protection Act, the Freedom of Information Act, the Privacy and Electronic Communications Regulations and the Environmental Information Regulations. The ICO also provides guidance to organisations and individuals.

The ICO rules on eligible complaints and can take action when the law is broken. Reporting directly to Parliament, the Commissioner's powers include the ability to order compliance, using enforcement and decision notices, and prosecution.

For more information on the ICO visit its website at www.ico.gov.uk

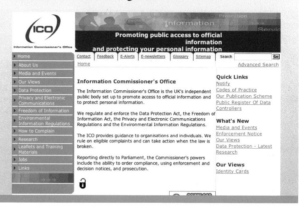

The legal framework

As you can see from the introduction, the government takes data security issues sufficiently seriously to have set up the ICO. Businesses should similarly take data security seriously. What are the issues? Any business must:

- conform to legal and self-regulatory constraints, and comply with legislation

- comply with the Freedom of Information Act if appropriate (or use the information that it obliges organisations to make available)

- supply accurate data to HM Revenue and Customs and Companies House for accounts and other statutory returns, including VAT, national insurance and PAYE

- safeguard commercially sensitive or confidential information useful to competitors

- keep paper-based back-up for legal and taxation purposes of data held on computers.

The main legal statutes that apply to the use, processing and storing of information are the Data Protection Act, Computer Misuse Act, Copyright Designs and Patents Act, Health and Safety (Display Screen Equipment) Regulations, and the Freedom of Information Act.

Data Protection Act

The Data Protection Act 1998 sets out eight principles for handling personal data, and protects the right of the individual to privacy and against misuse of personal information. The law applies to any business (or organisation) that holds data on individuals. Any personal data held by a business must be:

- secure

- accurate

- processed for limited purposes that are registered with the ICO

- fairly and lawfully processed

- adequate, relevant and not excessive

- not transferred to countries without adequate data protection law

- processed in line with an individual's own rights

- not kept for longer than is necessary.

If a business is storing personal data, then it needs to apply and register the details with the ICO. This applies to your bank, your doctor and dentist, your school, and any shop where you might work at weekends. The ICO needs to know who is storing the data, and be provided with a description of the type of data held, the purpose to which it will be put, and details of how the data will be kept safe and secure. The ICO also needs to be informed if the organisation has any plans to pass on the data to others or to transfer it out of the country.

If your data is held by an organisation then you have several rights under the Act. You can:

■ see a copy of the data

■ change any mistakes

■ prevent processing if it might cause you some distress

■ prevent the details being used for direct marketing, such as junk post or junk e-mail

■ prevent automated decisions such as in credit application

■ get compensation if data has been misused, lost or disclosed to other parties

■ complain to the ICO.

Computer Misuse Act

The Computer Misuse Act 1990 covers hacking, computer fraud and causing damage by spreading a virus. Of course, businesses are much more likely to be the victims of these crimes rather than the perpetrators, and in Topic 8 we look at the ways that any business can protect its data from these new types of external threats. The main provisions of the Computer Misuse Act concern:

■ hacking, by accessing programs or data without permission – you might do this "just for fun" to see whether you can get into a system, but it's illegal

■ fraud, by accessing programs or data with intent to commit a crime – if someone manages to make unauthorised changes to individuals' credit card or bank details so that money is paid into the fraudster's account, this is a crime and is just the same as stealing

■ unauthorised modifications, by writing or deliberately spreading a virus – if you develop a virus, or knowingly pass on one that you have received, again this is a crime.

Copyright, Designs and Patents Act

Next time you download a free software package such as Adobe Reader, look through the end user licence agreement (you can find this on Adobe's website, www.adobe.co.uk). Even though the software is free, there are still terms and conditions that protect the software manufacturer. The Copyright, Designs and Patents Act 1988 is designed to offer greater protection to an individual's or an organisation's intellectual property. It covers:

■ copying of software and manuals

■ using illegally copied software and manuals

■ using legally copied software but with an inadequate licence.

Health and Safety (Display Screen Equipment) Regulations

This law is particularly relevant to any business in which employees spend a considerable amount of time working at computers, such as call centres and telesales companies. The Health and Safety (Display Screen Equipment) Regulations 1992 cover issues such as design and positioning of the computer screens and chairs, lighting and ventilation. A business also has a general duty to ensure the safety of all electrical equipment.

Freedom of Information Act

The Freedom of Information Act 2000 came into force on 1 January 2005. It applies to public authorities which function in England, Wales and Northern Ireland. Anybody can request information and be told whether or not the public authority holds that information, and if so, to have that information communicated to them. It might be relevant, for example, for a company to want to know what planning applications are in process at the local authority that might affect its business, or where a new motorway might be built, or what new environmental regulations might be introduced in the areas in which it operates.

Financial accounts and statutory returns

A business is required by law to complete annual accounts. Sole traders and partnerships must compile accounts so that HM Revenue and Customs can assess the owners' income tax liabilities. Private and public limited companies must complete accounts for corporation tax purposes, and must file financial statements at Companies House. Obviously the data used in compiling these financial statements should be accurate, and a business must follow standard accounting procedures. Creative accounting can distort figures from year to year.

Any business that has employees is also required to submit tax (PAYE) and national insurance information on all its staff, taking the appropriate deductions from employees' salaries and making payments to the tax authorities. If a business is registered for value added tax (VAT) – and any business with a annual turnover above a minimum level set by the government must register – then it must submit quarterly returns to HM Revenue and Customs and make appropriate payments. Again, all this must be accurate.

A business must also ensure that all data on which its income tax returns are based is protected. This data must be stored for a period of at least six years, so that the authorities can investigate previous years'

returns. A business must keep paper back-ups of all financial and employee records that it uses to meet its taxation requirements.

Confidentiality agreements

Data and equipment needs protecting so that confidential information about customers, suppliers and the business doesn't fall into the wrong hands, either inadvertently or deliberately. As we discuss in Topic 8, there are a number of ways of controlling access to electronic data. Electronic and paper-based back-ups also need protecting. Confidential waste in the form of printouts of data, production reports, financial cash flows, etc. needs shredding and disposing of properly.

Staff need to be screened for suitability if they are likely to have access to sensitive information, and many organisations require employees to sign confidentiality agreements. Contracts may carry obligations not to join a rival company on leaving under certain conditions, for example.

Any negotiations with new clients or suppliers should also be covered by a confidentiality agreement. If a business hires an external information systems consultant, and provides data so that the consultant can design and test a new system, it doesn't want to find that the data has been passed to a competitor down the road. If it is taking out new professional indemnity insurance, and needs to release expected turnover figures to an insurance broker, it would expect this information to go no further.

---

stop and think

Two thirds of UK companies think the tax system has become more complicated over the last five years, a poll of business leaders revealed in 2006.

Richard Baron, head of taxation at the Institute of Directors, said: "Complexity in the tax system absorbs resources, clouds commercial decisions and can make the UK a less attractive investment location. Along with over-regulation, complicated tax rules are choking the life out of small businesses."

What do you think about this statement?

---

stop and think

How safe do you think laptops and palm-held devices such as the BlackBerry are?

Make some suggestions about how you could protect the information held on laptops and other portable devices.

---

assessment practice
Portfolio work

For your business activity or idea, draw up a list of relevant data security issues. How would you deal with them? Consider what documentation you need to put together for different end users in the business.

The Cottage Loaf now has three full-time members of staff. It is a private limited company. James is conducting an audit to check that the business is meeting all its legal obligations in respect of the way it holds and uses information. He is using the Business Link website to asses whether the business needs to register with the Information Commissioner's Office.

Access the Business Link website at www.businesslink.gov.uk/bdotg/action/ and click on "IT and e-commerce" and use the tools on the right-hand side of the page.

A Identify what data The Cottage Loaf needs to hold and submit to the government to meet its legal and statutory requirements.

B What impact would the Data Protection Act have on the business? Use Business Link's interactive tool to investigate whether James needs to apply to the ICO to register the business's activities.

Protecting data, users and equipment

Setting the scene: Firefox sorts out security flaws

This BBC report illustrates not only how you need to keep defence up to date against computer attack but that even the security programs themselves may not be perfect. The lesson is that any business should have more than one line of defence against hackers and bugs.

Computer users are being urged to update the Firefox web browser to close serious security holes. Some of the security lapses in Mozilla software, which Firefox is based on, could allow malicious hackers to hijack computers. There have been a total of 21 security flaws in various versions of Firefox, according to security firm Secunia.

Users are urged to download the latest versions of all Mozilla programs to protect their computers from attack. The Mozilla Foundations have released a new version of Firefox and Thunderbird which contains fixes to some of the security flaws.

Programs like Firefox have been thought to be more secure than other browsers such as Microsoft's Internet Explorer because of its links to the open-source software community.

There have been more than 100 million downloads of the Firefox software since its launch in 2004. However, Internet Explorer is still the world's most popular browser, with over 80 per cent of the market. Last year both browsers were hit by the same security bug.

Source: BBC News website, 20 April 2006

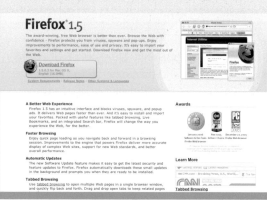

Safeguarding electronic data

When all data was in hard copy of some sort – personal record cards, financial accounts, reports, etc. – then a business could lock it in a fireproof filing cabinet. The cabinet could be locked in a room in a locked building with security staff, CCTV cameras and alarms linked to the police station. You can still do this to protect any hardware, but what about the software and the data within computerised information system? This is a very real issue for every business as it is likely to have at least some electronic data and is also likely to use electronic means of communication. Even the vast government systems are not immune from hackers. The tax credit computer system of the HMRC was targeted by gangs of organised criminals in 2005, which led to the closure of the online tax credit application system.

People have a number of reasons for trying to get access to a computer system:

KEY TERMS

A **virus** is a program that causes damage to a computer's data files or programs.

Spam is unsolicited junk e-mail, usually sent to thousands of e-mail addresses.

A **worm** is a special type of virus that replicates itself and uses up memory.

- criminal activity – gaining money by accessing individuals' bank accounts and credit card details

- revenge – from ex-employees or business partners who want to steal or destroy information

- sabotage – by students or "anoraks" who just want to see whether they can beat the system

- vandalism – to incapacitate a system for industrial or political reasons, such as when animal rights activists attack a pharmaceutical company's system, or just to be destructive

- industrial or political espionage – gaining commercially sensitive or politically sensitive information.

Someone – or some team – needs to take responsibility for managing data security issues within an information system. Otherwise, there are likely to be security breaches and someone in the system may allow non-authorised access. Small businesses suffer particularly with security breaches, as they often don't have the time, cash or expertise to bother with proper measures. According to a 2006 UK government information security breaches survey, on average small businesses suffer eight incidents a year, each one costing around £12,000 to put right.

Virus protection

A virus is a program that is designed to cause damage or destruction to a computer. It may erase data, or cause the system to crash, or it may be harmless until a certain date. Specific virus types include spyware that monitors the actions of the user, and Trojan horses that hide in apparently harmless programs to get into a computer and then emerge to cause damage. Viruses are often introduced as attachments to e-mails or buried within e-mails, and are commonly spread through junk e-mails or spam.

The "I Love You" virus which went round the world in May 2000 came as an e-mail attachment. When opened, the virus sent the same message to every address in the infected computer's Microsoft Outlook address book, and also deleted certain graphics and music files. Because of the widespread corporate and home use of Microsoft Outlook, 45 million users were affected. In the UK, it was estimated that the virus infected around 10 per cent of organisations to some extent, including the House of Commons, BT, Vodafone and Barclays Bank. Some businesses were forced to shut down for a short period to control the spread of the virus. Since this type of virus sends messages to addresses in an address book, then a recipient is likely to think that the message is legitimate – it comes from someone whose address you hold, so you open it!

Virus protection software, such as Norton AntiVirus and McAfee VirusScan, scans for and blocks incoming viruses. It is good practice to use an internet service provider (ISP) or e-mail service that provides virus, content and spam filters. You can use a firewall, which stops people accessing the computer without permission while it is connected to the internet. This can be installed on each PC in a network, and you can install a hardware router with a built-in firewall between your modem and your PC or the network.

Virus software needs continuously updating – on a weekly or even daily basis – as new viruses are developed, so new detection means have to be deployed. These updates are available as downloads from the software manufacturers' websites and need to be installed on each PC.

business practice
Spam

Statistics from security firm Sophos show that China is fast catching up the US as a source of junk e-mail. According to Sophos, 23.1 per cent of spam comes from computers in the US and 21.9 per cent comes from China. [See Figure 13.9 for the top ten spam nations.]

Graham Cluley, Sophos' senior technology consultant, said that in 2004 more than half of all the spam in the world was coming from the US. This has dropped, he said, because the US was making efforts to find and prosecute prolific spammers. More than 70 per cent of the 13.2 billion spam messages sent every day are now believed to be relayed via hijacked home computers of unsuspecting net users.

Many of the malicious hackers controlling these herds of so-called zombie computers rent them out to spammers who want to hide the origins of their unwanted e-mails. In a typical month half of the most active computer viruses are those tailored to find vulnerable home computers and turn them into zombies.

"It's imperative that computer users worldwide put better defences in place to prevent their computers from being converted into spam-spewing zombies," said Mr Cluley.

Source: BBC News website, 20 April 2006

Figure 13.9: Top spam nations

United States	23.1%
China (inc. Hong Kong)	21.9%
South Korea	9.8%
France	4.3%
Poland	3.8%
Spain	3.3%
Germany	3.0%
Brazil	2.9%
Japan	2.0%
United Kingdom	1.9%

Source: Sophos

Not all viruses come through spam: others can be introduced through data transfer. An employee might copy some information on to a CD-ROM from their home computer and bring it in to their work PC. The CD-ROM may be carrying a virus that the employee's home computer virus protection software didn't pick up – perhaps the employee hasn't got round to downloading the latest security patches and updates. This virus will be copied on to the work PC, and then will be able to access all PCs in the rest of the business through the network. Users should avoid transferring data in this way.

Users should also not download material from unknown or disreputable websites, or download unexpected attachments from addresses they know. Forwarding e-mail alerts and chain letters to others can help spread viruses.

Password protection

A common way of protecting data and an information system is through a password and user name system. Password protection can restrict access to information and programs to specified users or specified PCs. You can restrict access also by specifying which users or files can run particular programs (execute rights), read programs (read rights) but not change or amend data (write rights), or delete files (delete rights). Other protocols can restrict the installation of hardware or new software so that control of the information technology is maintained in one area. You may not want individual staff in functional areas trying to install new software.

Perhaps your school or college has an information system that you can access using your user name or number and your password. Perhaps you have another user name and password to use your local library facilities, or to access your e-mail account on a home computer.

Passwords are not foolproof! Others can gain access to networks if passwords are too easy to steal or to work out. Users, and this means you as an individual too, should use good practices:

- don't write passwords down anywhere near the computer or in your wallet with your bank card

- don't use a word found in a dictionary

- don't use the names of people, places or pets or birth dates

- share a password with a colleague or a friend

- don't use the same password for more than one account

- don't use the default password provided by the vendor

In large organisations operating in environments such as banking and finance, security is taken to another level. The reputation of these businesses demands:

- confidentiality – data accessible to authorised personnel only

- integrity – data has not been tampered with

- non-repudiation – the data has been sent by the sender and received by the recipient

- authentication – hardware, software and people are as they say they are.

These businesses will have a security infrastructure that uses encryption technology. This converts data into an illegible form (encrypts) which can be converted back to its original form (decrypts) by a unique public and private key system. It is used to ensure confidentiality and integrity. Digital signatures might be used. These are electronic signatures that authenticate the originator of the message in much the same way as a handwritten signature. They can be used with an encrypted message where confidentiality and identity are required. Some organisations also issue digital certificates. These are similar to credit cards and they are issued by a certification authority. Each certificate contains detailed information about the user.

Scams

There are many scams used by criminals to try to get access to your online personal banking details and other confidential information. For example, some criminals design e-mails that look as though they come from your bank, with an e-mail address that looks authentic. They will ask you to confirm your banking details for some (spurious) reason, directing you to a bogus website, and then, of course, they can use these details to gain direct access to your bank account.

Watch for other scams, especially in small businesses. If The Cottage Loaf receives a letter requesting money to renew its domain registration, James should not send the money without checking that this is actually from the company with which he registered the domain name. It may be bogus.

Equipment security

Hardware needs to be secure in an office environment, just like any other valuable equipment. Apart from the obvious lock and key and security guards approach, a business can introduce measures such as access controls. This means that only authorised users gain access to the business premises, by using "swipe cards", electronic keypad codes, smart cards, or biometric devices such as iris or fingerprint recognition.

Other measures might include:

- bolting and chaining computers to desks or floors

- storing back-up files in fireproof and bombproof safes, or in different "safe" locations

- infrared identification markers

- intruder detection systems such as internal and external CCTV cameras and monitoring

- motion detection alarms.

Data storage

All the data in the information system must be backed up regularly. These back-ups should be stored in a protected environment, safe from fire, loss or theft. It's pointless storing the back-ups in the same place as the original computer – if one is lost, then the other will be too. Regular backing up might need to be undertaken on an hourly or daily basis, depending on the business.

If the organisation is dependent on the data in the system to carry out its business, then it must have back-up files that are absolutely "bullet-proof" and can be immediately activated. The business needs to have a disaster plan it can put into operation if the worst happens. Some businesses may even need to duplicate their IT facilities completely in a separate location.

The Buncefield oil depot disaster in 2005 wrecked the many offices and warehouses in the immediate area – some were completely destroyed. And given the unstable nature of the remaining buildings left standing, staff were not allowed to recover any equipment. The companies affected had to depend on information that was not held on the site. The effects of the disaster were far-reaching – appointment booking systems for some regional hospitals and payrolls for many organisations were affected, as these systems were outsourced to companies that operated near the Buncefield depot.

To help large organisations manage information security issues and put in place appropriate policies and procedures, there is an internationally recognised Information Security Management Standard ISO 17799. Published in 2000, this offers guidelines on best practice. A business can use this standard to develop and manage its own information security. It also indicates to other organisations that it has adopted good data management standards and practices.

stop and think

What insurance would a business need to cover a disaster and the subsequent loss of data and facilities? How easy do you think it would be to get cover for all eventualities?

Completing your portfolio

Using information from www.getsafeonline.org on "protect your PC", "protect yourself" and "protect your business", write some guidance for the individual or department that has responsibility for the information system that underpins your business activity. This should cover data and equipment security. Devise documentation for users on procedures to be followed for collecting and accessing electronic data in the system.

You should now have a complete picture of the information system for your business activity or idea including:

- overall objectives of the information system and the business

- data required and how it is collected

- information needs of the business and end users

- security needs of the system

- organisational responsibilities and issues

- information flow

- processes and procedures for all parts of the information system with documentation

- design of the system

- management, maintenance and updating of the system.

You need to evaluate the suitability of your proposed information system and assess its ability to support your business activity or idea. You also need to identify the costs and benefits of the system, and the implications of implementing the system within the organisation. Is the sophistication – and the cost and complexity – of what you propose out of proportion to the overall objectives?

Measures of system success in supporting the business activity might include:

- systems quality – is it reliable and does it function properly

- information quality – is it useful, accurate and up to date

- information use and flow – does it get to the right people in an efficient way

- user satisfaction – are people happy working within the system at all levels from data collection to decision-making

- business impact – does the business have the right information for decision-making at all levels?

The Cottage Loaf

The Cottage Loaf has grown. It now has an office area with four networked PCs and various peripherals. There are three full-time staff and a number of part-time staff that may access the data, which includes information on sales, suppliers and staff.

Katie and James are considering making the café a wireless environment, so they can operate their own operations more easily and can access data from their laptops throughout the building. They also have in mind that they will use the wireless network to attract customers who want to continue working while they have lunch.

A Write a business security plan for The Cottage Loaf. You might find the Department of Trade and Industry IT risk assessment tool helpful. You can find it on the Business Link website (www.businesslink.gov.uk)

B What are the security issues of introducing a wireless environment?

THIS UNIT EXPLORES THE TYPES OF CHANGE THAT businesses might encounter. The major focus of the unit is change in small businesses, but it also considers the types of change experienced by large companies as well as not-for-profit organisations such as schools and hospitals.

We look at the possible causes of change that might affect a business. Change can be caused by internal factors as well as those outside the business – a new managing director or chief executive can create huge changes within an organisation. We consider what the business is seeking to gain as a result of change. A business is much more likely to manage change effectively if all employees are clear on what the organisation is hoping to achieve from the process.

To understand the process and nature of change it is essential to understand the potential effects of change. The starting point is research: the business must investigate how change might affect the business. The human dimension of change management is vital. This unit examines the importance of teams to manage projects, as well as other human dimensions such as creating a consensus for change.

Project plans are necessary to manage change, and this unit considers the techniques that can be used assist project planning. Effective management of change also requires that managers can identify the major factors that might prevent change, and propose and effect contingency plans. The concluding topic addresses these issues.

Managing change

Topic 1

Topic 1 | The internal causes of change

Setting the scene: Herbert Engineering

Herbert Engineering is a small company in Norfolk that was established in 1972. By 2005, it had grown to employ 130 people with an annual turnover of £9 million.

The company is best known for designing and manufacturing machinery to handle potatoes and other vegetables. However, managers have taken the decision to diversify the company's product range. Perhaps influenced by the increasing popularity of air travel and rising concerns about security, Herbert Engineering is to build specialist baggage conveyors for use in airports.

Herbert's conveyor system, called Pathfinda, automatically moves bags into the centre of the conveyor belt so that they can pass through the X-ray machine. If bags are not positioned centrally, existing scanning equipment will not work. Until now they have had to be positioned by hand.

Pathfinda can be slotted into existing conveyor belt systems and has potential for sales throughout the world. The system can handle up to 14 bags each minute and is designed to speed up the process of clearing passengers' baggage through security at airports.

What is change?

The dictionary defines change as "to become different or to alter". This has many meanings for organisations. Businesses encounter change at many levels. Indeed, change is continuous for most businesses. An important element of a manager's work at any level within an organisation is planning for, overseeing and dealing with the consequences of change.

KEY TERMS

Retrenchment is a contraction in the activities of a business. This could entail the closing down of a factory, office or shop, or maybe just a minor reduction in staffing.

Organisational growth is an increase in the scale of operations of a business. It could be shown by higher levels of sales, and possibly an increase in resources.

Diversification occurs when businesses produce an increased range of goods and services, possibly selling these in new markets.

A **driver of change** is simply a factor which promotes change, such as changing consumer tastes.

At the outset of this unit, we will consider the causes of change and the issues that it can create within an organisation. We can split change into two categories: strategic change and tactical change.

Strategic change

Strategic change is large-scale change that affects all elements of the business over a long period of time. This type of change is normally handled by senior managers within the organisation.

Let's consider an example. In February 2006 Tesco, the UK's largest retailer, announced that it was to invest £250 million to create a number of convenience stores (small supermarkets) in the United States. The project was being driven by a team under the leadership of Tim Mason, Tesco's marketing and property director. There are a number of factors which have promoted this change at Tesco. The company is committed to growth as a corporate objective, and it has been criticised for holding a too dominant position in retailing in the UK – so growth overseas is a logical strategy.

Strategic change is not limited to large businesses such as Tesco. Small businesses can experience strategic change as well. A local bakery might decide to open a café to increase sales of its bread, cakes and pies. This will have significant implications for the staffing, finance and marketing of the business as well as its operations. This wide impact on the business makes it a strategic decision.

Tactical change

Tactical change is usually on a smaller scale, and only affects a part of the business. Thus the bakery might experience tactical change when its employees are required to complete a course of hygiene training because of a change in the law. This would impact on the bakery's employees, but the effects would only be short-term during the period of training.

Large businesses can also experience change at a tactical level. Tesco might experience problems with the supply of oranges from its usual growers due to a poor harvest. This might require the company to source oranges from different suppliers in another country or to increase its supply of other fruit. This change only affects certain parts of the business and is likely to be short term.

Identifying when change is necessary

A driver of change is simply any factor which promotes change. In this topic, we focus on internal drivers of change, leaving a consideration of external drivers of change to Topic 2. Whatever the cause of change, whether it is internal or external, businesses have a number of ways of identifying that change is needed.

Feedback from customers

Businesses aim to satisfy customers, and evidence of customer dissatisfaction is clearly a worrying sign. Businesses can receive feedback from dissatisfied customers in a variety of ways. A rise in customers' complaints may indicate that the product quality is declining or inadequate. A small restaurant may, for example, find that increasing numbers of customers are sending food back or complaining to waiters. This tells the restaurant manager that some change is necessary to improve the quality of the food.

More formal systems such as market research may also indicate that change is required. Lloyds TSB (see "A change of script" panel) used market research to reveal customer dissatisfaction with the service supplied by its call centres. As a consequence, the bank's managers implemented a programme of change which was supported by all staff.

Employees at call centres operated by Lloyds TSB have been told by their managers to abandon the scripts they normally work from when talking to customers. The managers conducted research with customers and had discovered that the use of scripts was a major cause of annoyance.

The decision was approved by 86 per cent of call staff employees. Many claimed that the change would allow them to carry out their jobs more efficiently and to deal with enquiries more quickly. Lloyd TSB's managers were convinced that the decision would improve the bank's service. Martin Dodd said: "By ditching the scripts we are giving staff the freedom to treat every caller as an individual and build a much closer rapport with customers."

Employees

Employees who have close and frequent contact with customers are often best placed to identify that change is needed. This is particularly true of staff who work in customer services or who are part of an organisation's sales force. These employees are in a good position to identify any limitations in the organisation's products – say, for example, in comparison to products supplied by competitors – or changes in consumer tastes and fashions.

Even employees who have relatively little contact with customers can identify the need for change. Managers might notice that staff are not being used efficiently or effectively. They might suggest ways that technology might be introduced in the business to allow staff to be used more effectively. For example, by introducing automated telephone answering equipment, a business might allow its reception staff more time to deal with personal enquiries or to carry out a wider range of duties.

Suggestion schemes and quality circles (groups of employees who make proposals to improve the business's performance) are other ways in which the need for change can be identified within the business.

Analysing data

Unexpected changes in costs, sales figures or other performance data may indicate the need for change. This might be particularly true if results are very different from budgets, suggesting that the business is failing to meet (or perhaps exceeding) expectations. In 2006 many UK hospital trusts discovered that their wage bills had increased more than expected and were forced to reduce staffing levels. For example, the James Paget Hospital in Gorleston, Norfolk announced in April 2006 that it was to make 300 employees redundant after its spending exceeded its annual budget by £4 million.

Internal causes

Internal change is normally initiated by the organisation itself. Managers take decisions to expand or contract the business, to diversify its product range, to trade in new markets. Internal change should not be a surprise: it is possible to prepare and plan for this type of change.

Organisational growth and contraction

Many organisations have growth as a primary aim. Decisions on expansion can have profound effects throughout organisations. In March 2004 the northern-based supermarket group Morrisons bought one of its rivals Safeway, which was at the time a slightly larger company. In the months that followed this acquisition, the consequences were felt in all areas of the business. Morrisons had to close some existing branches, make radical changes to its supply systems and refit over 300 supermarkets to match the Morrisons brand.

The cause of this strategic change was internal. Morrisons' board of directors took the decision and was entirely responsible for the changes which the business was required to undertake. However, the Morrisons case also illustrates the long-term nature of some change. Two years after the takeover, the newly enlarged company was in financial difficulty. The costs of the takeover had exceeded budgets, and the company was making employees redundant following the announcement of a £313 million loss for the financial year. The management team recognised that some job losses were essential to reduce costs and restore the company to profitability.

Change can be an experience that lasts a period of years, rather than a short-term event, as the takeover of Safeway by Morrisons illustrates. This case also highlights the fact that expansion and contraction (or retrenchment) can both be drivers of change within an organisation.

Organisational growth is equally important for small businesses. The change in the licensing laws allows owners of public houses more freedom regarding the hours that they open. Relatively few licensed premises have opted to change opening hours significantly, but a manager might believe that the potential for substantial rises in sales revenue exists if the pub's opening hours are extended. The driver for change in this case could be the desire to increase the business's turnover and profits.

Leadership and management styles

Leaders and managers can use a variety of styles to carry out their work. Some managers retain tight control over information and decisions – this style is termed autocratic or authoritarian leadership. In contrast, other managers give subordinates a major role in decision-making, and empower their staff so that they have a major degree of control over their working lives. In between these two extremes there are many other leadership and management styles. (For a fuller discussion of leadership styles, see Unit 12 pages 164–68.)

Given this variety of styles, the appointment of a new manager or leader can have considerable implications for how the business operates and for the working lives of the organisation's employees. Indeed, it is unlikely that two leaders will employ identical, or even similar, leadership styles. For example, a move towards a more democratic style of leadership may mean that junior employees are given more complex tasks to complete and are expected to take more decisions.

In 2006 one of the UK's best known retailers, Body Shop, was taken over by the global cosmetics manufacturer L'Oreal. Body Shop is recognised for its ethical approach and the distinctive style of its founder and former chief executive Anita Roddick. Body Shop's 6,900 employees are likely to experience changes following the takeover, some of which will relate to a different management style.

Focusing or diversification

A business that focuses its activities identifies the most important part of what it does, and ceases other work that may be less profitable or peripheral to its core operation. In 2006, for example, Marks & Spencer sold its shops in the United States to allow it to focus on its retailing operations in the UK. Focusing on core activity in this way can allow a business to concentrate on what it is best at, and may reduce the workload on staff at all levels in the organisation. Businesses that are experiencing periods of poor performance (declining profits, for example) may be most vulnerable to this type of change.

The change introduced by Marks & Spencer would have had implications for the company's staff in the UK, particularly those who directly administered the operation in the United States, and also for its UK-based suppliers. It may have resulted in job losses and changing roles for the company's employees.

Diversification is the opposite approach to focusing on core operations, and can be an important internal driver of change. Diversification is pursued by businesses as a means of growth, possibly when existing markets are saturated. Tesco has diversified into selling clothes and electrical products as well as financial services because growth of sales in its core grocery market has slowed. Other businesses diversify to spread risk. Operating in different markets makes a sudden slump in sales less likely.

Some attempts at diversification can be highly imaginative. A farmer in Kent has responded to low prices in agricultural markets by growing a field of maize – a very tall crop – and then constructing a maze within the field. Visitors pay to enter the maze and take on the challenge of finding its centre. The farmer who created the maize expects to attract 30,000 to 40,000 visitors during the summer. At the end of the summer, the remaining crop will be harvested as usual.

Some businesses almost constantly diversify, using a common brand name. Virgin and the easyGroup – the firm behind easyJet, easyCar, easyCinema, etc. – are examples of companies that operate in this way. The impact of change in this type of organisation can be lessened by creating a separate company for each new element of the enterprise.

Business implications

Internal factors driving change have several implications for businesses. They need to consider the personnel, resource and information issues.

Human issues

Change can result in employees being required to undertake different duties: they may be called upon to take on more demanding tasks, to exercise new skills or to work in a new location. Change may also break up existing work groups and replace them with new teams. Some employees may be uncomfortable with the changes in their working lives, and this may create some resistance to the organisation's plans. It can require significant skill on the part of managers to overcome this resistance.

Resource issues

Expansion or contraction has implications for the amount and mix of resources needed by a business. Buildings, machinery and other assets may need to be purchased or sold. A change in leadership may result in different assets being required. When Arun Sarin replaced Sir Christopher Gent as chief executive of Vodafone he sanctioned the building of a major new head office in Newbury. Bringing the company's administration together in one building reflected his more consultative management style, but involved heavy expenditure by Vodafone.

Information issues

A changing business will have different information needs. Expansion into a new market requires market research to understand the needs of new customers. The farmer who installed a maze at his farm will have had to research consumer needs as well as the health and safety issues surrounding his proposal. He will have had to investigate what other services visitors might require, such as guides and a café. This would be vital to manage the change process successfully.

Pat Marshall manages *Natural Fare*, a vegetarian café in Frome in Somerset. Pat's café has an excellent reputation and is mostly full on the six days it is open. Pat has decided to extend the café into an adjoining property which she owns. This will double the café's capacity and hopefully will increase its profitability. Identify the cause of change in Pat's business. What issues might it create? You should consider staffing, physical resources, customer reactions and information needs.

a s s e s s m e n t p r a c t i c e
Starting work on your portfolio

This unit is assessed through a portfolio. You are expected to work as part of a team to produce a programme for managing change within a specific business scenario.

Your piece of research should be a practical activity for a team of people. It should be manageable to enable you to complete it successfully. The best portfolios are likely to come from exploring links with small local businesses or possibly with the school or college. Suitable projects should not be too ambitious and should offer you the chance to carry out a number of practical activities. Examples of feasible projects include:

■ considering how a local garden centre might improve its marketing in response to a new competitor opening nearby

■ improving school or college finances by making school facilities available to the local community during evenings and weekends.

Your portfolio must have four elements.

Part A – You should explain the change that is to take place such as improving the business's marketing, the factors that are driving change and sources of possible resistance to change, and set out how the proposed change programme will affect customers, employees and the business itself.

Part B – You must prepare a presentation for a proposal for change. Your proposal must include details on the aims and objectives of the change programme and its individual tasks. You need to set out how the business will organise people and other resources. There should be a clear statement of your individual contribution to the change process.

Part C – This element is part of the planning for the presentation required in Part B. You will need to analyse the activities that are required to complete the change programme. In relation to the marketing of a local garden centre, this may include activities such as researching customers' needs and the offerings of the new competitor, and assessing the business's current marketing. You will need to divide the tasks amongst the members of the team. The responsibilities should be allocated to distribute the workload evenly between team members.

Part D – You need to evaluate the effectiveness of the project undertaken and its chances of success. You should also evaluate the performance of the team, and how this might have affected the likelihood of the change project succeeding.

Even at this early stage in the development of your portfolio evidence, there are tasks that you can carry out in preparation for later activities. The first thing that you may wish to consider is the team that you are going to be a part of to complete this portfolio activity. You should start to discuss this as soon as possible with your teachers and fellow students.

Your team should be made up of people with different skills. You might need people who are good with IT, people who are confident in interviewing the employees of a business, people who are organised and can organise others, and possibly someone with leadership skills to ensure everything gets done.

The external causes of change

Setting the scene: a changing role for telephone boxes

Mobile phones are a social phenomenon. They change the way we communicate with one another. This social change has affected a number of businesses, not least the telecommunications group BT. It has seen a substantial decline in the usage of phone boxes.

Phone boxes are slowly becoming redundant. BT has seen a 40 per cent fall in revenues from payphones over the past few years, and as a result BT has removed some boxes which are little used.

However, the company has come up with other responses to this particular type of change. BT has installed ATMs (cash machines) in several phone boxes in Cardiff to get greater use from the facilities

The company has other ideas for the phone box. It plans to move the phone to the exterior of the box, allowing it to install vending machines inside the phone boxes. The vending machines will dispense chocolate, crisps and soft drinks. The new idea was piloted in the West Midlands.

Can you suggest other uses for BT's underutilised telephone boxes? What issues might the company face as a result of your proposals?

The types of external change

External change is caused by drivers outside an organisation's direct control. External change is normally imposed upon an organisation, but this does not mean that this change always has negative consequences. On the contrary, many businesses have benefited from social and economic changes that have boosted their sales and profits. In this topic, we review four major types of external change.

KEY TERMS

Interest rates are the price of borrowed money.

Exchange rates are the price of one currency expressed in terms of another. For example, at April 2006, £1 was equivalent to €1.44 and $1.75.

Taxation is a charge imposed by governments on the trading activities of organisations and individuals.

1 Political change

Political change results from the actions of government. In the UK, there are four sources of new legislation and regulation:

- the central government at Westminster

- national governments in Wales, Scotland and Northern Ireland (subject to political agreement)

- local governments throughout the UK

- the European Union (regulations and directives).

The UK and EU governments pass a variety of laws that affect how businesses operate. These laws often have disproportionate effects on small businesses. Since 2003 the UK government has either passed or confirmed EU laws that:

- limit the hours that drivers can work each day

- impose strict controls on the ways in which businesses dispose of waste products

- allow fathers two weeks' paid leave on the birth of a child.

In November 2005, the provisions of the Licensing Act 2003 came into force, which allowed supermarkets, pubs and nightclubs to sell alcohol for extended hours (including, in some cases, up to 24 hours per day). The effects of this new law were felt by many businesses according to research by the BBC. The BBC survey found that over 60,000 businesses had applied for extensions in the hours that they were selling alcohol. Only 1121 had applied for 24-hour licences, allowing them to trade all day and night. Many pubs and clubs will just open for longer hours on Friday and Saturday nights, while a small number of supermarkets (mainly in cities) have taken advantage of the new laws to trade beyond midnight.

The implications of this change fall mainly in the area of staffing. Premises selling alcohol will need more staff to work the longer hours they remain open, often until the early hours of the morning. It can be difficult to recruit staff to work these anti-social hours, and they may need to pay higher wage rates to attract and retain employees. This can increase the business's costs and may make the extension in trading hours less profitable than managers might have expected.

Political change can also impact on businesses without the introduction of new legislation. The government is currently promoting healthy diets for UK citizens. This results from growing concerns about increasing levels of obesity, especially among children. The government has engaged in discussion with food manufacturers to persuade them to voluntarily reduce the amount of fat and salt in processed foods. Some businesses have responded to this by altering their products. In 2006 Walkers Snack Foods Ltd launched a new range of crisps with significant reductions in the fat and salt content.

stop and think

Have the meals provided at your school or college changed recently? Is it possible for you to select a meal which contains large amounts of fruit and vegetables and small amounts of fat?

2 Economic change

Economic change can take a variety of forms. We will look at four of the most important factors – interest rates, exchange rates, taxation and incomes. Note, however, that other economic factors such as government spending, unemployment and inflation (the rate at which prices increase) also impact on business. Changes in any of these economic factors can have profound effects on individual businesses.

Economic changes are not always predictable. They can occur quickly and their effects can be considerable. Small businesses in particular are vulnerable to changes in the economic environment because they do not have the financial strength to survive rising costs or sudden slumps in demand.

Interest rates

A change in interest rates can increase or reduce the costs of borrowing for businesses and consumers. This can have a substantial direct effect on a business's costs and an indirect impact on its sales. A rate rise may lead to a small hotel paying higher interest charges on its loans. At the same time, the hotel may find that business begins to decline because a rise in the cost of mortgages means that consumers have less disposable income to spend on luxuries such as short breaks staying in hotels.

The basic interest rate (the base rate) is set by the monetary policy committee at the Bank of England. The committee has a remit to set interest rates to ensure that the economy meets the government's inflation targets. It meets each month to decide whether to change the base rate. The interest rates set by other lenders, such as mortgage companies and the high street banks, usually alter in response to changes in the Bank of England base rate.

Exchange rates

An exchange rate is the price of one currency expressed in terms of another currency. A rise in the exchange rate of the pound (for example, from £1 = €1.44 to £1 = €1.60) means that any imported products are cheaper, and UK exports are more expensive for overseas purchasers. This can have substantial effects on a business's operating costs.

If exchange rates for the pound rise, then UK importers benefit but exporters face potential difficulties. For example, a small-scale manufacturer of garden furniture might find that, in these circumstances, its costs of imported hardwood fall. This might provide the business with the opportunity to lower prices or make higher profits on each sale.

However, a small UK hotel mentioned earlier might suffer as tourists from abroad will find that its services are more expensive (more of their currency is required to exchange for each pound). As a result, the hotel might attract fewer guests unless it can offer foreign visitors a special price.

stop and think

Suppose the pound falls in value against the dollar. How might this affect:

- a travel agent that organises holidays to Florida
- a stately home in Oxfordshire that has many visitors from the United States?

Taxation

Taxation is a charge imposed by governments on the trading activities of organisations and individuals. Individuals and sole trader businesses pay income tax. Companies pay corporation tax on their profits. Individuals and businesses pay value added tax (VAT) on purchases of goods and services.

An increase in taxation can generally be expected to worsen trading conditions for most businesses. Increases in income tax mean that consumers retain less of their income. This means that their spending on non-essential and luxury products is likely to fall. A jeweller may experience a large fall in sales following a decision by the government to increase income tax. In contrast, a reduction in rates of corporation tax may boost spending by businesses as they retain a larger share of their profits, which they might use to spend on investment or in paying dividends to shareholders.

Incomes

Average incomes in the UK have doubled since 1975, and the pattern of spending by UK consumers has changed accordingly. This economic change has resulted in increasing demand for a range of services including foreign travel, meals in restaurants, electrical and technological products, and personal services such as cleaners and gardeners.

3 Social change

Social change is continuous and is particularly relevant for businesses in many consumer sectors. Changes in tastes and fashions can affect the clothing industry, all stages of the food industry as well as music, entertainment and the leisure industry. These industries are also affected by the social trend towards healthier lifestyles.

It is impossible to cover all the social changes that are impacting on UK businesses in a relatively short section of this book, and indeed social change is not constant, with new factors emerging regularly. However, these examples give some idea of its importance as a driver of change.

- Consumers are increasingly concerned about food quality. They are choosing "healthy" foods, leading to increasing sales of low-fat products, organic foodstuffs, and fruit and vegetables. This change offers opportunities for small businesses selling high-quality foodstuffs. Some farms have switched to organic production to meet rising demand. One benefit for farmers is that they are able to charge premium prices for high-quality organic products.

- Changes are taking place in the ways in which people travel. More people are travelling overseas. Some have taken advantage of cheap air travel to buy second homes overseas near to airports. Companies such as Ryanair are the most obvious beneficiaries, with rising sales and profits, but there are implications for the UK tourist industry and estate agents selling property overseas.

- Increasing numbers of people are living alone in single-person households. The government estimates that by 2021 more than 35 per cent of households will contain a single person. This requires more homes, and it is estimated that there will be a 20 per cent increase in the number of UK homes to nearly 25 million.

The UK's population is changing. The birth rate fell from 14.1 births per thousand women in 1975 to 11.4 in 2002. The UK's population is expected to rise to 67 million (from its current figure of 60 million) by 2050 before declining. The number of young people as a proportion of the overall population will decline, and a higher proportion will be of retirement age. This social change offers opportunities for businesses supplying products associated with older people.

stop and think

Identify three small businesses that might be affected by the estimated 20 per cent increase in the number of homes in the UK over the next fifteen years. In each case, explain the likely effects on the business.

The UK's card shops are carrying a larger stock as society changes. The latest cards carry far from traditional messages. Today, you can buy cards with messages such as:

■ For you, Mummy and Daddy, on your wedding day

■ Congratulations on your divorce

■ To a special Step-Mum.

These cards reflect the complexity of modern society. Don Lewin, chairman of Clintons, the UK's largest greeting cards retailer said: "We live in a changing world, and the messages on the new cards reflect this."

Since 1976 the divorce rate has more than doubled, with 154,000 couples separating in 2004. Over two million couples cohabit, and the proportion of children born outside wedlock has risen to 41 per cent. These social changes have offered opportunities for the designers of greeting cards.

Source: adapted from Daily Mail, 2 May 2005

4 Technological change

The pace of technological change has accelerated during the last twenty years, and this has huge implications for businesses. The key aspects of technological change can be separated into three categories: processes, products and communications.

Processes

All businesses have greater opportunities to use technology in supplying goods and services. Many manufacturers have installed robots on their production lines. Robots offer advantages in terms of 24-hour production and uniform quality. They also avoid issues involved in employing people, such as training, illness and industrial disputes. However, the use of robots as part of a manufacturing system involves a substantial investment, and a business may require skilled staff to operate and maintain this automated technology. It is not just manufacturing that can benefit: technology helps smaller businesses in the service sector too. Small shops can use technology to record sales and simultaneously monitor stock levels. It is possible to extend this system to allow automatic reordering of items.

Products

Technology has thrown up many new products. Obvious examples include MP3 players, chip and pin credit cards, games consoles and mobile phones. The impact of these changes on large companies is apparent. Nokia, the Finnish manufacturer of mobile phones, and Vodafone, one of the world's largest suppliers of mobile phone services, have both expanded enormously following the introduction of mobile phones.

New technologically advanced products drive change in other smaller businesses. A number of small companies have emerged to write games to be played on games consoles. Charities have used competitions based on text messages to raise money. Many shops have been set up across the UK to sell mobile phones.

Communications

Changes in technology have revolutionised business communications. Many businesses sell their goods and services on the internet, and the value of online sales is rising rapidly. In 2005, UK consumers spent £8,200 million online, a rise of 28.9 per cent on 2004. In the same period, sales growth in retail shops was virtually static. Large businesses such as Amazon have embraced this change, but it has benefited a huge range of small businesses. For example, owners running small hotels and bed & breakfast accommodation throughout the UK have benefited by being able to advertise their services online.

The development of affordable online communication has allowed small businesses flexible access to a large market with no geographical limitations, offering the prospect of increased sales and profits. Many companies have grown with the rise in use of the internet. For example, in 1993 the budget airline easyJet only carried 30,000 passengers who booked online. But it has used the internet to drive sales, and by 2005 it has approaching 30 million passengers.

Technological change creates issues for all organisations. Using technology requires staff to learn new skills. If they cannot be retrained, a business may need to recruit new people with the specific technological skills and experience. Technology can affect the way in which a business operates. It may, for example, allow people to be replaced by machinery. The growth of online banking has enable the UK's banks to reduce the numbers of staff employed in branches.

Technology creates opportunities for entrepreneurs. It encourages the development of new products and new ways of doing business. Even small estate agents

Martyn Clarke is the golf professional at Great Yarmouth and Caister Golf Club in Norfolk. Martyn provides lessons to golfers but also runs the club's golf shop, selling a wide range of equipment and clothes for the game.

Martyn is concerned about the future of his shop due to the increasing sales of golf equipment on the internet and through auction sites such as eBay. Martyn fears that many small club shops will disappear as customers focus on price and ignore the benefits of specialist advice that he, and other golf professionals, can offer. Club professionals can

advise customers on clubs to suit their particular style of play, can let them "try before they buy", and will provide after-sales service.

The impact of internet sales could destroy the club professional, says Martyn. "To be brutally honest, I feel that in the next five years there will be far fewer pro shops. Clubs will just have a little shop selling maybe balls and tees." However, Martyn is using technology to fight back. He is designing his own website to promote all aspects of his work.

Source: adapted from Eastern Daily Press, 18 March 2005

---

are able to maintain websites showing potential house buyers their portfolio, with virtual tours providing many views of the properties. However, technological change also brings problems. Costs may

rise because of the purchase of the equipment and the need to retrain staff. Redundancies may need to be made as machinery replaces people.

---

assessment practice
Pat's café

Pat Marshall manages *Natural Fare* a vegetarian café in Frome in Somerset. Pat has agreed to expand her café due to its increasing popularity. However, she is worried that there are so many external factors that could affect her café that the expansion might not be wise.

A Identify one social and one economic factor that could affect Pat's café and force her to introduce changes. In each case, explain the nature of the change and how it might affect Pat's business.

B Do you agree with the view that Pat's café is unlikely to be affected by technological change? Explain your answer.

---

assessment practice
Deciding upon a business

In the assessment practice at the end of Topic 1, you were advised put together a team to begin your portfolio work. Once you have created a team, the next stage in building your portfolio of evidence is to decide upon a business and an aspect of change that you wish to investigate.

At this stage you have studied the internal and external causes of change, and this equips you to analyse likely scenarios on which to base your portfolio. Choose a business and a project that is small and manageable. This is not a time to be too ambitious. A small-scale change that might be part of a larger change would be ideal. You should look at local businesses and perhaps your school or college for inspiration.

Topic 3 Organisational aims and change

Setting the scene: Morgan Design is going green

Morgan Design is a small manufacturing business in Salisbury, Wiltshire. The company makes high-quality bespoke furniture, and has a reputation for being one of the best in its field in the UK.

The business's philosophy is to act as a model of environmental care for other small organisations and workshops in the community. The aim of being environmentally friendly is a tough challenge for the business, but one which it intends to meet.

Managing director George Martin said: "We work with wood, the most environmentally friendly product there is, and we source all timber from sustainable forests and use any off-cuts to heat our workshops. To finish the manufacturing process, we use materials that are environmentally friendly." To finish products, the company uses cellulose, polyesters and acrylics.

George Martin is torn between quality and the aim of making his business as environmentally friendly as possible. He says that the company has been building its environmental aims into its business planning for the last two years.

This has become more challenging because of changes in waste disposal legislation. Under laws

introduced in 2005, Morgan Design has to make sure it has the right procedures in place for the storage, treatment and disposal of potentially harmful substances. George admits that the company cannot simply throw away surplus chemicals. "There are better ways that would fit in with the new legislation and our commitment to the environment," he acknowledges.

Sources: adapted from Independent on Sunday, 11 December 2005

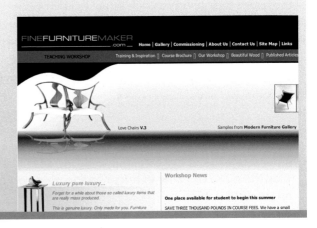

Aims and objectives

The aims of a business should give it a clear sense of purpose that guides and stimulates the organisation. An aim is a long-term goal from which other targets can be derived. Aims help to shape the way in which an organisation develops, and are usually expressed qualitatively. Aims can vary between organisations in the public and private sectors.

Tesco is the UK's largest retailer and sets out its core purposes or aims on its website: "Our core purpose is to create value for customers to earn their lifetime loyalty." This is a commercial aim linked to gaining and retaining customers.

In contrast, the government set up National Health Service Trusts in 2003 to allow local communities to run their own hospitals. According to the government: "The establishment of NHS Foundation Trusts aims to bring about improved access to higher quality services for NHS patients by incentivising

innovation and entrepreneurialism." The focus here is on quality of service.

Business objectives are medium-term or long-term goals and targets that provide a sense of direction. Objectives should be measurable and have a stated timescale – for example, to boost market share from 24 per cent to 33 per cent over the next four years.

Organisations may have a number of objectives, such as profit maximisation, survival, growth or improving product quality. The establishment of objectives is intended to provide guidance to managers, departments, teams and individual employees in decision-making. Objectives enable organisations to delegate authority as they provide a framework within which subordinates can take decisions.

Aims of the change process

There are a number of reasons why a business might implement a programme of change. In this section, we consider some examples of these underlying aims.

1 To reduce waste

Businesses in the UK spend an estimated £15,000 million each year disposing of waste. Cutting the costs of waste disposal could be an important aim for a manufacturing business. However, businesses in other sectors may also pursue similar aims. Retailers may wish to reduce product packaging or to manage perishable stock carefully so that less has to be thrown away because it is out of date. Some schools and colleges seek to reduce the number of textbooks that they throw away by arranging for them to be sent to less developed countries where teaching materials are in short supply.

New legislation introduced by the European Union and ratified by the UK government has put increased pressure on businesses to reduce waste. The European Hazardous Waste directive specifies new rules on disposing of hazardous waste. It bans the disposal of hazardous waste by mixing it with non-hazardous waste in landfill sites. All businesses disposing of hazardous waste are responsible for dealing with it properly. This can be a particular burden for small businesses, and it encourages them to minimise the waste that they generate, especially hazardous waste such as chemicals.

2 Increasing profitability

Profits are an important aim for many businesses in the private sector. They represent a reward to entrepreneurs and shareholders. A programme of change that has higher profits as an aim is likely to satisfy shareholders and managers, though other stakeholders such as employees may be dissatisfied if the changes result in job losses or less attractive working conditions. Consumers may react favourably

to changes which increase the quality of a business's product or increase its availability.

Businesses of all sizes implement change programmes with the aim of increasing profits. Over the last few years BT has expanded its provision of broadband and mobile telephone services. The success of this policy was demonstrated by a 25 per cent rise in the company's profits in 2005 at a time when the profitability of BT's traditional services was declining. Small retailers and restaurants introduce changes such as extending opening hours in the expectation of increasing profitability.

3 Providing high-quality services

One of the prime aims of change programmes in the public sector is the desire to improve the quality of public services like health and education. In 2006 Parliament passed the Education and Inspections Act which set out the government's commitment to deal with what it calls "failing schools". Under this legislation, schools that do not achieve educational targets are liable to be closed down. In some cases new schools may be opened to replace them. The intention is to improve the efficiency of schools and to provide better-quality education for students.

Private sector organisations also implement change programmes to improve the quality of services on offer. For example, in 2006 the Rose Hill Pharmacy in Normanton, Derby confirmed that it was to extend its opening hours in an attempt to reduce the pressure on the out-of-hours services offered by doctors. The pharmacy will be open for 100 hours each week and will offer a range of services including medical advice, blood pressure checks and diabetes services.

Advantages of setting aims

Setting aims at the outset of any programme of change offers a range of benefits to an organisation and its stakeholders.

Aims provide a focus for all employees within the organisation and can help to ensure that decisions taken as part of the change process contribute to the achievement of the agreed target. By involving employees in the process of setting aims, it is possible to encourage and develop ownership, which can increase commitment to the change process.

Aims help and encourage detailed planning of the change programme. The overall targets can be considered at each stage of the planning process to ensure that the plan continually addresses the aims of the project.

Aims give businesses a measure against which to judge the success of the change process. At its simplest, if the programme meets the objective, it can be judged to be a success. So, the success of Rose Hill Pharmacy's decision to extend its opening hours may be seen in the impact it has on doctors' surgeries elsewhere in Derby. If fewer patients attend these surgeries, the policy may be considered to be successful.

business practice
Milk vending scheme for schools

The Milk Development Council is working with the Health Education Trust to implement an initiative to introduce milk and dairy products into vending machines in schools throughout the UK. The two organisations are hoping to engage the support of schools, dairy companies, local authorities and vending companies.

The machines will sell milk and dairy products such as yoghurt. The aim of the project is to improve the health of schoolchildren by encouraging a diet that is less dependent on chocolate, crisps and sugar-based drinks. They believe that schools should play a central part in encouraging children to eat a healthy diet.

assessment practice
Pat's café

Pat Marshall manages *Natural Fare* a vegetarian café in Frome in Somerset. She has decided to extend her café into an adjacent building so that she accommodate more customers during busy times of the week. Pat is applying for a bank loan to finance some of the necessary building work. She is unsure how to answer a question on the application form about the aims of her project.

A Pat thinks that the aims of her project could be to increase the business's profits or to provide a better service. Explain why each of these aims could be appropriate to Pat's business.

B Why do you think that the bank has asked a question about the aims of the project for which the loan is required?

Objectives and change

Setting the scene: Braveheart

Over half a million people in Scotland suffer from heart disease, with 180,000 people requiring treatment for the condition. Although the death rate for heart disease is decreasing, Scotland still has much higher levels of heart disease than most other Western industrialised countries.

The Braveheart project aims to improve heart health in Lanarkshire – the area with the poorest heart health record in Scotland – and prevent a range of heart-related diseases such as strokes and diabetes.

The campaign message is that heart disease is preventable. If Lanarkshire people make small changes to their lifestyle, this could have a significant effect on the number of people who suffer and eventually die from this disease.

The project is providing health checks and advice for those at risk. The nurses on the project provide information on stopping smoking, healthy eating, taking exercise, safe drinking and weight management.

The Braveheart project has four objectives:

- to promote awareness of and identify the risks of heart disease, diabetes and related illnesses

- to identify lifestyles which make people vulnerable

- to provide education to equip people with the knowledge, attitude and motivation to effectively change or modify their lifestyle to maximise their health

- to use the evidence from the project to develop guidelines to assist medical staff in identifying the early stages of heart disease.

Source: adapted from www.nhslanarkshire.co.uk

Business objectives

Objectives are targets or goals that must be achieved in order to fulfil the aims of an organisation, department or team. The objectives pursued by organisations shape the policies they implement. Objectives should be measurable and have a stated timescale – for example to boost market share from 19 per cent to 28 cent over the next three years.

The major objectives of private sector organisations include survival, profit and growth. Non-profit-making organisations are likely to have rather different objectives such as protecting the well-being of less fortunate members of society. However, the precise objectives of any organisation will depend upon the aspirations of its owners, the strength and actions of its competitors, and the financial position of the enterprise. Organisations are likely to have a hierarchy of objectives, with the main organisational objectives informing team objectives, and team objectives in turn informing individual objectives.

Types of project objectives

An organisation's primary objectives are those which must be achieved if the organisation is to survive and be successful. These normally relate to issues such as profit levels and market share. Secondary objectives tend to measure the efficiency of the organisation. They may affect the chances of success, but only in the long term. So, for example, initiatives to improve administrative efficiency and labour turnover rates would be regarded as secondary objectives. These distinctions between primary and secondary objectives are not fixed for all time. In recent years, customer care has assumed greater importance for many businesses, and improvements in customer care are likely to be classified as a primary objective rather than a secondary objective.

The objectives of a change project can be exactly the same as the objectives for the organisation as a whole. However, project objectives can also be more specific, as in the case of the Braveheart project (see the introduction to this topic). Project objectives might focus on any (or all) of these concerns:

- budgetary issues – relating to cutting costs or achieving a specific level of profits

- market-related issues – this type of objective could be expressed in terms of market share, or changing the opinions of a proportion of the population

- engineering – to develop a new product and new equipment for use on a production line

- organisational issues – to change the structure or size of the workforce

- technological issues – to use new technology, say to replace employees or to improve quality.

Project objectives, like organisation objectives, can be divided into two categories. The main objectives are the reasons for carrying out the project. The secondary objectives are benefits that are achieved "by the way" but not as the major reason for carrying out the project.

SMART objectives

The objectives for any project are more likely to be effective and assist in the successful completion of the change programme if they are expressed in SMART terms. SMART objectives are specific, measurable, achievable, relevant and time-specifc.

Specific

Objectives should be clear and easily defined. This helps both project team members and their managers, as the team member knows what is expected of them and the manager is able to monitor and assess actual performance against the specific objectives. The objectives of a project may well include a scope description, which includes details of what is within the scope of the project and what is not included.

Measurable

A measurable project is a quantifiable one: for example, the objective might be to reduce labour costs by 10 per cent. Progress towards a change programme's objectives should be to be monitored throughout the project. It is also very useful to know when that work has been done and the objectives are completed. A measurable objective helps project managers in this respect.

Achievable

Project managers should be aware that teams may not be able to achieve an objective simply because it is unrealistic. This might be for various reasons, such as lacking the necessary skills, having insufficient resources (computers and people, for example) or by not having the support of senior managers. Achievable objectives should prove challenging but not impossible. Furthermore, achievable objectives should not conflict with other objectives pursued by the business or by its departments and teams.

Relevant

An objective should help to achieve the aims of the organisation as a whole rather than merely serve the needs of the project. For example, by setting an objective to introduce computerised systems for recording council tax payments within three months, the team is setting an objective that both provides impetus and focus to the technology project but which also will assist the council in providing high-quality services to local residents.

Time-specific

Descriptions of objectives should also include information on start and finish dates. Giving a timescale adds an appropriate sense of urgency, and ensures that the objectives do not continue over an unreasonably long period.

The use of SMART objectives helps to ensure that the managers of the change programme think carefully about the goals that they are setting. It should ensure that project objectives do not conflict with the organisation's overall aims. It can be useful to allow team members to play some part in setting the objectives, as getting wide support for a project can be a vital element in managing change.

From objectives to targets

Some objectives can seem large and daunting. To make them easier to achieve, it is useful to divide these objectives into a number of targets. In turn, these individual targets can be allocated to the teams or individuals who have responsibility for carrying out the programme of change. If each of the teams and/or individuals meets their own targets within an agreed timescale, then the overall objective should be met.

With a large change project there may be many different objectives and it may involve many employees. In this case, the project becomes more manageable by breaking it down into smaller elements. However, this process can also apply with small projects, as it enables project managers to provide individuals with definite goals that can improve motivation as well as providing a clear focus.

To illustrate the process of breaking down objectives into targets, consider this example. In 2006, one of the UK's leading printers moved its printing works from a site in Norwich to a location outside the city. This programme of change entailed setting a series of objectives for all involved. One objective might have been to complete the fitting-out of the new building by a certain date. This objective is substantial and would benefit from being split into a number of targets such as:

- complete decoration of the building
- equip building with necessary security equipment
- install new printing machinery
- carry out staff training on new equipment.

One way of breaking down objectives into a series of tasks is to decide what criteria will signal success in terms of meeting the project's objective. In turn, this "success criterion" can be given an indicator which will signal success. The use of a success criterion translates an objective into a more operational form to which an indicator can be assigned. The indicator of success can be translated into a target which is a precise goal that needs to be met within a given time period. Figure 14.1 illustrates this process, using as an example one objective for the project to transfer the printing operation to a new location.

Meeting an objective is more likely to be successful if it can be broken down in this way into a number of discrete tasks or targets that need to be completed. These tasks or targets can be allocated to teams of employees or even to individual workers. The completion of all the individual tasks will allow the objective to be fulfilled, and if all objectives are met, the programme of change should be completed successfully.

Planning for change

The process of translating objectives into smaller targets is an important part of the planning process. Any change project should have an accompanying plan. The plan will contain a range of important data.

- It should list the aims and objectives of the project.
- It should set out who has overall responsibility for the project as well the persons or teams responsible for the individual elements.
- It should list resources that are available to the managers and teams leading the change.
- It plan should set out a time frame for completion of the project.
- It plan should contain the project budget. It is vital that the programme of change is carried out within agreed budgets, as financial resources are certain to be limited.

Many change projects rely upon external finance for their completion. In these circumstances, a business plan will be required to persuade external parties such as banks and venture capitalists to take a risk and invest money into the project. Clear and detailed planning assists potential investors in assessing the risks involved in the project, and the business plan will help them make a decision on whether the potential returns are worth the risks involved.

A note for your portfolio

You should explore the idea of aims and objectives as fully as possible before considering your own project. To help you to do this, think through the issues associated with Pat's café (see the assessment practice on the next page). In addition, you might want to look at the O2's corporate social report (see box next page) to see how a real business uses aims and objectives in managing change. This report can be downloaded from O2's corporate website, or viewed at www.o2.com/cr/report2005/index.asp.

Figure 14.1: Breaking down objectives into targets

Objective	Success criterion	Target
Complete staff training on new printing machinery by 23 October	1 Meet existing work schedules throughout training period	1 Design schedule of training to allow existing printing to continue without interruption
	2 Equip staff to operate new printing machinery flexibly	2 Arrange schedule of training to ensure that all employees receive training in full range of printing machinery
	3 Complete training by 23 October	3 Design and carry out training programme to meet a series of intermediate dates

O_2 is one of the UKs leading providers of mobile telephone services. It was acquired by the Spanish telecommunications company Telefonica in 2006. O_2's corporate social report sets out how the company seeks to meet the needs of all stakeholders through its activities rather than just focusing on the needs of shareholders. In other words, it is a document that presents the company as a good citizen.

One key element of O_2's corporate social report relates to its plans to change its operations to reduce its impact on the environment. Figure 14.2 shows how O_2 has broken down one of its key aims into objectives and targets. This extract reproduces some its objectives and targets.

> We have identified the main ways our business affects the environment, and have put an environmental policy in place, supported by the board, to mitigate them. The key issues are:

- energy consumption and the associated greenhouse-gas emissions that come from running our networks, our buildings and transport

- disposal of redundant handsets

- waste management of our offices, shops and networks

- engaging with our supply chains

- reducing ozone-depleting substances used in our offices and by our networks

- controlling the risk of local pollution from storage of fuel oil.

Source: O_2 corporate responsibility report 2005

O_2's environmental targets are broad and wide-ranging. Can you see why these should be broken down further into a series of smaller tasks?

Figure 14.2: O_2's aim to reduce air emissions

Aim	Objective	Target
Reducing air emissions	Seek to lower levels of energy use	Reduce electricity consumption by 5 per cent in offices by 2007
		Reduce electricity consumption by 5 per cent in call centres by 2007
	Reduce transport fuel consumption and emissions	Reduce emissions associated with business transport by 5 per cent by 2007

Source: adapted from O_2 corporate responsibility report 2005

assessment practice
Pat's café

Pat Marshall manages *Natural Fare*, a very popular vegetarian café in Frome in Somerset. She is in the process of planning the extension of her business into a neighbouring property so that she can increase her café's seating capacity. The aim of the expansion of the café is to make it more profitable.

A What objectives might Pat set for the expansion of the café to help her to fulfil her overall aim of increasing the business's profitability? Explain your choice.

B Why might setting SMART objectives help her to manage this change project?

Preparing for change

Setting the scene: Dell and BuzzMachine

Blogs are online diaries. Internet users record their experiences in a blog on a variety of topics. Many blogs are personal, but some bloggers use the platform to make political comment and to criticise businesses that they think perform badly.

One company that discovered the negative potential of bloggers is the global computer manufacturer Dell. In 2005, Jeff Jarvis recorded his experiences with a Dell laptop that was not working properly. A very dissatisfied customer, he criticised the response of the company's customer services department to his complaints. Jarvis used his blog website BuzzMachine to set out his frustrations with the US company.

Jarvis's postings attracted hundreds of responses, and inspired comments by other bloggers. Ultimately, the whole affair influenced public perceptions of Dell to such an extent that market researchers concluded Dell had "sustained long-term damage to its brand image".

A joint report by three marketing firms – Market Sentinel, Onalytica and Immediate Future PR – found: "Bloggers used Jeff Jarvis' shorthand 'Dell Hell' to collaboratively spread negative comment about Dell's customer service – weakening Dell's reputation where the company used to be so strong."

Dell responded to the controversy by admitting that "Mr Jarvis' experience could've been handled better" and saying that it had begun monitoring blogs, with a view to contacting dissatisfied consumers directly. Blogs offer a new way for businesses to collect information on customer opinions and, as in the case of Dell's customer service department, can lead to real change

Source: adapted from BBC News website, 10 April 2006

Assessing the impact of change

Managers implement many changes that affect consumers. Decisions that impact on customers include altering a business's opening hours, changing the price of a product, or introducing a new product range. A wise manager will not take these types of decisions without investigating the likely reactions of consumers to the planned change. For example, a decision by the manager of a charity shop to raise the prices on all goods by 10 per cent might result in many former customers turning to other shops to look for better bargains; on the other hand, the shop's customers might be willing to pay the higher prices as they know that the money is used for a good cause. By researching customers' opinions as part of the planning process, it is possible to discover the likely response to the price increase before implementing the change.

Managers may need to research the views of other stakeholders – not just customers – when contemplating change. Before deciding to sell a wider range of greenhouse plants, a garden centre would need to ensure that suppliers can deliver the quantities it needs to meet expected sales. A business that decides to extend its opening hours will want to get the views of employees on the proposed change.

Qualitative research is detailed research that investigates the reasons behind people's views, attitudes and reactions.

Quantitative research uses predetermined questions to discover numerical information from large numbers of people.

A **questionnaire** is a set of questions in written form designed to collect information from large numbers of people.

Observation is a method of market research in which consumers' behaviour is observed and recorded.

It would want to know whether they would be willing to work longer hours. The managers proposing the change will need to assess the additional wage costs incurred through operating for longer hours. They would need to consider whether the business needs to recruit more employees to implement the change successfully.

Managers involved in a change decision will also need to consult with other managers within the business to assess the likely impact of their proposals on the operation of other aspects of the business. For example, the manager of a supermarket planning to open an in-store bakery would need to discuss the implications with colleagues. The decision would clearly impact on the operation of other aspects of the supermarket. Sales of other bread products would be affected, and there may be less floor space to sell other products. The supermarket may also need to recruit bakers to staff the new operation.

Making a decision on whether to implement change can be difficult. The manager(s) responsible for the decision obviously hope that the change will help the organisation to achieve its objectives. By investigating the views of stakeholders on the proposed change as part of the planning process, they take an important step towards taking the "right" decision regarding change.

stopand**think**

A head teacher plans to update the school's website. Suggest which groups and people the head teacher might need to speak to before implementing this change.

Methods of collecting information

Several techniques can be used to collect information from people who are likely to be affected by an organisation's decision to change some aspect of its operations. The research methods used will depend upon the information that is required.

1 Qualitative research methods

A business may conduct qualitative research to determine the impact of a decision. Qualitative research investigates the reasons behind people's views, attitudes and reactions. It can be used, therefore, to assess people's likely reaction to any proposed change. There are a number of techniques available to a manager wishing to elicit this type of information.

Interviews

Interviews are an effective way of gathering detailed information on the opinions of consumers, employees, suppliers, creditors and other stakeholders with an interest in a programme of change. The downside is that interviews are a time-consuming and, hence, expensive process, and cost considerations are likely to restrict the number of interviews that can be undertaken.

Interviews are scripted to some extent, with those carrying them out expected to ask a series of questions. However, they also offer the opportunity to ask follow-up questions and to explore further the answers of those interviewed. This can help to uncover the reasons that lie behind particular views and opinions, and to gain greater insight into the impact that the proposed change may have. This helps a business assess the overall impact of the change.

Focus groups

Focus groups provide a structured opportunity for small groups of employees, customers or other people affected by a decision to discuss their views on a particular change proposal. The sessions require careful and skilled leadership to ensure that the discussion remains focused and that there is chance to explore the reasons that lie behind people's opinions and attitudes. As with interviews and other methods of qualitative research, focus groups can provide detailed information, but from a relatively small number of people.

Another means of getting information on customer attitudes is the Delphi technique. This involves assembling a panel of experts to provide long-term forecasts, particularly on market trends. The Delphi technique relies upon the panels reaching a consensus.

2 Quantitative research methods

Quantitative research uses predetermined questions to discover key numerical information from large numbers of people. This research can be conducted by the business – or a research company on its behalf – or it could draw on the many existing information sources that can provide quantitative data relating to a particular decision. In some cases, these sources can also offer some qualitative information.

Questionnaires

A questionnaire is a set of questions in written form designed to collect information from large numbers of people. A carefully constructed questionnaire can provide valuable information. This is a frequently used research technique. Customers are often sent questionnaires through the post by companies for completion and return to the research team. Some customer questionnaires are handed out at the point of sale or included as part of a product's packaging. Questionnaires can also be an appropriate method of assessing the views of employees towards a change programme, especially if many employees are likely to be affected.

Questionnaires can be a relatively cheap form of research; however, businesses do not have much control over responses. Response rates for questionnaires sent to a random group of customers

rarely exceed 10 per cent, which is why many research companies offer incentives (such as entry into a prize draw) to encourage more responses, though a business would expect a much higher return for an employee questionnaire.

Observation

Observation involves watching people in a variety of situations. It can provide information on how consumers react to in-store displays, prices, or the locations of products. Managers considering changing the layout of a store or introducing new products may observe how customers react to the existing layout or to a limited number of changes before making a final decision.

Organisational records

Most enterprises keep extensive records relating to sales, production, finance, employees, etc. An organisation considering investing heavily in updating its employees' skills through a training programme may look back on production and sales data relating to a previous time period during which it invested heavily in training. This may help managers to judge the likely impact of training on the performance of employees as well as on the entire organisation.

Official data

The government collects and publishes vast amounts of detailed information, including key annual publications such as *Social Trends* and *Regional Trends*. These can provide information on expected or actual changes in income or population levels – important information for managers considering, for example, launching a new range of products. Most government data is now available online. Visit the National Statistics website (www.statistics.gov.uk) for more information.

Another useful source of data is trade associations and trade journals. These can supply valuable and quite specific information on market trends as well as the cost of purchasing assets such as machinery.

Which methods to use?

The methods that a business uses to collect information prior to making a decision will depend upon a number three principal factors.

The type of decision

A business considering using a new supplier may have to engage in qualitative research, talking to suppliers about prices, quality, delivery dates, credit terms, and

Rolls-Royce, the UK manufacturer of aerospace engines, announced plans in 2005 to change the way it pays pensions to its employees once they have retired. The proposals involve ending the final salary system, a scheme in which a pension is based upon a proportion of an employee's final salary.

Under the new scheme, employees' pensions would depend upon the success of the company in investing the money put into the pension scheme through contributions (from the company and the employees) during employees' working lives.

Rolls Royce has nearly 120,000 employees and ex-employees within its current pension scheme. Under the company's new proposals only new employees would go on the new scheme: existing employees would remain on the final salary scheme.

The company is consulting its employees on the new pension system. These discussions have continued for some time, and the company says it will not proceed with its plans unless they receive the agreement of its workforce.

so on. In contrast, the manager of a sports club contemplating a decision to offer a new type of exercise class may want to collect information from a large number of potential customers about times and durations of the class, and the prices they might be willing to pay.

Budgets

The research instruments used by a business will be constrained by the budget it has available for the exercise. Qualitative information is more detailed, and reveals why people hold certain views or attitudes, but it is expensive to collect, even from small numbers of people. Quantitative information is cheaper, takes

in data from larger numbers of people, and may be more readily available from existing information sources. Managers with very limited budgets may be forced to rely on quantitative information to take the decision.

The timescale

If a quick decision is essential, managers may not be able to conduct qualitative research, as carrying out interviews and setting up focus groups can be time-consuming. It may be that, in these circumstances, sources such as the internet are used to collect numerical information on the likely impact of changes such as increasing or reducing prices.

assessmentpractice
Pat's café

Pat Marshall manages *Natural Fare*, a very popular vegetarian café in Frome in Somerset. She is in the process of planning the extension of her business into a neighbouring property so that she can increase her café's seating capacity.

A Identify four stakeholder groups that Pat should discuss her plans with prior to implementing them. In each case, explain why she should research the views of the chosen stakeholder group.

B Explain the advantages that Pat might receive from researching the likely effects of her plans in this way. Could she go ahead with her changes without carrying out this research?

The impact of change

Setting the scene: a tax on plastic bags

Interested parties in Scotland are debating a proposal by members of the Scottish Parliament to impose a tax on 10p on each carrier bag handed out by retailers.

The proposal was made by Scottish Liberal Democrat MP Mike Pringle. Arguing in its favour, he said that the tax would reduce Scotland's litter problem as fewer bags would be thrown away and the money raised could be used to finance environmental projects.

However, research commissioned by the Scottish Executive questioned the benefits that might result from the tax. This research revealed that plastic bags accounted for less than 1 per cent of litter, and found that a tax on plastic bags would have limited impact on Scotland's overall litter problem.

The study acknowledged that there would be environmental gains, but noted that paper bags had a greater effect on the environment than conventional plastic carrier bags. "If paper bags are excluded from the levy, as currently proposed, we estimate that paper bag usage will increase by 174 million bags per year to 213 million per year," said the report. "This will have associated environmental implications in terms of increased energy use, transport costs, storage space and waste disposal."

The Carrier Bag Consortium, a group of businesses that manufacture plastic bags, are strongly opposed to the proposal and doubt its ability to raise substantial amounts of money for environmental projects.

A spokesperson for the consortium said: "The proposed tax level of 2000 per cent is higher than any other tax in the world, but it would not raise any significant funds. Such a tax is fundamentally self-defeating. Experience in the Republic of Ireland indicates that the usage of plastic carrier bags has declined by more than 90 per cent – but the residual funds (estimated to be 10 million euros) generated by those prepared to pay for carrier bags is estimated to be far less than the cost borne by the authorities in administering the scheme."

Sources: Carrier Bag Consortium (www.carrierbagtax.com) and BBC News website, 29 August 2005

Categories of impact

Change has the potential to affect most, if not all, aspects of the operations of an organisation. This is true of even relatively small changes, such as the decision by a department store to start selling carpets. In this example, it is possible to identify three different elements of the impact that this change has on the department store.

- **The technical impact**. The department store would need to purchase equipment to display carpets – possibly on large rolls, or metal frames on which to hang rugs and mats. It would also need to stock associated products such as grippers to fix carpets to floors.

> ### KEY TERMS
>
> A **business culture** is the attitudes, ideas and beliefs that are shared by employees within the organisation.
>
> **Innovation** is the act of creating new products, new production processes and new ways of delivering products.

- **The human impact**. The company may need to recruit people with experience in selling carpets, or to retrain some of its existing staff. It may find some existing employees become demotivated if their sections lose some selling space to make way for the new enterprise.

- **The systems impact**. The department store might need to create a separate section for carpets, and it may decide to operate this section as a profit centre. This could have an effect, for example, on the financial management systems used by the business. The store might negotiate a deal with a local carpet-fitting firm to take responsibility for this section and to operate an after-sales service for customers.

We will use these three headings to consider the impact of change in more detail.

1 The technical impact

The technical effects of change depend on the type and size of the business and on the nature of the change that is implemented. This is best illustrated through some examples.

It is increasingly common for UK businesses to use automated telephone operating systems to answer and route calls within the organisation. This reduces the need to employ reception staff to answer calls, and can help to reduce costs as well as providing an answering service at all times of the day. However, this change usually requires an investment by the business in new technology as well as in the operating software.

Computerised technology must be installed and adapted to meet the precise requirements of the business. Messages have to be set up on the system to guide callers to the correct person, and the system may need to be linked with the mobile phones and computer systems already in use within the business. These operating systems are increasing sophisticated. ContactPortal technology (see box) supplied by Telephonetics, a small company based in Hertfordshire, relies upon speech recognition rather than callers selecting from options. It is regarded as being more user-friendly, as well as more efficient, than conventional systems.

Productivity is an important measure for manufacturing businesses, and a common aim of many change programmes is to increase their levels of productivity. If they can increase the amount produced per hour or day, then it offers the chance to sell more cheaply or to enjoy higher profit margins.

Many businesses look to drive productive improvements by introducing technology on to the production line. This can take the form of machinery to control the operation of the production line. This allows different types of products (varying designs or colours, for example) to be manufactured simultaneously. Businesses may also use robots on the production line (termed computer-aided manufacture, or CAM) to speed up production and achieve consistent levels of quality.

For smaller businesses, change might have a simpler technical impact. The expansion of a delivery business could require the purchase of more vehicles or computers to manage the process. A petrol station

business practice
ContactPortal®

The ContactPortal® is an innovative speech-driven virtual operator that answers calls quickly and professionally 24 hours a day, seven days a week, with specific time-of-day greetings. Opportunities for contact with new business prospects are maximised, and members of staff also enjoy the benefits of working in a more productive and efficient environment.

The solution has been developed by Telephonetics to be simple to use, requiring very little training, and easy to administer using a web interface. ContactPortal® has been designed to be integrated with an existing PBX and any third-party equipment including paging systems and call loggers, therefore protecting existing and future investments in telephony infrastructure.

Chosen by industry-leading organisations to handle all external and internal calls, features include:

- auto-attendant
- speed-dial and personal speed-dials
- multi-site variant
- configurable time-of-day greetings
- call screening
- missed call notification by SMS, e-mail and voice
- intelligent contact disambiguation and synonym support.

Source: www.telephonetics.co.uk

may decide to open for longer hours, and as a consequence install closed circuit television (CCTV) to provide security for employees who work the late-night shifts. Similarly, the technical impact of a decision by a farmer to grow sugar beet might be the purchase of specialist equipment for harvesting this new crop.

2 The systems impact

Systems are the processes of methods used by an organisation as part of its day-to-day work. Common examples of systems used by businesses would include financial systems, communication systems and delivery systems.

Expansion is likely to have significant effects on the systems used by a business. The Business in Practice feature below can be used to illustrate the impact of growth on systems.

The move into manufacturing could have had significant implications for the systems used by Tyrrells Court Farm. In terms of finance, the farm may need separate budgets and financial records for the two elements of the business: growing potatoes and manufacturing crisps. Certainly William Chase would have wanted financial systems that would enable him to assess the profitability of his new venture. He may have run the two enterprises as profit centres.

Distribution has changed over time. When selling locally, it was possible to deliver the crisps to retailers

business practice

William Chase's story

William Chase owns and manages Tyrrells Court Farm in Herefordshire (see Stop & Think above). This is his story of how the business changed from growing potatoes to manufacturing crisps.

> I have been farming potatoes at Tyrrells Court for the last twenty years. Most of the potatoes I supplied to supermarkets, which often left me feeling detached – without any feedback or thanks from my end customers. With the continual price pressure from the supermarkets, I realised I had to change direction. I wanted to remain in farming and produce a great-tasting product from our potatoes.

> My aim was to produce the tastiest hand-fried chips in the UK with a pedigree – using my years of knowledge and ability to grow the raw product here at Tyrrells Court. I'm in control from seed to chip.

> I spent spring 2002 travelling the world in search of the equipment and recipes I needed to make the very best product possible. Summer 2002 was spent in one of

the old potato sheds with a small fryer, making and refining the very first packets of Tyrrells potato chips.

> As a result of the fantastic response to these early chips, and as demand increased, we decided to convert one of our own large potato stores into a modern, fully accredited production facility. We now have a small team here at Tyrrells, all fully trained in all aspects of the chip-making process. Everyone enjoys being part of a growing company and we all contribute individually to the success of the company.

> We distribute direct to independent retailers throughout the UK, ensuring total freshness. We are very proud of our potato chips, so we package them in transparent bags, cushioned with air for better transportation. Once our products began to be sold throughout the UK, we used other businesses to distribute the crisps to customers.

Source: Adapted from www.tyrrellspotatochips.co.uk

using the farm's own vehicles. However, as the business expanded, selling throughout the UK (including to prestige stores like Harrods) and overseas, the systems used for delivery had to change. The business brought in other companies to deliver its products, and it needed to have the administrative systems in place to organise distribution, to monitor its effectiveness and to ensure that customers were satisfied with the service. Selling overseas involved developing the administrative systems to meet the requirements of exporting. These include trading in different currencies and meeting the laws relating to food in Norway and Germany, for example. As a simple example, the company had to produce packaging in different languages.

Communications systems have also changed as the Tyrrells Court Farm business has developed. There is a greater need for internal communications between the farming – potato growing – and the manufacturing sides of the business. This is essential to ensure that the supply of potatoes matches the expectations and needs of the team responsible for manufacturing the crisps. However, the company has had to improve its external communications to deal with customers and other interested parties. It has developed a website and appointed reception staff with responsibility for dealing with all aspects of external communications.

Smaller changes can also impact upon the systems used by a business. As an example, a restaurant introducing a new menu might need to deal with different suppliers. These new suppliers may not offer credit, but require payment on delivery. This could have significant implications for the management of the business's cash flow as well as its administrative systems. The menu change may also impact on the production systems used in the kitchen. It may not be possible to store some of the new items on the menu, so the dishes may have to be made freshly each time a customer places an order.

3 The human impact

In many ways, the human impact is perhaps the most obvious and the most publicised aspect of any change. A programme of change may result in more or fewer employees. Even if it has no implications for overall staff numbers, a business may need different skills. Preparing for the human dimension of change is the responsibility of the human resources department, and is part of its workforce planning. In smaller businesses, there may not be a separate human resources department and responsibility will fall to general managers.

Developing new skills

Many types of change require employees to gain new skills if they are to be successful. In a very small business, a programme that produces growth may require some staff to develop managerial skills as they assume responsibilities for looking after other employees. New technical skills are required if the business is introducing new technology. A move into e-commerce could require employees to undertake training in website design and, if this involves selling goods or services overseas, they may need to develop their language skills.

New skills will require training. It may be possible to organise training within the business. In-house training can ensure that it meets the precise needs of the business. However, some training needs can only be met by outside agencies, most probably through off-the-job training. This type of training can be expensive. Identifying training needs is an important element of planning for change, and these needs must be satisfied before change can be implemented successfully.

stop and think

What training needs do you think were required by (a) William Chase and (b) other staff at Tyrrells Court Farm as a result of the decision to start manufacturing potato crisps?

Creating a new culture

A business's culture is the attitudes, ideas and beliefs that are shared by employees within the organisation. Certain types of change demand that a business develops a new culture. Introducing new products, expanding a business or moving into new markets may require a more innovative and entrepreneurial culture. Entrepreneurial employees can assist the development of a business in several ways. They can propose ideas for new products, and question existing customers about their future needs. In an entrepreneurial culture, employees may be willing to try out new approaches and systems, and there is likely to be less resistance to change.

How do businesses develop a new culture? A variety of approaches may be necessary. First, senior managers and/or the owners of the business must champion, and be seen to lead, the change. Their views and actions are likely to influence other employees within the business. Second, training may be required. It is unrealistic to expect employees to take on new roles without some support. Third, the structure of the organisation can also assist the process of changing a culture. By offering employees further down the structure great authority, a business will be encouraging its staff to become more entrepreneurial and show greater initiative. Fourth, the introduction of quality circles can aid the process of developing a change-oriented and entrepreneurial culture as people become accustomed to proposing ideas.

A further key element is communication. A business undergoing change of any type is likely to benefit from effective two-way communication between managers and junior staff. A combination of good communication and a degree of employee participation in decision-making not only assists in effecting a change in the organisation's culture but can also ease the process of change by helping to overcome employee resistance. Employees who are informed and involved throughout the planning and implementation stages will be more willing to make the necessary alterations to their working lives and will adapt more readily to the new culture. Influencing employees' attitudes helps to change cultures and prepare them to work in a different environment.

assessment practice
Pat's café

Pat Marshall manages *Natural Fare*, a very popular vegetarian café in Frome in Somerset. She is in the process of planning the extension of her business into a neighbouring property so that she can increase her café's seating capacity. She has completed her plans for the expansion and is about to assess the impact of these changes on her business and its stakeholders.

A Identify and explain three possible effects that the expansion may have on her business.

B To what extent do you agree with the view that the human impact of the change will be the most important?

assessment practice
Developing your portfolio

You are now in a position to make some real progress with your evidence for the portfolio for Unit 14. At this stage you have covered sufficient of this unit to compile the evidence needed for requirement A (see part A in the assessment practice, Topic 1, page 240). This means that you should be able to explain:

■ the nature of the change

■ the factors driving and resisting this change

■ how the change will impact upon the organisation and its stakeholders.

You should also begin to analyse the nature of the change and its likely impact on people and the organisation.

Topic 6 The impact of change

Topic 7 Key decisions in managing change

Setting the scene: Olympic and project champion

In July 2005 it was announced that the city of London's bid to host the 2012 Olympics had been successful. This was the final stage in a project which began in 2002. The key figure was Sebastian Coe, who led the team from 2004 and became the champion of the project to bring the games to London.

Coe was delighted by the last-minute success of the London team. "This is almost entirely on a different planet to winning the gold medals," Coe said. The London team's bid was initially rated third behind Madrid and favourites Paris. But with the timing that he showed so often in an illustrious running career, Coe helped London produce the late charge which saw it pip its French rivals. His CV was perfect for the job. Not only did he have the necessary public profile, but his knowledge of sporting politics gave him massive influence with those who would decide London's fate.

Coe had been a member of various British sporting committees as well as winning a place on the ruling council of athletics' governing body, the IAAF. And with quiet determination, Coe began to turn the fortunes of London's bid around. "I felt our natural instinct was to make our strategy based around sport and getting more young people involved both domestically and internationally," he said.

With a unity of purpose and an inspiring vision, London started to make inroads. Emphasis was made on the legacy of the games for London and Britain. The use of stars such as David Beckham, Matthew Pinsent and Steve Redgrave gave the bid an air of authority that was hard to ignore.

Coe saved his finest masterstroke for the closing moments when he delivered a very personal speech to IOC delegates during London's final presentation. "When I was 12 years old I was marched into a large school hall with my classmates and we watched grainy pictures from the 1968 Mexico Olympic Games," he told the delegates. "Two athletes from our home town were competing. John Sherwood won a bronze medal in the 400m hurdles. His wife Sheila just narrowly missed gold in the long jump.

"By the time I was back in my classroom, I knew what I wanted to do – and what I wanted to be. Thirty-five years on, I stand before you with those memories still fresh and still inspired by this great movement." His speech, in the final moments of an incredibly close battle, turned the race in London's favour.

Source: adapted from BBC News website profile, 31 December 2005

What is project management?

Project management is a series of techniques used to deliver an agreed result on time and within the stated budget. It involves achieving the change that is desired, using the available resources and within the timescale that has been negotiated. Good project management is the most efficient way to manage change processes.

The first stage in the process of managing a project is to decide to who should take management responsibility. An organisation needs to decide whether a project should be managed by one or more of its own employees, or whether to invite an outside agency such as a management consultancy to lead and oversee the project. This decision depends upon three main factors.

■ **The scale of the change project**
The larger the project, the more likely it is that an organisation will involve outside agencies in at least some elements of project management. A substantial project, such as to relocate part of the business to an overseas location, is likely to draw on external expertise. In contrast, a project to delayer the organisational structure of a business and empower relatively junior employees might be managed internally.

■ **The finance available to the business**
Small businesses with limited funds and weak cash flows may not be able to afford the substantial fees that are charged by companies providing project management services. However, some businesses may decide that this investment is worthwhile and use their scarce financial resources in this way.

■ **The skills available within the business**
If managers believe that employees possess the necessary skills to manage the project, they may decide not to seek any external support. They would look for employees with skills in managing budgets and resources (including time), with experience in using project management software, and with the capability to promote and encourage a change culture.

The human dimension

There is obviously a strong human dimension in project management – the ability to manage and motivate can be crucial to the project's success. The

major human elements that need to be addressed as part of the process of managing a change project are:

■ building a project team

■ identifying and preparing a project champion

■ creating a change culture within the organisation

■ gaining the commitment of the workforce to the change project.

1 Building a project team

An organisation benefits in several ways from using a team to carry through a change project. Teams can draw on a range of different and complementary skills, leading to greater creativity, ingenuity and imagination. Together, the talents of a team are more likely to be successful and, furthermore, they are likely to collectively provide a network of support and commitment.

Setting up a team is not in itself a guarantee that the project will be completed successfully. Assembling the right balance of team members is essential. Managers responsible for recruiting team members need to think about the skills that the team will require and the tasks that have to be carried out to complete the project. A successful team is likely to have a number of important characteristics.

Size

A team should have a small and manageable number of members. An ideal number is between four and eight people. This is a practical number – the team will be easier to build, and there is less likelihood of conflict and group factions developing.

Complementary skills

The team should have a range of complementary skills. It should have a range of technical, functional and professional skills appropriate to its task. Thus Seb Coe's team needed language skills, presentational skills, IT skills and knowledge of the sporting world to mount a successful bid for the 2012 Olympics.

Well-balanced teams contain people that can solve problems and make decisions. They should be able to approach a task systematically, decide on actions, and use appropriate techniques to carry them out. They need a good range of interpersonal skills so that all participants act as team players. To hold the team together, there must be team communication and cohesion, and all must be willing to contribute. Successful teams demonstrate synergy – that is, the output and results of the team working as a whole is greater than that which could be achieved by its members working as individuals on their own.

Clear purpose

The team must have a common and agreed purpose. Teams need clearly defined objectives and an agreed timescale. The corporate, team and personal objectives must fit with the common purpose, which should be expressed in clear well-designed performance goals. This will give a clear focus for actions, help communication as the team has one framework for understanding the task, and minimise conflict.

Authority and accountability

The team must have the authority and be empowered to make decisions. This should motivate the team, as it offers the opportunity to meet ego needs as identified by Maslow and Herzberg's motivators (see pages 175–6). The team must be willing to work together and take collective and individual responsibility for their results and objectives. This mutual accountability for results encourages all team members to take part in the decision-making process.

Resources

The team must have sufficient resources available to carry out task – including manpower, finance, physical resources and research capability. A team given the task of selling an established product in an overseas market would need finance, human resources and, possibly, property and vehicles.

> ## stop and think
>
> In 2006 a project team was established by the Manx government to improve road safety on some of the mountain roads that run across the Isle of Man. The team was given a budget of £200,000. What resources might it have purchased to complete its objectives?

business practice
Decommissioning Sellafield

A number of small businesses located in west Cumbria near to the Sellafield nuclear site have been told that they must work together if they are to win bids to carry out the work necessary to decommission the nuclear site. The government has estimated that the cost of decommissioning and cleaning up Sellafield will be about £33,000 million over the next ten years.

Over 80 businesses have had meetings to find out how local skills and services can be used as part of the clean-up process. The message from British Nuclear Group which runs Sellafield is that the businesses need to team up to make sure that they offer a range of complementary skills which can be used efficiently. There are 1500 businesses that currently operate on the Sellafield site, supplying everything from meals to specialist nuclear services.

Leadership

A team needs the leader to keep a focus on the task and motivate team members to achieve common, team and individual goals. The leader will need to have the ability to assess the situation and manage in appropriate styles to take forward the project. At times, this might require an "autocratic" approach; at other times, possibly when complex decisions have to be made, a democratic or participative approach will be more appropriate.

A capacity for evaluation

The team should be able to evaluate its success. The team needs to regularly assess how it is performing and analyse any issues that may be interfering with its effectiveness.

How does a team become effective? Psychologist BW Tuckman developed a model in the 1960s stating the four stages a team needs to go through to become productive.

Forming

When someone first starts to work with a team on a project, he or she is unlikely to know all the members of the team well, and might feel a bit embarrassed about discussing ideas with other team members. This can be a stressful time, as each member of the team wants to show who they are and establish their personality within the group.

Storming

After a while, team members will start to feel more confident with one another. There might be some disagreements, as each member has a different opinion on how best to tackle the project. This is an important stage as it helps members to trust and understand each other, learn to negotiate and channel conflict, and decide the realistic aims and objectives of the project.

Norming

At this stage, members are learning how to work together as a team, and will be deciding how to behave and how to make decisions together, and are developing shared views. They will probably feel like a team and will be more accepting of each others' ideas and opinions.

Performing

By now, members will be really getting down to business. They will be working well together as a team and focused on achieving the team's goals. Some teams never make it this far. Members should make sure they use their disagreements productively and think about the best solutions for the team as a whole.

2 Project champions and project managers

A project champion is crucial to the success of a project. The project champion's job is to drive a project forward, advocating its benefits, assisting the team and helping to navigate any problems to keep the project on track.

A project without a champion may lack focus and clear targets, face difficulties in getting decisions made and the project may be at risk. The project champion will always come from within the organisation and won't get involved in the day-to-day planning, co-ordination and management of its implementation. It is beneficial if the project champion comes from the ranks of middle to senior management as the champion needs to have authority to make decisions or to encourage others to do so.

Every major project, in particular, needs a cheerleader or champion – someone who will advocate its benefits, assist and mentor the team and navigate any roadblocks to keep the project on track. The role of a project champion involves displaying initiative, diplomacy and tact. Project champions generally have positive attitudes, are able to motivate other members of the team as well as being able to generate enthusiasm and co-operation.

In contrast, a project manager is responsible for the day-to-day operation of the project. Project managers will be focused on achievement and completing the project within the agreed timescale and within budget. They could be described as a proactive "doer". Figure 14.3 sets out some ground rules for being a successful project manager.

Figure 14.3: The dos and don'ts of being a project manager

Dos	Don'ts
Have a clear idea of what you want to achieve	Don't be single-minded
Understand the business objectives driving the project	Don't compromise on the right action
Research the problem thoroughly	Don't forget to keep the long-term objectives in mind
Ensure that the whole team is involved and enthusiastic	Don't over-commit and then under-deliver
Plan and budget well	
Measure your progress and success	
Communicate with all stakeholders	

3 Creating a change culture

A business's culture is the attitudes, ideas and beliefs that are shared by employees within the organisation. Leadership style plays a key role in developing an organisational culture that will accept change. A manager who holds McGregor's Theory Y view of his or her employees will attempt to involve employees and give them some ownership of the process. This is likely to help to reduce the degree of resistance to change and to ensure that the project team receives support from people across the organisation.

Communication is important in gaining the support and commitment of the workforce. At the outset of the change process, and before project teams are assembled, it is vital for senior managers to ensure that employees know the reasons for and the objectives of the change programme. Involvement at this early stage helps to prepare employees for change and to gain greater acceptance for the process. Opposition is more likely if employees feel that they are being foisted with a programme for change without explanation and consultation. Employee involvement in planning and executing the change programme, even to the extent of providing information on progress, can assist in gaining acceptance for change.

It is difficult, however, to change an organisation's culture and to gain the support of the workforce throughout this process. Although communication is vital, there are other actions management can take to ease the process. In the initial stages of any project, managers should aim to convince employees to participate and embrace change. This requires managers to:

- establish the current attitudes held by employees

- identify staff who are "opinion formers" and able to influence the views and actions of others

- assess how much resistance to change is likely to occur.

This initial investigation can identify the possible barriers to change as well as bring on board people who may be able to aid the process. Beyond this stage, managers should aim to establish an environment in which trust, creativity and the desire for innovation are actively encouraged and rewarded.

They need to make sufficient resources available to ensure that the change plan can be implemented properly. These resources may be financial, human and material. Employees may be sceptical about, and lack commitment to, any change programme that is under-resourced. Additional staffing may be necessary to allow the business to conduct its normal functions alongside the change project. Further human resources may be required to carry out any in-house training that is needed.

It is important to ensure that the expectations of employees match the reality of the change process. This avoids speculation and rumour, which can develop into hostility and opposition. As with many facets of project management, communication plays a key role in this respect.

Throughout the process, managers must monitor and evaluate the plan to make sure that the project is going as expected. Flexibility may be required to make changes so that the overall objectives are realised and crises are averted. Crises can lead to a sudden and dramatic loss of support for the change process.

assessment practice
Portfolio evidence

Following on from the work you did at the end of the Topic 6, you might want to consider the roles and tasks that are allocated to your team and who might carry out each role. Make a start by identifying your objectives and what has to be achieved to complete the overall project.

Consider the individual strengths of your team members, and the tasks to which they may be best suited. Part of your portfolio evidence should be an analysis of the roles and tasks allocated to your team.

Project plans and change

Setting the scene: Tesco's US expansion

Tesco has reached a decision to open convenience stores in the United States following several years researching the North American market. The UK's largest retailer had a project team in the United States completing the investigation before announcing its decision.

The company's project team, lead by Tim Mason, the company's marketing and property director, will oversee the retailer's start-up in the world's most wealthy market. The project team will use the company's experience of operating Express stores in the UK in designing its new US convenience shops.

Tesco will face tough competition in the United States. Many retail analysts believe that Tesco will find the US market hugely competitive and that the company may struggle to succeed. However, it's a growing market. Tesco's research has revealed that the US grocery market is worth over £340 billion a year, and analysts expect it to grow by 40 per cent by 2011.

Tesco's rival Sainsbury failed in an attempt to move into the US market, selling its Shaw supermarket chain in 2004. Tesco chief executive Terry Leahy has no doubts, however. "We have committed serious resources to developing a format that we believe will be really popular with American consumers. We've put a strong team together, led by Tim Mason and drawing on the wealth of skills and experience within the group," he said.

Sources: BBC News website, 9 February 2006 and Tesco press release, 9 February 2006

Drawing up a project plan

The main focus of this unit is small tactical change rather than major strategic change. However, in this topic we temporarily suspend this constraint to consider the full potential and uses of project plans in achieving the objectives of a change process. We shall look at the stages involved in creating a project plan for use in a change programme.

1 Getting started

Writing a plan for a project provides the necessary framework for thinking about how it will deliver on its aims. The first stage of any project, therefore, is to define what change you are hoping to effect. This is called the initiation stage. There should be a clear business reason for undertaking the project. The opening elements of the plan should state what the project needs to accomplish – that is, it should set out its aims and objectives.

> ### KEY TERMS
>
> **Project management** is the process of delivering the agreed result on time and within the set budget.
>
> A **project team** is a group of people assembled for a clearly defined purpose and for the duration of the project.
>
> A **project plan** is a formal, approved document used to guide the carrying out of the project, and to monitor and control its progress.

The aim of the project is a statement of the change that it is intended to complete. The objectives, as we discussed in Topic 4, should be derived from the aim, but are more specific and can be measured.

2 Making a plan

The people writing the project plan need to consider which strategies and methods might be used to achieve the change objectives. There is likely to be more than one way to achieve objectives, so planners

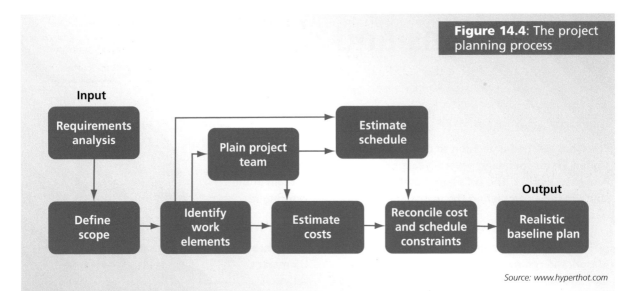

Figure 14.4: The project planning process

Source: www.hyperthot.com

stop and **think**

Who will be involved in drawing up the project plan you are producing for your portfolio evidence? Will you involve everyone in your team, or will one or two people do it? What are the advantages and disadvantages of involving a larger number of people?

must assess the advantages and disadvantages of each approach and decide which is likely to be the most successful. They also need to answer several important questions.

■ What will be covered by the project plan? This is called the scope and boundaries. It is important to be clear about the scope and boundaries to ensure there are no misunderstandings down the line. The team should know what lies outside the scope of the project. One way to think about scope is in terms of who, what, when, where, how.

■ What factors are critical to the success of the project? For example, if the project is to design a website then usability is likely to be a critical success factor.

■ Who is going to be involved in the project team? What are their strengths and areas of expertise? What roles are they most suited for?

■ What budget is available for the plan? Projects can involve expenditure on wages and salaries, travel, equipment, resources such as equipment and buildings, and specialist services from other businesses such as IT support.

■ What are the project outcomes? This can be physical things – tangible deliverables such as websites, reports, products – or intangible knowledge and experiences.

It is essential to ensure that a project is satisfactorily completed on time and within budget. Writing a project plan will force all members of the team to discuss their ideas and make decisions about how to proceed. The project plan details how the project will be completed, by when, by whom, and how much it will cost. The plan should demonstrate that all facets of the project have been carefully considered.

stop and **think**

Think about the following issues in relation to your project plan.

■ What are the issues that are essential to its success?

■ What is the timescale within which you have to complete it?

■ How will you know if your plan has been successful?

3 Work breakdown structure

Having decided what the project intends, the next task is to decide what the project team needs to do, and how to do it. You need to think of the project as a set of sequenced tasks. Any project can be broken down into a set of simpler tasks, which when carried out in sequence will achieve the desired outcome. This process is given the rather grand name of work breakdown structure.

If any task is too complicated to organise easily, then it should be broken down into a series of smaller and less complex tasks. Managers can then provide clear instructions about what is to be done, and estimate the time and resources required. Work breakdown structure helps project managers to include all the little details of a change project which can be easily forgotten at the planning stage.

4 Task allocation

The next stage is to decide who will be responsible for carrying out the individual tasks that have been identified. At this stage, it is important to know when each task needs to be completed to ensure that tasks are carried out in the right sequence.

Task allocation can be a complex task for a team manager. The manager has to make sure that team members given responsibility for particular tasks are capable of completing them. This requires matching the skills and experience of the team member to the demands of the specific tasks.

However, there is a more subtle aspect to the process of task allocation. The project manager needs to consider the development of the team. In some circumstances, it may be beneficial in the long term to give tasks to people of which they have little experience and possibly limited skills. The manager may justify this decision on the grounds that the team member has the potential to complete the task and it will contribute to the member's personal development. This will help to make the team member a more valuable employee in the future.

Managers try to guesstimate how long it will take to complete each task. This is added to the work breakdown structure, as it will help schedule and allocate tasks. As we will see later in this topic, there are techniques and tools that can be used to aid this process.

stop and think

Think how you are going to allocate the tasks in your project.

- Will you give tasks to the people who are best suited to them?

- What will you do if this places too much work on one or two individuals?

- What will you do if there are tasks for which team members are not skilled?

5 Executing the project

Once the project is underway, you must build in regular points to review progress and ensure you are still on track. There are two major elements used by managers to control their projects.

- Milestones – clear targets (short-term goals) of what you will deliver by when. If these are not met, managers will take corrective action to put the project back on time.

- Effective communication – it is essential to have an early warning system for any problems to allow you to take corrective action. All team members should report back regularly on progress, and meetings may be arranged for this purpose.

6 Project evaluation

Evaluating the success of a project plan requires that a number of important questions are answered.

- Were the objectives of the project met?

- Was the outcome of suitable quality, and did it meet the needs of the project's stakeholders?

- Was enough time allocated?

- Did everyone understand the project definition and their roles within it?

- What lessons did we learn from our mistakes and successes?

The case study on page 270 shows how one business put this planning process into practice.

Project scheduling tools

To ensure that your team has the right resources available at the right time, it is essential that the project has a schedule. There are many tools available to help managers schedule project tasks. In the next section, we consider two of the most widely used tools: Gantt charts and critical path analysis

Gantt charts

Gantt charts are a visual way to analyse, plan and sequence activities within a change project. A Gantt chart is really a bar chart with activities listed on the vertical axis, and the timescale on the horizontal axis. Horizontal lines or bars are drawn for each activity, and the length of these bars shows the time taken to complete each activity. A Gantt chart is drawn up by following the stages listed on page 271.

This case study sets out some aspects of a project plan drawn up by a medium-sized business that was relocating its printing operation. The company used two teams to oversee this move: a design team which was engaged in the planning process, and a smaller project team that actually carried through the change programme.

The full design team consisted of:

■ planning consultant (to help to gain planning permission for the development)

■ quantity surveyor (to cost the project)

■ project manager (project champion)

■ architect (building and landscape design)

■ structural engineer (ground surveys, specialist engineering calculations and design)

■ builder (construction of building)

■ mechanical and electrical consultant

■ mechanical and electrical contractors (installation of factory systems)

■ planning supervisor (health and safety issues).

The project team consisted of three full-time members as well as some part-time members The team members, and their responsibilities, were:

■ project manager (full-time, managed activities, set priorities, liaised with directors)

■ project engineer (full-time, responsible for press and factory system design and installation)

■ project co-ordinator (full-time, produced plans, maintained cost forecasts, maintained records)

■ operations director (strategic direction, financial authorisation, liaison with other directors)

■ operations managers (operational and personnel issues).

Liaison with external agencies
During the course of the project, liaison was required with various external organisations as well as the contractors and suppliers working on the project. These included customers, the company's regular suppliers, council planning authorities, local authority environmental agencies, the Health and Safety Executive and utility companies.

Internal communication
How was the change presented to the workforce? The directors presented the high-level details of the change during briefing sessions with the workforce. The operations managers provided more details through regular meetings and daily contact with staff. The project manager issued a monthly project summary on the factory notice boards.

Project timescales
The overall timescale of the project had depended on whether a new factory was built, or an existing building adapted. In the event, a new factory was built and the plan allowed 36 weeks for construction following the signing of a contract with the builders. After construction, the first press could be installed. Up to 25 weeks was scheduled into the plan for the fit-out process (installing all factory systems and moving equipment). Overall the plan had a timescale in excess of one year.

Project management tools
A hierarchy of Gantt charts was used to plan and control the project.

■ Level 1 – outline plans (main events against a long-term timescale)

■ Level 2 – task plans (key tasks in more detail against a medium-term timescale)

■ Level 3 – activity plans (key activities in detail against a short-term timescale).

Spreadsheets were used to forecast anticipated expenditure on factory fit out equipment and services, and to record and categorise actual costs. A detailed filing system was maintained to ensure that all documents, specifications, drawings and plans were available quickly when required.

How were blocking factors evaluated?
A process called risk management was used to identify issues that could prevent targets being reached. Once the main risks were identified, a risk register was produced, and owners were assigned for each risk. The objective was to review each risk to eliminate it if possible, or reduce the effect if elimination was not practical. Project meetings were used to monitor progress on the risk register, and to identify what actions needed to be taken.

Listing and classifying activities

An essential part of project planning is to recognise that some activities are dependent on others being completed first. These dependent activities need to be completed in sequence, with each stage being finished before the next activity can begin. These are sequential tasks. However, some activities can be completed at any time as they are not dependent on other tasks. These are called parallel tasks.

For each activity or task in the project, managers should show the earliest date it needs to start, estimate how long it will take to complete, and assess whether it is a parallel or sequential task. If tasks are sequential, it is necessary to list the other activities upon which they depend.

Plotting the activities

On graph paper or using a computer, managers should draw the project time intervals on the horizontal or x-axis. They plot each task on the chart, showing it starting on the earliest possible date. It is drawn as a bar, with the length of the bar being the duration of the task. Above the task bars, the time taken to complete them is clearly marked. At this stage, project managers do not schedule the activities, or determine when each one will be completed.

Scheduling the activities

It is at this stage that the draft Gantt chart can be used to schedule actions. There are several important considerations in drawing up the schedule.

■ Any sequential actions must be carried out in the required sequence.

■ If possible, managers should schedule parallel tasks so that they do not interfere with sequential actions. This can assist in using scarce resources efficiently. In essence, this means fitting in parallel tasks during a "quiet" period in the project.

■ While scheduling, managers should aim to make the best use of the resources available, and should not be too ambitious in what can be completed in a limited time.

■ Managers should build some slippage time into the schedule. This allows for unforeseen problems, and can avoid a situation in which stakeholders become dissatisfied because a project is not finished when a project manager said it would be.

Presenting the analysis

The outcome of the process of drawing up a Gantt chart should be something like Figure 14.5. This chart shows when activities should start and finish. As the

Figure 14.5: A Gantt chart for the launch of a new product

Tasks	Time (Months)								
---	J	F	M	A	M	J	J	A	S
Customer survey									
Design									
Developing prototype									
Setting up production line									
Staff training									
Promotion									

activities on the Gantt chart are completed, the bars are filled in. Used in this way, Gantt charts help you to plan a list of tasks that need to be completed. They assist you in scheduling when these tasks will be carried out, and in allocating the resources that you will need to complete the project. Gantt charts also help you to monitor the progress of a project, and see which stages are on schedule.

Critical path analysis

Critical path analysis (CPA) similarly breaks down a change project into a series of separate activities. The time required to complete each of these activities is estimated, and judgements are made as to whether individual activities have to be completed before, after or at the same time as other activities. It is recognising what activities in a complex project can be carried out at the same time that is at the heart of CPA.

Critical path analysis uses a diagram (called a network) to show all the activities which make up a project. The CPA diagram shows the sequence in which the tasks or activities must be completed, the length of time taken to complete each activity, the earliest time at which each activity can start, and the latest time at which activity can finish without delaying the whole project.

We look at critical path analysis in detail in Unit 16. On pages 391–4, we set out how to draw a critical

business practice
Microsoft project planner

Managers use IT extensively in planning and monitoring change projects. The software is designed to help project teams cope with all aspects of project management. Probably the most used software is Microsoft Project Planner. This package assists project managers in developing plans, assigning resources to tasks, tracking progress of all tasks within the project, managing budgets and analysing workloads. Microsoft Project Planner can draw up critical path networks. The outcome is shown as a Gantt chart. Resources (people, equipment and materials) can be shared between projects. Each resource can have its own calendar, which defines what days and shifts it is available. Resource rates are used to calculate resource assignment costs which can be summarised as part of the budget.

Many other businesses produce project planning software. See, for example, Atlantic Global software (www.atlantic-ec.com).

path network, as well as highlighting the strengths and weaknesses of the technique.

assessment practice
Pat's café

Pat Marshall manages *Natural Fare*, a very popular vegetarian café in Frome in Somerset. She is in the process of planning the extension of her business into a neighbouring property so that she can increase her café's seating capacity. Pat has drawn up her plan for the expansion and is keen to complete this as quickly as possible because the building work will be disruptive.

A In what ways might Pat benefit from breaking down the project into a series of smaller tasks?

B Do you think that she should draw a Gantt chart for this project? Explain your decision.

assessment practice
Portfolio work

At this stage you should be able to draw up your own project plan. You can draw up the plan, setting out its aims and objectives, breaking down the project into tasks, and detailing the organisation of human, financial and other resources. The only missing element is contingency plans – these are covered in Topic 9.

Risk, uncertainty and change

Setting the scene: Coca-Cola gets it wrong

Dasani was launched in the United States in 1999 as purified bottled water. It was a great success and became the market leader for bottled water. Coca-Cola decided, unsurprisingly, to repeat a successful formula by launching Dasani in the UK.

Dasani is different from most bottled water sold in the UK. It is not a mineral water that has been drawn from deep springs and wells – its source is tap water. Once drawn from the tap, the water is purified three times and minerals are added, but nonetheless Dasani does come from a tap, and British consumers were not used to paying for tap water in this way.

Coca-Cola launched Dasani in February 2004, with few people aware of its source. The decision to launch in the UK was part of the company's strategy to diversify into products that cannot be linked to obesity. Most consumers assumed that it was mineral water like the other bottles on the supermarket shelves. Initially all went well.

However, within weeks, the tabloid newspapers had discovered (from an article in *The Grocer*) the true source of Dasani – it was tap water from Sidcup in Kent. The result was inevitable. Headline writers had fun at Coca-Cola's expense. *The Sun* called it "The real sting", a play on Coca-Cola's advertising strapline "The real thing".

The publicity was disastrous. Sales of Dasani slumped when consumers realised they were paying nearly £1 a bottled for tap water. Despite this, Coca-Cola continued its advertising campaign. It fought back by explaining that the product was the purest drinking water on sale in the UK. However, the company was about to face another disaster.

In mid March it was revealed that at least one batch of Dasani exceeded the UK's legal limit for bromate, a chemical linked with cancer. Bromate is found in the calcium which is added to Dasani during the purification process. The UK's legal limit is 10 parts per billion, but Dasani had between 10 and 22 parts per billion. (EU standards are less stringent at 25 parts per billion.)

Coca-Cola's executives bowed to the inevitable. Within one week of the bromate scare, half a million bottles of Dasani had been withdrawn from shops throughout the UK. There has been no attempt to launch the brand again in the UK.

Factors that can prevent change

It is impossible to drawn up a comprehensive list of all the factors that might prevent a business implementing a change programme. In this unit, we look at some of the most common problems that can derail a change programme

1 Unclear or unrealistic aims and objectives

Unclear aims can result in internal difficulties within a business, and represent a threat to successful change from the outset of the process. Aims provide all employees with a sense of direction. In particular, senior employees (directors of companies and the owners of small businesses) use them as a guide

A **contingency plan** is a document which sets out how a business will respond to unwanted or unlikely events such as a fire or the bankruptcy of a major supplier.

Risk is the possibility of a business incurring misfortune or financial loss.

Aims are the long-term intentions of a business.

Objectives are targets or goals that must be achieved in the medium term if the organisation's aims are to be realised.

when setting objectives. If a business has unclear or contradictory aims, managers may experience difficulties in deciding and setting the quantifiable objectives that they and more junior employees should pursue.

Implementing change with vague aims such as "improving the business's performance" are unclear in the sense that employees will be uncertain as to which aspect of the business's performance should be the focus of any action. Should they set objectives to enhance the business's profitability (which might entail cutting costs as an objective) or to improve its record on environmental responsibility (which may result in increased operational costs)?

Unclear objectives can pose similar problems in change programmes. They make it difficult for project managers to determine the tasks that need to be completed and to allocate those tasks to members of the project team.

There are several steps that managers can take at this stage to avoid problems with imprecise or unclear objectives.

- Sufficient time and resources must be devoted at this early stage of the management of a change project. This might include the use of employees with specialist skills to help, for example, in setting timescales that are realistic.

- The statement of aims and objectives of the change project must be simple and direct.

- The team should set objectives that meet the SMART criteria to avoid any ambiguities.

Businesses can assess the likelihood of unclear aims or objectives blocking change by considering the experience of the project team managing the change. An experienced team is more likely to have encountered these difficulties in the past and will use this knowledge to avoid any recurrence.

Change projects which are complex or which take several years to complete may be more at risk of

having unclear aims and objectives. By assessing these risk factors at the outset, managers can increase the probability of writing clear and unambiguous aims and objectives.

2 Lack of commitment from management or staff

Uncommitted managers or staff can pose a major threat to the success of a project, because change projects normally are a time when more is expected of employees within a business, and especially those in the project team. To complete a change project on time, employees may be expected to work additional hours (sometimes without receiving additional pay). Members of the project team may be required to carry out tasks or take responsibilities that may not be within their normal working routine. Other employees may be expected to cover for those working on the change project.

What makes employees likely to be uncommitted in the face of change? A conventional view is that older employees tend to oppose change. However, research does not bear this out. A lack of commitment is more likely to be the result of other factors.

Threat of job losses

Many change programmes lead to redundancies. The introduction of machinery on to a production line or the introduction of internet banking have led to job losses in the manufacturing and banking industries. The possibility of job losses is not a reason for deciding not to introduce change, but it does mean that the project has to be handled sensitively. It makes the need to communicate with employees and their representatives paramount.

Time pressures

Some projects set a timescale for change which places employees under undue and unnecessary pressure. By setting tight deadlines, say for introducing a new product on to the market, a business might feel it can quickly increase sales and profits. However, if employees feel that it is not possible to complete the project successfully in the time allotted, they may lack commitment. In these circumstances, precious time and energy may be spent arguing about timescales rather than making progress with the project.

Lack of consultation

Employees are more likely to be committed if they feel some ownership for the change project. In a small business, it may be possible to hold meetings at which employees can make direct contributions to deciding upon and planning change. In bigger organisations, this approach may not be feasible because a business may have too many employees and may operate in numerous locations. However, it is possible to forewarn employees of the need for change and to keep them informed of the nature and progress of the change programme.

Lack of training

Many change programmes involve the introduction of information technology into the workplace. Employees are more likely to be committed (and possibly enthused) if they can appreciate the potential of technology to improve their working lives and if they feel confident in their ability to operate the technology effectively. Training is the key to creating these types of positive feelings.

---

business practice

Prudential

Prudential is a financial services company, offering personal banking, insurance and pension products, with operations in Asia, the UK and Europe, and the United States. In April 2006, the company announced that it was to close some of its offices in Belfast, Bristol and London. Some 700 jobs will be transferred to other locations in the UK as well as to offices in India.

One objective of this change programme is to contribute to an annual £40 million reduction in the company's costs. Managers at the company plan to avoid any compulsory redundancies before the end of 2006, and the relocation programme will take two years to complete.

The announcement provoked great opposition from employees, and trade unions have threatened strike action. David Fleming, an official of the union Amicus said: "Amicus is prepared to fight these proposals, and we will support our members in any action they choose to take to protect their jobs. We have told the company in no uncertain terms that we do not accept their proposals and that they are making no attempt to avoid compulsory redundancies."

The union added that it had signed an agreement with Prudential back in 2002 which stipulated that no compulsory redundancies would be made at the firm as a result of offshoring.

---

stop and **think**

What actions might Prudential take to reduce the amount of opposition to its change programme? Which single action do you think might be most effective?

3 Failing to draw up effective implementation plans

Project plans are at the heart of any successful change programme. The failure to identify the tasks that make up the entire project, to identify key milestones by which success can be measured and monitored along the way, and to allocate adequate financial and human resources to a change project can all contribute to its failure.

Several factors can lead to the creation of project plans which do not stand up to the rigours of implementation. A lack of experience in the project planning team may result in a plan that lacks detail, is incomplete or contains inconsistencies. It is vital that some of the team have experience in planning as well as implementing change projects. This is especially true of the project manager or champion. It is not enough for this person to have enthusiasm for the project; success is more likely if he or she has experience of the process.

A range of tools is available to support managers when drawing up project plans. We have considered the uses and benefits of techniques such as Gantt charts, critical path analysis and software tools such as Microsoft Project Planner. These tools can reduce the workload at a time of considerable pressure, as well as assist in scheduling tasks, managing time effectively and monitoring progress. However, relying on these approaches does not eliminate the possibility of producing a project plan that is not robust. Managers still have to identify the tasks that are necessary to complete the change programme and to allocate sufficient resources at the right times.

The appointment of suitably skilled and experienced staff to the project team, and the provision of adequate resources, are the key actions that businesses can take to help ensure that they produce robust project plans at the outset of the change process.

4 Risks and changing circumstances

All projects, no matter how carefully planned and fully resourced, are subject to a number of risks.

Threats to the project's timescale

Delays can result from many events. Suppliers may fail to deliver materials or provide specialist staff at the expected and agreed time because of internal problems. Bad weather, natural disasters and mechanical failures can all result in unexpected delays. Longer, more complex projects are more vulnerable to threats to meeting deadlines, as in the case of the new Wembley Stadium (see box below).

Threats to project tasks

Employees are critical to the completion of the tasks that make a change project. Any project can suffer if key staff get ill or leave the business during the course of the project. These problems can be more acute within a small business, where there is less likely to be cover for absent employees and staff may not be multiskilled. External factors can mean that some tasks become irrelevant or other new tasks become necessary. During the building of the new Wembley Stadium, sewer pipes below the site collapsed. The construction team had to divert resources to repair the pipes before the project could continue.

Threats to the project's budget

It can be a challenging task to forecast the costs of a change project. Unexpected delays obviously add to costs, but other factors such as rising prices can also push costs upwards. In some cases, change projects can exceeded budgeted costs by large amounts. The cost of the new Parliament building in Edinburgh was originally estimated at £40 million; the final cost was £431 million.

Managers can reduce the threats to projects by building in time to allow for delays to the project plan, by avoiding relying too extensively on a single supplier, and also by training employees to enable them to take on a variety of tasks.

Employing other businesses to carry out part of the work of a project can also increase the risk of delays, as these business may have other objectives and commitments. Some organisations impose heavy penalty fines on suppliers that deliver late to reduce the risk of delays.

business practice
Wembley Stadium not completed on time

The factors causing the construction of Wembley Stadium to be completed late included subcontractors' performance, changes in design, relations with trade unions representing workers on the site, and the weather. Finishing the roof on the stadium's south side also caused a problem. Windy conditions delayed the removal of steel cable supports to settle the roof into its final position.

But there is one reason above others that Wembley was not be ready on time, according to one industry commentator. "The real reason why it was ready on time is because of the dispute with steelwork firm Cleveland Bridge in summer 2004," said David Rogers, deputy news editor of *Construction News*.

"Wembley is basically steel," he said. Cleveland Bridge was contracted to source, fabricate and install the steel. A long-bubbling dispute over money with Multiplex (the Australian company building the stadium) saw Cleveland Bridge end its agreement. The result was months of work time lost, David Rogers said. "They had to try to claw back five months and they didn't have enough wriggle room."

"The delay did have knock-on effects, causing problems with other subcontractors, such as electricians, as the company tried to make up the time. But they all relate to the fact that if Multiplex wasn't having to rush to get the job finished, they wouldn't have had all these problems."

Unconfirmed newspaper reports say that Multiplex has overspent its construction budget by a huge amount, some say by more than £100 million.

Source: BBC News website, 21 February 2006

Contingency plans

A contingency plan is a document which sets out how a business will respond to unwanted or unlikely events such as a fire or the bankruptcy of a major supplier.

All plans, and especially long-term plans, can go wrong. It is important for businesses to prepare for this eventuality. They should also plan for the unexpected. When the unexpected does happen, it is essential that the organisation is prepared. A central element of the business's response should be to put a contingency plan into operation.

There are many circumstances in which a contingency plan is required to assist in the completion of a change programme. Here are just a few threats.

- The failure of a supplier – a supplier may cease trading due to financial problems, perhaps leaving the project without essential materials or human skills.

- Becoming the object of the attentions of a pressure groups – change programmes may pose a threat to the environment and be the focus of protests.

- Competitor actions – a plan to launch a new product may be undermined by a rival bringing out a similar product first.

A business constructing a contingency plan as part of the overall project plan should make sure that it nominates key personnel with responsibility for implementing the contingency plan. One employee should be given overall responsibility. Sufficient resources must be available deal with a problem – the team may need financial resources, communications technology and access to experts to cope with the unexpected. There must be effective communications to identify the nature and causes of the problem as well as to prepare appropriate responses.

Building in flexibility to the project can help to deal with a range of unexpected events. Flexibility can take several forms.

- Staffing should be as flexible as possible. If employees can carry out a range of tasks, then the loss of one member of staff, no matter how important, should be easier to cover.

- The project schedule should build in some allowance for delays. This can reduce pressure on managers and allow them to handle the consequences of delays more effectively.

- By including milestones as often as possible, project planners can take action before the project is too far advanced and delays become inevitable. Milestones are points in the project plan at which progress can be assessed and remedial action taken if necessary.

assessment practice
Pat's café

Pat Marshall manages *Natural Fare*, a very popular vegetarian café in Frome in Somerset. She is in the process of planning the extension of her business into a neighbouring property so that she can increase her café's seating capacity. She has completed her plans for the expansion but is concerned about whether her plan will be completed on time.

A Identify and explain three possible factors which could delay Pat's project plan

B What actions can Pat take to minimise the chances of her plan not working out as expected?

assessment practice
Portfolio work

This is the final topic in Unit 14. When you have completed this topic, you have all the necessary subject knowledge to complete your evidence for the portfolio. By this stage you should already have completed most of the requirements. This topic allows you to complete the final element of requirement, assessing the risks and uncertainty associated with the change your team is planning.

THIS UNIT EXAMINES HOW BUSINESSES MANAGE and review their finances. It considers the purpose of financial statements and the underlying concepts that underpin their compilation. It also looks at the systems used by businesses to try and ensure that reported information is accurate, and how this information is then analysed to provide a key source of data on business performance.

It introduces the main accounting concepts, the basic rules followed by accountants when preparing financial information. These provide a framework to ensure that the final accounts of a business present a true and fair view of that business's financial position regardless of the accountant who actually produced them.

It explores the purpose and use of different financial documents, how they flow between and around business organisations, and how large volumes of transactions are recorded to make sure that mistakes and inaccuracies do not occur.

This unit introduces the two main financial statements – the profit and loss account and the balance sheet – which can be used to examine a business's financial performance and prospects. We examine how businesses can use this information to review and monitor their performance by calculating key financial ratios.

Financial accounting for managers

Setting the scene: financial information for stakeholders

There are many different stakeholder groups who are interested in the financial performance of a business. As Figure 15.1 suggests, it is not just the owner(s) and managers that need to know how well a business is doing.

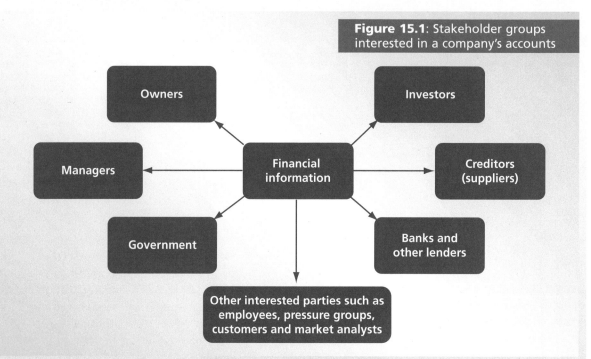

Figure 15.1: Stakeholder groups interested in a company's accounts

Owners

Investors

Managers

Financial information

Creditors (suppliers)

Government

Banks and other lenders

Other interested parties such as employees, pressure groups, customers and market analysts

It is important therefore that all accounts follow a common format so that the different interested parties can understand what the information means. It shouldn't matter if a business's accounts are prepared by, say, an accountant in Aberdeen or by one in Oldham, the accountants should both arrive at the same figures and report the same information.

In order for this to be achieved, accountants follow standard rules and guidelines when preparing financial information, so that comparisons can be made between a business's performance year on year or so that the financial performance of two companies can be assessed on a like-for-like basis.

The fundamental rules for how accountants should treat financial transactions when preparing financial information are laid down by the ASB (Accounting Standards Board). This provides a system for producing financial accounts that everybody can agree to, and these fundamental rules are known as the "accounting concepts".

Key concepts

In this topic, we set out the standard concepts that underpin the preparation and presentation of financial accounts. These concepts help to set the ground rules that we shall see applied when we look at the preparation of accounts and financial statements in later topics in this unit.

Going concern

The concept of a going concern is mainly concerned with how a company values its assets. It requires that accounts should be prepared on the assumption that the business will continue to be a viable trading concern into the foreseeable future. If the business is viable, then the assets that it uses to produce goods

Going concern is the assumption that the business is going to continue trading into the foreseeable future.

Accruals (or matching) concept is the practice of placing costs incurred and revenues generated by a business in the financial periods in which goods and services were used and products were sold. This is not necessarily when payments were actually made.

Consistency is the application of a uniform approach to accounting policies when presenting accounts.

Prudence is an approach that accounts for losses as soon as they are anticipated – that is, immediately – but accounts for profits only when they are realised.

Realisation is the concept that recognises that revenue and profits have only been earned when the actual ownership of goods has been exchanged, and cash or credit payment agreements are in place.

Materiality assesses the impact of individual items on the presentation of accounts. Items with a low monetary value are not recorded separately.

Duality covers the principle that every business transaction has two effects, and gives rise to both a debit and a credit entry in the accounting system.

Business entity concept considers the accounts of the business and its owner(s) to be two totally separate legal entities. In other words, the assets and liabilities of the owner are kept separate from those of the business itself.

Money measurement refers to the underlying principle that financial accounting is only concerned with recording items that have a definite measurable monetary value.

and services have some value. In other words, the idea is that the productive assets of a business that is a going concern are worth more than those of a business that is about to close down.

Consider a company like the Ford Motor Company. Assuming that it is going to keep manufacturing models such as the Mondeo, the assets (machinery) used to produce these cars have an intrinsic value to the company. However, if Ford is to stop trading, what use – and, therefore, value – are the machines used to make Ford Mondeos to another company?

If a business is assumed to be a going concern, the value of its assets are listed at their current worth to the business. If a business is to cease trading, the assets are only worth what they could feasibly be sold for to another company or to a scrap merchant.

The accruals or matching concept

The accruals concept highlights the fact that profit is not simply the measurement of cash in minus cash out. It states that the measurement of profit is the difference between the revenues the business has earned and the costs (expenses) involved in earning those revenues during the financial period being considered. Notice that this statement does not say that these costs must have been paid for. To consider what this means in practice, consider two examples.

Businesses need electricity to run their offices, computers, lights, machinery, etc. In many cases, electricity bills are paid quarterly (every three months) by businesses. They are usually paid in arrears – the business pays the utility company for what it has consumed in the previous period. The accruals

concept means that when calculating profit, it doesn't matter that a business may not receive and pay the electricity bill for several more months or weeks, it has used the electricity now and therefore this cost should be included in the profit calculation.

Similarly, suppose one of the business's customers may buy some goods on credit terms and agree to pay the bill in two months' time. Even though the customer has not yet paid for the goods, the business has still sold them. So the sales revenue has been earned and is included in the calculation of profit, despite the fact that the business has not yet received the money.

These examples explain why this concept is also known as the matching concept – the practice is to match a cost or revenue to the financial period when the transaction took place, not when the payment changes hands. A key application of this concept is the theory of depreciation (covered in Topic 8). Depreciation spreads the cost of a fixed asset over the years the asset will be kept and used by the company, rather than including the whole cost in the accounts covering the year the asset was purchased.

stop and think

Consider the Ford Motor Company in the context of the accruals concept. How do most private buyers purchase a new car? What would be the effect on Ford's profits for the year if it only recorded the amount it received in payment from customers?

Consistency

In some cases, accountants may face a choice as to how they should treat certain items and transactions. The reason this occurs is due to the fact that every business is unique, so the way a particular item might be treated for one business is not the same as how it may be treated for another. Consider, for example, that most companies would regard a vehicle as an asset that they would keep and use over a number of years. However, for Ford, a vehicle would represent a stock item that it intends to sell. It makes sense, therefore, that the treatment (classification) of vehicles is different in Ford's accounts and those of a business that uses a vehicle as part of its operations.

In simple terms, the consistency concept states that once a firm has decided upon a method for how an item should be treated, similar items should be treated the same way. The same method should also be applied year on year, so that the accounts produced are consistent and comparable. This concept has particular application when companies are choosing how best to depreciate fixed assets.

Prudence

In many cases, the actual value of an item may not be completely clear-cut. Suppose, for example, a business has some outstanding debts – it is owed money by one customer, and every time the business asks, the customer promises that the debt will be paid. However, after a period of time, no payment has yet been received. In this case, should the accountant be optimistic and assume the customer will pay given further time, or should the accountant be pessimistic and assume that the company will never actually be paid? This is where the concept of prudence comes into effect. It states that potential losses should be accounted for as soon as they are anticipated – that is, as soon as it is thought that losses are going to be incurred – but, conversely, a profit is only recognised when it has happened in reality.

The reason for this practice is that it would be unwise for an accountant to overstate the profits or value of a business. The owners or potential lenders might think that the business is performing better than it

Unit 15 Financial accounting for managers

stop and think

What might the owner of a small business like an independent newsagent do if she potentially thought the business was making more profit than it actually was?

actually is, and this could cause the business to overextend itself or for people to lend it money when its not really such a safe prospect.

The realisation concept

The realisation concept ties in with the idea of prudence. Profits are only recognised once they have happened in reality – in financial terms, this called being realised. For a profit on a transaction to be considered as realised, four criteria must be met:

- goods or services have been provided to the buyer
- the monetary value (price) of the goods or services has been agreed
- the buyer either pays for the goods or accepts responsibility (under, say, a credit contract) to pay for the goods at a future date
- the buyer will be in a situation to be able to pay for the goods or services received.

Again using our example of Ford, if it sold a car to a customer who agreed to make monthly payments for three years to purchase the vehicle, and the customer discovers that he is unable to afford the repayments after having taken possession of the car, Ford would be able to repossess the vehicle as the customer is not in a position to pay. Ford would not be able to record the whole amount of profit it would normally have made on the sale as, in reality, that profit will not be realised as the customer did not in fact pay the agreed price.

Materiality

The fundamental basis of accounting is that the information it is providing to the various interested stakeholder groups should be meaningful and worthwhile. If the cost of providing this information is greater than the benefit that can be derived from having the information, then it could be argued that gathering and presenting that information is a waste of time. This is the concept of materiality: accountants recognise that being absolutely precise about every single expense would actually cost the business more time and money than any benefit gained.

The accruals/matching concept states that the cost of an item should be matched to the financial periods in which it is used. If we take this literally, then the cost of an A4 ring binder costing 89p should be divided up and spread across the number of years the ring binder is going to be used. This will affect the profit declared by the business by a few pence per year, but the amount spent in wages for calculating and distributing this expense would cost ten times as much. In this case, the cost of the action outweighs the benefit gained. This type of exercise would therefore be deemed immaterial – in other words, it is useless and would be pointless.

As a general rule, if any stakeholder could be misled by the exclusion or inclusion of an item in the accounts, then that item is regarded as being important and therefore material. However, businesses should not waste their time in the sophisticated recording of trivial items.

The duality concept

The duality concept (or dual aspect) concept outlines the view that every financial transaction has two effects, one creating a positive response for the business and one creating a negative response.

Suppose a customer walks on to a garage forecourt and agrees to buy a new car:

- the positive aspect is that the business has made a sale and will receive payment

- the negative aspect is that the business has to give the customer a car – it now has less stock and will need to get some more.

The underlying assumption here is that the two effects are always exactly equal in value, and thus will always balance. From this assumption, we derive an important relationship called the accounting equation.

The accounting equation is the formula that forms the basis for the balance sheet and all balance sheet operations. It is this formula that actually means that a balance sheet will balance. The formula states that:

assets = capital + liabilities

To begin with let us simplify this to:

assets = capital

What this formula says is that all the resources or assets in the business are equal to the amount of money or resources that the owners have invested. For example, imagine that someone is about to establish a business as a window-cleaner. This is a fairly simple (and cheap) form of enterprise. The person starting the business is able to put up all the capital required themselves. This start-up capital is then going to be used to pay for ladders and equipment, and any money left over would be put into a bank account to pay expenses and bills as the business starts trading.

Let's introduce some actual figures at this point. Suppose Bill Godfrey starts his window-cleaning business with £500 that he has managed to save over the last few months. He buys a set of ladders costing £250, several buckets costing £40, some cleaning fluids costing £35 and a squeegee sponge costing £15. He then puts £140 into a business bank account and holds £20 in change. Using the formula, we can present this as a simple equation.

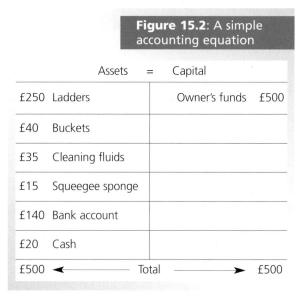

Figure 15.2: A simple accounting equation

Assets		=	Capital	
£250	Ladders		Owner's funds	£500
£40	Buckets			
£35	Cleaning fluids			
£15	Squeegee sponge			
£140	Bank account			
£20	Cash			
£500	←	Total →		£500

Figure 15.2 shows a very simple balance sheet in operation. As can be seen, the two sides balance at £500. Expanding the equation back to its original form, we can now consider the effect that liabilities might have on the situation. Suppose Bill Godfrey decides his window cleaning business would be much more successful if he could get to see more clients. To do this he needs to purchase a van to transport himself and his equipment. However, he used all his own savings to start the business so he approaches the bank for a loan. He manages to obtain a loan for £3,000 repayable over the next two years and buys a van costing £2,700. Figure 15.3 shows the position now. Note that the extra £300 from the loan has been deposited in Bill Godfrey's bank account.

Figure 15.3: The expanded accounting equation

Assets		=	Capital + Liabilities	
£250	Ladders		Owner's funds	£500
£40	Buckets		Two-year loan	£3,000
£35	Cleaning fluids			
£15	Squeegee sponge			
£440	Bank account			
£20	Cash			
£2,700	Van			
£3,500	←	Total →		£3,500

We can see that the accounting equation will always hold true, as any money invested in the business is either spent, in which case we record what it was spent on, or it is left in the form of bank or cash deposits. This in turn gives rise to the format of recording financial transactions known as double entry.

Business entity concept

The business entity concept describes the idea that the financial affairs of the business and the owner are separate. When preparing a business's accounts, we are only concerned with recording the financial transactions of the business itself, not the actions of the owner. Therefore, we ignore private transactions made by the owner(s) and also any transactions regarding their personal assets or liabilities.

Money measurement concept

This concept states that only transactions that can be measured in monetary terms are recorded in a business's accounts. What this means in practice is that a set of accounts is limited in the information it contains, and can never provide you with everything you may need to know about a business. For example, staff motivation is a key factor in business success, but can you measure commitment in monetary terms?

stop and think

Using Figure 15.1, choose three stakeholder groups. List information that they might be interested in knowing that could not be recorded in monetary terms.

assessment practice
Mary's florists

Mary Brooke has just started her own business as a high street florist. She has hired an accountant to produce a set of interim accounts at the end of her first three months' trading. However, she is somewhat puzzled by the results the accountant has produced. She has approached you for some advice in explaining what her accountant has done and why.

A In each of these scenarios, explain to Mary the accounting concept her accountant has applied and why.

i   Mary bought several types of fixtures and fittings to help display the flowers in shop. These ranged in cost from £8 for some vases to £400 for shelving and display units. However, her accountant does not seem to have treated all of these items as fixed assets.

ii Mary has kept detailed records of the amounts of money she has received each day and paid out, but her calculations of the amount of money she has made don't agree with the figure the accountant has calculated for profit. The accountant appears to have even included some amounts she hasn't even paid yet.

iii The accountant appears to have charged Mary's own account (drawings) with the

value of some flowers she took from the shop for her mother's birthday.

iv Mary has received an order from a respected local dignitary to supply flowers worth £600 for the upcoming mayoral dinner. This takes place next month. She has no concerns that the client won't pay, and so she doesn't understand why the accountant has not taken this sale into account.

v   Mary knows that her stock of flowers and associated items is worth at least £7,000 in retail value. However, the accountant appears only to have valued it at £4,300, the same amount that Mary paid for it. She wishes to know how such a wide discrepancy could occur.

B Explain to Mary why she is not allowed to value her business as being worth more than a local competitor because she argues her staff are more polite, happier and better at dealing with customers.

Recording transactions and the financial accounting system: part 1

Setting the scene: why record financial transactions?

Money is the lifeblood of any business. Money is required to set up and establish a new business, to purchase equipment and supplies, and to pay for ongoing running costs. It is vital, therefore, that businesses have systems for controlling and recording the movement of money, and operate these systems accurately.

Financial transactions involve a range of documents, each of which needs to be accurately completed and recorded. The use of written documents allows both buyer and seller to have a clear understanding of the trading arrangements. They confirm each stage of the transaction: the buyer's requirements, the price to be paid to the seller, the delivery of the goods or services, the amount owed by the buyer, the time within which payment must be paid and, finally, the amount paid. These documents constitute legally binding evidence in cases of dispute.

The majority of financial transactions involve either purchases or sales. These need to be recorded in order to calculate the organisation's profit (or loss) when the final accounts are drawn up. It is essential that every transaction be recorded in order to generate complete and accurate accounts. Everything the business has bought or sold must be taken into account when calculating the profit (or loss). Everything the

business owns or is owed by others (its assets) and everything it owes to others (its liabilities) must be shown on the balance sheet. In this way, the final accounts achieve their purpose – to give a "fair and true view" of the financial affairs of the business.

Good record-keeping is also essential to manage cash flow. Purchases and sales on credit need to be recorded in such a way that a business knows what money is owing, both to its suppliers and by its customers. Without accurate records, payments to suppliers may be overlooked or delayed, possibly resulting in supplies being stopped and legal action being taken to recover the debt. At the very least, this will damage relations with the supplier. Likewise, credit customers may delay settling (or fail to pay) their invoices. These outstanding debts cannot be followed up if credit sales are not accurately recorded at the time they are made.

Finally, note that all businesses are required to keep financial records in order that any tax liability can be accurately determined. Information must be recorded and made available to HM Revenue and Customs. This body has the legal right to inspect the accounts and check that they are accurate and represent a fair and true view of the business.

Financial documents

The introduction (above) explains why financial transactions need to be recorded. Now we are going to look at the documents used in the process. Most of these documents are required when goods are purchased and supplied on credit. This is because, as there is a delay between the exchange of goods and payment being made, an exceedingly accurate record needs to be made and maintained by both suppliers and customers.

Note that you might not come across these documents when you are out shopping. In most day-

to-day transactions, you pay for the goods when you receive them. However, the retail sector is only a relatively small part of UK business and industry. The vast majority of businesses supply goods and services to other businesses, and a significant amount of this trade is supplied on credit terms.

Purchase orders

The purchasing process begins when the customer sends an order to a supplier, detailing what the individual or the purchasing organisation wants to purchase. Figure 15.4 (page 286) shows a purchase order for a supply of stationery.

Purchase orders are documents used to initiate or confirm the placing of an order for goods or services from a supplier.

Delivery notes are documents issued by suppliers to customers for signature confirming the delivery of goods made. They are dispatched with the goods.

Goods received notes are internal documents used by the receiver of goods to confirm what has been received by the business. These can be matched against the original purchase order.

Invoices are documents sent from the seller to the buyer that detail the payment required for goods or services exchanged.

Remittance advice slips are sent by customers to suppliers advising them of payments made.

Debit notes are documents sent to customers to notify them that the original invoice is undercharged. These aresometimes used by customers when returning goods to suppliers.

Credit notes are issued by suppliers when customers have returned goods, to act as a discount against any payments still outstanding or to be set off against the customer's next purchase.

Statements of accounts are documents that summarise all transactions between a buyer and a seller over a given period of time (usually one month).

Cheques are blank forms issued by a bank that when completed act as instructions to the bank that the holder of an account wants to transfer a stated sum of money to a named person or business.

Figure 15.4: A purchase order

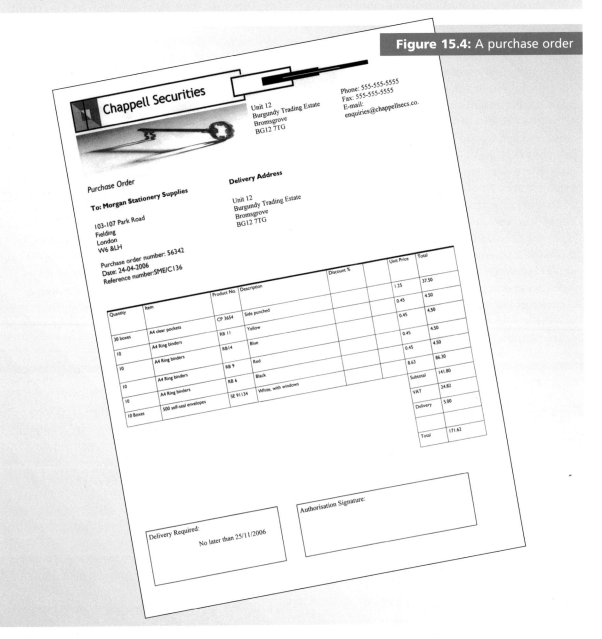

Unit 15 Financial accounting for managers

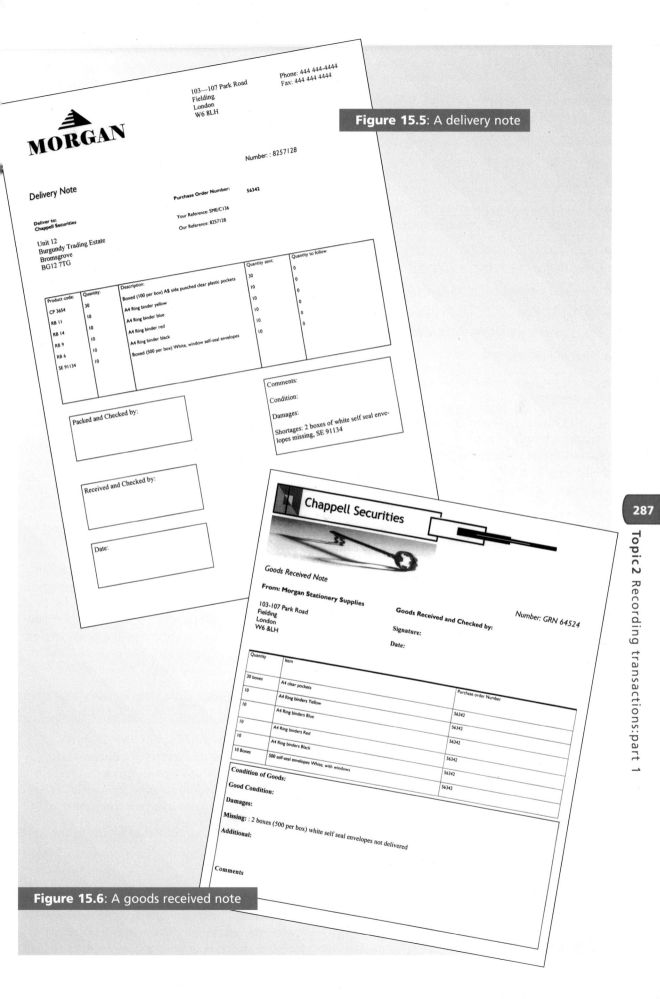

Figure 15.5: A delivery note

Figure 15.6: A goods received note

Each puchase order form shows this information:

- customer's name, address and telephone number
- delivery address (if the goods are to be sent to a different address such as a warehouse)
- unique order number – used for reference on subsequent documents and for filing
- date of order
- a full description of the goods required, including any product code or catalogue numbers
- the quantity required, including units where applicable (such as box of 20, pack of 2)
- unit and total price(s), as quoted by the supplier
- authorised signature – the order must be signed by someone authorised to place orders
- required delivery date
- whether quality and/or certification documentation is required.

Figure 15.4 shows an order placed by Chappell Securities with one of its suppliers, Morgan Stationery Supplies Limited. Look at the list of features that should appear on a purchase order form (set out above) and locate them on this example.

Orders are normally checked and approved by an authorised person, who has both the authority to approve purchases and the responsibility for justifying why they were made. The authorised person then signs the order, making it official. Authorised persons may be the managers of departments, the owners of small businesses or, in some large organisations, a central purchasing department that issues and authorises all orders.

A signed order form is a legal commitment to purchase what has been ordered, so errors can be very expensive. If a business makes a mistake and orders the wrong goods, that business, in turn, may be unable to supply its customers on time. This could prove even more expensive, especially if its customers find a new (and more reliable) supplier and stop buying from the business.

Delivery notes

Having received an order, the supplier checks that the goods are available and arranges for them to be delivered, with an accompanying delivery note. This is issued by the supplier and lists the items that are being delivered. Figure 15.5 (see page 287) shows an delivery note that Morgan Stationery Supplies might have sent following Chappell Securities' order.

When a delivery arrives, the customer checks the goods to ensure that what is listed on the delivery note has actually been delivered in good condition, and then signs the delivery note to confirm receipt of the goods. If the goods are packaged in such a way that a full inspection is not possible at the time of delivery, the person receiving the goods should write "unexamined" on the delivery note before signing it. In this way, the customer retains the right to notify the supplier if goods are later found to be faulty or missing when the packaging is opened.

Once the goods have been signed for, there is a legal obligation to pay for them. It is important, therefore, that the number, specification and condition of the goods are checked against the original order and match the delivery note before the delivery is accepted. This responsibility usually rests with the warehouse supervisor or manager.

Goods received notes

During the purchasing process there could be problems with orders that have been placed, such as:

- missing goods – when the goods received are not in the same quantities as those originally ordered
- additional goods – when the supplier company delivers extra goods to those originally ordered
- damaged or faulty goods – goods that are not fit for the purpose they are intended for.

For this reason, some organisations also prepare an internal document called a goods received note. This lists what has actually been received and is used by the accounts department to check that the purchase invoice, when it arrives, is correct. The goods received note illustrated in Figure 15.6 (see page 287) would have been drawn up by Chappell Securities.

stop and think

Why would an organisation like Chappell Securities draw up its own goods received note? Can you think of two groups of staff at Chappell who would need to know the information contained within this note?

Invoices

Having confirmed receipt of the goods, the customer (Chappell Securities) can now expect to receive an invoice from the supplier (Morgan Stationery Supplies), stating how much money needs to be paid.

Figure 15.7: An invoice

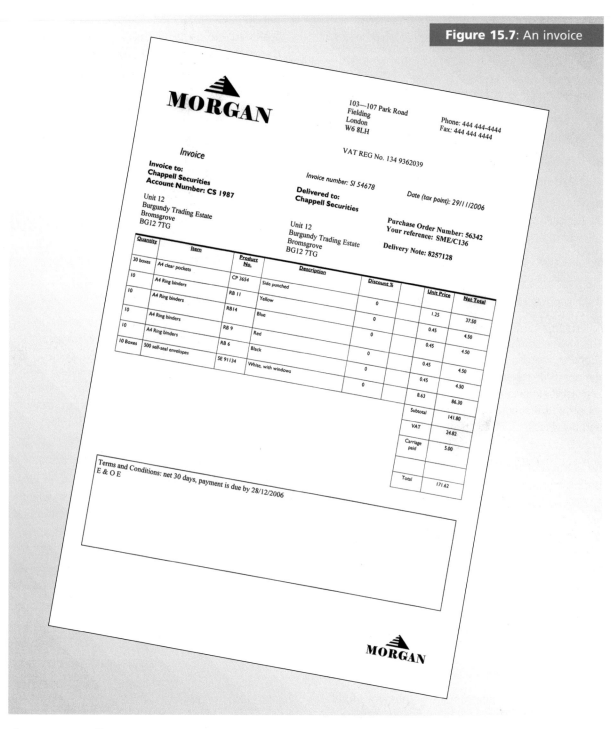

MORGAN

103—107 Park Road
Fielding
London
W6 8LH

Phone: 444 444-4444
Fax: 444 444 4444

Invoice

VAT REG No. 134 9362039

Invoice to:
Chappell Securities
Account Number: CS 1987

Unit 12
Burgundy Trading Estate
Bromsgrove
BG12 7TG

Invoice number: SI 54678

Delivered to:
Chappell Securities

Unit 12
Burgundy Trading Estate
Bromsgrove
BG12 7TG

Date (tax point): 29/11/2006

Purchase Order Number: 56342
Your reference: SME/C136

Delivery Note: 8257128

Quantity	Item	Product No.	Description	Discount %		Unit Price	Net Total
30 boxes	A4 clear pockets	CP 3654	Side punched				
10	A4 Ring binders	RB 11	Yellow	0		1.25	37.50
10	A4 Ring binders	RB14	Blue	0		0.45	4.50
10	A4 Ring binders	RB 9	Red	0		0.45	4.50
10	A4 Ring binders	RB 6	Black	0		0.45	4.50
10 Boxes	500 self-seal envelopes	SE 91134	White, with windows	0		0.45	4.50
				0		8.63	86.30
					Subtotal		141.80
					VAT		24.82
					Carriage paid		5.00
					Total		171.62

Terms and Conditions: net 30 days, payment is due by 28/12/2006
E & O E

MORGAN

These are normally sent by mail, and usually arrive a few days after the goods are received.

As far as the supplier (Morgan) is concerned, this document is a sales invoice. However, from the customer's viewpoint, it is an incoming purchase invoice detailing what has been bought and how much is due to the supplier. In other words, the same document serves two purposes depending on which side of the transaction you are: buyer or seller.

The invoice shows details about the supplier, the customer, the date of sale, the details of goods or services supplied, and the terms of trade. It has names and addresses:

■ of the supplier

■ of the customer – to whom the invoice should be sent

■ to whom the goods were delivered (if different from the above).

The invoice date is the start of the credit period. It therefore determines when payment is due. If VAT is included, the invoice date is also known as the "tax point" because it is the date at which the sale officially takes place, and at which VAT is charged for tax purposes.

The invoice usually has several reference numbers. These include:

■ invoice number, an unique number – usually pre-printed

■ order number(s), enabling the customer to match the invoice to the original order form(s)

■ delivery note number(s), enabling the invoice to be matched to the delivery note(s) and goods received note(s)

■ customer's account number (for reference in the supplier's accounting system).

If the supplier is registered for VAT, the invoice must also show the supplier's VAT registration number.

The invoice contains details of the goods and services supplied, including the code or catalogue numbers of the goods delivered (as shown on the original orders and delivery notes), and the quantity of each item supplied (this should agree with the quantity ordered and delivered).

The invoice should clearly set out how the final price for goods and services has been calculated. It should do this by setting out:

■ unit price of each item

■ total price per item (unit price multiplied by quantity)

■ trade discount – the percentage of trade discount allowed (usually given to regular customers in the same line of business)

■ net amount due after the deduction of trade discount

■ goods total – the total of the net amount column

■ cash discount – a percentage of the goods total which may be deducted by customers if they pay within specified terms (see below)

■ value added tax (VAT) – a tax (currently 17.5 per cent) on most goods and services, which is applied to the total remaining after the deduction of any cash discount

■ invoice total – the final amount due after everything has been taken into account.

Finally, the invoice shows what terms for payment apply to the supply. This is where the supplier indicates the credit and payment terms that are being offered For example, if ithe invoice states:

■ net 30 days – this means that the supplier expects the invoice to be paid in full (with no cash discount taken) within 30 days of the invoice date

■ 10% 7 days – this means that the customer can deduct a 10 per cent cash discount (as shown on the invoice) if the invoice is paid within seven days of the invoice date

■ carriage paid – means that the price of the goods includes the cost of delivering them

■ E & O E – stands for "errors and omissions excepted", which means that if there is a mistake on the invoice, or something has been left out, the supplier reserves the right to correct the mistake and demand the correct amount.

Credit notes

Sometimes goods do not arrive in good condition. They may have been damaged or lost in transit, or the supplier may have sent the incorrect items or quantities, or they may simply be faulty. When this occurs, the supplier sends the customer a credit note. A credit note is very similar to an invoice but, instead of increasing the customer's debt to the supplier, a credit note reduces the debt. In other words, it is the opposite of an invoice for accounting purposes.

Credit notes detail very similar information to invoices, usually with the addition of an explanation of why the credit is being issued. To avoid confusion, credit notes are often printed in red so that they are easily

Figure 15.8: A credit note

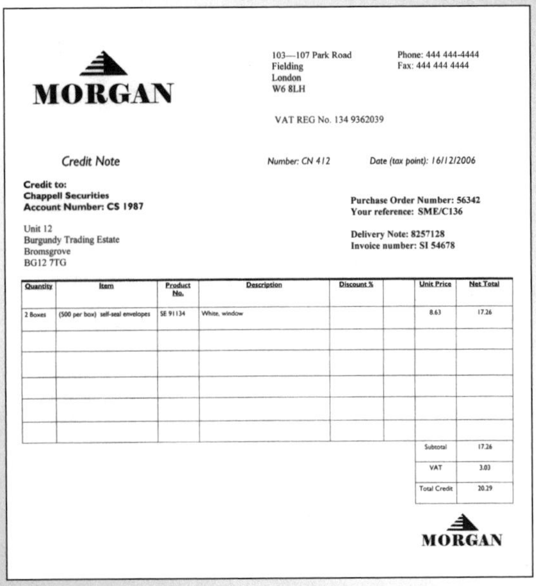

Figure 15.9: A statement of account

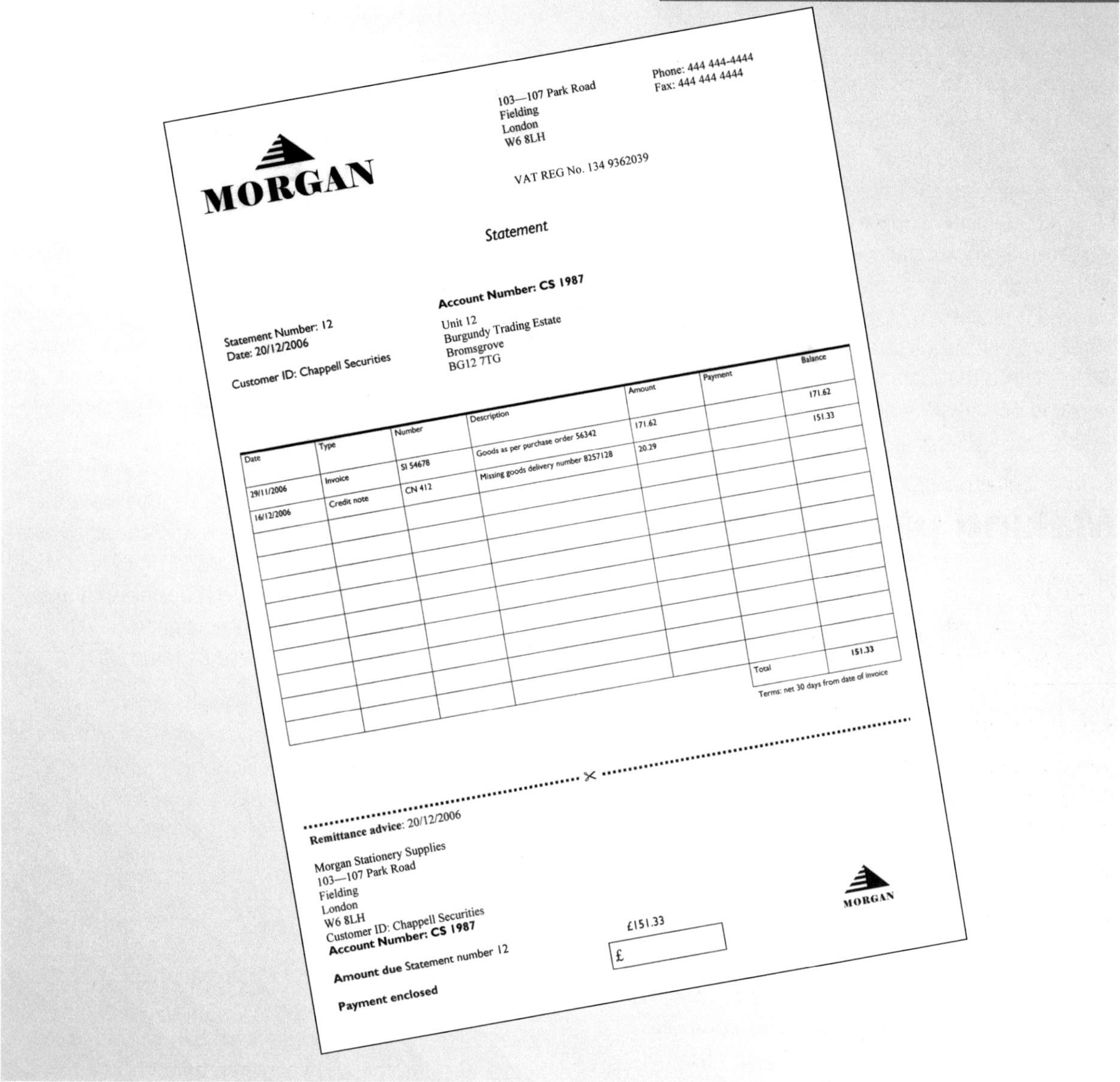

103—107 Park Road
Fielding
London
W6 8LH

Phone: 444 444-4444
Fax: 444 444 4444

MORGAN

VAT REG No. 134 9362039

Statement

Account Number: **CS 1987**

Statement Number: 12
Date: 20/12/2006

Customer ID: Chappell Securities

Unit 12
Burgundy Trading Estate
Bromsgrove
BG12 7TG

Date	Type	Number	Description	Amount	Payment	Balance
						171.62
			Goods as per purchase order 56342	171.62		151.33
29/11/2006	Invoice	SI 54678	Missing goods delivery number 8257128	20.29		
16/12/2006	Credit note	CN 412				
					Total	151.33

Terms: net 30 days from date of invoice

Remittance advice: 20/12/2006

Morgan Stationery Supplies
103—107 Park Road
Fielding
London
W6 8LH
Customer ID: Chappell Securities
Account Number: **CS 1987**

Amount due Statement number 12

Payment enclosed

£151.33

£

MORGAN

---

recognised by the customer's accounts department and not mistaken for invoices.

Credit notes are also issued if the customer has been overcharged on an invoice or if the customer has decided not to purchase some of the goods (provided the supplier is prepared to take them back). Occasionally deliveries are incomplete or damaged. Morgan left two boxes of envelopes off Chappell's order. Figure 15.8 represents a refund in recognition of this fact and means that Chappell does not have to pay for this part of the order.

Debit notes

Debit notes are sometimes also used when goods are being returned. These are issued by the customer to the supplier. They are sent with the goods being returned to detail the amount of allowance (refund) the customer thinks it should receive. They form a useful record for the customer's accounts of goods that were ordered, delivered and received but which are actually no longer in the company's possession as they have been sent back (returned outward) to the supplier. In appearance, a debit note looks very similar to a credit note but it obviously would have the customer's name and logo as the main details.

Statements of account

At the end of each month, a supplier often issues a statement of account to each of its regular customers. This lists all the invoices and credit notes that have been sent to the customer during the month, together with any payments that have been received from the customer. The total of the statement, therefore, is the outstanding amount currently due to be paid by the customer. In effect, the statement is a summary of all the transactions that have taken place between the two organisations during the month, and a reminder to the customer of how much remains to be paid.

Figure 15.9 shows the statement received by Chappell Securities in respect of the order it placed with Morgan Stationery Supplies. Chappell may pay on receipt of a regular statement such as this rather than paying each invoice. In practice, it is likely that a statement received by Chappell would contain details of a number of invoices rather than a single one. You will also note that details of any credit notes are also recorded on this statement.

Making payments

Before any payments are made in response to an invoice or statement of account, checks are carried out to ensure that the goods were ordered by an authorised person and received in good condition. Usually, this is done by matching the invoices received from the supplier to the original purchase orders and delivery notes (and goods received notes if used). Any discrepancies or errors are notified to the supplier, and the invoice is held until the matter is resolved (usually upon receipt of a credit note or the outstanding goods). These security checks ensure that no supplier is paid in error.

Provided that everything is in order, the invoices will be approved for payment. A senior accountant or manager usually has responsibility for approving payments. Sometimes an "authorisation box" is rubber-stamped on the front of the invoice, which is signed when it is approved for payment. Ensuring that different people are responsible for the receipt of goods and the payment for goods reduces the opportunities for fraud within a business. This is known as segregation of duties.

Cheques

A cheque instructs a bank to pay a specified amount of money to a named person (or organisation). The bank issues pre-printed cheques to its account holders to use when they need to pay money to other people or businesses. The cheque has the name, address and sort code of the bank at which the account is held, together with the account holder's name and account number.

The person writing out the cheque is known as the drawer, and the person to whom it is payable is known as the payee. Cheques must be written clearly, in ink, with the amount written in both words and figures. The name of the payee must appear, and the cheque must be dated and signed by the drawer. Any changes made on the cheque must be initialled by the drawer. In the UK, the life of a cheque is six months, after which time it becomes invalid.

Most cheques are marked "A/C Payee only". This means that the cheque can only be paid into a bank account held in the payee's name. This provides some measure of security against fraud and allows cheques to be sent safely through the post. Payments can normally only be authorised by senior staff, and only authorised signatories can sign cheques. The authorised signatories give the bank specimens of their signatures, and the banks will not validate the cheque or make a payment unless it is signed by one or more of the recognised authorised officers of the company. Some banks specify that business cheques must be signed by two authorised signatories to reduce the risk of embezzlement or fraud.

Note that although cheques are still used by many businesses to settle their debts, an increasing number of businesses prefer to use electronic transfer and/or internet banking to pay their creditors. This eliminates the risk of cheques being lost in the post and the threat of cheque fraud.

Remittance advice

When the customer receives the statement of account, it is checked to ensure that it is correct. If the customer is satisfied that it is accurate and there are no items under dispute, then payment can be authorised and payment is sent to the supplier to settle the account.

Sometimes the statement includes a tear-off section called a remittance advice (see Figure 15.9, page 291), which is detached and returned by the customer with payment to confirm exactly which invoices or items are being paid. If this form is not provided with the statement by the supplier company, some customers prepare their own remittance advices to be sent with their cheques.

Some customers prepare their own remittance advices to be sent with their cheques. Any business that uses electronic transfer to pay its supplier would, as a matter of course, issue a remittance advice so that the customer knows that funds have been transferred by the business into the customer's account.

The Palace Hotel is situated on the Grand Promenade, Chiltern-by-Sea. It was bought by David and Debbie Blythe-Clarke in 2003. Their initial vision was to create a quality hotel experience, with standards and prices to match some of the larger hotel chain operators, while retaining the warmth and welcome of a family-run operation.

David had 16 years' experience in hotel management, having worked for both the Radisson and Marriott hotel and resort groups at different stages in his career. Debbie came from a marketing and public relations background, so between them they thought that they should be able to create a well-run and successful hotel.

David is fond of telling any new member of staff employed by the hotel that "the key to success in the hotel trade is to have happy satisfied customers who come back time and time again, and who enjoy their experience so much they recommend us onward to family and friends".

In many respects David and Debbie have realised their vision: the hotel is profitable and has many regular customers who return frequently. Debbie is excellent at coming up with ideas for off-peak periods, and the hotel bar and restaurant are patronised by local townspeople as well as hotel residents, so the business always has a regular weekly turnover.

However, while David and Debbie are regarded as being good hotel managers and hospitable owners, they do not have a good reputation with their suppliers for their financial administration aspects of the business. Suppliers often complain of not being paid on time or being paid incorrect amounts.

The Palace Hotel is currently in dispute with one of its key restaurant suppliers, Stones Catering Services, over an invoice for goods which includes some items David claims the hotel never received. David is not overly concerned, he does his best to keep friendly relations with all the people he deals with, he knows the business is profitable and, at the end of the day, any problems get resolved and all suppliers eventually get paid. So he can't really see that there is any difficulty with the way the Palace Hotel is managed.

A State two reasons why it would be important for the Palace Hotel to keep accurate financial records.

B Purchase invoices are important business documents. Explain how they may help the Palace Hotel to manage its finances.

C David Blythe-Clarke maintains that the hotel only ever received 60 serviette holders from Stones Catering Services, and so refuses to pay for the 80 serviette holders listed on Stones' latest invoice. David has no records to prove his

claim. Explain two documents that should have been completed as part of this transaction that would have prevented this problem from occurring.

D David "can't really see that there is any difficulty with the way the Palace Hotel is managed". Consider the arguments for and against this view, and decide which is correct. You should justify your opinion.

Recording transactions and the financial accounting system: part 2

Setting the scene: the role of accounting

Accounting is a service that is required by each and every business. In fact, every individual uses a vague form of accounting when they plan what they want to do with their money.

Accountancy formalises the process by which organisations record, analyse and communicate financial information. This information is then used by managers or other interested parties to monitor and control the business's performance or make decisions.

Many stakeholder groups have an interest in the financial performance of an organisation. You should consider how different stakeholder groups could be adversely affected by the miscommunication of inaccurate financial information.

Figure 15.10: The accountancy process

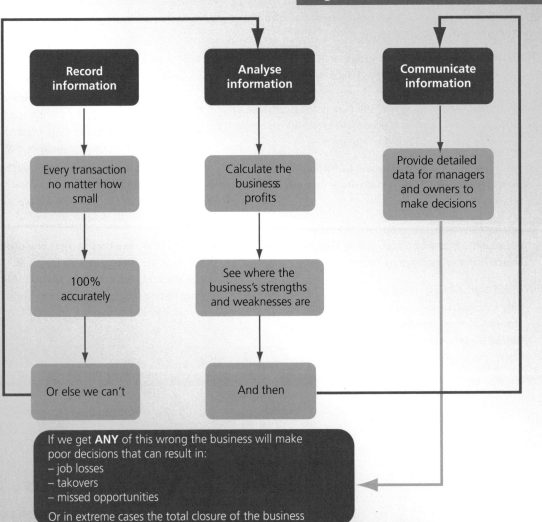

Record information

Every transaction no matter how small

100% accurately

Or else we can't

Analyse information

Calculate the businesss profits

See where the business's strengths and weaknesses are

And then

Communicate information

Provide detailed data for managers and owners to make decisions

If we get **ANY** of this wrong the business will make poor decisions that can result in:
– job losses
– takovers
– missed opportunities
Or in extreme cases the total closure of the business

Purchases journals (also known as the **purchases day book**) contain a chronological list of all credit purchases. These are compiled from invoices received from creditors (suppliers).

Purchases returns journals (also known as the **purchases returns day book**) contain a chronological list of all purchases subsequently returned to suppliers (returns outwards). These are compiled from credit notes received.

Sales journals (also known as the **sales day book**) contain a chronological list of all credit sales. These are compiled from invoices issued by the company to debtors.

Sales returns journals (also known as the **sales returns day book**) contain a chronological list of all sales subsequently returned to the company by customers (returns inwards). These are compiled from credit notes issued by the company.

The **journal** (also known as the **journal proper**) is used to record entries such as the purchase or sale of fixed assets or the correction of errors.

Purchase ledgers are part of the double-entry system. These contain the individual personal accounts of a business's credit suppliers (creditors). The main entries in the purchases ledger are posted from the purchases journals and the cashbook.

Sales ledgers are part of the double-entry system. These contain the individual personal accounts of a business's credit customers (debtors). The main entries in the sales ledger are posted from the sales journals and the cashbook.

General ledgers are part of the double-entry system. This ledger contains all the impersonal (nominal or real) accounts of the business, such as fixed assets, expenses, sales and purchases accounts.

The **cashbook** is a book of original entry and a part of the double-entry system. This contains details of every transaction that takes place using the company's bank account or cash funds.

The financial recording system

With the amount of interest taken, and the seriousness of the level of decisions to be made, it is important *above all else* that financial information is as *accurate* as it can be. The first thing an accountant must therefore learn to do is record data. This is done using the double-entry system of bookkeeping. This system records each transaction twice: once on the left-hand side of the accounts, and once on the right-hand side.

Figure 15.11: Simple double entry

£	£
400	400
200	200
100	100
£700	£700

The purpose of double-entry system bookkeeping is to try and ensure that the financial information communicated at any point in time is correct. This is quite simply achieved by the fact that at the end of the financial period under examination, if the left-hand side and the right-hand side are equal in total (they balance) then "hopefully" the accounts are correct.

However, just making two lists of numbers is meaningless. Large volumes of numerical information can be difficult to understand. The information recorded needs to be classified in categories, so that like items are placed together and analysis can be undertaken. This makes information that is useful to the business. Therefore, the information on financial transactions that have taken place needs to be summarised as well as classified so that it is easy to understand.

All numerical transactions that take place in a business can be classified under particular areas of activity – that is, they can be grouped together under certain headings. These are:

- sales
- purchases
- other income
- expenses
- fixed assets
- current assets
- current liabilities
- long-term liabilities
- capital.

Figure 15.12: Each transaction has two effects

Transaction	Good effect	Bad effect
Sell goods for £400 to a customer	The business receives £400	The business had to give the customer some stock
Buy a new company vehicle for £16,000	The business now has a new vehicle	The business no longer has £16,000 in its bank account
Buy £370 of stock on credit from a supplier	The business now has stock it can sell to customers	The business is now in debt to the supplier by £370

Having classified financial information into different types, this can then be recorded, analysed and communicated in a meaningful way to those stakeholder groups that need access to the information.

The double-entry system

The double-entry system is based on the idea that every transaction that takes place has two effects; one that can be regarded as being good or bringing a benefit to the business, and one that can be regarded as being bad or bringing a burden to the business. Figure 15.12 gives some examples.

Each transaction is recorded twice on two different accounts. Every individual area of activity the business undertakes has its own account. The good effect of the transaction is recorded in every account on the right-hand side (known as the debit or Dr side), with the bad effect of the transaction recorded on the left-hand side (known as the credit or Cr side),

Books of original entry and ledgers

The documentation that arises from a business's transactions (examined in Topic 2) is first of all recorded in books of original entry, and then at a later date transferred to the individual accounts in the ledger. The reason for this is that the sheer volume of financial transactions means that if all the information were to be kept in one place, it would become very difficult to access the information needed. Large businesses have more than one accountant or

Figure 15.13: The books used in recording financial transactions

Books of original entry	Ledgers
These are not part of the double-entry system	
Sales journal (credit sales only)	Sales ledger (personal accounts or debtors only)
Purchases journal (credit purchases only)	Purchase ledger (personal accounts of creditors only)
Returns in journal (goods returned by customers to us)	Returns in a/c kept in general ledger
Returns out journal (goods returned by us to suppliers)	Returns out a/c kept in general ledger
The journal (for other items)	General ledger (for remaining double-entry accounts such as expenses, fixed assets and capital)
	Note the sales a/c and purchases a/c are kept in the general ledger.
Does form part of the double-entry system	
Cashbook (for receipts/payments of cash and cheques)	

Purchases Journal (page 22)				
Date	**Description**	**Invoice ref.**	**Folio**	**Amount**
12/10	L. Bones	624	PL 22	670
13/10	K. Smithers	625	PL 35	1,180
14/10	M. Hodgers	626	PL 10	120
24/10	L. Barker	627	PL 14	510
Transferred to purchases account			GL 2	1,480

To personal accounts in Purchase Ledger (credit entries)

GL - General Ledger
PL - Purchase Ledger

To the purchases account in the General Ledger (debit entry)

bookkeeper to keep track of the information, and therefore they have specialist areas that they work on, so it makes sense to keep separate books. To keep matters simple, similar transactions are listed in particular books, so all sales are listed in one book, all purchases in another, and all bank and cash transactions in a separate book.

Books of original entry are more commonly referred to as journals or day books, and the books where individual accounts are kept are called ledgers. The books of original entry are therefore just lists of events in chronological order. We then transfer these lists to the various ledgers (each transaction twice) to fulfil the double-entry requirements.

Purchases journal

The purchases journal is only used for recording a list in chronological order of those purchases that are made on credit terms. This allows a business to keep a record of the suppliers to which it owes money. Cash purchases are not entered here. For any credit purchase that is transacted, the seller should provide the buyer with an invoice – an invoice is a purchase invoice when it is entered into the accounts of the buyer – and these are then recorded in the purchases journal as shown in Figure 15.14.

The information from the purchases journal will then be posted, as indicated in Figure 15.14, to the purchases account in the general ledger and the individual creditor accounts in the purchase ledger at a later date.

Sales journal

The sales journal is only used to list sales that are on credit terms. Cash sales are not entered here, as there is no need to know the names and addresses of people and other businesses that pay when goods are actually exchanged – they don't owe the company any money. For each credit sale, the seller should provide the buyer with a sales invoice. Sales invoices should run in numerical order, and the seller should make a copy of all sales invoices processed and enter up the details of sales made into the sales journal.

The information from the sales journal will then be posted, as indicated in Figure 15.15, to the sales account in the general ledger and the individual debtor accounts in the sales ledger at a later date.

Returns journals

Returns journals look exactly the same as purchases and sales journals – they just contain credit notes not invoices. Figure 15.16 shows the returns in and out transactions.

The journal proper

Any other items are usually much less common than purchases and sales transactions. These can therefore be rather more complicated, and they are listed in the journal proper.

Due to the uncommon nature of these non-purchase and non-sale items, these entries are far more detailed than entries in the other journals. For each

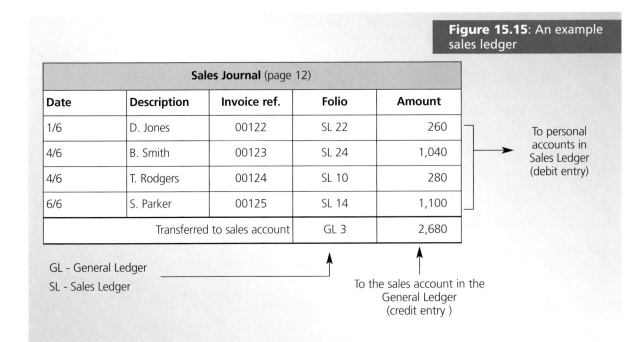

Sales Journal (page 12)				
Date	Description	Invoice ref.	Folio	Amount
1/6	D. Jones	00122	SL 22	260
4/6	B. Smith	00123	SL 24	1,040
4/6	T. Rodgers	00124	SL 10	280
6/6	S. Parker	00125	SL 14	1,100
Transferred to sales account			GL 3	2,680

To personal accounts in Sales Ledger (debit entry)

GL - General Ledger
SL - Sales Ledger

To the sales account in the General Ledger (credit entry)

transaction, the entry in the journal proper records:

- the date

- the name of the account to be debited and the amount

- the name of the account to be credited and the amount

- a description of the transaction taking place – this is called the narrative

- a reference number of the source documents giving proof of the transaction.

The journal is not used by all businesses, as many would have too few extraordinary items to warrant a separate book. However, the use of a journal lessens the chance of fraud by bookkeepers and reduces the risk of errors in accounting. It is good practice to use the journal to record:

- purchase and sale of fixed assets (see Figure 15.17)

- the correction of errors (see Figure 15.18)

- any other exceptional item.

Note that in the example in Figure 15.17, the entry for NJ Equipment Ltd is listed in the purchases ledger as this is the *personal* account of a *creditor*; the business owes NJ Equipment the money for the machine (hence shown as a credit entry). The machinery account itself is in the general ledger, and is shown as a debit entry as this is the benefit (a new machine) from this transaction.

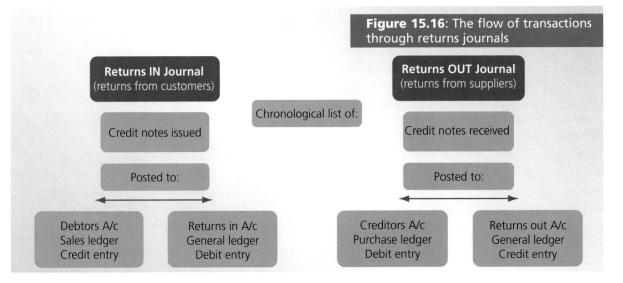

Figure 15.16: The flow of transactions through returns journals

Returns IN Journal (returns from customers)

Credit notes issued

Posted to:

Debtors A/c
Sales ledger
Credit entry

Returns in A/c
General ledger
Debit entry

Chronological list of:

Returns OUT Journal (returns from suppliers)

Credit notes received

Posted to:

Creditors A/c
Purchase ledger
Debit entry

Returns out A/c
General ledger
Credit entry

Figure 15.17: Record of purchase of a fixed asset on credit

The Journal				
Date	Description	Folio	Dr	Cr
1/6	Purchase of new lathe on credit Capital purchases invoice 3456 from NJ Equipment Ltd			
	Machinery	GL 14	650	
	NJ Equipment Ltd	PL 26		650

Figure 15.18: Error of omission (forgot to enter a transaction completely)

The Journal				
Date	Description	Folio	Dr	Cr
15/6	Correction of error of omission sales invoice 234 M. Bailey			
	Sales	GL 4		34
	M. Bailey	SL 6	34	

A note about folio numbers

Folio numbers are a tracking device used by accountants and auditors to let them know where the opposite side of an entry is located and where it originated. Simply, every journal or ledger has a two-letter code:

purchase ledger	PL
sales ledger	SL
general ledger	GL
sales journal	SJ
purchases journal	PJ
returns in journal	RI
returns out journal	RO
journal or journal proper	JP

Every account has its own page. Therefore, SL 34 is the account on page 34 of the sales ledger.

Folio numbers are useful as they allow any transaction to be traced through the accounts right back to the original document that caused the transaction to be originated. They are highly useful when trying to trace errors, or when a company is being audited – that is, during an independent check on its accounts.

The cashbook

The cashbook shows a business's bank and cash accounts side by side. This has one prime advantage, other than just being more convenient to use, in that by having the two together it allows managers to see how much money has been paid out or received in any one day and how much the business has available to use at any point in time.

The cashbook is both a book of original entry and part of the ledger systems. This is due to the fact that the business needs to keep a chronological list of payments made and money received (the original entry) as well as a record of who and where money came from or went to (the double entry). Figure 15.19 shows a typical cashbook.

Sometimes, for whatever reason, a business may well want to take cash out of the bank and put it into its

Figure 15.19: An example cashbook

Cashbook							Page 3
Debit							Credit
Details	**Folio**	**Cash**	**Bank**	**Details**	**Folio**	**Cash**	**Bank**
		£	£			£	£
Balance		200	1,060	Wages	GL 16		600
Sales	GL2	75		Electricity	GL 27		210
Loan	GL27		4,000	K. Smithers	PL 35		400
Sales	GL2		600	Petrol	GL 22	45	
Cash	C		150	Bank	C	150	
B. Smith	SL 24		1,000	Purchases	GL 3		2,300
The debit side shows the benefit gained by the business – that is, money being received				The credit side shows the burden gained by the business – that is, money being paid out			

cash account, or vice versa. When this happens, because we are not referring to another ledger (both transactions take place on the same page of the cashbook), we do not need a folio number. This type of transaction is termed a contra item, and as such we enter the letter C in the folio column. This tells us that the second entry is on the same page.

Purchase ledger

The purchase ledger is used to hold all the individual accounts of suppliers from whom a business has bought goods on credit. This keeps a record for the business of which suppliers it has used to buy goods, how much it owes them, how and when they have been paid, and if any goods were returned at any point for refunds. Figure 15.20 shows an example of a creditor's account in the purchase ledger.

The purchase ledger is also useful to the business in aiding cash flow management. By totalling up the amounts outstanding on the individual accounts, the company would generate a figure for total creditors – the amount of money it is due to pay out to suppliers in the short term.

Note, the purchase ledger does not contain the purchases account itself, this is entered in the accounts within the general ledger.

The Purchase Ledger					Page 35
Debit		K Smithers Account			Credit
Details	**Folio**	**Amount £**	**Details**	**Folio**	**Amount £**
Bank	CB 2	600	Purchases	PJ 22	1,180
Bank	CB 3	400			
Returns out	RO 4	180			

The Sales Ledger					Page 25
Debit			**B. Smith Account**		Credit
Details	**Folio**	**Amount £**	**Details**	**Folio**	**Amount £**
Sales	SJ 12	1,040	Bank	CB 3	1,000
			Returns in	RI 2	40

Sales ledger

The sales ledger is used to hold all the individual accounts of customers that have bought goods on credit. This keeps a record for the business of which customers have bought what goods from them, how much it is owed, how and when it has been paid, and if any goods were returned by customers at any point for refunds.

The sales ledger is also useful to the business in aiding cash flow management and credit control. By totalling up the amounts outstanding on the individual accounts, the company would generate a figure for total debtors – the amount of money it is due to receive from customers (debtors) in the short term. The individual accounts also allow the business to see which customers owe it money, how much and for how long. This can assist the business by indicating when to send statements to customers demanding payment or to restrict customers whose accounts show outstanding balances that are too large. This helps prevent non-payment for goods by customers, as the business is able to monitor the position of each debtor's account on an individual and detailed basis.

Note, the sales ledger does not contain the sales account itself; this is entered in the accounts within the general ledger.

The general ledger

The general ledger contains all other account classifications involved in the running of an individual business. It contains all the accounts for:

■ fixed assets – land, premises, machinery, fixtures and fittings, furniture and vehicles

■ expenses – wages, advertising, petrol, heat and light, stationery, cleaning, depreciation, bad debt, rent, insurance, repairs, etc.

■ income – interest received, rent received and commission received

■ other – discounts received or allowed, carriage on goods (delivery charges), returns in and out, and the sales and purchases accounts.

The accounts held in the general ledger vary from business to business, depending on the type of activity they undertake. They have a common factor in that they are termed as impersonal accounts – they are not the accounts of real people or other businesses but the accounts of items that the business owns or uses.

Private ledgers

Some companies keep details of capital (money invested by the owner) and drawings (money taken out by the owner) in what is called a private ledger; this is so that office staff cannot see details of items that the proprietors want to keep secret.

stop and think

Businesses such as credit card companies use 16-digit identification (account) numbers to recognise individual customers as well as their names. Why is it that they consider the identification of individual customers to be so important?

AJ Solutions is a private company that specialises in providing training, guidance and advice to small businesses on how to increase the effectiveness of their operations. One area where small business people are notoriously weak is at keeping track of their financial information, and the amounts of money they owe or are owed.

You have been asked by AJ Solutions to produce a series of brief presentations on financial recording systems for people wishing to set up their own business. A colleague has started to prepare a slide demonstrating the flow of financial information through the various journals and ledgers. You have been asked to complete this slide. Complete the chart (Figure 15.22) by filling in the shaded boxes with the correct information.

Figure 15.22: Partially complete slide for business seminar

Source document	Book of original entry	Ledgers	Accounts
		Cashbook	
Cheque received in payment from a credit customer	Cashbook		
			Debtor
		General ledger	
Invoice received for purchase of stock on credit			
			Creditor
		Cashbook	
Purchase of stationery items for cash			
			Stationery
			Bank
Cheque sent to supplier for payment	Cashbook		
		Purchase ledger	
		General ledger	
Purchase of a new vehicle on credit			
			Creditor
		Purchase ledger	
Return of damaged goods to a supplier, credit note received			
			Returns out account
Sale of goods on credit to a customer	Sales journal		
		General ledger	

The trial balance and errors

Setting the scene: accounting error increases General Motors' loss to $10.6 billion

US car producer General Motors was been forced to increase its reported losses in 2005 by $2 billion (£1.1 billion) due to accounting errors. General Motors is also going to have to restate its results for the years 2000 to 2004 due to the same error. It also declared that it had further incorrectly accounted for some supplier payments.

Business analysts commented that the declaration of this level of accounting errors would be yet another blow to the credibility of a firm that is struggling to turn around its fortunes. An analyst for JP Morgan (a leading financial services firm) said the multitude of accounting errors raised concerns about the company's internal accounting controls and struggling management.

After correcting for the errors, General Motors restated its 2005 losses as $10.6 billion. The company's shares dropped in value by 4.9 per cent after the news. General Motors is cutting 30,000 jobs in the US to slash costs, and has announced 900 job losses at Vauxhall's Ellesmere Port plant in Cheshire.

Source: adapted from BBC News website, 17 March 2006

The trial balance

Inaccurate accounting can have wide-ranging effects on a business, and can threaten its success. If owners and managers are supplied with incorrect information, then any decisions they make based on that information are unlikely to be sound. This can have knock-on effects for various stakeholder groups, such as employees and shareholders. As the General Motors case shows, jobs can be lost and investor confidence is damaged. If a company wrongly declares its profits – or provides wrong information

that understates its tax liability say – it faces possible sanctions from the government and the agencies that regulate stock exchanges. This could lead to legal action being taken against the company and serious fines being imposed. In the most extreme cases, inaccurate and incorrect information could lead to the eventual closure of the business.

As we have explained, the key to double-entry bookkeeping is that every transaction has two effects – it is recorded twice, once on the debit side of an account and once on the credit side of a separate account. At the end of a financial period, the two sides should add up to the same amount: they should balance. This works as a self-checking system, because if the two sides do not balance it is obvious that there are some errors present. However, it would be extremely time-consuming to add up every single individual transaction that has taken place over an accounting year. Imagine how many buying and selling transactions take place nationwide in an organisation such as Tesco, even in just one hour.

The solution accountants adopt is to make checks throughout the year. The trial balance is an independent check that the information held within the books of account is correct before the company goes on to prepare its final accounts (declaring its profit and loss account and balance sheet). It allows a company to know that its declared financial position is as accurate as possible.

A trial balance is easily constructed. As we have seen, all accounts balance off on one side or the other, unless they balance completely and close off. We can check our double entry by adding up the all the Dr balance b/f and all the Cr balance b/f. If we have used double entry correctly, then Dr b/f should equal Cr b/f. If this is the case, it balances. This is formally known as a trial balance

Figure 15.23 shows how a trial balance is laid out. The first item of a trial balance is the title. This must read: "Trial balance for *company name* as at DD/MM/YY". The trial balance is laid out directly underneath. It is constructed by transferring all the individual Dr and Cr balance b/f's from the ledger accounts. Once this is complete, you total the Dr column and the Cr column.

Errors

The key use of the trial balance is to check whether

there are any errors present in the records of account (the ledgers). Obviously, if the trial balance doesn't balance, then there are errors present and the accounts need to be double-checked so these errors can be traced and corrected.

If the trial balance does balance, this is a fair indication – but not a guarantee – that the accounts are correct. For complete accuracy, every transaction that takes place needs to be entered in the right type of account, with the right name, the correct amount and on the right side (debit or credit). This needs to be done on both the accounts affected by the transaction. There are several errors that could occur in a business's record-keeping that a trial balance will not flag up. Managers need to understand that a trial balance provides one check of accuracy, but it does not guarantee that the accounting information is totally error-free. Errors that can occur are now examined individually in detail.

Error of commission

This occurs when the correct classifications of account have been used, the correct numbers have been entered and on the correct sides, but the entry has been put under the wrong person's or company's name. For example, a commission error would be entering a sale of goods of £300 to P Talbot on credit terms on the records of C Talbot by mistake. As the numerical information is all correct, the trial balance would still balance. However, obviously the accounts of P Talbot and C Talbot are wrong.

Error of omission

This occurs when quite simply a transaction has taken place but no record of it has been made anywhere in the accounts. The net effect of this then is zero, as no information appears anywhere and the trial balance

Figure 15.23: Trial balance formal layout

	Debit	Credit
	£	£
Capital		10,000
Bank	3,500	
Cash	400	
Vehicles	6,000	
Loan		4,000
Electricity	450	
Stationery	650	
Wages	1,000	
Sales		8,455
Purchases	9,000	
Returns in/out	170	240
Carriage In	375	
Carriage out	200	
Debtors		
M. Frost	1,670	
N. Jones	480	
Creditors		
F. Willoughby		880
K. Clarke		320
	23,895	23,895

Closing balances from ledger accounts Balance b/f

Figure 15.24: Types of error

Type of error	Correct amount	Correct account names	Correct account classification	Correct sides
Commission	✓	✗	✓	✓
Omission No entry made at all	✗	✗	✗	✗
Principle	✓	✓	✗	✓
Original entry	✗	✓	✓	✓
Reversal	✓	✓	✓	✗
Compensating	Compensating errors can consist of any type of more than one error that act to cancel each other out.			

will still balance. However, again the trial balance is not 100% correct as this transaction has been missed out.

Error of principle

This is similar to an error of commission in that the correct numbers have been used and entered on the correct sides. However, in this case, the transaction is assigned to the wrong classification type. So, for example, a purchase of a new machine for £230, which should have been entered as a fixed asset, is mistakenly entered as a machinery expense. Here the trial balance will still total up to the correct amount, but the accounts will be wrong. By entering this item as an expense in the profit and loss account rather than a fixed asset (which should appear on the balance sheet), the effect will be to lower the profit declared by the business.

Compensating error

This is one of the most difficult errors to spot, because it occurs when several errors have been made which, when taken together, have the effect of coincidentally cancelling each other out. For example, suppose a mistake is made in totalling an account so that it is recorded as £15 too much on the credit side, and then later a similar mistake is made with a different account (with the same error of £15) but on the debit side. These two entirely separate errors actually balance each other, and so the trial balance would also appear to be accurate.

Error of original entry

This occurs when the original figure used is actually wrong. A common example is when figures are transposed (swapped around) when entered in the ledger – say, a cash transaction of £67 for the purchase of stationery items is actually entered as £76. The double-entry process is followed correctly, with the transaction being entered on both the stationery and cash accounts, but the wrong number is used on both accounts. Yet again, the trial balance would appear to be correct, but some of the actual figures are wrong.

Error of reversal

This occurs when the correct number, classifications of accounts and names are used, but the transaction is entered on the wrong side of each account. So there is a debit and a credit entry (thus the trial balance will still balance) but the transaction has been recorded so that it has debited the account to be credited, and vice versa.

Correction of errors

Despite not being shown by the trial balance, most errors are found at a later date and many will often turn up on their own. For example, if a business had made the error of commission above (attributing a credit sale to P Talbot to the account of C Talbot), as soon as it sent C Talbot his statement he would contact the company and to inform it of the mistake. Similarly, so would any supplier if it had been paid an incorrect amount because the business's records were inaccurate.

When an error is discovered, it is not good policy to alter the ledger records by crossing things out or painting entries out – this may give the appearance of fraudulent practice taking place. Instead, these errors need to be formally corrected using the proper double-entry system. However, as these errors arose because of a mistake, there is no source document to act as proof of the transaction, so the journal is used. By using the journal, we are able to write a brief description of what has occurred – a narrative explaining the error made and the actions taken to correct it. In this way, someone examining the accounts can see what amendments have been made to any accounts, and why. The actions to be taken are:

- write a narrative describing the error made

- show the corrections to be made to the accounts affected – which account is to be debited and which to be credited, and with what amount

- correct the ledger accounts by completing the double entries described in the journal.

A worked example

Consider how we might correct the error of commission described above: where a sale of goods of £300 to P Talbot on credit terms was actually entered on the records of C Talbot. To correct this error the journal would appear as Figure 15.25. It shows we are taking £300 out of C Talbot's account and placing it in P Talbot's account, where it should have been. Note, P Talbot's account is a debit entry as he becomes a debtor for the goods he has purchased on credit terms.

Figure 15.25: A correction in the journal

The Journal		
Description	**Debit (Dr)**	**Credit (Cr)**
Correction of error of commission		
C Talbot		£300
P Talbot	£300	

assessment practice
Mike's Music

Mike Divine owns and runs a specialist music shop buying and selling second-hand, rare or collectors' edition vinyl LPs, CDs and DVDs. He compiled his trial balance several weeks ago, and after several attempts was very pleased to finally get it to balance.

So, believing all his financial records were correct, he sent the information to his accountant to prepare his final accounts at the end of his trading year. However, several errors have subsequently come to light, and Mike now needs to correct them and send the amended information to his accountant. These errors have been found.

- Mike introduced £2000 of new capital into his business, but this has been entered in the sales account by mistake.

- A cash sale of £390 has been incorrectly entered in both the cash and sales account as £360.

- Mike purchased stock costing £465 from JV Trading, but has entered this under Java Trading in his creditor records in the purchase ledger by mistake.

- Mike banks his takings for the week every Friday night. However, he discovered that one week's takings of £1,560 have been incorrectly credited to his bank account and debited to the cash account in error.

- Mike sold an extremely rare CD to a collector for £320, but in his excitement about the sale he forgot to make any entries in his accounts at all.

A Give the journal entries necessary to correct these errors.

B In each case, state the type of error being corrected.

Profit and loss accounts and balance sheets: part 1

Setting the scene: the importance of measuring profit

Without the potential of making a profit, why should individuals and companies commit time and resources to a business? It is the profit motivation – the reward to be gained – that drives many people towards starting out in business in the first place.

Profit is one of the main ways a business monitors its success or failure. Profit is therefore one of the most important goals businesses possess. It is not just owners that are interested in profits: there is a legal obligation on all companies to report their profits each year in returns to Companies House. Even non-incorporated businesses – sole traders and partnerships – must file their profits with HM Revenue and Customs.

A profit and loss account measures the profitability and financial performance of a business over a period of time (nearly always one year). This is useful so we can see how well the business is doing. The balance sheet shows us what the business has managed to achieve over its entire existence. It shows the assets that have been built up over time, sets out the value of what the company actually owns, and gives the source(s) of the finance that has been used to purchase these assets. A balance sheet tells you about a business's financial strength.

By studying a balance sheet we can also obtain a rough idea of what the business is worth, by comparing how much an individual company actually owns with how much it owes to creditors. Many stakeholders make important decisions based on the information contained within the balance sheet – from a supplier deciding whether to supply goods on credit to a bank assessing whether to lend money to a business that wants a loan to build a new factory.

Profit and loss accounts

In this topic, we look at how profit and loss accounts and balance sheets are put together. Throughout, we use the format that would be adopted by a sole trader. In Topic 6, we shall examine the formats used by other types of businesses, with a focus on limited company accounts.

A profit and loss account is the method by which a business determines its level of profit. As profit is important to so many different stakeholder groups, it is vital that it is calculated accurately. Guidelines set out how a profit and loss account should be calculated. The idea is that it shouldn't matter who prepares the profit and loss account, the same set of underlying transactions (revenues, expenses and costs during the accounting period) should produce the same answer.

There are four stages to calculating the profit (or loss) made by a business in a period, which is usually one year but can be a longer period at the owners' discretion. We shall consider each stage in turn.

1 Turnover

A profit is made if a business generates more revenue than the costs it incurs. Usually this revenue comes from providing goods and services for sale. Sales revenue earned by a business in a period can be calculated from the number of items sold (or services provided) and the price at which they are sold. Put simply:

sales revenue = quantity of goods sold x selling price per unit

However, some customers may have bought goods and then returned them. These must be taken off sales revenue to reflect the fact that some of the business's sales over the period may well have been refunded. So, if a business has sales of £470,000 in the period but goods worth £8,000 are returned, then its net sales (called turnover) is £462,000. Again this can be expressed as a simple formula:

turnover = sales less returns

KEY TERMS

Profitability is a measure of a business's ability to generate more revenue from its activities than it actually costs to undertake those activities. Profitability is usually measured in the profit and loss account.

A **profit and loss account** is a statement that shows a firm's revenue generated over a trading period and the relevant costs (expenses) incurred in earning that revenue.

Revenue is the total value of income made from selling goods and services over a given period of time.

Expenses are the costs that are incurred by a business in its day-to-day running. These are items that are bought by the business to be used (not to be resold), such as stationery and employees' labour.

Profit is the difference that arises when a firm's revenue is greater than its total expenses.

Gross profit is the difference between the revenue generated by sales and the cost of the products which have been sold. It measures the profit made on buying and selling activities.

Net profit is the actual amount left after all other costs associated with running the business are taken into account, including expenses such as marketing costs and electricity.

A **loss** occurs when revenue is less than the total cost of providing goods and services and the associated expenses.

Liquidity is an assessment of a business's ability to be able to pay its short-term debts. It is a measure of whether the business has enough cash available to pay bills and invoices as they come due for payment. It is assessed from the balance sheet.

A **balance sheet** is a statement that shows a business's assets and liabilities on a particular day. In effect, it shows what a business owns and how it is financed.

Assets are the resources owned by a business that have a monetary value.

Liabilities are debts owed by a business to other parties. Liabilities are sources of finance, and provide the means by which some of the company's assets have been bought.

Capital (or share capital) is the money invested by the owners into the business. This is used by the business to purchase assets and help finance operations. It is called share capital as company owners invest money by buying shares. Shareholders are paid dividends out of a business's profits.

Shareholders' funds are made up of reserves that have been accumulated by the business over the years it has been operating. Prudent owners will keep some of the profits their business makes each year in the company. This retained profit belongs to the shareholders, but is reinvested to help the business grow and become stronger.

2 Cost of sales

In calculating the cost of sales, we are trying to work out how much it costs to make (or buy) the products that the business has sold in the current financial period. In most cases, a business will actually start a financial period selling stock that was made or bought in the previous financial period (this is called its "opening stock"). The cost of making this stock is therefore brought into this financial period as this is when it is going to be sold.

On to this cost we add the cost of any stock the business makes over the period – as, although it may have had stocks at the beginning of the period, these are not going to last forever. So a business must purchase new stocks or more raw materials with which to make further products. From this figure, however, we deduct "returns out" – we take off the value of any purchases the business made but then sent back to suppliers because the stock was faulty or damaged in some way.

When calculating cost of sales, it is also necessary to add on carriage in. This is the cost of having the business's purchases delivered to its premises. This is because if it didn't pay for them to be delivered, it wouldn't get them.

Lastly, for our calculation we need to subtract "closing stock". This is similar but opposite to opening stock. It follows that if at the beginning of a period a business is selling stock that was left over from the last period, at the end of this current period it may well have stocks left that have not yet been sold. These leftover stocks (closing stock) need to be taken off the cost of goods sold, as the business hasn't actually sold them. They will probably be sold in the next financial period.

A key point to take into account here is that closing stock at the end of the current financial period becomes opening stock for the next period.

3 Calculating gross profit

This is the first of the profit calculations. It is a measure of how much profit the business has made on its buying and selling activities – in other words, it shows how good it is at trading. Gross profit is calculated by deducting the cost of sales from the turnover. This is done by using a formal layout called a trading account (see Figure 15.26).

Trading, profit and loss account for Johnston's year ending 31/12/2005

	£000s	£000s
Sales	870,200	
Less *Returns In*	(30,210)	
= Turnover		839,990
Less *Cost of sales*		
Opening stock	50,200	
Add *Purchases*	430,240	
Less *Returns out*	(10,700)	
Add *Carriage in*	20,100	
Less *Closing stock*	(84,000)	= 405,840
Gross profit		434,150

4 Accounting for expenses

So far we have calculated how much revenue the business made, and deducted the cost of providing the goods and services that it has sold. However, there is more to running a business than just buying and selling, and these other aspects (costs) need to be considered so the final profit can be calculated. These additional costs are the expenses.

Expenses are overheads or indirect costs that a company incurs that are not directly involved in production, buying or selling activities. Expenses are characterised as items which the business has paid for and "used up" in conducting its activities. Typical expenses are:

- wages and salaries
- rent and rates
- advertising/marketing expenses
- utility bills
- motor expenses
- warehouse costs
- depreciation
- distribution costs
- administration expenses
- finance costs.

These expenses are added to the formal layout after gross profit and used to calculate the net profit for the period. An example is shown in Figure 15.27.

Note that it is not necessary for every category of expenses to be present. Some expenses do not apply to some businesses.

5 Calculating net profit

This is the second calculation of profit, often termed the bottom line, as it is the final entry on the formal profit and loss account. It is the measure of how much overall profit the business has made after taking into account all relevant costs that have been incurred. As Figure 15.27 illustrates, it is found by deducting the expenses total from the gross profit figure.

stopand**think**

Why do we calculate two types of profit? How does this help a business? Consider the value of these calculations in terms of:

- finding strengths and weaknesses
- making comparisons with previous years
- taking management decisions
- making comparisons with competitors.

Balance sheets

A balance sheet, like a profit and loss account, is a formal document that states in detail the assets, liabilities and capital structure of a business. It is split into six main parts.

Trading, profit and loss account for Johnston's year ending 31/12/2005

	£000's	£000's
Sales	870,200	
Less *Returns in*	(30,210)	
= Turnover		839,990
Less *Cost of sales*		
Opening stock	50,200	
Add *Purchases*	430,240	
Less *Returns out*	(10,700)	
Add *Carriage in*	20,100	
Less *Closing stock*	(84,000)	= 405,840
Gross profit		434,150
Less *Expenses*		
Administration expenses:		
Wages and salaries, advertising, marketing, rent, utilities and finance costs	80,288	
Distribution costs:		
Motor expenses, warehouse, wages and salaries and depreciation	60,760	= (141,048)
Net profit/(Loss)		293,102

1 Fixed assets

The first part of a balance sheet is a list showing the value of those items owned by the business that have a long-term function and can be used repeatedly, such as vehicles and machinery. These are assets the business plans to keep and use for more than one year. This shows anybody looking at the accounts what the business actually possesses and intends to keep. Fixed assets are listed in order of permanency; the ones the business intends to keep longest are listed first.

Figure 15.28 shows an example of a balance sheet for a sole trader business. The fixed assets are shown at the top of the sheet, and are organised under four headings:

- land and buildings
- machinery and equipment
- fixtures, fittings and furniture
- vehicles.

These are all tangible assets. However, some businesses may have various other fixed assets that are termed intangible assets. These are items that the business owns that also have a value, but not a physical presence. A good example of an intangible asset would be a brand name. These are also listed on the balance sheet as fixed assets.

stop and **think**

The Virgin group of companies operates in many different market sectors. List all the different types of Virgin products that come to mind. How does a brand name like Virgin add value to a product and the Virgin group as a whole? How easy do you think it would be to put a value on this intangible asset?

Figure 15.28: A sole trader balance sheet

Balance sheet Johnston's as at 31/12/2005			
	£	£	£
Fixed assets: tangible			
Land and buildings	600,000		
Machinery and equipment	245,000		
Fixtures, fittings and furniture	47,000		
Vehicles	98,000		990,000
Current assets			
Stock	84,000		
Debtors	32,000		
Prepayments	8,700		
Cash at bank	24,320		
Cash in hand	3,340	152,360	
Current liabilities: debts due within one year			
Creditors	42,000		
Accruals	12,300		
Short-term loans or overdrafts	9,000	63,300	
Working capital (net current assets)			89,060
Capital employed			1,079,060
Financed by			
Long-term liabilities: debts due after one year			
Loans	148,000		
Mortgages	310,000		458,000
Capital as at year start	501,340		
Add net profit	293,162		
Less drawings	(173,442)		
Capital as at year end			621,060
			1,079,060

2 Current assets

The next section in the balance sheet shows the value of items the company owns that are likely to be turned into cash before the next balance sheet is drawn up. These are short-term assets, and the value (or amount held) of these assets will change during the course of one year. The business does not intend to keep these assets, but intends to use them to help run its everyday operations.

Current assets are cash or near-cash equivalents that the business has or will have available in the next few months in order to pay bills and invoices received. They are listed in order of liquidity – this is a measure of how easy it is to turn the items into cash, with the most illliquid listed first. Figure 15.28 has five entries under the currents assets heading:

- stock – this will not turn into cash until the goods have been sold

- debtors – these are customers that have bought goods on credit terms, so this line represents money owed to the business that it expects to receive in due course

- prepayments – these are bills or invoices paid in advance

- cash at bank – the funds available in the business's bank account

- cash in hand – the actual amount of notes and coins in its possession.

3 Current liabilities

Current liabilities are the business's debts that are due within one year. In this segment of the balance sheet, the business totals all debts, bills and invoices it has to pay within the next twelve months. These are the debts that it will have to pay using its current assets (its cash or near-cash equivalents).

This section therefore shows how much money the business will have to pay out in the short term. Two terms on this section of the balance sheet may be unfamiliar:

- creditors – these are suppliers from which the business has bought stock, services or raw materials on credit terms, so this line represents money that the business owes to its suppliers

- accruals – these are items that the business has used but not yet paid for, such as electricity and employees' wages (many salaried employees get paid a month in arrears).

4 Working capital

Working capital (also known as net current assets) is the first measure of the financial strength of the company to appear on the balance sheet. This is a measure of the liquidity of the business – its ability to be able to pay its short-term debts. This is found by comparing the value of its current assets with the

value of its current liabilities. In other words, we are looking at how much cash the business has currently got (or will have soon) against how much cash the business has currently got to pay out (or will have to pay soon).

The calculation is a straightforward subtraction of total current liabilities from total current assets. In Figure 15.28, for example, we subtract £63,300 (current liabilities) from £152,360 (current assets) to get working capital of £89,060. This resulting figure is called working capital as it shows how much finance the business has available for day-to-day operations even after all its short-term debts have been paid.

stopandthink

Consider what would be the implications for a company like Sainsbury's if its current liabilities were actually greater than its current assets. How might suppliers (creditors) or employees react to this situation?

5 Long-term liabilities

This section of the balance requires a business to provide information regarding any debts, loans or mortgages it has borrowed from external agencies like a bank in order to help it purchase its fixed assets.

We can make an assessment of the business's financial strength by comparing the value of the assets owned to the amount borrowed. By comparing the amount actually owed to other parties with the business's total fixed assets, we can determine how much of the business's fixed assets it actually owns. Obviously, it is better if the company has not borrowed too much money but has acquired many assets.

6 Capital and reserves

The final section of the balance sheet shows the capital invested by the owner and the funds retained in the business in the form of reserves. This is therefore telling us how much of the business's resources or asset strength have actually been financed by investment rather than borrowing. This states how much money the owner has invested, how much the company grew from making profits, and finally how much the owner then took out of the business (drawings).

Jackson's is a small business owned by Chris Jackson who manufactures professional sports equipment. It is a well-known company with a reputation for expensive but high-quality goods. The business has been in operation for over 40 years and is regarded as being one of the leading manufacturers in the field of high-performance rackets for sports such as squash, badminton and tennis.

Recently it has been experiencing problems with one of its suppliers, partly because Jackson's wants to upgrade its processes and this current supplier is unwilling or unable to meet its desires. Chris wants to approach a new supplier to discuss possible terms, but is aware that any new supplier will probably want to see his accounts. Jackson's is only a relatively small business, and any new supplier would need some sort of security before offering to do business with him on credit terms.

Figure 15.29 shows financial information for Jackson's at 31 March 2006. The business's closing stock has been counted and valued at £9,000.

A Prepare the end of year final accounts for Jackson's.

B Using your calculations from part A, and any other relevant analysis, make an assessment of the strengths and weaknesses of Jackson's short-term and long-term balance sheet position.

C Jackson's has approached Micromesh plc, a company that produces high-quality plastic netting. It wishes to place an order for £15,700 of Micromesh products for use in making squash and badminton rackets. Jackson's has asked for two months' credit before paying for these goods to be ordered. From the perspective of Micromesh's financial adviser, write a memo to the managing director of Micromesh advising whether the company should accept Jackson's order.

Figure 15.29: Jackson's financial data, as at 31 March 2006

	Dr £	Cr £
Equipment	15,000	
Debtors	4,200	
Three-year loan		8,000
Advertising	250	
Sales		50,300
Loan interest	200	
Premises	60,000	
Purchases	48,000	
Wages	1,000	
Heat and light	2,400	
Furniture	8,000	
Cash	390	
Creditors		1,910
Drawings	22,000	
Vehicles	15,000	
Printing	150	
Insurance	1600	
General expenses	400	
Bad debts	100	
Capital		60,000
Bank	800	
Fuel	720	
Mortgage		60,000
	180,210	180,210

Profit and loss accounts and balance sheets: part 2

Setting the scene: the finances of large organisations

Consider three well-known organisations: Cancer Research UK is a medical research organisation, O_2 is a leading provider of mobile phone services, and ICI is one of the world's largest speciality chemical and paint manufacturers.

All three organisations have multi-million pound operations, and they have a responsibility to all their stakeholders to record, monitor and report their finances correctly. However, they are very different types of organisation.

- O_2 is a wholly-owned subsidiary of Telefónica, the Spanish telecommunications company.

- Cancer Research is a charitable not-for-profit organisation.

- ICI is a manufacturing organisation quoted on the London Stock Exchange.

It would be unreasonable to assume that all three companies would produce and present their profit and loss accounts and balance sheets in exactly the same way. For example, as a charity Cancer Research UK doesn't even make a profit, yet its total income for 2005 was £384,232,000. Any organisation with this level of financial resources at its disposal must ensure that its financial records are accurate.

Consider the different legal forms of O_2, Cancer Research UK and ICI. Think about the different stakeholder groups each takes into account when compiling their financial records. What are the key elements and features that stakeholders would wish to see in each case?

KEY TERMS

Limited liability provides protection for the owners of a company (normally the shareholders). It means that the financial risk taken by an owner is limited to the amount they have invested in the company. Their personal private assets cannot be seized should the company go into liquidation owing millions of pounds.

Unlimited liability means that the owners have full responsibility for all debts or losses incurred by their business. In the event of the business having to close, the owners may be forced to use their personal private assets to cover any outstanding debts.

Surplus is the term used by a not-for-profit organisation to describe any excess of income over expenditure.

Debentures are a form of loan stock (long-term liability) issued by companies as a means of raising finance. The company pays a fixed rate of interest to the debenture holder for an agreed period of time.

Share capital is the money invested by the owners into the business in return for a shareholding.

Dividends are the rewards paid to shareholders out of a company's profits. These are made in proportion to their shareholding, and are usually paid annually.

Variations in financial statements

In Topic 5 we showed how a basic profit and loss account and balance sheet would be prepared for a sole trader business. In this topic, we look at the main financial statements of other legal forms of business organisation. The profit and loss account and the balance sheet remain the main instruments, but there are variations to reflect the financial fundamentals of different types of businesses.

Trading organisations

A trading organisation is exactly as the name suggests – it is a business that has as its main activity buying and selling goods. This can take several forms, but the most common example is a retail operation like most high street stores and the major supermarkets. Retail companies do not manufacture products themselves, but they purchase their product lines direct from producers (such as clothes manufacturers, farmers, etc.) or from wholesalers, and then offer them for sale to the next link in the chain of distribution, frequently to end users and consumers. However, a trading organisation could also be a bulk importer of goods in bulk, which then sells onwards to the retail outlet, that in turn trades with the end consumer.

The accounts of trading organisations look similar to those presented in Topic 5. Gross profit is first calculated via a trading account, by finding the difference between the sales value of the goods and the cost of those sales. Trading organisations, then, have accounts that are very similar to those considered in Topic 5 – however, this is not the case for the other types of organisation considered in this topic.

Service providers

Service providers do not offer a tangible physical product for sale to their customers. Nevertheless, they provide something that customers are prepared to pay for. These services are often based on the skills and knowledge possessed by the providers: for example, people visit or employ hairdressers, accountants, solicitors and dentists for the specialist skills and expertise. None of these businesses actually exchange goods with their clients, the basis of the transaction is purely intangible in nature.

Figure 15.30: An example profit and loss account for a service provider

Peter Skelton and Co. profit and loss account for the period ended 30 April 2002

	£	£
Fees received		186,420
Less expenses		
Wages and salaries	43,046	
Motor expenses	11,842	
Rent	4,700	
Heat and light	3,479	
Post and packing	1,840	
Advertising	1,460	
Insurance	2,200	
Bad debts	850	
Provision for bad debts	62	
Depreciation	1,240	
Sundry expenses	1,040	71,759
Net profit		114,661

This means that some parts of a standard profit and loss account and balance sheet are simply unnecessary. For example, if the company does not buy or manufacture goods to sell on to customers, then it obviously does not possess opening or closing stocks, nor under the accounting definition has it made any purchases (goods bought with the specific intention of reselling). Thus the entire trading account section of a standard profit and loss account becomes redundant, as does the entry for stock under current assets on the balance sheet. Figure 15.30 shows a typical profit and loss account for a service provider such as an accountant.

Manufacturing organisations

Let's now consider how to compile a profit and loss account and balance sheet for companies that don't just buy and sell goods but which, like ICI, actually manufacture their own products. The essential difference is that really there isn't a figure for purchases on the trading account, as instead of buying finished products to resell, the company is going to make them.

As its first step, the business must calculate the cost of manufacturing all items across a financial year. This value is inserted in place of purchases on the profit and loss account. Note, though, that this is not cost of sales; it is the production cost of goods completed. What we now have to take into account is the fact that even though products have been made, this does not necessarily mean they have been sold – we still have to account for opening and closing stocks of finished goods. To calculate the production cost of goods completed, a formal account called a manufacturing account is drawn up. Figure 15.31 shows an example of a manufacturing account. The final figure for the production cost of goods completed is inserted on a normal profit and loss account in place of purchases (as in Figure 15.32).

Another difference for manufacturing companies comes on the balance sheet under the current asset section. Normally the first item here shows the stock of unsold goods that the business is carrying into the start of the next financial period. A manufacturing organisation, though, won't just have one type of stock; it would possess stocks of raw materials and components that haven't been used in manufacture yet, stocks of work-in-progress – partly-made products that are not yet through the production process – and stocks of finished goods that have been made but not yet sold. Figure 15.33 shows how the current asset section of a balance sheet would appear for a manufacturing company.

Figure 15.31: An example manufacturing account

Manufacturing account for Slater Industries year ending 31/12/2006

	£	£
Opening stock of raw materials	240,000	
Purchases of materials	2,352,000	
Carriage Inward	8,000	
Closing stock of raw materials	270,000	
Raw materials consumed		3,230,000
Direct wages		1,012,000
Direct expenses		18,000
Prime cost		4,260,000
Factory overheads		
Indirect labour	460,000	
Heat, light and power	512,500	
Factory expenses	234,000	
Depreciation of machinery	95,000	1,301,500
Factory cost		5,561,500
Work in progress @ year start	67,000	
Work in progress @ year end	(64,000)	3,000
Production cost of finished goods completed		5,564,500

Figure 15.32: Profit and loss account for Slater Industries

Profit and loss account for Slater Industries year ending 31/12/2006

	£	£
Sales	12,000,000	
Less Sales returns	(400,000)	11,600,000
Less Cost of sales		
Opening stock of finished goods	65,000	
Cost of finished goods transferred	5,564,500	
Less Closing stock of finished goods	(123,000)	(5,506,500)
Gross profit		6,093,500
Less expenses		
Distribution costs	430,000	
Administration expenses	327,000	(757,000)
Net profit		5,336,500

Balance sheet for Slater Industries year ending 31/12/2006		
	£	£
Current assets		
Closing stock of raw materials	270,000	
Work in progress @ year end	64,000	
Closing stock of finished goods	123,000	
Debtors	46,000	
Prepayments	24,300	
Bank/cash	37,200	564,500

Limited companies

A limited company is so called because its owners are protected by limited liability. In contrast, owners of sole trader businesses and partnerships have unlimited liability. Limited companies are required by law to lodge their accounts at Companies House. This allows them to be accessed and analysed by potential shareholders, possible financiers (banks, building societies, etc.) and by competitors.

A limited company will prepare a profit and loss account purely for internal use – for use by its directors and management. This will look very similar to those shown in Topic 5. However, when the accounts are for publication the company tries to include as little information as possible – it certainly doesn't want to put information in the public domain that could be exploited by its competitors. The Companies Act 1985 lays down specific instructions as to the minimum information that must be included and the layout in which it should be shown.

Figure 15.34 shows an extract taken from BT's published accounts. You can see that the external account provides less information than you would expect to see in an internal profit and loss account. This minimises the information its competitors could use to gain an advantage. However, companies do not have to publish to the minimum standard. They can include any extra information they wish, but not less.

Not-for-profit organisations

Organisations like charities, clubs and societies do not make profits, they are non-profit-making organisations. These organisations do not record "profit" and "loss" using a profit and loss account. Instead, they record their surpluses and deficits of income over expenditure. This results in a financial statement called an income and expenditure account, that has the same broad function as a profit and loss account.

The top half records income and the bottom half expenditure. The key here is that not-for-profit organisations can receive income from all sorts of different areas. For example, an organisation might receive income from:

Figure 15.34: Extract from BT's summary group profit and loss account 2005

	£m
Group turnover	18,623
Group operating profit	2,866
Profit on sale of property fixed assets	22
Net interest payable	(801)
Profit before taxation	2,085

Notes: for year ending 31 March 2005
Source: BT annual review and summary financial statement 2005

Incoming resources	£'000
General donations	83,954
Legacies	125,102
Corporate fundraising	6,462
Regional and national fundraising	58,627
Grants	7,956
Income from technology developments	21,098
Retail income	61,889
Investment income	8,891
Other income	10,253
Total incoming resources	384,232
Expenditure	
Total cost of generating funds	111,680
Total charitable expenditure	217,014
Total expenditure	328,694
Excess of income over expenditure	55,538

Notes: for year ending 31 March 2005
Source: Cancer research annual report and accounts 2004/2005

- subscription fees from members
- donations and grants, such as National Lottery money
- revenue from ticket sales for a concert or charitable event
- fund-raising activities

stopandthink

Many companies do not include any more information in their published accounts than required by law, so that they do not give away potentially sensitive or useful financial information. Imagine that you are in business and you could tell from one of your competitor's financial accounts that they were struggling badly: what might you do? What actions would you advise your company to take that might allow it to capitalise on this situation?

- revenue from profit-making enterprises run as part of their operation.

Expenditure is exactly the same as expenses on a standard profit and loss account. This records all the expenses associated with running the not-for-profit organisation. This can include depreciation and bad debts (members who have not paid subscription fees, for example) and all the other usual categories. Figure 15.35 shows an extract from the published accounts of Cancer Research UK.

Income less expenditure then generates either a figure for a surplus or a deficit (not profit or loss) that is carried forward to the balance sheet. It is added on in the "financed by" section, exactly as we would do with net profit in a company's balance sheet. Remember, though, that nobody owns a not-for-profit organisation so there is no capital account. Instead, these organisations have an accumulated fund – this shows the money the organisation has built up over the years. The rest of the balance sheet appears exactly the same as a normal company balance sheet.

For the last five years, Morgan White has been managing director of Eve's, a chain of successful beauty salon and spa treatment centres. He has shown particular flair in personnel management techniques and quality standards. He has recently been headhunted by Burghley Engineering Limited to bring some extra motivation and consistency to its own workforce and factory practices.

Initially Morgan has been asked to consider the financial side of the company so he can get a feel for the scope and depth of its operation. He has been provided with the financial information in Figure 15.36.

Morgan is quite happy to admit that he does not fully understand accounts, so he has asked you to prepare the information in a format he can understand. Martin (the financial director) has suggested drawing a manufacturing account as this would enable Morgan to see the scale of operations.

A Prepare the manufacturing account as requested, clearly showing prime cost, factory cost and the cost of finished goods completed.

B Using your calculations from task A, and any other relevant information, prepare the trading account for Burghley Engineering stating the gross profit made.

C Write a short memo to Morgan explaining why the accounts you have prepared are different in format to the ones he was used to seeing when he worked at Eve's.

Figure 15.36: Burghley Engineering financial information

	£
Costs	
January 1st opening stock of materials	300,000
December 31st closing stock of materials	312,000
Purchases of raw materials	1,850,000
January 1st work in progress	150,000
December 31st work in progress	159,000
Direct wages	614,000
Supervisory wages	74,000
Fuel and power	7,250
Direct expenses	6,700
Carriage on materials	18,000
Depreciation on machinery	42,000
General factory expenses	12,100
Factory security and insurance	19,700
Other information	
January 1st stocks of finished goods	211,000
December 31st stocks of finished goods	187,000
Sales for the year	3,670,000

Accruals and prepayments

Setting the scene: profit versus cash

The key to understanding accounting is the realisation that profit and cash are not the same thing. Cash in accounting terms represents the amount of money a business currently has available to spend (notes, coins and bank deposits in its possession). Profit is a measure of a business's performance over a given time period.

So, although when recording transactions in ledger accounts we are mainly concerned with payments made and received – money in versus money out – this is not the correct basis for calculating profit, nor for recording the financial position of the firm on the balance sheet.

Consider a company like Comet – the electrical goods retailer – that offers many products on a "buy now, pay later" basis. Suppose a customer purchases a widescreen plasma television from its store. The television has a selling price of £898, and it cost Comet say £600 from its wholesaler. The customer can choose to pay in various ways:

- pay the whole £898 immediately

- spread the cost of the television over 12 monthly instalments at £87.24 per month (including interest)

- pay a 10% deposit of £89.80 now, and the balance in 10 months (interest-free)

- pay a 10% deposit now, have ten months interest free and then pay the balance by monthly instalments.

In each case, the customer is free to leave the store with the television. In each case, the amount Comet would receive in payment from the customer during the financial year is different. However, the amount of profit it has made is the same in each case. No matter how the customer pays for the television, Comet still sold it for £898 and still bought it for £600. Therefore, it makes £298 profit on the sale regardless of how, when and what form the customer's payment actually takes.

This means that information from the company's ledgers extracted to the trial balance needs to be adjusted so that the profit and loss account actually represents the real substance of the transactions that have taken place during the financial period, rather than just showing the form those transactions took. In other words, the financial accounts must show a true and fair view of events, not simply money in and money out.

stop and think

Consider if a company like Dairy Crest invested in new machinery for its production line of milk cartons. The form of the transaction may be that they'd pay £47,000 to the manufacturer in a one off bank payment, thus all the payment occurs in one year. However, the machinery is to be kept and used over the next six years by the business. What would be a true and fair way of representing the cost of this machinery in each years accounts.

The accruals concept

The accruals or matching concept states that costs and revenues are to be accounted for in the financial period in which they are incurred and realised, not when they are paid for. So when calculating the level of expenses (costs) and revenues for a profit and loss account, we cannot just take the figures from the ledger accounts that are used for the trial balance, as these numbers are records of actual transactions – that is, they state what has been paid, not what has been used.

Accruals

An accrual occurs when an item has been used by the business but not yet paid for. Therefore although the item has been used, it won't have been recorded in

Accruals are amounts owed by a business for services it has used during an accounting period but not yet paid for. They represent those expenses that remain unpaid at the year end when the financial accounts are being prepared.

Prepayments represent amounts paid by the business during the accounting period under consideration, for services or expenses that have not been used yet – that is, they have been paid for in advance and will actually be used in the next financial period.

the books of original entry or ledgers as no financial transaction has yet taken place. A simple example is wages. In most jobs it is expected that you work first and get paid afterwards. In many cases, you will be paid weekly or even monthly in arrears. The information on your pay is entered into the wages account in the ledger when and as it is paid by the company. Assume it is the month of May and you get paid £250 per week every Friday, for working five days a week. Figure 15.37 shows how this would be recorded in the wages account in the general ledger for the month.

So at the month end (31 May) we would transfer the figure of £1,000 to the trial balance. However, this figure does not represent the amount of your labour the company has actually used, because you might have worked Saturday (29 May), Sunday (30 May) and Monday (31 May). You are not due to be paid for this work until the end of the week, which would be Friday (4 June).

The accruals concept means that for the profit and loss account we *must* enter the amount used, not the amount paid. So assuming that you usually work Monday to Friday and have the weekend free, this means that you would have worked Monday 31 May, and at £250 per week for a five-day week this equals £50 for that one day. The company owes you this money as, by the end of Monday 31 May when we move into the new month of June, you have done the work for that day. As the company owes you this money it is termed as being an accrual.

Effectively then, the value of the labour you supplied to the company during May was £1,050. This was earned as follows:

Figure 15.37: Wages account in the general ledger

Dr		Your Wages Account				Cr
May		£				£
7th	Bank	250				
14th	Bank	250				
21st	Bank	250				
28th	Bank	250	31st	Bal c/f	1,000
		1,000			1,000
31st	Bal b/f	1,000			

Figure 15.38: The adjusted ledger account

Dr		Your Wages Account				Cr
May		£				£
7th	Bank	250				
14th	Bank	250				
21st	Bank	250				
28th	Bank	250	31st	Transferred to P&L	1,050
31st	Bal c/f	50			
		1,050			1,050
			31st	Bal b/f	50

1–7 May	£250
8–14 May	£250
15–21 May	£250
22–28 May	£250
29–31 May	£50

The ledger account and trial balance value now need to be adjusted to show the true situation rather than just the amount of money paid. This is done by inserting a balance c/f and b/f figure to make the account add up to the now corrected totals. There are two viewpoints here.

- The original accounts figure was too low (as it did not include the work done on Monday 31 May), so it needs increasing. As an expense, this is done by inserting the required figure on the debit side.

- Alternatively, when we start June the company actually already owes you some money for the work you did in May. Therefore we need to start June with a credit (bad) balance showing.

Figure 15.38 shows the adjusted ledger account following the action suggested by the second viewpoint. From this we can see two effects. First, the amount transferred and used for the profit and loss account is not the original figure of £1,000 as would have appeared on the trial balance, but £1,050, the amount of wages and labour used during the period. Second, final entry on the account shows a credit balance bought forward. This means that the company would go into the next financial period owing money from this period. This balance represents a short-term debt that must be paid soon.

Obviously, from the example given, £50 is not a massive amount. However, consider the same situation for a company like ICI employing thousands of people across the country, all of whom are paid in arrears. The outstanding accrual for wages in this instance would definitely have a material impact upon profits.

Note that although we have used wages as the example here, an accrual will occur on any item the business typically pays for in arrears – that is, anything that it uses first and then pays for at a later date.

Effect on the final accounts

Accruals will decrease the profit a business declares, as the amounts owing are added to expenses on the profit and loss account. Accruals are also added to the current liability section of the balance sheet, so they also have the effect of reducing the working capital figure and, therefore, the overall capital employed by the business.

Prepayments

Prepayments are exactly opposite in nature to accruals – they represent items the business has paid for but not actually used. Therefore they do not affect this year's profit, as they will actually be used in the next financial period.

Consider a business that starts on trading on 1 August 2006. After a couple of months, it realises that a delivery vehicle would be a useful addition, so on 1 November it purchases and insures a small van. The best quote for insurance is £420 for the year, payable as a one-off payment on 1 November 2006. As can be seen from Figure 15.39, the insurance paid for runs over the company's financial year-end by three months. However, the insurance ledger account (see Figure 15.40) would show that the whole payment for the insurance has been made.

We know at 31 July 2007 (the business's financial year-end) that £420 is not the correct amount, as this is not the value of the insurance used in the financial year. Three months of the insurance paid for will be used next financial year. Therefore, obviously we need to calculate the amount used. This is done by working out the monthly premium: £420, the cost of insurance each month, divided by 12 is £35 per month.

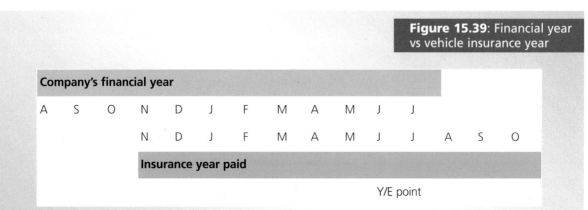

Figure 15.39: Financial year vs vehicle insurance year

Figure 15.40: Insurance ledger account

Dr		Insurance Account		Cr
Nov	**2006**	£		£
1st	Bank	420		

This means the business has used £315 worth of insurance in its financial year to 31 July 2007 (9 x £35), and has £105 worth of insurance it has not yet used (3 x £35). We now need to make the ledger account reflect the *true* amount. Again, there are two viewpoints.

■ The original accounts figure was too high (as it included the total payment made), therefore it needs decreasing. As an expense, this is done by inserting the required figure on the credit side, thus lowering the account.

■ Alternatively, when we start the financial year in 2007 the business actually has already paid for three months' insurance in advance. Therefore, we need to start August 2007 with a debit (good) balance showing. This is shown in Figure 15.41.

In subsequent years, therefore, it is possible that we might start the year with a balance already showing on one of our accounts.

Effect on the final accounts

Prepayments will increase the amount of profit a company declares, as the amounts prepaid are deducted from this year's expenses on the profit and loss account. Prepayments are added to the current asset section of the balance sheet, so they also have the effect of increasing the working capital figure

and, therefore, the overall capital employed by the business.

Other income

One other issue to be aware of is a "receivable" account. This is a revenue account, not a cost, and so the entries are reversed. Suppose a customer has prepaid rent to a business, then the business owes the customer the use of the premises for which they have paid in advance. So a prepayment opening balance on a receivable account would be a credit entry and an accrual would be a debit.

Further adjustments

A final consideration that needs to be taken into account is if the owners of the business have taken stock or goods for their own use, or used the business account to pay for private purchases. These items should be accounted for in any profit calculations or balance sheet valuations, as they are now no longer part of the business's operations – they have been taken from the business by the owners. In these circumstances, the relevant trial balance figures and ledger accounts should be adjusted by removing the value of the items from the account concerned and recording the value as part of the drawings taken by the owners.

Figure 15.41: The adjusted insurance ledger account

Dr		Mary's Insurance Account				Cr
Nov	**2006**	£				£
1st	Bank	420	31/8	Transfer to P&L		315
				Bal c/f		105
	2007	420				420
31/8	Bal b/f	105				

Note the transfer to P&L on the credit side of the accounts; this is because we are about to prepare a set of final accounts at the year end (P&L and balance sheet).

Phil Ellis set up in business twelve months ago. His year-end date is 30 September and he has asked you to help him prepare his profit and loss account and balance sheet.

Figure 15.42 is information available from Phil's trial balance. You also know that:

- his closing stock has been counted and valued at £12,000

- Phil has prepaid his insurance by £150

- wages are paid in arrears, and currently Phil has £350 owing to his employee

- stocks of stationery items to be carried forward to next year total £40.

Phil has also fallen behind with the rental payments for his premises. He currently owes August and September rent at a total of £840.

A Prepare Phil's end of year final accounts as requested.

B Explain to Phil why accruals and prepayments must be accounted for when preparing final accounts.

C Phil pays himself £1,150 every month and cannot understand why his drawings are listed at £17,000. Explain two ways in which this situation may have occurred.

Figure 15.42: Phil's trial balance

	Dr	Cr
	£	£
Machinery	20,000	
Debtors	4,200	
Five-year loan		10,000
Advertising	250	
Sales		80,000
Loan interest	2,000	
Rent	6,000	
Purchases	42,000	
Rates	1,000	
Heat and light	2,000	
Fixtures and fittings	8,000	
Cash	95	
Creditors		4,000
Drawings	17,000	
Vehicles	12,000	
Stationery	120	
Insurance	500	
General expenses	885	
Wages	4,000	
Capital		33,600
Bank	6,800	
Petrol	750	
	127,600	127,600

Depreciation and bad debts

Setting the scene: reasons for depreciation

Fixed assets such as machinery, vehicles and premises do not last for ever. They have a limited useful life to the business that has bought and uses them.

Consider a business such as a local painting and decorating firm that purchases a new van for £16,000 and then subsequently sells it four years later for £5,000. The value of the van can be regarded as having fallen by £11,000 in the four years that it has be owned by the business. Depreciation is a way of representing this drop in value of an asset over time.

However, depreciation also serves another purpose: that is to help a business comply with the underlying accounting principle of providing a true and fair view of its reported profits each year and its balance sheet value. Depreciation is a method by which the cost of a fixed asset is allocated across the financial periods in which the cost of the asset will be incurred.

Think about how this might be done. What was the actual cost to the painting and decorating

business of owning the van for four years (excluding running costs)? Did this cost occur in one particular year? How should the cost of owning the van be treated in each of the four years the company had the van in its possession?

Unit 15 Financial accounting for managers

Depreciation

Depreciation is the method by which the cost of a fixed asset is allocated to the accounting periods in which that asset will be used by the business. It can be used to allocate costs for all the major categories of fixed assets, including:

- machinery
- equipment
- furniture
- fixtures
- premises
- vehicles.

All these fixed assets are likely to be used by a business for more than a year. A vehicle might be replaced every three or four years, an office block might serve a useful function for decades. In order to produce a true and fair view of the business each year – and the costs it has incurred and, therefore, the profit it has made – it makes sense to spread the cost of these fixed assets over the years in which they will be used. This is the

basic idea behind depreciation: we write off some of the value of the fixed asset each year.

Consider, for example, a fixed asset costing £100,000 and which is going to last four years. If that cost is spread over the asset's life, it would "cost" the business £25,000 each year (£100,000/4). This appears as an expense on the profit and loss account. This charge is called depreciation. It is not a cost, it is a provision. This means it is not a real transaction.

In reality, the business bought an asset for £100,000, and it has £100,000 less in its bank account. But if we charged the whole of this cost to year one (the year in which the asset was bought), it might look like the business hardly made any profit at all that year. Whereas, for the next three years, it would look like it was suddenly making huge profits (because it would be getting the benefit of the asset without incurring any charge for it). Depreciation is therefore used to allocate the cost of the asset over the amount of time it serves a productive function for the business. It spreads the cost of the asset over its useful life, despite the fact that the business actually paid £100,000 before the asset was put to use.

Depreciation is not a method of saving up for a replacement machine (that is a separate decision to be taken independently). In effect, depreciation reduces the book value of an asset. This is a statement of what it is worth to the business. The book value does not have to reflect the true market value of the asset, it simply represents how much use the asset has left to the business that owns it. The only time that depreciation can be accurately calculated is when the firm disposes of the asset – this allows the difference between its purchase cost and the amount received on disposal to be calculated. However, this may not be known for years in advance and so is impractical for accountancy purposes.

Before looking at different methods of calculating depreciation, it is worth considering some of the reasons why fixed assets decline in value over time. These include:

- wear and tear – through use, the asset eventually wears out

- decay – rust, rot, erosion, etc.

- obsolescence – eventually a machine will be replaced by faster, more efficient, models although the old machine may still be in perfect working order

- inadequacy – an asset is no longer useful to a company due to changes in company size or structure

- passage of time – some assets such as patents and leases actually have a set legal lifetime and therefore lose value as time passes (this process is more properly known as amortisation)

- depletion – some natural assets such as quarries and mines will run out, therefore they can be depreciated in value.

Of course, some assets may well increase, not decrease, in value – this is called appreciation. Normal accounting practice is to ignore appreciation as it is contrary to the cost and prudence concepts, and in many cases value is very subjective. Some people may pay £30 million for a Van Gogh picture of sunflowers, where others may think it worthless. However, anybody who owns a Van Gogh knows that the value of these paintings continues to rise on the international art market.

Methods of depreciation

Although the concept of allocating the cost of a fixed asset across its useful lifetime is a sensible and equitable idea, there is no single approved method for doing so. In this topic, we shall examine two of the main methods in current business use.

Straight line method

This is the simplest and easiest method of depreciation. It reduces the value of the asset by the same amount each year over the asset's useful life. In other words, the depreciation charge each year can be expressed as this formula:

$$\text{depreciation charge per year} = \frac{\text{cost of asset} - \text{expected residual value}}{\text{useful life (in years)}}$$

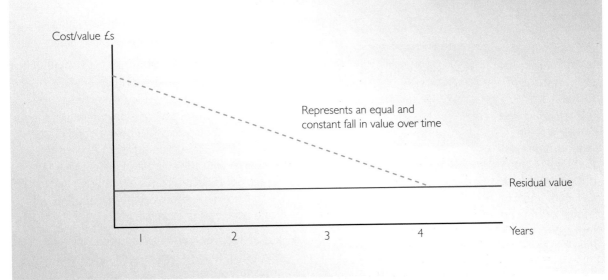

Figure 15.43: Straight line depreciation

Cost/value £s

Represents an equal and constant fall in value over time

Residual value

Years

So if a machine costs £10,000, and is expected to be used for four years, when the company hopes to sell it for £4,000, the depreciation charge is £1,500 per year: (10,000 − 4,000) = 6,000; 6,000/4 = 1,500.

The straight line method has the advantage of simplicity, and is useful when the business is expecting constant returns over the life of an asset.

Reducing balance method (declining)

This method recognises the fact that few assets decline in value by the same amount each year, so we reduce the value of the asset each year by using a fixed percentage. This means that the depreciation charge is higher in the early years and lower in the asset's later years. The reducing balance method takes into account that as a machine grows older it will require more maintenance and repairs. Costs, therefore, are liable to increase as its earning power decreases.

Suppose we depreciate a £10,000 car at 20 per cent per year. These calculations show how its value declines:

> Year 1 depreciation = 20% of current value
> £10,000 = £2,000
>
> Year 2 depreciation = 20% of current value
> £8,000 = £1,600
>
> Year 3 depreciation = 20% of current value
> £6,400 = £1,280
>
> Year 4 depreciation = 20% of current value
> £5,120 = £1,024

After four years, its value is £4,096 (£10,000 less £2,000 + £1,600 + £1,280 + £1,024). The car is worth less than half of its purchase price.

stop and think

If a company buys a Vauxhall Vectra at a list price of £18,500, how much would that car be worth second-hand just two weeks later? Consider what is the difference in value between a 15-year-old Vauxhall and one that is 16 years old. Which choice of depreciation method most accurately represents how the value of a car may decline over time?

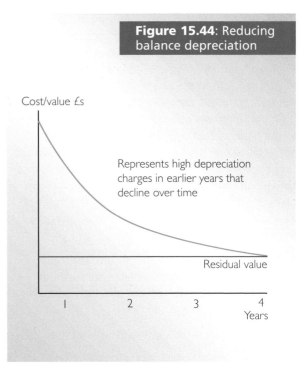

Figure 15.44: Reducing balance depreciation

Cost/value £s

Represents high depreciation charges in earlier years that decline over time

Residual value

Years

Using depreciation in the accounts

According to the accruals or matching concept, firms should allocate costs to the period in which they were incurred. The concept of depreciation enables us to do this – the amount depreciated each year is charged to the profit and loss account (as part of expenses) and the unallocated portion (the cost of the asset less the total depreciation charged to date) is treated as an asset and appears on the balance sheet. Figure 15.45 shows how depreciation is treated on the balance sheet.

Figure 15.46 shows a template (without numbers) for the treatment of depreciation in the profit and loss account. We only put the depreciation charge for the current year in the profit and loss account. In contrast, the balance sheet records "accumulated depreciation" – this year's charge plus all other years to date.

There is no hard and fast rule as to which method of depreciation should be chosen. However, once an asset has been depreciated using a particular method, the consistency concept means that we must continue to use that method (unless we have a good reason not to). A general guideline is to try to match the method used with the amount of benefit received in each year. So, expected consistent returns use straight line, and high initial returns gradually reducing use reducing balance. For example:

■ a chair receives constant use over its life – we don't sit in it more because it is new – so use the straight-line method

Figure 15.45: Treatment of depreciation in balance sheet

Balance sheet for S Smith as at 31/12/06			
Fixed assets	**Cost**	**Accumulated depreciation**	**Net book value**
Motor van	£10,000	£3,000	£7,000
Machinery	£5,000	£2,000	£3,000
			£10,000

Trading, profit and loss account for   **period ending**   /   /

	£	£
Sales	xxx	
Less Returns in	(xxx)	XXX
Less Cost of goods sold		
Opening stock	xxx	
Purchases	xxx	
Less Returns out	(xxx)	
Carriage inwards	xxx	
Less Closing stock	(xxx)	XXX
Gross profit		YYY
Expenses		
Heat and light	xxx	
Wages	xxx	
Carriage	xxx	
Depreciation		
Machinery	xxx	
Equipment	xxx	
Fixtures	xxx	
Furniture	xxx	
Vehicles	xxx	XXX
Net profit		ZZZ

- we tend to use a new car or machine more than we would an old one – so use the reducing balance method.

Bad debts

A bad debt occurs when a customer that has bought goods on credit (therefore a debtor) is unable to pay their account. If the business is unable to collect this debt, it is going to lose money on the transaction as it will not get paid for the goods it has sold.

When the business sold these goods originally, it did not know that this customer would be unable (or refuse) to pay, so the transaction was recorded in the books as normal. The transaction would have been included in the sales account. It will increase the business's sales and, hence, the level of profit it would declare at the end of the year.

However, if it is not going to get the money, it should not have to declare this "income" as part of profit. So when a business knows that a customer is unable to pay a debt, it can write off the amount of money still owing as a bad debt. The total bad debts for a year are then deducted on the profit and loss account as an expense (cost), reducing the level of profits made and reflecting the fact that although the business sold the goods it never received the money it was owed.

Provision for bad and doubtful debts

Bad debts exist – and experience tells any business that no matter how carefully it applies credit checks on customers, some are still going to turn bad. This means that at the end of a financial period a business will have debtors that owe it money, and that some of them are unlikely to pay. However, it doesn't know who, or how many.

The problem is similar to bad debts. Sales have been recorded, increasing profits, but if debtors don't pay up, the business actually loses money. However, at the point when the profit and loss account and balance sheet are due to be drawn up, it doesn't know what this amount might be. The provision for bad debt is a best guess, and it is deducted from the profit and loss account as an expense.

Again, this is an application of the accruals or matching concept, as the sales were made in this financial period, so any non-payment also needs to be accounted for in this financial period. Even though debtors may actually turn bad at a later date, we account for the possibility now. This is also reflecting the prudence concept in that we are recognising the potential for a loss in profit as soon as we are anticipating it might happen. This amount is added to the expense sections of the profit and loss account to reduce declared profits. It is also deducted from debtors on the current assets section of the balance sheet because, if a business doesn't think all its debtors are going to pay, how can the total sum be recorded as an asset?

stop and think

Would every type of industry suffer from the same degree of debtors going bad? Consider businesses like Tesco, a local newsagent, car sales and a furniture retailer like MFI. What factors would a business need to consider when trying to estimate its provision for bad (doubtful) debts for the year?

Jenny Harris set up in business two years ago. Her next year-end date is the 31 November 2006 and she has asked you to help her prepare her profit and loss account and balance sheet.

Figure 15.47 gives some financial information for the business. You also know that her closing stock has been counted and valued at £12,000.

Jenny has told you her policy on depreciation.

- Machinery is depreciated at 20% per annum on the reducing balance method, and the machinery is already one year old (provision for depreciation already exists in Figure 15.47).

- Fixtures and fitting are depreciated at 10% per annum straight line, and the fixtures are already one year old.

- Vehicles are depreciated at 25% per annum reducing balance and the vehicle was bought on 1 September 2006 – it is Jenny's pratice to depreciate these assets monthly.

As far as accruals and prepayments are concerned, Jenny has wages totalling £350 outstanding for the year, and her insurance policy actually covers the twelve months up to 31 December.

A Prepare Jenny's end of year final accounts as requested.

B Explain two fundamental concepts that are being applied when calculating depreciation.

C Differentiate between bad debts and the provision for bad (doubtful) debts.

Figure 15.47: Jenny's trial balance

	Dr £	Cr £
Machinery	20,000	
Provision for depreciation		4,000
Debtors	5,200	
Opening stock	6,000	
Five-year loan		14,000
Advertising	250	
Sales		84,275
Loan interest	4,000	
Rent	6,275	
Purchases	42,000	
Wages	3,000	
Heat and light	1,600	
Fixtures and fittings	8,000	
Provision for depreciation		800
Cash	490	
Creditors		3,800
Drawings	19,000	
Vehicles	12,000	
Stationery	120	
Insurance	300	
General expenses	190	
Bad debt	200	
Capital		30,100
Bank	6,925	
Petrol	1,425	
	136,975	136,975

Setting the scene: reasons for ratio analysis

The function of financial information is to provide an insight into how a particular organisation has performed over a period of time. Ratio analysis represents one way business performance can be assessed.

Final accounts, such as the profit and loss account and the balance sheet, are used for three main purposes:

- financial control
- planning
- accountability.

Ratio analysis can help in interpreting this financial information and assist managers in achieving these. However, the results gained using ratio analysis techniques mean absolutely nothing unless the organisation's objectives are also considered.

Not all businesses have the same objectives. A sole trader with a net profit of £500,000 is likely to be quite satisfied with such a healthy return. However, neither a major plc such as Sony nor a leisure centre such as The Dome in Doncaster may be satisfied with this financial result. Sony has a range of objectives, including maximising profits, maintaining market share and/or market leadership, and corporate growth. Sony would not regard £500,000 profit as an adequate return on its investment.

The Dome's mission statement states: "We manage the leisure and entertainment experience to improve the lives and wellbeing of our clients and their communities." It may well be trying to achieve the objective of providing an efficient service to the whole community, while still remaining within its given budget. Profit is not a key objective for the organisation.

So when interpreting financial results it is important to consider what the organisation is trying to achieve. What are its objectives? These will have an influence on whether we consider the financial results to be acceptable or unacceptable.

Methods of financial analysis

For mangers to gain the information they need, the analysis of the final accounts is not undertaken randomly. A well-ordered and structured process needs to be followed.

- **Initial reading**
  Used to gain a broad understanding of the business's financial position. You should find out the type of industry and the market in which it is operating, and gain a rough idea of its recent financial performance.

- **Vertical analysis**
  This considers the interdependence of one figure on another. For example, gross profit is not only affected by the level of sales but also by the cost of sales.

- **Horizontal analysis**
  Compares current financial statements with statements from previous years. This is done on an item-by-item basis, to determine whether there have been any particular areas of change. For example, you will want to find out if sales have risen or fallen compared to last year.

- **Trend analysis**
  The current figures are compared with those from several consecutive previous years in an attempt to determine the presence of any significant trends. This can be done on a horizontal or a vertical basis, or both. For example, we could use horizontal analysis to see if there had been any consistent change in the level of sales over three or four years. We could then also use vertical analysis to see if there had been a secondary effect on the level of gross profit reported.

■ Ratio analysis

The use of financial ratios to compare and interpret financial statements. This method allows for in-depth monitoring of financial performance from one period to another, comparisons over time, comparisons with other companies, and analysis of current financial performance.

Figure 15.48 shows an extract from the accounts of J Sainsbury plc. From a simple horizontal analysis, it can be seen that gross profit has fallen between 2004 and 2005. However, what managers and other stakeholders may actually want to know is:

- for every pound of stock that Sainsbury has sold how much profit does it make, and is this rising or falling year on year

- is the company turning over as much stock as in previous years, or is this too decreasing

- is it keeping the cost of buying stock under control?

Figure 15.48: J Sainsbury plc financial results		
	2005 £m	2004 £m
Turnover including VAT and sales tax	16,573	18,239
VAT and sales tax	(1,164)	(1,098)
Continuing operations	15,202	14,440
Discontinued operations	207	2,701
Turnover excluding VAT and sales tax	15,409	17,141
Cost of sales (including exceptional costs)	(14,726)	(15,658)
Gross profit	683	1,483

Source: J Sainsbury plc Annual Report 2005

Liquidity ratios

Liquidity ratios (also known as solvency ratios) are concerned with the financial stability of a business. They mainly involve investigation of the organisation's working capital to review whether it is being managed effectively. Working capital is needed by all organisations to finance their day-to-day activities such as buying stock and paying running expenses. Too little, and the business may not be able to pay all its debts and bills. Too much, and it may not be making the most efficient use of its resources.

Although profitability is important for most businesses, it is often a short-term lack of cash (liquidity) that causes a firm to fold (liquidate). An unprofitable business can survive in the short term so long as it still has sufficient financial resources to pay debts as they become due.

The current ratio

The current ratio looks at the relationship between current assets and current liabilities; it is often referred to as the working capital ratio and examines the liquidity position of the firm. It is given by the formula:

$$\text{current ratio} = \frac{\text{current assets}}{\text{current liabilities}}$$

This is expressed as a ratio, for example 2:1 or 3:1. So, for example, if a business has current assets of £30,000 and current liabilities of £10,000, its current ratio is 30,000:10,000, which we would show as 3:1.

Understanding the result

This result shows that there are three times as many current assets as current liabilities. This means that the business has £3 of short-term assets available to pay for every £1 of short-term money owed. This company is therefore in a comfortable position to pay its debts.

Accepted knowledge is that an ideal current ratio should be around 2:1 – that is, £2 of assets for every £1 of debt. Any higher, and the organisation has too many resources tied up in unproductive assets. For example, it might be holding too much stock, which could be invested more profitably. A low result, something like 0.7:1, means a business may not be able to pay its debts as they fall due. In this case, the business only has 70p of current assets available to pay every £1 it owes.

Managing the ratio

This is dependent on the direction the business wishes to go. If the business is holding far too many resources in either stocks, cash or money at the bank account, or has too many debtors, then the current ratio may be too high. This can easily be solved by converting some of these liquid assets to cash and investing it back in the business, such as buying better machinery or training employees.

If the ratio is too low, the business may well have to sell off some of its fixed assets – or arrange a sell and leaseback deal – to obtain a more liquid position. Alternatively, it might look for additional long-term finance, through say selling more shares or obtaining a long-term loan. This would enable it to inject cash into the business so that it is then able to pay debts when required.

The acid test

The acid test is sometimes called the quick or liquid ratio. It too examines liquidity by comparing current assets and liabilities, but it removes stock from the total of current assets. This is done because stock is the most illiquid current asset – it is the hardest to turn into cash without a loss in its value. In many cases, in order to convert stock into cash or bank deposits, a business reduces it prices to achieve some quick sales. It can take a long time to convert stock into cash at its full value. Consider, for example, how long it would take a car showroom selling BMWs to clear every car off its forecourt.

Furthermore, stock held in warehouses may be old or obsolete, and thus unsellable. With the removal of stock from the equation, we are able to directly relate cash and near-cash equivalents (cash, bank and debtors) to short-term debts. This therefore provides a much more accurate measure of the firm's liquidity than the current ratio. And again it is expressed in ratio form, such as 3:1, and is given by the formula:

$$\text{acid test} = \frac{\text{(current assets} - \text{stock)}}{\text{current liabilities}}$$

Understanding the result

An ideal result for the acid test is around 1.1:1, showing that the firm has £1.10 to pay every £1 of debt. The business could pay all its debts, and has a 10 per cent safety margin. A lower result, such as 0.7:1, indicates that the firm may well have difficulties meeting short-term payments. However, some businesses are able to operate with a very low level of liquidity, such as supermarkets like Asda and Tesco that have the majority of their current assets tied up in stock.

stopandthink

The information in Figure 15.49 can be used to assess Sainsbury's liquidity position. Calculate the company's current ratio and acid test. In your opinion, is Sainsbury really in danger of business closure through liquidity problems?

Figure 15.49: Sainsbury's liquidity position

Current assets	
Stocks	559
Debtors	
Retail debtors	271
Sainsbury's Bank debtors	2,615
Assets held for resale	87
Investments	114
Cash at bank and in hand	673
Total	4,319
Current liabilities: creditors amounts falling due in one year	(5097)

Source: J Sainsbury plc Annual Report 2005

Managing the ratio

The same types of action can be taken as with the current ratio. Again, businesses may wish to convert current assets to productive investment if the result is considered too high, or seek methods of injecting cash resources into the firm if the result is too low.

Gearing

Gearing is included in the classification of liquidity ratios, as this ratio focuses on long-term financial stability rather than short. It measures how much of the total capital employed by the business has been borrowed in the form of long-term debts. Gearing is found by using the formula:

$$\text{gearing} = \frac{\text{long-term liabilities} + \text{preference shares}}{\text{total capital employed}} \times 100$$

Where:

total capital employed = ordinary share capital + preference share capital + reserves + debentures + long-term loans + mortgages

long-term liabilities = long-term loans + debentures + preference shares

Understanding the result

The gearing ratio shows whether a company is a risky investment. If loans represent more than 50 per cent of capital employed, the company is said to be highly geared. A highly-geared firm has to pay interest on its borrowings before it can pay dividends to ordinary shareholders or retain profits for reinvestment. The higher the resulting figure for gearing, therefore, the higher the degree of risk.

Ordinary shareholders should enjoy a greater rate of return from lower-geared companies. Low-geared companies – those under 50 per cent – should therefore provide a lower risk investment opportunity. Lower-geared companies should also be able to negotiate new loans much more easily than a highly-geared company, as they are not already financed by a high proportion of debt.

Managing the ratio

The gearing ratio can be altered in several ways, depending on whether the organisation wishes to raise or lower its gearing figure. If it wishes to raise gearing, it can:

- buy back ordinary shares
- issue more preference shares
- issue more debentures
- obtain more loans.

If it wishes to reduce gearing, it can:

- issue more ordinary shares
- buy back debentures (redeeming)
- retain more profits (increase reserves)
- repay loans.

It might be tempting to think that raising finance by increasing gearing (taking more loans) is bad. However, the advantage of raising gearing as a method of increasing capital employed – rather than, for example, issuing more shares – is that loans will eventually be paid back. By issuing shares, the company is diluting the ownership of the business, and it creates a permanent commitment – new shareholders will expect to receive annual dividends for as long the company is in existence.

Profitability ratios

Most private business enterprises have making a profit as one of their main objectives. However, it is not sufficient just to measure the absolute amount of profit a business makes. Consider this example. Company A and B both trade in the same market, and at the end of the year:

- company A reports profits of £400,000
- company B reports profits of £1,000,000.

In your judgement which is the better company? It would be reasonable to argue that company B looks the better option. However, now consider some additional information in Figure 15.50.

	Company A	**Company B**
Figure 15.50: Returns for company A and company B		
Profit	£400,000	£1,000,000
Capital invested	£800,000	£5,000,000
% return	50%	20%

We can see that Company A has actually made a much higher return compared to the amount of money tied up in the business compared to Company B. As you can see, it is not only the quantity of profit that matters, but also the amount of assets required to generate this profit. Profitability ratios allow us to examine these relationships in detail. In Topic 5, we made a distinction between various types of profit. Because of the different types of profit, there are several ratios for measuring profitability.

Gross profit margin

Gross profit margin examines the relationship between the profits made on trading activities only. It measures the level of gross profit against the level of turnover (sales made). The result is expressed as a percentage, and is given by the formula:

$$\text{gross profit margin} = \frac{\text{gross profit}}{\text{turnover (sales)}} \times 100$$

Understanding the result

The higher the gross profit margin, the better. However, the level of gross profit margin made will vary considerably between different markets and products. For example, the gross profit percentage put on clothes (especially fashion items) is far higher than that put on food items. So any result must be looked at in the context of the industry in which the firm operates. However, any business should be able to make comparisons with previous years' figures to establish whether its trading position has become more or less profitable.

Managing the ratio

The gross profit margin can be improved by:

- raising sales revenue while keeping the cost of sales static – that is, increasing prices

- reducing cost of sales made while maintaining the same level of sales revenue – that is, purchasing or manufacturing goods for less

- or a combination of these two methods.

Net profit margin

This ratio measures the relationship between the net profit (profit made after all other expenses have been deducted) and the level of turnover or sales made. Again it is expressed as a percentage, and it is given by the formula:

$$\text{net profit margin} = \frac{\text{net profit}}{\text{turnover (sales)}} \times 100$$

Understanding the result

As with gross profit, a higher percentage result is preferred as this shows the business is more profitable overall. The net profit margin is used to determine how well the firm has controlled its day-to-day running costs. It should be compared with previous years' results and with other companies in the same industry to judge relative efficiency. A rising net profit margin would suggest that the company is becoming more efficient year on year.

The net profit margin should also be compared with the gross profit margin. If the gross profit margin has improved but the net profit margin declined, this shows that profits made on trading are becoming better – however, the expenses incurred in running the business are also increasing but at a faster rate than profits. This means that efficiency is declining. This can be investigated further by measuring each category of expenses over sales to determine where the problems are occurring. If any category of expenses has risen disproportionably compared with previous years, this may be a good indicator of the cause of the problem.

Managing the ratio

The net profit margin can be improved by:

- improvements in the gross profit margin, such as increasing sales while maintaining costs

- reducing expenses while maintaining the same level of sales revenue.

Return on capital employed

Return on capital employed (ROCE) (primary ratio) is often considered to be one of the most important ratios. It measures the efficiency of funds invested in the business compared to the generation of profits. This ratio is different for sole traders and companies because of the different ways these types of business can raise their capital.

For a sole trader, return on capital employed is given by the formula:

$$\text{sole trader ROCE} = \frac{\text{net profit}}{\text{capital employed}} \times 100$$

For a limited company, the formula is:

$$\text{limited company ROCE} = \frac{\text{net profit before interest and tax}}{\text{total capital employed}} \times 100$$

Where again, as with gearing:

total capital employed = ordinary share capital + preference share capital + reserves + debentures + long-term loans + mortgages

For each type of company the idea is to determine how much profit has been made compared to the total amount of assets employed by that business. For example, to make £100,000 profit when you have £1 million to invest is somewhat easier than making the same £100,000 profit when you've only got £50,000 of total capital employed by your business.

Tax and interest charges are ignored when calculating ROCE for a limited company, as these items will fluctuate according decisions made by the government and the Bank of England, and they are therefore outside the direct control of the business.

Understanding the result

As with the other profitability ratios examined so far, the higher the value of the ratio the better. A higher percentage provides owners with a greater return on the money they have invested. Inevitably again, this figure needs to be compared with previous years and other companies to determine whether the result is satisfactory.

The result also needs to be compared with the percentage return offered by interest-bearing accounts at banks and building societies. For example, what is the point of a sole trader investing all his or her money in the business, working very hard all year and making a return on capital employed of

7 per cent if more profit could be earned by investing in a savings account earning 10 per cent interest? Although there are non-financial benefits from being your own boss, ideally the ROCE should be higher than any return that could be gained from interest-earning accounts.

Managing the ratio

The return on capital employed can be improved by:

- increasing the level of profit generated by the same level of capital invested

- maintaining the level of profits generated, but decreasing the amount of capital it takes to generate that profit.

Efficiency ratios

Efficiency ratios are sometimes called activity ratios or asset utilisation ratios. They are concerned with measuring how an organisation manages and uses its resources. Mainly they investigate how well managers control the current situation of the business. They consider stock, debtors and creditors, and the use of assets.

Stock turnover

Stock turnover measures the number of times in one year that a business turns over its stock of goods for sale. From this figure, we can also establish the average length of time (in days) that stock is held by the company. It is given by the formula:

$$\text{stock turnover} = \frac{\text{cost of goods sold}}{\text{average stock}}$$

Where:

$$\text{average stock} = \frac{(\text{opening stock} + \text{closing stock})}{2}$$

Note, the stock turnover ratio cannot be used for service businesses as they do not buy or sell stocks of goods.

Understanding the result

This ratio needs to be interpreted with knowledge of the industry and market in which the firm operates. For example, recalling the BMW business, if we were examining the accounts of a car sales business we would not expect it to turn over its entire stock of cars and replace them with new ones every week. A good result might be to turn over its stock about once

a month or every five to six weeks, therefore we would see a result round about 9 or 10 times (a year).

As usual, we can also compare this year's result with previous years or other similar-sized firms in the same market. As a general rule, the quicker a business is selling its stock, the quicker it is going to realise profits, so the higher the rate of stock turnover the better. A falling stock turnover figure can indicate falling sales or that the company is holding a large amount of obsolete or slow-selling items. It could also result from an inefficient purchasing system that isn't effectively matching purchasing to selling. A note of caution though: the rate of stock turnover can be increased by firms selling off stock cheaply (below the normal market price). This could be undesirable, so stock turnover results should be closely compared to gross profit margin.

Managing the ratio

The stock turnover ratio can be improved by:

- reducing the average level of stocks held, without losing sales

- increasing the rate of sales, without raising the level of stocks.

Debtor collection period

The debtor collection period is designed to show how long, on average, it takes the company to collect debts owed by customers. Customers who are granted credit are called debtors. Expressed in days, the formula for this ratio is:

$$\text{debtor collection period} = \frac{\text{debtors}}{\text{credit sales}} \times 365$$

Often the figure for credit sales is not actually provided on the profit and loss account. In this case, the sales/turnover figure should be substituted and used instead.

Understanding the result

Different industries typically allow different amounts of time for debtors to settle invoices. Standard credit terms are usually for 30, 60, 90 and 120 days. The debt collection period figure should therefore be compared against the *official* number of days the business allows for debts to be settled. This has important implications for cash flow as it shows how effective an organisation's credit control system is at collecting the money it is owed. The nearer the result to the actual period allowed by the organisation's standard credit terms the better. Poor results over the period show that while the company may be good at selling goods, it is not so good at collecting the money owed.

Managing the ratio

The debtor collection period can be improved by:

- reducing the amount of time credit is offered, say reducing credit terms from 90 to 60 days

- offering incentives for clients to pay on time, such as cash discounts

- stepping up the efficiency of the credit control department – if there is a real problem in this area, some companies may consider debt factoring as a solution.

Creditor payment period

The creditor payment period shows how long, on average, it takes the company to pay debts owed to suppliers. The formula for this ratio (expressed as days) is:

$$\text{creditor payment period} = \frac{\text{creditors}}{\text{credit purchases}} \times 365$$

Again, the exact figure for credit purchases is not actually provided on the profit and loss account. In this case, the purchases figure should be substituted and used instead.

Understanding the result

This ratio shows how good a company is at actually paying its suppliers. So if a supplier offers 30 days' credit they can use this ratio to forecast whether or not they are likely to be paid on time by the company asking for the credit terms. Companies with poor credit payment periods therefore may find it hard to negotiate and receive new credit agreements in the future. A key area for analysis here is the comparison between debtor and creditor periods; obviously it would be better for most businesses if debtors pay sooner than creditors fall due, thus ensuring cash flow is present to enable payments to suppliers to be made.

Managing the ratio

The creditor payment period can be improved by:

- ensuring invoices from suppliers are paid on time

- improving cash flow and working capital management to ensure funds are available to meet payments as they fall due.

Return on assets

Return on assets, like the ROCE ratio, is a very important ratio. Instead of relating the return made by the business to the total amount of capital invested in it, this ratio looks at the relationship between net profit and net assets. It compares profits generated to the assets used, not capital.

You may recall that net assets is one of the key figures on a limited company's balance sheet. This ratio is designed to show how hard a company's assets are working. It is pointless to have money tied up in assets that are not beingn used productively. The return on net assets is expressed as a percentage and given by the formula:

$$\text{return on net assets} = \frac{\text{net profit before tax and interest}}{\text{net assets}} \times 100$$

Where:

net assets = fixed assets + (current assets – current liabilities)

Understanding the result

A higher percentage compared to previous years or with other companies would indicate that assets are being utilised effectively in the generation of profit. Therefore, the higher the figure, the harder the company's assets are being made to work. This is generally preferred to a lower result.

Managing the ratio

The net assets ratio can be improved by:

- raising net profit while keeping net assets constant

- reducing net assets while maintaining the same level of net profit – the fewer assets required to generate a given profit the better.

Limitations of ratio analysis

Ratio analysis is a very useful tool for managers to employ in running companies. It can show how efficiently the business is working and what its profit performance is, as well as indicating the long-term and short-term financial stability of the organisation. From this analysis, managers can pinpoint areas of weakness and thus try to remedy or remove problems that could potentially threaten business survival. The analysis also highlights areas of key strength which can then be built upon to improve future business performance. However, ratio analysis results, in themselves, can be relatively meaningless unless they are compared to previous years or current competitors' results. This comparison establishes whether the results obtained in the current year are satisfactory.

Ratio analysis is a very powerful tool in the interpretation of financial accounts. It can allow for inter-firm comparisons, appraisal of financial performance and the identification of trends, and can be a great help in financial planning and decision-making. However, because of its usefulness and the range of possible applications, there is a

tendency too attach to much importance to the results: other types of analysis exist, and there are sometimes more important issues at stake than just financial performance. Remember, ratio analysis does not provide any information on these key aspects of a business's operating environment:

- state of the market – such as whether it is about to enter a recessionary period

- morale and motivation levels of the workforce

- legal environment – is the business affected by changes in government legislation

- supply chain relationships

- the future plans of the management for the business.

assessment practice
Considering investment opportunities

In your capacity as a financial adviser, you have been approached by one of your clients asking you to assess two possible investment opportunities. Study the financial statements in Figure 15.51 before tackling the tasks that follow.

A For each company, calculate its:
- return on capital employed
- net profit margin
- rate of stock turnover
- gross profit margin
- debtor collection period
- current ratio.

B Using the acid test, comment on the liquidity position of each company. Why is liquidity an important factor for businesses to consider?

C Explain three other factors you would also need to know before making an informed recommendation to your client.

D Including any other calculations you consider relevant, write a report to your client clearly analysing the two companies and stating your recommendation.

Figure 15.51: Returns of company A and company B

	Company A £	Company B £
Net profit	10,000	20,000
Capital employed	50,000	100,000
Sales	500,000	200,000
Cost of sales	110,000	45,000
Opening stock	20,000	4,000
Closing stock	15,000	5,000
Debtors	30,000	8,500
Creditors	15,000	7,000
Bank/cash	12,000	(5,000) overdrawn

Practice external assessment

Praha 1

Praha 1 is a popular Czech café situated in the heart of Manchester. It offers takeaway snacks and sandwiches as well as an eat-in service. Dobromir and Claire Capps opened Praha 1 in 2002 as a limited company, with members of Dobromir's family contributing as shareholders. They have built up a regular clientele, as well frequently attracting new customers and tourists, especially as the restaurant has received several very good reviews in the local press and tourist guides. It is popular with business people and has a thriving evening trade.

Dobromir is a skilled chef, while Claire tends to handle the lighter side of the menu such as sandwiches, but neither is skilled at keeping financial records. Praha 1 at one point had several corporate customers who would book the whole restaurant for business events and entertaining clients. However, after having Dobromir send out several incorrect invoices to various clients – generating numerous complaints – this area of business has started to decline recently.

To combat this decline, Claire wants to launch a delivery service during lunchtime for local business people. This would involve setting up a website so that customers could log on in the morning and pre-order their favourite lunchtime snack or sandwich. This would be ready for collection or, for a small surcharge, it could be delivered direct to the customer's office. Dobromir's cousin Capeka is willing to work part-time during the week as a delivery person. However, the scheme would require Dobromir and Claire to approach the bank to ask for a loan to finance their plans.

Figure 15.52: Invoice to Westland Finance plc

Invoice

Praha 1

42 Oxford Street
Manchester
M60 7HA

Phone: 0161 288 7439
Fax: 0161 288 7438

VAT REG No. 234 7342039

Invoice number: 205   Date (tax point): 29/7/2006

Invoice to:
Westland Finance PLC

Purchase Order Number: WF/PO 21393

Trafalgar House
Whitworth Street West
Manchester
M60 3BJ

Quantity Description		Net Total
Hire of restaurant premises for private function		230.00
To provide cold buffet style lunch for 25 at £8.50 per person on 14/7/2006		242.50
To provide tea/coffee refreshments for 25 at £1.40 per person		35.00
	Subtotal	507.50
Terms and Conditions: net 30 days	VAT @17.5%	138.00
E & O E		
	Total	645.50

Figure 15.53: Document flow chart

Source document	Book of original entry	Ledger accounts involved	Where account appears in final accounts
		Purchases	
Invoice received for purchase of stock on credit			
			Balance sheet Current liability
		Cash	
Purchase of stationery items for cash			
			Profit and loss account Expenses
			Balance sheet Current asset
Cheque sent to supplier for payment	Cashbook		
		Creditor account	
		Vehicle account	
Purchase of a new vehicle on credit			
			Balance sheet Current liabilities
Sale of goods on credit to a customer	Sales journal		
		Sales account	

1 Identify two of Praha 1's stakeholders. For each stakeholder, explain what interest they would have in Praha 1's financial information.

2 In July, Dobromir sent an invoice to Westland Finance plc (see Figure 15.52), one of Praha 1's best corporate clients. Westland subsequently complained about the amount it had been charged. Using Figure 15.52, calculate the correct value of the invoice Dobromir should have sent.

3 Explain which document Dobromir would send on behalf of Praha 1 to Westland to correct an error in an invoice such as in Figure 15.52. Explain the importance of invoices to the managers of Praha 1.

4 Copy and then complete the document flow chart in Figure 15.53 by filling in the shaded squares. Remember that each source document gets recorded in a book of original entry, and this transaction is recorded in two ledger accounts. These accounts are then used to compile the profit and loss account and the balance sheet (the final accounts).

5 After completing the flow chart in Figure 15.53, Dobromir is still uncertain about the exact purpose of a sales journal (sales day book). State what information is used to prepare the sales journal. Explain one reason why a business should have a sales journal.

Kingsways

Emily Hewett owns and manages Kingsways, an up-to-the-minute music, DVD and magazine retail outlet. Aimed at attracting 18–25 year olds, the store has a relaxed atmosphere, modern appearance and up-to-date merchandise.

As Emily has a knack for spotting and sourcing innovative and fashionable products, she also acts as a supplier to several smaller independent traders that do not directly compete with Kingsways as they are spread across the country.

Emily has recently being thinking about totally refurbishing her premises and introducing a cafeteria, coffee and social area. As part of her plans, the bank has asked for her final accounts for the year before granting approval on any loans.

James (the financial manager) has extracted the trial balance (see Figure 15.54) from the books of account.

He has done this to check the accuracy of their accounting records and make the preparation of the final accounts easier. He has also provided these notes:

■ closing stock at 31/12/2006 was valued at £56,494

■ depreciation policy is:

– motor vehicles 20% straight line method

– plant and machinery 10% straight line method

– premises are not depreciated

■ insurances prepaid at 31/12/2006 totalled £120

■ general expenses owing at the end of year were £220

■ the provision for doubtful debts is to be increased to £1,500.

Figure 15.54: Kingsways trial balance as at 31/12/2006

Kingsways trial balance as at 31/12/2006		
	Debit £	**Credit £**
Capital		114,120
Drawings	15,920	
Plant and Machinery at cost	70,000	
Motor vehicles at cost	30,000	
Debtors	28,000	
Premises at cost	40,000	
Creditors		42,000
Bank	28,000	
Cash	1,010	
Loan (5 years)		18,000
Stock as at 1/1/2006	50,400	
General Expenses	22,040	
Purchases	329,528	
Sales		466,768
Loan Interest	1,800	
Fuel and power	650	
Wages and Salaries	40,000	
Maintenance	18,670	
Insurance	600	
Returns Inwards	420	
Returns Outwards		340
Provisions for Depreciation:		
Plant and Machinery		34,000
Motor Vehicles		20,480
Electricity	11,400	
Telephone	2,600	
Carriage Inwards	640	
Provision for doubtful debts		1,200
Advertising	1,960	
Rent	3,270	
	696,908	696,908

Figure 15.55: Draft Kingsways profit and loss account

Kingsways
Trading, profit and loss account for Year Ended 31/12/2006

	£	£
Sales	466,768	
Less Returns In	(420)	
Less Cost of Sales		
Opening Stock	50,400	
Add Purchases		
Less Returns Out	(340)	
Carriage In	640	
Less Closing Stock		
Gross Profit		
Less Expenses		
General Expenses		
Loan Interest	1,800	
Fuel and Power		
Wages and Salaries	40,000	
Maintenance	18,670	
Insurance		
Electricity	11,400	
Telephone	2,600	
Provision for doubtful debt	300	
Advertising	1,960	
Rent	3,270	
Provision for depreciation:		
Plant and Machinery	7,000	
Vehicles		
Net Profit/(Loss)		

Figure 15.56: Draft
Kingsways balance sheet

Kingsways balance sheet as at 31/12/2006

Fixed Assets	£ Cost	£ Acc Depn	£ NBV
Premises	40,000	Nil	40,000
Plant and Machinery	70,000		
Vehicles	30,000		
Current Assets			
Stock			
Debtors	28,000		
Less provision for doubtful debt	(1,500)		
Expenses Prepaid			
Bank	28,000		
Cash	1,010		
Less Current Liabilities:			
Creditors	42,000		
Accruals (expenses owing)	3,220		
Working Capital			
Capital employed			139,424
Financed by			
Long-term Liabilities:			
Loan (5 years)			18,000
Capital			
Capital as at 1/1/2006	114,120		
Add Net profit	23,224	137,244	
Less drawings		(15,920)	
Capital as at 31/12/2006			121,424
			139,424

activities

1 Identify and explain one error that Emily could have made in her financial records that would not have been identified by the preparation of a trial balance.

2 It was discovered that an amount for fuel and power of £3000 was outstanding at 31 December 2006. Using the trial balance in Figure 15.54, calculate the amount for fuel and power that should be included in the profit and loss account. State how the outstanding amount of £3000 for fuel and power would be treated on Kingsways' balance sheet.

3 Using the trial balance from Figure 15.54 and the notes James prepared, complete the trading, profit and loss account (see Figure 15.55). You should take into account the adjustment for fuel and power (question 2). The information should be entered in the shaded boxes.

4 Using the trial balance from Figure 15.54 and the notes James prepared, complete the balance sheet (Figure 15.56). You should take into account the adjustment for fuel and power (question 2). The information should be entered in the shaded boxes.

5 Explain two accounting concepts that would have been applied when accounting for the depreciation charged on the fixed assets owned by the company.

Figure 15.57: Financial information for Strikers at 31/12/2006

Indicator	Result
Gross profit margin	37%
Net profit margin	12%
Return on capital employed	6%
Rate of stock turnover	29 times
Current ratio	1.9:1
Acid test	0.85:1
Debtors collection period (see note 1)	56 days
Creditors payment period (see note 2)	85 days
Sales	£242,000
Purchases	£130,000
Gross profit	£89,540
Net profit	£29,040
Capital employed	£484,000
Debtors	£3,700
Creditors	£30,300

Note 1: Only 10 per cent of Strikers total sales are on credit terms, and debtors receive 30 days to pay.

Note 2: All Strikers purchases are on credit, and suppliers offer 60 days.

Strikers

Like many industries and markets, the retail sector has its own specialist magazines. Emily subscribes to *Retail Updates*, a monthly publication which investigates new products and reports on upcoming events and conferences. There are often adverts for job vacancies and business opportunities, as well as adverts from suppliers.

In this month's issue, Emily noticed that Strikers, one of her nearby competitors, is up for sale. Emily is seriously considering the option of putting in a bid to buy Strikers as this would mean that she would not need to refurbish and expand Kingsways. Strikers has all the facilities Emily wants already in place.

Kingsways is already profitable, and Emily has a large amount of capital invested in the business. Emily envisages that she can sell Kingsways to raise the majority of the money needed to purchase Strikers and borrow the rest from the bank. Alternatively, depending on the exact financial circumstances, she may be able to buy Strikers using mainly borrowed money, and then run both businesses.

Emily has asked James to investigate the financial position of Strikers in order to recommend whether he thinks Emily should buy the business.

activities

1. Using the information in Figure 15.57 assess:
   - the solvency (liquidity) position of Strikers
   - the profitability of Strikers
   - the efficiency of Strikers.

2. Using your answers to question 1, discuss whether Emily should consider buying Strikers.

THIS UNIT CENTRES ON THE DECISIONS THAT MANAGERS have to take before starting to produce a good or a service. It concerns the decisions a manager faces before allowing production to commence and how these considerations vary between different industries and different types of business. Factors include where the business is located and what methods of production the business intends to use.

Most businesses aim to produce goods and services as efficiently as possible using the least resources. This allows them to be competitive. You will examine the techniques that businesses can use to maintain and enhance their productive efficiency. You will study the issues that managers face regularly during the production process, such as ensuring that products meet consumers' quality expectations and that stocks of raw materials are available for use in production.

This unit is assessed through a portfolio of work investigating the way in which a business (of your choice) organises its resources to plan, manage and improve the efficiency of its production.

Managing resources

Introduction to managing resources

Setting the scene: business resources

The term "resources" has a wide meaning in business. The term covers financial resources as well as a wide range of physical, labour and intellectual resources.

Other units in the course look in detail at how businesses should manage their finances – see in particular Unit 3 in the AS course and Unit 15 in this textbook. This unit, therefore, focuses on how businesses manage the non-financial resources needed to produce goods and deliver services.

These resources, as the following list shows, range from physical assets through to the ideas that underpin products, from tangible property to intellectual property.

Property such as factories and offices
Many businesses own properties, others choose to lease or rent premises. It is important that a business has the right property in the right location.

Ideas for products
Pharmaceutical companies such as GlaxoSmithKline spend huge sums of money discovering new drugs, and then protect their ideas so that competitors cannot copy them.

Skilled labour
Businesses such as Microsoft and Google are competitive because they have highly skilled employees developing new products that will be attractive to consumers. Organisations like hospitals simply cannot function without appropriately trained medical staff – without them, they cannot provide health care to patients. That is why managers in many UK hospitals have responded to skill shortages by recruiting nurses and doctors from overseas.

Machinery and vehicles
Few modern manufacturers can operate without using technology on their production lines. Airlines, railways and bus companies all use vehicles as a central element of their mix of resources.

Raw materials
Raw materials are used in manufacturing and in a range of service industries. Nestlé uses cocoa beans to make chocolate, Norwich Union uses vast amounts of paper in providing a range of financial services to its customers. Businesses need to manage both their stock of raw materials to ensure continuity of production – though some only keep a very small quantity – and their stock of finished products to ensure continuity of supply to customers.

Being competitive

Using resources effectively assists a business to operate efficiently and to remain competitive. A competitive business produces products that consumers want, at prices that they consider good value for money. If a business can use the resources available to it more efficiently than its rivals, then it is likely to be highly competitive.

This unit will examine the ways in which businesses can use resources effectively to improve their competitiveness through:

- planning production

- managing production

- efficient production.

Planning production

Planning how resources are to be used is a vital part of being competitive. A well-managed business undertakes research to develop products that will be attractive to its customers. A competitive business finds ways to produce those products as efficiently as possible. This includes finding the right location – typically the cheapest location available that is fit for its purpose and function.

Adidas, the global sportswear manufacturer, has introduced a new running shoe which is made to order for customers. Shoppers in Europe and North America can order shoes by selecting from a range of designs and colours. Orders are submitted electronically to factories in Asia, and the finished shoes are airfreighted back to the customer.

Managing production

Production is an ongoing process, and businesses must attempt to maximise consumer satisfaction while keeping their costs under control. This is a balancing act. Businesses aim to supply high-quality products to their customers – products that meet (or exceed) customers' expectations. At the same time, businesses seek to use their resources as efficiently as possible.

Successful businesses find ways of managing production so that they achieve savings without sacrificing quality. For example, some businesses manage to reduce production costs by not holding stocks of raw materials or of finished goods. This approach to managing production can reduce costs by eliminating the need for buildings and staff to store and manage stocks.

Efficient production

Efficient production is the goal of many managers and businesses. If a business can manage its operations efficiently, this means that it uses a minimum of resources. This enables it to control costs tightly, offering the opportunity to be price-competitive. In many markets, this gives a business a crucial competitive advantage.

Some businesses encourage efficient production by training employees to high levels. Others attempt to use the resources available as intensively as possible. Ryanair's strategy of keeping its aircraft in use for the maximum amount of time possible is an example of intensive use of resources. This is one of the factors that allows the company to have an average fare below £50.

Some businesses aim to become efficient by producing on a large scale. The US company Wal-Mart is the largest retailer in the world. In 2004/05, its global sales exceeded £160,000 million – the company's tills take over £300,000 every minute of every day. Wal-Mart can sell cheaply because it has the power to buy cheaply. In the retail business, price is an important measure of efficiency.

How is this unit assessed

This unit is assessed through a portfolio. You need to produce a piece of work that investigates the way in which a specific business manages its resources. Your investigation should examine how this business uses its resources to plan, manage and improve the efficiency of its production.

Your piece of research should:

■ explain the importance of planning production to make a business competitive

■ include and explain a proposal by which the business could improve its competitiveness

■ analyse how this proposal might improve the business's competitiveness

■ evaluate whether your proposal is a viable way for the business to improve its competitiveness.

Methods of production

Setting the scene: made to measure

Savile Row in London is the home of English tailoring. It contains a number of well-known tailors with a reputation for providing high-quality suits specifically made for individual customers.

Steven Hitchcock has been working in Savile Row since he was 16, and he now runs his own business. Steven's suits are hand-made using a technique called "soft tailoring". The advantage of soft tailoring is that the cloth is draped over the shoulders, then tailored and manipulated to achieve a very comfortable, stylish and unique-looking coat.

All Steven's suits are hand-cut and hand-made by skilled individual tailors right down to the flower and button holes. Steven takes great professional pride in his business and personally oversees the whole suit-making process from concept to completion.

Steven's suits have a unique individuality. Steven cuts and fits all his own garments from the finest materials available. He also cuts a paper pattern for each customer; therefore ensuring further orders will fit in the same way. Suits will take between four and six weeks to make.

Steven's suits are priced competitively when compared to the charges made by other Savile Row tailors. As you might expect, however, you pay good money for this level of quality and attention to detail. In 2005, prices for Steven's two-piece suits start from £1,690, and suits in "luxurious super 100's cloth" start from £1,950.

Source: adapted from www.stevenhitchcock.co.uk

KEY TERMS

Job production is a method of production in which a product is supplied in response to a specific order from a customer. For example, in a high-quality restaurant a meal will only be cooked on receiving an order, and it will be prepared to meet the precise requirements of the customer.

Batch production is the manufacture of a limited number of identical products. Each stage of production is completed for the entire batch before moving onto the next stage of the production process. Bakeries often make bread in batches.

Flow production is the continuous production of a product in large quantities. Flow production usually involves a production line. This style of production is also termed mass production.

Cell production is a method of production in which the manufacturing process is organised into independent teams (or cells) that each produce a significant part of the finished item.

Productivity measures the efficiency with which a business converts inputs into outputs. The most commonly used productivity measure is labour productivity, which assesses the efficiency of labour in the production process.

What is production?

Production is the process of taking resources such as labour, fuel and raw materials and changing them into products. It is the process of using resources to meet the needs of customers. Production is not simply about manufacturing – businesses that supply services such as insurance and health care must produce those services, just as manufacturing firms produce goods.

In a factory, manufacturing starts with the purchase of raw materials from suppliers, and continues through the process of assembly to checks on quality and delivery to customers. In contrast, the process of production in supplying car insurance begins with the response to an enquiry from a potential customer, and includes collecting data on the customer and vehicle, providing a quotation and issuing documentation.

stopandthink

What effect has the internet had on the production process of car insurance companies?

Methods of production

There are a number of methods of production that are available to businesses. Each method of production has advantages and disadvantages, and there are circumstances in which each may be the best option for a business.

1 Job production

Job production is the creation of an item or items of output for a specific customer. The product made is likely to include specific features to meet the needs of the individual customer.

This is the method used by Steven Hitchcock (featured in the introduction to this topic). He designs and prepares suits for individual customers. A huge range of businesses produce for individual customers in this way. Small businesses such as hairdressers and solicitors provide services geared to the specific needs of individual customers.

At the other end of the scale, construction companies commonly build to the needs of individual customers. In December 2003, the M6 toll road opened. This is a 27-mile motorway around the north of Birmingham which was built at a cost of £900 million. Similarly, the Millennium Dome was designed for a specific purpose – to host an exhibition celebrating the millennium. This might explain partly why it proved so difficult to find a further use for the dome, although it is now been redeveloped by a new owner and will be a venue in the 2012 London Olympics.

Job production offers a number of benefits to businesses and their customers.

- Each job is a unique product which exactly matches the requirements of the customer, often from as early as the design stage. This means that the customer is more likely to be satisfied with the end product and may place repeat orders.

- Employees can derive considerable satisfaction from working on different projects to meet the needs of individual customers. An IT consultant may be more motivated by designing different IT systems tailor-made for individual businesses than producing standard off-the-shelf software. In this way, job production can be creative and challenging.

- Specifications for the job can change during the course of production to meet the customer's changing needs. For example, printers commonly supply initial drafts of publications – known as proofs – and customers can alter details and tweak the design up until the final print run.

The potential downside to job production is that it can be resource-intensive, and it is therefore normally an expensive method of production. Labour productivity can be low when using this method of production, because each job can require a considerable staff input in design and planning. This means that customers can usually expect to pay high prices, or businesses can find that their profit margins are squeezed.

Job production is an appropriate method of production when a business wants to distinguish itself from competitors, when customers' demands are highly individual, and when few benefits exist from producing a standard product in large quantities.

2 Batch production

Batch production involves the manufacture of a limited number of identical products at the same time. Each stage of production is completed for the entire batch before beginning the next stage. Typically, as one batch finishes, the next one starts. This method is sometimes known as intermittent production, as each partly-completed batch is often stored between the various stages of production. It is common for a business to switch from job production to batch production as it grows and its output increases.

Batch production offers businesses a number of benefits. Batch production allows employees to specialise in particular aspects of production, leaving other stages of production to be completed by other employees. It is also possible to utilise machinery effectively in the production process by organising production carefully. For example, in a kitchen a team of chefs can utilise all the catering equipment to prepare batches of vegetables, main courses and desserts for diners over the next few days. This method of production allows businesses to benefit from some economies of scale.

Batch production also has some drawbacks. It can take careful planning to ensure that the various batches move through the production process smoothly without delays. Unless employees operate at similar levels of productivity, delays are inevitable, and partly-completed work – known as work-in-progress – may build up. This can tie up the business's cash. Despite these problems, batch production is probably the most common method of production for small to medium-sized manufacturing businesses.

3 Flow production

Batch production, as we noted above, is also known as intermittent production and is characterised by irregularity. If the rest period between the different stages of production in batch production disappeared, it would then become flow production. This type of production is the continuous production of a product in large quantities, normally using a production line.

In flow production, as an individual product completes each stage of the production process it passes immediately to the next stage without waiting for the batch to be completed. Flow production is more effective when each stage of production takes a similar amount of time, so that delays do not occur. It is more likely to be successful if demand is stable.

Flow production is used in the manufacture of small, relatively cheap products such as chocolates, as well as more expensive items such as televisions and DVD players. Although flow production systems were designed to make standardised products, new technology has made it possible to produce more varied products using the same basic system. Computer-aided production allows production to cope with differences in, for example, colour and finishes within a flow system. Many car manufacturers now produce cars to meet individual customer's needs using a flow method of production. One of Hyundai's high-tech car production lines is shown below.

For flow production to be efficient, planning is essential to make sure that raw materials are purchased and delivered on time, that sufficient labour is employed and that there is continuous attention to maintaining and improving quality throughout the production process.

Flow production is attractive to some producers as it offers the opportunity to produce items at very low cost. Producing similar items through flow production allows a business to produce large quantities each day. A business is therefore able to record high levels of productivity – achieving high levels of outputs from its inputs of labour, machinery and raw materials. Managers aim for a high level of productivity because it keeps costs of production low and enhances price competitiveness.

The Nissan factory in Sunderland has the highest level of productivity amongst car manufacturers in Europe. It achieves labour productivity levels in excess of 100 cars per employee per year by using flow production techniques on a high-technology production line. This helps Nissan to be extremely price-competitive in European markets.

Flow production is appropriate when a business faces a steady and high level of demand for its products. The most obvious application of flow production is for a manufacturing business producing large quantities of a standard product. However, modern production line technology has allowed businesses to use this method of production to produce a range of products designed to meet the individual needs of customers.

stop and think

Do you think it is possible for an insurance and financial services company such as Norwich Union to make use of flow production? Give reasons for your answer.

4 Cell production

Cell production is a refinement of flow production. It splits flow production into a series of self-contained units. Each part or "cell" in the production process produces a substantial element of the final product. It is important under cell production that each cell produces a "complete item" with which the workers can identify. This can assist in improving the motivation of employees on the production line.

Cell production uses teams in each of the cells to share the production of their element of the production process. It is common for the teams to be empowered to decide on their own targets and to choose the best ways to achieve these targets.

Cell production was designed to overcome some of the problems associated with flow production. It aims to give employees the opportunity to carry out jobs that are less monotonous and contain a greater variety of more demanding duties.

For example, Volvo implemented cell production in its factory in Uddevalla in Sweden, organising its workers into teams with responsibility for completing specific elements of the assembly of the company's cars. This was intended to reduce boredom, to motivate the company's workforce and to reduce the previously high levels of absenteeism in the factory. Through the use of cell production Volvo hoped to improve the productivity of its workforce as well as the quality of cars manufactured.

Cell production is not appropriate for all businesses. For it to be successful, a business must be able to:

- produce a sufficient level of output to make cell production feasible – it is unlikely to be appropriate for small-scale production

- plan the work of the cells so that each one takes a similar time in the production process – businesses must avoid a situation in which one cell builds up a big stock of partly-finished products

- arrange the design of the factory or office (assuming there is sufficient space) so that cells are able to operate independently.

business practice
Cell production in Sunderland

In 2005 Nissan, the Japanese-owned car manufacturer, announced that it was creating "a factory within a factory" at its facility in Sunderland. The Sunderland plant builds the Nissan Micra C+C which features a folding glass roof. This roof is manufactured by a German supplier, Karmann GmbH.

The two companies have agreed "for reasons of quality and speed of manufacture" to create a Karmann production cell within the Nissan Micra production line to supply the glass roofs directly. The cell will run two shifts a day, and have the capacity to produce up to 20,000 glass roofs each year.

What benefits might Nissan receive from having the Karmann production cell within its factory? Why might Karmann expect its cell to achieve high levels of productivity and quality?

assessment practice
Maxwell's cakes

Richard Maxwell had turned a hobby into a small business. He had always loved cooking but had been employed as a painter and decorator. However, his love of cooking won out and he started a small cake business

Operating at first while continuing his full-time job, Robert started making wedding, birthday and other celebratory cakes for friends and family. As his talent became better known, orders started to flood in. Eventually he gave up his job as a painter and decorator to concentrate on the growing cake-making business.

For the first year, Richard made his cakes to order. He coped with variations in demand by working very long hours when necessary, and enjoying the occasional quiet periods. As the business continued to grow, he knew he would have to consider a different method of production.

He asked a small business adviser for help. She suggested making the cakes in batches and then icing them to order.

A Richard currently uses job production. How does this help to make his business competitive?

B He is thinking about moving to use batch production. Will this make his business more competitive? Explain your views.

Setting the scene: Dyson benefits from move east

In 2002 James Dyson took the decision to move the manufacturing of his company's distinctive vacuum cleaners to Malaysia. By 2005 this appeared to be a good decision for the company's shareholders, if not the 600 employees who lost their jobs as a result of the move from Wiltshire.

James Dyson, the company's sole shareholder, said that "it was the right decision". The results for Dyson tend to bear out his views. Profits more than doubled to £103 million in the 2004–5 financial year and revenues rose 54 per cent to £426 million.

The success of the move to Malaysia in reducing the company's costs is shown by the increase in the company's profit margin on each sale. This was achieved despite entering the highly competitive US market for vacuum cleaners. In the final quarter of 2004 Dyson achieved 21 per cent of sales in the US, overtaking Hoover in the process, only two years after entering the market.

Dyson confirmed that the company plans to

Figure 16.1: UK and Malaysia, key cost comparisons

	UK	Malaysia
Labour cost per hour	£9	£3
Office rents (per square metre per annum)	£114	£38

Source: Economist Intelligence Unit

boost spending in the UK on research and development by £10 million to £50 million in 2005 and to employ an additional 100 people in this role in Wiltshire.

Source: adapted from The Daily Telegraph, 23 February 2005

Resource factors

In this topic, we look at the various factors that influence where a business locates its operations. We start by considering resource factors.

1 Energy

Energy can be a significant cost for businesses, particularly for manufacturing concerns such as car manufacturers. Energy-intensive businesses therefore want secure and relatively low-cost energy supplies. In the twenty-first century, businesses can obtain electricity, gas and coal in most parts of the world. However, costs can vary and, in the long term, the energy supply in some regions may not be reliable.

In the UK, manufacturers often complain about the high costs of energy. They argue that UK firms even face higher energy bills than their competitors in neighbouring European countries such as Belgium. In 2005, a dramatic rise in the price of gas forced Ineos, a manufacturer of chemicals based in Cheshire, to reduce production to cut back on consumption of gas. If high differentials in energy prices continue in the long term, businesses will consider relocating to countries where energy is cheaper.

2 Skilled and unskilled labour

Most businesses need some employees with specialist skills, and the workforce in many firms is vital to their competitiveness. Some manufacturers may use a large number of relatively unskilled workers, but these will be supplemented by a number of employees with specialised skills to support the work on the production line. Manufacturers are likely to require employees with skills in engineering, electronics, information technology, marketing and languages. In some service industries – banking, insurance and health are good examples – a high proportion of staff may require specialist skills which need updating through regular training.

For many businesses, then, an effective workforce is an essential competitive weapon, and any shortage of labour with the necessary skills poses a real problem. The UK has suffered at times from shortages of certain types of skilled labour. One response by business is to recruit employees from overseas. For example, the National Health Service has appointed doctors, nurses and dentists from many other countries. Another possible reaction to labour shortages is to move operations to another location in the UK or overseas.

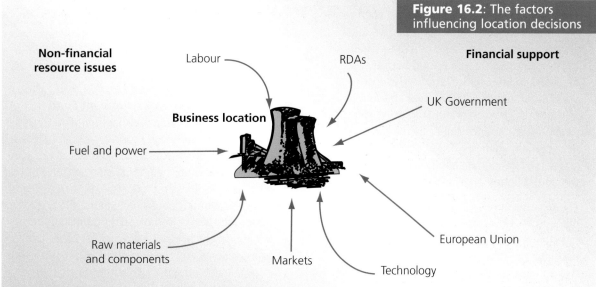

Figure 16.2: The factors influencing location decisions

Non-financial resource issues

Labour

RDAs

Financial support

UK Government

Business location

Fuel and power

European Union

Raw materials and components

Markets

Technology

Other factors

Factors influencing location

Few economies suffer from a shortage of unskilled labour, but its cost can have a major impact on the competitiveness of a business. In recent years many businesses have opted to move at least part of their operations from the UK because wage costs are lower overseas. A range of companies including Norwich Union, Mars, HSBC and BT have opted to relocate parts of their businesses overseas, principally because of lower wage costs (see Figure 16.1, for example). The financial services industry (insurance, pensions and banking) is forecast to move 155,000 jobs overseas between 2006 and 2010. This trend highlights the importance of minimising costs to remain competitive.

3 Raw materials and components

The availability of raw materials is a major determinant of the location of primary industries – businesses involved in mining and quarrying, for example – and it also influences the location of manufacturing industry.

A primary industry such as the oil industry operates wherever it can find viable deposits, and will often locate processing plants nearby to turn the crude oil into saleable products.

There is less need for a manufacturing company to locate near to the source of its raw materials, but manufacturers commonly opt to operate near to businesses that supply their components. In this way, they minimise transport costs and reduce the need to hold stocks of components on their premises – both these factors can help to enhance price competitiveness.

Financial factors

All governments are keen to encourage businesses to locate in their countries. They bring jobs and help to create wealth. Government agencies at all levels – local, national and international – therefore provide incentives to encourage business development. There are limits on the amount and types of state assistance that can be offered, however. Countries within the European Union are constrained by the rules established in EU treaties that are designed to ensure fair competition between all businesses.

1 The UK government

The government's regional policy aims to influence the location of business within the UK. The intention is to assist poorer areas of the UK to attract new businesses, and hence to increase prosperity. Although this is a less important aspect of government policy than in the past, the government retains considerable power to influence where businesses locate themselves. Two key elements of the UK's government regional policy are enterprise zones and regional development agencies.

■ **Enterprise zones**
  Most enterprise zones are located in depressed inner-city areas. Businesses locating in enterprise zones can receive grants, subsidised premises, and they face fewer restrictions on development. By promoting vigorous activity by the private sector in this way, the idea is that enterprise zones will help revitalise the local area. An enterprise zone is designated for a period of ten years.

- ### Regional development agencies

  There are nine regional development agencies within England, and similar bodies covering Northern Ireland, Scotland and Wales. These are the key agencies for influencing business location decisions. In the Chancellor of the Exchequer's pre-Budget report in 2005 it was announced that Manchester, Newcastle and York were to be promoted as "science cities" by the regional development agencies. These cities were joined by Bristol, Nottingham and Birmingham following the 2005 Budget.

  The regional development agencies in England also manage the government's Selective Finance for Investment scheme. The scheme is restricted to businesses that are in assisted areas. The UK has two categories of assisted area, as agreed with the European Union.
  - **Article 87 (3)(a)** areas have households with incomes of less than 75 per cent of the EU average. Businesses setting up in these areas are entitled to a maximum grant of 35 per cent of the cost of capital investment.
  - **Article 87 (3)(c)** areas have other social or economic problems, and businesses establishing in these areas may receive a maximum grant of between 10 and 20 per cent of the cost of capital investment.

The Selective Finance for Investment scheme is designed for businesses that are thinking of investing in an assisted area but need financial help to go ahead. The scheme offers financial assistance to small and medium-sized businesses to:

- establish a new business

- expand or modernise an existing business

- set up research and development facilities

- take the step from development to production.

2 The European Union

The European Union (EU) has a considerable impact on location decisions by UK and foreign businesses. As we noted, EU rules limit the amount of regional aid that the UK – and other member states – can give to businesses locating within assisted areas in any member state. The EU also places further restrictions on regional aid – for example, it must be used to create new jobs (not simply relocate existing ones), and must not lead to overcapacity in the industry.

The EU also operates its own funding schemes to promote regional economic development in the poorer areas of Europe. Increasingly, these schemes will be used to assist economic reconstruction in the former Eastern bloc countries that joined the EU in 2004, such as Poland and the Czech Republic. However, in the past, the poorer regions of the UK have been major beneficiaries of the schemes. There are two principal funds.

- ### European Regional Development Fund

  The European Regional Development Fund was set up in 1975 to stimulate economic development in the least prosperous regions of the EU. It provides financial and other help for businesses, and as well part-finances infrastructure projects such as roads and telecommunications. Between 2000 and 2006, the UK received over £3,000 million from this fund, which was used, amongst other things, to assist small and medium-sized businesses invest in capital equipment, carry out research and development, and provide job-related training.

- ### European Social Fund

  This provides money for training and other schemes designed to solve labour market problems and to help businesses to flourish. It can help to attract businesses to less prosperous regions.

3 Local authorities

Assistance from the local level of government varies from authority to authority. It can include grants, loans or guarantees for borrowing. Local authorities might also advance loans or invest directly in a business to enable it to be established or to grow. Much support offered by local authorities is given to small businesses. In practice, however, support from local authorities is limited. This is for two reasons. First, local government has many competing demands for its resources, and authorities have fewer tax-raising powers than central government. Second, all support offered by local authorities must still conform to EU rules on business assistance.

Other factors

There are a range of other factors that businesses consider when taking decisions on location. They need to think about their customers and their distribution chain, and they also need sites and premises that suit their operational requirements.

Many firms need to be close to their markets. This can be an important influence in the location decision, particularly for those businesses that supply bulky goods. Similarly, firms supplying services or perishable goods need to locate close to their markets. Retail businesses clearly need many different locations if they want as many customers as possible to visit their stores. The US coffee shop chain, Starbucks, currently has over 6,000 locations worldwide. As UK firms expand and begin to supply international markets, their locations can develop globally to fit in with their new markets. In part, this explains the move of Dyson to Malaysia, as the company sought to sell its vacuum cleaners in markets around the world.

The characteristics of any particular site are important. There is a big difference between a newly completed factory unit on a modern industrial estate, an old factory in need of modernisation, and a renovated warehouse offering retail possibilities. Managers responsible for location decisions will consider the cost relative to other sites, the amount of space available for current needs, and the potential for expansion.

Another key issue is the availability of planning permission. This is important if a change of use of premises is required. Businesses will also seek good infrastructure, with efficient transport and communication links. Many businesses will also want to consider the waste disposal facilities.

Recently many firms have moved to greenfield sites. These are locations usually found on the outskirts of towns and cities which have not been built on before – hence their name. Land here tends to be cheaper and easier to develop. However, the use of greenfield sites frequently attracts opposition from environmentalist pressure groups, and access can be a problem. The government is keen to encourage businesses to develop on brownfield sites, areas of land that have been developed before.

International location

Throughout the developed world the size of firms is growing, principally through mergers. This means that an increasing number of firms have locations in more than one country. Businesses which operate (as opposed to just selling) in more than one country are known as multinationals.

International location operates on exactly the same principles as domestic location theory. Multinationals seek the lowest cost location to maximise profits. They often use their power and influence to persuade host governments to offer grants and benefits as a condition of locating in the country.

The UK spends considerable sums to attract inward investment. In 2004, over 40 per cent of the financial support offered by the UK government was given to foreign firms. This has been successful in attracting many foreign businesses. The United Kingdom is the most popular country for foreign investment in Europe. It receives around 40 per cent of Japanese, US and Asian investment into the EU. The reasons for its popularity include:

■ easy access to the EU single market (the world's largest market, with 450 million consumers)

■ a highly skilled English-speaking workforce

■ a low-cost environment that allows business to prosper (see Figure 16.3).

The Economist Intelligence Unit measures the attractiveness of the business environment in the major industrial countries. It produces a regular set of global business rankings, using a model that considers 70 factors across seven categories which affect

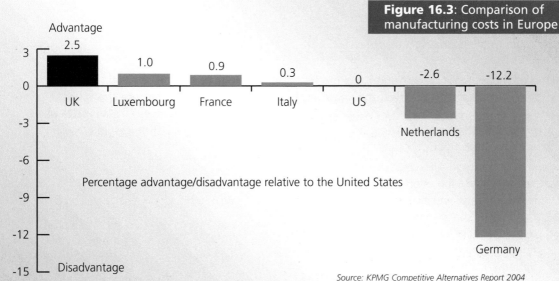

Figure 16.3: Comparison of manufacturing costs in Europe

Advantage

Percentage advantage/disadvantage relative to the United States

Disadvantage

| UK | Luxembourg | France | Italy | US | Netherlands | Germany |
| 2.5 | 1.0 | 0.9 | 0.3 | 0 | -2.6 | -12.2 |

Source: KPMG Competitive Alternatives Report 2004

opportunities for the conduct of business. They include policies on enterprise, investment, tax, exchange controls, labour, infrastructure and finance. In 2005, the UK held fifth position in the rankings, scoring well across a range of business categories – top position was held by Denmark, followed by Canada, the United States and the Netherlands.

In general, multinationals taking location decisions place importance on:

- effective communication and transport networks
- trained labour available at competitive rates of pay
- low rates of taxation levied on business profits
- grants and support available from local and national governments to support heavy investment
- support services (such as R&D) readily available.

Technology and location

In many respects technology, and in particular IT, has made it easier to locate a business. The most important technological influence on business location has been the internet. This has freed businesses from seeking particular locations and has allowed a more flexible approach. Possibly the biggest beneficiary of this development is the retailing sector. Online sales in the UK are currently rising by 40 per cent per annum and were estimated to be £14,500 million in 2005.

The rapid growth of Amazon, the US-owned online store, shows how the internet has affected the location decisions of retailers. In the UK, Amazon dispatches books and other products to customers from three huge warehouses. Amazon utilises its website to communicate with its customers rather as a traditional book retailer uses its network of stores. Its technology permits online customers to browse selected pages of books in which they are interested.

Technological developments have had a considerable impact on the locations of other businesses too. We saw earlier that many businesses in the financial services sector have moved part of their operations overseas to benefit from lower wage costs. HSBC is one business that has adopted this approach.

business practice
HSBC

HSBC is one of the UK's most profitable businesses. In 2004, the bank announced record profits of close to £10,000 million. Despite this massive profit, HSBC is planning to move another 12,000 administrative jobs from the UK to India and the Philippines.

HSBC has four global service centres in India, three in China and one each in Malaysia, the Philippines and Sri Lanka. These centres carry out a range of administrative tasks for the bank. HSBC is estimated to save £10,400 per annum for each job it moves from the UK to Asia.

However, the move of these jobs to locations thousands of miles away has only been possible because of modern communications technology. Large amounts of data can be transferred instantaneously and securely via the internet, and satellite communications have reduced the cost of international telephone calls to the point where businesses can use them routinely.

assessment practice
Investigating support for business

One of the major factors influencing the location decisions of businesses is financial support from local authorities, the UK government and the EU. Investigate the types and levels of support that are available to the UK by using the Business Link website at www.businesslink.gov.uk. There are a number of pages on this site that you may wish to explore during your research.

   A **You should use this information to prepare a leaflet for small and medium-sized businesses that may be considering expansion or relocation. Your leaflet should emphasise how financial support from governments can assist a business in improving its competitiveness.**

Research and development

Setting the scene: the UK National Sizing Survey

Nearly 11,000 people took part in the UK National Sizing Survey in 2001 and 2002. The results were announced in 2004, providing a comprehensive profile of the typical shapes and sizes of British residents of all ages.

The survey was organised by SizeUK, a collaboration between the UK government, 17 major UK retailers, leading academics and technology companies. It used the latest body scanners to take 130 separate measurements to profile the size of the volunteers. Data was collected at a range of centres across the UK, including colleges of further education as well as at some high street shops.

This was the first body-scanning survey carried out since the 1950s, and that only measured women using a tape measure! As a result of this work, the UK has gained a world lead in the use of body scanning in the clothing industry. For clothing companies, the data can be used to:

- improve the fit and specification of garments for customers

- maximise the percentage of the target customer profile that can fit retailers' clothes

- increase sales by understanding the demand for untypical size categories, such as outsize and petites

- reduce the number of clothes returned because they do not fit

- ensure that branches have the right size clothes for their particular customers.

This survey has important implications for other industries. For example, it will help the National Health Service to understand the impact of modern lifestyles on body shape, and to assess the potential health problems that might be generated as a consequence. The transport industry will also benefit from a greater understanding of the shape and size of consumers when designing seats for cars and aircraft.

R&D in business

Research and development has two distinct and separate components. Research is the scientific investigation that is necessary to discover new products and to find new ways of making products. It includes diverse techniques such as laboratory research and brainstorming. Development is the technical work necessary to ensure that the new products or processes are suited to consumers' needs.

Innovation is essential if a business is to benefit from its research and development. One aspect of innovation is finding new methods of production that can result in efficiencies, allowing a business to reduce its costs or lower prices, or improvements, allowing a business to increase the quality and/or range of products available to consumers. The use of robotic technology on production lines is an example of this type of process innovation: robots can be more accurate, producing better-quality products, and they can be cheaper, once a business has paid the installation costs.

KEY TERMS

Research and development is the systematic approach to product development, and the process of bringing new products to the market.

Innovation is the process of using novel ideas to develop new products or new methods of production.

Patents grant individuals or businesses the sole right to gain benefit from an invention for a specified period.

Copyright is the legal protection of the work of authors, composers and artists.

The better-known aspect of innovation is turning new ideas into saleable products. For example, new satellite systems can be used to identify someone's precise location. This technology has been used by enterprising businesses to design global positioning systems (GPS) that aid car drivers to find their way to unfamiliar destinations. Many new cars are now fitted with satellite navigation systems (so-called "sat-nav") which offer spoken directions to drivers.

The process of research and development

Research and development (R&D) can be a very time-consuming process. For example, the development of Lusec, a drug that treats stomach ulcers, took over twenty years. However, R&D normally involves a number of identifiable stages.

- **The generation of ideas**

  Firms may generate the ideas for research and development internally or externally, informally or formally. Ideas may simply come through discussion, say by getting employees together to come up with ideas. Managers in some industries believe that generating new ideas is the responsibility of everyone within the organisation. Alternatively, suggestion schemes – from employees or from customers – might be the source of ideas for new products. At a more formal level, ideas for new computer software or for new pharmaceuticals to use in medical treatment are likely to follow prolonged laboratory research.

- **The screening of ideas**

  Few ideas generated through the various forms of scientific, technological and market research have the potential to become a saleable product or an efficient process of producing a product. The ability to identify the potentially viable ideas from the totality of ideas thrown up at the generation stage is a key part of the R&D process, and is an important stage in the development of desirable new products. Ideas for new products and processes that are simply unworkable or too expensive or costly to produce must be eliminated to avoid unnecessary expenditure. The screening process might involve discussions with consumers or people with expertise in the area.

- **Developing prototypes**

  Once the worthwhile ideas have been identified, the next stage is to develop them further into prototypes that can actually be tested. This can be a costly and prolonged stage in the development of new products and processes. James Dyson famously spent many years developing his now world-beating vacuum cleaners. Before he produced a marketable product, Dyson made 5,127 prototypes. This enabled him to find and eliminate faults, so that when the product was finally launched it was suitable for consumers to use.

- **Launch**

  This is the final stage of the research and development process. The new product is made available to consumers, or a new process is introduced into the production of an existing good or service. Obviously a business wants the product just right at launch, but some products then undergo a serious of additional modifications after launch to improve them further – this, typically, is what happens with computer software.

The importance of research and development

As Figures 16.4 and 16.5 suggest, investment in research and development is particularly important in some industrial sectors. In the UK, the pharmaceutical, biotechnology and computer software industries are the major spenders on research and development. These industries spend heavily on R&D because scientific advances offer the opportunity for new products.

The pharmaceutical industry accounts for nearly 30 per cent of spending on research and development in the UK. The development of new drugs on a continuous basis – GlaxoSmithKline was running about 150 separate research projects in 2005 – is an essential element of maintaining competitiveness and market share in the pharmaceutical industry. A successful new drug can generate high levels of sales and income for many years ahead. A notable example

Figure 16.4: Top five UK firms spending on research and development, 2004

Company	Industry	R&D spending	As a percentage of sales
GlaxoSmithKline	Pharmaceuticals	£2,800 million	13.0
AstraZeneca	Pharmaceuticals	£1,900 million	18.3
BAE Systems	Defence technology	£1,100 million	13.1
Unilever	Consumer goods	£800 million	17.7
BT	Telecommunications	£300 million	2.3

Source: The Times, 25 October 2004

here is Viagra, the anti-impotence drug produced by the US pharmaceutical company, Pfizer. When Viagra was launched in 1998, Pfizer's share price doubled and the market for the drug is now estimated to be worth £2,000 million each year. Importantly for Pfizer, this revenue generated by Viagra provides a constant flow of cash to fund further research into new products and to maintain its competitive advantage over rivals.

The importance of R&D to the pharmaceutical industry is suggested by the series of mergers that have taken place in recent years. Larger companies have more resources to devote to R&D, so there is a competitive advantage for drugs companies to merge. In 2000, Glaxo Wellcome and SmithKline Beecham merged to form GlaxoSmithKline, the UK's largest pharmaceutical company. Previously, Smith Kline had merged with Beecham in 1989, and Glaxo with Wellcome in 1995, as the benefits – and costs – of investing in drug R&D became increasingly apparent to pharmaceutical companies.

The case for investment in R&D is equally strong in some other industries. Computer software is a growing market, especially the computer gaming segment. Computer software companies currently spend about 7 per cent of their sales revenue on R&D, and this figure is rising. Many smaller businesses have been unable to keep pace with the R&D spend of the larger software houses, and they have found it difficult to compete successfully as a consequence.

Some very successful computer games were produced by relatively small companies in the past. But as the computer games industry has matured, and the games have become ever more complex and involved, the budget required to produce a high-quality product has grown considerably. In 2005, Eidos, the company that developed the Lara Croft computer games, was taken over by SCI Entertainment. In turn, SCI Entertainment is considering mergers with other games companies. Tomorrow's games will be produced by companies with the financial resources to afford the significant R&D spend necessary to develop the products that gamers want.

s t o p a n d t h i n k

Why is spending on R&D a long-term strategy for any business?

Protecting R&D results

Investing in R&D is a risky business. Businesses can spend enormous sums of money on projects that fail to create marketable new products. In 2005, Pfizer received considerable criticism for its failure to come up with a new best-selling drug despite spending

Figure 16.5: Top five world firms spending on research and development, 2004

Company	Industry	R&D spending	As a percentage of sales
Ford	Car manufacturer	£4,200 million	3.8
Pfizer	Pharmaceuticals	£4,000 million	18.1
DaimlerChrysler	Car manufacturer	£3,900 million	5.1
Siemens	Electronics	£3,900 million	17.7
Toyota	Car manufacturer	£3,500 million	4.0

Source: The Times, 25 October 2004

nearly £12,000 million on R&D in the previous three years. The problem was compounded by the fact that Pfizer profits also fell when sales from its arthritis drug Celebrex slumped following a health scare associated with the use of the product.

Even when R&D results in a successful product, things can go wrong. Competitors may bring out a rival product, and they may even be able to develop a better and cheaper product if they can build on the innovation without incurring the costs involved in the initial research. Until 2005 pharmaceutical companies in India had freedom to copy drugs produced by companies elsewhere provided they used a different method of production. The companies that had originally researched the products faced a substantial loss of sales because they could not match the prices charged by the manufacturers of these "generic" drugs. Companies that invest heavily in R&D have to recoup that investment through the price they charge for their products; businesses that merely copy other people's inventions do not have to incur R&D costs.

Having spent enormous sums on innovating new products, businesses understandably therefore wish to protect their investment. They have some recourse to law, as many governments offer legal protection to encourage research and development, but the same legal safeguards do not necessarily apply throughout the world. However, businesses in the UK can use a range of measures to protect the results of R&D.

■ **Patents**
Patents are documents granting individuals or business the sole right to gain benefit from an invention for a specified period. They provide protection for products and processes for a period of up to 20 years. Patents can be taken out on a wide range of products, ranging from computer processors and MP3 players to drugs and vacuum cleaners. Companies have the right to sue the businesses that infringe their patents.

■ **Copyright**
Copyright law offers protection for the creators and owners of material such as books, films, music and cartoons. Copyright can last for up to 70 years after the death of the author and is granted automatically.

■ **Trademarks**
Trademarks grant legal ownership of recognisable signs and symbols for an indefinite period. Firms such as Adidas use trademarks to protect their symbols, and Perrier prevents rivals copying the shape and colour of the bottles in which it sells its mineral water.

■ **Registered designs**
Registered designs are employed to confirm legal ownership of shapes and forms. Fashion clothing is protected from pirate copies through the application of registered design.

R&D and marketing

Firms that spend heavily on R&D to produce new goods, services and processes will seek to exploit their investment through marketing. R&D offers the promise of new products, different from those supplied by competitors – at least for a period of time. This differentiation allows businesses to promote a unique selling point (USP) in marketing campaigns, and to charge premium prices for their products.

The strategy employed by some innovative companies is to keep one step ahead of competitors. In 2005 the technology company Apple launched the latest version of its iPod player, introducing a model which could store and play televisions clips and films as well as music. Owners of the new iPods are able to download videos, including television shows such as *Desperate Housewives*, using the company's iTunes program.

Successful R&D has the potential to provide a range of benefits for consumers which can be emphasised in marketing campaigns. Effective R&D can improve the reliability and durability of products. It can also enhance a product's design and appearance, which can be particularly important in fashion industries such as clothing and music. R&D can also improve the process of producing products, reducing costs and allowing businesses to lower prices.

Market research can work alongside R&D. It is not unusual for market research to identify a need amongst a substantial number of consumers, which is subsequently met as a result of R&D. Market research played a part in revealing the potential for selling teeth-whitening kits to consumers. A number of companies developed teeth-whitening kits that could be used at home (rather than relying on the skill of a dentist), and a significant market has developed since the late 1990s.

stop and think

In what ways might Barclays Bank use R&D to make it more competitive against the other major banks in the UK?

assessment practice
Richer Sounds

Richer Sounds is a hi-fi retailer. It was set up by Julian Richer in 1978, and is now one of the most successful retailing operations in the UK. By 2005, the company had 45 stores across the UK that sold a range of video and hi-fi equipment.

Julian Richer, the founder and chairman, was 19 when he opened his first store in 1978. He now has a national retail chain, as well as a mail order and e-commerce business. Although the company has changed dramatically over the years, Richer still maintains a presence and ensures that his employees are kept motivated. Survey figures substantiate his effort: 91 per cent have faith in his leadership.

Richer strongly supports the company's suggestion scheme. All employees are given a book to record their ideas when starting employment with Richer Sounds, and are encouraged to attend regular after-work meetings to brainstorm new ideas. There is a cash bonus, of at least £5 for each idea and quirky incentives for the best, and the scheme has been remarkably successful, producing on average 20 suggestions a year from each employee. Richer ensures that his managers respond to all staff suggestions promptly, and praise those who offer good ideas as well as giving financial rewards.

Before attempting the tasks, find out more about Richer Sounds by visiting the company's website at www.richersounds.com.

A How might Richer Sounds use its employees' ideas as part of the company's marketing?

B In what ways can simple R&D, such as that used by Richer Sounds, help to make a retailer more competitive?

Topic 4 | Stock control

Setting the scene: Microsoft unable to meet Xbox demand

The Xbox 360 was launched by Microsoft in May 2005. When the console was unveiled on MTV by *Lord Of The Rings* star Elijah Wood, the company said the new Xbox would be in the shops for Christmas.

By November 2005, it was clear that there was a problem matching supply with demand. UK High street retailers reported that they were running out of supplies of Xbox 360s because the manufacturer has been unable to meet their demands. HMV said it had twice as many orders as it had stock; Dixons had been forced to stop taking orders for the Xbox 360.

The severe shortage meant that many consumers were unable to purchase the product until after Christmas. Microsoft lost out on sales at the most important time of the year, and potentially lost customers to competitors. UK retailers reported that rival products such as Sony's portable PlayStation (PSP) were selling well, with supplies sufficient to match demand.

Microsoft launched the new model of the Xbox simultaneously throughout the world in an attempt to compete with Sony's new PSP.

However, in the short term, the company did not build up sufficient stocks to meet demand. Neil Thompson, Microsoft's UK director responsible for the Xbox 360, acknowledged that it would be "hard to find" in the run-up to Christmas. Microsoft was trying to find "regular replenishment", but expected that it might take six months to match demand and supply.

Source: adapted from reports in The Times, 24 November 2005

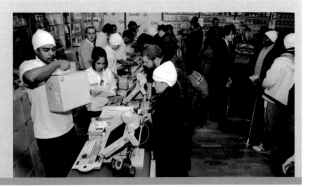

A model of stock control

A business's stocks can take several forms. A business needs the physical resources to make its goods or deliver its service – so a manufacturing concern will require stocks of raw materials, components and work-in-progress (half-finished products in the process of being manufactured). A business also requires a stock of finished goods to ensure that consumer demand can be satisfied. Some businesses will also require stocks of ancillary items, such as tools and spare parts for the maintenance of essential machinery and equipment.

Stock control is the process of managing and regulating the quantity of stock held by a business. The systems of stock control in use vary, but all seek to minimise the costs of holding stocks while ensuring that materials, components and finished goods are available when required. The modern practice in stock control is for firms to hold smaller quantities of stocks – or none at all, in some cases – to reduce production and operating costs. For this approach to work, firms must organise their supply chain to ensure that they

KEY TERMS

Stocks are the raw materials, components, part-completed products and finished goods held by a business at a given time.

Buffer stocks are raw materials or finished goods kept by businesses to guard against supply problems or unexpected increases in demand.

Lead time is the interval between the placing of an order by a customer and the delivery of the goods or service to the customer.

have ready access to raw materials, components and other inputs to avoid delays in production or in getting goods to the customer.

stop and think

The Malmaison chain operates eight luxury hotels in major UK cities. What stocks might this business hold?

Figure 16.6 illustrates one method by which a business might control its stocks. This model shows the key features of a stock control system.

■ The **buffer or minimum stock level** – this is a minimum stock level held by the firm, designed to protect against unexpected increases in demand or delays in supply.

■ The **reorder quantity** – this is the amount the business purchases from its suppliers each time it places an order.

■ The **maximum stock level** – this is the buffer stock level plus the reorder quantity. Firms will ensure that they have the storage capacity to house the maximum stock level, but exceeding this level may incur heavy additional costs.

■ The **reorder level** – this is an amount which acts as a trigger to place an order for further stock from suppliers. It usually takes some time for new stock to arrive, and the reorder level is set to ensure that the business does not run out of stock.

■ The **lead time** – the time that elapses between placing an order and the arrival of the stock.

Although it illustrates principles, this model of stock control is a simplification of the real world. First, it is unusual for businesses to use up stocks at a uniform rate, as shown by the steady reduction in stocks over time in Figure 16.6. In reality, stocks would be used at different rates. Second, supplies of new stocks do not always arrive at the precise time they are expected. Lead times can vary because suppliers face problems with production or with transportation.

stop and think

What would happen to the chart in Figure 16.6, if the business:

(a) used its stock twice as quickly following delivery of a stock order

(b) if delivery of stock took twice as long

(c) if the reorder quantity was halved due to supply problems?

Key decisions

There are several important questions that managers must consider in relation to holding stocks. These apply to many businesses, but are especially relevant for manufacturers.

1 How much stock to order?

Managers must take into account the costs of delivering stock as well as the cost of storing stock when deciding on the amount they will purchase on each occasion. (This is the reorder quantity shown in Figure 16.6.) These two costs can be used to calculate the economic order quantity (EOQ). It can be calculated by using this formula:

$$EOQ = \sqrt{\frac{2P \times D}{C}}$$

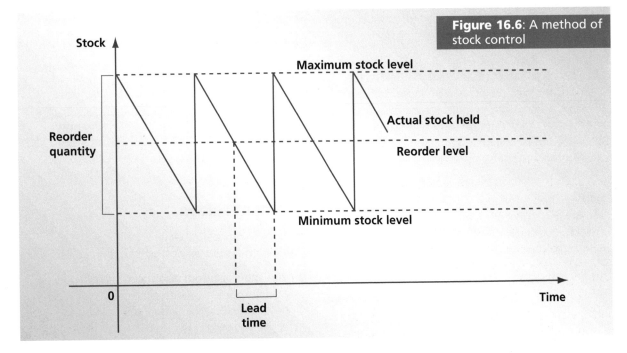

Figure 16.6: A method of stock control

Where:

P = the cost of a single delivery of stock

D = the business's annual demand for stock

C = the cost of storing a single unit of stock.

The economic order quantity is that quantity of stock at which the cost of holding stock equals the cost of raising and holding a delivery of stock. However, the EOQ model has a major flaw in that it ignores the potential costs incurred by a business that runs out of stock and is unable to meet customers' orders.

2 How much stock to hold?

Managers will take into account the costs and benefits of holding stocks when deciding on the optimal amount to hold. Some businesses incur considerable costs by holding stocks of raw materials, components or finished goods. There are a number of factors that can affect the cost of storage.

- **Security**
  Stocks need to be stored and insured. Some stocks are expensive to store. Jewellery needs high levels of security to avoid theft. Some foods need to be frozen to prevent them perishing.

- **Opportunity cost**
  If a business holds £500,000 worth of stock, then it will lose around £25,000 a year in interest it could have earned from keeping this money in a bank account with a 5 per cent interest rate.

- **Warehousing**
  Buildings are frequently needed to store stocks. These buildings are not only expensive to maintain, but could also be used for production if the business held lower quantities of stock.

- **Labour costs**
  There are labour costs associated with holding stocks. Businesses employ warehouse staff to manage stocks and to transport them as necessary. Administrative staff may also be required to place orders, arrange transport and monitor the stock to ensure that it is in good condition.

However, there a number of benefits to businesses from holding stocks of raw materials and finished products. Essentially these occur because there are costs involved in not having enough stock.

Holding sufficient stock of raw materials means that a business will be able to produce continuously, and it should not be forced to stop production, leaving expensive labour and machinery idle.

A business that holds buffer stock will be able to meet sudden and unexpected orders from customers without any delays, thereby achieving greater levels of customer satisfaction.

Businesses that hold buffer stocks can also benefit from lower purchase costs due to the discounts available when buying in bulk.

Possibly the greatest cost is the potential loss of sales if the business is unable to meet customers' orders. Microsoft's revenues would have benefited greatly if it had organised adequate supplies of the Xbox 360 for the 2005 Christmas rush.

Figure 16.7 shows the contrasting financial effects of the costs and benefits of holding stocks. It is clear that as the level of stock held by a firm rises, the costs associated with having inadequate levels of stocks decline, while the costs of holding stock increase. Together these two effects create a U-shaped cost curve for holding stocks. Profit-maximising businesses should plan to hold enough stocks to keep these costs to a minimum. By holding stocks equivalent to OX in the diagram, a business will minimise stockholding costs and enhance its competitiveness.

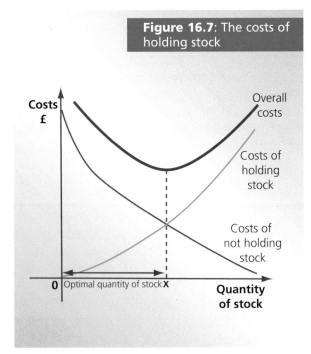

Figure 16.7: The costs of holding stock

3 Other factors

There are a number of factors that influence a business's decisions on holding stocks.

- **The type of goods produced or sold**
  Despite high costs of stockholding, jewellers tend to hold relatively large quantities of stock to give customers choice.

The type of business and its financial position

In August 2005, Tesco held stocks valued at £1,351 million. Tesco can afford to hold this level of stock as it is a highly profitable business, but it also makes commercial sense. A supermarket chain needs large quantities of stocks, both in its stores and in its warehouses, to meet customers' needs. Without sufficient stocks on a day-to-day basis, customers would go elsewhere. One of the problems faced by Sainsbury in the past was a shortage of some products: shelves were left empty and customers got dissatisfied. This, in part, explains Sainsbury's poor performance in recent years and loss of market share.

Stability in demand

If a business can be reasonably sure that it will face stable levels of demand over a period of time, it may feel more confident operating with lower stock levels. It will not need a buffer stock supply to cope with surges in demand.

Certainty of supply

If producers are reasonably confident that they will receive supplies regularly and promptly, they may be persuaded to hold relatively low levels of stocks. However, doubts over the reliability of supplies may have the opposite effect.

---

business practice
Computerised stock control

Businesses frequently hold details of their entire stock on a database. All additions to, and uses of, stock are immediately recorded. This allows up-to-date stock levels to be found instantly and detailed on a stock print-out.

Through use of the barcode system, supermarkets monitor sales of stock, and each sale is subtracted from the total stock level held. When the barcode is passed over a laser at the checkout, the sale is recorded on a database. This system makes it much easier to compute the day's takings as well as adjusting the stock level.

This type of stock control system can be linked to automatic ordering systems, which are triggered once stocks fall to the buffer stock level (the reorder level). However, technology does not always work. Sainsbury invested many millions of pounds in a computerised system in the years after 2000, but it failed to improve the company's ability to meet the needs of its customers.

---

stop and think

What are the major stock control issues facing (a) a greengrocer (selling fruit and vegetables) and (b) a manufacturer of fireworks?

Increasing stock control efficiency

The method of stock control illustrated in Figure 16.6 can be described as "just-in-case". Businesses hold stocks of materials, components, work-in-progress and finished goods just in case they are needed. This offers managers some security but involves additional storage costs. Businesses using the just-in-case approach are also regularly forced to lower prices to shift surplus stock. This approach to stock control does not assist a business in operating efficiently.

In the 1960s and 1970s, Japanese businesses began to challenge the just-in-case method of stock control. Japanese managers believed that this was not an efficient method as it required expenditure on storage, insurance and staffing. The Japanese approach was to reduce and, if possible, eliminate all stocks of raw materials, components and finished goods. They began to operate a system under which stocks arrived at the precise moment they were required. This method of stock control was termed "just-in-time" stock control.

Just-in-time stock control offers obvious advantages in terms of reducing costs, increasing financial efficiency and improving competitiveness. A just-in-time approach, in principle, allows a firm to produce the same level of output with fewer buildings, lower insurance costs and fewer employees. However, the just-in-time method has some potential drawbacks. The most worrying problem is that if supplies are delayed – for whatever reason – the firm is unable to continue production. Keeping resources of labour and capital idle, even for a short period of time, can be very costly. Manufacturers can reduce this risk by signing contracts with local suppliers. Honda, in Swindon, opted for this approach when it introduced a just-in-time method of stock control.

Another drawback is that purchasing stocks under a just-in-time approach means that businesses tend to buy small quantities of stock. As a result, they lose the benefits of bulk-buying and can pay a relatively high price per unit. This can offset some of the financial gains associated with the method of stock control.

Just-in-time stock control is an integral part of the just-in-time system of production. This is examined in detail in Topic 5.

assessment practice
Highways Agency builds up stocks of salt

The Highways Agency is part of the Department of Transport. It has responsibility for maintaining and operating the UK's major road network. One of its tasks is to respond to bad weather, to ensure that traffic can move as freely as possible in all conditions.

Over recent years the Highways Agency has been criticised for failing to react quickly enough to weather forecasts for snow – critics claim that gritters and snowploughs are not sent out in time. During 2005 the agency took steps to improve its efficiency in keeping the main roads open during the winter.

In autumn 2005, the Meteorological Office was predicting a very cold winter. The Highways Agency responded by building up stocks of salt ready to de-ice roads. By late November 2005, it held 500,000 tonnes of salt across the UK, with 5,000 tonnes available for use in Birmingham alone. The agency also kept gritters and snowploughs on round-the-clock standby when periods of bad weather were forecast.

A What are the drawbacks to the Highways Agency in using a "just-in-case" system of stock control?

B What factors might have persuaded the Highways Agency to increase the stocks of salt it holds?

C How might effective control of stocks help the Highways Agency to be more efficient?

assessment practice
Building your portfolio

By this stage of Unit 16 you are in a position to choose your business that will be the focus of the assessment for this unit. It is important that this choice is made in conjunction with your teacher. Indeed your teacher may suggest some suitable businesses for you to use.

The business that you choose should meet a number of requirements. It should allow you to be able to consider how planning production is important in determining the competitiveness of the business. It should permit you to analyse how the business might improve its competitiveness by planning and managing production, and by increasing the efficiency of production. You should be able to evaluate the extent to which your proposals might improve the business's competitiveness.

You do not have to choose a manufacturing business; service businesses can be used too. Ensure you select a business for which you can gain relevant information. This is more likely in the case of a local business where you may have personal contacts. National businesses are glamorous, but unlikely to divulge the sort of information you require.

Once the choice is made, you can complete the first requirement (set out below) of the portfolio.

A Explain the importance of planning production to the competitiveness of your chosen business. You answer should consider the business's location, research and development, and method of production.

Just-in-time production

Setting the scene: just-in-time gas?

As recently as 2004, the UK was self-sufficient in gas, exporting roughly the same amount of gas as it imported. But dwindling UK North Sea reserves and rising demand means that in the future the UK will be a net importer of gas.

To meet the anticipated demand, the world's longest underwater gas pipeline is being constructed to link the UK to the Ormen Lange gas field in the Norwegian sector of the North Sea. The 1,200 kilometre long Langeled pipeline will be used to pump 20–25 billion cubic metres of gas each year to the UK from a hi-tech underwater installation off the coast of Norway, via an onshore processing centre.

When it comes on-stream in 2007, it is estimated that the Langeled pipeline could supply 20–25 per cent of the UK's demand for gas, operating on a "just-in-time" basis. The facility should help to reduce concerns that Britain's gas supplies might fail to meet demand during extreme cold spells or in the event of other energy supplies being disrupted through, say, a terrorist attack.

And yet, even with the Ormen Lange connection, some analysts still think that the UK may be at risk of untimely power shortages. A parliamentary report into the UK's gas supplies questions the wisdom of using "just-in-time" production to deliver gas to the UK. The report doubts whether just-in-time production can be expected to cope with surges in demand or other unforeseen circumstances.

The JIT philosophy

Traditionally many businesses produced goods and then stored them in the hope that they would be sold at some point in the near future. This is a "push" system: first produce goods, then wait for (or encourage) orders which can be met from the stockpile of finished products. The philosophy of just-in-time (JIT) production has superseded this approach for many manufacturers.

JIT is a "pull" production system, in which an order from a customer instigates production. It is a production system in which raw materials, partly manufactured goods and finished products are delivered at the precise time they are required. Finished goods are produced just in time to be supplied to the consumer, and components and materials arrive just in time to be used in the production process.

Figure 16.8 highlights the essential features of just-in-time production. It entails co-ordinating exactly the supply of materials and components with production, eliminating the need to hold buffer stocks of components, raw materials or finished goods. New deliveries of raw materials and components are taken directly to the production line on arrival, so there is no need to use warehouses to store supplies. This can be highly cost-efficient, but requires reliable suppliers who will deliver materials and components on time.

JIT production is not only about the management of stocks. The philosophy behind JIT is one of reducing costs by eliminating waste. The principal aim of just-in-time is to reduce waste and inefficiencies in the production process by using the smallest possible amounts of materials, parts, factory and office space, and workers' time to produce high-quality products – every time.

JIT production systems focus on value-added activities within a business rather than non-value-added activities.

KEY TERMS

Just-in-time (JIT) production is a management philosophy that involves having the right items of the right quality in the right place at the right time. Raw materials, partly manufactured goods and finished products are delivered at the precise time they are required.

A pull system of production is one where a business only produces products once an order is received.

A push system of production operates by producing goods and stockpiling them to await customers' orders.

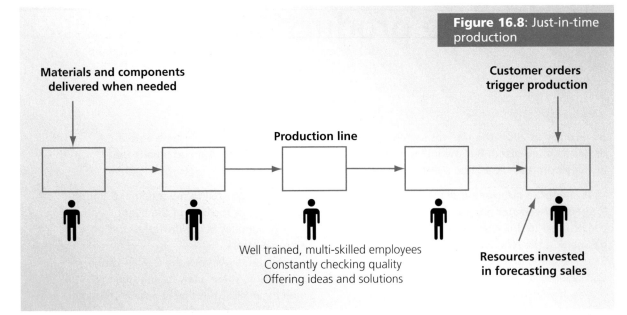

Figure 16.8: Just-in-time production

Materials and components delivered when needed

Customer orders trigger production

Production line

Well trained, multi-skilled employees
Constantly checking quality
Offering ideas and solutions

Resources invested in forecasting sales

- Value-added activities are those which actually involve working on raw materials and components as part of the manufacturing process. These activities occur on the production line.

- Non-value-added activities include storage, quality inspection and repairing faulty products. During these activities, raw materials, components or finished products are lying idle.

Many traditional factories spend up to 90 per cent of time on non-value-added activities. In contrast, JIT production aims to eliminate non-value-added activities from the manufacturing process. Firms employing JIT systems focus upon reducing the non-value-added time, thus helping to eliminate all forms of waste.

stopandthink

How might just-in-time production help a car manufacturer to reduce its costs of production?

JIT has the potential to offer many benefits to a business. The greatest benefit is arguably a significant reduction in operating costs, thereby enhancing a business's competitiveness. The system can also improve the quality of product as well as reducing manufacturing times and shortening delivery dates. Figure 16.9 summarises two benefits enjoyed by the computer manufacturer Hewlett Packard as a result of introducing JIT production methods in the assembly of PCB circuit boards – the company reported vastly reduced lead times and a significant reduction in the amount of capital tied up in stock.

Figure 16.9: Some benefits of JIT production at Hewlett Packard

	PCB assembly manufacturing time by company	Value of stock held
Before JIT implementation	15 days	$670,000
After JIT implementation	0.47 days	$20,000

The implications of JIT production

JIT production encourages businesses to concentrate on long-term strategies, even though it may result in increased expenditure in the short term. JIT is not a short-term strategy that businesses can adopt on a whim. It requires significant amounts of preparation and investment in a range of human and other resources. It requires businesses to change many aspects of the production process and, as we discuss in this section, its implementation can have considerable implications for managers.

The first consideration is space. As JIT production can eliminate many, if not all, stocks of raw materials, work-in-progress and finished goods, businesses can operate with smaller factories. Put simply, less space is needed for the storage of stocks. This means that a business may be able to expand production at a particular site – possibly allowing it to close other locations – or to put the surplus buildings to other productive uses.

The next consideration is technology. Flexible technology is needed on the production line, as production equipment must be able to be switched from one use to another at short notice. For example, car manufacturers using JIT production in a global market have to operate production lines which can cope with a range of styles and models, switching between different colour cars, or left-hand and right-hand vehicles, or even between different designs, such as estates and saloon models. Computer-aided manufacturing (CAM) techniques help businesses automate a production line and configure it to handle differentiated products.

Although JIT is fundamentally a pull system of production, businesses adopting a JIT approach can help production planning by improving the quality of their sales forecasts. This may require investment in training or hiring additional staff with expertise in this area. By improving this aspect of production planning, it is possible to keep suppliers better informed about requirements and to reduce uncertainty, which is an enemy of JIT production systems.

Businesses also need to consider employment issues. Under JIT production the layout of the factory is arranged for maximum flexibility. Businesses therefore want employees with a wide range of skills, who can readily switch from one job to another when necessary. Many businesses also want employees that can take some initiative in their work: managers delegate more authority to junior employees to deal with problems and hold-ups in production, and to spot and solve potential difficulties in advance. By empowering employees in this way, and by having a multiskilled workforce, a business is better able to operate with minimal planning and maximum responsiveness to customers' needs. This means that a business may need to invest heavily in training to ensure that employees have a sufficient range of skills. It may have to negotiate new contracts with employees to allow more flexible working practices. Some businesses adopting JIT production use more temporary and part-time employees to cope with short-term increases in workload – and that requires reaching agreements with the existing workforce if good labour relations are to be maintained.

Good relationships with suppliers are another essential ingredient of a successful JIT production system. Efficient communication systems must be established. Orders for supplies will be placed at short notice, and it is vital that suppliers receive these quickly to permit them to respond promptly. Often this is achieved by use of an intranet – an electronic communications system which can link several businesses. However, it is also important that suppliers are sufficiently flexible to deliver immediately an order is received. This may require the suppliers to hold stocks of materials.

Finally, any business introducing JIT production needs to consider quality issues. This is such an important concern – and covers such a wide area – that it is the subject of the next two topics in this unit. We consider two key aspects.

- **Continuous improvement**
  Continuous improvement – kaizen in Japanese – is an integral part of JIT. Employees at all levels in the organisation should be encouraged to offer ideas and solutions to problems. This process should be ongoing in an attempt to continually raise standards. The ideas behind kaizen are developed in Topic 6.

- **Meeting customer needs**
  Quality means meeting the needs of each and every customer every time. Under many JIT production systems, every employee engages in inspection to ensure that their work is of high quality and will satisfy the final customer. If this process is conducted at each stage of production, the final product should be of high quality. This aspect of quality is considered further in Topic 7.

Potential problems

JIT production offers businesses many benefits, particularly through the efficient use of resources. However, it requires careful management. Initially its implementation requires thorough planning, and the commitment of substantial sums of money to train employees and to purchase the necessary equipment and software to make the system a success. The training of employees, the reconfiguring of production and the testing of new equipment are all large projects, meaning that it can take a considerable time to plan and implement JIT production systems. It is essential to have the wholehearted support of the organisation's senior managers from the outset.

Once in operation the greatest potential threat comes from a break in the supply chain that halts production. This becomes a more likely scenario if the business using JIT production methods relies on a single supplier or uses suppliers at some distance from its factory. In 2003 Toyota and other Japanese car manufacturers experienced difficulties following a strike by dock workers in the United States. The companies, which all use JIT production systems, ship parts from Japan to their factories in the USA. The strike closed many US ports, interrupting the flow of supplies. In response, the car manufacturers were forced to use air transport to supply their US factories – production resumed and continued during the dock strike, but at great financial cost.

assessment practice
GKS Bicycles Ltd

GKS Bicycles is one of Britain's last bicycle manufacturers. The company employs 350 people at its factory in Hereford, and it has a reputation for high-quality production.

The system of production used by the company relies heavily on the use of supervisors. Employees receive little encouragement to take decisions on their own initiative. The company does use some robots on the production line, and has purchased some up-to-date software to operate this equipment, although it does not make full use of technology's capability.

GKS Bicycles makes the frames and wheels for the bicycles in-house, but the company buys in components such as tyres, gears, brakes and saddles from five different suppliers located in other regions of the UK. Demand for the company's products is rising slowly, but the level of orders is predictable, with seasonal increases in the spring and in the run-up to Christmas.

A new chief executive has just been appointed. He is considering a number of changes to the company, one of which is the introduction of a JIT production system.

A Make a list of the steps that GKS Bicycles will need to take prior to introducing JIT production.

B Explain how the use of JIT production might help GKS Bicycles to become more competitive in the long run.

assessment practice
Building your portfolio

At this stage, you can continue to build up evidence for your portfolio by starting to develop evidence for requirement C. This requires you to collect evidence on your chosen business, focusing in particular on how it plans, manages and attempts to improve the efficiency of production.

This analysis should consider the business's current methods and techniques, and provide the evidence for you to outline an improvement in one or more of these areas. For example, if your chosen business holds stocks, this might be an appropriate stage to consider whether improvements in stockholding methods could be implemented. You may want to consider the merits of the JIT system in reducing stock levels. Alternatively, you may want to consider the wider issue of JIT production in relation to your chosen business. Would the advantages from this approach merit the costs of implementing and operating the system?

Continuous improvement

Setting the scene: the Toyota Production System

The Toyota Production System (TPS) is a "pull" production system, which asks workers to use their heads. It was developed and continues to be used by Toyota, one of the world's largest car manufacturers.

For Teruyuki Minoura, a former director with Toyota, the way the company's system of production develops people is its greatest strength. "Under a 'push' system, there is little opportunity for workers to gain wisdom because they just produce according to the instructions they are given. In contrast, a 'pull' system asks the worker to use his or her head to come up with a manufacturing process where he or she alone must decide what needs to be made and how quickly it needs to be made."

"An environment where people have to think brings with it wisdom, and this wisdom brings with it kaizen (continuous improvement)," notes Minoura. "If asked to produce only one unit at a time, to produce according to the flow, a typical line worker is likely to be confused. It's a basic characteristic of humans that they develop wisdom from being put under pressure. Perhaps the greatest strength of the Toyota Production System is the way it develops people."

This is why, when Minoura explains TPS, he says that the T actually stands for "thinking" as well as for Toyota. Recalling being asked to solve problems by Taiichi Ohno, the creator of the Toyota Production System, Minoura says: "I don't think he was interested in my answer at all. I think he was just putting me through some kind of training to get me to learn how to think."

This approach mirrors the way that Harvard Business School uses the case study method to develop business thinkers. Harvard professors never tell students the answers, because the point of the exercise is to develop their capacity for independent thought. And, as Minoura says: "Developing people is the starting point for *monozukuri* (making things) at Toyota."

Source: adapted from www.toyotageorgetown.com

Kaizen in the context of lean production

Kaizen aims at continuous improvement throughout a business. Kaizen aims for a series of small improvements in methods of working, each one improving the efficiency of the business in some way.

Businesses that adopt a kaizen philosophy encourage their workers to suggest ideas for improving the way they operate. In this way, they hope to generate and implement suggestions that will lead to a series of improvements in efficiency, quality and competitiveness. Some businesses formalise the process by forming kaizen groups – drawn from all areas of the workforce – to encourage suggestions, ideas and solutions to problems. Others rely on a

KEY TERMS

Kaizen is a management philosophy that aims at continuous improvement in all aspects of the operation of a business.

Lean production is a term used to describe a series of management techniques intended to make the most efficient use of resources within an organisation, thereby minimising waste.

more informal culture of enterprise and initiative. The aim in both cases is identical: to achieve small but continuous change that has a positive impact on the competitiveness of the business, and that can be achieved without incurring large capital expenditure. Figure 16.10 summarises the intended benefits of the kaizen approach.

Kaizen is an important part of a wider approach to management known as lean production. This is a term used to describe a series of management techniques intended to make efficient use of resources within an organisation, thereby minimising waste. Lean production may include the use of kaizen and just-in-time production techniques, and it places great emphasis on producing high-quality products. Businesses using lean production techniques require multiskilled workers – employees who are able to carry out a variety of activities and who are highly responsive to consumers' needs. Lean production produces what the consumer wants when it is wanted, using as few resources as possible.

Lean production contrasts with the more traditional resource-intensive approach of mass production. Companies that engage in mass production produce large quantities of standard products, which may not meet the precise needs of individual consumers. Typically mass producers engage in occasional major improvements in production, often involving heavy investment by the businesses. This approach frequently involves acquiring new technology for use on the production line or in providing services. As an example, many of the UK's most popular banks have invested in providing internet banking services, sometimes accompanied by a branch closure scheme.

Figure 16.11 outlines the main differences between lean production and mass production, and suggests the possible effects the different approaches have on the levels of efficiency of the businesses.

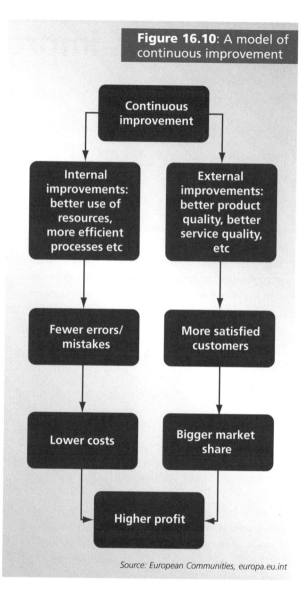

Figure 16.10: A model of continuous improvement

Source: European Communities, europa.eu.int

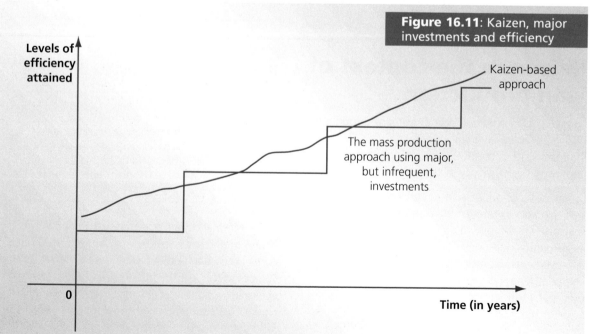

Figure 16.11: Kaizen, major investments and efficiency

The operation of kaizen

Kaizen relates to an enormous range of business activities, not just production. Improvements can be achieved through kaizen in customer service, training methods and internal communication as well as activities on the production line. Many service businesses have implemented kaizen schemes with the aim of improving their performance.

stop and think

Can you think of any (relatively minor) steps that your local branch of Tesco might take to improve the performance of the store?

Businesses using kaizen need to gain the support of their entire workforces if the approach is to be effective. Employees will be required to contribute to the operation of kaizen in a variety of ways. All employees are encouraged to seek ways to improve their performance. This is not a one-off initiative, but should be seen as a continuous process. It may involve adopting new approaches and techniques, or it may involve relatively minor changes in the workplace.

The kaizen approach is based on the idea that employees are in the best position to assess how to improve their work. Most employees are "experts" at their particular jobs, and this gives them a perspective on the work which may not be shared by their managers. This means that they are able to generate excellent ideas for improvements as well as specific solutions to problems; both can be invaluable in helping a business improve its performance.

For many businesses, the major challenge of kaizen is to decide how to fit in the problem-solving and idea-generating sessions alongside the ongoing demands of production. Most experts suggest that kaizen is unlikely to work unless given sufficient time and status by managers. Most businesses opt for one of these two approaches.

Some businesses opt to remove employees from the workplace for a few days (a week at a maximum). The intention is to generate a range of ideas and solutions to problems which can be considered at leisure later. This approach is normally repeated every year or two. Businesses using this approach normally set targets and challenges at the outset – such as how can we reduce the amount of stock we hold by 50 per cent – in order to focus the minds of those taking part.

Some businesses fit kaizen activities into their day-to-day activities. Advansa, a polyester manufacturer, uses this approach. Chris Lakin, one of its managers, notes: "It is often possible to integrate the kaizen activity with the day-to-day workload [by taking advantage of] quiet times. I prefer this, because it encourages a culture in which continuous improvement is ongoing and involves everyone, rather than being specifically targeted through [one-off] events."

Teamworking is an integral element of continuous improvement. Teams – known as kaizen groups – can be formed specifically to provide ideas and solve problems. Often a business will put together a kaizen group by selecting staff from different areas of its operations to insure a wide mix of skills, knowledge, experience and perspectives. Such a combination can help to generate imaginative and creative ideas.

However, kaizen is more likely to be productive if employees are properly empowered and have a degree of control over their working lives. So some businesses organise their workforces into permanent teams, giving them responsibility for their area of work. This means the team has to meet performance targets, and has to look for continuous improvement, but is given the freedom to decide how it is to achieve its set goals. This kind of responsibility can enthuse employees to come up with ideas to improve the organisation's performance.

Training is an important component of kaizen. Employees need new skills if they are to fulfil a number of roles within their teams. Training will also assist teams in planning their work and implementing their decisions with minimal disruption to production.

Introducing any system of Kaizen can offer indirect benefits to businesses. One obvious advantage is that it can raise employee motivation and morale. Employees are consulted more under a system of kaizen, and they have the opportunity to become involved in problem-solving, possibly meeting their esteem needs (as identified by Maslow, see page 175) as a consequence. In addition, the training associated with kaizen can also have a positive effect. The business is seen to be investing in its employees, and the workforce is likely to respond by being more committed to the business.

Potential problems

Some businesses can experience problems in operating any system of kaizen. For example, industries that operate in markets in which there are regular changes in consumer tastes and fashions may not be well suited to kaizen. The fashion clothes industry requires major rethinks on a regular basis to maintain consumer interest.

It can be difficult to involve employees from all areas within the business, if some managers are obstructive. Not all managers support kaizen ideas. Some believe that it detracts from their authority. Some are "old school", and take the view that managers manage and subordinates follow orders.

Some businesses have problems sustaining kaizen. There is a view that the impact of kaizen lessens over time. Partly this is because the more obvious ideas and improvements are implemented quite early on in the process, and partly it is because staff enthusiasm often diminishes over time. In response, managers have used financial incentives to maintain continued enthusiasm for kaizen. This can, however, lead to further problems such as deciding who to reward: the originator of the idea, or the team that developed the idea into a workable method of improving the production process or the product, or both.

A note for your portfolio

Kaizen is still a relatively new management approach in the UK. Many businesses do not take advantage of the benefits that kaizen can bring. These benefits can be substantial, and the system can be introduced even into small businesses. This could be an aspect of managing resources that the business you have chosen for your portfolio exercise may use to improve its competitiveness. You might consider the potential – and the possible pitfalls – of kaizen for your business when you are analysing ways in which it could improve its operations.

business practice
Kaizen at Aimia Foods Ltd

Aimia Foods is a privately owned, family-run business. Founded by Gary and Ian Unsworth in 1981, today Aimia Foods is a £40 million turnover company with over 300 employees working at its site on Merseyside. Aimia Foods supplies an extensive product range including coffees, teas and other beverages as well as many foods. The company also provides a range of hot and cold beverage vending machines.

The company takes employees away from their day-to-day work to engage in kaizen activities. However, it also encourages employees to come up with ideas for improving products and processes within their ordinary working day.

Malcolm Dowling, Aimia's operations director, says: "We reward different things, such as 100 per cent attendance as well as kaizen-related achievements. We have a company villa in Spain and a luxury caravan in Devon to offer as part of special award holidays, and there are gifts of turkey and wine for all employees at Christmas. Employees can also nominate a colleague to receive a trip on Eurostar, and there are monthly awards for the best improvement team. Our heritage is as a family-owned business, and that people-based culture remains strong."

Source: adapted from www.aimiafoods.com and www.themanufacturer.com

assessment practice
Advising a leisure group

Fitness Central England operates around twenty gyms in the Midlands. The gyms contain a range of sporting and fitness facilities as well as restaurants and shops selling sportswear and beauty products. However, Fitness Central England faces tough competition from other companies such as Ballantynes and Greens.

Janet Damen, managing director of the company, has been involved in discussion with fellow directors on ways to improve the competitiveness of the business. The directors believe that kaizen might work for them, and they have agreed that Janet should investigate the possibilities. In turn, she has approached you for information and has asked to discuss:

■ how staff can be encouraged to support a kaizen approach

■ what preparations may be necessary before implementing kaizen

■ the possible roles that teams may play in implementing kaizen.

A In your role as a business adviser, prepare some notes for use in the meeting with Janet.

Quality

Setting the scene: "customer delight" at Kwik-Fit

The Kwik-Fit brand is distinctive, well known, and used by more than three million motorists each year. The Kwik-Fit Group operates from more than 600 service points in the UK and provides an increasing range of products and services, including new tyres, batteries and exhausts, windscreens and other car maintenance services.

Over recent years, Kwik-Fit has recorded growth and has been bought and sold by venture capital companies for its business growth potential as a group and at an individual centre level. Consistent marketing over time, across all media, has helped consumers understand the Kwik-Fit brand and its values.

Consistent marketing over time, across all media, has helped consumers understand the Kwik-Fit brand and its values. Convenient, friendly, helpful, fast, affordable and professional values have been a fundamental part of Kwik-Fit's communications.

The iconic Kwik-Fit fitters have established the brand but the advertising has moved on in the last 12 years to demonstrate that it can think national, but act local when it comes to range, product availability, low prices and crucially, quality.

Within the automotive industry, Kwik-Fit has set new standards of customer care, promoting, at every opportunity, its aim of delivering 100 per cent customer delight. This commitment to customers has been driven forward by Kwik-Fit since it was set up in 1971.

The company seeks not just to satisfy customers, which is the aim of many businesses in relation to quality. Instead, the company seeks to "delight" its customers in the expectation that they will want to purchase again in the future.

Source: adapted from www.newspapersoc.org.uk

KEY TERMS

Quality assurance systems use a preventative approach to ensure that all products meet certain quality standards by checking quality at every stage of production.

Quality control is a system for checking the quality of products at the end of the production process to make sure they meet agreed standards.

What is quality?

It is not easy to define quality. For some, a quality product is a good or service that has features that meet customers' needs. On the other hand, a good quality product might delight its customers as Kwik-Fit aims to do – that is, it might exceed customers' expectations. In a highly competitive market, a quality product might be one that is better than those of rivals. In a technological market, it may be one with more sophisticated and advanced functions. Quality can also encompass the actual buying experience (the advice offered before purchase, for example) and after-sales service. Quality can, therefore, take a number of forms.

- **Durability**
  Durability means that products last for at least as long as expected, and possibly longer. Companies that produce batteries for use in electrical products aim for durability – the brand name Eveready used by one battery manufacturer emphasises this aspect of quality.

- **Reliability**
  Reliable products do what the consumer expects, and is considered a mark of quality. Ronseal uses

the strapline "It does exactly what it says on the tin" in its adverts for products that stain and protect wood. The strapline clearly and wittily emphasises the reliability of quality.

- **Design**

  Some products are purchased because they look good. Apple's iPod Nano has proved very popular with many consumers because of its small size and cool image. The iPod Nano is about the same size as a credit card.

- **Functions**

  A high-quality product may have functions or features that others do not possess. High-quality cars have satellite navigation systems and cruise control mechanisms that allow a constant speed to be maintained on motorways.

- **Compliance to legal standards**

  Some aspects of quality are defined by the law. Electrical products have to meet rigorous safety standards, as do cars. Foods have to be fresh and free from contamination. People providing financial services have to be qualified and must follow strict rules regarding impartiality. Many businesses operate according to quality guidelines such as BS EN ISO 9000, which we shall look at in more detail later.

Quality is not just a concept that can be applied to tangible goods; it applies equally to the provision of services. Indeed, quality is an important competitive weapon for businesses that supply services.

Consumers may not return to a restaurant or visit a hotel again if they believe that the quality of food or accommodation was below what was expected. Banks, supermarkets and other providers of services aim to provide the highest-quality service that their budgets will allow.

Quality management

Quality is perhaps most commonly used in reference to a particular standard. Is a product fault-free and does it operate as expected? Is a service provided to an appropriate standard? However, as we have discussed, quality can be used to describe several other attributes of a product. And just as there is no single definition of quality, there is no single approach to quality management.

1 Quality control

Quality control takes place after the production process is complete. It is used to establish whether products are of sufficient quality before they are made available to customers. In other words, the quality control check is used to see if products attain defined standards. So, for example, quality control inspectors are employed by car manufacturers to make sure that the cars do not contain faults such as leaking water seals on windows or slight dents in the bodywork. If faults are discovered, the faulty products are returned to the production line to be brought up to the expected quality. This process is known as reworking.

Other techniques can be used for quality control, including statistical process control. This method, as the name suggests, uses statistics in monitoring quality. The idea is to measure or test aspects of products – or a sample of products – and monitor deviations which might indicate quality problems. For example, a food company that makes jam might monitor the weight of each jar it produces. If jars are recorded above or below a specified acceptable weight range, then the manufacturer would investigate the problem – it might be that there is some fault in the production process, it may only indicate that it is filling jars with a consistent shortfall in quantity. Service providers can also use statistical techniques, for example by monitoring the level of complaints. They would take action, if there is an increase of complaints above what is "normal" and considered acceptable by managers.

A major weakness of quality control is that it assumes that defects are inevitable. In fact, it is a system of quality management that is designed to intercept defects rather than prevent them in the first place. This weakness has led a large number of UK businesses to adopt quality assurance systems.

2 Quality assurance

Businesses use quality assurance systems to prevent the production of any substandard products, or at least to minimise the possibility of defects in goods or services occurring. Some quality control systems recognise that human error is evitable, so managers set a "defects per million" standard, meaning that there should just be a few faulty products per million products produced.

The quality assurance approach emphasises the importance of employees producing goods and services conforming to the business's standards on quality on each and every occasion. Under most quality assurance systems, considerable importance is placed on employees checking their own work. Employees have a responsibility to avoid passing substandard work to the next stage of production or service delivery. The aim is that by checking for quality at every stage of production, the likelihood of substandard products being delivered to consumers should be zero. Businesses using quality assurance

systems should not require quality control inspectors.

Quality assurance is also relevant in the service sector. The "whole workforce" philosophy is the same too. In a services environment, if each employee provides a level of service designed to meet or even surpass the expectations of customers, then the overall experience should be of high quality. Quality assurance in a hospital, for example, would require that all staff – medical or non-medical – should meet agreed levels of service.

One feature of quality assurance systems is the use of quality circles. These are groups of employees drawn from all levels and areas within the organisation that meet regularly to identify problems in working processes and to propose solutions. Quality circles can tackle the causes of defective products, and also suggest improvements in production methods.

Businesses can achieve a British Standards BS EN ISO 9000 award for operating specified quality assurance systems. This sets out the quality management systems that firms must implement. Businesses achieving these standards can display the award on their marketing literature and product packaging. A large number of UK businesses insist that their suppliers are accredited to the BS EN ISO 9000 standard, as they do not want to receive supplies or services that are poor quality. This is particularly important for businesses that operate just-in-time production systems, as they do not hold stocks of raw materials and components to use in the case of a faulty batch arriving from suppliers.

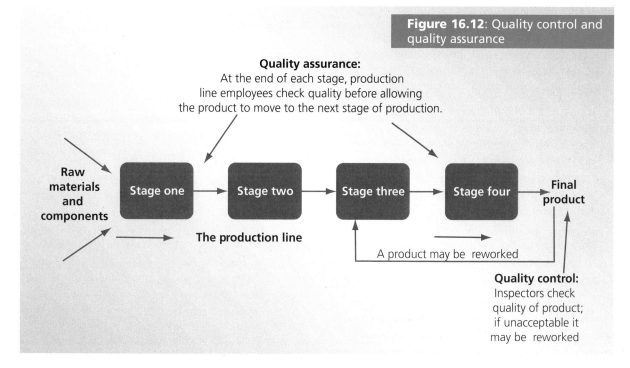

Figure 16.12: Quality control and quality assurance

Quality assurance:
At the end of each stage, production line employees check quality before allowing the product to move to the next stage of production.

Raw materials and components

Stage one → Stage two → Stage three → Stage four → Final product

The production line

A product may be reworked

Quality control:
Inspectors check quality of product; if unacceptable it may be reworked

3 Total quality management

Total quality management (TQM) is the attempt to establish a culture of quality that permeates the attitudes and actions of every employee. TQM operates internally and externally. Businesses aim to meet the needs of their external customers by providing high-quality, well-designed products. This can enable them to gain a competitive advantage. The German car manufacturer, BMW, is an example of a business that has achieved success through its reputation for quality.

However, TQM also has an internal dimension. It recognises that a business's ability to generate and sustain quality advantages arises from its internal operations and processes. Most businesses comprise a network of departments. Under TQM, each department is viewed as a customer and/or supplier of other departments. Departments are expected to meet high standards in this "internal market". This covers the flow not only of raw materials, components and partly manufactured goods, but also of supporting services such as research, marketing, reception and finance. TQM seeks to create a commitment to the highest possible standards in each internal transaction. This is seen as a way of guaranteeing high standards for external customers.

4 The human dimension

Employees are vital in providing quality services. To provide a service or a good that meets the expectations of consumers requires that staff have the relevant skills and correct attitude. Well-managed businesses do not take this for granted.

Training is an essential part of providing quality products. Employees cannot be expected to recognise – and be able to meet – consumers' expectations without some preparation. This training can take a number of forms.

- **Basic training**
  Shop assistants need to know the range of stock held by the store and to have sufficient knowledge to advise consumers. Production line employees need to know how to assemble products, and how to avoid making errors resulting in faulty products. Doctors should have a broad medical knowledge to spot symptoms, but also be trained to refer patients to specialists when necessary. Employees cannot be expected to possess these abilities naturally – training is necessary. Basic training can be lengthy and costly, especially when high levels of skills are needed, as in the case of doctors.

- **Training in design**
  Design, in all its forms, is an aspect of quality. Training employees to improve the design quality of goods and services and to improve their reliability can enhance the customers' experience and boost a business's competitiveness.

- **Training in quality procedures**
  Specific training in quality is clearly essential to minimise the chance of product defects. Employees require training in how to spot defective products and in what actions to take if a faulty product is identified. This is important if employees are to engage in "self-checking" to spot poor-quality products. With quality assurance systems most, if not all, employees require these skills.

- **Training in customer services**
  Inevitably mistakes occur and products fail to meet expectations. Employees may need training in customer service to ensure they know how to deal with dissatisfied customers and to resolve difficulties as quickly and amicably as possible.

Broader training can also be required. Employees may require training in teamworking as part of a move to quality assurance. It is common for businesses adopting a quality assurance approach to use teams in the production process as part of the self-inspection process. Team members need some understanding of each others' roles to be able to assess the quality of their work. Employees may need training to enhance their skill range, so that they are properly multiskilled and able to carry out a range of duties.

5 The financial implications

Quality costs money. Any business that makes a serious commitment to delivering high quality needs to recognise that it can require significant investment. However, this can work out cheaper in the long run than the costs incurred in correcting errors and quality defects once products have been received by customers.

First, businesses must consider the human resource costs. It often requires training to implement quality systems, some of which can be costly. External training courses can cost hundreds of pounds per day, and the business also has to cover for the absent employees. In-house training is cheaper but can be very disruptive to day-to-day operations. Training also brings indirect costs. Trained employees may demand higher wages, and may be more likely to leave as they will be attractive to other businesses. Even quality circles – which can drive substantial quality improvements – can be costly, if only in lost working time when team members are at meetings.

Second, businesses must consider the cost of materials and other inputs. The provision of high-quality goods and services is likely to lead to increased costs for materials, components and accommodation. A high-quality car may have relatively expensive materials such as wood and leather for its interior furnishings. Cheaper alternatives exist, but may detract from the quality of the product. A hotel providing a high-quality service requires well-designed, attractive and functional furniture. It also has to be housed in a suitable building in an appropriate location which fits with the quality image it is projecting. Inevitably, this increases its costs.

Finally, a business needs to consider the cost of changing its production methods. Introducing new methods of production can be a highly effective way of improving quality standards. A manufacturer might introduce robots to automate some operations on the production line. An insurance services company might introduce a telephone answering system that can deal with multiple calls simultaneously. However, these types of changes in production and operations involve an initial investment which can be significant, especially in manufacturing environments.

Importance of quality

There is little doubt that quality has become a more important issue over recent years. Consumers are more aware of quality, and they more likely to complain if products fail to meet their needs. As a consequence, quality has become a key issue with managers and directors, and increasingly it is used by businesses as a competitive weapon.

Quality has short-term and long-term dimensions. In the short term, it can lead to an increase in costs. This may lead to shareholder unrest, particularly from those who are seeking a short-term returns in the form of dividends. However, lack of quality also imposes costs in the short term. For example, potteries suffer financially from poor-quality work – it forces them to scrap a proportion of their output and to sell other substandard products as "seconds" at low prices.

The pursuit of quality can produce long-term benefits. It offers businesses marketing advantages. Quality products are likely to have a longer product life cycle, and quality can be used as a USP in promotion. A reputation for quality enables a business to charge premium prices, increasing its profit margin. Quality products also encourage brand loyalty, and enable "word-of-mouth" promotion to take place.

business practice
Number of UK product recalls rises

The number of product recalls in the UK has shot up 16 per cent over the last year according to research by Reynolds Porter Chamberlain, the City law firm. A product recall takes place when a business is forced to withdraw (usually temporarily) a product that it has already sold to its customers because of quality problems.

There were 166 recorded product recalls in the year to October 2005 compared with 143 the year before. The biggest increase has come from the pharmaceutical sector with a 250 per cent rise in recalls and safety alerts.

Mark Kendall, a solicitor at RPC said: "This dramatic rise in product recalls is caused, in part, by … the fear of becoming involved in any crippling compensation claims, and is leading firms to recall products where there is only the slightest chance of there being a liability."

Although product recalls can be very costly, they are usually far less expensive than the compensation claims that might result if the

product is proved to be dangerous and the company negligent. For example, Merck, the pharmaceutical company, estimates the cost of its recent Vioxx recall to be £71 million, yet analysts forecast that the full bill for Merck including legal fees and compensation claims could be as much as £11,300 million.

According to Mark Kendall the rise in the number of recalls also demonstrates the increasing emphasis firms are putting on brand reputation. "We are seeing a rise in the number of product recalls taking place for reasons of reputation rather than for strictly health and safety reasons.

"Companies invest a lot of money in developing a strong brand and they are unwilling to have it damaged by goods which, although not dangerous, are of a quality below what consumers expect from the brand. Whilst the costs of recalling a product are high, the cost to brand image of a below-standard product can be far higher."

Source: Reynolds Porter Chamberlain press release, 12 December 2005

assessmentpractice
Gucci

The Gucci Group is based in the Netherlands and has 11,655 employees worldwide. It is one of the world's leading multi-brand luxury goods companies.

The group owns a number of fashion brands including Gucci, Yves Saint Laurent, Boucheron, Sergio Rossi, Bédat & Co, Roger & Gallet, Alexander McQueen, Stella McCartney and Balenciaga. The Gucci Group designs, produces and distributes high-quality personal luxury goods. These include:

- handbags
- luggage and small leather goods
- shoes
- timepieces and jewellery
- ties and scarves
- perfumes, cosmetics and skincare products.

The Gucci Group directly operates stores in major markets throughout the world and sells products through franchise stores, duty-free boutiques and leading department stores.

A The Gucci Group describes itself as selling "high-quality personal goods". What do you think the company means by the term "quality"?

B Describe one single aspect of the company's work that is most important in allowing it to sell goods it describes as "high-quality". You should justify your choice.

assessmentpractice
Building your portfolio

What represents quality in your chosen business? You should investigate this facet of your business's operation, using this topic help you to make this judgement.

- Does your business offer high-quality product(s)?
- Does the company use quality control or quality assurance systems?
- Can the company make improvements in this area, and hence improve its competitiveness?
- Will the possible costs outweigh the likely benefits?

In this topic, we have reported that quality is an increasingly important issue for many businesses in the service and manufacturing sectors. This could be a fruitful area for further research.

Productive efficiency

Setting the scene: Nissan's productive factory

The latest car to be produced at Nissan's Sunderland factory rolled off the production lines in January 2006. The Nissan Note has resulted in the creation of 200 jobs and has safeguarded 800 existing posts at the Nissan's factory. It is the fifth Nissan model to be built at Sunderland.

Nissan's operations in Sunderland began in 1984, with the first vehicle coming off the production line in 1986. The factory currently employs about 4,000 people. The production lines use the latest technology, with over 250 computer-operated robots helping the workforce assemble and weld car bodies.

Nissan hopes that the factory's record of high productivity will be maintained in manufacturing the Note. Sunderland has achieved the highest productivity rates of any European car manufacturing plant, with levels as high as 100 cars per worker per year This figure is calculated by dividing the factory's annual output of cars by the average number of workers used to manufacture cars.

A Nissan spokesperson paid tribute to the employees' role in achieving the impressive productivity figures. "High productivity is the by-product of good manufacturing practice, and reflects how successfully you run the whole business. However, the skill and adaptability of our workforce remains the biggest factor in our success."

The production process

All organisations take inputs, transform these in some way and produce outputs – this is the production process. A pottery uses clay, paint and other materials to produce the finished pots, vases and plates. In contrast, an advertising agency takes the ideas and creativity of its employees, along with computer and camera technology, and produces an advertising campaign.

The inputs into any production process include:

- people, including employees' skills and ideas

- capital equipment such as tools and equipment

- raw materials and components

- energy for heat and lighting and to power machinery

- finance, to buy the materials and hire employees for example.

The outputs of a firm may be in the form of goods, such as furniture and personal computers, or services such as teaching and health care.

KEY TERMS

Productivity is the relationship between the inputs (labour and machinery, for example) in the production process and the resulting outputs. The productivity of labour is calculated by dividing the level of output produced over a time period by the number of workers employed.

Capacity is the maximum level of output a business can attain by using its factories, workforce and other resources to their fullest extent.

Capacity utilisation measures the extent to which a business uses the resources it has available. It is normally expressed in percentage terms.

A competitive firm is likely to succeed in its chosen market because it can at least match the performance of rival businesses. Competitiveness can take a number of forms dependent upon the type and size of business. Competitive businesses normally aim to achieve one or more of the following objectives.

- Producing more reliable goods with fewer faults. Firms will delight consumers if their products last longer than expected.

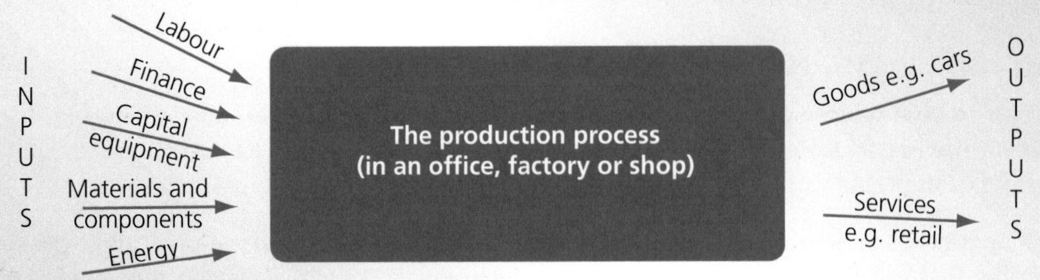

Figure 16.13: The production process

Reducing the cost of producing its goods or services, so that it is able to lower its prices. In 2006, Asda, one of Britain's major supermarket chains, announced that it was cutting prices to improve its competitiveness against rivals such as Tesco. The company said its price cuts would mean that a typical customer would spend 2 per cent less on a visit.

■ Providing better-quality goods that meet the needs of customers more effectively than other firms. The mobile phone company O_2 has enjoyed strongly rising customer numbers partly because its network coverage has improved, offering users a much better signal.

■ Producing goods and services faster than the competition, so they can get them to customers more quickly. If a firm can speed up its production process so it can deliver goods and services faster than its competitors, it will have found another way of delighting customers.

■ Developing new products quickly, so that customers are offered new models or new varieties ahead of the competition.

In this topic, we are going to focus on the second of these objectives. We look at ways in which firms can reduce the cost of producing goods and services, either by using fewer inputs or by achieving increased levels of outputs from a given amount of resources. By increasing productive efficiency in this way, businesses have the opportunity to reduce prices. However, remember that simply being able to cut prices as a result of an increase in productive efficiency is not likely to be an effective long-term strategy if it can only be achieved by compromising quality.

Measuring efficiency

Productive efficiency measures the cost of producing an item in terms of the resources used to produce that item. If a firm increases its productive efficiency, it lowers the cost per unit; conversely, if it becomes less efficient, it increases the cost per unit.

The efficiency of a business also depends on the productivity of its resources. This can be measured in relation to the labour or capital equipment (machinery) that is used in the production process. Businesses commonly measure labour or capital productivity – that is the output per person or per machine each hour, day or week.

1 Labour productivity

Labour productivity measures the output per worker. As the workforce becomes more productive, fewer employees are needed to produce any given level of output. So provided wage rates are unchanged, higher labour productivity leads to a lower labour cost per unit. Labour productivity can be calculated by:

$$\text{labour productivity} = \frac{\text{output per time period}}{\text{number of employees}}$$

Taking Nissan as an example (see the introduction to this topic), if the Sunderland plant had a workforce of 4,000 employees on average over the year and it produced 396,000 cars in that time, then its level of productivity would be 99 cars per employee per year.

$$\text{labour productivity at Sunderland} = \frac{396,000 \text{ cars}}{4,000 \text{ employees}} = 99$$

2 Capital productivity

Businesses are increasingly using technology within their production processes, as is the case with Nissan. To some extent, this invalidates the use of output per worker per time period as a measurement of productivity. An alternative is to measure the productivity of machinery used by the business. This is called capital productivity. It is calculated using a similar formula to that used for labour productivity.

$$\text{capital productivity} = \frac{\text{output}}{\text{capital employed}}$$

To continue with Nissan's Sunderland factory, if it achieves an output of 396,000 cars per year using 250 robots on the production line, then its capital productivity is 1,584 cars per robot per year.

$$\begin{array}{l}\text{capital productivity} \\ \text{at Sunderland}\end{array} = \frac{396,000 \text{ cars}}{250 \text{ robots}} = 1,584$$

Both capital and labour productivity measures do not fully assess the efficiency of an enterprise, since each considers only a single input in relation to final output. Nissan's production of cars is the result of combining a number of inputs, including labour and capital equipment. A fuller assessment would require that all inputs are considered in relation to final output.

Influencing factors

To increase productive efficiency, any business needs to consider the factors which influence its productivity.

1 Capacity utilisation

Capacity is the maximum level of output a business can attain if it uses its factories, workforce and other resources to their fullest extent. Over time, a firm is likely to adjust its capacity to meet the demands of the marketplace.

The productive efficiency and the competitiveness of a business depends partly on its current level of output compared to its maximum output. In other words, it depends upon the extent to which the business uses its capacity, or its capacity utilisation. This is measured in percentage terms, with 100 per cent representing the total use of available capacity.

As capacity utilisation increases, a business's fixed costs are spread over more units of production, and the cost of producing an average unit of production (the unit or average cost) falls. Thus the business

becomes more productively efficient. Figure 16.14 shows this relationship between capacity utilisation and efficiency.

Capacity utilisation is calculated by comparing the extent to which resources are used to the maximum extent to which they could be used.

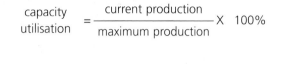

$$\begin{array}{l}\text{capacity} \\ \text{utilisation}\end{array} = \frac{\text{current production}}{\text{maximum production}} \times 100\%$$

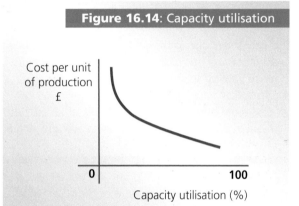

Figure 16.14: Capacity utilisation

For example, if easyJet carries 117 passengers on one of its Airbus A319 flights that has a seating capacity of 156 people (see box on page 388), then its capacity utilisation will be 75 per cent.

$$\begin{array}{l}\text{easyJet capacity} \\ \text{utilisation}\end{array} = \frac{117}{156} \times 100\% = 75\%$$

2 Training

Training is the process of improving an employee's work-related knowledge and skills. Businesses can improve an employee's skills and knowledge by providing on-the-job training. This might involve learning within the workplace, perhaps through working with a more experienced employee. Alternatively, training can be supplied off-the-job by sending employees to attend courses or other training events run by specialist organisations.

Training can help to give a business a competitive advantage through providing employees with the skills to become more productive. It can help improve a business's productive efficiency by reducing error and wastage, as a well-trained workforce is less likely to produce defective products.

More generally, training can eliminate the so-called skills gap – see Figure 16.15 – by giving employees the skills and knowledge necessary to perform to their

EasyJet is one of the UK's best known airlines. It operates between 67 European airports on 224 routes across the UK, France, Spain, Switzerland, the Netherlands, Denmark, Italy, Czech Republic, Greece, Germany and Portugal. EasyJet was launched in 1995. In its first year, 30,000 passengers travelled in the company's bright orange planes – by 2005, passenger numbers had risen to nearly 30 million.

The cornerstone of the company's success has been its low-price, no-frills policy. In 2004, the average price paid by an easyJet passenger was £48.70. These low prices have driven a rapid increase in passenger number. The average cost of an easyJet flight in 2004 was £5,591. So, with average income

of £48.70 per passenger, easyJet would need an average of 115 passengers on each flight to break even. Greater numbers would earn the company a profit, and possibly allow it to reduce prices further. This is an important part of the company's strategy if it is to compete with other low-price airlines such as Ryanair.

EasyJet has updated its aircraft fleet by purchasing 120 Airbus A319s. These planes can carry a maximum of 156 passengers. By getting nearer to the magic 156 passenger figure on each flight, easyJet can increase its productive efficiency. The company admits to attaining 88 per cent utilisation – if it can increase this figure, it may be able to set its prices even lower.

---

full potential. A survey in 2004 by the trade union Amicus revealed that 60 per cent of UK businesses believed that their employees lacked some of the necessary skills to do their jobs effectively. Amicus commented that lack of skills was a major reason why UK firms lagged behind those of France and Germany in terms of productivity and competitiveness.

The UK government recognises the importance of training in improving business competitiveness. In 2001, it established the Learning and Skills Council (LSC) to take responsibility for funding and planning further education and training for adults (16-year-olds and older) in England. The LSC has a target that by 2010 young people and adults in England will have knowledge and productive skills matching the best in the world. The LSC has an annual budget of £8,000 million. Its work includes identifying specific training needs, and funding appropriate training and education programmes in further education and

sixth form colleges. The LSC also provides information and advice on work-based training for adults.

3 Investment

Investment in fixed assets, such as buildings and vehicles, is essential for any business if it is to be able to produce goods and services. Many businesses see fixed assets, and particularly new technology, as the key to productivity. Many have sought to improve their productive efficiency by investing in fixed assets such as computer-based machinery.

In a manufacturing plant, new machinery to create large improvements in efficiency and competitiveness can cost millions of pounds. For example, some manufacturers have purchased a computer-aided manufacturing (CAM) capability. This is a form of automation in which computers communicate work instructions directly to machinery on the production line. A single computer can control banks of robotic

Figure 16.15: Bridging the skills gap

Actual performance — TRAINING → Desired performance

Current skills / Current knowledge — Required skills / Required knowledge milling machines, lathes, welding machines and other tools, moving the product from machine to machine as each step in the manufacturing process is finished.

CAM systems are easy to reprogram, permitting quick implementation of design changes. The most advanced systems, which are often integrated with computerised design systems, can also manage tasks such as parts ordering, scheduling, maintenance and tool replacement. They reduce the number of employees needed on a production line, and increase labour productivity as a result. However, businesses opting for automation are likely to face substantial interest charges on loans they incur to finance this investment, which add to the costs of production.

Significant improvements in productive efficiency and competitiveness can also be achieved with much smaller investments. For example, many businesses have invested in websites to sell products directly to consumers. This has reduced costs significantly, as well as making products available to a global audience. Other relatively small investments in broadband, laptops and mobile phones enable key employees to work away from the office and to keep in contact when visiting customers, which can lead to greater efficiencies and allow better use of office space.

A note on your portfolio

When you complete this topic, you can begin to examine ways in which your chosen business might improve its productive efficiency and competitiveness.

business practice
Dating on the internet

Marriage or dating agencies have been around for a long time. In the 1930s, they existed to find spouses for people who were working abroad in jobs associated with the British Empire. By the 1960s they had become more common, with organisations like Dateline using personality testing to pair people up.

The internet has changed the dating agency industry. Darren Richards is the founder of the UK's most popular online dating service Dating Direct. He started his business in 1999 after looking in vain on the internet for UK dating sites. "That was the eureka moment," says Mr Richards. He recognised that the internet represented a safe and efficient way for people to browse and look for potential partners.

In total, 3.5 million people have posted their profiles on Richards' site. A relatively small investment has transformed the efficiency of an industry that had existed for many years.

You might want to consider whether improving labour or capital productivity might be appropriate. Both of these could require an investment: either in training or capital equipment. You might also think about the extent to which your business uses its resources. Is it possible to increase capacity utilisation?

assessment practice
The corner shop

David Ward is a businessman under pressure. He owns and manages a small corner shop in north London selling groceries, sweets, tobacco products and newspapers. The shop has been in his family for 60 years, but is facing intense competitive pressure.

"When the first supermarkets opened in the 1960s, my grandfather was running this business. He couldn't compete with them on price, so he found other ways to be efficient," David says. "For a long time that was enough. However, the opening of 'local' stores by the supermarkets poses the greatest-ever threat to my livelihood." Over 2,000 independently run corner shops closed in 2005.

A In what ways can a corner shop such as that run by David Ward be efficient?

B Propose and explain one action that David Ward might take to improve the efficiency of his business and its competitiveness.

Setting the scene: London's Olympic Stadium

The success of London in winning the right to host the 2012 Olympic Games means that the city will see a number of major building projects over the next few years. Pride of place will go to the new Olympic Stadium which will be at the southern extreme of the Olympic Park. The stadium will stage the opening and closing ceremonies, as well as the athletics events.

The design of the stadium is based on the human body, with a roof designed to wrap around the complex like a set of muscles. The stadium will have a capacity of 80,000, and the construction cost is estimated to be £225 million.

The construction of the new stadium will be a complex and lengthy enterprise. Some of the key elements of the construction project are:

- clearing of the land on which the stadium is to be built
- designing the new stadium
- constructing components to be used in the stadium such as 80,000 seats
- building foundations for the stadium
- developing road and rail transport links to the stadium
- installing thousands of miles of cabling for telecommunications
- building a running track and associated athletics facilities
- installing boxes for journalists
- constructing the stands for spectators

- building changing rooms for athletes and judges
- landscaping the surrounding area
- painting and decorating the stadium.

The team responsible for building the Olympic Stadium will be under extreme pressure to deliver on time. The stadium must be ready, with approved safety certificates, for the opening ceremony in July 2012. Effective time management will be essential. The construction team will have to recognise which aspects of the construction process can be carried out simultaneously. Planning the process will be a vital element of a successful project.

KEY TERMS

Critical path analysis is a technique of analysing and organising the tasks needed to undertake a complex project to determine the quickest and most efficient means of completing that project.

Activities are parts of a project requiring time and resources, and they are indicated by an arrow in a critical path analysis diagram.

Nodes represent the start or end of each activity, and are drawn as circles.

The critical path shows the sequence of activities that must be completed on time if the whole project is not to be delayed.

What is critical path analysis?

Critical path analysis (CPA) was first used by the Du Pont Corporation in America in 1957 as a means of improving its management of projects. It is a method of calculating how complex projects can be completed as quickly as possible. Effective time management is the principal reason why managers use CPA, and it is ideal for projects, such as building London's Olympic Stadium, where is it essential to meet deadlines.

We start this topic by reviewing and building upon the introduction to critical path analysis presented in Unit 12, Topic 7 (see pages 188–90). As we explained in that part of the textbook, CPA breaks down even the most complex project into a series of separate activities. The time required to complete each of these activities is estimated, and judgements are made about whether individual activities have to be completed before or after, or can be undertaken simultaneously with, other activities. Recognising the activities in a complex project that can be carried out at the same time is at the heart of CPA.

CPA is essentially a type of network analysis. Employees carry out a simple form of network analysis when carrying out day-to-day activities at work. For example, a busy shop assistant might enter a customer's debit card into the shop's electronic system and allow it to process the transaction, while removing any security tags from the goods and packing the customer's purchases. These activities can be carried out simultaneously, saving time and reducing queues at the tills. In other situations, employees make judgements about which activities have to be completed first, and how long these activities are likely to take. These are the essential elements of carrying out critical path analysis.

The nuts and bolts of CPA

Critical path analysis uses a diagram (called a network) to show all the activities which make up a project. The CPA diagram shows:

- the sequence in which the tasks or activities must be completed

- the length of time taken to complete each activity

- the earliest time at which each activity can start and finish.

Any CPA network has two elements. First, it has activities. This is any part of a project requiring time and almost certainly some resources, such as labour, materials and cash. The arrows (running from left to right) show the sequence of the tasks, with activities that can be completed simultaneously represented by parallel arrows placed above each other in the same vertical plane.

Activities are frequently given letters to avoid cluttering the diagram and to denote the order of tasks – the first task would be given the letter A, the second B, etc. These letters are normally written above the relevant activity or arrow. The duration of each task is normally written below the arrow.

The second element of any CPA network is the nodes. These represent the start or end of each activity, and are drawn as circles. They represent stops and starts, and they do not require any resources. The circles are numbered starting from the left. Some nodes can have more than one activity drawn into them, as shown in Figure 16.16.

Constructing simple network diagrams

Figure 16.17 shows the first steps in drawing a network diagram. Activity A is expected to last 6 weeks, while activity B is expected to last 8 weeks. The diagram shows that activity B can only be started

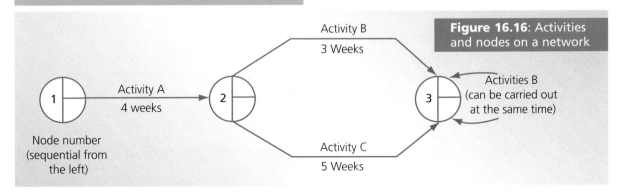

Figure 16.16: Activities and nodes on a network

Activity B
3 Weeks

Activity A
4 weeks

Activities B
(can be carried out
at the same time)

1

2

3

Node number
(sequential from
the left)

Activity C
5 Weeks

Figure 16.17: The start of the network

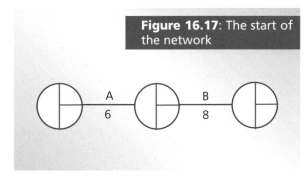

Figure 16.17: The start of the network

Figure 16.20: A network table

Activity	Preceded by	Duration (weeks)
A	-	6
B	A	8
C	B	5
D	B	2
E	C and D	9
F	-	8
G	F	11
H	E and G	7

when activity A is completed; this is why activity B follows on from activity A.

Figure 16.18 shows that activities C and D can only be started when activity B has been finished. Because they are drawn parallel to one another – in the same vertical plane – it shows that they can be carried out simultaneously. It is only possible to start activity E once C and D are both finished.

In Figure 16.19, more activities have been added. This is a more complex network, but a more realistic one as more activities are able to be carried out simultaneously. Activities F and G can be carried out alongside other activities. Activity F can be started at the same time as activity A; it must be finished before activity G can be started.

All the information in Figure 16.19 can be summarised in a network table. Figure 16.20 shows the network table for the network represented in Figure 16.19.

There are a number of rules that apply when constructing a network.

■ Start by drawing the activities which have no precedents (A and F in th3 case of the network in Figure 16.19).

■ Then draw subsequent activities using a network table such as Figure 16.20 as a guide to sequences.

■ Do not draw the end node for any activity until you know what follows it.

■ Lines showing different activities must not cross.

■ The network should start and end with one node.

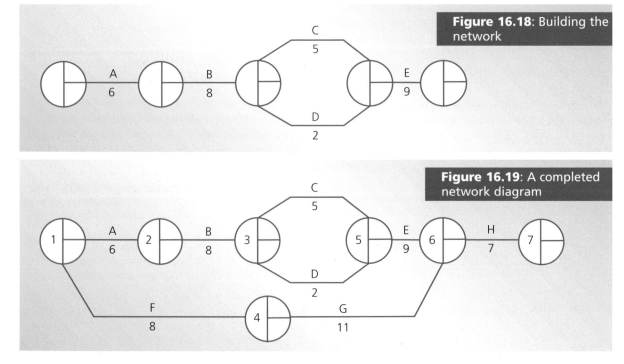

Figure 16.18: Building the network

Figure 16.19: A completed network diagram

Figure 16.21: A network table for a test project

Activity	Preceded by	Duration (weeks)
A	-	6
B	A	4
C	B	3
D	B	4
E	C and D	12
F	B	2
G	F	7
H	B	14

Recording data in a node

As we saw noted above, nodes should be numbered sequentially from left to right. This number should be entered in the left-hand half of each node, and it acts as a reference number. The right-hand half of each node is divided into two quadrants, which are used to record the earliest start times and the latest finish times.

Earliest start times

The earliest start time (EST) is shown in the top right-hand quadrant of each node, see Figure 16.22. The EST shows the earliest time at which the activity – or activities – which immediately follow the node can commence. The EST is calculated by adding the duration of the activity preceding the node to the EST of the previous node. This is perhaps easiest to understand by looking at an example.

We shall use Figure 16.19 to illustrate how ESTs are calculated. The first node is straightforward – it has an EST of week 0 as this is when the project starts. So we enter 0 in the top right-hand quadrant of node 1. The duration of activity A is 6 weeks, so the EST recorded in node 2 is 6 + 0 = 6 weeks. Similarly, the EST recorded in node 3 is 6 + 8 = 14. Node 5's EST is slightly more complicated. There are two activities leading into node 5. When calculating the EST of activity E it is necessary to add the longer duration of

the two activities (C and D) to the EST shown in node 3. In this case, the longer activity is C, which takes 5 weeks, so the EST in node 5 is 14 + 5 = 19. This figure is entered in the top right-hand quadrant of node 5. Figure 16.23 shows all the ESTs associated with the project represented by the network diagram in Figure 16.19.

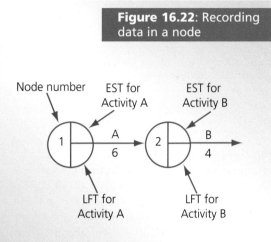

Figure 16.22: Recording data in a node

Node number   EST for Activity A   EST for Activity B

LFT for Activity A   LFT for Activity B

By identifying the earliest start times in this way, managers know when resources are required. Raw materials, components and/or specialist labour can be ordered to arrive just in time. This can help to minimise costs and make the project more cost-efficient. For example, Figure 16.23 shows that the resources and materials needed for activity H will not be required until the start of week 28.

Latest finish times

The latest finish time (LFT) records the time by which an activity must be completed if the entire project is not to be delayed. The LFT is shown in the bottom right-hand quadrant of the node.

Latest finish times are calculated by moving from right to left in a CPA diagram, starting with the node that marks the completion of the project. They are calculated by subtracting the duration of a given activity from its latest finish time, to get the latest finish time of the preceding activity. In circumstances, where two activities run parallel to each other, such as C and D in Figure 16.19, it is normal to subtract the longer duration.

In Figure 16.23, node 7 is the end of this project. The LFT of this node is the same as the EST – 35 weeks. The LFT of activity E is calculated by subtracting activity H's duration (7 weeks) from activity H's LFT. So the LFT of activity E is 35 – 7 = 28 weeks. Similarly, the LFT of activity C is 28 – 9 = 19 weeks.

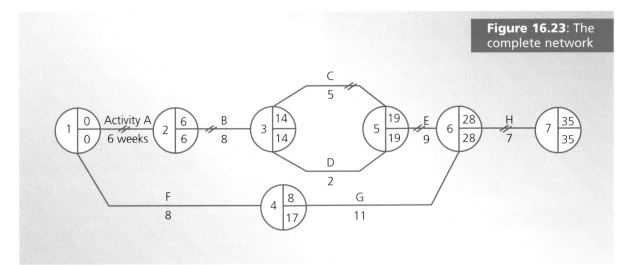

Figure 16.23: The complete network

The critical path

The nodes in which EST = LFT make up the critical path for the project. The critical path shows those activities that cannot be delayed without delaying the entire project. Activities off the critical path can delayed – at least for a period – without pushing back the finish time of the whole project. In this sense, they are not critical.

The critical path highlights those activities that take the longest to complete, and helps managers to recognise the key activities on which they must concentrate if the project is to be completed on time. The process of concentrating on a small number of vital activities is called "management by exception". In Figure 16.23, the critical path is A-B-C-E-H. This is shown by a series of double lines.

stop and think

Add the ESTs and LFTs to the network you drew in response to the Stop and Think exercise on page 393. (This was based on the information in Figure 16.21.) Identify the critical path.

Why businesses use critical path analysis

CPA has a wide range of applications for businesses in the manufacturing and service sectors. It is used to manage major building projects, as we suggest in the introduction to this unit, but it has many other applications as well. These include:

- introducing new products – Unilever has used CPA to manage the release of new food products

- implementing marketing campaigns – ensuring that key activities, such as national advertising and large-scale production, are co-ordinated

- planning relocations of factories and offices – careful time management is important to minimise the disruption to the business and the impact on customers

- overseeing major R&D programmes

In all these situations CPA can offer benefits to managers and can help to improve a business's productive efficiency. Time is an important resource for many businesses. Critical path analysis, by identifying activities that can be carried out simultaneously, helps managers to complete projects on schedule. By completing two or more activities at the same time, projects can be completed quickly and efficiently, offering commercial advantages to businesses. This can be particularly important when introducing new products. Bringing a new product onto the market quickly, a business can get an earlier return on its investment. The business may also be able to charge premium prices if it has a lead over its rivals, thereby enhancing potential profitability.

Effective management of time can help businesses in other ways. Businesses that do not complete projects on schedule will incur extra costs, as they are using valuable resources, such as skilled labour, for longer periods of time. They may also incur penalties if contracts state that a project must be completed by a given date. Multiplex, the Australian company building the new Wembley Stadium in London, is threatened with substantial financial penalties for failing to complete the £757 million stadium by the agreed date of March 2006. It has been reported that Multiplex would have to pay a penalty of £1 million for each week the project overran the agreed completion date.

Many networks that are drawn up to represent real business projects are highly complex. They can contain thousands of activities and nodes. Some of the projects may have durations in excess of one year. The network diagrams would be too complex to draw by hand.

It is for this reason that computers are used to draw up many of the networks that are used in CPA and similar techniques. Project management software developer Clarity released the latest version of its Open Workbench desktop project manager in December 2005. The California-based company, formerly called Niku, also provides a wide range of other software for managing projects.

Clarity's Open Workbench program supports a range of project management functions including critical path analysis, and it can be used to estimate the time to completion of a project. Project managers can view their networks on computer screens and make adjustments as necessary. Clarity claims that there are over 100,000 users of Open Workbench inside major companies such as BT, Phillips, HSBC, Unilever and Visa.

Further savings in costs, and hence improvements in efficiency, are possible through the use of critical path analysis. The technique can assist managers in minimising the amount of resources they need to hold at any one time, as critical path networks identify when particular resources are required. For example, a critical path network for building an extension to a restaurant would identify when skilled labour, such as bricklayers and plasterers, are needed. This helps to minimise wage costs, as labour can be hired when it is needed. The more efficient management of resources can also assist businesses in managing working capital. Purchasing resources at the precise time that they are needed means that scarce cash is not tied up in idle resources.

Critical path analysis can also be used to manage delays. When a delay occurs on an activity, the network shows the impact on other subsequent activities. The network makes it easier for managers to see the implications of the delay and to reschedule the remaining activities to ensure that the overall delay is minimal. It enables businesses to tell customers about the probable timescale of any delays that do occur. This can help to improve customer service.

Weaknesses

Although critical path analysis offers businesses many benefits, the technique has several drawbacks. The major weakness in using critical path analysis is that it is difficult to estimate the durations of activities accurately. If these are incorrect, the whole network is of limited value. A more sophisticated method of project management, called the program evaluation and review technique (PERT), overcomes this problem to some extent by attaching probabilities to the estimations of the durations of the activities.

Another problem with CPA is that it requires specialist software to apply the technique to large projects. This means that project management skills are becoming more specialised, and many smaller businesses are unlikely to have project managers with the necessary abilities.

The software also has limitations. Highly complex projects, such as building Terminal Five at Heathrow airport, can contain so many activities that it becomes very difficult to manage the CPA network even using a computer. However, recent improvements in software have helped managers to cope more easily with complex networks. Essentially, the latest CPA technology allows managers to focus on small parts of a project at a time, while keeping an overview of the bigger picture.

A final weakness of CPA is that it can breed complacency. The process of drawing up a network is only the first stage of project management. Some managers may believe that once the network is planned and mapped out, the project should progress smoothly. However, plans can go awry, and any project needs managing throughout its life. The network will often need updating throughout the project to reflect actual experience on the ground. Managers need to guard against becoming complacent, resulting in delays in critical activities.

Launching a new product

Anglian Drinks Ltd is planning to launch a new brand of flavoured water. The directors want to have this product on the market within twenty weeks.

Figure 16.24 shows the stages in the development of this new product. The company's project manager has considered which activities are dependent upon others, and has estimated the times (in weeks) necessary to complete each of the activities.

A Draw the network for this project. You should calculate the ESTs, LFTs and the critical path, and include this information on your network.

B Can this project be completed within the time available of twenty weeks?

C Do you think that drawing up this network will help the company to be more efficient in developing this new product? You should explain your answer.

Figure 16.24: The flavoured water project

Activity	Preceded by	Duration (weeks)
A: Research flavours	-	8
B: Investigate types of bottles	-	5
C: Refit existing production line	A, B	3
D: Train employees	A, B	2
E: Plan marketing campaign	A, B	8
F: Carry out test run of production	C, D	2
G: Design final marketing campaign	E, F	1

Building your portfolio

You may like to consider whether your chosen business could improve its productive efficiency by using critical path analysis to manage a project in which it is involved. For example, if it is introducing computer technology into its production process, CPA could help to minimise the length and cost of the changeover period, and help the business meet customers' needs as fully as possible.

It is possible that smaller businesses may not be aware of CPA or of the software that is available to help managers use the technique. This could be an area for consideration. If your business manages its time more effectively, it arguably should become more competitive.

CPA could be used as part of your evaluation of the viability of a proposal to improve the business's competitiveness. If this proposal would take a long time to implement, or cannot meet an essential deadline, then it may not be viable. CPA may be able to focus in on key areas that might cause delay.

The scale of production

Setting the scene: Wal-Mart – the world's biggest

The cash tills at any one of Wal-Mart's giant retail stores are rarely quiet. Customers bought more than £153,000 million worth of goods from the world's largest retailer in the year to the end of January 2005.

Why are shoppers attracted to Wal-Mart? "We shop here because the prices are great and the service is wonderful," raves one customer at a Wal-Mart store in New Jersey. Consumers are enthusiastic about the value for money it affords and the wide range of products that it sells. The sheer size of the company is staggering.

- Wal-Mart's tills take well over £250,000 every minute of every day.

- The company employs more than 1.5 million people across the world

- It has more than 3,600 stores in the US, and more than 1,500 in Mexico, Puerto Rico, Canada, Argentina, Brazil, China, South Korea, Germany and Britain (where it trades as Asda).

- In just three months, it sells the same value of goods as its nearest US competitor, Home Depot, sells in a year.

Wal-Mart has its roots in a town called Bentonville, in Arkansas. From there, the company's founder, Sam Walton, sowed the seeds that would grow into the world's largest retailer and enable the Walton family to amass a fortune thought to be worth around £102,000 million.

Wal-Mart has not performed as well as expected at times over recent years. The company has seen rising sales, but growth has been lower than anticipated. Some of its rivals have been more successful in the same period, achieving higher rates of growth in sales and profits. This has led business analysts to speculate that Wal-Mart's problems run deeper.

Robert Buchanan, an analyst at AG Edwards, told the business television network CNBC that the retailer's "dismal" performance suggested problems with management and staff morale as much as short-term issues like bad weather keeping shoppers at home. Many of the problems, analysts argue, are to do with the company's size.

Analysts such as Buchanan argue that Wal-Mart is not a very responsive company. It does not always respond quickly to changes. For example, the company held virtually no stocks of Apple's iPod in the months before Christmas 2004. At the same time, rivals were selling tens of thousands of the music players.

As Wal-Mart has grown, it has attracted a lot of criticism and has generated much negative publicity. It has come under fire for its employment practices – it is accused of paying low wages and of banning trade unions – as well as for always seeking very cheap products. It will not be easy for such a large business to change policies and to promote a more positive image across the globe.

Sources: adapted from reports on the BBC News website, 25 February 2005, and The Guardian website, 13 May 2005.

KEY TERMS

Total costs of production are the sum of all expenses involved in producing goods or services, including fixed and variable costs.

Average cost of production is the expense incurred in producing a single unit of output. This is calculated by dividing the total costs of production by the number of units of output.

Economies of scale occur when an increase in the size of the firm's operations results in a fall in the average cost of production.

Diseconomies of scale are the financial disadvantages that can result from the growth of a business. These are shown by a rise in the average cost of production

Globalisation is the trend for markets to become worldwide in extent. The markets for an increasing number of goods such as computers and services such as insurance are now global.

Production costs

The total costs of production are calculated by summing all the expenses involved in producing goods and services, including fixed and variable costs. The formula for calculating costs of production is:

total costs = fixed costs + variable costs

Total costs are calculated for a given period of time, normally one month or a year. Fixed costs are those costs, such as rent and rates, that do not change when the level of production or output alters. Variable costs, as the name suggests, vary directly with the level of output. For example, if a business increases its level of production, it is likely to incur higher wage and energy costs, and so its variable costs of production will increase.

It is common for managers to calculate total costs in relation to different levels of production. This enables them to work out the average cost of production at any level of output using the formula:

$$\frac{\text{average (or unit)}}{\text{cost of production}} = \frac{\text{total cost of production}}{\text{output in units}}$$

To illustrate the value of these concepts of total and average costs of production, consider the example of Chet Boats that follows.

business practice
Chet Boats Ltd

Chet Boats constructs up to 100 cruisers each year for the UK holiday trade. The company's boatyard is at Loddon in Norfolk, and many of the company's boats are regularly seen on the Norfolk Broads.

The company faces quite high fixed costs such as interest payments on a mortgage on its boatyard and offices. The construction of each cruiser involves expenditure on a wide range of raw materials as well as skilled labour.
Figure 16.25 sets out Chet Boats' annual costs for different levels of production. Chet Boats sold 72 cruisers in its last financial year.

Chet Boats trades in a very competitive market, and the management team realise that it is important to increase the company's productive efficiency. Manufacturing on a larger scale might be a way to achieve some efficiencies. The company is considering increasing production to 110 cruisers a year. At this level of production, its variable costs will be £6,600,000.

What will be the average cost of producing a single cruiser, if the company increased production to 110 cruisers a year? Would you advise the company to increase its scale of production based on this evidence?

Figure 16.25: Annual costs of production for Chet Boats

Annual level of production	Fixed costs (£)	Variable costs (£)	Total costs (£)	Average costs (£)
10 Cruisers	800,000	750,000	1,550,000	155,000
20 Cruisers	800,000	1,450,000	2,250,000	112,500
30 Cruisers	800,000	2,100,000	2,900,000	96,667
40 Cruisers	800,000	2,700,000	3,500,000	87,500
50 Cruisers	800,000	3,250,000	4,050,000	81,000
60 Cruisers	800,000	3,750,000	4,550,000	75,833
70 Cruisers	800,000	4,200,000	5,000,000	71,429
80 Cruisers	800,000	4,600,000	5,400,000	67,500
90 Cruisers	800,000	5,050,000	5,850,000	65,000
100 Cruisers	800,000	5,700,000	6,500,000	65,000

Average costs provide managers with useful information. The average cost of production can be a guide in making pricing decisions. If a business sets its prices higher than its average costs of production, it will make a profit on each sale. The weakness of this approach is that it ignores the market. If competitors sell similar quality products at lower prices, then it may be difficult to achieve high sales.

It is common for average costs to fall as levels of production increase. However, at some point they normally rise again. In the rest of this topic, we examine the causes of the reductions and increases in average costs of production.

Economies of scale

When businesses grow, many enjoy the benefits of economies of scale. This means that production unit costs fall and productive efficiency should improve.

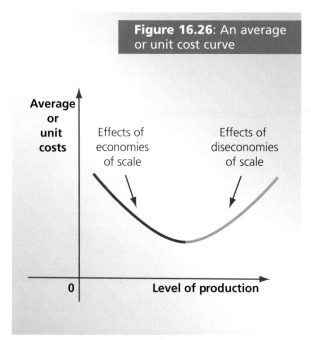

Figure 16.26: An average or unit cost curve

Internal economies of scale

Economies of scale are those factors which reduce average costs as a business increases the scale of its operations. Economies of scale can be divided into two distinct types. Internal economies of scale benefit a single business, rather than the entire industry. Internal economies of scale can arise for a number of reasons.

Technical economies of scale

As a business grows, it becomes possible to afford more efficient production technologies that reduce unit cost of production. For example, a business may

be able to replace employees on the production line with computerised technology. This will enable the firm to reduce the unit costs of production. One reason that Nissan's factory in Sunderland is one of the world's most efficient manufacturing plants is that there are over 250 robots on the production line.

Financial economies of scale

Small businesses often experience problems in raising finance. Banks are unwilling to lend money to small firms because of the high risk: the businesses are less secure, and there is a greater possibility that the loan will not be repaid. If a bank decides to take the risk and make a loan to a small business, it is likely to charge high rates of interest. As a business grows, it becomes easier to negotiate loans and to get more competitive (that is, lower) interest rates. These factors help to reduce the costs of gaining finance.

Managerial economies of scale

As firms get bigger, they are able to employ people that specialise in different aspects of management. Instead of having managers trying to do several jobs at once – or having to pay other companies to do specialist work – they can hire their own people to concentrate on particular areas of the business. For example, as a business becomes bigger, it might have enough internal demand to make it worthwhile employing its own IT specialists or market researchers. By using their own specialists rather than incurring the greater cost of buying in services, firms find that their labour costs do not rise in proportion with output.

Marketing economies of scale

Many businesses spend heavily on marketing. Expenditure on advertising and sales teams is costly for all firms, but the burden falls more heavily on smaller businesses. The impact of marketing spend on the average costs of a large business will be much lower because it has a much greater number of units of production to spread those costs across. A relatively small firm may find a £1 million advertising campaign a real burden if it only sells 100,000 products a year. A larger firm is in a better position to finance this type of campaign. Its very size may allow the firm to get a better deal with the media that carry its adverts.

Purchasing economies of scale

As firms get bigger, they will need to buy more supplies. As a result, they should be able to negotiate better deals with suppliers, and negotiate a better price on components and raw materials. This type of economy of scale is sometimes called bulk-buying economies of scale. Many suppliers are willing to give discounts because they don't want to risk losing a major customer. Large firms are also more likely to obtain better terms when dealing with distributors.

External economies of scale

Some economies of scale benefit all businesses in a particular industry. These are called external economies of scale. They often arise when an industry is concentrated in a particular geographic area. All businesses benefit from being able to draw on a pool of highly skilled labour. Similarly, all businesses benefit if there are high-quality transport links that allow products to be transported cheaply and efficiently to markets. Other types of external economies include the close proximity of suppliers, allowing raw materials, components and specialised labour to be provided cheaply and efficiently, thereby contributing to a further reduction in unit costs.

The value of economies of scale

Economies of scale can be important because reducing the average cost of producing a unit of output can have a significant impact on a business's productive efficiency and its competitiveness.

If a business can reduce its unit costs by increasing its scale, it might choose to keep its prices at the same level. This allows it to make more profit on each sale. This increased profit can be reinvested in developing new products or in improving methods of production. Either approach can increase the business's productive efficiency further in the future. Alternatively, It can choose to pass the cost saving on to the customer by cutting its prices. This may enable the business to offer better value than its competitors. In turn, this may lead to further increases in sales, prompting further growth and further economies of scale. This may allow the company to cut prices further. This is the approach used by Amazon, the internet retailer.

Diseconomies of scale

Diseconomies of scale occur when a firm's average costs of production rise as it increases its level of production. There are a number of reasons why diseconomies of scale can occur.

Communication diseconomies

As a business grows, it has more employees and, possibly, more levels of hierarchy. These developments can make communications more difficult. Despite

In 1994, a 30-year-old New Yorker called Jeff Bezos read about the internet. He moved to California and in a year had set up an internet bookshop. When the orders came in, he packed and posted books from his garage.

By 2005 Amazon had become the world's largest internet retailer. Its sales reached £1,000 million and were growing at an annual rate of more than 25 per cent. The company has transformed itself from a bookseller into an online retailer selling everything from DVDs to diamonds.

Scale has played a part in the company's growth. Jeff Bezos believes in what he calls the "virtuous circle". As Amazon's sales have grown, Bezos has resisted the temptation to cash in by taking higher profits. Instead, he has used his increasing size and leverage to obtain lower prices from his suppliers. This has allowed the company to reduce its prices and to achieve further increases in sales – continuing the virtuous circle. This approach does have a downside: in its first seven years, Amazon did not make a profit.

developments in information technology, such as e-mail, voicemail and intranets, it can still be quite difficult to make sure everyone in a large business knows exactly what they need to know at the appropriate time, and to ensure that messages find their intended recipients successfully. Communication problems can become more pronounced within multinational businesses. Employees may speak different languages and work in different time zones, making communication difficult.

Co-ordination diseconomies

In a large business, it can be difficult to ensure that everyone is working efficiently towards the same goals. As a company expands and sets up new parts of the business, it is easy for employees to work in different ways to different objectives. Sometimes problems arise because growth is not properly resourced – if managers are unable to delegate work, they can become overburdened and less efficient. Sometimes problems arise if a business grows by merging with, or taking over, other companies – unless this process is handled properly, there can be duplication of roles and a lack of clarity about objectives, leading to inefficiencies.

Motivation diseconomies

In a large business, senior managers are less able to stay in day-to-day contact with all staff, especially if the business is based in a number of locations. Junior employees may feel less involved in the business and remote from its decision-making. In a small business, it is more likely that employees will receive recognition from senior managers for their efforts. This is a major motivator and can improve employee performance. If big businesses become too impersonal and fail to find ways of building morale and motivation, they can suffer diseconomies and higher unit production costs.

Responding to diseconomies

Globalisation offers businesses the opportunity to achieve economies of scale, but also makes it more likely that diseconomies will emerge, especailly those relating to communication and co-ordination. Multinationals are particularly vulnerable. Their size can be a problem, but operating in many countries adds to the challenge. So how can multinationals address these problems?

Consider the case of HSBC. This is one of the largest banks in the world. The company has its headquarters in the UK, but has over 10,000 outlets in 76 countries. HSBC's strategy for tackling diseconomies of scale is to operate as a series of local businesses with varying degrees of decentralisation. HSBC is divided into three "core" areas: Europe, Hong Kong and North America. Within these core areas, smaller "businesses" operate. Thus the UK's branches of HSBC trade as a separate business, giving it more of small business "feel".

Creating businesses within businesses allows greater use of delegation, giving junior staff the authority to take a broader range of decisions. Providing each business element has a clear understanding of the aims of the organisation, this approach can avoid co-ordination diseconomies. Organising multinationals in this way can also tackle problems associated with poor communication and demotivation. In the UK, HSBC employees find it easier to identify with their business element, and are more likely to have contact with senior managers. They will be more motivated by being given more responsibility.

Completing your portfolio

By this stage, you should be able to complete requirements B and D for this unit. Requirement B asks you to consider how a business might improve its competitiveness. You will need to consider all aspects of this unit, and its three main themes of planning production, managing production and improving the efficiency of production. You do not need to write in detail on all aspects of each theme, but you need to think about which are most relevant to your chosen business. You must link ideas to your proposals on how the business might improve its competitiveness.

Requirement D asks you to evaluate your proposal. This entails weighing up its likely impact on the competitiveness of the business. Think about the advantages and disadvantages of your proposal. It may be that your ideas add to the business's costs, for example. You may want to use this approach of weighing the pros and cons to structure arguments.

assessment practice
Cadbury Schweppes

Cadbury Schweppes is a multinational company selling chocolate products and soft drinks in more than 200 countries. The company operates 133 factories across the world and employs over 50,000 people.

In 2005 Cadbury Schweppes' worldwide sales rose 7 per cent to £6,510 million. As a result, the company's share of the global confectionery market rose to 9.9 per cent. Cadbury Schweppes has set itself a target of overtaking Mars in the world rankings. In recent years the company has sold many of its soft drinks brands to Coca-Cola and has concentrated more on confectionery products. In 2005, it bought Green & Blacks, a manufacturer of high-quality organic chocolate products.

A What economies of scale might Cadbury Schweppes benefit from as a result of selling chocolate products in 200 countries?

B Why is Cadbury Schweppes vulnerable to diseconomies of scale?

C What might the company do to reduce the likelihood of it being affected by diseconomies of scale?

THIS BUSINESS PLANNING UNIT IS DIFFERENT FROM the other units that make up the A2 GCE in Applied Business course in that it is a synoptic unit. Synoptic means that the unit is a summary of what you have learnt. It is an opportunity for you to apply skills and knowledge that you have learnt from your AS units. You will also be able to apply knowledge from other A2 units.

The introductory topic explains the importance of business planning. It sets out a way of structuring a business plan into a main document and a set of detailed appendices. The rest of the unit explores the issues you need to consider when completing each stage of the plan. This provides the framework – to undertake the work to produce detailed proposals for each element of a business plan you will need to draw on knowledge and learning gained throughout the Applied Business course.

The assessment for this unit requires you to produce a business plan. This could be to support a proposal for a new business start-up, or a proposal by an existing business that is, say, considering launching a new product. Your business proposal could also be for a not-for-profit organisation that, say, wishes to launch a new charitable venture to serve a section of the community. Throughout this unit, the assessment practice session at the end of each topic helps you to gradually build up your portfolio.

Business planning

Setting the scene: business failure

Start-up businesses have a very high failure rate in the UK. As many as one in two failing in their first two years. Of course, the reverse side of the coin is that almost a half survive and go on to prosper.

There are many reasons for business failure. However, one of the main reasons that many new businesses don't succeed is a failure of business planning. Too many people start businesses with either a poor business plan or no business plan at all.

It is often said that "failing to plan is planning to fail". A business plan should cover aspects such as marketing, finance, sales and promotional plans, as well as detailed breakdowns of costings and profit predictions.

According to the business advice website Start Business (www.startbusiness.co.uk), many start-up businesses cannot see how important it is to write a business plan. However, try this for a sobering statistic: over 90 per cent of businesses that fail didn't have a business plan.

Why business planning is important

Business planning is vital not just for new business start-up enterprises, it is equally important for established businesses introducing a new product or just maintaining their current operations. Not-for-profit organisations and social enterprises also need business planning. Producing a business plan has two main functions in creating or maintaining a successful business: an external function and an internal function.

The external function of a business plan is to help attract and maintain funding for the business. An external funder, such as a bank, will need evidence that the business has the ability to meet interest payments and eventually pay back the loan. Investors will want solid evidence that the business is going to be profitable.

The internal function of a business plan is to contribute to a process that will help a business achieve its goals. The plan provides a focus, helping the whole organisation move in the same direction.

The external function

If a business does not have sufficient funds from its owners to start up or to expand its activities, it will have to raise finance from outside the business. Sources of external finance include:

- banks, which may provide a loan to the business at an agreed rate of interest

- venture capitalists, who may provide finance in return for a share in the business

KEY TERMS

Business plans describe the nature of a business and the activities it will engage in, and set out how it will be structured, and how it will make money or achieve its goals.

External users are people or organisations outside the business that use the business plan to decide whether to support the business by, for example, lending money or making grants.

Internal users are people within a business that use the business plan to help make decisions and to monitor and control the activities of the business.

Venture capitalists provide investment finance to companies to help them grow and expand. In exchange, venture capitalists expect a share in the ownership of the company. Venture capitalists look to invest in high-growth businesses, and they usually expect a high rate of return (in excess of 20 per cent).

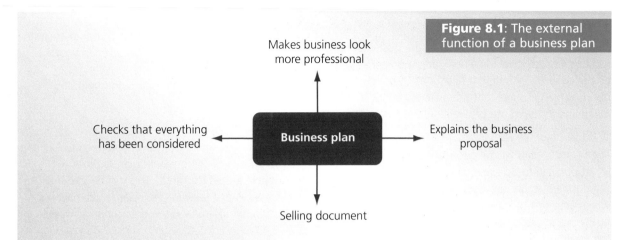

Figure 8.1: The external function of a business plan

Makes business look more professional

Checks that everything has been considered

Business plan

Explains the business proposal

Selling document

- government agencies, which may give loans or grants under certain circumstances

- corporate or charitable foundations, which may make grants to not-for-profit organisations to fulfil their community or charitable activities.

External funders provide business finance in the right conditions, but demand for funds always outstrips supply so they require reasons why they should provide funds to a particular business. The business plan can provide these reasons.

Many providers of finance require a business plan before they will even consider making funds available. The plan shows that the applicant is "businesslike". It is used to check that a business has considered all the main aspects of the business proposal such as:

- aims and objectives

- type of business ownership

- management of the business

- location of the business

- human resources needed by the business

- market research

- customers and competition

- the marketing mix

- operations planning

- legal requirements

- financial analysis and planning.

The business plan is used to explain what the business is about, and it should give a reader an idea of the business's likely success and viability. It is also a selling document that will persuade funders to buy into the business idea. Business plans for new enterprise or new business ideas should have a "wow" factor that really sparks the interest of the provider of finance.

s t o p a n d **t h i n k**

Innocent Drinks (www.innocentdrinks.co.uk) is a relatively young firm. Visit its website, and suggest what is the business's "wow" factor.

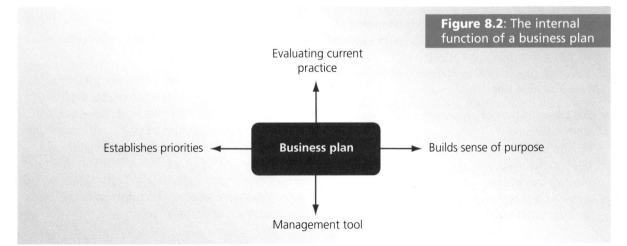

Figure 8.2: The internal function of a business plan

Evaluating current practice

Establishes priorities

Business plan

Builds sense of purpose

Management tool

The internal function

The business plan gives direction to the business. For any business, particularly a new one, it is very easy to be pulled in many different directions. A good business plan ensures that the business builds and maintains a clear sense of direction and has a clarity of purpose.

The business plan will help to establish priorities, as it is not possible to do everything at once. This will help the business to decide which activities to focus on and which activities to leave until later. If everybody in a business is included in the business planning process, the final business plan can also help to bring the whole business together in order to achieve a common goal.

For an existing business, a business plan can be a good way of evaluating where a business is, what it does well and what could be improved upon. It is a powerful management tool that, combined with budgets and forecasts, can help keep control of the business.

How is this unit assessed?

To pass this unit, you have to research, prepare and write a business plan. You need to select a business proposal which can form the basis of this plan. This could be:

■ a proposal to start a business

■ a proposal to develop an existing business, say by launching a new product

■ a proposal to submit to a local authority or to the National Lottery to develop a community project.

Your portfolio will be assessed using four criteria called assessment objectives (AO).

■ **AO1 Knowledge, skills and understanding**
For this assessment objective, you need to explain your business proposal – its activities, its aims and objectives, the form of ownership and the key personnel required.

■ **AO2 Application of knowledge skills and understanding**
For this assessment objective, you need to develop the marketing, operations and financial plans of the business proposal, explaining how these achieve the aims and objectives of the business proposal.

■ **AO3 Research and analysis**
For this assessment objective, you should analyse the key research findings to be used in your marketing, operations and financial plans in order to quantify and develop an integrated business plan.

■ **AO4 Evaluation**
For this assessment objective, you need to evaluate the viability of the business plan in order to support a case for funds. This will be based on an assessment of relevant financial ratios, payback period, what-if analysis and contingency plans.

Choosing a suitable business proposal

The choice you make for the business proposal that you are going to plan is very important in helping you to achieve a high grade. You should start now by selecting the business proposal around which you will base your business plan. There are several questions to consider.

Has the proposal got "legs"?

Obviously, by developing your business plan, you will be deciding if your business proposal is viable. But there is a dilemma here. If the business proposal is not viable, why are you planning to start it? Before you finalise your choice for your business plan, you need to be sure that it will have a good chance of being a success, so this needs to be considered before you put in all your hard work.

You need to draw up a shortlist of ideas and ask yourself (and other people) "will it work?" – just because you think something would be a brilliant choice does not mean everybody else will.

Will it allow you to get good marks?

You should aim for the top, and try to achieve full marks for each assessment objective. This means aiming for mark band 4.

Mark band 4 for assessment objective 2 asks for "a business plan which contains comprehensive marketing, operations and financial plans" and "an in-depth explanation of how these could achieve the aims and objectives of the business proposal". Consider two different businesses that you could start up: a window cleaning round and takeaway sandwich shop. Which would allow you to access all the marks for assessment objective 2?

The window cleaning round does not really fit the bill here. What could you actually write about? The only physical resources it requires would be a ladder, bucket and sponge. On the other hand, a takeaway sandwich shop allows you to consider so much more. For example, you need to consider premises (are you going to rent or buy?), equipment such as cookers and fridge (are you going to lease or buy these?), and, possibly, a delivery van.

Your proposal needs to be sufficiently "rich" to allow you to demonstrate the planning that could get you good marks. Your teacher will be able to advise you here.

Is the proposal something that you could do?

When you are considering a possible business proposal, do you have an idea what is involved, and would it be something that you could do now or in the future? If you consider the takeaway sandwich shop, you probably have a good idea of what will be required, and you probably think that with some financial backing and training you could operate this type of business. On the other hand, setting up a haulage firm importing and exporting to Eastern European countries, for example, might not be something that you can readily understand or expect to be able to operate.

Does the proposal interest you?

If the business proposal interests you – and you think that you might want to do something similar in the future – you are likely to enjoy what you are doing. There is a health warning to be considered here: because it interests you, it does not mean that your idea interests everybody else. Is there a market for your proposal? You need to test your idea against the other questions listed here.

Does it need funding?

Your proposal must be big enough to require funding. This is very important in allowing you to access good marks, particularly for assessment objective 4 that asks you to "evaluate the viability of the business plan in order to support a case for funds". Funding does not necessarily need to be from a bank, but it does require you making a case to some external source of business finance.

Once you have decided on your business proposal, you should work through each section of this unit, building up the appendix and then completing the relevant sections of the business plan.

Preparing a business plan

It takes time, and much research, to write a business plan. The final business plan should be concise, and structured under several different but related headings. It should include:

- an explanation of the business – the aims and objectives of the business, the owners, the type of business ownership, where the business is located

- a marketing plan that covers market research, customers and competition, the marketing mix and sales forecasts

- an operations plan, including both physical and human resources

- a financial plan, including budgets and forecasts

- an evaluation of the business idea, including viability and risk assessment.

You should present your plan in two sections, the actual business plan and a set of appendices that you will use to support the business plan.

The business plan should be short; you should focus on what the potential funder wants to know. In practice, a funder does not have time to read through all the details. If you are worried about the business plan being short, remember that it is harder to write a short focused piece of work than a long rambling piece of work. Make your business plan look professional. Put a front cover on it, give it a title and include a contents page. The appendix can be longer, but do not include research that you do not use or irrelevant diagrams and charts.

You might like to use this suggested structure for your plan, but note that the final order suggested is not the order that you would work through the proposal.

The main business plan

- **Executive summary**
  This should outline the business proposal. This section will be the last section to be written as you are summarising the whole plan. This summary should cover your product (its advantages, your niche in the market), aims and objectives (make them SMART), your management team, key financial projections, funding requirements.

- **The business**
  This should provide background information. It should include the location, ownership structure and key personnel of the business. If it is an existing business developing a new product, mention the track record of the business.

■ **Market research**

This should include the findings of your market research. It needs to be focused; you should take the opportunity of including key information represented in tables, diagrams or charts.

■ **Marketing planning**

This should be an overview of your marketing plan with a rationale. It will include information on customers and competitors, the marketing mix and sales forecasts.

■ **Operations plan**

In this section, present your rationale for your operations plan. It is important to make an evaluation as to why you have arranged operations the way you have. Make sure you include a financial summary of the operations plan. The plan will include an overview of both the physical and human resources required for the business.

■ **Financial planning**

In this section, you should use key information and diagrams from the financial planning section from the appendices. Remember, you need to make this section persuasive to a potential lender.

■ **Evaluating the business plan**

You need to evaluate your business plan. You have a choice to make here. If you choose to embed the evaluation throughout the business plan this section will be quite short, really just a summary. If you have not embedded the evaluation, then this section will require a longer, more detailed rationale.

The appendices

■ **Personnel**

CVs of the management team and the key personnel involved in the project.

■ **Location**

Details of the location of the business. Include a map.

■ **Ownership**

Information on how you decided on a type of ownership. This should not be a list af advantages and disadvantages of each type of business ownership: this would be irrelevant information. The research could consider what types of ownership are common to the type of business that your proposal is about; this would narrow down the options. Decide criteria for the final choice, and then give reasons for the choice.

■ **Market research**

This should set out the information that you have collected and selected. It should include your primary and secondary research, with reasons why you chose the particular research types. Include tables, diagrams and charts. Focus on the relevant findings you have discovered and assess their value to your business. Avoid including multiple copies of questionnaires and tables, diagrams or charts that do nothing to enhance your research. For example, just because spreadsheet packages can generate graphs, does not mean you have to overuse this facility.

■ **Marketing planning**

This section builds on your market research, and it is possible that the two sections will merge. Include details of customers and competitors. Show the research that you use to identify the marketing mix for your business proposal. You should consider and weigh up alternative combinations of the 4Ps. Detailed workings for the sales forecast need to be included. Explain your assumptions and estimates.

■ **Operations planning**

Set out your research on physical and human resource requirements. All resources need to be costed. Research into physical resources needs to cover premises, equipment, vehicles, office equipment and stock. If relevant, you will need to explain your stock control methods. Describe how the business will be operating and how it will guarantee the quality of your product. Include all relevant legislation. Set out the staffing requirements, including any training needs (and how this will be delivered).

■ **Financial planning**

These could include start-up budget, running costs, cash flow forecast, breakeven analysis, contribution, projected profit and loss account, and projected balance sheet. This information is likely to be detailed, but you may have to estimate some figures. You might also include a what-if analysis with cash flow forecasts.

■ **Evaluating the business plan**

In this section you should select relevant techniques to evaluate the business plan. These techniques include ratio analysis, payback, what-if analysis, risk assessment and contingency planning, SWOT and PEST analysis. You should be using these techniques to meet assessment objective 4 "evaluate the viability of the business plan in order to support a case for funds".

Explaining the business

Setting the scene: an Innocent business

Take a fledgling idea for a company, run by three young friends, with no sector experience, no financial backing and no clear leader. Sound like a sound investment?

Perhaps unsurprisingly, the venture capitalists approached by the founding members of Innocent smoothies weren't that keen either. "We broke every rule in the investment manager's handbook," says Richard Reed, one of the founders.

Launched in 1999 by three Cambridge graduates, the smoothies were a relatively new concept. Perishable, with a very short shelf life, and at almost £2 a bottle, the odds seemed stacked against them.

Innocent's founders were also determined to run a very different kind of company, one where "the image and the product are the same", with aspirations of spending company profits on sponsoring cycle lanes in London rather than on high art.

Four years and over £10 million worth of squashed fruit sales later, critics could be reviewing their scepticism.

Source: BBC News website, 9 July 2003

Aims and objectives

Innocent has continued to grow since the BBC report in 2003 (see introduction). By 2005, it had around 60 employees and a turnover of £16.7 million. The success of Innocent drinks has been based on the determination of its owners. They have a very clear aim of what the business wants to do, where it wants to be in the future and how it wants to get there. The owners of Innocent drinks want to grow a profitable business making fruit smoothies with fresh and natural ingredients. They want to run the business in a socially responsible way, treating their staff and customers ethically, and making charitable donations.

All successful businesses need to have an aim. This is the primary goal, something to work towards and keep the business "on track". Potential lenders will expect to see a statement of the business's aims before considering lending money to a business. It is not enough for a business just to have aims, it also needs objectives to give the business targets that will help it achieve its aims. Setting objectives:

- allows the business to plan

- sets targets

- motivates staff and employees

- provides a means to measure success.

For objectives to be really effective they need to be SMART (specific, measurable, achievable, relevant and time-specific) objectives.

Specific – objectives need to be precise about what the business is going to achieve. For example, a business might want to achieve a particular percentage share of the market.

Measurable – objectives need to be quantifiable or expressed in such a way that managers can assess whether they have been achieved. For example, Innocent drinks could have set a target of £10 million worth of sales

Achievable – objectives need to be practica, there is little point in setting an objective that the business could not reasonably achieve. Trying to do too much can result in not achieving anything. The objectives must reflect the resources (physical, human and financial) that the business has available.

Relevant – objectives should help to achieve the wider aims and goals of the organisation.

Time-specific (sometimes called time-bound or timely) – objectives should have a timescale, a date by when the objective should have been achieved. For example, Innocent drinks could have set an objective to obtain a 30 per cent share of the smoothies market by 2007.

Aims and objectives are an opportunity to explain what the business is about, and they should appear at the beginning of the business plan. It is important that these aims and objectives are finalised and agreed before the remainder of the business plan is written.

stop and think

Bully Free Zone is a charity based in Bolton that tries to tackle issues surrounding bullying. Visit its website (www.bullyfreezone.co.uk). What are the aims and objectives of the organisation? Try and formulate its objectives using SMART techniques.

Bully Free Zone, launched in 1996, has become one of the leading peer support projects in Britain. The project aims to raise awareness of alternative ways of resolving conflict and reducing bullying.

Bully Free Zone is a registered charity (number 1076258). Website designed by Ichameleon.

Business ownership

There are several ways in which a business can be set up. The most appropriate type of ownership depends on factors such as:

- do the business owners require limited or unlimited liability

- is the business a profit or not-for-profit enterprise

- is ownership to be restricted to the people who started the business

- are shares in the business to be offered in return for capital investment?

Unlimited liability

In a business that has unlimited liability, the owners have full responsibility for the contracts entered into by the business, and are fully liable for the debts of a business. This means that if the business gets into debt, the owners are responsible (jointly and severally) for the debts and will need to meet this liability from their own money. They can be required to sell their possessions, including their homes, to raise money to pay the debts. If the business is found negligent in its business dealings, then the owners are fully responsible and can be fined or imprisoned.

Why would anybody choose to set up an unlimited liability business? One reason is that it is much easier to start this kind of business, and there are fewer costs involved in administering the business. Although unlimited liability seems potentially quite serious for the owners, providing that the business trades within the law, takes appropriate public liability and professional indemnity insurance, and does not run up high levels of debt, liability is not an issue.

There are three main types of unlimited liability businesses: sole traders, partnerships and unincorporated associations.

Sole traders

A sole trader business has one owner, although there can be any number of employees. The main advantage of being a sole trader is that it is the easiest and cheapest type of business to set up. The owner has full control, and keeps all the profits. The business does not have to publish information about itself that could be used by competitors. It is a suitable type of ownership for an individual starting a business that sets out to make a profit. The main disadvantage of a sole trader is that the owner has unlimited liability.

Partnerships

Partnerships have at least two owners who set up a business jointly with a view to making a profit. Most partnerships normally have no more than 20 partners, although some professional partnerships such as firms of accountants can have more.

A partnership requires a deed of partnership. This is an agreement between the partners that sets out how much capital each partner will put into the business and how the profits and losses will be shared. It will also cover issues such as bringing in new partners to the business, and how and in what circumstances the partnership will be dissolved.

Entering into a partnership allows more people to contribute to the capital of the business. Partners can bring different skills to the business, and they help to spread the risk. Like sole traders, partnerships are relatively cheap and easy to set up.

The disadvantages of partnerships include the fact that the partners have unlimited liability. Profits need to be shared between partners. There is a possibility of disputes between partners, particularly over money, that might cause the business to suffer or to close.

Unincorporated associations

Unincorporated associations are similar to partnerships, but this type of ownership is more suitable for not-for-profit organisations or businesses with charitable aims. Unincorporated associations are joint ventures or projects set up by two or more people. A constitution will be drawn up which sets out the aims of the association and how it will operate. It provides for a framework to allow the organisation to be run by a committee on behalf of its members. An unincorporated association is cheap and easy to set up, but like sole traders and partnerships has the disadvantage of unlimited liability.

Limited liability

In a limited liability business (called a limited company), the owner's liability is restricted to the amount of capital they have invested in the business. For example, if someone invests £1000 in a business, the most that they could lose is £1000. Limited liability obviously looks to be more attractive than unlimited liability; however, there is a financial and administrative cost associated with setting up and running a limited liability company.

In a limited liability company, the owners of the business are called shareholders, as they buy shares in the business. Their liability is limited to the amount of money they have paid for their shares. The shareholders elect a board of directors to run the business on their behalf.

There are three main types of limited liability companies: private limited companies, public limited companies and companies limited by guarantee.

Private limited companies

This type of business is the most common type of company. Shares cannot be sold to the general public, so this potentially restricts the amount of capital that can be raised. But this form of ownership does have some advantages over public limited companies.

- It is easier and cheaper to set up than a public limited company.

- It is less vulnerable to takeover as it requires the agreement of the shareholders before shares can be sold.

Public limited companies

The shares of public limited companies are freely traded – usually on the London Stock Exchange – and can be bought by the general public. Public liability companies have access to large amounts of capital, which is the main reason why private limited companies become public limited companies. It is why the largest types of business tend to adopt this form of company. It is also easier for public limited companies to raise money from banks and other lenders.

There are disadvantages to becoming a public limited company. First, it is expensive to become a public limited company, so it may be better to consider alternative sources of finance. Second, public limited companies face the threat of takeover. As the shares are available for anyone to buy, it is possible that the original shareholders can lose control of the business. Third, public limited companies have to disclose more information than private limited companies. This information could be of use to competitors and possible takeover bidders.

Companies limited by guarantee

A company limited by guarantee is special type of private limited company that is commonly set up by not-for-profit organisations and charities. A guarantee company does not sell shares but has members who are guarantors rather than shareholders. Liability takes the form of a guarantee from members to pay a nominal sum in the event of the business being wound up (this can be as little as £1).

A company limited by guarantee is a useful structure for not-for-profit organisations that want to have the benefits of limited liability. The organisation will want to enter into contracts – when employing staff, buying premises or contracting to deliver a service – so its members and trustees, who are likely to be involved on a voluntary basis, need some financial protection.

In a company limited by guarantee, profits are not distributed to members but are retained in order to be used for the future activities of the organisation.

Ownership and objectives

All businesses, regardless of whether they are profit-making or not-for-profit, have survival as an objective. However, other objectives of businesses will vary, but some objectives are likely to be related to the type of ownership adopted by the business.

Sole traders, partnerships, private and public limited companies all aim to make a profit, so they will have objectives such as profit maximisation – they try and make as much profit as possible. They may also aim to achieve sales growth as a way to ensure survival. Private limited companies and public companies are focused on profit maximisation, as their shareholders are likely to demand high returns on their investment.

Sole traders and partnerships sometimes do not pursue profit maximisation as an objective, but profit "satisficing" instead. This means they merely work to obtain the minimum amount of profit that serves their needs. As owners they may enjoy working for themselves, and providing they are happy with the profits they are making, they do not want to work longer hours just to drive up profits further.

Social enterprises will have a profit motive, but the profits will be kept within the business to invest in local communities and worthy causes. Similarly, not-for-profit organisations and charities will have aims and objectives based on the reasons they started.

Increasingly, all types of businesses are adopting ethical and socially responsible objectives. In other words, businesses try to ensure that their operations don't harm the environment or local communities.

Management

Potential funders are going to want to know about the people involved in the business that they are going to fund – not just the owners but also the key personnel. They want to be reassured that those involved in setting up and running the business have the necessary skills and qualities to make a success of the venture and, of course, to protect their investment. Business plans should therefore have a

section explaining how the business will be managed. The could be illustrated in several ways including

- a chart showing the business's management structure

- pen portraits of the management team, giving brief details of their past business experience

- CVs of all managers – these would probably be included in an appendix

- job descriptions of employees (current posts and posts that the business expects to create) including qualifications sought – again in an appendix.

Location

For many businesses its location is vital, as it needs to have access to suppliers and to sufficient numbers of customers. Funders will be very interested to know where a retail business is located, and to see whether the area is likely to attract the right level of custom. For other businesses, location is less important – e-commerce businesses, for example, do not need to be located close to their customers.

stopandthink

Have any shops closed recently near to where you live? Could the problem have been location? Is there enough passing trade and parking? Find out the reasons for any closures.

Why doesn't IKEA, the Swedish furniture superstore, open more large stores in the UK?

assessmentpractice
Starting your business plan

You should have already chosen your business idea – now is the time to make a start on your business plan. For your chosen business activity, open a word processing document and put headings for:

- aims and objectives

- type of ownership (sole trader, partnership, etc.)

- owners and management

- location.

You can start to add content to the headings after reading through this topic, but remember you will not finalise the "explaining the business" section of

your business plan until you have completed the research required in each topic.

You should also start a series of appendices that you will submit with your business plan. These will help to justify decisions that you make, but do not include anything in the appendices that you do not use or refer to in the business plan.

Market research

Setting the scene: Enjoying the curry mile

Home to every variety of curry dish known to man, Rusholme's "curry mile" is nothing less than poppadam paradise.

With more Asian food outlets than anywhere else in the UK, and the highest concentration of Eastern eating establishments in Europe, this bright and bustling part of Manchester is among the city's most popular attractions. Over 50 restaurants, takeaways and sweet houses compete to offer the delicacies of Bangladesh, Pakistan, India and Iran.

Manchester's student population and locals provide a loyal fanbase for Rusholme, while coach-loads of curry-lovers arrive from all over the country. It is estimated that around 65,000 diners a week visit Rusholme to enjoy this unique eastern experience.

Every taste and wallet is catered for here. Cheap and cheerful takeaways provide dishes for those on a strict budget. All-you-can-eat buffet restaurants allow diners to experiment, while lavish marble and gilt curry palaces cater for the more discerning and extravagant.

The competition for business in Rusholme ensures choice, keen prices and award-winning quality wherever you choose to eat. Many restaurants have bring-your-own alcohol policies, and vegetarians are amply catered for.

Whether you've an appetite for the curry or the culture, Rusholme is unrivalled for ambience and cuisine. To get your own taste of the action, just head for the golden glow.

Source: adapted from the Manchester Evening News

Why undertake market research?

Market research is the first test of the likely success of a business. Will anybody want to buy the goods and services that the business provides? It is vital that the owners of a business know this, so that they don't waste money on a venture that is not going to work. The business will also need to be able to convince potential lenders of money that there will be sufficient customers for the business to succeed and repay the investment.

Market research is a structured approach to gauging likely business success. It should support the business plan. It needs to ask the right questions with the aim of identifying:

- how big is the market for the product a business is planning to offer – for example, are there already too many restaurants on Manchester's "curry mile"

- how big a share of this market can the business capture – for example, how many customers will be attracted to this new restaurant

KEY TERMS

Primary market research is the gathering of information directly from customers or competitors within the target market.

Secondary market research is the gathering of information about customers and competitors from already published data such as government statistics.

- what is the value of that market share – will this share of the market be enough to make the required profit?

stop and think

Would the information in the article in the *Manchester Evening News* (see introduction) make it more or less likely that a prospective restaurant owner would want to open a new restaurant on the "curry mile" offering Asian cuisine?

Market research focuses on two groups: customers and competitors. A business will need specific information about its potential customers.

- Who are the target customers – is it a specific group, such as students, or is it everybody?

- How much money does the target group have to spend?

- What does the target group want from the product the business plans to offer?

A business will need to know the level of competition that it will face.

- How many other businesses are offering the same or similar products, and where do they operate?

- What prices are these competitors charging – will a strategy of undercutting these prices get a foothold in the market?

- Is there a gap in the market that does not appear to be met by other businesses?

stop and think

If you were considering opening a new restaurant on the "curry mile", how would you identify your customers and competitors?

Types of market research

A business can either carry out its own market research or it can use a specialist market research company to undertake research on its behalf. In each case, it needs to decide on an approach, and there are two types of market research that can be conducted, primary research and secondary research.

Primary market research

Primary market research involves gathering information directly from customers and competitors. Primary research is sometimes called field research, and it can be undertaken in a number of ways.

Surveys

An obvious way to find out about customers is to ask them directly about their needs, opinions and tastes. This can be done either face-to-face, by telephone or by post using a questionnaire. Increasingly, businesses are asking customers to complete surveys online through their websites. Depending on how many consumers are surveyed, this can be a cheap and relatively quick method of market research.

Observation

Observation can be either a quite simple or very complicated method of market research. At it simplest, it could involve recording how many people pass by the spot that a business is considering locating in, or counting how many people an hour enter a competitors' premises. On a more complex level, supermarkets analyse video recordings to observe customer behaviour.

Consumer panels

A consumer panel, or focus group, involves inviting people from the target customer group to a meeting and asking them for their opinions on the products a business provides (or is planning to offer). A fee is usually paid to anyone attending these consumer panels as an incentive to take part. Consumer panels can provide in-depth market information.

Test marketing

Test marketing is an expensive form of market research. It involves "testing" a new product on part of the target market. This could be in one part of the country by, for example, advertising the product on regional television. The results of this test marketing will determine if the product should be launched to the national market. If a business decides not to go ahead, it will have potentially wasted the investment in the product development as well as the cost of the test marketing exercise.

Competitor scans

A competitor scan has elements of observation. It involves visiting a competitor's premises as a customer, observing the popularity of the business, and collecting useful background information such as price lists.

Secondary market research

Secondary market research is sometimes called desk research, because it involves gathering intelligence from existing published information sources rather than obtaining new information through field research. Useful market information can be found in libraries, and increasingly is available on the internet. Some data is free, other information sources may have to be purchased.

Government statistics

Government departments collect and produce many statistics. These can be used by businesses, social enterprises and not-for-profit organisations. Key publications include *Regional Trends* and *Social Trends*. Most data produced by the government can be accessed free of charge from National Statistics Online (www.statistics.gov.uk).

Commercial research reports

There are several companies that specialise in producing market information, such as Mintel, Key Note and Dun and Bradstreet. Many reports focus on specific industries or market sectors, and report on market size, the market share held by leading business, market trends, etc. These research reports are expensive, but some can be found at larger public libraries and university libraries.

Newspaper articles

The broadsheet newspapers regularly report on business and consumer issues, and are a useful source of market information. Many reports can be accessed free from their websites (though some content requires a subscription). The most useful sources are the *Financial Times, The Times, The Guardian, Daily Telegraph* and *The Independent*.

Trade associations

Many industries and retail sectors have trade associations that publish market information and occasionally undertake market surveys. Some information is only available to members of the respective associations, some is available on trade association websites.

---

stopandthink

You will need to market research your business idea. Identify three examples of primary market research that it would be useful to undertake to research your idea.

Visit the government's statistics website (www.statistics.gov.uk), and identify three items of market information about your chosen business.

Planning market research

Market research helps the business planning process by providing the evidence (and the confidence) that there is a large enough market for the business to be a success. It can convince groups external to the proposed business that the business is worth backing. To do this, market research has to be very carefully planned.

Whatever the type of market research that is being conducted, it must be clear at the outset what the research is trying to achieve. For example, if a questionnaire is being devised to find out about customers, it would be useful to apply the five Ws: who, what, when, where and why.

- Who are the customers? The questionnaire needs to collect information about target customers, such as age range, sex and income.

- What do they buy, and how much do they buy?

- When do they buy? For example, is the product seasonal or is it bought at a particular time of the day?

- Where will they buy? This will help decide the location of the business.

- Why will they buy the product? What is it about a product that will make the customer buy from a particular business?

Care needs to be taken in designing the questionnaire to ensure that the questions provide accurate and helpful answers. It is worth testing the questions on a small sample first to see what works and what doesn't, and then producing a final version.

Care also needs to be taken that the right people are surveyed. Often people starting new businesses include all their friends and family in the survey. This group is likely to give the answers the researcher wants to hear. It is not an unbiased sample.

Analysing market research

Once the market research information has been collected, information has to be selected and analysed. The first stage in analysing data is to group the information into a usable format. This will mean focusing on grouping together respondents by key characteristics using sensible categories. For example, you might produce separate tables for different groups of customers, arranged say by age, occupation and income.

Once market research information has been grouped, it needs to be presented so that judgements on the likely success of the business can be made. The presentation can also be used to persuade potential investors that the business is viable.

There are several ways market research information can be presented. It is important that the right type of presentation is used and that only relevant information is used. The main types of presentation are tables, diagrams, graphs and charts. These types of presentation are used to show relationships, comparisons and changes. Figure 8.3 sets out the advantages and disadvantages of different types of presentation.

stop and think

If you have conducted a survey using a questionnaire on potential customers in the "curry mile", how might you group students into categories for analysis?

Figure 8.3: Ways of presenting data

Presentation	Advantages	Disadvantages	Frequent mistakes
Table	Good when a number of different results need to be displayed alongside each other. Shows detail.	Not visually appealing, not directed to key information.	Poor labelling of rows and columns.
Diagram	Shows key relationships, ideas, facts, plans, concepts, processes and sequences.	Can become too complex and confusing. Not good for displaying different results together.	Easy to get carried away and over-elaborate.
Graphs and charts	A pie chart is good for dividing a whole into component parts, showing proportions. Bar graphs helps to show relationships between two or more things. Line graphs are a good way to show trends.	Easy to make mistakes when comparing values, particularly for small segments. Limits to the number of different results that can be displayed alongside each other. Limits to the number of trends that can be displayed on one chart.	Programs such as Microsoft Excel have charting functions, but it is very easy to get carried away with the variety of styles available. There is also the temptation to draw a chart for everything.

assessment practice
A market research plan

You should set out an explanation of what your business is about. The next heading in your business plan should be market research. This will be completed when you have undertaken your market research.

In order to complete the market research section of your business plan, you will need to construct a market research plan. You can use the appendix to show the details of your market research. You need to set out

- what type of primary research you are going to use, and justify your choice

- details of your primary research

- details of your secondary research.

You may include a copy of any questionnaire that you use in undertaking primary research. There should be an explanation of why you have chosen to ask the questions in your survey.

Once you have completed your market research, you will need to include your findings. You will need to consider how you want to present this market research information. Consider whether to use tables, diagrams, charts, or a combination of all three, to complement your written findings.

Market planning

A marketing plan is that part of a business plan that outlines the market and the marketing strategy for a product. It includes information on the product, pricing, target market, competitors, marketing budget and promotional mix. Like the overall business plan, the marketing plan needs to be constructed with aims and objectives.

It needs to be designed to devise strategies that attract customers to the business. To do this, a business needs to determine the level of competition for the product and to identify how it might establish a competitive advantage.

The marketing plan will identify the correct marketing mix for the product: the mix of price, product, promotion and place. Based on customer and competitor behaviour, and the chosen marketing mix, the plan should contain a quantified sales forecast.

The purpose of planning is to "plan to succeed", and a business needs to understand exactly what it wants to achieve. This will determine the objectives of the marketing plan. The objectives should be SMART objectives (specific, measurable, achievable, relevant and time-specific). Objectives for a marketing plan could include

- to capture 10 per cent of the market in the first year of trading
- to ensure that prices are 5 per cent lower than competitors
- to ensure that 90 per cent of customers return to buy within two months of their first purchase.

Once the objectives have been determined, strategies can be decided on. These are the bigger ideas that will help achieve the business objectives. These bigger ideas will be broken down into individual actions or tactics that will be used to achieve objectives.

Components of the marketing plan

The marketing plan should be organised under a number of headings. This will help to clarify your thinking and structure your proposals.

KEY TERMS

Market segmentation is the division of potential buyers into groups with similar characteristics.

The **marketing mix** is the 4Ps – product, price, promotion and place – used by businesses to influence customers' buying decisions.

Customers

The marketing plan should identify the target customers – who they are and why they would be prepared to buy the product. It must also identify the projected number of customers and their buying behaviour. It is usually helpful to group information about customers. This grouping is called market segmentation. Customers can be segmented into many categories. Here are some typical ways of segmenting populations.

Age

The demand for some goods or services may be linked to age, so it may be necessary to identify different age ranges for some markets. For example, city centre bars will have a younger clientele than a country pub.

Sex

Businesses can target their products for either both sexes or one sex only. In any city centre, there are clothes shops that cater for both men and women, such as Marks & Spencer and Next, and those that cater for one sex, such as Dorothy Perkins that sells to women and girls.

Socioeconomic factors

Social class and income can segment markets. An individual's occupation is an indicator of social class, as is education. Social class is likely to be related to income, and it is obviously important to know how much a customer has to spend.

Lifestyle

Segmentation by lifestyle involves analysing individual patterns of behaviour and spending. Lifestyle will include the activities, interests and opinions of customers.

Not all businesses sell to the general public – many operate in business to business markets (B2B); their customers are other businesses. These businesses could be segmented by:

- product
- turnover
- size
- location.

Competitors

The marketing plan should include an assessment of the competition. This should set out to answer:

- who they are
- how many businesses are in the market
- what products do they offer
- what their prices are
- where they are based
- what their strengths and weaknesses are
- howthey promote their products
- what their market share is.

Marketing mix

Once a business understands its market through segmentation and competitor analysis, it can target customers where it has an advantage over the competition. If this group of customers is large enough and has enough spending power, then the marketing plan can target this group.

The marketing mix is a combination of activities that are under the control of a business. Because they are under the control of the business, they can be altered to meet the marketing objectives of the business. This mix is known as the 4Ps.

Product

Obviously a business has control over the goods and services it offers. This also includes additional services offered to the customer, such as installation of the product, after-sales support, maintenance contracts and computer software upgrades.

Price

A key question is to determine the price of products. Set the price too low, and the profit margins will be low, but setting it too high could deter customers from buying. Research will need to consider how sensitive the market is to price changes, and the relationship between the business's profit margins and its volume of sales. Determining the price involves considering the three Cs:

- cost – prices need to at least cover the cost of producing the product
- competition – the price charged by the competition
- customers – the price customers are willing to pay.

Promotion

It doesn't matter how good the product is if nobody knows about its availability. Promotion is a mix of marketing activities required to attract the right type of customers in sufficient numbers and at the right time to make the business a success.

There are several elements to the promotional mix. These include advertising, sales promotions, merchandising and public relations.

A business can pay for advertising in newspapers, on television and radio, and on the internet in order to communicate with existing and potential customers. Advertising can be informative, increasing consumer awareness, or persuasive, by seeking to convince consumers that its product is better than the competition. It is, however, often expensive.

Sales promotion is a form of financial incentive to customers to encourage them to buy a business's products. It includes money-off offers such as "buy one, get one free", competitions and loyalty cards.

Merchandising is a tactic in retailing. Shops are encouraged to locate a business's products in advantageous locations, such as near a cash till. Businesses offer shops incentives to display their products favourably, and will supply in-store display stands and product-branded chiller or freezer compartments.

Public relations can be used to portray the business in a favourable light by good publicity. The aim is to get customers to view the business positively. Some examples of public relations involve charitable donations, sponsoring sporting and cultural activities, and school visits. Businesses of all sizes can engage in this type of promotion. A small business might sponsor a local amateur football team through shirt sponsorship, large companies might sponsor Premiership football teams.

Place

Customers need to be able to find the products of a business. Place will depend on whether the product has to be sold from a fixed physical location or if it can be sold by mail order or through the internet. It will depend on the target customers – are they local or will they be national or even international?

How a business chooses to "place" its products will depend on the nature of the particular goods and services it offers, and the size (or scale) of the business. A large business, such Kellogg's, has to place its products into every town and city in the UK through a distribution network. A local hairdressing business will just have its shop.

Sales forecasting

Marketing planning must include a sales forecast. So many factors depend on having an accurate sales forecast. A sales forecast will determine how much the business needs to produce or supply. This has consequences for critical decisions on:

- the number of workers to employ
- the fixed assets required, like buildings, machinery, and fixtures and fittings
- the levels of stock and working capital that need to be maintained
- the amount of money that needs to be borrowed.

Marketing research will be needed to provide the information required to underpin a sales forecast. Once the information has been obtained, it needs to be turned into a forecast.

Suppose that you have decided to open a hairdressing business for women. From the marketing mix that has been produced, you know what price you are going

to charge for each hair styling, where you are locating the business, and the type of customer that you are targeting. You will also know how often these customers tend to go to the hairdressers. You need to be able to quantify the market and find the actual numbers of customers that could visit your salon. This will be an estimate – it is safer to underestimate the numbers at this stage.

Next, you need to identify how many other hairdressers there are in the area offering the type of service you are opening. This should be a precise figure. You now need to estimate how much your market share will be; again, it is better to underestimate rather than be too optimistic.

Let's put some numbers in to see how the forecast might be constructed. Use these figures.

- There are 6000 women in the target group each visiting a hairdressers eight times per year.
- There are currently four hairdressers that provide the same type of service you intend to provide.
- You expect that you will capture only 10 per cent of the market in the first year – even though you intend to charge lower prices than your competitors, you expect many customers to stay loyal to their existing hairdresser.
- The average price you will charge will be £25.

Figure 8.4: Sales budget for the first six months of operating

	Jan	Feb	Mar	Apr	May	June
Sales value (£)	10,000	10,000	10,000	10,000	10,000	10,000
Sales (units)	400	400	400	400	400	400

Now you can begin to produce a sales forecast. First calculate the total market. There are 6000 customers visiting hairdressers eight times a year. So the total annual market is 48,000 (6000 x 8).

You expect a 10 per cent share of this market, so you would expect 4,800 customers a year (48,000 x 0.1 = 4,800). To get a monthly forecast, divide this number by 12, so that will be 400 customers a month. And now calculate your monthly revenue: with 400 customers paying £25, that brings in £10,000 a month. This forecast would be the basis of a sales budget or target for the next year or next period. It could be set out in a table, as Figure 8.4.

It is now important to refine the forecast. It is not likely that you would capture the 10 per cent share of the market as soon as the salon opens. Again, you will need to make a reasonable estimate (based on research). Suppose you estimated that, in the first two months, sales would be 25 per cent below the 10 per cent market share, and in the following three months 20 per cent below your expectation of a 10 per cent market share, before reaching this estimated market share in June. Figure 8.5 shows the revised forecast. Note that you might even be sophisticated, and adjust the forecast for seasonal factors (again based on research).

Figure 8.5: Revised sales budget for the first six months of operating adjusted for start-up

	Jan	Feb	Mar	Apr	May	June
Sales value (£)	7,500	7,500	8,000	8,000	8,000	10,000
Sales (units)	300	300	320	320	320	400

assessment practice
Marketing plan

You now need to have a heading for marketing planning in your business plan and in the appendix.

You should include your research into your customers and competitors. It is likely that there will be detailed primary and secondary research on both customers and competitors. The appendix should also show the research that you use to identify the marketing mix for your business idea. For each of the 4Ps, you need to consider alternatives before you decide on the final mix. So the research should be used to assess the advantages and disadvantages of different options, and your plan should describe how you have weighed up alternatives.

Include detailed workings for the sales forecast in the appendix. You will have to make estimates here. Make sure you do not overestimate sales but try to be realistic. Remember to include any assumptions you have made.

In the business plan, you should present your findings with a rationale for your marketing mix.

Operations planning

Setting the scene: Pret a Manger

Pret opened in London in 1986. College friends, Sinclair and Julian, made proper sandwiches using natural, preservative-free ingredients. There are 150 Pret shops at the moment, most in the UK. The company has a turnover of around £150 million.

Pret's founders admit that when they started out they had woefully little experience in the world of business. But they had a clear business vision: they wanted to create the sort of food they craved but couldn't find anywhere else. This is how they describe their business ideas on the Pret website.

★ PRET A MANGER ★

★ HOME ★ OUR FOOD ★ FIND A PRET ★ DELIVERIES ★ ABOUT OUR COMPANY ★ JOBS ★ CONTACT US ★

It is important our sandwiches and salads taste better than everybody else's. To achieve this, we build a beautiful sandwich kitchen in every Pret. We get vans every night to drop off our good natural ingredients. Our chefs get cracking early in the morning.

We don't like big food factories, depots and processing places. We make our stuff fresh (it's old-fashioned but works well). We'd rather offer our sandwiches to charity than keep them over to sell the next day. Because we make in-house and sell them the same day, you won't find "shelf life" dates and "display until" on our salads and sandwiches. We simply don't need to sell old food.

Because Pret is private we don't face the same pressure to grow that a public company does. We will develop slowly, one shop at a time. We would like to make 9 per cent profit, but haven't yet. One day we will.

Source: adapted from www.pret.com

Without superb operations planning, the business will never achieve its 9 per cent profit target. There are two resources to be planned: physical resources and human resources. This includes ensuring that fresh ingredients are delivered to 150 shops every working day and that unsold stock is kept to a minimum.

Staff will need to be employed in each shop. When each new shop is added, it will need to fitted out to the company's exacting standards and a "beautiful sandwich kitchen" installed.

Physical resources

Determining the physical resources for any business venture is a key task in operations planning – a very detailed list needs to be drawn up and costed. The exact list will vary from business to business, although there are likely to be common elements (or headings) in any business.

Premises

The most common physical resource, and probably the most expensive, is likely to be premises. This could be a shop, warehouse, office or factory, singly or in any combination. The key decision about premises is whether to buy or to rent. As Figure 8.6 shows, there are advantages and disadvantages to each choice.

Fixed costs are costs that do not vary with the level of output. Fixed costs are incurred even if a business is not producing goods or services.

Variable costs are costs that vary directly with output.

Fixed reorder stock level is a method of stock control based on buying stock to arrive before minimum levels of stock are reached.

Economic order level is the stock level that balances money tied up in stock with the costs of ordering stock.

Just-in-time (JIT) is a method of stock control in which the lowest possible levels of stock are maintained, and stock is only ordered to arrive just when it is needed.

Finding commercial premises can be achieved by internet searches, or by visiting a commercial estate agent. Information on mortgages can be found on the websites of banks.

Note that the business will incur additional premises costs regardless of whether the buildings are bought or rented. These costs include insurance, electricity, business rates, water rates, etc.

Equipment

The equipment and machinery needed by a business will vary from enterprise to enterprise. In addition to identifying its requirements, a business needs to decide whether to buy or lease the equipment. A lease can be used to finance the purchase of many fixed assets, including equipment. It is a contract in which the asset is rented by a business (lessee), for the duration of the lease period, when it is then given back to the lessor.

There are advantages to leasing – it spreads the cost of the equipment over a period of years, which helps with cash flow, and it allows a business to acquire assets without making a large initial cash outlay. The disadvantage to leasing is that the business does not own the asset at the end of the lease period, although it could be argued that this does not matter as there may be little value left in the asset at the end of this period. Leasing payments do not attract capital allowances that allows a business to reduce its tax bill.

Vehicles

Depending on the operational needs of the business, it may need cars, delivery vans or other vehicles. Vehicle costs have two components: fixed costs that will remain the same whether the vehicle is used or not, and variable cost which will vary with use. The fixed costs include:

■ lease payments, purchase price or loan repayments

■ vehicle insurance

■ road fund licence

■ MOT

■ annual service and maintenance

■ subscription to recovery organisation such as the AA and the RAC

Figure 8.6: Rent or buy?

	Advantages	Disadvantages
Buy	Business owns an asset that will rise in value	Responsible for maintenance
	Mortgage repayments likely to be cheaper than rent	Unlikely to get a 100 per cent mortgage, so a large deposit needed
	More control over budget because rent cannot be increased	Difficult to relocate if premises need to be sold
	Fixed rate mortgage will make budget-setting easier	
	Interest rates on a commercial mortgage are tax-deductible	
Rent	Landlord responsible for maintenance	Business does not own premises
	Rental deposit likely to be less than mortgage deposit	Rent likely to be more expensive than mortgage repayments
	Easier to relocate	Rent may increase

- garaging
- salary and training of drivers.

The variable costs include:

- fuel – petrol, diesel, etc.
- cleaning
- parking
- repairs.

Office costs

All businesses will require an office, however small, in order to run the business. These costs will need to be identified and estimated. The costs associated with running and equipping an office include:

- computers, including software, printers, toner and maintenance contract
- photocopiers – purchase or lease costs and maintenance contracts
- telephone system and internet connection
- desks and filing cabinets
- stationery including paper, envelopes, compliment slips, business cards
- first aid box, cash box and safe.

Stock

If the business involves manufacturing, buying or selling a product, then stock is a very important resource. There are many ways in which stock can be bought and managed. Any business needs to have good stock control procedures to ensure it is using its resources efficiently.

Buying stock

Stock has a significant impact on the cash flow position of a business. Stock is expensive, and while it is being held in the warehouse or shop premises of a business it is not generating revenue that could be used to pay bills and creditors.

Stock could be bought for "cash", which in effect means paying the supplier upfront before (or at the point of) delivery. However, the most common method of buying and selling between businesses is trade credit. With trade credit, a business sends a purchase order to a supplier to buy stock. The supplier sends the stock to the customer. An invoice is then sent to the customer who has 30 days in which to settle the invoice; this is known as the credit period. No interest is charged on trade credit.

One way of improving cash flow is to try and negotiate a longer period of trade credit from suppliers. Of course, while this benefits the business receiving the goods, it does not help the cash position of the supplier. If the business is selling on credit, then obviously waiting to receive payment is not helping its cash flow situation. One way to improve the cash flow in this situation is to offer a discount (usually 5 per cent) to customers if they pay promptly. This is known as a cash discount.

It can be difficult for new businesses to obtain trade credit, as they have not yet established a reputation for settling their bills.

Controlling stock

As stock is expensive to hold, it is important not to buy more than is needed. However, there must always be enough to satisfy the needs of customers. A manufacturing business needs to ensure that it has enough stock of raw materials to meet production requirements, but it also needs to control its stock of work-in-progress (production part-way through the production process) and finished goods. There are three main methods of stock control that can be used by a business, including fixed reorder stock level, economic order quantity and just-in-time production.

- **Fixed reorder stock level**
  A business decides the lowest or minimum stock level it needs to meet likely demand, and reorders before stocks reach this level. When it reorders will depend on how long it takes for new stock to be delivered (called lead time); this is called the reorder level. A maximum stock level also needs to be set so that the business can determine how much to reorder.

- **Economic order quantity**
  This method of stock control is based on striking a balance between holding the optimum level of stocks against the money tied up in stock, the space taken up by stock and the costs of ordering stock. A business may get a better deal if it orders more stock at the one time.

- **Just-in-time production**
  Stocks are kept as low as possible and new stocks of raw material are ordered when they are needed – hence the name just-in-time. This is obviously an ideal situation, but it requires close co-operation between the business and its suppliers. There may be additional costs involved to guarantee delivery just in time.

Human resources

People are essential to any business. An operation plan needs to identify the personnel requirements of a business. It should highlight the key personnel – and provide background information for the business plan on their experience, attributes and roles within the new business – and give an indication of the total personnel requirements to operate the business.

Personnel may need to be trained and developed, both at the start of a business and as it develops. A provider of finance would be interested to know that the owners or key personnel had been trained in running a business. This might involve attending courses on business start-ups covering aspects such as legal requirements, basic bookkeeping and marketing.

There may be legal requirements that staff must meet. For example, if the business is operating in the food industry, then staff would need to have basic food hygiene certificates. As the business develops, all personnel should have continuous professional development to maintain and update their skills. Increasingly, employees consider this as part of their employment package. The business will need to include training in its budget.

The costs associated with recruiting and employing people include:

- recruitment costs – advertising, interviews, applicant expenses

- employment costs – salaries, national insurance, pension contribution, training costs.

The operations plan

All the information – including cost estimates – relating to the physical and human resources of a business needs to be brought together in an operations plan. The operations plan will identify the monthly quantity of goods and services provided. The quantity will have been determined by the marketing plan and sales forecast.

In Figure 8.5 (see page 420), we showed a sales budget for a hairdressing salon. This indicates how many haircuts it is forecast would be provided in each month in the salon's first six months of trading. The operations plan will need to deliver this quantity and show how much this would cost. This should be presented in a similar way to the sales budget.

The operations plan should also describe the different stages of production or operations required to deliver the product in a saleable form. This description should include detail on how the business will ensure product quality.

The operations plan must also recognise the main legal requirements and legislation that impact on the business's operations, and should set out how the business intends to meet these requirements. If staff need to be trained to meet legal requirements, this should be indicated in the plan.

Figure 8.7: Production budget for first six months of trading

	Jan	Feb	Mar	Apr	May	June
Operations (units)	300	300	320	320	320	400
Salaries						
Shampoo, etc.						

assessment practice
The operations plan

You now need to have a heading for operations planning in your business plan and in the appendix.

Your appendix should be quite detailed, with headings where appropriate for:

■ premises – if you have identified suitable premises in your research, you might like to include a photograph or estate agent details about the property

■ equipment – you might want to explain why you have chosen particular types of equipment

■ vehicles (if needed by the business)

■ office equipment and office costs

■ stock – if possible decide what method of stock control you are using, and why

■ recruitment costs associated with employing staff

■ salaries of staff – remember to include national insurance and pension costs

■ training – you will need this to ensure that you include a budget for training.

You need to put a monetary figure on each of these items. Try and make this as accurate as possible for the larger items. It is acceptable to group smaller items together and make an estimate for the totals.

Make sure you can describe the business's operations in some detail, using diagrams if necessary. It is important to indicate what training will be required, and to set out how this will be delivered. The appendix should also show how you plan to guarantee the quality of the product. It should include a summary of all relevant legislation.

In the business plan itself, you need to present your main findings together with a rationale for your operations plan. It is important to make an evaluation as to why you have arranged operations the way you have. Make sure you include a financial summary of the operations plan.

Financial planning and analysis

The financial plan is arguably the most important part of the business plan – money matters. Financial planning and analysis are central to all business ventures, from new business start-ups to those developing a new product, or enterprises just continuing their day-to-day business operations.

The financial plan brings information together from the marketing and operations plans – which should have already been written – to see if a business proposal will work. The operations plan gives a picture of the physical and human resource requirements of the business proposal, and the sales forecast gives an estimate of monthly and annual sales. This provides the core information to produce a financial plan.

The aim is to produce a document that clearly states the funding requirements of the business and could be used to persuade potential funders that the business is a sound proposition. The plan will include financial statements and provide tools to analyse the likely performance of the business.

Financial planning toolkit

There are several financial statements and techniques that it can use to develop and analyse the financial plan. The particular financial statements produced – and techniques deployed – depend on what the business needs to demonstrate. It is useful to think of

these statements and techniques as a "toolkit", see Figure 8.8. A business will select the tools it needs for the particular job it needs to do.

Start-up budget

When either starting a new business or developing a new product for an existing business, a start-up budget helps to establish the financing requirements for the venture. There will be a variety of costs that will be incurred by the business before it provides a service or produces goods for sale.

Most of the start-up costs should have been identified in the operations plan. They include not only physical resources such as premises and equipment, but personnel requirements such as advertising for staff. A business needs to list these costs and determine the total finance needed to begin the venture. This total will determine whether the business needs to obtain a

stop and think

A hairdressing salon has been operating for several years. The owner has decided to offer new services to customers. These will include manicures and pedicures.

Identify items that should appear in the start-up budget for the new manicure and pedicure services that the salon will offer.

KEY TERMS

Start-up budget is a summary of those costs which must be met before a business can start operating.

Running costs are the day-to-day costs of a business. They need to be paid on a weekly or monthly basis.

Cash flow forecasts are detailed estimates of when and how cash is expected to flow into and out of a business.

Fixed costs are costs which do not vary with the level of output. Fixed costs exist even if a business is not producing any goods or services.

Variable costs vary directly with output.

Semi-variable costs are costs that have both fixed and variable elements.

Contribution is the difference between the selling price per unit and the variable price per unit. It is an amount that can be used to make a "contribution" to covering fixed costs and making a profit.

Breakeven is the point at which a business sells exactly the right number of products so that its revenue equals its costs.

A **profit and loss account** is a financial statement that calculates and shows the net profit made by a business.

A **balance sheet** shows the financial position of a business at a given point in time.

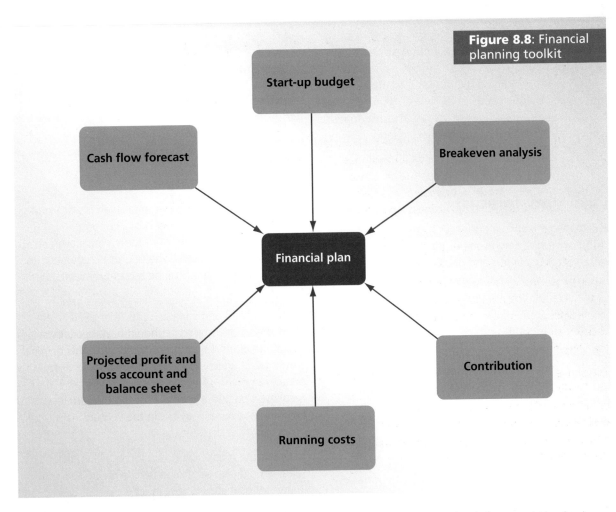

Figure 8.8: Financial planning toolkit

- Start-up budget
- Cash flow forecast
- Breakeven analysis
- Financial plan
- Projected profit and loss account and balance sheet
- Contribution
- Running costs

loan to finance the new venture. The total will also be included in the cash flow forecast for the business.

If the business plan being produced is for a new business, the start-up budget will be very comprehensive, as the business will be starting from scratch. If the business plan is for an existing business, premises and other assets may already have been acquired, so the start-up budget will need to consider the cost of adapting existing resources as well as buying new physical assets.

business practice
Super Skaters

Jan has started a new business called Super Skaters making skateboards, which she sells to shops. She has worked out that after she has covered costs, she should make a profit of 40 per cent on each skateboard. So the business will be profitable.

Jan has taken out a loan to pay for the start-up costs of the business, and needs to pay back some of the loan with interest each month. She will employ two workers who will be paid each week.

Jan has offered trade credit to her customers – the shops that will sell her skateboards to consumers – so she will not be paid until at least 30 days after

she has delivered the goods. Because Super Skaters is a new business, Jan's suppliers will not offer her trade credit, so all raw materials need to be paid for before they are delivered.

In the first few months of operating, Super Skaters received twice as many orders as expected. After six months' trading, the business is in serious financial difficulties. It cannot afford to buy new materials to fulfil orders, pay its staff and meet the repayments on the bank loan, because it is waiting for its customers to settle their invoices for last month's sales.

Running costs

In addition to its start-up costs, a business needs to identify its running costs. These are the day-to-day costs incurred in running the business. In the long term, sales revenue needs to be greater than running costs, otherwise the business will fail. The information gained from identifying, and then estimating, running costs will be used to construct the business's cash flow forecast.

Cash flow forecast

The management of a business's finances through cash flow forecasting is one of the most important activities for managers and owners. Cash flow forecasting helps to ensure that a business can meet its debts when they become due. Having a positive or negative cash flow is not the same as making a profit or a loss.

The situation facing Super Skaters is very common for new businesses. It is called overtrading, and a business is more likely to avoid this situation if it produces a cash flow forecast. The information required to produce a cash flow forecast should be available from sales forecasts and the operations plan. The information just needs to be brought together.

Figure 8.9 shows that Super Skaters does not have enough cash to be able run the business during the first four months of trading. As a result it will have to amend its plans. There are several options that could be explored. It might be possible to lease rather than buy any equipment that it needs to begin operations. It might be able take out the bank loan over a longer period of time.

stop and think

Can you think of two actions that Super Skaters could take to help reduce the cash flow problems that it has experienced in its first four months of trading?

Breakeven analysis

The use and construction of breakeven charts was covered in Unit 3 (see pages 130–3 of your AS textbook). It is useful to include a breakeven chart in a financial plan, as it is a quick way of showing to potential funders the business's profit targets

The first step in breakeven analysis is to sum the business's fixed and variable costs, identified in the operations plan, to find total costs. These total costs should be plotted on a graph with total sales revenue. The point at which the two lines intersect is called the breakeven point. Any level of sales below the breakeven point represents a loss to the business, and anything above represents a profit.

The margin of safety, which is the difference between the breakeven point and the likely level of sales, should also be shown on the chart. This is important as it shows how much sales can drop before a loss is made.

The breakeven point can also be calculated using the formula:

$$\text{breakeven point} = \frac{\text{total fixed costs}}{\text{selling price} - \text{variable cost per unit}}$$

Figure 8.9: Cash flow forecast for Super Skaters

	January	February	March	April
Cash In				
Bank loan	60,000			
Credit sales		14,000	16,800	21,000
Total inflow	60,000	14,000	16,800	21,000
Cash Out				
Payments for raw materials	10,000	12,000	15,000	18,000
Wages	3,400	3,400	3,400	3,400
Start-up costs	60,000			
Bank repayments	1,750	1,750	1,750	1,750
Other costs	800	850	900	1,000
Total outflow	75,950	18,000	21,050	24,150
Net monthly cash flow	(15,950)	(4,000)	(4,250)	(3,150)
Opening balance	16,000	50	(3,950)	(8,200)
Closing balance	50	(3,950)	(8,200)	(11,350)

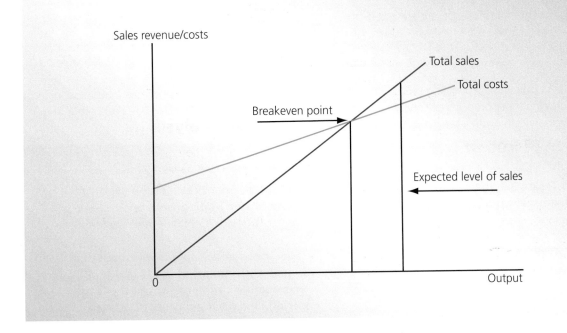

Figure 8.10: Breakeven chart

Sales revenue/costs

Total sales

Total costs

Breakeven point

Expected level of sales

Output

0

Breakeven analysis does not show the profits of a business, only the profits that would be made at given prices, costs and outputs. If the breakeven chart and breakeven calculations are produced using a spreadsheet, it is easy to explore the effect of changing figures such as fixed cost, variable cost and selling price. This allows a business to test the sensitivity of its profit forecasts to its various cost assumptions and to consider the implications of different pricing options.

There are limitations to breakeven charts. They are really intended for single product line businesses. It is also difficult to show semi-variable costs in the charts and calculations.

Contribution

The contribution approach uses the same financial information as breakeven analysis, but it is a more useful technique for a business that offers more than one product. Contribution can be calculated using the formula:

contribution = selling price − variable cost per unit

If the answer is positive (selling price is greater than variable costs), it means that a contribution is being made to covering the business's fixed costs. If a business is producing or selling more than one product, as long as each product is making a contribution then it is worthwhile providing that product, providing this does not stop the business providing a product with a bigger contribution.

Profit and loss accounts

Any potential finance lender such as a bank will want to see a projected (forecasted) profit and loss account for a new business. This will be used to check that the business is expected to make sufficient net profit to pay back the loan plus interest.

A profit and loss account is used to identify the net profit of a business. In addition to giving a final profit figure, profit and loss accounts can be used to provide data for ratios that are used to evaluate the success of a business. A full explanation of profit and loss accounts is given in Unit 15 (see pages 308–11). Here, therefore, we shall simply restate the basic principles. A profit and loss account is based on two simple formulas:

gross profit = sales revenue (turnover) − cost of sales

net profit = gross profit − expenses

If the business plan is for an existing business that wants to develop other products or services, it would be appropriate to provide a profit statement for the new product or service rather than a full projected profit and loss account. If the business plan is for a not-for-profit organisation, it should include an income and expenditure account rather than a profit and loss account.

Balance sheets

As with the projected profit and loss account, a bank or other lender will want to see a projected balance sheet. Balance sheets provide data for ratios that are used to evaluate the solvency of a business. Lenders will use the balance sheet to assess whether the business is solvent and to see if there are assets of the business that can be used to secure a loan. Again, a full explanation of the balance sheet is given in Unit 15 (see pages 310–13).

If the business plan is for an existing business that wants to develop other products or services, it may not be necessary to provide a projected balance sheet.

stop and think

Consider Figure 8.9, the cash flow forecast for Super Skaters. What items would be included in the balance sheet at the end of the first four months of trading? Which items are assets, and which are liabilities?

Bank loans

Banks provide different types of loans to small businesses.

■ **Business loans**
These loans can be for a variable amount and duration with a variable interest rate.

■ **Fixed and capped rate loans**
With these loans, the interest rate does not vary, or does not go above a particular value. This can be good for cash flow.

■ **Commercial mortgages**
Like domestic mortgages, commercial mortgages are loans taken out over a long period of time in order to buy property such as premises. The rate of interest can be fixed or variable.

There are a number of ready reckoners available on the internet that can be used to work out monthly repayments on loans. These enable a business to provide data for cash flow forecasts and profit and loss statements.

stop and think

Visit the payment calculator page of the Office of Fair Trading website. This is at www.oft.gov.uk/Consumer/money/loan.htm.

If you need a loan for your business plan, type in the amount of the loan, the APR and number of the months of the loan period, and let the payment calculator do the sums.

assessment practice
The financial plan

You now need to add a heading for financial planning in your business plan and in the appendix.

Your appendix will be quite detailed, with headings from the financial planning toolkit where appropriate for:

■ start-up budget

■ running costs

■ cash forecast

■ breakeven analysis

■ contribution

■ projected profit and loss account or profit statement

■ projected balance sheet.

In the business plan, present key information and diagrams from the financial plan. Remember, the business plan should have a rationale for your financial plan. You need to make this section persuasive to a potential lender. You only need to use the relevant tools from the financial planning toolkit.

Setting the scene: a business plan toolkit

The process of putting a business plan together involves, as we have seen, market research and planning marketing, operations and finance. This will provide an insight into how likely it is that the business proposal will succeed.

A business plan must formally evaluate the business proposal's chances of success. This is to ensure that the owners of the business do not lose their investment, and to convince potential lenders that their money is safe.

As with financial planning, there is a toolkit of evaluation methods that can be used and, where appropriate, applied to a business proposal.

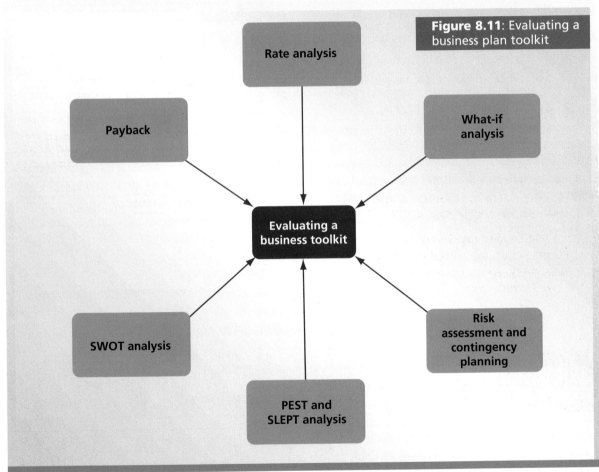

Figure 8.11: Evaluating a business plan toolkit

Evaluation techniques

In this topic, we shall consider each of the techniques that can be used to evaluate a business proposal.

Ratio analysis

Ratios are used to analyse the financial performance of a business by examining the profit and loss accounts and balance sheets, or the projections of these statements for a new business.

Ratio analysis establishes and makes use of relationships that exist between the information contained in the profit and loss account and the balance sheet. The information required for ratio analysis from the profit and loss account is:

- sales and purchases

- opening and closing stock

- cost of sales

- expenses.

Ratio analysis makes use of information in the profit and loss account and balance sheet to analyse the financial performance of a business.

Payback is a project appraisal tool that measures how long it takes to recover the outlay on an investment.

What-if analysis considers what would happen if variables such as costs changed. It is best conducted using computer software such as spreadsheets.

Risk assessment is a technique for measuring the possible risks of an activity.

SWOT analysis is a technique for understanding the strengths, weaknesses, opportunities and threats to a business.

PEST and **SLEPT analysis** consider the impact of political, economic, social, technological and legal factors on a business.

The information required for ratio analysis from the balance sheet is:

- fixed assets

- current assets, including stock, debtors and cash

- current liabilities, including creditors and bank overdrafts

- long-term liabilities, including loans and mortgages

- capital employed.

Ratio analysis is explored in detail in Unit 15, Topic 9 (see pages 332–9). In this topic, we shall illustrate how ratio analysis can be used with a brief example. Suppose you have two businesses: business A made a net profit of £10,000 and business B made a net profit of £100,000. There is very little that can actually be said about these businesses from this information, other than that business B has made more profit than business A. In order to establish which business is more profitable, more information is needed.

	Business A	Business B
Figure 8.12: Two businesses		
Net profit	£10,000	£100,000
Capital	£50,000	£1,000,000

Figure 8.12 contain a little more information on the two business from their balance sheets. A relationship can now be established: the return on capital. In other words, how much profit has been made from the money invested in the business. The relationship can now be quantified.

Business A $\qquad \dfrac{£10,000}{£50,000} = 1:5$

Business B $\qquad \dfrac{£100,000}{£1,000,000} = 1:10$

This analysis suggest that business A is more profitable than business B (1:5 is greater than 1:10). It would be better to express these ratios as percentages. Business A is making a return of 20 per cent and business B a return of 10 per cent. By expressing the relationship as a percentage, the return on capital can be compared with prevailing interest rates – as a minimum, investors would want a greater return than they could get by simply keeping their money in an interest-bearing bank account. On this basis, not only does business A appear to be more profitable than business B, but both businesses are profitable in the sense that they are generating greater returns than interest rates (which are around 4 per cent at the time of writing).

Ratio analysis is used to evaluate performance in three crucial areas:

- profitability

- solvency

- efficiency.

Profitability

There are three main ratios used to evaluate the profitability of a business:

- gross profit margin

- net profit margin

- return on capital employed (as used in our example above).

Solvency

Solvency (or liquidity) ratios indicate the businesses ability to meet its debts. They can be short-term or long-term measures. There are three main ratios here:

- the current ratio (short term)

- the acid test (short term)

- the gearing ratio (long term).

Efficiency

There are four main ratios used to measure the efficiency of a business:

- stock turnover – shows how quickly stock is sold

- debtor collection period – shows how quickly the business collects money from debtors for credit sales

- creditor payment period – shows how quickly the business pays its creditors

- return on assets – shows how much money is made from assets.

Ratio analysis is more effective when the results are compared with the results of competitors or with a business's previous years to establish trends. Full details of all these ratios are in Unit 15 (pages 332–9).

Similar analysis can be applied to not-for-profit organisations. The concept of "best value" has developed ratio-like performance indicators for all activities of local authorities, for example. Many best-value indicators are not strictly financial, and they provide ways of developing not-for-profit measures. For example, these measures could include indicators of:

- project quality

- user satisfaction.

Payback

Payback is the name given to a method of project appraisal. It is usually applied to the purchase of capital items such as fixed assets like machinery, although it can be applied to whole projects. The technique shows how long it takes for the initial outlay on the project to be repaid, and is useful when comparing alternative machinery purchases.

Look at the data in Figure 8.13. The payback for machine A is 2 years and the payback for machine B is 2 years and 3 months. With this method of project appraisal, preference is given to projects with the faster payback period, in this case machine A. However, over the course of five years, note that machine B actually generates more cash flow.

Figure 8.13: Two machines		
	Machine A	**Machine B**
Cost of machine	£80,000	£100,000
Net cash flow		
Year 1	£30,000	£40,000
Year 2	£50,000	£50,000
Year 3	£40,000	£40,000
Year 4	£20,000	£30,000
Year 5	£10,000	£20,000

The advantages of the payback method to project appraisal include:

- it is easy to understand and calculate

- it concentrates on earlier cash flows that are likely to be the most accurate.

The disadvantages of payback include:

- cash flows after the payback period are ignored

- it ignores the timing of cash flows within the payback period.

What-if analysis

What-if analysis is a technique in which financial statements are set up in a software package, usually a spreadsheet, and the numbers (or variables) are altered to assess what would happen if circumstances change. It is a good way of checking out best-case and worse-case scenarios. The technique can be used with several financial statements and analyses.

- **Cash flow forecast**
  Once the forecast is set up on a spreadsheet, several variables can be changed. A business might want to assess the affect of generating fewer or more sales than expected, of debtors not paying on time, and of leasing rather than buying assets.

- **Breakeven analysis**
  What-if analysis can be used to measure the effects of changing fixed costs, variable costs and prices.

- **Profit and loss account**
  The effects of changes in sales, purchases and costs can be modelled to see the impact on profit.

- **Balance sheet**
  Changes in the profit and loss account will have a knock-on effect in the balance sheet.

Risk assessment and contingency planning

There are risks associated with all business proposals. It is sensible therefore to identify risks, to assess the chance of them happening, and to identify action to manage the risk. This is called risk assessment.

Although risk assessments are often associated with health and safety, they can be carried out on any aspect of a business. In a business plan, risk assessment could investigate the risks attached to operations, marketing and finance plans, such as:

■ workers cannot serve as many people as expected

■ sales are lower than expected

■ debtors are taking too long to pay for goods

■ a worsening economic climate.

A risk assessment framework, such as Figure 8.14, should be used to assess each risk against:

■ the likelihood of it happening – this should be graded high, medium or low

■ the potential impact

■ action needed to prevent the risk

■ contingency plans to manage the risk if it occurs.

stop and think

Look back at the Super Skaters business in Topic 5. This business manufactures skateboards. Complete a risk assessment worksheet for two risks for her business.

SWOT analysis

SWOT analysis is a technique for evaluating the strengths and weaknesses, opportunities and threats that face a business proposal. One way of presenting this analysis is to complete a worksheet, such as Figure 8.15. In this diagram, we have included some questions that you could use to generate ideas about the strengths, weaknesses, opportunities and threats of your business proposal.

It is important to get the balance right when completing the worksheet, and not to concentrate too much on the weaknesses and threats. It is helpful to complete the analysis individually before having a meeting in a larger group to agree the SWOT.

PEST analysis

PEST is a way of characterising and mapping the external environment of a business. This helps managers understand the issues that could affect the strategic development of a business. Like SWOT, PEST is an acronym standing for:

■ political – for example, this could include environmental regulations and protection

■ economic – for example, this could include inflation and exchange rates

■ social – for example, this could include fashion and lifestyle

■ technological – for example, this could include developments in information technology.

PEST analysis is similar to SWOT analysis in that it is quick, easy to understand and uses four key questions or perspectives. PEST analysis is more concerned with

Figure 8.14: Risk assessment check list

Risk	Likelihood	Potential impact	Action needed to prevent it	Contingency plan
Debtors are slow to pay for goods purchased	Medium	Possible solvency problems	Ensure invoices and statements are sent out promptly	Arrange bank overdraft facilities
Risk 2				
Risk 3				

Figure 8.15: SWOT worksheet

Strengths

- What are the advantages of the business proposal?
- What will the business do better than anyone else?
- What is unique about the proposal?
- Why will this proposal allow the business to be better than the competition?

Opportunities

- Are there any new services that could be provided?
- What are the interesting trends in the market for the product?

Weaknesses

- What could you improve?
- What should you avoid?
- What can competitors do better?

Threats

- What obstacles does the business face?
- What is the competition doing?
- Could any of the weaknesses seriously threaten the business?

the overall market, whereas SWOT analysis is concerned with an individual business. PEST factors are external to a business, so it makes sense to undertake this analysis before a SWOT analysis, which includes internal and external factors. A PEST analysis can be presented by using a worksheet similar to Figure 8.15.

You may also come across SLEPT analysis. This is another acronym, and stands for social, legal, economic, political and technological. Like PEST, it is a way of looking at the external factors on a business. The difference is that SLEPT separates out legal influences, although it could be argued that these should be included in the political part of PEST.

assessment practice
Evaluation

You need to ensure that the evaluation of your business proposal is evident in your business plan. A heading for evaluating your business proposal needs to be included in the appendix.

Your appendix will be quite detailed with headings from the evaluating the business plan" toolkit. You should only use the tools from the evaluating a business plan toolkit that are relevant, so you may have some (or all) of these headings:

- ratio analysis

- payback

- what-if analysis

- risk assessment and contingency planning

- SWOT analysis

- PEST or SLEPT analysis.

You should make use of the resources in this topic in compiling your appendix. For example, use the risk assessment worksheet (Figure 8.14), and try to

identify at least six risks for your business proposal and indicate your contingency plans for each risk. You should also include examples of different cash flow forecasts and breakeven scenarios.

In the business plan, you have the choice of either embedding your evaluation throughout the plan or showing it as a separate heading. Embedding means including the evaluation throughout the plan. For example, you could mention the what-if analysis of the cash-flow forecast when you are considering cash flow in the financial planning section of your business plan.

Once again you need to remember that one of the functions of the business plan is to persuade funders to lend the money needed to start or develop the business.

Index

Applied Business A2 for AQA

Applied Business A2 for AQA

Applied Business A2 for AQA